Human Antiquity

An Introduction to Physical Anthropology and Archaeology

Third Edition

Kenneth L. Feder

Michael Alan Park

Central Connecticut State University

Mayfield Publishing Company
Mountain View, California
London • Toronto

To my parents, who ignited my sense of wonder
To Melissa, whose love makes life wonderful
To our children, first Josh and now Jacob, who are wonders

To Joyce, Gabby, Stanley, Emma, Cassie, Max, and Zoe,
who kept me company and provided a
sometimes humbling perspective
on the human species.
And to Jan
who knows why.

This is the story of how we begin to remember.
                                        —Paul Simon

Library of Congress Cataloging-in-Publication Data

Feder, Kenneth L.
   Human antiquity: an introduction to physical anthropology and
archaeology / Kenneth L. Feder, Michael Alan Park. — 3rd ed.
      p.   cm.
   Includes bibliographical references and index.
   ISBN 1-55934-684-1
   1. Physical anthropology. 2. Archaeology. 3. Man, Prehistoric.
I. Park, Michael Alan. II. Title.
GN60.F43 1996
573—dc20   96-21880
                                                                CIP

Manufactured in the United States of America
10 9 8 7 6 5 4 3 2 1

Mayfield Publishing Company
1280 Villa Street
Mountain View, California 94041

Sponsoring editor, Janet M. Beatty; production editor, Lynn Rabin Bauer; manuscript editor, Dale Anderson; art director, Jeanne M. Schreiber; art manager, Robin Mouat; text and cover designer, Jeanne Calabrese; illustrators, Joan Carol and John and Judy Waller; photo researcher, Brian Pecko; cover photograph, © Peter Menzel; manufacturing manager, Randy Hurst. The text was set in 10.5/12 Berkeley Book by American Composition and Graphics and printed on 50# Chromatone LG by The Banta Company.

To the Instructor

—m—

Physical (biological) anthropology and archaeology, two subfields of anthropology, are really two starting points on the road to a common goal—the understanding of the human past. Both authors of this book research human antiquity: Feder is an archaeologist who conducts surveys, excavations, and analyses aimed at understanding the native inhabitants of southern New England. Park is a biological anthropologist interested in the application of evolutionary theory to the biological history of our species. But a full understanding of the human past is simply not possible without the kinds of research *both* of us do. Our approach in this book, then, is to truly combine the ideas, methods, and knowledge from our two subfields into the unified effort they really are.

Features

• *Accessibility* This book is written for students. It does not assume prior knowledge of archaeology or biological anthropology. We *explain* the material we present in clear, straightforward language, including, where appropriate, colloquialisms and personal comments; we want our readers to know this was written by real people.

We have attempted to at least touch on all relevant topics within this broad subject and to discuss all reasonable points of view around individual issues, giving the pros and cons of each and indicating our leaning—and the reasons for it—where we have one. Some items, naturally, will be left out or will not be covered as completely as some may wish. We can only say that our goal here is to help our readers understand what is known about the human past and *how* we have come to know it.

We have also included various study aids to help introductory students navigate their way through what must often seem like an overwhelming amount of new information. These study aids include definitions of key terms on the page where they first appear as well as in a comprehensive glossary at the back of the book; chapter summaries, study questions, lists of key terms, and suggested readings at the ends of chapters; a taxonomic glossary with pronunciation; and an extensive bibliography.

• *Science made interesting and relevant.* Although *we* think all the topics in this book are inherently fascinating, they may not be to students, many of whom find the very idea of science rather daunting. So we include subjects that we have found, over the years, seem to naturally pique students' interest. Chapter 1, for example, consists of a unique discussion of three creation myths compared to scientific explanations for human origins. Throughout the text we introduce the chapters with subjects or ideas that capture student interest—the Piltdown fraud, for example (Chapter 8), or the story of Archbishop Usser and his dating of the Creation (Chapter 2). And to demonstrate that the study of the past can apply to the present, "Contemporary Issue" sections show how the anthropological investigation of the human past can be applied to current concerns.

• *Use of narrative and analogy.* Stories are often easier to remember than lists of facts, so we present our material as orderly and logical sequences of causality. In some places, this takes the form of a chronological narrative. In Chapter 3, for example, we provide a unique overview of the evolution of the universe, focusing, of course, on the latter stages of earth's history. This brief chapter accomplishes several things. It shows students that history—evolutionary as well as cultural—is made up of contingent series of events. It provides a perspective on the time scale involved in the history of our universe, and a sense of the relative temporal placement of individual important events. Most importantly, it places the human story within a universal time frame. This chapter shows students that the evolution of humanity is not separate from the evolution of everything else, but is, rather, just one story line within a much larger epic. And, for that portion of history that is the topic of this book, Chapter 3 previews and outlines what is to be detailed in the subsequent chapters about human evolution.

In other places, the "narrative" approach is accomplished simply by relying on the logic of the scientific method—developing inductive hypotheses and then deductively testing them. We show how scientific reasoning works (Chapter 1) and then apply it throughout the book. Chapter 8 describes and tests various explanations and scenarios about the evolution of hominid bipedalism. Chapter 12 applies an explicitly deductive approach to the question of the origins of anatomically modern human beings. Chapter 14 does the same with eight different hypotheses that have attempted to account for the origins of agriculture; and Chapter 15 presents our current understanding of the evolution of complex civilizations using this same deductive approach.

We also recognize the importance of analogy. For example, in Chapter 3, we help instill a sense of time by comparing the history of the universe to a calendar year (with thanks to Carl Sagan). In Chapter 6 we discuss the comparison of human behaviors to those of other primates and some non-primates, and of contemporary human foragers to ancient hunter-gatherers, stressing the limitations involved in all such comparisons. In Chapter 7, on methodology, the archaeological dating technique of seriation is explained using the analogy of changes in automobile styles. And in Chapter 10 we help students appreciate the rigors of the Pleistocene ice ages by describing a New England winter storm.

Organization

We begin in **Part One: Thinking About the Past** with some examples of mythological explanations of the past and a discussion of how these explanations differ from those offered by science. After discussing the nature of the science of anthropology, we give a brief account of some early scientific attempts to study and explain the human past. The part ends with a narrative overview of what is now understood about evolutionary history to help give the reader a sense of time and the sequence of events.

Part Two: The Study of the Past focuses on the tools—material and intellectual—that we apply to our study of the human past. We include here, in separate chapters, a discussion of genetics and evolutionary theory, the evolution of the primates, the use of animal behavior in developing models of the behavior of our evolutionary ancestors, and the research methods used by archaeologists and paleoanthropologists.

Part Three: The Story of the Human Past chronicles what we have learned so far about human antiquity. We begin with the origins of the human family and trace our evolutionary journey through the beginnings of civilization.

We conclude with **An Evolutionary Afterword** in which we show how the scientific information about our past may be applied to improving our present and, perhaps, to ensuring that our species' tenure on this planet lasts a little longer.

What's New in This Edition

Our understanding of the human past changes at a dizzying rate. New discoveries, new methods of analysis, and new interpretations of old data cause a more or less constant reassessment of our models of human antiquity. Though intellectually exhilarating, the pace of change can be frustrating to authors of textbooks. We have made every effort to bring this book up-to-date by adding new material on many topics.

Chapter 1: Frameworks now includes a description of the science of anthropology, moved from its former location in Chapter 7.

Our discussion of the development of an evolutionary view of the planet in **Chapter 2: Eden Questioned: Historical Perspectives**, now includes a broader discussion of the archaeological discoveries and interpretations that contributed to a uniformitarian paradigm.

Chapter 3: Evolution: An Overview has been revised to reflect the latest dating of important events in earth history, and we have replaced the visual timeline of earth history with a thoroughly recalculated version of Carl Sagan's "cosmic calendar."

Chapter 4: Understanding Change: Modern Evolutionary Theory contains a revised discussion of the relationship between gradualism and punctuated equilibrium and includes some of the latest research (such as that on Darwin's finches) regarding the short-term operation of natural selection on specific populations. This chapter also introduces the idea of "racial" variation within a species.

The discussion of genetic research to determine the evolutionary relationships among the primates (formerly in Chapter 8) now appears in **Chapter 5: Learning About the Past: The Primates.** Also in this chapter is a revised discussion of primate evolution that includes new fossil material and the latest ideas on the relationships among the early hominoids.

Chapter 7: Learning About the Past: The Material Record now includes a brief presentation of the problem of identifying and classifying extinct species and a discussion of the analysis of fortuitously preserved ancient bodies (for example, the Ice Man).

Chapter 8: The Emergence of the Human Lineage has been completely rewritten to include new fossil evidence and hypotheses for the evolution of bipedalism. *Ardipithecus ramidus, Australopithecus anamensis,* and the newly christened *Australopithecus bahrelghazalia* from Chad have been added to the discussion of early hominid fossils in this chapter and in **Chapter 9: The Human Lineage Established.** The "Contemporary Issue: Our Cousin, the Chimp?" (Chapter 8) has also been expanded to better describe cladistics and show how it can be applied to the primates.

Chapter 10: The Human Lineage Evolves and **Chapter 11: On the Origin of Our Species** incorporate the newest information on the Atapuerca hominids including discussions of the 780,000-year-old fossils at Gran Dolina (Chapter 10) and the 300,000-year-old pre-Neandertals at Sima de los Huesos (Chapter 11).

The discussion of the ongoing debate over the origins of modern *Homo sapiens* in **Chapter 12: The Evolution of Modern Humanity** has been revised to more clearly explain the complex arguments in favor of and against competing schools of thought. Included is new cultural evidence of early anatomically modern humans from Zaire and Kenya. Coverage of modern human biodiversity (previously a separate chapter) is now at the end of Chapter 12 to provide closure and a contemporary context for our chronicle of human biological evolution.

The Upper Paleolithic now has its own chapter, **Chapter 13: New Ideas, New Worlds: Life in the Upper Paleolithic.** It includes expanded discussions of the intellectual leaps that help define that period, and offers a far more detailed presentation of the peopling of Australia and the New World.

Chapter 14: The Origins of Agriculture presents a more inclusive and thorough description of hypotheses proposed to explain the origins of food production with a more detailed discussion of the Old World Mesolithic and New World Archaic periods. This chapter also includes a greatly expanded discussion of North America's independent agricultural revolution.

Chapter 15: The Evolution of Civilization presents a broadened discussion of levels of socio-political complexity. There is also an expanded discussion of African civilization south of Egypt, and thoroughly updated presentations on the development of complexity in Mesoamerica, South America, and North America.

Finally, to make the book more pedagogically useful, we've provided thought-provoking questions in the captions accompanying chapter-opening art that offer insight into chapter contents. We've also added **Study Questions** at the end of each chapter. Our hope is that students will use them as self-tests to help assess their understanding of each chapter's facts, theories, and issues.

Supplementary Material

Available with *Human Antiquity* is a complete package of ancillary materials to enhance both teaching and learning.

The *Instructor's Manual* includes a test bank of more than 500 multiple-choice and short-answer/essay questions, as well as chapter summaries, learning goals, suggested activities, and lists of key terms.

A *Computerized Test Bank* is available free of charge to qualifying adopters. It is a powerful, easy-to-use test-generation system that provides all test items on computer disk for IBM-compatible or Macintosh computers. You can select, add, or edit questions, randomize them, and print tests appropriate for your individual classes.

A set of color transparency acetates is also available for use on an overhead projector. Included are charts and diagrams from this text as well as other illustrations to help elaborate on text material.

We have replaced our *Human Antiquity Newsletter* with a Web site (http://wwwas.ccsu.ctstateu.edu/depts/anth/human_antiquity/) to provide up-to-date information on the topics covered in the book. We will include new fossil and archaeological finds, new theoretical ideas, important new references, teaching suggestions, and anything else we think will help make our text the most useful teaching and learning tool available. If you'd like to contribute, please contact us at: feder@ccsu.ctstateu.edu or parkm@ccsu.ctstateu.edu.

Acknowledgments

We particularly wish to thank those of you who responded on the comment cards supplied with the second edition. Many colleagues were generous with both praise and criticism, and we genuinely appreciate these responses and value the wise counsel contained therein. We would also like to thank those colleagues who went even further and wrote to us with specific suggestions on how to improve this edition of the book.

Thanks again to all those who supplied photographs and artwork. They are acknowledged with their contributions.

Once again, all the people at Mayfield Publishing Company have done a marvelous job in helping make our idea a reality. In particular, we thank Jan Beatty, sponsoring editor, who has now been with this book through three incarnations and has been a true partner in our work. Special thanks also to Lynn Rabin Bauer, production editor; Brian Pecko, photo researcher; Dale Anderson, copyeditor; Jeanne Schreiber, art director; Robin Mouat, art manager; and Jeanne Calabrese, designer.

We would also like to thank those colleagues who reviewed the manuscript and provided specific advice and criticism for this edition: Russell J. Barber, California State University, San Bernardino; John E. Blank, Cleveland State University; David L. Carmichael, University of Texas at El Paso; Nancy R. Coinman, Iowa State University; Bill Engelbrecht, Buffalo State College; Lucille Lewis Johnson, Vassar College; Heather McKillop, Louisiana State University; Peter Robertshaw, California State University, San Bernardino; Raymond Scupin, Lindenwood College; Joan C. Stevenson, Western Washington University; and Jim Wanner, University of Northern Colorado. Any errors, of course, remain our responsibility.

To the Reader

—∽∽—

Very simply, this book explains what we now know about the most basic questions regarding our species: Where do we come from? Why do we behave as we do? Why do we look like we do? What is our place in nature? What exactly has happened to us during our 5 or 6 million years on earth? And, just as important, this book tells *how* we have arrived at our answers.

Obviously, many academic disciplines focus on aspects of humanity's long tenure on this planet. Our perspective in this book is the perspective of *anthropology*—the field that broadly studies the entire human species and that looks for the connections between our past and our present, between one culture and another, and between human cultural behavior and biological endowments.

The two areas of anthropology most concerned with the human past are physical (or biological) anthropology, whose starting point is the biological nature of human beings, and archaeology, whose focus is the human cultural past. Commonly considered separate fields, these two anthropological subfields are clearly interrelated. One cannot fully understand the history of human culture without understanding how our ancestors lived *before* they had acquired culture, and how the biological nature of our complex brains makes our cultural behavior possible. Similarly, one cannot understand how and why our biology changed over time without understanding how our behavior, especially our cultural behavior, helped us adapt to the various environments we have encountered during our 5-million-year evolution.

The study of the interrelationship of human biology and human culture is achieved by integrating the methods, the data, and the conclusions of *both* physical anthropology and archaeology, and it is this approach we use here to answer the questions posed at the beginning of this section.

How to Use This Book

We have tried to make the text readable and easy to use. Each chapter begins with a photograph and a caption that asks the questions we will address within the chapter. Important terms are in **boldface** in the text and are listed under "Key Terms" at the end of each chapter. These terms are defined in three places: in the text itself, in a running glossary found in the margins, and in the main "Glossary of Terms" at the back of the book. Although the wording of the definitions of a term may differ in these three places, they all carry the same meaning; we hope that defining a term in several slightly different ways will help you more fully grasp its meaning.

Scientific names of living and extinct primates are in boldface in the text where they first appear and are defined (with a pronunciation key) in a second glossary, the "Glossary of Human and Nonhuman Primates."

All references within the text are in parentheses, giving the author's last name, the date of publication, and page numbers where applicable. Details of these references may then be looked up at your convenience in the "Bibliography." For each chapter, a "Summary" is provided where the key concepts and ideas of the chapter are briefly discussed. Following this is a list of "Study Questions" that focus on key issues of the chapter and will allow you to assess your understanding of the chapter contents. Each chapter ends with a section called "For More Information" where we list some additional works we think would be helpful should you wish to do further reading on a particular topic. Full references to these works are also in the "Bibliography."

Many of our chapters contain a "Contemporary Issue" section. Here, we have applied the perspective gained in our study of the human past to some modern concern. The data of human antiquity are not merely interesting bits of information—fascinating, but esoteric and essentially useless. The perspective gained from understanding our roots is uniquely important to our full comprehension of ourselves, past and present.

Contents

**PART THREE
THE STORY OF THE HUMAN PAST**

How do these native South Americans explain the origin of humankind? In what ways is their explanation like that of Europeans prior to the eighteenth century? How do these explanations differ from those offered by science? *(Napoleon Chagnon/Anthro-Photo)*

1

Frameworks

—m—

"*Where do I come from?*"

This is a question most of us, as children, ask our parents. Eventually, we come to understand that we haven't always been here; we had a beginning, we developed and changed, and we will continue to do so. Finally—hardest to comprehend—we realize that we will not always exist.

Human groups are also curious about their origins, their development, and their fates. "Where do *we* come from?" we ask as conscious, intelligent, curious beings. We attempt to answer that question in a number of different ways.

FIGURE 1.1   The Yąnomamö live in villages that consist of a large circular building, surrounded by a log palisade and covered around the edges by a thatched roof, seen here in the background. The people in the picture are visitors to this village, waiting to be welcomed by their hosts for a ritual feast aimed at promoting political alliance and trade relations between villages. *(Napoleon Chagnon/Anthro-Photo)*

Human Origins: The Framework of Myth

For much of the history of our species, people have addressed the question of where we came from with **myths**—stories involving magic and gods. For a long time these supernatural accounts, taken on faith, provided satisfying answers to this most profound of questions. For many, they still do.

Virtually every culture has had its own myth explaining the creation of the earth, of plants and animals, and of human beings. **Science**, through a different process, attempts to explain the same things. To better understand the process of the scientific investigation of human origins and development, and to comprehend how it differs from mythological explanations, we will look at three origin tales, one of which you likely know. We will begin with the creation story of the Yąnomamö, Native Americans living in southern Venezuela and northern Brazil (Figure 1.1).

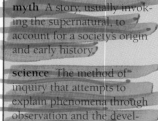

myth A story, usually invoking the supernatural, to account for a society's origin and early history.

science The method of inquiry that attempts to explain phenomena through observation and the development and testing of hypotheses.

The Yąnomamö

The Yąnomamö hunt and farm in the jungles of the Orinoco River. They tell of their past this way (Chagnon 1977): In the beginning, they say, the cosmos was made of four layers (Figure 1.2). The top layer once had a function, but now it is empty. The undersurface of the next layer is the visible sky. The layer below that is the earth, a huge jungle dotted with countless Yąnomamö villages. Even foreigners, who degenerated from the Yąnomamö, live in such villages. The bottom layer contains a single village inhabited by spirit people who sometimes travel up to earth to capture and eat the souls of children and so must be constantly guarded against.

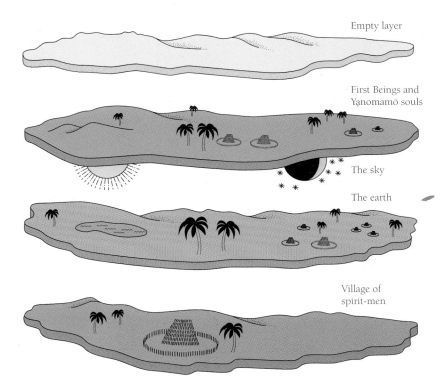

Empty layer

First Beings and
Yąnomamö souls

The sky

The earth

Village of
spirit-men

FIGURE 1.2   A schematic diagram of the Yąnomamö image of the cosmos. The layers resemble the layers of the rain forest canopy in which the Yąnomamö live.   (*Redrawn from Verdun P. Chagnon in Napoleon A. Chagnon,* Yąnomamö: The Fierce People, *2d ed., New York: Holt, Rinehart and Winston, 1977, p. 27. Reproduced by permission of the publisher.*)

The First Beings—the Yąnomamö gods—originated along with the layers of the cosmos. Each Being is credited with a specific function, usually the creation of something useful in Yąnomamö life—important plants, tools, fire, animals, knowledge of farming.

The Yąnomamö themselves were created when one of the First Beings, Periboriwä, came to earth to eat the souls of children. Two other Beings shot at him with arrows as he ascended to the second layer. One arrow found its mark, and Periboriwä was wounded. The wound bled, and each drop of blood that hit the earth became a Yąnomamö man. Because they were originally created of blood, all Yąnomamö men are, to this day, fierce warriors. One of the men created in this way became pregnant in his legs, and from his legs were born other men and a new type of being, woman. Unlike the men created from blood, these new Yąnomamö people were timid and docile. Later, all the First Beings became spirits and now dwell, along with the souls of departed Yąnomamö, on the second layer, a replica of the "real-world" third layer.

The Ancient Hebrews

The ancient Hebrews told two different versions of their creation story. One told of an all-powerful Being who brought order to a chaotic world of water. Over six days he created, in succession, light; Heaven; the earth with its dry land, oceans, and plants; the sun, moon, and stars; aquatic animals, flying creatures, and land animals; and finally, in his own image, man and woman. This Being—God—told the man and woman that all his other creations were for their use, instructing them to "be fruitful, and multiply." He placed humanity at the apex of his creation, telling the first man and first woman to "replenish the earth, and subdue it" and granting humans "dominion over the fish of the sea, and over the fowl of the air, and over every living thing that moveth upon the earth."

The second version of the Hebrew creation story concerns both the origin of humans and the early history of the Hebrew people. In this story, a fallible, humanlike god creates water on a dry world and produces a man out of "the dust of the ground." He plants a garden in a place called Eden for the man to care for and eat from. Feeling that the man needs a partner, God begins creating all sorts of beasts and fowl, which the man names, but none proves to be a suitable companion and helper. So God puts the man to sleep and makes a woman from one of his ribs.

All is well in the garden until one day, while walking there, God discovers that his two human creations have eaten from the forbidden tree of knowledge. Now they are too much like gods themselves because they know good and evil. Angry, God curses them, condemning women to the "sorrow" of bearing children and to the rule of men and punishing men by forcing on them the hard labor of farming the land to acquire food. He expels them from the garden (Figure 1.3). Generations pass, during which their descendants become increasingly sinful. God realizes he has erred and produces a catastrophic flood that destroys all his creations except Noah and his family and a few representatives of each other kind of living thing, saved on the ark Noah builds according to God's directions. The story then describes in great detail how these survivors produced all the generations that became the Hebrews and related peoples.

The Maya

The Maya are indigenous to Central America. Beginning more than 2000 years ago, they developed a complex civilization with magnificent pyramids, a sophisticated calendar, and far-reaching trade networks. The Maya also developed a writing system, and it is from one of their few remaining books, the *Popol Vuh,* that we can learn about their creation story (Savaria 1965).

Before creation, according to the *Popol Vuh,* there were no people, animals, birds, fish, crabs, trees, or stones. There was only the calm sea. The creators, K'ucumatz and Tepew (Figure 1.4, p. 6), first made the earth with its mountains, plains, and rivers and then made animals such as deer, jaguars, and snakes. The creators assigned each animal its own place to live in the newly created world.

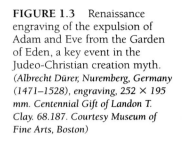

FIGURE 1.3 Renaissance engraving of the expulsion of Adam and Eve from the Garden of Eden, a key event in the Judeo-Christian creation myth. *(Albrecht Dürer, Nuremberg, Germany (1471–1528), engraving, 252 × 195 mm. Centennial Gift of Landon T. Clay. 68.187. Courtesy Museum of Fine Arts, Boston)*

The creators next ordered the animals to speak so that they might praise the creators for their work; the animals, however, could not speak. The creators then decided to make creatures that could; these would be people. The first people, made of mud, could speak, but they had no minds and merely dissolved in the water. Then the creators made people out of wood. These people multiplied and spread across the earth. They could speak but lacked blood and minds, and they did not remember the creators who made them. K'ucumatz and Tepew ordered that they be

FIGURE 1.4   In the Maya creation story in the *Popol Vuh*, the
creators, K'ucumatz and Tepew,
first made the earth and its
mountains, plains, and rivers.

destroyed; birds plucked out their eyes, and jaguars devoured their woody
flesh. Some of these wooden men, nevertheless, managed to escape into
the jungle where all that remains of them today are the monkeys. According to the Maya, this is why monkeys are similar to human beings.

Finally, the fox, the coyote, the parrot, and the crow told the creators
about the yellow and white corn that grew on the earth (Figure 1.5). The
creators ground and mixed the yellow and white corn; from this corn
meal, they made the flesh and blood of the first true people. These people
had blood and minds, and they worshiped the gods who created them and
the world in which they lived.

Creation Myths

These stories are what we call **creation myths**. Every culture has one or
more of them. A creation myth performs several functions. It provides an
account of the origin of the world. It tells the story of a people's beginnings
and their early history. It lays out the society's world view and belief system. It explains the origin and meaning of a people's rules of social behavior. In having these functions, creation myths ultimately serve to codify,
rationalize, justify, and stabilize a given social system—generally under the
auspices of some supernatural power.

Consequently, a creation story reflects the environment, history, and
cultural system of the society that tells it. The mythical layers of the

creation myth   A myth that
explains the origin of the
world and its inhabitants.

Yąnomamö cosmos, for example, resemble the ecological layers of the rain forest canopy in which they live. Yąnomamö men see themselves as—and indeed they are—fierce warriors who regularly wage war on neighboring villages and generally lead lives centered around violent conflict. Such wars and conflicts have, of course, perfectly concrete explanations. But the Yąnomamö explanation—the abstract justification that maintains this behavior—is found in the creation story of men formed from drops of blood. The subservient position of women in Yąnomamö society and, presumably, the presence of a few men who are not fierce warriors are nicely accounted for by the story of the creation of the timid, docile Yąnomamö from the pregnant legs of one of the first men born from drops of blood.

Similarly, the *Popol Vuh,* the creation story of the Maya, represents the world in which they lived. It includes animals that were important inhabitants of their world and accounts for the vital role played by corn farming in their culture.

The same sort of analysis, of course, can be applied to the creation myths of the ancient Hebrews. We have come to know these stories well, and they have exerted a great deal of influence on Western culture. They were written down and make up the book of *Genesis*—the first book in the Jewish Torah and the Christian Bible. Parts of these stories have been traced to the creation myths of the Babylonians and other peoples living in the Middle East at about the same time as the Hebrews. But the specific details of the Genesis stories, and even the fact that they were written down, are direct results of the environment and history of the Hebrew people at specific times.

For example, Biblical scholars now think that the basic Hebrew creation story of the first man and woman was first put into writing about 3000 years ago by a man or men we know only as J^1 as a political protest against King David's having moved the seat of government to a new location (Asimov 1969; Buttrick 1952). J^1's reasoning was that such a document would reinforce in the Jewish people the ideas of their common bond, heritage, and commitment to God. About 100 years later, in response to a subsequent political split between northern and southern Hebrew groups, a man or men we call J^2 added the details of the second creation story—the one about the humanlike god, the garden, and the flood. Like J^1, he was trying to demonstrate the common heritage of his people in order to reunite them.

This attempt failed, and the divided Jews were conquered by the Assyrians and the Babylonians. When the Babylonian captivity ended in the sixth century B.C., the Jews needed to establish their uniqueness and identity and to formalize their history and cultural heritage. To help accomplish this goal, a group of priests we now call P edited the old writings of J^1, J^2, and others. They took out some internal contradictions and added some of the history that had taken place since. They also wrote a "preface" to the story of the garden and the flood: the account of the six-day creation

FIGURE 1.5 Here, from the *Popol Vuh,* the parrot tells one of the Maya creators about the yellow and white corn. The creator then uses the corn meal to make the flesh and blood of the first true people.

by an all-powerful god, taken largely from a then-popular Babylonian myth called the *Enuma Elish*.

It is this Hebrew creation myth that is of direct concern to us here. As the very beginning of the basic document of Judeo-Christian tradition, it has had an important impact on many aspects of the development of Western civilization—including the ways in which people asked and answered questions about the history of their physical world and its inhabitants. This creation myth, in other words, has deeply affected the way in which Western peoples have studied the past.

Human Origins: The Framework of Science

In this book, we focus on the *scientific* study of the origin and development of the human species—in essence, on the **evolution** of humankind. Anthropologist Misia Landau (1991) justifiably asserts that scientific narratives of human evolution—the "stories" scientists devise for how they think human evolution transpired—are similar in their configuration to traditional folktales. The structure of these narratives, however, is not as important as how they develop, how they are used, and their intent. A scientific investigation of humanity differs fundamentally from mythic constructs of human origins of the sort just outlined.

Myths are highly variable and idiosyncratic, differing from culture to culture. The contents of myths may or may not be based on observations of the real world. The point of mythmaking is the construction of satisfying stories aimed at explaining some aspect of reality and reinforcing or maintaining a social or political order. The creation myths of the Yanomamö, the ancient Hebrews, and the Maya are just this—tales that perform valuable functions, but have no necessary grounding in fact.

In contrast, the **scientific method** is always predicated on observations of the real world, generalizations from those observations, and tests of those generalizations. Creating general explanations of how things work based on specific observations is called **induction**. The general explanations, the "educated guesses" at the rules that govern the way things work, are called **hypotheses**. Scientists, however, do not stop with seemingly plausible explanations for how things like volcanoes, the weather, or human behavior operate or for how things like stars, planets, plants, animals, or people came into being. Science goes beyond its own reasonable, credible guesses to rigorously test those hypotheses. Science always asks the question: If a hypothesis induced from concrete observation is valid, *if* it accurately describes or explains how some part of reality functions, *then* what new, specific data can be predicted and what further study can test that prediction? This process of suggesting what specific data should be found if a general explanation is to be supported is called **deduction**.

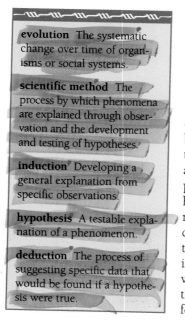

evolution The systematic change over time of organisms or social systems.

scientific method The process by which phenomena are explained through observation and the development and testing of hypotheses.

induction Developing a general explanation from specific observations.

hypothesis A testable explanation of a phenomenon.

deduction The process of suggesting specific data that would be found if a hypothesis were true.

Consider the story about chimpanzees and gorillas told in the nineteenth century by the Mpongwe people of Gabon in coastal Africa. Just as the Maya perceived similarities between monkeys and people and explained this in their creation myth, the Mpongwe recognized both the physical and behavioral similarities between apes and human beings and the differences between the two African apes, and they attempted to explain these through their myths. They viewed chimps as the physical incarnation of the departed souls of highly intelligent and peaceable people; in other words, they thought of chimps as reincarnated Mpongwe. They perceived gorillas as the embodiment of the souls of less intelligent but fiercer forest peoples. Thus, a curious similarity between people and apes was explained within the context of a belief system that included the mobility of the soul and the Mpongwe's feeling of intellectual superiority.

In contrast to the Mpongwe explanation, scientists hypothesize that chimpanzees, gorillas, and human beings are so similar because we share a relatively recent common ancestor; in other words, we are evolutionarily closely connected in time. That sounds reasonable, but scientists don't stop there. *If* the hypothesis is correct that humans and these apes are biologically closely related, *then* our genetic codes should be quite similar (see Chapter 4), reflecting our recent divergence (see Chapter 8). In addition, the fossil record should show increasing similarity between human ancestors and the African apes as that record goes back in time (see Chapter 5), and behavioral studies of apes and humans should show detailed and specific similarities (see Chapter 6). As you will see in these subsequent chapters, this is precisely what has been found. Thus, scientists are not content merely to suggest what seems like a reasonable, pleasing, or congenial explanation for the perceived similarity of humans and apes. They predict what must be true if the hypothesis is valid, and then go about the task of seeing if those predictions pan out.

In the scientific method, if experimentation or data collection produces new data that contradict the predictions derived from a hypothesis, that plausible guess must be rejected and an attempt made to develop a better explanation. If, on the other hand, the predictions are supported, scientists keep the hypothesis (although they never say they absolutely "prove" it), unless and until someone develops something better—that is, an explanation that is superior at predicting, explaining, or encompassing new data. Such constant critical testing and refining are the hallmarks of science and distinguish science from myth.

Eventually, a hypothesis that holds up under rigorous testing is elevated to the status of a **theory.** Scientists have developed many such theories; the theory of gravity and the atomic theory are two developed by physics. As you will see, evolution, as an explanation of how life developed and changed on this planet, is a scientific theory from the field of biology. It is a hypothesis that has held up so well and for so long under scientific scrutiny that scientists are virtually certain of its validity in a general sense.

theory A hypothesis that has been well supported by evidence and experimental testing.

Although evolution is a general theory of the development of life, scientists are still testing many specific hypotheses that seek to explain particular aspects of how evolution operates. This book presents the data and arguments that have been generated by the extensive testing of the many specific hypotheses concerning human evolution.

The general theory of evolution, as well as some specific hypotheses concerning how evolution may have happened, developed within a cultural environment where the Judeo-Christian creation myth was important and influential. In the next chapter we will outline how the theory of evolution itself evolved within that context.

Anthropology: Studying Ourselves

The specific science that focuses on humanity, including its biology, behavior, culture, and history, is **anthropology.** Anthropologists investigate humanity's origins and subsequent biological and cultural development. In simplest terms, anthropologists' focus is on the past and present nature of the human **species.**

To use an analogy, anthropology studies humans much the way a branch of biology, say entomology, studies its subjects (although anthropologists focus on a single species). Anthropologists try to make generalizations about that species of organism. They look for connections between the present condition and past history of the organism. Anthropology assumes that all facets of human anatomy, physiology, behavior, environment, and evolution are interrelated and can only be fully understood in terms of those interrelationships. Thus described, anthropology is the **holistic** study of people. Anthropology studies the whole species and all its features in interaction with one another.

Such a broad subject is necessarily divided into a number of specialties or subfields. Perhaps the most characteristic feature of our species is cultural behavior with all its various manifestations. The specialty of **cultural anthropology** focuses on this behavior, seeking to understand the nature of culture and its variety among different societies. In its most general definition, **culture** is the sum total of those things people have invented or developed and have passed down to later generations. Culture is our *extrasomatic* (nonphysical, literally "beyond the body") means of adaptation.

Whereas most other animal species rely on very specific physical adaptations or adjustments to their environment, people, through culture, produce their own means of survival. In other words, culture constitutes all aspects of the human strategy for survival that people, as a result of their intelligence, have been able to think up. Cultural anthropology attempts to describe various cultural systems and to explain the variations these systems exhibit (Figure 1.6). It also searches for processes that account for change in culture through time. Cultural anthropologists characteristically study living societies.

anthropology The holistic and integrative scientific study of the human species.

species A group of organisms that can produce fertile offspring among themselves but not with any other group.

holistic A study that views its subject as a whole made up of integrated parts.

cultural anthropology The branch of anthropology that focuses on cultural behavior.

culture The nongenetic means of adaptation; those things people invent or develop and pass down.

FIGURE 1.6 Raymond Hames using a battery-powered computer and printer gathers data from some Yąnomamö villagers about the history of their settlement patterns. *(Raymond Hames)*

Because language is unique to human beings and such an important part of what makes us different from other animals, some anthropologists focus on linguistics, the nature and structure of human language. **Anthropological linguistics** focuses on issues like the evolution of speech, the historical connections between the many and various human language systems, and the ways in which language affects our perception of the world.

But cultural systems also have a past. **Archaeology** is the branch of anthropology that studies this past (Figure 1.7, left). Much of the evidence to be presented in this book has been obtained through the study of the human cultural past.

Finally, we are, of course, living organisms, subject to the same biological processes that affect all other organisms. The study of how these processes apply to people is the subject of **physical**, or **biological, anthropology** (Figure 1.7, right). Some specialists in this subfield gather biological

anthropological linguistics The branch of anthropology that focuses on language.

archaeology The branch of anthropology that focuses on cultural evolution through the study of the material remains of past societies.

physical (biological) anthropology The branch of anthropology that focuses on humans as a biological species.

FIGURE 1.7 *(Left)* Ken Feder conducting a field excavation along the Farmington River in Connecticut as part of the Farmington River Archaeological Project. *(Right)* Biological anthropology applied: the excavation of an early New England grave (at the family's request) and the study and eventual reburial of the bones. Nick Bellantoni, Connecticut state archaeologist, hands Michael Park a bone for identification.(*L K. L. Feder; R photo by William F. Keegan; courtesy Nicholas Bellantoni*)

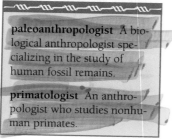

paleoanthropologist A biological anthropologist specializing in the study of human fossil remains.

primatologist An anthropologist who studies nonhuman primates.

data from living human populations. Others focus on groups of the past, represented by fossil remains; these are **paleoanthropologists.** Still others, **primatologists,** study the biology of our closest relatives, the other primates.

Our subject in this book is human antiquity. In terms of the field of anthropology, this book focuses on the data and methods of archaeology and paleoanthropology—the "anthropology of the past." Remember, though, that in a real sense the subfield designations in anthropology have limited meaning. They refer not to separate disciplines but to starting points or focuses in the general process of trying to understand the human species. Our subject—people—does not divide itself neatly into discrete categories such as present, past, cultural, and biological. Neither does anthropology. All branches of anthropology work together toward a common goal: understanding the human species.

Summary

People use two basic frameworks for explaining the past. Myths are stories created to explain some aspect of the world as a group of people sees it at a given time. Myths satisfy the need to place events in chronological order and in a sequence of causality, and they address the basic questions of how, what, who, when, and why. Many myths, like the three described, specifically attempt to account for a people's origins, for their early history, and for their present lifestyle.

Science also seeks to answer these questions, but with a methodology that requires skepticism, testing, and continual reexamination. Science uses observations of real-world data to generate hypotheses. It then tests these hypotheses in an attempt to derive theories—generalizations based on factual data—about the hows, whats, whos, whens, and whys of the world in which we humans live, including our origin and our past.

What follows in this book is an account of what the scientific method has told us so far about the origin and early history of the human species.

Study Questions

1. What are creation myths? How do the three myths described account for the origins of the cultures that tell those myths?
2. What is the scientific method? How does it differ from the use of myth in accounting for human origins and evolution?
3. How does science generate its hypotheses, and how does it test them? What do we mean by *theory* in science?
4. What is anthropology, and why is it described as a holistic study? What are the subfields of anthropology?

Key Terms

myth	deduction	anthropological
science	theory	linguistics
creation myth	anthropology	archaeology
evolution	species	physical (biological)
scientific method	holistic	anthropology
induction	cultural anthropology	paleoanthropologist
hypothesis	culture	primatologist

For More Information

The best book on the Yanomamö remains Napoleon A. Chagnon's *Yanomamö.* A useful summary of the archaeology and history of the Maya is *A Forest of Kings: The Untold Story of the Ancient Maya* by Linda Schele and David Freidel. There are many interpretations of the Bible story. A standard is G. A. Buttrick, ed., *Interpreter's Bible.* See also Isaac Asimov's *Asimov's Guide to the Bible* and John Romer's *Testament: The Bible and History.*

For more detailed discussions of scientific methodology, see *Science and Unreason* by Daisie Radner and Michael Radner and *Frauds, Myths, and Mysteries: Science and Pseudoscience in Archaeology,* Second Edition, by Kenneth L. Feder.

Features of the landscape, like the eroded spires of Bryce Canyon in Utah, were interpreted by some geologists as evidence of a young earth afflicted by natural cataclysms. Others saw such features as evidence of an ancient, uniformly changing planet. How did the modern scientific view of an ancient and changing earth arise? How did scientists in the centuries before our own view the place of humanity in their chronological schemes? *(K. L. Feder)*

2

Eden Questioned
Historical Perspectives

—m—

So much of what is now known about the past was not known just a few hundred years ago. For most Europeans in prior centuries, the biblical framework of history—including the Judeo-Christian creation myth discussed in Chapter 1—was the only acceptable way of looking at the past. The stories of the six-day creation, the garden of Eden, Adam and Eve, and Noah's flood were all regarded as genuine history. These stories clearly defined and constrained Western understanding of the past.

In the same way that the Maya and the Yąnomamö looked to their myths and legends for information about their worlds, Europeans invoked the Bible as the ultimate source of knowledge, even concerning specific questions of earth history. For example, many Europeans were curious about the actual age of the world. Based on an interpretation of the Bible, in past centuries it was commonly believed that the earth was less than 6000 years old. When in the play *As You Like It* William Shakespeare had his heroine Rosalind state, "This poor world is almost six thousand years old," he was repeating what had become a generally held opinion when the play was written in the 1590s.

The best known seventeenth-century attempt to determine the precise age of the earth was that of Archbishop James Ussher, an Irish cleric. In 1650, through reference to biblical detail, astronomical cycles, and historical records, and after not just a few interpretive leaps, the archbishop determined that the world was created in the year 4004 B.C. "upon the entrance of the night preceding the twenty-third day of October" (from Archbishop Ussher's *Annales* as cited in Brice 1982:18). Ussher's calculation was widely accepted, and this date was printed in the margins of many English language Bibles beginning in 1701.

Although Ussher was wrong, he was not as irrational as some modern writers suggest. After all, he arrived at his figure by careful calculation; there was no claim of divine revelation. His result derived from simple math and historical analysis, although it was based in part on a literal interpretation of the Bible.

Some Europeans and Americans of the seventeenth, eighteenth, and nineteenth centuries, though still believing in God, began to seek enlightenment about the world around them from a source other than the Bible—that is, from nature itself (Greene 1959). Calling themselves *natural scientists* or *natural philosophers,* they began a vigorous exploration of various natural sources of information about the earth and the heavens. In 1691, the natural scientist and theologian Reverend John Ray expressed the view of many scientists in the title of his book; the proper role of science was to reveal *The Wisdom of God Manifested in the Works of the Creation.*

Uniformitarianism: The Contribution from Geology

Many of these early natural scientists accepted Ussher's claim of a recent divine creation, but when they looked directly at nature they saw evidence for extensive physical change in the earth itself. The new science of geology described natural features that clearly indicated the earth had undergone vast amounts of change in its appearance. How, then, to reconcile this evidence with the accepted biblical interpretation that the earth was created in its then-present form less than 6000 years before?

The answer for some thinkers was to view the earth's appearance as the result of a series of natural catastrophes. Noah's flood was seen as the latest—and maybe the most catastrophic—of these occurrences, but not the only one. Many natural scientists believed that these catastrophes—floods, earthquakes, volcanic eruptions, operating not just locally but on a global scale as well—accounted for the diverse layers of rock and other evidence of substantial change that they had observed. Those who adhered to this general interpretation were called, appropriately enough, **catastrophists.**

Opponents to this view emerged. Geology was developing as an empirical science in which hypotheses proposed for explaining the condition of the earth were based on observation, but global catastrophes of the size and impact necessary to support the catastrophist view had never been observed or recorded. Instead, geologists observed mostly slow-acting, steady processes of change. Some interpreted this to mean that these slow-acting processes, not planet-wide cataclysms, had produced the present appearance of the earth. For example, Reverend Thomas Burnet, writing in 1681, suggested that the condition of the earth could best be explained, and its age determined, by reference to ordinary, slow-acting, noncatastrophic natural processes of erosion by ice, wind, and water. Still, he concluded, the world was very young. He argued that if the earth had been ancient, erosion would already have worn away even the tallest mountains. Burnet was unaware that mountain building was still taking place, but he was on the right track by looking strictly at natural phenomena even if his conclusion of a young earth was incorrect.

Robert Hooke, another seventeenth-century English scientist, was fascinated by fossils (Figure 2.1, p. 18). Whereas others contended that fossils were mere tricks of nature, Hooke correctly interpreted them as the remains of animals and plants that no longer existed. He contended that organisms became extinct because the earth was always changing. These changes were only partly a result, he said, of Noah's flood; they were also caused by long-term phenomena—ordinary occurrences such as erosion that went on all the time in nature.

Hooke was more correct than he knew. The geological and biological records are indeed the results of slow, ordinary, long-term phenomena *and* catastrophic events. For example, the extinction of the dinosaurs 65 million years ago appears to have been initiated by the impact of an asteroid with the earth, which radically altered the planet's climate. One difference between the modern understanding of such events and the catastrophism of the seventeenth and eighteenth centuries lies in the early thinkers' assumptions that these catastrophes had a divine origin and that all of the earth's features were the result of a regular *series* of catastrophic events.

Like Burnet, however, Hooke also believed that the earth was quite young. He was confused by the fact that ancient histories, such as those of Egypt and China, did not contain descriptions of fossilization actually taking

catastrophist An adherent of the idea that the world was changed over time by a series of catastrophic events.

FIGURE 2.1   Early depiction of fossil hunters recovering ancient animal remains in a cave. The seventeenth-century natural scientist Robert Hooke was one of the first to recognize that fossils were the remains of extinct plants and animals. *(From Buckland 1823)*

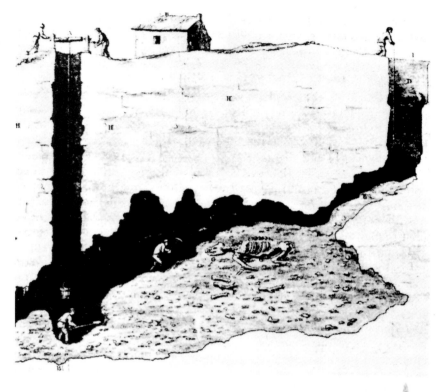

place. He failed to realize that even the most ancient of human histories were far too recent to have borne witness to that process.

By the late eighteenth century, however, some scientists began doing what had heretofore been inconceivable—actually calling into question the historical accuracy of the Genesis account. In 1774, the first volume of *A Natural History*, by the French scholar Georges Buffon, was published. In this work, a perspective called **uniformitarianism** was articulated. In essence, Buffon stated that in trying to explain the present appearance of the earth and to determine its age,

> We ought not to be affected by causes which seldom act and whose action is always sudden and violent. These have no place in the ordinary course of nature. But operations *uniformly* repeated, motions which succeed one another without interruption, are the causes which alone ought to be the foundation of our reasoning [emphasis ours]. (as cited in Greene 1959:55)

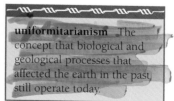

uniformitarianism The concept that biological and geological processes that affected the earth in the past still operate today.

What Buffon was saying was simple and straightforward: To learn about the earth, study the earth. The world looks the way it does because of known, natural, observable processes, not because of catastrophic events that no one has ever witnessed. Rivers cut channels, wind and rain wear away mountains, and waves bite into the shore. These simple, every-day processes can be observed all around. Given enough time—far more time than Ussher, Burnet, or Hooke had reckoned—rivers could eventually create vast canyons, tall mountains could be worn away leaving flat plains, and coasts could be entirely redrawn.

The implications of Buffon's work were not entirely lost on those who still maintained that the world, exactly as it presently appeared, was the very recent creation of God. In fact, as pressure mounted on Buffon, by the fourth volume of *A Natural History* he felt obliged to retract just about everything he had said about the age of the earth in the first three volumes. Twenty-five years later, however, in *Epochs of Nature,* Buffon tried to accommodate the biblical story of Genesis with his uniformitarian perspective. He suggested that the world was indeed ancient and that earth's history could be divided into six distinct epochs. Although he estimated the duration of each epoch in thousands of years, the six epochs clearly echoed the six days of creation in the Bible.

Perhaps the most important eighteenth-century work on the uniformitarian approach was that of the Scottish geologist James Hutton. In *Theory of the Earth* (1788), Hutton explicitly advanced the notion that by studying natural, slowly working, repetitive processes—that is, uniform, natural processes such as erosion and weathering—we could explain the earth's geology and geography. Again, the key element was time. Given enough time—counted in at least hundreds of thousands of years, not merely thousands—the present appearance of the earth could be understood and explained.

According to Hutton, God had created the earth as a self-regulating system. The slow erosion of mountains produced the soil in which plants could grow, which, in turn, could feed animals and humans, for whom it was all created (Figure 2.2, p. 20). The pressure of this soil on the surface of the earth would, over a long period of time, push up more mountains, ultimately providing new sources of soil on which more plants could grow, and so on. Hutton presented uniformitarianism in a way that made it appear even more to glorify the creator who had produced such a clever, self-sustaining system for the benefit of his crown of creation, humans. For such a system to work, a 6000-year time span was simply insufficient, which is why Hutton suggested that the earth was at least hundreds of thousands of years old. Even this radical suggestion, however, greatly underestimated the actual age of the earth.

The English geologist Charles Lyell was, perhaps, the most eloquent nineteenth-century advocate for the uniformitarian perspective. It was Lyell who uttered the memorable statement, "The present is the key to the past." In other words, the key to understanding the past rests in the study of "causes now in operation": those geological processes that can be observed in the present. By examining geological data, Lyell could estimate the age of specific features of the earth. For example, because the present

FIGURE 2.2 Bryce Canyon in southern Utah reflects some of the processes of erosion that eighteenth-century natural scientist James Hutton recognized. (*K. L. Feder*)

rate of deposition of silt at the mouth of the Mississippi River (Figure 2.3) can be measured and because the total size of the existing deposit in the Mississippi Delta can be estimated, the amount of time required for the delta to be formed can be approximated, assuming a uniform rate of deposition. Lyell's figure was about 100,000 years (1873:44–47). (The current delta is actually not that old; deposition rates are not as constant as Lyell thought, nor were available measuring techniques precise enough.)

Many people were shocked at the time spans proposed by Hutton and Lyell. Their work was attacked, partly on scientific grounds, but largely on the basis that it contradicted the accepted interpretation of Genesis. Then, early in the nineteenth century, a respected English cleric, Reverend Thomas Chalmers, accepted Hutton's work on the principle of uniformitarianism, proclaiming, "The writings of Moses do not fix the antiquity of the globe" (Howard 1975:69). Many other scientists followed suit and, eventually, almost all viewed the hypothesis of an ancient earth as contradicting only Archbishop Ussher, not the Bible itself. The work of Buffon and especially Hutton and Lyell had opened the door for the concept of an old earth—an earth that had existed long enough for the slow erosion of mountains, the cutting of great canyons, the changing of animal species, and even, perhaps, the evolution of humanity.

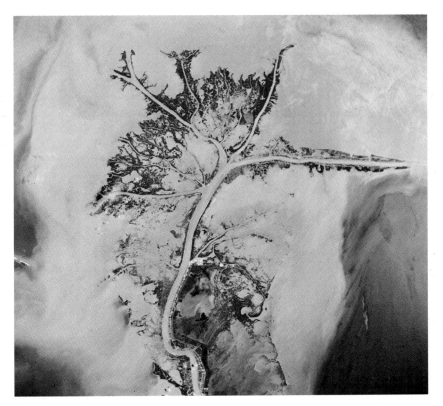

FIGURE 2.3   Aerial view of the Mississippi Delta. By estimating the amount of material deposited in the delta, nineteenth-century geologist Charles Lyell concluded that the delta was 100,000 years old. (*Courtesy NASA*)

Natural Selection: The Contribution from Biology

It was shocking enough for people of the late eighteenth and early nineteenth centuries to realize that the earth on which they lived had undergone significant change. At the same time, they learned that the earth was far older than 6000 years and that the vast changes recorded in the geological record were the result not of a series of supernatural catastrophes but of mostly rather mundane, everyday processes. What may have been most shocking, however, was another implication of these ideas: Life on earth, including human life, may also have undergone change.

Despite the mounting geological evidence for a changing earth, some biologists still denied the possibility of biological change. Like some geologists, however, many were willing to go beyond the Bible and into nature to seek support for divine creation. They sought to glorify creation by studying it. Perhaps the most famous was the Swedish botanist, Karl von Linné (1707–1778), better known to us by his Latinized name, Carolus Linnaeus.

Linnaeus was a strict **creationist**; he believed the world and all its inhabitants had been divinely created all at once and had undergone no change (or perhaps only limited change) since the creation. But he also observed that living things resembled or differed from one another to varying degrees. A bear and a deer, for example, have far more features in common (they are warm-blooded, give birth to live offspring, suckle their young) than either has with an earthworm. There was, Linnaeus felt, a system to God's creative works, and he set out to describe it scientifically.

Linnaeus looked at the varying degrees of similarity and difference among organisms, a process today called **comparative biology.** Based on these comparisons, he devised a system of categories and names that identified living things and indicated their physical similarities as he felt God had planned them. Linnaeus's system of classification—a **taxonomy**—was published in final form in 1758. Scientists still use his system today, and we'll show you how it works in Chapter 5.

Although Linnaeus thought he was describing a static, unchanging world of living things, he was actually setting the stage for a more complex interpretation. The similarities and differences Linnaeus recorded might reflect not simultaneous creation but a series of biological relationships. That is, the reason bears and deer are similar in certain ways is that they are biologically related, having once had an ancestor in common—much as you and your cousin are related in that you share the same set of grandparents. In other words, one could infer from Linnaeus's descriptions that life on earth had indeed undergone change—and many people were beginning to infer just that.

The hard evidence of the fossil record finally made the study of living things completely "natural." Robert Hooke and others had recognized that some fossils represented the remains of creatures that no longer existed (Figure 2.4). Clearly, this showed that life in general was anything but static. Other fossils showed that particular kinds of creatures had undergone change over time; modern elephants did not look exactly like the ancient, extinct elephants as indicated by their fossil bones.

Moreover, fossils were often found in identifiable layers of rock and soil. Scientists call these layers **strata** (singular, **stratum**) and their study **stratigraphy.** The strata indicate a sequence of geological events, the deeper strata representing older events and those closer to the surface more recent ones (Figure 2.5). Thus, the fossils embedded within the strata reflected a history of life on earth.

As with geological change, the rapidly mounting evidence for biological change quickly became irrefutable, and by the late 1700s the idea had been fairly well accepted within the scientific community and by much of the educated public. The big question, as the 1800s began, was not if change had occurred, but how.

Even in their attempts to answer this question, some investigators still tried to include an aspect of stability. If living things themselves could not

creationist One who believes that a supernatural power was responsible for the origin of the universe, the earth, and living things.

comparative biology The study of the similarities and differences among plants and animals.

taxonomy A systematic classification based on similarities and differences.

strata (singular, **stratum**) Layers of different rock and soil types.

stratigraphy The arrangement of rocks and soil in sequential layers.

FIGURE 2.4 The discovery of the fossils of extinct animals showed natural scientists of the seventeenth and eighteenth centuries that life on earth was not static but changing. These dinosaur bones are from Dinosaur National Monument on the Utah–Colorado border. (*K. L. Feder*)

FIGURE 2.5 The stratigraphic layers exposed by the Green River in Dinosaur National Monument represent millions of years of deposition and erosion. (*K. L. Feder*)

be stable and unchanging, they seemed to think, at least the process that brought change about could be stable, dependable, and predictable. One of the first popular proposals for a regular mechanism of biological change was made by Jean-Baptiste de Lamarck (1744–1829).

Lamarck, who coined the term *biology,* was a French naturalist. In the early years of the nineteenth century, he proposed an explanation for how and why plants and animals had changed—in modern terms, how they had evolved. One part of his idea was absolutely correct; the other two parts were wrong. He correctly recognized that organisms and their environments have an intimate and dynamic relationship: Plants and animals are **adapted** to their environments, that is, they possess physical characteristics and patterns of behavior that help them survive under a given set of natural circumstances. When environments change (as the geological record shows they continually do), organisms must alter their adaptive characteristics if they are to survive.

Lamarck went astray, however, in his overall concept of the direction of evolution and in the specific mechanism he proposed for it. He believed that evolution was **progressive,** causing organisms to become increasingly complex and thus more perfect. It followed from this that no organisms would become extinct; creatures represented only by fossils were simply creatures that had undergone so much change they existed today in unrecognizably different forms. Of course, if all organisms were evolving to become more complex, you might logically ask why very simple organisms still exist. Lamarck would have answered by saying—against a great deal of evidence to the contrary—that new, and therefore simple, living things were always being naturally created.

Progressive evolution is really the heart of Lamarck's idea, but it is not what he is remembered for. His name has come to represent the second erroneous part of his evolutionary concept, his mechanism for change. Lamarck supported an idea that had been around for some time called the **inheritance of acquired characteristics.** His own words in *Philosophie Zoologique* (1809) describe this theory best:

> When the will guides an animal to any action, the organs which have to carry out that action are immediately stimulated to it by the influx of subtle fluids. . . . Hence it follows that numerous repetitions of these organized activities strengthen, stretch, develop and even create the organs necessary to them. . . . Now every change that is wrought in an organ through habit of frequently using it, is subsequently preserved by reproduction. . . . Such a change is thus handed on to all succeeding individuals in the same environment, without their having to acquire it in the same way that it was actually created. (as cited in Harris 1981:116–17)

When the environment changes, said Lamarck, organisms perceive the change and use, cease using, or even create the organs necessary to alter their adaptation. The effects of this use or disuse, or the new organ, are automatically passed on to succeeding generations (Figure 2.6).

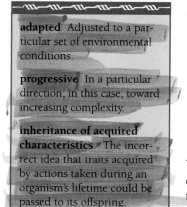

adapted Adjusted to a particular set of environmental conditions.

progressive In a particular direction; in this case, toward increasing complexity.

inheritance of acquired characteristics The incorrect idea that traits acquired by actions taken during an organism's lifetime could be passed to its offspring.

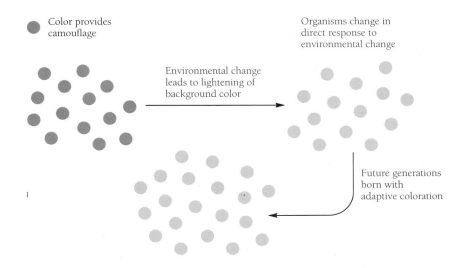

Color provides camouflage

Environmental change leads to lightening of background color

Organisms change in direct response to environmental change

Future generations born with adaptive coloration

FIGURE 2.6   Schematic diagram of Lamarckian evolution. (Compare with Figure 4.6.)

Lamarck's scheme doesn't work, of course. Traits acquired during one's lifetime cannot be inherited by one's offspring. A bodybuilder's children will not be born with bulging muscles. Furthermore, how can simple creatures or plants have some sort of will that allows them to know which organs to use and which not to use, or even to create new organs? How can a butterfly will itself to change color? How can a sightless creature sense the need for eyes and then develop them? These were the very sorts of objections many people voiced during Lamarck's time.

The hypothesis, though, maintained some popularity. First, nobody had come up with anything better. Second, it was a comfortable idea that if organisms were going to change, at least they were changing progressively and had some direct control over the process. Indeed, the supposed evolutionary impact of the use (or disuse) of particular muscles or organs and the inheritance of acquired characteristics seem to keep popping up in the history of evolutionary thought.

The scientific objections remained, however, and so the search was still on to explain why and how living things evolved. Enter Englishmen Charles Darwin and Alfred Russel Wallace. The story of these two scientists is fascinating in itself. (Consult the sources at the end of the chapter for a fuller account.) For our purposes, suffice it to say that Darwin (1809–1882) and Wallace (1823–1913), as a result of separate worldwide travels, observations, and readings, independently became aware of two important facts that had seemingly been overlooked by their predecessors.

First, both noticed that individual organisms within a species exhibit variation. Not every member of a species looks like every other member. Just look around your classroom. If Lamarck's idea were correct, you would expect very little variation because all members of a species would have used, not used, or created the same characteristics.

Second, both men expanded the inference from Linnaeus that similarities and differences among organisms represent biological relationships resulting from their descent from previous organisms. Species, they concluded, descend from other species, as members of your family descend from earlier members. Darwin and Wallace pictured life on earth as a gigantic and complex family tree.

Given these assumptions, how did Darwin and Wallace think evolution actually worked? Their theory, developed independently by each man, is known by the name Darwin gave it: **natural selection.** Like Lamarck's concept, natural selection is based on the premise that organisms are adapted to their environments and undergo adaptive change when the environments change. But the theory differs from Lamarck's in its explanation of the nature and source of variation.

The theory of inheritance of acquired characteristics requires variation to arise *when it is needed.* The theory of natural selection, on the other hand, requires that variation *already* exists (Figure 2.7). Neither Darwin nor Wallace understood why variation existed within species because the nature of the genetic code had yet to be discovered, but they realized that this variation was important. Nature "selects" from the existing variation within a species in the sense that those individuals who, by chance, are best adapted to environmental conditions are the most reproductively successful—produce the most offspring who survive—and so pass on their adaptive traits to more offspring. As a result, the most adaptive traits of a species tend to increase in frequency within the species; the less adaptive traits tend to decrease.

It follows that evolution has no particular direction. Organisms do not all evolve into more complex forms, as Lamarck had suggested, or into bigger or smarter ones. Rather, populations of organisms evolve to become better adapted, or at least to stay adapted, to their environments. There is no overriding principle of progression. Further, the variation from which nature selects is random, not willed by the organism.

It follows that if populations from one species are geographically separated, the separate populations, in their different environments, will face different selective pressures. Because changes are selected for and accumulate through time, the populations may eventually become so different that they constitute separate species—that is, they will not be able to interbreed and produce fertile offspring. Thus, not only can a single species change through time as a result of environmental change, but it can also generate new species. This thinking is reflected in the title of Darwin's most famous book, published in 1859, *On the Origin of Species by Means of Natural Selection.*

Finally, it must be understood that such a process, using random variation as its raw material, can't always ensure that species successfully adapt. Sometimes there is simply no variation available that is adapted to

natural selection Evolution based on relative reproductive success of individuals within a species due to the individual's adaptive fitness.

FIGURE 2.7 Variation within a population represents the raw material for natural selection. The tiger swallowtail butterflies (*upper right* and *bottom*) are members of the same species. The dark one is a mimic of the pipe-vine butterfly (*left*) that is protected from predation by its foul taste. (*Robert F. Sisson, © National Geographic Society*)

a particularly extensive or rapid environmental change. In such a case, a species becomes extinct. This, in fact, is the norm. Perhaps more than nine-tenths of all species that have ever existed are now extinct.

Wallace, younger and brasher than Darwin, was willing to go public with his new idea right away. But Darwin, who actually thought of natural selection some twenty years before Wallace, kept the idea a secret from all but his closest colleagues; even his wife didn't know about it. Darwin was finally talked into publishing by his friends only after Wallace had made his version known. Why had he kept quiet for so long?

Darwin's delay was not—as popular opinion has it—because he feared public reaction to his support of the *idea* of evolution. That concept had been accepted for some time. Rather, Darwin was afraid that his *mechanism* for evolution, as confident as he was about it, was everything that Lamarck's was not and so would not be well received. Natural selection was not progressive, it did not involve the organism's conscious control, and it freely acknowledged extinction. And Darwin, a recluse who suffered poor physical and mental health and feared any sort of unpleasantness or controversy, may have been wise to delay. The world may not have accepted natural selection when he first came up with the theory, around 1836. As the second half of the century began, however—a period marked by rapid and extensive social, political, technological, and economic change—the Western world was ready. The first printing of Darwin's book sold out in a single day and was, for the most part, hailed as a major scientific break-through. One scientist of the time is said to have remarked, "How stupid of me not to have thought of that!"

In this way, the scientific revolution brought about by the work of geologists and biologists, put together so well by Charles Darwin, altered forever the scientific view of the past. The past was now seen as a series of events, often caused initially by random change, that were linked to each other through time and linked to the present by uniformitarian processes. This new concept even changed the view of human behavior.

Cultural Evolution: The Contribution from Anthropology

The Discovery of "New" People

Darwin and Wallace focused on variation in plants and animals, but what about a concept taken for granted today—variation in people and their cultures? We are aware that some people live in industrialized, technologically complex societies while others live in societies of farmers who plow their fields with oxen. Still others (at least until fairly recently) relied on hunting animals and gathering wild plants for their subsistence. Most of us realize that different cultures representing different ways of life coexist in the modern world.

Before the Renaissance and the Age of Exploration, however, Europeans were unaware of the diversity of the world's cultures. They knew only a few cultures beyond their own—the Arabs to the south, for example, and the Mongols to the east whom Marco Polo described in the thirteenth century. Most of the peoples living in Africa and Asia were unknown to Europeans. On maps before the sixteenth century, these areas are labeled *terra incognita*—literally, "unknown land" (Figure 2.8). The Americas remained largely unexplored by Europeans until the sixteenth, seventeenth, and eighteenth centuries.

Europeans looked to the Bible to explain the existence of those other cultures of which they were aware. Remember, the Judeo-Christian creation myth was accepted as a factual account of human history. Adam and Eve, the first people, were the ancestors of all human beings. After their eviction from the garden of Eden, their direct descendants spread across the land. These people were simple, hard-working farmers, but eventually they strayed from the righteous life and were destroyed by God in a great flood. Only Noah, his family, and the animals aboard the ark were saved from destruction. It was the view of most Europeans in these centuries that all living animals could be traced to those saved on board the ark and all living people could be traced to one of Noah's three sons. Sometime after Noah's flood and the dispersal of Noah's sons and their families, the Bible maintains, God became angry at a group of people attempting to build a great tower, the Tower

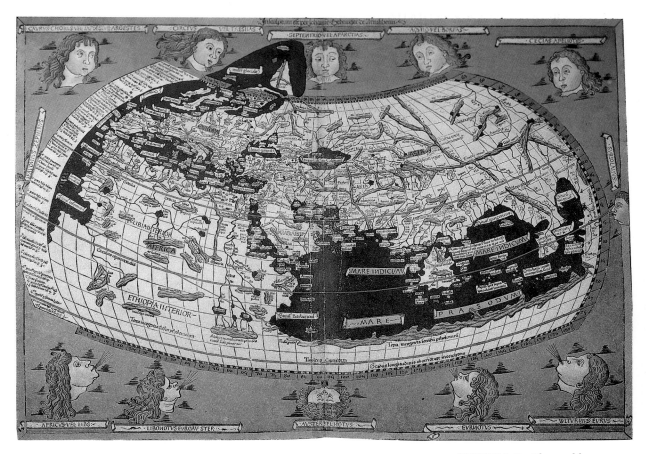

FIGURE 2.8 The world as perceived by Europeans in the fifteenth century. This popular map of the world is from the second-century geographer Ptolemy's *Geography*. Much of Africa is labeled *terra incognita*, literally "unknown land." (© *The Granger Collection, New York*)

of Babel, up to heaven. He caused them all to speak in different languages, ruining their plans by destroying their ability to communicate.

This is how the Bible accounts for the origin of language differences and, by inference, the origin of separate cultures. The European interpretation of subsequent history is derived from this biblical framework. The Egyptians, the Greeks, and others were each seen as having originated at Babel. Within this framework, human history was fairly neat and simple; it conformed to the Bible and could be accommodated within a 6000-year-old universe.

Imagine the Europeans' surprise when early explorers brought home stories of previously unknown peoples—peoples not mentioned in the Bible. They didn't look like Europeans, and some lived very differently. For example, Portuguese sailors who explored the coast of Africa encountered societies of dark-skinned people who knew nothing of the Bible. Looking for a route to the East Indies, Christopher Columbus sailed west and instead came upon an unknown world with unimagined cultures and peoples, none of which were described in the Bible (Figure 2.9, p. 30). These new peoples and their cultures simply did not fit neatly into the accepted biblical chronology of human societies.

29

FIGURE 2.9 A seventeenth-century Spanish version of a 1594 engraving (by de Bry) depicting Columbus's first contact with natives of the New World. (© *The Granger Collection, New York*)

Many European thinkers were perplexed by these discoveries. Initially, they assumed that the newly encountered peoples of Asia and Africa were descendants of Noah's sons, Shem and Ham. (Europeans were supposed to be the descendants of the third son, Japheth.) The so-called simpler cultures of Africans and Asians were explained as the result of intellectual degeneration of the descendants of Noah's less worthy offspring.

Unfortunately, this neat arrangement left no ancestor for the native peoples of the New World, a circumstance that gave rise to a tremendous amount of speculation about who, exactly, the Native Americans were and how they fit into the biblical chronology (Feder 1996; Williams 1991). Practically every European and Asian culture was proposed, at one time or another, as having given rise to Native Americans sometime after Noah's flood (Huddleston 1967). One idea was that a group of sailors or fishermen—perhaps Greeks, maybe "Hindoos," possibly even Norwegians—was lost at sea long ago, fortuitously washed up on the American shore, and established a population. Over the years they changed in appearance, forgot their religion, and became the Indians that Columbus encountered. For a while it was also popular to believe that American Indians were the Lost Tribes of Israel—groups of biblical Hebrews historically unaccounted for. Even the mythical lost continent of Atlantis was suggested as a source of American Indian culture. Europeans were indeed having a hard time trying to make an ever-expanding world fit within their creation myth.

The Discovery of Mysterious Artifacts

While some Europeans were exploring unknown lands and encountering unknown cultures, others were examining the soil beneath their own feet and discovering some rather strange looking stone objects. Though the symmetry, sharp edges, and beauty of these flaked pieces implied that they had been manufactured by human beings, most writers denied the possibility that these objects represented human craftsmanship.

This interpretation was firmly rooted in biblical literalism. The Bible did not mention the existence of a primitive stage of human development, certainly not one in which people made tools of stone and knew nothing of metal. In fact, reference is made in Genesis to a seventh-generation descendant of Adam, named Tubalcain (a brother or half-brother of Noah), as the "instructor of every artificer in brass and iron" (Genesis 4:22). With metallurgy traceable to this early a time in biblical history, there seemed no reason to believe that there had been a historical period when human beings relied on stone tools. Many thinkers in the seventeenth, eighteenth, and nineteenth centuries concluded that these toollike objects of stone must have been tricks of nature. (Remember that fossils were also explained this way by those seeking to deny the earth's antiquity.) Some suggested that such objects were the handiwork of fairies and elves while others declared them to be the natural result of lightning striking the ground. Still others did accept the objects as made by humans; they believed, however, that the makers of such simple stone tools must have been some degraded form of humanity that existed just before Noah's flood, but after Tubalcain's invention of metallurgy.

The Evolutionary Explanation

At the same time, other thinkers challenged these Bible-based interpretations. Some thinkers in the seventeenth century—for example, the French naturalist Isaac de la Peyrère—explicitly suggested that finely worked stone objects found deep in the earth must have been the result of ancient human manufacture. In the late eighteenth century, a young Englishman, John Frere, published a short note in the journal of the London Society of Antiquaries recounting his discovery of finely chipped stone axes at a great depth in a quarry in Hoxne, England (Figure 2.10, p. 32). These tools were found beneath the bones of extinct animals, suggesting great antiquity for the period of their manufacture "by a people who had not the use of metals" (Frere 1800:204).

In *The Geological Evidences of the Antiquity of Man,* first published in 1863, Charles Lyell, the ardent uniformitarianist met earlier, presented de-

FIGURE 2.10 Woodcut of one of the hand axes discovered in Hoxne and reported on by John Frere to the London Society of Antiquaries in 1797 (and first published in 1800). The hand-axes from Hoxne were important because, perhaps for the first time, such artifacts had been found in stratigraphic position, deeply buried in the soil, and in association with the bones of extinct animals. All this implied a great age for these specimens—and for the humans who had manufactured them. (*The Society of Antiquaries of London*)

tailed evidence for the association of some stone tools with the fossilized bones of extinct animals and even humans.

> For the last half-century, the occasional occurrence, in various parts of Europe, of the bones of Man or the work of his hands, in cave-breccias and stalagmites, associated with the remains of the extinct hyaena, bear, elephant, or rhinoceros, has given rise to a suspicion that the date of Man must be carried further back than we had heretofore imagined. (1873:1–2)

The discovery of stone tools at great depth and in direct association with the bones of extinct animals strongly supported the argument for the great antiquity of these artifacts (Grayson 1983; Van Riper 1993).

A "Stone Age"

De la Peyrère, Frere, Lyell, the French customs official turned scientist Jacques Boucher de Perthes, and others agreed that chipped-stone artifacts were the handiwork of people living in more primitive ways in the distant past. Some thinkers went on to propose that such tools were direct evidence of a previous and primitive stage of universal human **cultural evolution**—a stone age through which all people, including Europeans, had passed.

Evidence of previous stages of human cultural development mounted as more and more ancient artifacts were unearthed. The evidence became so compelling that in 1836, Christian Jurgensen Thomsen of the Danish National Museum in Copenhagen produced a guidebook describing the museum's collection of artifacts in which he organized the museum's collection into three such prehistoric ages—stone, bronze, and iron. Inherent in Thomsen's three-age system was the notion that human culture had changed through time in a patterned and comprehensible way. Thomsen's ages were thought to reflect increasing technological sophistication through time, a progression of better tools made from increasingly difficult-to-work raw materials.

Others applied the notion of cultural evolution even more broadly. Anthropologist Edward Burnett Tylor, in his book *Primitive Culture* (1871), argued that the persistence of primitive—that is, less technologically complex—societies into the nineteenth century could be explained in one of two ways. Either culture was created more or less as is and primitive societies represent degeneration; or modern civilization developed over a very long period of time from an initial state of "barbarism" and modern primitives, for whatever reason, were still living in a stage of development that the rest of humanity had long ago left behind. For the former theory, Tylor concluded that there was absolutely no evidence. He championed the latter and became one of the first cultural evolutionists.

Lewis Henry Morgan, an American anthropologist and cultural evolutionist, followed Tylor's idea and suggested, in *Ancient Society* (1877), that all cultures change through time, evolving through stages of "savagery," "barbarism," and "civilization." Cultures could get stuck at a particular level if certain key inventions and advances were not made—the bow and arrow, the domestication of plants and animals, the smelting of iron. Modern primitives were such frozen societies.

Tylor and Morgan's schemes of cultural evolution were **unilinear.** Their view was that all cultures eventually pass through the same fixed stages of increasing technological complexity. Modern anthropologists no longer accept such simplistic schemes, viewing cultural evolution as **multilinear,** with different cultures passing through different possible sequences of change. Nevertheless, Tylor and Morgan are important early theorists because they recognized that human beings and their cultures have undergone great change, just as plants and animals have done. They showed that cultures have evolved and that processes of cultural change can be identified and understood.

Evidence for the great age of and change within humanity was mounting in the newly developing field of anthropology. As with geology and biology, the interpretation of the anthropological evidence virtually required that both the earth itself and the human race were ancient and always changing. Science was supplying enormous amounts of new data about human history and the world. And these data simply could no longer be contained within a 6000-year-old, static universe (Figure 2.11).

cultural evolution Changes in cultural patterns through time.

unilinear The now-discredited notion that all cultures pass through the same sequence of change.

multilinear The accepted notion that different cultures pass through any one of a number of possible sequences of change.

FIGURE 2.11   Timeline showing the chronology of key thinkers and events in the intellectual history of research into the age of the earth and the evolution of life on the planet.

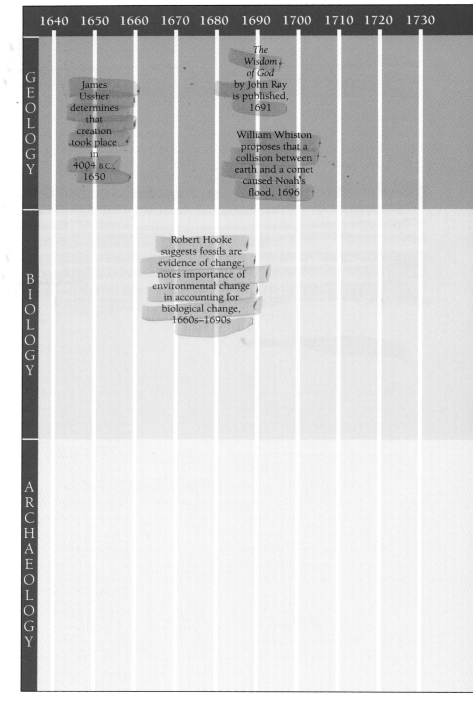

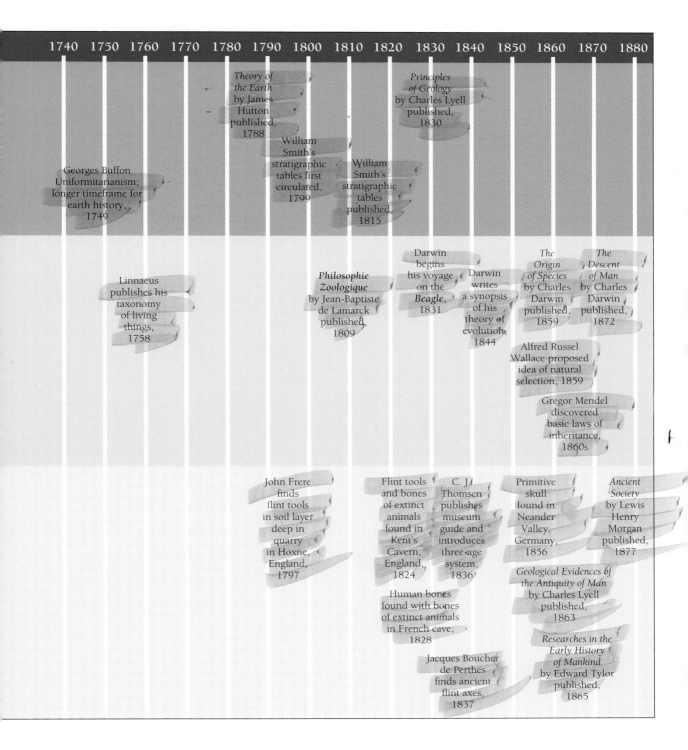

1740 1750 1760 1770 1780 1790 1800 1810 1820 1830 1840 1850 1860 1870 1880

Theory of the Earth by James Hutton published, 1788

Principles of Geology by Charles Lyell published, 1830

William Smith's stratigraphic tables first circulated, 1799

William Smith's stratigraphic tables published, 1815

Georges Buffon Uniformitarianism; longer timeframe for earth history, 1749

Linnaeus publishes his taxonomy of living things, 1758

Philosophie Zoologique by Jean-Baptiste de Lamarck published, 1809

Darwin begins his voyage on the *Beagle*, 1831

Darwin writes a synopsis of his theory of evolution, 1844

The Origin of Species by Charles Darwin published, 1859

The Descent of Man by Charles Darwin published, 1872

Alfred Russel Wallace proposed idea of natural selection, 1859

Gregor Mendel discovered basic laws of inheritance, 1860s

John Frere finds flint tools in soil layer deep in quarry in Hoxne, England, 1797

Flint tools and bones of extinct animals found in Kent's Cavern, England, 1824

C. J. Thomsen publishes museum guide and introduces three-age system, 1836

Primitive skull found in Neander Valley, Germany, 1856

Ancient Society by Lewis Henry Morgan published, 1877

Human bones found with bones of extinct animals in French cave, 1828

Geological Evidences of the Antiquity of Man by Charles Lyell published, 1863

Jacques Boucher de Perthes finds ancient flint axes, 1837

Researches in the Early History of Mankind by Edward Tylor published, 1865

Contemporary Issue

Scientific Creationism: An Old Idea in a New Form

The belief that the universe and everything in it were created by a divine being did not die out when the theories of uniformitarianism and natural selection were developed. These theories took many years to gain acceptance, and even today many people continue to have faith that their god or gods had some hand in designing the world.

For most Westerners, no conflict exists between such a belief and the actual processes of earth history and evolution so laboriously learned and described by science. Most Jews and Christians, for example, simply believe that God created those processes along with everything else. But a sizable minority still holds that the Judeo-Christian creation myth is factual. Like most Europeans in previous centuries, they take the stories in Genesis literally.

Scientific knowledge involves a rational, logical attempt to understand the physical world. It is based on the scientific method described in the previous chapter. In honest science, this method of inquiry is continuous; no idea is ever accepted as proven for all time. Rather, it is tested, retested, refined, and changed as new evidence and new ideas accumulate. As the evolutionary scientist John Maynard Smith puts it, science tells us "what is possible" (1984:24). Or, in the words of Pope John Paul II (quoting Galileo), the function of science is to instruct us "how heaven is."

The other type of human knowledge consists of belief systems, which are not open to testing and experimentation. They are taken on faith, accepted as given. A belief in God, for instance, or a disbelief in God for that matter, simply cannot be subjected to the scientific method. What is the concrete evidence? How is it tested? What person, believing in a supreme deity, is going to change his or her mind in light of some scientifically derived theory about the physical world? What sort of rational thinking would convince someone that human life is not sacred? Rather than serving to describe the physical world,

belief systems function to tell people how to behave toward one another and toward that world. They also serve to define the meaning of life. They tell us, says John Maynard Smith, "what is desirable" (1984:24), and instruct us, say Galileo and Pope John Paul II, "how to *get* to heaven."

To the majority of people who hold them, religious beliefs usually fall into a category of knowledge that also includes ethical precepts, moral values, and philosophical tenets. There is no inherent conflict between this kind of knowledge and the kind labeled science. Indeed, the two usually live in harmony with each other.

In fact, these two spheres of knowledge—rather than being eternally in conflict with each other, as they are all too often seen—must interact harmoniously for any society to thrive and prosper. People require scientific knowledge, based on the scientific method, to tell them how to hunt animals, grow plants, make tools, and program computers. They also require rules of behavior, taken on faith, to ensure unity, cooperation, and harmony within societies. It is perhaps part of the human condition to wonder why we are here, and belief systems also help answer this sort of question. Again, science tells us what is possible; belief systems tell us what is desirable.

Sometimes, however, the harmonious interaction of these spheres of knowledge is broken when they are forced into conflict with one another—when science attempts to challenge a belief system or when a belief system claims its tenets are scientifically valid. The latter occurred in Tennessee in 1925, when a bill was passed in the state legislature that declared it illegal to teach, in a state-supported school, any theory that denied the biblical creation story and claimed humans were descended from some "lower order of animals." Initially, the bill was not taken seriously (except by its sponsor, of course), but the governor signed it as a demonstration of Christian faith. No one thought it would be enforced.

William Jennings Bryan *(right)* and Clarence Darrow at the Scopes trial. *(© AP/Wide World Photos)*

In Dayton, Tennessee, however, teacher John T. Scopes and some of the town leaders thought that a deliberate violation of this act would put their town on the map. While substitute teaching in a biology class, Scopes assigned a text section dealing with evolution and so was arrested and charged. Then things got out of hand. People came from all over the country to watch the trial, not so much because of the issue but because the attorney for the prosecution was William Jennings Bryan, fundamentalist speaker and failed presidential candidate, and the lawyer for the defense was Clarence Darrow, perhaps the best-known and most successful lawyer of his time.

(continued)

Contemporary Issue *(continued)*

The town of Dayton took on a circus atmosphere, though the trial itself turned out to be rather unspectacular and boring. Convicted and fined $100, Scopes later had his conviction overturned on a technicality. But the trial did feature a memorable and now-famous confrontation between Bryan and Darrow—which did not become part of the formal record. In an unprecedented move, Darrow put prosecutor Bryan on the stand and questioned him about his views on the literal truth of the Bible. During this exchange, which demonstrated the wit and oratorical skills of both men, the separate natures of science and religion became clear as Bryan was unable to support his interpretation of creation with anything other than faith. Here is a brief excerpt (Appleman 1970:543–44):

DARROW: [*asking about the accepted date of 4004 B.C. for the creation of the world*] Don't you know that the ancient civilizations of China are 6,000 or 7,000 years old, at the very least?

BRYAN: No; but they would not run back beyond the creation according to the Bible, 6,000 years.

DARROW: You don't know how old they are, is that right?

BRYAN: I don't know how old they are, but probably you do. I think you would give preference to anybody who opposed the Bible, and I give the preference to the Bible.

As this exchange became part of American folklore, the common interpretation was that science had "won." In fact, both science and religion suffered.

One result of the trial was to draw attention to a conflict that didn't necessarily exist. Shortly after the trial, the topic of evolution began to disappear from textbooks, where previously it had occupied a prominent place. It only reappeared after 1957, when the Soviet launching of the Sputnik satellite prompted the United States to reexamine the quality of its science education.

We might see the story of this trial (called the "monkey trial" because of the implications of Darwin's theory for our ancestry) as an amusing little bit of Americana but for its larger implications and present-day echoes. The issue the trial brought to the public's attention has lingered, and recently creationism has returned in a particularly complex and disturbing form.

Called **scientific creationism**, this latter-day notion has as its basic tenets (1) that real scientific evidence exists to support the biblical creation story, and (2) that no evidence exists to support evolutionary theory. The Bible, according to this view, is a scientific and historical document as well as a religious one. Moreover, it posits that if evolution can be shown to be false, then scientific creationism *must* be true.

As we have outlined briefly and will discuss in detail later, an enormous quantity of evidence supports the ideas of biological evolution. That is why these topics are part of mainstream science. Not one shred of scientific evidence supports scientific creationism.

One of the corollary ideas of the scientific creationists is that, as a science, creationism should be given equal time in schools alongside evolution as an equally viable scientific hypothesis. This argument has gained some support in the United States and in other countries. With a very basic national belief in religious freedom and tolerance, Americans are reluctant to deny people access to an idea with religious (especially Judeo-Christian) connections.

The fact is, though, that equal time is for equal things, and creationism is not the equivalent of evolution. Scientific creationism is based on one group's interpretation of the content and message of the Bible. It is a belief system and thus is not even open to scientific investigation. But some of the specific claims of scientific creationism *are* open to testing—and they have utterly failed these tests.

For example, believing that the world is a mere 6000 to 10,000 years old, some scientific creationists have attempted to prove that dinosaurs and human beings lived during the same period of earth history and even that Noah saved dinosaurs on board the ark (Morris 1980). They deny the simple fact of **biostratigraphy,** wherein fossils often appear in a regular sequence of ancient soil and rock layers, or strata, from old (deeper) to recent (higher). Paleontologists and paleoanthropologists know that dinosaur and human bones are never found in the same layers (see Chapter 7) because dinosaurs and the immediate evolutionary ancestors of humans are separated by at least 60 million years. Scientific creationists rationalize the separation in this way: Dinosaurs who drowned in Noah's flood didn't float as well as humans who died in the flood, so humans are found in higher geological layers.

In one of the few examples of actual field work they have conducted, creationists excavated a series of fossilized footprints along the Paluxey River in Texas. They claimed that dinosaur footprints and giant human footprints were found side by side in the same layer, implying that dinosaurs and people lived at the same time. The so-called human footprints have been shown conclusively to be misidentified dinosaur footprints (Kuban 1989a and 1989b).

In its attempt to attribute scientific and historical accuracy to the Bible, scientific creationism is no less than a clever and insidious device for injecting a partisan religious view into public education. In fact, teaching the two models side-by-side in science classes would contradict the principle of religious freedom, for it would mean that one group's religious ideas were being taught as scientific theory to individuals who hold other religious views or no religious views at all. Furthermore, it would undermine the whole idea of free scientific inquiry and intellectual honesty.

We will describe a great many scientific hypotheses and theories throughout this book. We have no vested interest in whether any specific idea proves to be true or false. As scientists, we believe that our only vested interest is in seeking and understanding the nature of the world—*whatever* that may be. The strides made by science toward that goal and the resulting benefits to our species are only possible in an atmosphere of free inquiry and harmonious interaction between science and belief systems.

Summary

Until a few hundred years ago, most European thinkers sought to interpret the nature of the world in the context of biblical history. The more they looked into nature itself, however, the more the biblical framework became supplanted by ideas derived from use of the scientific method—the inductive development of hypotheses to account for observed data and the deductive testing of these hypotheses to generate theories.

Science thus altered the European view of the world. Where the earth had been seen as young and unchanging, Europeans came to see the earth as ancient and undergoing virtually continual change. The work of natural scientists like James Hutton and Charles Lyell and their principle of uniformitarianism provided evidence for this ancient and changing earth. Where living things had been seen as the unaltered creations of a supreme being, species were now viewed as the ever-changing products of natural processes. The work of Alfred Wallace and Charles Darwin in the nineteenth century explained the mechanisms for these processes of change. Even humans themselves came to be seen as a topic for scientific investigation and as a species whose history stretched far into antiquity.

Study Questions

1. How did the study of the human past begin to move from the realm of belief systems to the realm of science?
2. What is uniformitarianism? How did it develop, and how did it contribute to our understanding of changes in the earth and its inhabitants?
3. What were the major ideas about how life on earth evolved? How does natural selection operate, and what does it imply about how life has changed?
4. How were new peoples, discovered during the Age of Exploration, first accounted for? How did the science of anthropology explain the observed variation in human cultural systems?
5. What is scientific creationism, and why is it considered a threat to both science education and religious freedom?

scientific creationism The belief that scientific evidence exists that supports the religious claim that the universe is the product of divine creation.

biostratigraphy The patterned appearance of plant and animal fossils in strata. The fossils of more ancient organisms are found in older, deeper strata, while those of more recent organisms are found in younger, generally higher strata.

Key Terms

catastrophist
uniformitarianism
creationist
comparative biology
taxonomy
strata

stratigraphy
adapted
progressive
inheritance of acquired
    characteristics
natural selection

cultural evolution
unilinear
multilinear
scientific creationism
biostratigraphy

For More Information

Perhaps the most famous book on the history of evolution, which still holds up over thirty years after its publication, is John C. Greene's *The Death of Adam: Evolution and Its Impact on Thought.* Another treatment of the same subject, using excerpts from original writings, is *Evolution: Genesis and Revelations,* edited and with comments by C. Leon Harris. A collection of writings by Charles Darwin and many of his contemporaries, predecessors, and successors is *Darwin,* edited by Philip Appleman. A biography of Darwin that focuses on the man as well as the scientist is John Bowlby's *Charles Darwin: A New Life.*

Finally, paleontologist and science historian Stephen Jay Gould has written a number of essays on the history of evolutionary thought, many aimed at reexamining old ideas on the subject. They can be found in his books *Ever Since Darwin, The Panda's Thumb, Hen's Teeth and Horse's Toes, The Flamingo's Smile, Bully for Brontosaurus, Eight Little Piggies,* and *Dinosaur in a Haystack.*

This gaseous pillar in the M16 nebula is an incubator of new stars. Our own sun may have formed in just such a structure. What do scientists know about the history of the universe and the development of life on our miniscule part of it? (*J. Hestor, P. Srowen, and NASA, courtesy Space Telescope Institute, Baltimore*)

3

Evolution

An Overview

—◊—

In the remainder of this book, we'll be painting a picture of human antiquity. Our palette will be the methods of inquiry and investigation called science; some of these methods were described in Chapter 1. Our paints will be the hypotheses, theories, and facts that science has provided. The canvas we paint on will be the dimension of time.

Time can often be a problem for those who seek to learn about the past, who must deal with vast quantities of it. It is easy to conceive of a day, a week, a month, even a year. By stretching the imagination, it is possible to get a feel for the span of time that makes up an individual life. But it becomes increasingly difficult to imagine the time involved in the last few generations, or in the history of the United States, or the period of time since the ancient Egyptians built the pyramids more than 4000 years ago.

It gets even more difficult when thinking about the time since the invention of writing, since the beginnings of modern humans, and since the dawn of our evolutionary line. And it becomes a monumental task to conceive of the vistas of time back to the dinosaurs, to the first land animals, to the beginning of life on earth, and to the very origin of the universe.

But it's vital for someone interested in human antiquity to acquire a concept of the time involved in humans' tenure on earth and to appreciate just where that time fits into the broader scheme of events that makes up earth history. It's essential to understand that all the processes of evolution apply to all forms of life on earth and that the idea of evolution—systematic change through time—applies to the whole history of the universe.

In the chapters that follow, we'll present many details about human evolution. It's difficult, we think, to develop a concept of time working from the specific to the general; so, in this chapter we'll provide a brief narrative outline of evolutionary history, focusing on human evolution. Then, as you read about the detailed evidence and ideas, you'll have a context—of time and basic events—in which to place those details.

Big Bang to Big Dinosaurs

A number of hypotheses attempt to account for the origin of the universe. According to the majority of scientists, in the beginning—the very beginning—all the energy, space, and matter of the known universe were condensed into a dense, hot, inconceivably tiny speck of pure energy. The laws of physics as currently understood can't account for the existence of this speck, so science has yet to answer the question of where it came from. Some people turn to religion for an answer; some simply believe the universe has always been here, cycling through eternity; others wait, assuming science will one day be able to provide an explanation.

While science cannot yet determine where the universe came from or why it is here, science can account for most of the history of the universe by using the established fact that the universe is rapidly expanding. To this fact scientists apply the current laws of physics and astronomy and work backward, rather like running a movie of an explosion in reverse. They hypothetically shrink the universe and determine what would happen to all its matter and energy under conditions of decreasing size and increasing density and heat. They also devise a time frame for the events involved.

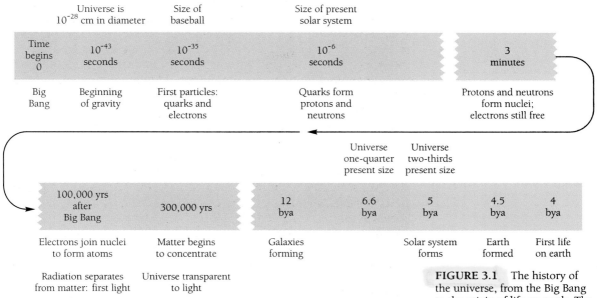

| Universe is 10^{-28} cm in diameter | Size of baseball | | Size of present solar system | | | |

Time begins 0	10^{-43} seconds	10^{-35} seconds		10^{-6} seconds		3 minutes
Big Bang	Beginning of gravity	First particles: quarks and electrons		Quarks form protons and neutrons		Protons and neutrons form nuclei; electrons still free

| | | | Universe one-quarter present size | Universe two-thirds present size | | | |

100,000 yrs after Big Bang	300,000 yrs	12 bya	6.6 bya	5 bya	4.5 bya	4 bya
Electrons join nuclei to form atoms	Matter begins to concentrate	Galaxies forming		Solar system forms	Earth formed	First life on earth
Radiation separates from matter: first light	Universe transparent to light					

FIGURE 3.1   The history of the universe, from the Big Bang to the origin of life on earth. The scale of the timeline changes because some events are condensed into incredibly small periods and others are stretched over unimaginable spans.

Through this procedure, scientists trace the chronology of a long series of events and processes set in motion somewhere around 15 billion years ago (bya) (Figure 3.1). (Estimates for the age of the universe vary greatly, but 15 billion is an average. For more detail on the evolution of the universe and life, see Attenborough 1979, Calder 1983, Lewin 1982, and Sagan 1980.) It was then that the tiny speck began to expand. This event is called the *Big Bang* although it wasn't really an explosion. It was more like a balloon being rapidly inflated, a balloon that contained both energy and space.

A fraction of a second after the expansion began, the space–energy speck, now the size of a baseball, began cooling off, and matter began to condense from energy. The first matter was in the form of the smallest sub-atomic particles, but as the infant universe continued to grow and cool, increasingly larger particles formed. By three minutes after the Big Bang, atomic nuclei appeared—but it took another 100,000 years to form the first atoms. They were atoms of hydrogen, the element with the simplest atomic structure.

To make a *very* long story short, expansion continued and the cooling universe eventually saw simple elements condense to form galaxies and their stars. The first stars were made mainly of hydrogen, but in the nuclear furnaces of these stars heavier elements with larger, more complex atoms were formed. When these early stars died in tremendous explosions called supernovas, these new elements were shot out into the universe, ultimately contributing to the formation of more galaxies, stars, and planets

FIGURE 3.2   This spectacular photo, taken by the Hubble Space Telescope in 1995, shows huge pillars of gas in the M16 nebula in the constellation Serpens. Such pillars are the incubators for new stars, which form in the tips of the pillars by a process called "photoevaporation." Each pillar in this picture is about one light-year (6 trillion miles) long.   (*J. Hestor, P. Srowen, and NASA, courtesy Space Telescope Institute, Baltimore*)

FIGURE 3.3   The whole earth from space, showing Africa and the Arabian Peninsula. The island of Madagascar is just right of center. *(NASA)*

(Figure 3.2). On one planet at least, the atoms formed inside stars provided the raw material that eventually evolved into living creatures. When astronomer Carl Sagan (1980) says we are "star stuff," he is being literal.

By a little over 4.5 bya, the universe was about half its present size. At about this time, our star, the sun, was formed, and the earth took shape shortly thereafter (Figure 3.3). The early earth contained only inorganic (nonliving) molecules, but about 4 bya some of these were rearranged and formed organic molecules, those that make up living organisms. Figure 3.4 (p. 48) summarizes what is known about the timing of important events in the evolution of life on earth.

Although creating living molecules out of nonliving ones may sound like magic, it's not. Scientists have been producing a simple version of this reaction in laboratories for over forty years; all they do is add water to the chemicals that made up the early earth atmosphere and subject the mixture to a source of energy like electricity. Among the molecules that result are amino acids, the raw materials from which genes form proteins. These are the building blocks of all known life.

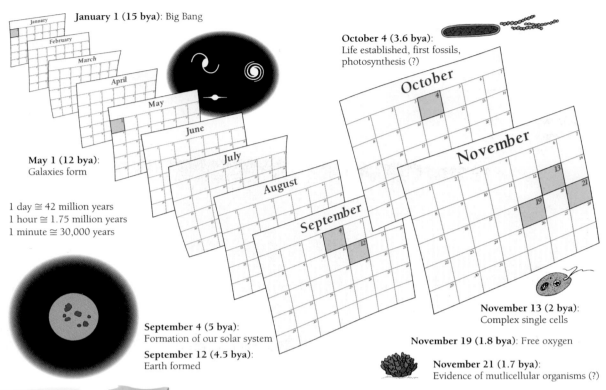

January 1 (15 bya): Big Bang

October 4 (3.6 bya):
Life established, first fossils,
photosynthesis (?)

May 1 (12 bya):
Galaxies form

1 day ≅ 42 million years
1 hour ≅ 1.75 million years
1 minute ≅ 30,000 years

September 4 (5 bya):
Formation of our solar system

September 12 (4.5 bya):
Earth formed

November 13 (2 bya):
Complex single cells

November 19 (1.8 bya): Free oxygen

November 21 (1.7 bya):
Evidence of mutlicellular organisms (?)

FIGURE 3.4 Astronomer Carl Sagan likened the history of the universe to a single calendar year in his 1975 Pulitzer Prize—winning book *The Dragons of Eden*. This calendar has been recalculated to show the currently accepted dates for important events. Numbers in parentheses are actual dates given in billion years ago (bya) or million years ago (mya). One calendar day equals approximately 42 million years. (*Adapted from Sagan, 1975*)

An amino acid, though, is still a long way from a living organism, and another 500 million years were required for these and other organic chemicals to react in just the right ways to form living, reproducing creatures. Scientists know that these reactions occurred because they have found fossils of bacterialike cells—among the simplest of living things—in 3.6 billion-year-old strata exposed by various geological processes in Greenland, southern Africa, and Australia (Figure 3.5, p. 50).

The earth's first creatures were all asexual—that is, they reproduced by splitting or budding, making copies of themselves. Change was very slow because it relied solely on mutations, but it still took place. Evidence shows that 3.6 bya the first single-celled organisms appeared that could photosynthesize—or make nutrients from water, sunlight, and carbon dioxide—as modern green plants do. A waste product of photosynthesis is oxygen. Originally, no free oxygen was present in the earth's atmosphere, but as a result of photosynthesis it appeared by 1.8 bya. Shortly thereafter came the evolution of organisms that could use it. A new branch of the evolutionary tree had begun.

December

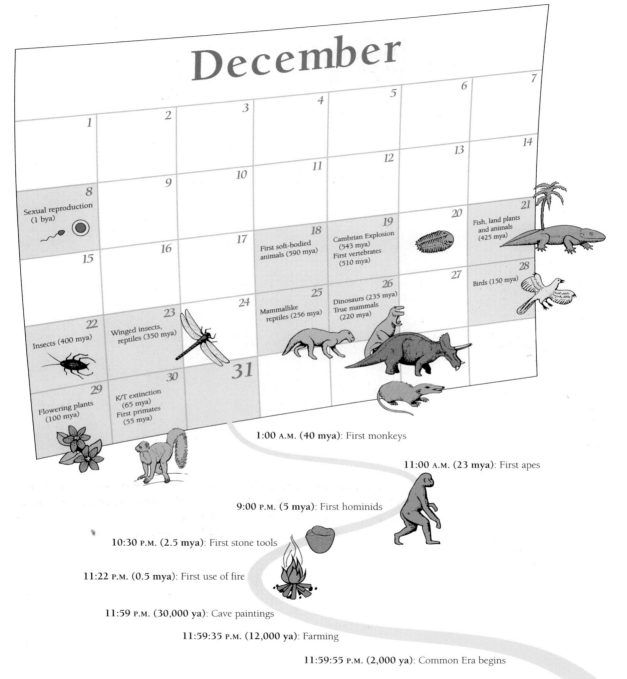

| 1 | 2 | 3 | 4 | 5 | 6 | 7 |
| 8 | 9 | 10 | 11 | 12 | 13 | 14 |

8 Sexual reproduction (1 bya)

15 | **16** | **17** | **18** First soft-bodied animals (590 mya) | **19** Cambrian Explosion (543 mya) First vertebrates (510 mya) | **20** | **21** Fish, land plants and animals (425 mya)

22 Insects (400 mya) | **23** Winged insects, reptiles (350 mya) | **24** | **25** Mammallike reptiles (256 mya) | **26** Dinosaurs (235 mya) True mammals (220 mya) | **27** | **28** Birds (150 mya)

29 Flowering plants (100 mya) | **30** K/T extinction (65 mya) First primates (55 mya) | **31**

1:00 A.M. (40 mya): First monkeys

11:00 A.M. (23 mya): First apes

9:00 P.M. (5 mya): First hominids

10:30 P.M. (2.5 mya): First stone tools

11:22 P.M. (0.5 mya): First use of fire

11:59 P.M. (30,000 ya): Cave paintings

11:59:35 P.M. (12,000 ya): Farming

11:59:55 P.M. (2,000 ya): Common Era begins

11:59:59 P.M. (500 ya): Renaissance

FIGURE 3.5 Stromatolites in Australia, formed when mats of blue-green algae, single-celled organisms, are covered with sand, silt, and mud, which the algae cement down and then grow over. Fossil stromatolites, and thus the organisms that made them, have been dated to 3.5 billion years ago. (© *Fred Bavendam/Peter Arnold, Inc.*)

Evidence from the stratigraphic record shows that by 2 bya cells that were more complex than bacteria had evolved. These cells had a nucleus and functionally differentiated internal parts. Multicellular organisms may have evolved as early as 1.7 bya. And around 1 bya, something new appeared: sex. With sexual reproduction came more possibilities for change because the genes of two parents were now recombined in the production of offspring. Natural selection had more variation from which to choose, and evolution accelerated as a result.

By the beginning of the Cambrian period, 570 million years ago (mya), the world contained many new and different kinds of creatures—complex multicellular animals such as jellyfish and worms. About 543 mya came the sudden appearance of animals with hard outer coverings, forerunners of creatures like clams and lobsters. This has been called the Cambrian Explosion. And 510 mya saw the first vertebrates, creatures with internal skeletons. We, of course, are vertebrates.

The pace of change continued to accelerate. Around 425 mya, fish evolved, and plants and simple animals began to colonize the land. Insects appeared 400 mya and evolved winged forms 350 mya. Reptiles first showed up 350 mya, and the form of reptile that would give rise to mammals appeared about 256 mya.

During all this time, the earth didn't look as it does now. The continents that seem so permanent today aren't. They move or, in the term used by geology, drift. The process that explains continental drift, called **plate tectonics,** is complex, but basically the hard outer shell of the earth, the crust, is made up of about sixteen plates that fit together like a jigsaw puzzle. The continents are the portions of these plates that protrude above the oceans. The plates are in constant interaction with the inside of the earth, which is made up of liquid rock continually in motion. As this liquid moves, it adds solid rock to some parts of the crust and melts away solid rock from other parts, causing the plates with their continents to drift slowly but constantly around the surface of the planet (Figure 3.6). Where the plates meet, they grind against one another, producing the tremendous forces that are largely responsible for great geological events like volcanoes, earthquakes, and mountain building.

About the time the dinosaurs were evolving, around 235 mya, landmasses that are part of all the present continents were drifting together to form a single supercontinent called **Pangea** (literally, "all lands"). This supercontinent was fully formed by 210 mya. Similar fossils of early dinosaurs and other organisms have been found in such diverse places as the Gobi Desert in China, the Badlands of South Dakota, and Antarctica because these were all part of one unbroken landmass.

Mammals first appeared around 220 mya, and about 150 mya a small upright dinosaur with feathers heralded the beginning of the birds (see Figure 4.11). Flowering plants appear only about 100 mya. By this time, however, Pangea had broken up, and it is here that the story of human evolution really starts.

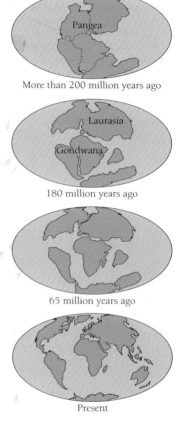

More than 200 million years ago

180 million years ago

65 million years ago

Present

FIGURE 3.6 Movement of the earth's landmasses over the last 200 million years, caused by the process of plate tectonics.

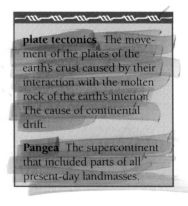

plate tectonics The movement of the plates of the earth's crust caused by their interaction with the molten rock of the earth's interior. The cause of continental drift.

Pangea The supercontinent that included parts of all present-day landmasses.

FIGURE 3.7 Humans are not typical primates. These rhesus monkeys from Asia are perhaps as close as one could come to an "average" primate. The rhesus has been important in medical and behavioral experimentation. The Rh positive and negative blood types were named after it. (© *Fred Whitehead/Animals Animals*)

Grasping Hands and Big Brains

Pangea broke up into six landmasses that are approximately the present-day continents, although they were not then in the same locations they are today. As these new lands drifted over the globe, a greater variety of separate environments was produced, offering a greater opportunity for the evolution of new types of living things.

One new evolutionary line began perhaps 65 mya on a large northern landmass called **Laurasia,** made up of parts of modern North America and Eurasia. It consisted of a group of mammals whose fossilized skeletons are reminiscent of rodents. But their multipurpose teeth, the beginning of grasping hands and feet, and other details of their anatomy were not rodentlike. They were more like the features of the **primates,** the group of mammals that today includes monkeys, apes, and humans (Figure 3.7).

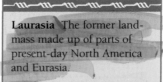

Laurasia The former landmass made up of parts of present-day North America and Eurasia.

primate A large-brained, arboreal mammal with stereoscopic color vision and grasping hands and (often) feet.

FIGURE 3.8 Of all living species, this Asian tree shrew, though not a primate, most closely resembles what we think the first primates looked like. (© *Doug Wechsler/Animals Animals*)

Like the other mammals at the time, the early primates were mostly small, inconspicuous, nocturnal creatures (Figure 3.8). This was largely because the dinosaurs, one of evolution's most successful groups, dominated the world's major environments. Add the fact that many dinosaurs were carnivores who certainly included mammals on their menu, and it is understandable why mammalian evolution was slow at first.

But about 65 mya, something happened that we can probably thank for our very existence: Dinosaurs became extinct. A major and rapid environmental change took place to which the dinosaurs were unable to adapt, and they disappeared (Figure 3.9, p. 54). The only direct living descendants of the dinosaurs are the birds; snakes, lizards, and other living reptiles had a separate evolution.

The extinction of this major and widespread group opened the world up for the evolution of other organisms, especially the mammals. No longer forced to compete with the dinosaurs, the mammals flourished. Shortly after the extinction of the dinosaurs, the fossil record begins to show fossils of most major kinds of mammals—creatures as diverse as bats, whales, and primates. Mammals spread rapidly, filling in the ecological gaps left by the dinosaurs.

By 45 mya, North America and Eurasia drifted apart, and the Western and Eastern Hemispheres were formed. This split the populations of living things that had once inhabited Laurasia, setting the species in each hemisphere off on separate evolutionary courses.

As North America and Eurasia drifted northward toward their present locations, their climates began to get cooler and increasingly inhospitable to many of their inhabitants, adapted to tropical life. South America and Africa, then farther south than today, were also drifting northward and by 30 mya had joined their respective northern partners. Now warm-climate animals like the early primates, the **prosimians,** had somewhere to go. In

prosimian A member of the group of primates with the most primitive features.

FIGURE 3.9 This painting, by the late Rudolph Zallinger, reflects some now out-dated ideas about the appearance and behavior of the dinosaurs. It does show, how-ever, some of the variety of these creatures as they existed over 170 million years of time *(from left to right in the mural)*. The dinosaurs once dominated the earth's environ-ments but became extinct about 65 million years ago. It is now thought that the cause of their extinction was an enormous asteroid that crashed into the earth where the Mexican Yucatán peninsula is now, leaving a crater perhaps 200 miles across. The resulting explosion caused a series of events that blocked sunlight, cooled the earth, started huge forest fires, and may have initiated volcanic eruptions. Perhaps 75 per-cent of the earth's marine species became extinct, along with many land animals.
(The Age of Reptiles, a mural by Rudolph F. Zallinger. Copyright © 1966, 1975, 1985, 1989, Peabody Museum of Natural History, New Haven, Connecticut, USA)

the Old World, some prosimians evolved into more **arboreal** (tree-living), larger-brained, leaf-eating primates—the monkeys, who were successful and began to spread and diversify. They pushed the Old World prosimians into isolated areas. Most living prosimians now inhabit the island of Mada-gascar and the isolated islands of Southeast Asia (Figure 3.10). What hap-pened in the New World is an involved topic which we'll take up in Chapter 8. For now, suffice it to say there are at present only monkeys, no prosimians, in Central and South America.

Continental drift and climatic change continued, and more new niches resulted. The primates responded to these, and around 23 mya another new group evolved in the Old World. They were larger than the monkeys, had bigger brains, were tailless, spent more time on the ground, and were adapted to a more varied diet that included some sea-sonal foods like nuts and fruits and maybe even some meat. These were the first apes, smaller, more monkeylike forerunners of present-day chimpanzees, gorillas, and orangutans.

Between 23 and 14 mya, various species of apes flourished across Eu-rope, Africa, and Asia, which by this time occupied almost their present-

arboreal Adapted to life in the trees.

54

FIGURE 3.10 A ring-tailed lemur, one of the living prosimians from Madagascar.
(© *Zoological Society of San Diego*)

FIGURE 3.11 The savannas (open grasslands) of present-day Africa are sufficiently similar to those of 6 mya to give us a glimpse into what life was like at that time for its inhabitants, including our earliest ancestors. (© C. W. Perkins/Animals Animals)

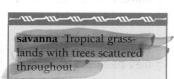

savanna Tropical grasslands with trees scattered throughout.

day positions. Ape species ranged in size from that of a large monkey to a giant grain eater from India and China, larger than modern gorillas. But the heyday of the apes began to end about 10 mya. Many ape species became extinct. Populations of an ape that survived in the forests of Africa gave rise to modern-day chimps, bonobos, and gorillas. Another group, probably living where forest met **savanna**, changed in a different direction and became adapted to life on the vast and dangerous open plains (Figure 3.11). These were our ancestors.

Data are scarce at present, but scientists can make an educated guess about when the human evolutionary line split from that of the apes. Based on existing fossil and geological evidence and on the genetic similarities between humans and chimpanzees, the human ancestor apparently diverged from the ape line 5 or 6 mya. By the time the fossil record starts to provide more substantial evidence, a little over 4 mya, a new creature emerges, one with the face and brain size of an ape, but with an added feature that sets it off from all other primates that had ever existed: It walked upright (Figure 3.12).

FIGURE 3.12 The importance of bipedal locomotion for our species can be seen in the drive of infants to master upright walking. (*K. L. Feder*)

It seems as if the most important and earliest human adaptive response to life on the African plains was upright, or **bipedal**, locomotion. This adaptation, seen in rudimentary form in modern apes, allowed our earliest ancestors to move efficiently over great distances and to carry things at the same time. On the savannas, where food sources were more widely scattered and less varied than in the forests and where numerous creatures lurked who were ready to make meals out of small mammals, this ability was particularly important. It was a successful adaptation, for fossil evidence of these early humans is found all over eastern and southern Africa. In broad evolutionary perspective then, bipedalism is our most distinguishing feature because it was first. In Chapter 8, we'll explore some ideas about just how and why this adaptation took place.

Our earliest ancestors, the topic of Chapter 9, are called australopithecines. The term means, literally, "southern ape," a holdover from the fact that the man who first identified one of their fossils and named them, in 1925, recognized but wasn't quite ready formally to admit they were **hominids**, part of the human lineage. But they were.

About 3 mya, another evolutionary event took place. The australopithecines diverged. Two branches, called the robust early hominids, seem to have evolved toward an increasingly vegetarian diet. These branches became extinct about 1 mya.

A third branch evolved a different adaptation. These hominids had bigger brains, smaller, more modern-looking teeth and chewing muscles,

bipedal The ability to walk on two feet.

hominid The bipedal primate; modern humans and their ancestors.

and a new and important behavior: They made stone tools. As a result, they are given the scientific name *Homo habilis,* "the skillful people." *Homo habilis* began to be a major factor in the savanna environment. With their big brains and more complex intellect, and with the tools that they produced as a result, they could exploit savanna food sources more efficiently than other hominids. We'll examine them in detail in Chapter 9.

Now the big brain became the adaptive focus of hominid evolution. By 1.75 mya, the brains of our African ancestors approached in size the lower limit of modern humans. Their heads and faces were notably different from ours today, but from the neck down their skeletons were essentially of modern form. These hominids are called *Homo erectus,* the topic of Chapter 10. This name, which means "the people who stand upright," is a holdover from the time when these fossils were thought to be the oldest humans and thus the first bipeds. It's only recently that scientists have realized that hominids were walking erect at least 2 million years before *Homo erectus* appeared.

Bigger brains allowed *Homo erectus* to improve on toolmaking and probably to devise schemes for social organization and cooperation. Their populations increased, and they began to spread rapidly. *Homo erectus* fossils appear throughout Africa and in Europe, Southeast Asia, and northern China. Their adaptations, originally geared for life on the savannas of Africa, turned out to be useful all over the Old World.

For the next million years, human evolution seems to have stabilized. To be sure, various populations of *Homo erectus* devised different sorts of tools and other cultural adaptations specifically geared to their environments from the savannas of Africa to the tropical forests of Southeast Asia to the temperate woodlands of Europe and China, then at times much colder than today (see Chapter 10). But so successful were their basic adaptations—shelter, clothing, fire, and perhaps organized hunting—that, despite the unstable climates, we see relatively little biological or cultural change until about 400,000 ya.

At that time, there was another burst of change in human evolution: an increase in average brain size to that of modern people. What caused this development is unknown. Natural selection, operating with the trend already begun and proven successful, may have promoted the reproductive success of those humans with still bigger, more complex brains. These people may have had a slightly better ability to think up answers to the problems of survival. This point, at any rate, marks the beginning of *Homo sapiens* ("the wise people"), the species to which all living humans belong. In Chapter 11, we will describe the beginnings of our species.

After this turning point, it becomes harder to generalize about our evolutionary history. The adaptation of culture, made possible by humans' big brain, allowed for great diversity in behaviors. Humans spread all over the Old World, fitting tools and social organizations to the specific problems the various environments posed. But these humans were to some extent still at the mercy of the climatic fluctuations of the ice ages, and environment still had some effect on biology.

Evidence for this effect can be seen in a striking set of physical features possessed by one variety of fossil humans, the Neandertals. Appearing in the fossil record from before 100,000 ya to 35,000 ya, they displayed some unique traits that distinguish them from other hominids living at the same time who were more probably ancestral to modern humans. The Neandertals were, however, responsible for a number of innovative and important inventions—activities like burial of the dead. The exact relationship between the Neandertals and modern people remains controversial. We will examine the story of the Neandertals in Chapter 11 and the controversy in Chapter 12.

New evidence indicates that the earliest fully modern humans can be traced back to at least 100,000 ya. In Chapter 12, we will discuss the continued success of the modern human species as it entered new habitats and populated new worlds. Around 40,000 ya, humans entered Australia and about 15,000 ya the Americas, crossing over a broad land connection between Siberia and Alaska. *Homo sapiens* now inhabited nearly the entire globe, and it was probably at this point that the species began to evolve the physical variation that characterizes people today (and that seems to present us with so many social problems). We will discuss the topic of race at the end of Chapter 12.

Culture change continued to accelerate; people increased their populations and adapted to new and increasingly specific ecological niches. Sometime after 12,000 ya, some populations found it necessary to use their vast knowledge of their environments to gain more control over their food resources. They invented farming and animal domestication (Chapter 13). With this came even more cultural diversity and a whole host of new cultural adaptations: cities, metallurgy, warfare, complex political and economic organization, and writing—the beginning of the historical record (Chapter 14).

Thus, the canvas of time on which we will paint the picture of human antiquity begins with the very first primates and continues to the recent past.

Summary

We hope this brief narrative will provide you with a basic context into which all the details of the next chapters can be easily fit. We also hope it has demonstrated three other general ideas. First, you should see that the story of human evolution, as complex as it is, takes up only the smallest fraction of time in the whole history of the universe; it is just the latest tick

FIGURE 3.13   All that our species has achieved—from observing the universe to its actual exploration, from the efficient transmission of knowledge to the drive of children to understand and participate in their world—all can be traced back to the Big Bang some 15 bya. *(Telescope, National Optical Astronomy Observatories; astronaut, NASA; computer kids, K. L. Feder; boy, K. L. Feder)*

of the evolutionary clock. We find that a rather humbling thought (Figure 3.13).

Second, though we use terms like *beginning* and *origin,* notice that the whole story contains only one *real* origin: that tiny, dense speck of energy and space that started the whole thing. Since then, nothing brand new has entered the picture. There have only been rearrangements of what already existed: matter condensing from cooling energy; large particles formed from combinations of smaller ones; stars and planets coming together from cosmic dust; inorganic molecules shuffling their parts and producing the molecules of life; the genes of living things recombining in a nearly infinite variety of ways to evolve the wondrous array of creatures that have inhabited the earth. Indeed, *uniformitarianism* has a broader meaning than James Hutton and Charles Lyell could have imagined. We are all truly "star stuff."

Third, the specific history of the universe, the earth, and life on earth could have happened in countless other ways. Each event in the story is contingent upon preceding events. Even the evolution of our species is dependent upon a specific sequence of events. If those events had been different, *we* would probably be different—or we might not be here at all. What if that asteroid had not hit the earth 65 million years ago? The evolution of human beings—or any other species—was not inevitable. We're lucky we're here.

Study Questions

1. What are the major events in the history of the universe, the earth, and earth's living forms? When did these events occur?
2. What general ideas may we perceive from this history about the nature of evolutionary change?

Key Terms

plate tectonics   primate   savanna
Pangea   prosimian   bipedal
Laurasia   arboreal   hominid

For More Information

The evolution of the universe is one of the themes of Carl Sagan's *Cosmos*. The evolution of life on earth is described in narrative fashion in *Life on Earth*, by David Attenborough. Both these books accompanied public television series of the same names. For a good discussion of the science behind our understanding of the history of the universe, see Timothy Ferris's *Coming of Age in the Milky Way*.

The evolution of life is covered in more detail in Roger Lewin's *Thread of Life: The Smithsonian Looks at Evolution*, and in the lavishly illustrated *The Book of Life* edited by Stephen Jay Gould. For a more technical but still highly readable treatment, try Richard Cowen's *History of Life*.

These moths, one clearly visible and the other camouflaged, demonstrate the operation of natural selection, the central process in the evolution of life on earth. How does evolution work? *(© Michael Tweedie/The National Audubon Society Collection/Photo Researchers, Inc.)*

4

Understanding Change
Modern Evolutionary Theory

———————————————————— —w— ————————————————————

CHAPTER CONTENTS

Genetics • The Genetics of Populations • The Processes of Evolution • The Origins of Species •
Contemporary Issue: The 3 Billion Names of Humanity •
Summary • Study Questions • Key Terms • For More Information

Chapter 2 ended with a discussion of scientific creationism and evolution. We said that the theory of evolution, unlike creationism, is supported by a massive amount of interrelated evidence gathered and interpreted according to the scientific method.

What is the evidence for evolution as we understand it today? How does evolution work? What does it have to do with human beings?

Genetics

As we noted in Chapter 2, neither Charles Darwin nor Alfred Wallace understood the biological variation that was so crucial to their theory of natural selection. They knew that variation existed, but, as Darwin admitted, such variations "seem to us in our ignorance to arise spontaneously" (1898:239).

Why did Darwin fail to understand this principle? The answer is that he was operating without knowledge of **genetics.** Adhering to the notion current in his day, he thought inheritance worked through some sort of "blending"—a mixing of parental substances in the offspring. There seemed to be ample evidence for this idea from plant and animal breeding, where offspring often exhibited traits that appeared to be 50:50 mixtures of their parents' traits—pink flowers from a cross of red-flowered and white-flowered parents, for instance.

Plenty of traits, of course, don't show this equal mixture of parental traits. Organisms inherit their sex from their parents and, with few exceptions, are not 50:50 blends but are either male or female. Traits that seem to blend, though, like flower color, appear to have been more influential in early thinking about the mechanism of inheritance.

Ironically, at about the same time Darwin was writing *The Origin of Species,* an Augustinian monk named Gregor Mendel (1822–1884), working in a monastery in what is now the Czech Republic, established that inheritance did not operate by blending but rather was **particulate.** By conducting breeding experiments with the pea plants in the monastery garden (the culmination of many years of experimentation with plants and mice), Mendel showed that an organism's traits are passed from generation to generation by individual particles, which Mendel called *factors*—what we now call **genes.**

As a further irony, Mendel's work was neither widely read (Darwin never read it) nor fully appreciated by those who did know about it. They failed to see any implications beyond some interesting facts about pea plants. After Mendel's death, his work fell into obscurity, and it was not until 1900 that it was rediscovered. By then the implications of his experiments were clear, and so the stage was set for the series of discoveries that led to our modern understanding of genetics.

The Genetic Code

We now understand that a gene is actually a chemical code for the production of a **protein.** Proteins make up the basic structure of the cells of living things and, in the form of **enzymes,** are responsible for the cells' functions. Because organisms are made up of cells, it's safe to say that, in a sense, living things *are* proteins. Humans can produce at least 100,000 different proteins.

genetics The study of the mechanism of inheritance.

particulate The idea that biological traits are controlled by individual factors rather than by a single hereditary agent.

gene The portion of the DNA molecule that codes for a specific protein.

protein The family of molecules that makes cells and carries out cellular functions.

enzyme A protein that controls chemical processes.

The genetic code is made up of a variable sequence of bases (a family of chemicals) that are part of a long chemical strand called **deoxyribonucleic acid (DNA)**. The individual strands of DNA are themselves arranged in longer strands called **chromosomes,** found in the nuclei of all cells. Four bases are involved in the code: adenine (A), thymine (T), cytosine (C), and guanine (G). Chemical bonds between these bases hold the DNA molecule together, but the bases are only bonded in A-T or T-A and C-G or G-C pairs.

The first function of this pairing is to enable the DNA molecule to make copies of itself during cell division. The DNA molecule is shaped like a ladder with the ends twisted in opposite directions, a configuration called a double helix. During cell division the helix unwinds, and each strand, with its now unpaired bases, picks up the proper complementary bases, which are in solution in the cell. This is called **replication.** Thus, when the whole cell divides, each new daughter cell has a complete set of DNA base pairs.

The sequence of the DNA bases is divided into groups of three. These are called **codons.** Think of them as three-letter words. Each codon "word" is the code for a particular **amino acid,** and a sequence of words— a genetic "sentence"—puts together a chain of amino acids. A chain of amino acids is a protein or enzyme—one of the chemicals that make up and run the body's cells. To complete the analogy, some codons also act as capitalization and punctuation, beginning and ending the sentences.

A gene can thus be thought of as that portion of the DNA molecule that carries the codon sentence for a particular protein. We call that portion a **locus** (plural, **loci**), a term more specific than, and so preferable to, gene.

Our current understanding of how proteins are manufactured according to the genetic code is a process known as **protein synthesis** (Figure 4.1, p. 66). Follow along in the diagram as you read the description.

The genetic code is "read" by **messenger ribonucleic acid (mRNA).** The DNA unwinds, as it does during replication, exposing the bases of the one strand that carries the actual code. The mRNA, with uracil (U) replacing thymine (T), transcribes the code, its bases matching up with their complements on the DNA molecule. The mRNA then moves out of the cell's nucleus and acts as a template for the translation of the code into a protein. **Transfer ribonucleic acid (tRNA)** molecules, carrying bases in the original code words, pick up the proper free-floating amino acids (from about twenty different ones) and line them up along the mRNA, the bases paired up as in the original DNA molecule (with U still replacing T). The amino acids bond, and a protein is synthesized. The protein can then serve its specific function in the cell and the cell can now perform its specific roles in the structure and function of the organism.

The measurable, observable chemical or physical traits of an organism are the results of the actions of proteins that have been manufactured by

deoxyribonucleic acid (DNA) The molecule that carries the genetic code.

chromosome A strand of DNA in the nucleus of cells.

replication The copying of the genetic code during the process of cell division.

codon A section of DNA that codes for a particular amino acid.

amino acid The chief component of proteins.

locus (plural, **loci**) The location on a chromosome of the genetic code for a specific protein.

protein synthesis The process by which the genetic code puts together proteins in the cell.

messenger ribonucleic acid (mRNA) The molecule that carries the genetic code out of the nucleus for translation into proteins.

transfer ribonucleic acid (tRNA) RNA that lines up amino acids along mRNA to make proteins.

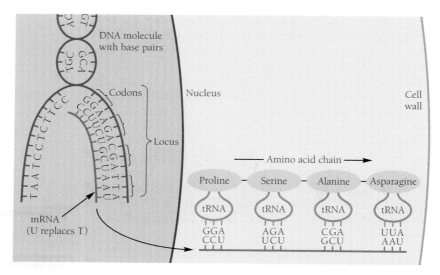

FIGURE 4.1 What genes are
and how they work. The portion
of a DNA molecule (*left*) shows
four codons. The DNA unwinds,
and mRNA translates the code
and then moves out of the cell
nucleus to act as a template
along which tRNA, carrying specific amino acids, lines up. The
resulting string of amino acids,
in their proper order, becomes
one of the proteins responsible
for some structure or function in
the cell. In reality, no protein is
only four amino acids long (the
average protein contains 1000
amino acids), but the process
works exactly as shown.

the cells according to genetic instructions. Some traits, such as the blood
component hemoglobin, are chemically simple. Hemoglobin is a protein
made up of two paired amino acid chains and thus is determined by two
loci. Skin color is made up of many proteins and is thus coded for by
many loci.

Each species has a characteristic number of chromosomes. Bacteria
have a single chromosome. Humans have forty-six; chimpanzees, forty-
eight; and wheat, forty-two. Obviously, no necessary relationship exists
between the number of chromosomes and the complexity of an organism.

In sexually reproducing species, chromosomes come in pairs. An organism inherits one chromosome of each pair from each parent and thus
gets half its genetic material from each parent. It follows that the genetic
loci also come in pairs, so each organism has two of every locus.

The catch is that a genetic locus can have variants, called **alleles**, each
with a slightly different set of codons. The alleles of a locus influence the
same trait but may produce different expressions of that trait. For example,
for blood type in the ABO system, there are three possible alleles, *A, B,* and
O. Whether you have blood type A, B, AB, or O depends on which pair of
alleles is present at the locus that codes for the amino acid chain determining blood type. Each allele codes for a version of the chain with a different
specific sequence of amino acids. Your allele pair is your **genotype** for that
locus.

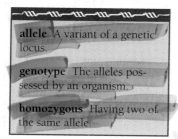

allele A variant of a genetic
locus.

genotype The alleles possessed by an organism.

homozygous Having two of
the same allele.

The Inheritance of Characteristics

An organism has two of the same allele, a condition called **homozygous**,
when both parents have contributed the same allele of that genetic locus.

An organism has two different alleles, called **heterozygous**, when the loci contributed by the parents carry different codes. Alleles are products of **mutations**, genetic mistakes that alter the code and thus may transform one allele into another.

The expression of a genotype—the trait that results from the genetic code—is called the **phenotype.** In homozygotes both alleles are the same, so the way the trait is expressed is simply in accordance with these alleles. There is no alternative. In heterozygotes, the situation is more complex. In many, the influence of *both* alleles is expressed in the phenotype. This is what gives rise to the appearance of blending. But on occasion, the expression of one allele in heterozygotes may be hidden. Such alleles are said to be **recessive**. The other member of the pair, the one expressed, is **dominant.** The words *dominant* and *recessive* carry no implications of value, no significance for adaptation. Dominant alleles are not necessarily better than recessive alleles.

When an organism reproduces, it obviously cannot pass on *both* alleles of each pair to its offspring. If this were the case, the offspring would end up with twice the proper number of genetic loci. Instead, organisms produce reproductive cells that are different from the cells that make up the rest of the organism. These are the sex cells, or **gametes** (sperm and egg, for instance). Gametes are produced through the process of meiosis, which splits the chromosome pairs—and thus the allele pairs—so that each gamete only has one of each locus (Figure 4.2, p. 68). Mendel called this effect **segregation.**

When a sperm from the male parent fertilizes an egg from the female, the resultant **zygote** once again has proper pairs of chromosomes and thus pairs at each genetic locus. But because the members of each pair have two different sources, the combination of loci in each pair may well be different from that of either parent. This effect is called **recombination** and produces genetic variation among individuals of the same species and, in fact, among offspring of the same parent.

These principles can be demonstrated in a concrete example. Sickle cell anemia is a genetic disease of the blood often associated, erroneously, only with African Americans. The association results from the disease being found in high frequencies in a band across central Africa, a region from which most American blacks trace their ancestry. That association is erroneous because sickle cell anemia is also found in southern Europe, the Middle East, India, and Southeast Asia.

Sickle cell anemia is the result of a mutation affecting hemoglobin, the protein on the red blood cells that carries oxygen from the lungs to the body's tissues. Hemoglobin is made up of two paired amino acid chains, an alpha chain of 141 amino acids and a beta chain 146 amino acids long. If, through a mutation, an incorrect amino acid is substituted for the correct one at position 6 on the beta chain, the disease results. In terms of the genetic code, this means that the mutation is one wrong "word"—a mistake in one codon—in a sentence of 146 words. This is a **point mutation.**

heterozygous Having two different alleles in a pair.

mutation A change in an organism's genetic material.

phenotype The chemical or physical results of the genetic code.

recessive An allele of a pair that is not expressed.

dominant An allele of a pair that is expressed.

gamete The cell of reproduction.

segregation The breaking up of allele pairs during gamete production.

zygote A fertilized egg before cell division begins.

recombination The reconstitution of allele pairs at fertilization.

point mutation A mutation of a single codon.

FIGURE 4.2 Cell division occurs in two ways. Mitosis produces exact copies of the parent cell and is the most common form of cell division. Meiosis results in four daughter cells, each with one-half the genetic content of the parent cell. Meiosis is the process by which gametes, or sex cells (sperm and egg), are manufactured. It ensures that when fertilization occurs, the new individual has a complete set of genes, one-half from each parent.

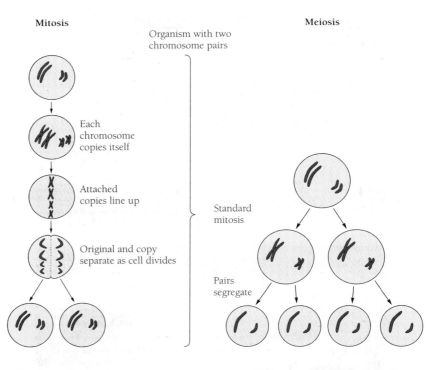

Mitosis

Each chromosome copies itself

Attached copies line up

Original and copy separate as cell divides

Daughter cells are copies of parent cell

Meiosis

Organism with two chromosome pairs

Standard mitosis

Pairs segregate

Each gamete has half the normal number of chromosomes

When the abnormal hemoglobin is present and stress, high altitude, or illness lowers an individual's oxygen supply, the red blood cells take on peculiar shapes. Some resemble sickles (Figure 4.3). In this condition they cannot carry sufficient oxygen to nourish the body's cells. Results can include fatigue, retarded physical development in children, miscarriage in pregnant women, fever, severe pain, and increased susceptibility to infection. People with sickle cell anemia frequently die before their twenties; even if they live longer, they have a very low reproductive rate. In terms of evolutionary success, sickle cell anemia may be considered nearly 100 percent lethal.

The abnormal allele for sickle cell acts like a recessive in the sense that a person must have the homozygous genotype to be afflicted with the disease. Heterozygotes, however, still carry the sickle cell allele. When two individuals carrying one allele each for sickle cell mate, they have a one-quarter chance of producing an offspring with the sickle cell anemia

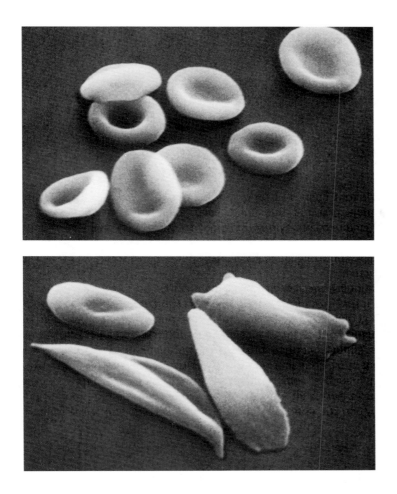

FIGURE 4.3   Normal red blood cells (*top*) and those showing the abnormal shapes (*bottom*) that result from the presence of hemoglobin with one incorrect amino acid. Such cells fail to transport oxygen properly to the body's tissues. (© *AP/Wide World Photos*)

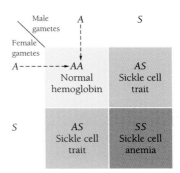

FIGURE 4.4   Punnett square showing sickle cell inheritance. (*A* is the normal allele; *S* is the sickle cell allele). Two individuals, each heterozygous at the hemoglobin locus, produce gametes with normal and abnormal alleles in about equal numbers. When they mate, they have a one-quarter chance of producing a child with normal hemoglobin, a one-half chance of producing a heterozygote like themselves, and a one-quarter chance of producing a child who will almost certainly die from sickle cell anemia.

phenotype. A device called a Punnett square shows how this process works (Figure 4.4).

Sickle cell anemia also demonstrates some of the complexity of genetics and its intricate relationship to the environment and to evolution. The sickle cell allele is not completely recessive. Heterozygotes possess about 40 percent abnormal hemoglobin, and, under extreme conditions of low oxygen, they experience sickle cell symptoms, although not as severely as homozygotes. Indeed, complete dominance and complete recessiveness are the exception; the different alleles of most loci are both expressed to some degree. A heterozygote may be somehow intermediate between either homozygote or may show the phenotypes of both alleles. Alleles that exhibit these characteristics are said to be **codominant.**

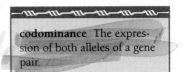

codominance The expression of both alleles of a gene pair.

The general rule is that in most cases the phenotype is not a clear-cut indication of the genotype. Besides various relationships among alleles, most phenotypic traits are simply not coded for by a single genetic locus (**monogenic**) but by many loci (**polygenic**). This effect becomes clear in complex traits like stature or skin color, where numerous individual cellular and chemical actions operate together to make up those phenotypes.

Moreover, not all loci are always in operation. Some are switched on by other loci in response to environmental changes or some internal timing. In other words, not all genetic loci are equally influential in producing phenotypic traits. In addition, many loci can influence several seemingly unrelated traits. Think of the many symptoms of sickle cell anemia—highly variable specific expressions all resulting from a point mutation.

Finally, the relationship between genotype and phenotype can be influenced by environmental factors, that is, any factor outside the codon-to-trait process just outlined. Your skin color, for example, though coded for in your DNA, can change noticeably depending on your health, how much sun you get, and even your emotional state. All these factors can be considered *environmental* in the broadest sense of the word. Heterozygotes for sickle cell anemia, who all have the same genotype, nonetheless vary greatly in the degree to which they exhibit the symptoms of the disease and in how easily those symptoms are triggered. This variation occurs because of a complex interaction of numerous features that affects the relationship between genotype and phenotype.

With the rediscovery of Mendel's work in 1900, an understanding of the mechanism of inheritance and of the basic source of variation was added to Darwin's framework for a theory of evolution. From this synthesis, over the next century, our current knowledge both of genetics and of the processes of evolution has developed.

The Genetics of Populations

The physical evidence for evolution is change in the phenotypic features of organisms through time. If evolution manifests itself as phenotypic change and if the genetic code is responsible for generating phenotypic traits, then evolution may be accurately regarded as genetic change through time. Because the overall genetic makeup of an individual doesn't change (except for isolated mutations), individuals don't evolve. The unit of evolution is the **population,** defined generally as a group within which mates are normally found. Technically, a whole species could be treated as a genetic population because members of a species, by definition, can only mate within that species. But most species are unevenly distributed within their range and so contain subunits of interbreeding individuals, often further defined by a particular locality and perhaps even particular adaptations and physical characteristics. These groups are called **breeding populations,** or **demes.** The evolution of the species can be seen as the collective

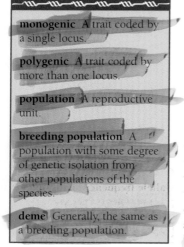

monogenic A trait coded by a single locus.

polygenic A trait coded by more than one locus.

population A reproductive unit.

breeding population A population with some degree of genetic isolation from other populations of the species.

deme Generally, the same as a breeding population.

evolution of the demes within that species, as they change independently and as they interact by exchanging genetic material.

A breeding population is characterized genetically by identifying how often a certain allele appears in the population relative to the other alleles at the same locus. This is called **allele frequency**. Thus, the essential definition of evolution is *change in allele frequency over time*. The processes of evolution, then, are all those factors that bring about changes in allele frequency.

To understand how this concept can help us study and explain the nature and operation of evolutionary processes, let's use sickle cell anemia in a hypothetical breeding population (Park 1996 from Relethford 1994). In a population of 145 individuals under study, the following numbers were found:

Phenotype	Genotype	Number
Normal	AA	35
Heterozygote	AS	100
Sickle cell	SS	10
Total		145

To study the population, it is necessary first to find the allele frequency. Because individuals with normal hemoglobin have genotype *AA*, there are twice as many *A* alleles as there are "normal" individuals. In addition, all heterozygotes possess one *A* allele, so this must be added to the total *A* allele count. Thus,

$$\text{Number of } A \text{ alleles} = (35 \times 2) + 100 = 170$$

Similarly, for the *S* allele,

$$\text{Number of } S \text{ alleles} = (10 \times 2) + 100 = \frac{120}{290}$$

Now, in order to calculate the frequency (the percentage) of occurrence of each allele, divide the number of each allele by the total number of alleles in the population. Thus, for the *A* allele,

$$170/290 = 0.59$$

Similarly for the *S* allele,

$$120/290 = 0.41$$

In a population of 145 individuals with 290 loci of the hemoglobin gene, the allele for normal hemoglobin occurs 59 percent of the time, and the allele for sickle cell occurs 41 percent of the time. These are the allele frequencies for that population.

Given those allele frequencies, we can now calculate the expected *genotype* and *phenotype* frequencies under conditions where no evolution is in operation. This procedure is called a *null hypothesis*. If you can state the condition under which nothing occurs, you can then compare it to situations where something *does* occur, observe the nature and direction of the

allele frequency The number of times (in percentage) that a particular allele appears in a population.

difference, and possibly discern factors that are responsible. With reference to the genetics of populations, the null hypothesis is specifically known as the **Hardy–Weinberg equilibrium.**

Using our two alleles, *A* and *S,* we designate the frequency of *A* as *p* and the frequency of *S* as *q*. (These letters are used because of a mathematical convention.) The probability of creating each of the possible genotypes is the product (the result of multiplication) of the frequencies of the alleles of that genotype. Thus,

Genotype	Product of Frequencies
AA	$p \times p = p^2$
AS	$p \times q = pq$
SA	$p \times q = pq$
	$q \times p = qp$
	$pq + qp = 2pq$
SS	$q \times q = q^2$

Because all genotypes are now accounted for,

$$p^2 + 2pq + q^2 = 1$$

(that is, 100 percent of the genotypes).

We can now return to our hypothetical population to see what its genotype frequencies would be if they were based solely on the frequencies of the alleles, if, in the terminology of population genetics, the population were in Hardy–Weinberg equilibrium.

Genotype	Expected Frequency	Expected Number	Observed Number
AA	$p^2 = 0.59^2 = 0.3481$	$0.3481 \times 145 = 50$	35
AS	$2pq = 0.59 \times 0.41 \times 2 = 0.4838$	$0.4838 \times 145 = 70$	100
SS	$q^2 = 0.41^2 = 0.1618$	$0.1618 \times 145 = 24$	10

The observed numbers are not in equilibrium. The allele frequencies have changed relative to the null hypothesis situation. Evolution, by definition, is taking place: There are fewer "normal" individuals than expected, more heterozygotes, and fewer sickle cell victims. An evolutionary trend seems to favor heterozygotes. Given what we know about sickle cell anemia, this makes perfect sense depending on the population in question. (We'll see why in the next section.) Indeed, data similar to this hinted at the nature of the disease and led to our understanding of it.

In real life, we would still have to run certain statistical tests on the above results because even if the expected and observed numbers do not match, they could still result from simple chance. One such test, called Chi-Square, showed that the results are probably not a matter of chance. They are, in mathematical terms, statistically significant.

What processes, then, can bring about changes in allele frequency in populations and thus alter the phenotypic nature of the group?

Hardy–Weinberg equilibrium The formula that shows genotype percentages under hypothetical conditions of no evolutionary change.

The Processes of Evolution

Natural Selection

As Darwin explained, from the physical and behavioral variation within a species, nature selects the characteristics best adapted to a particular environment. The measure of nature's selection is the relative reproductive success of the individual organisms that possess those characteristics. This is called **differential reproduction.** Individuals with the most adaptive traits tend to produce more offspring on the average, thus relatively more often passing on the alleles that code for their advantageous traits. In this manner, the better adapted traits accumulate over time and the poorly adapted ones become less frequent—even disappearing if their possessors fail to reproduce at all. The result is that the species as a whole stays adapted to its environmental **niche**—the particular set of environmental circumstances with which it comes in contact and to which it must adjust.

The traits that make an individual better adapted will, of course, vary with the species in question and with that species' particular niche. Bigger size, smaller size, bright colors, dull colors, speed, stealth, intelligence, reliance on built-in instincts—each can be adaptive depending on the species and niche.

In addition, selection of mating partners takes place in some species. Males may directly compete with one another for access to females. The famous head-clashing duels of bighorn sheep are an example. In other cases, females choose mates based on things like the establishment of a nesting site or colorful feather displays, as with the peacock (although the adaptive benefit of these displays is still not fully understood). This form of selection is called **sexual selection,** and as we'll see it may have played a part in early human evolution.

Thus, by ensuring that the more advantageous traits are passed to more offspring, natural selection maintains a species' adaptation to its environment. As we have seen, however, environments change. When this happens, traits that were once adaptively neutral or even poorly adapted may actually become better adapted. These traits will begin to occur in higher frequencies because their possessors are becoming increasingly reproductively successful. At the same time, once adaptive traits may become increasingly rare and perhaps even eventually nonexistent. Even under new environmental conditions then, the species can remain viable and adapted, though its adaptive features may be different.

A classic example of differential reproduction in changing environments is the peppered moth (Figure 4.5, p. 74). When first described in England before the Industrial Revolution, most members of this species were multicolored. This coloration provided them with camouflage when they landed on lichen-covered trees, making them less easily seen by birds. Some uniformly dark moths appeared each generation, however, the results of a different allele (or alleles) for coloration. These members of the species

differential reproduction The differing reproductive success of individuals within a population.

niche The environment of an organism and its adaptive response to that environment.

sexual selection The active, rather than random, selection of mating partners by individuals within a population.

FIGURE 4.5 Peppered moths. Where trees are light and covered with lichens *(top)*, the light form obviously has a selective advantage through better camouflage. Where trees are blackened by soot, the dark form has the advantage. As pollution increased in England, the dark form of the peppered moth became more common. *(© Michael Tweedie/The National Audubon Society Collection/Photo Researchers, Inc.)*

were rare because they were highly visible and thus far less successful at staying alive to reproduce. In the nineteenth century, though, pollution from coal burning killed off the sensitive lichens and blackened tree trunks. The once-rare dark moths began to have an adaptive advantage. They—and the alleles causing their coloration—became more frequent, and the multicolored moths occurred less frequently. More recently, with less coal burning and better pollution control, the multicolored moths are once again becoming the most frequent type.

Note that in this case, as in any example of natural selection, the variation that proved useful under changed circumstances was *already present*. It did not appear when it was needed or because it was needed. This is the essential difference between Lamarck's inheritance of acquired characteristics and Darwin's natural selection (Figure 4.6).

A more complex example comes once again from sickle cell anemia. Despite the fact that it is so disadvantageous, sickle cell anemia is found in

Selection for   color

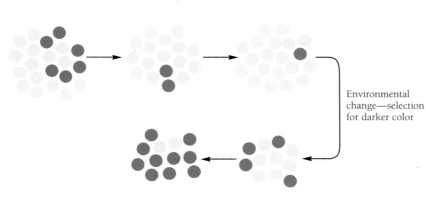

Environmental change—selection for darker color

FIGURE 4.6 Schematic diagram of Darwinian natural selection. As in the case of the peppered moth, an environmental change makes the darker individuals more reproductively successful, and they become the most common representative of their species. Compare with Figure 2.6, Lamarck's concept of evolutionary change.

high frequencies in certain areas of the world (Figure 4.7, p. 76). One would expect a lethal allele to disappear quickly, or in evolutionary terms, to be "selected out." But in some parts of West Africa, the sickle cell disease is found in at least one in every sixty-four people. There's clearly more to the persistence of this disease than first meets the eye.

The reason for the high frequency of sickle cell disease is that the heterozygous condition conveys an adaptive benefit. Besides not usually having severe symptoms of sickle cell anemia, heterozygote individuals also have a resistance to malaria, a potentially fatal disease caused by a parasitic single-celled organism and transmitted by mosquitoes. This resistance comes about because red blood cells with abnormal hemoglobin (heterozygotes have 40 percent abnormal hemoglobin) take on abnormal shapes when infected by the malaria parasite and die, failing to transport the parasite through the system. Sickle cell is found in highest frequencies where malaria is found in highest frequencies (Figure 4.8, p. 77). In no environment is there any advantage in being homozygous for the abnormal allele. In malarial environments, however, heterozygotes do have an advantage. As you saw in the Punnett square, when two heterozygotes mate, they have only a one-quarter chance of producing a homozygous child who will probably die at an early age from sickle cell whereas they have a one-half chance (twice as good) of producing more heterozygotes who carry the defense against malaria.

Adaptive fitness, then, is relative to particular environmental conditions. What is adaptive in one environment may not be adaptive in another. What is adaptive at one time may not be at another. A lethal allele may actually be adaptive in certain genotypic combinations within certain environments. The gene–environment relationship is a complex one.

This is something to keep in mind as we discuss the various phenotypic evolutionary changes our species has undergone. Few evolutionary

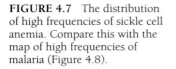

FIGURE 4.7 The distribution of high frequencies of sickle cell anemia. Compare this with the map of high frequencies of malaria (Figure 4.8).

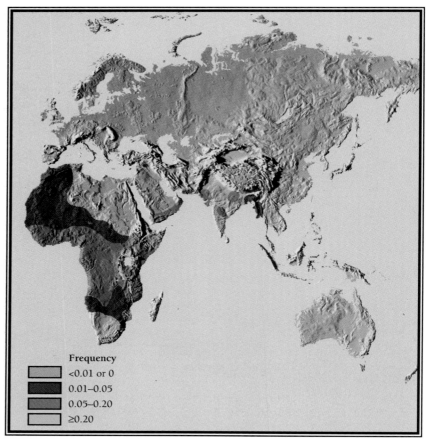

Frequency

	<0.01 or 0
	0.01–0.05
	0.05–0.20
	≥0.20

events are as simple as they first seem. When we discuss the evolution of our upright posture or our large brains, you should appreciate the complex genetic changes that must have occurred, as well as the complex interactions between genotype and phenotype and between phenotype and environment.

It is also important to remember that because it operates on variation already present in existing traits, natural selection is not always successful in maintaining the viability of a species. When some environmental change is too severe or too rapid, there may simply not be any variation within a species that enables some of its members to reproduce in quantities sufficient to perpetuate the species. Extinction is the result—indeed, it has been the fate of over 90 percent of all species that have ever existed.

For example, dinosaur species occupied a great diversity of niches and were around in some form for over 100 million years. Yet a rapid environ-

FIGURE 4.8 The distribution of high frequencies of malaria shows a correspondence with high frequencies of sickle cell anemia (Figure 4.7).

mental change occurred to which none of the dinosaurs (or too few to matter) had sufficiently adapted traits. The dinosaurs died out in a fairly short period of time. Human activity also constitutes a form of environmental change and can bring about the same kinds of results. Overhunting of passenger pigeons in North America, coupled with the felling of forests, resulted in the extinction, by 1914, of a species that once numbered in the billions.

Natural selection is not magic, nor is it the only process that changes allele frequency and thus contributes to evolution. Whereas natural selection produces change in the direction of better adaptation, other processes have no predictable adaptive direction. Because they cause the frequency of alleles to change through time, however, they are considered evolutionary processes (Figure 4.9, p. 78). These processes are mutation, gene flow, and genetic drift, which we will examine next.

FIGURE 4.9 The processes of evolution. A species is in an adaptive relationship with its environment. This relationship is maintained by natural selection. Environments, however, are constantly changing, so which characteristics are adaptive changes through time. In addition, the gene pool of a species is always changing, altering the phenotypes upon which selection acts. Processes that alter a species' gene pool are also, by definition, processes of evolution because they change allele frequency. Mutation provides new genetic variation. Flow and drift mix the genetic variation within populations.

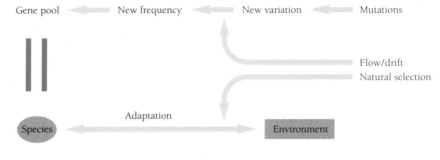

Mutation

Mutations are random—that is, unpredictable—changes in the material of inheritance. Mutations may affect individual genetic loci, as in the case of sickle cell anemia, the result of one wrong codon in a sequence of 146. Or they may affect a whole chromosome, or a portion of a chromosome, and therefore many loci. Mutations may occur spontaneously as a result of mechanical errors during the processes by which the genetic code copies itself during cell division or is translated into working proteins. Mutations may also result from certain outside stimuli such as cosmic or nuclear radiation, various chemical pollutants, and some insecticides.

Mutations are frequent. Some have taken place in cells somewhere in your body since you started reading this page. The only ones that matter to the evolution of sexually reproducing species, though, are those that occur in the sex cells or the cells that produce the sex cells. These are the mutations that can be passed on and can thus change the allele frequencies of a population through time.

Because mutations are sudden, random changes, they may logically be considered mistakes. As mistakes, many have deleterious effects. Such mutations tend to disappear because individuals having them are less reproductively successful. In other words, these mutations are selected *against*. Other mutations may produce alleles that are neutral in terms of adaptation—that is, at the time they occur they are neither more nor less adaptive than the original allele. And some mutations may even be more adaptive than other variations. In this case, natural selection is provided with new raw material that is selected *for*.

Mutation, then, is a source of variation upon which natural selection can act. It is also itself a process of evolutionary change because it alters the hereditary material of a species. The effect of a mutation on the species depends, of course, on just what traits are affected and on how important those traits are to the relative reproductive success of individuals possessing them. A small, inconsequential mutation has little or no effect on the individual. As a result, it may or may not be passed to a proportionately large number of offspring; *that* depends on the success of the individual based on other traits it possesses. A large mutation, or a small one with extensive effects (like the sickle cell allele), will be passed on to decreasing numbers of individuals if it is deleterious—but it may spread rapidly through the species in subsequent generations if it confers a distinct advantage on those who carry it.

Mutations are changes that affect the hereditary material itself. Natural selection operates on the physical manifestations of the hereditary material. Two other processes of evolution, **gene flow** and **genetic drift**, work at a level between selection and mutation. These processes change allele frequency by altering the frequencies of genotypes, that is, allele combinations. They work, however, *without regard* to their specific adaptive characteristics.

Gene Flow

Members of a species interbreed with one another. But species tend to be divided into breeding populations, or demes, that are delimited by geographic distance, a specific environmental range and niche, and social organization. Populations within a species may undergo natural selection for their particular environmental situations and may therefore exhibit minor differences among one another. So when members of different populations do interbreed through migration—when the genes of one "flow" into the **gene pool** of another—the offspring have new genetic combinations. New physical manifestations appear in the mixed population and provide even more raw material for natural selection on the species level.

When flow is extensive among populations within a species, it has the effect of reducing the genetic variation among those populations. This is the case, for example, in our own species, where our mobility and tendency to interbreed have blurred physical distinctions among individual populations.

Genetic Drift

Several distinct processes fall under the heading of genetic drift. **Fission** is the opposite of gene flow. When a population within a species splits, the new subpopulations will differ from one another and from the original population in the average phenotypes and genotypes. This may not seem obvious at first, but an example can demonstrate the point. Suppose you calculate the average stature of members of your anthropology class to be 5′ 9″ with a range from 5′ 1″ to 6′ 7″. If you divide the class into two groups without considering height, do you think the average stature and range for each new group will be the same as the original? Unless the class is extremely large—say, thousands of people—the laws of probability are heavily against it. The same applies to genes in natural popula-

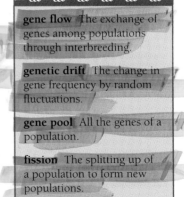

gene flow The exchange of genes among populations through interbreeding.

genetic drift The change in gene frequency by random fluctuations.

gene pool All the genes of a population.

fission The splitting up of a population to form new populations.

FIGURE 4.10 Diagram of fission and the founder effect where a population split produces new populations with distinct gene pools. Gene flow, which produces one new genetic population from two or more, can be pictured by reversing the direction of the arrows.

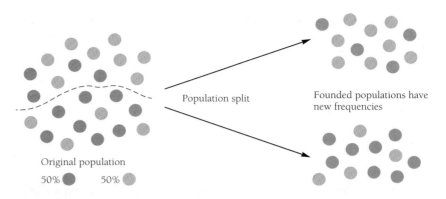

Population split

Founded populations have new frequencies

Original population

50%   50%

tions. Any population split—a common enough occurrence—will provide evolutionary change as well as new gene pools for selection to operate on (Figure 4.10).

This effect is enhanced when the split is uneven—when, for example, 10 percent of a population splits from the original and founds a new population. It is virtually impossible for that 10 percent to possess the same average physical traits, gene combinations, and allele frequencies as the original. This is known as the **founder effect.** It and fission are usually considered one form of genetic drift.

The other form of genetic drift is **gamete sampling.** When fertilization takes place in sexually reproducing species, the genetic material from two parents is mixed. The potential number of new genetic combinations in the offspring is enormous. You may resemble your parents, but you are not a "carbon copy" of either, and your specific genetic makeup is absolutely unique to you (unless you have an identical twin). With sexual reproduction, then, change occurs every generation, based solely on the laws of probability applied to the recombination of parental genes in their offspring. This change is not related to the adaptive fitness of the traits involved because it is produced at the time of fertilization, before the environment has a chance to act on the physical traits.

Recombination affects only the offspring of one set of parents, but the combined effects of this process at the population level, in many sets of parents and offspring, can bring about a great deal of change from one generation to the next. Especially if the phenotypes coded for by the new genetic combinations are adaptively unimportant, the specific expressions may change at random across generations, "drifting" in whatever direction chance takes them—hence the name of the process.

Suppose, for instance, two parents are both heterozygous for a certain locus, say, *Aa*. A Punnett square would reveal that they stand a one-quarter chance of producing an *AA* offspring, a one-half chance of producing an *Aa* offspring, and a one-quarter chance of producing an *aa* offspring. These figures, however, are probabilities, not certainties. Each fertilization

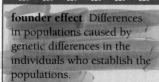

founder effect Differences in populations caused by genetic differences in the individuals who establish the populations.

gamete sampling The genetic change caused when genes are passed to new generations in frequencies unlike those in the parental population.

is an event independent of all previous fertilizations. They may, for example, produce nothing but *AA* offspring. In that case, all their *a* alleles are lost. In a large population, there is a good chance that two other parents of genotype *Aa* will produce only *aa* offspring, and it will all balance out. But in a small population, under 100, the chance of such a balance is very small. In fact, all forms of genetic drift have greater effects in small populations. In this way, some alleles may ultimately be lost and others may reach a frequency of 100 percent all with no necessary relation to adaptation.

As with the other processes, drift produces evolutionary change as well as new population variation on which natural selection may then operate. It may not, however, always be a positive process. A further threat to species already on the brink of extinction because of low population size is the fact that what little genetic variation they have left may be further depleted by the drifting of some alleles to high frequencies and others to low frequencies. The less genetic variation, the less chance a species has of containing enough individuals well enough adapted to reproduce in sufficient numbers. This is part of the current plight of cheetahs, African lions, gorillas, condors, and other endangered species.

The Origins of Species

Although natural selection was the cornerstone of Darwin's theory of evolution, it was not the phenomenon he ultimately sought to explain. What interested Darwin, and Wallace, was the question of where all the species of plants and animals had come from in the first place. Natural selection was the mechanism they proposed as the answer. Darwin, in fact, felt it was *the* answer. Natural selection, he said, brought about "the accumulation of innumerable slight variations, each good for the individual possessor" (1898:267). He added,

> What limit can be put to this power, acting during long ages and rigidly scrutinizing the whole constitution, structure, and habits of each creature,— favoring the good and rejecting the bad? I can see no limit to this power, in slowly and beautifully adapting each form to the most complex relations of life. (1898:267)

So, according to Darwin's view, new species arise as a direct result of constant adaptive change within existing species. Eventually, the species changes so much it evolves into a new species.

Such constant selection, Darwin said, will also produce variation among populations within a species in response to slight differences in their environments. He referred to these populations as "varieties." Eventually, selection brings about such marked distinctions that two or more new species branch from the old one. Species, said Darwin, "are only well-marked varieties, of which the characters have become in a high degree permanent" (1898:285).

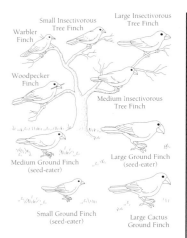

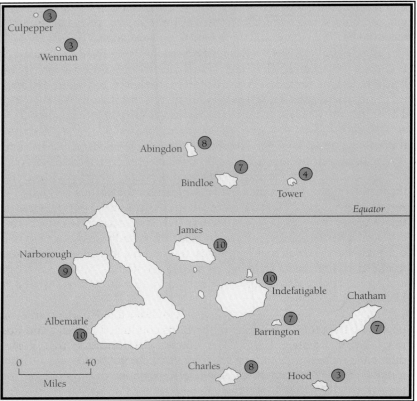

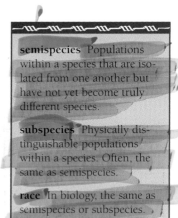

FIGURE 4.11 The various species of Darwin's finches evolved when small groups from an original species underwent adaptation to the varying environmental conditions found throughout the Galápagos Islands. The numbers on the map represent the number of finch species found on each major island.

semispecies Populations within a species that are isolated from one another but have not yet become truly different species.

subspecies Physically distinguishable populations within a species. Often, the same as semispecies.

race In biology, the same as semispecies or subspecies.

Darwin's "varieties" are what modern evolutionary scientists call **semispecies**—populations within a species that can still potentially interbreed within that species but which are, through variation and isolation, well on the way to becoming separate species. Synonyms for semispecies might be **subspecies** or **race.** When the term *race* is used at all in modern biology, it is often used in this way. (Thus, *on a biological level,* we may say that races don't exist within the modern human species because there are no populations within modern *Homo sapiens* that are so different from the rest as to be on the way toward becoming a separate species. See Chapter 12.)

Darwin, then, saw natural selection as more than a mechanism for the origin of species. To him it was the driving force behind the origin of species, constantly choosing from among innumerable small variations those best suited to an environment, and in the end turning one species gradually but inexorably into another or producing first new varieties within species and finally new species, forming in the process "an interminable number of intermediate forms . . . linking together all the species in each group by [fine] gradations" (1898:271–72). Evolution, according to Darwin, is a long string of small adaptive changes through time. This model of evolution is called **gradualism**, or sometimes Darwinian gradualism.

For example, thirteen species of related finches inhabit the Galápagos Islands in the Pacific. They are collectively known as "Darwin's finches" because he first described them, although, surprisingly, he did not realize that they provided a classic example of **speciation** (Gould 1985b, Weiner 1994). Later it was realized that all thirteen species were descended from a single South American species. Over a long span of time, individuals from the original population were blown out to sea from the mainland, and a few managed to end up on the dozen or so major Galápagos Islands where they adapted to the various niches on the islands. Natural selection to those niches, along with the relative isolation of the islands and long periods of time, allowed the finch populations to diverge to such a degree that they are now considered separate species, characterized by such features as differences in size and, especially, in beaks specifically shaped to aid in acquiring the foods each niche provides. Subsequent movement has resulted in a dispersal of the various species among the islands. Some of the larger and more ecologically varied islands of the group support as many as ten finch species (Figure 4.11).

That the finches could be an example of Darwinian gradualism is supported by the pioneering study of the birds conducted by Peter and Rosemary Grant (Weiner 1994). The Grants' data indicate that a slight difference in beak size among members of a finch species—as little as a millimeter or two—can be of adaptive importance during sudden, prolonged, or radical environmental changes such as droughts. In fact, small differences made the difference between life and death, and so, after such an environmental episode, the average beak size of an affected finch species could be significantly altered. When conditions—and, thus, food sources—returned to normal, the average beak size often returned to its previous measurement. Important traits of a species, then, may change back and forth as environmental conditions change. This is called "oscillating selection."

What the Grants' data show is that natural selection *can,* under certain conditions "scrutinize" (as Darwin put it) even what to us would seem the smallest of variations—*if those variations are important to the fitness of the species in question.* Thus, a species could gradually evolve what, over a long period of time, would be sufficient differences to classify the result as a new species. Or, perhaps, varieties within a species could slowly and gradually evolve differences that would eventually make them separate species. Indeed, although we recognize thirteen species names for the Galápagos finches, some of these species can interbreed when altered environmental circumstances cause their niches to overlap. In other words, they might be considered semispecies, still somewhere in the gradual process of becoming true species.

gradualism The view that speciation is slow and steady with cumulative change.

speciation The evolution of new species.

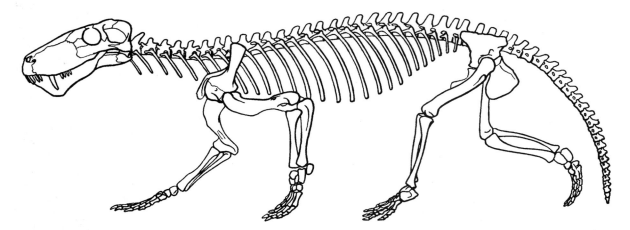

FIGURE 4.12 *Lycaenops*, a mammallike reptile from 240 mya. Its legs were long and under its body, allowing it to keep its body continually off the ground, like mammals in general but unlike earlier reptiles. *Lycaenops* also had long canine teeth like mammals, though its other teeth were reptilian. *(Neg. #2A3387. Courtesy Department of Library Services, American Museum of Natural History)*

Darwin was challenged, however, on one aspect of his model of speciation. If evolution were slow and gradual, where, some of his contemporaries asked, were all those "intermediate forms" in the fossil record? Darwin's answer was that the fossil record was "imperfect," that more time and study would reveal all the transitions. He was overly optimistic.

Although the last 100 years have brought to light fossils representing the transitions between major forms of life (reptiles to birds and reptiles to mammals, for example) (Figure 4.12), transitional forms between individual species have, for the most part, failed to appear. The concrete evidence does not fully support Darwin's model. Moreover, Darwin's gradualism itself presents a theoretical problem. If each small variation selected for is "good for the individual possessor," then we must account for the adaptive benefit of each small step toward the development of some completed characteristic. Could one-tenth of a wing, or one-hundredth of an eye—like a millimeter in the finch's beak—*always* convey to its possessor a reproductive advantage over the members of its species that lack this trait?

It seems more likely that new forms of a trait, or whole new traits, arise fairly rapidly in more complete form. The adaptive value of the new or radically changed characteristic is *then* acted on by natural selection. Selection will eliminate a trait that is not adaptive, ignore a trait that is neutral, or keep a trait that is adaptively advantageous. According to this view, the origin of a new species involves not a series of small steps but an initial big step.

This idea was first seriously proposed in the 1940s, but no genetic mechanism was generally accepted that could account for such large changes so rapidly. Mutations were thought to involve only slight alterations. Now, however, we recognize that not all genetic loci are of equal importance and that a mutation of large numbers of loci or of loci that code for important phenotypic traits can produce a major change in the

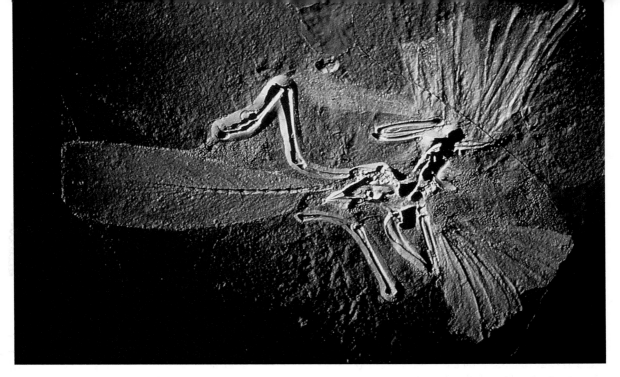

offspring of the organism that passes that mutation on. Such a mutation is called a **macromutation.** Sickle cell anemia is an example—a point mutation but with numerous and extensive phenotypic effects.

There are, in addition, loci influencing developmental changes that act on the individual at an early age but may have important consequences for the structure and function of the adult organism. There appears to have been one such change, more than 140 million years ago, that altered the development of dinosaur scales to produce featherlike structures, thus beginning the evolution of the birds (Figure 4.13). Differences of this sort may be responsible for distinguishing humans from chimpanzees, a topic we'll take up in Chapter 8.

With these theoretical perspectives, the "sudden change" idea of the origin of species could reemerge. It did so in 1972, proposed by paleontologists Niles Eldredge and Stephen Jay Gould (1972), who called it **punctuated equilibrium.** They say that the evolutionary histories of species are marked by equilibrium—long periods of little change—with natural selection acting largely in a conservative way to maintain the species' adaptation to its environment, mostly by selecting against maladaptive variations.

This equilibrium, however, is punctuated by bursts of change that occur when a mutation with extensive results—a macromutation—takes place, producing a variation of a trait or perhaps a whole new feature. If it is particularly adaptive, the characteristic can increase in frequency as new generations are produced, rapidly spreading through the species by means of differential reproduction. Or, in other cases, the new characteristic may arise in a small population isolated at the edge of a species' range. A new

FIGURE 4.13 The fossil remains of *Archeopteryx* ("ancient bird"), about 150 million years old. It is actually a small, bipedal dinosaur with feathers. These feathers, modifications of dinosaurian scales, are an example of a sudden but sizable alteration in a species' genetic makeup that eventually gave rise to a whole new group of organisms. (*Neg. #K12654. Courtesy Department of Library Services, American Museum of Natural History*)

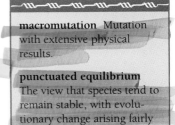

macromutation Mutation with extensive physical results.

punctuated equilibrium The view that species tend to remain stable, with evolutionary change arising fairly suddenly.

Contemporary Issue

The 3 Billion Names of Humanity

—————————————————— —m— ——————————————————

In Arthur C. Clarke's haunting short story "The Nine Billion Names of God," a group of Tibetan monks purchases a supercomputer to speed their task of compiling the 9 billion names of the Supreme Being. Once that compilation is accomplished, they believe, God's purpose will be achieved and the world will end.

In 1986 the U.S. Department of Energy (DOE) initiated, with the cooperation of a number of other agencies and institutions, an ambitious project to develop a "complete description of the human genome at the molecular level" (Woodhead and Barnhart 1988:v), ideally by the year 2000. This project, officially known as the Human Genome Initiative, is mapping the locations of the 100,000 human loci and will ultimately determine the exact sequence of the 3 billion bases that make up our genetic code. This "library" will then act as a tool to allow researchers to understand just how the genetic code functions to generate our various phenotypic traits. We may then be able to apply this knowledge to matters of human health, to the understanding of the diversity within our species and our evolutionary relationships to other species, and to the improvement of domesticated plants and animals.

As of mid-1996, the genetic mapping phase of the project was considered complete (Jordan and Collins 1996; Dib et al. 1996). Genetic maps show the order and relative positions of marker genes along the chromosomes. The physical mapping phase is projected to be complete by 1997. These maps describe the actual chemical make up of marker loci. The base-pair sequence map is expected by about 2003.

The participating agencies are trying to improve the computer and genetic technologies involved to greatly increase the number of bases that can be sequenced each year. Some researchers talk of the need to achieve a rate of 5000 bases per person per day in order to reach their goal in the projected time.

It all sounds ominously like Clarke's monks, and some people fear what might happen when the project is finished and scientists possess such intimate knowledge about just who and what we are. Are such fears warranted?

It should be clear that knowledge itself is not the problem; what we *do* with our knowledge is the concern. For starters, sponsorship of the project by the DOE is explained as "a logical extension of its long term commitment to investigating genetic damage from exposures to radiations and energy-related chemicals" (Woodhead and Barnhart 1988:v). One has to wonder just what the DOE's practical motivation is and exactly how that motivation will affect us in the future. Moreover, one participant in a conference on the project noted (not negatively) that there were financial benefits involved: "The first group or institution to achieve access to data contained in the human genome will be in a position to dominate the biotechnology and pharmaceutical industries for years" (McConnell 1988:2).

Other worries have been expressed as well. Might such detailed knowledge of the genetic differences between individuals and among various populations only fuel the problems of racism and bigotry that

adaptive trait will spread very rapidly through such a group and quickly set that group off on a new mode of life.

In time, a new species may evolve. This is not an instant process; it may take thousands of years, but it is not a gradual evolution marked by a long series of small transitional steps, as Darwin had proposed. It begins with a big step—a "jump," some call it—providing natural selection with something brand new and very different to work with.

still have not been solved? Could employers deny people jobs or insurance companies deny them coverage because of the presence of potentially harmful genetic codes? Will human dignity suffer when we have to acknowledge that we are the results of a bunch of chemical sentences that we can now read and manipulate?

All these results could occur, but it would not be the fault of the information. Rather, the responsible party would be us and the social and ethical environment in which we put this information to use. It is this we need to work on—because the potential benefits of the human genome project far outweigh these preventable deleterious results.

Through their understanding of genetics to date, scientists have been able to diagnose and treat a number of genetic illnesses and to identify persons who may fall victim to a genetic disease or may pass one on to offspring. They can use techniques commonly called genetic engineering—the human manipulation of the genetic process—to do such things as "trick" bacteria into producing real (rather than artificial) human insulin for the treatment of diabetes. Human growth hormone and interferon, a chemical that is part of the body's immune system, have also been manufactured in this way. Scientists have designed plants that are resistant to certain diseases or that can grow in climates to which they were not originally adapted. They have even created bacteria that can "eat" oil spills.

More detailed knowledge of the genome of humans and other organisms can lead to even more progress in these areas. Researchers have, for example, already discovered the base sequence for the AIDS virus. Although scientists have yet to cure or even treat this disease, a complete understanding of the organism that causes it is obviously essential and can guide new and specific experiments.

Understanding completely our genetic code can help physicians individualize medical care. Although many diseases have a single cause, many, like heart attacks, strokes, and cancers, are caused by multiple factors. Being able to read and understand the human genome will help in dealing with these diseases on an individual basis, allowing doctors to find genetic markers that may indicate a greater susceptibility to a particular ailment.

At the end of Clarke's story, the monks, with the aid of the new computer, complete their task in a few months. As the American computer technicians are leaving Tibet, they look up into the sky—and see the stars going out. Will that happen when the genome project has decoded the genetic code? Hardly. For one thing, even after all 3 billion bases are known, researchers will still have to figure out exactly how the protein products of our genes operate to produce all our traits and behaviors. Knowledge is never finished; there's always more to learn. But mostly it's clear that, if used ethically and with care and caution, the knowledge gained through the Human Genome Initiative will greatly benefit human health and general welfare.

After a new trait appears, it will itself begin to exhibit variation that natural selection can then use to "fine-tune" the new adaptive feature to the specific environment. The oscillating selection for beak size (and probably for other traits as well) among Darwin's finches is an example.

With this model in mind, the overall fossil record makes more sense. For instance, we don't find a long, gradual series of stages in the evolution of birds from dinosaurs. The first evidence of birds, from about 150 mil-

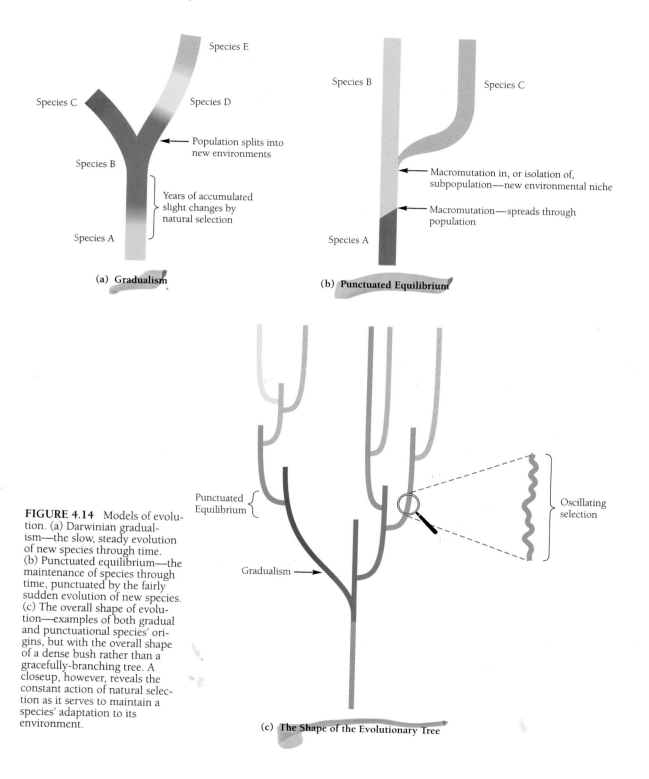

Species E

Species C

Species D

Population splits into
new environments

Species B

Years of accumulated
slight changes by
natural selection

Species A

(a) **Gradualism**

Species B

Species C

Macromutation in, or isolation of,
subpopulation—new environmental niche

Macromutation—spreads through
population

Species A

(b) **Punctuated Equilibrium**

Punctuated
Equilibrium

Oscillating
selection

Gradualism

FIGURE 4.14   Models of evolution. (a) Darwinian gradualism—the slow, steady evolution
of new species through time.
(b) Punctuated equilibrium—the
maintenance of species through
time, punctuated by the fairly
sudden evolution of new species.
(c) The overall shape of evolution—examples of both gradual
and punctuational species' origins, but with the overall shape
of a dense bush rather than a
gracefully-branching tree. A
closeup, however, reveals the
constant action of natural selection as it serves to maintain a
species' adaptation to its
environment.

(c) **The Shape of the Evolutionary Tree**

lion years ago, is in the form of a small, bipedal dinosaur with feathers (see Figure 4.13). These are not one-tenth feathers, but feathers nearly like those of modern birds. Even bigger changes, such as the evolution of mammals from early reptiles—although this took a long time to accomplish—still show a number of jumps rather than a long accumulation of minor changes.

Almost certainly, Darwinian gradualism has accounted for the beginnings of some species—such as the populations of Darwin's finches responding to the different environmental niches of the Galápagos. Natural selection is always in operation and responds, as Darwin suggested, to situations where species' environments undergo sudden and extensive changes. On the level of the day-to-day operation of evolution, natural selection is a powerful, ever-present force. The general record of evolution, however—the origin of all those species Darwin wondered about, and the shape of life's family tree—seems best depicted by punctuated equilibrium (Figure 4.14).

Summary

To fully account for the evolution of species, an understanding of the workings of genetics is vital. Genes code for the traits that make up the physical organism by giving instructions for the synthesis of proteins. Proteins make cells and control their functions, and cells, in turn, make up the tissues that make up the organism.

The gene pool of a species changes over time because of four processes that change the frequencies with which the alleles of genes appear. Mutations produce new alleles or, on the chromosomal level, new sequences or combinations of alleles. Gene flow shuffles the alleles of populations within a species to produce new genotypic frequencies. Due to genetic drift, new genotypic frequencies occur each time a population splits and each time a new generation is produced. And natural selection affects allele frequencies via the differential reproduction of the carriers of adaptive phenotypes.

A great enough degree of this change, under the right circumstances, can evolve new species out of existing ones. Charles Darwin thought this occurred as a result of the gradual yet inexorable force of selection changing each species every generation. We now understand that natural selection is more a conservative force than a creative one, largely acting to maintain the adaptation of a species to its environment. Speciation seems most often to occur when a sudden change, via a large or important mutation or the isolation of a small population within a species, provides natural selection with a new and important choice. If the new choice is adaptively advantageous, it can give a "head start" to the evolution of a new species.

Study Questions

1. What are genes and through what steps do they produce the traits that make up a living organism?
2. What are the basic laws of inheritance; that is, how are traits passed on from parent to offspring?
3. How may we study the genetic makeup of populations as well as genetic change in populations through the use of mathematics?
4. What are the processes of evolution? How do they interact to bring about evolutionary change?
5. How do existing species give rise to new species?
6. How is sickle cell anemia an example of all aspects of modern evolutionary theory?

Key Terms

genetics
gene
particulate
protein
enzyme
deoxyribonucleic acid (DNA)
chromosome
replication
codon
amino acid
locus (plural, loci)
protein synthesis
messenger ribonucleic acid (mRNA)
transfer RNA (tRNA)
allele
genotype
homozygous

heterozygous
mutation
phenotype
recessive
dominant
gamete
segregation
zygote
recombination
codominance
monogenic
polygenic
point mutation
population
breeding population
deme
allele frequency
Hardy–Weinberg equilibrium

differential reproduction
niche
sexual selection
gene flow
genetic drift
gene pool
fission
founder effect
gamete sampling
semispecies
subspecies
race
gradualism
speciation
punctuated equilibrium
macromutation

For More Information

Many excellent books on evolution and evolutionary processes are available. We recommend Mark Ridley's *Evolution*. The history of evolutionary thought, with excerpts from original sources, is covered in C. Leon Harris's *Evolution: Genesis and Revelations.*

A "must" for anyone interested in genetics—or, for that matter, the nature of scientific inquiry in general—is *The Double Helix* by James D. Watson, about the race to discover the nature of the genetic code and thereby win the Nobel Prize. The author was one of the winners. Also on genetics, try Daniel L. Hartl's *Our Uncertain Heritage: Genetics and Human Diversity* for a good general text. *Genetics: Readings from Scientific American,* edited by Cedric F. Davern, provides a wealth of original important articles, including some of historical interest (even one by Mendel). For information on genetic engineering, see "Changing Life's Genetic Blueprint," by Robert F. Weaver, in *National Geographic* (December 1984).

Darwin's finches—a fascinating example of natural selection in operation—and the people who study them are the subject of Jonathan Weiner's Pulitzer Prize–winning *The Beak of the Finch: A Story of Evolution in Our Time.*

The Southeast Asian tarsier is, like us, a primate. What do we have in common with this small tree-dwelling insect-eater—and with nearly 200 other living primate species? How is our species unique? (© *The Zoological Society of San Diego*)

5

Learning About the Past
The Primates

—⁓—

CHAPTER CONTENTS

Taxonomy • The Primates • A Primate Portfolio • The Human Primate • Genetics and Primate Relationships •
The Evolution of the Primates • Contemporary Issue: Why Save the Primates? • Summary • Study Questions •
Key Terms • For More Information

"What is man, that thou art mindful of him?" asks David in the biblical psalm. It is a question we must ask as well, but in a broader form: "What is a human being?" Before we embark on our journey through human evolution, we must understand modern humans, the species with which our journey ultimately ends.

Two problems are encountered in defining humanness. First, all modern human beings belong to a single species, and we lose perspective if we refer only to ourselves. Try describing any animal without referring to other organisms: "Well, a spider has body segments and jointed legs like an insect, only it has eight legs instead of six. . . ." Second, we are members of the very species we're describing. It's difficult to step back and see ourselves from an objective perspective. We have a tendency to focus on things that are important to us in a certain cultural setting at a certain time. For example, Carolus Linnaeus, the great eighteenth-century Swedish naturalist discussed before, listed as the distinguishing characteristics of *Homo sapiens* "diurnal [active during the day]; varying by education and situation." He then described five subspecies of humans using a combination of physical features and subjective European attitudes. Of the Native American, for instance, he said: "Hair black, straight, thick; nostrils wide, face harsh; beard scanty; obstinate, content free. Paints himself with fine red lines. Regulated by customs" (Kennedy 1976:25).

Clearly, we need to look at ourselves not from cultural perspectives like Linnaeus's but in terms of how we compare with other living organisms. Demosthenes, a fourth-century B.C. Greek orator, described us as "featherless bipeds"; twentieth-century biologist Desmond Morris dubbed us the "naked ape." These are better definitions because they are free from cultural values and recognize both our similarities to other organisms and our distinctive differences.

Taxonomy

Despite his obvious ethnocentric biases, Linnaeus did first recognize the importance of describing living organisms in comparison with each other. His **taxonomy,** or system of classification, placed living things in categories based on their similarities to and differences from other living things. The system uses a hierarchical set of nested categories: a few general categories, each containing a number of subcategories, each of those with subcategories, and so on down to the most specific, the species or individual interbreeding group of organisms (Table 5.1).

Humans, for example, fall into the group Animalia within the largest category, kingdom. We are animals because we ingest our nutrients, move about, and have sense organs and nervous systems. We are clearly not members of any of the other four kingdoms: simple single-celled organisms, complex single-celled organisms, fungi, or plants.

Within each kingdom are a number of phyla (singular, phylum). Among the animals, for example, are some thirty phyla—such groups as sponges, jellyfish, flatworms, roundworms, molluscs, insects, and chordates. We have backbones, a fairly distinctive feature in the animal kingdom, so we are members of phylum Chordata—animals with a **notochord,**

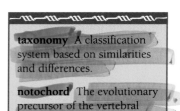

taxonomy A classification system based on similarities and differences.

notochord The evolutionary precursor of the vertebral column.

TABLE 5.1   Taxonomies of Four Familiar Mammals with Basic Features for Each Category

	Jaguar	Mountain Lion	Chimpanzee	Human
Kingdom	**Animalia** Ingestion Movement Sense organs	Animalia	Animalia	Animalia
Phylum	**Chordata** Notochord	Chordata	Chordata	Chordata
Class	**Mammalia** Hair Warm-blooded Live birth Mammary glands Active and intelligent	Mammalia	Mammalia	Mammalia
Order	**Carnivora** Meat eaters	Carnivora	Primates Arboreal Developed vision Grasping hands Large brains	Primates
Family	**Felidae** Retractable claws Furred feet Sharp vision	Felidae	Pongidae Large Tailless Brachiators	Hominidae Habitual bipeds
Genus	*Panthera* Larger roaring cats	*Felis* Smaller purring cats	*Pan* Smaller of African apes Open forest	*Homo* Toolmaking Omnivore
Species	*onca* Largest New World cat Only roaring cat Spotted	*concolor* Largest N. American purring cat Solid color	*troglodytes* Larger of two *Pan* species	*sapiens* Brain size 1000–2000 ml

a long cartilaginous structure running down the back for support—and subphylum Vertebrata—chordates whose notochord is replaced by a bony spine.

There are seven classes within the vertebrates: jawless fishes, cartilaginous fishes (sharks and their kin), bony fishes, amphibians, reptiles, birds, and mammals. We are obviously members of class Mammalia—vertebrates with constant body temperature, hair, live births, mammary glands for nursing young, and relatively large, complex brains.

While things have narrowed down quite a bit, there are still over 4000 species of mammals, everything from kangaroos to blue whales to bats. Where should the comparison be focused next? The key is to remember that the mechanism of natural selection is adaptation. What characterizes a group of organisms in nature is their adaptive behavior. Physical features are important, but the reason they are important is that they make possible a set of behaviors that allows a creature to survive in a certain way under a specific set of environmental circumstances.

Looked at this way, the taxonomic categories become statements about adaptation, with each level more specifically focused. Mammals, for example, are animals that adapt through active lifestyles, relying more than other creatures on learned behavior and thus requiring more care and nurturing of the young as well as a protected constant body temperature to maintain their activity level. But mammals have many different ways of using this general adaptation, and the next category, order, focuses to a great extent on these more specific adaptive strategies. Among the nineteen mammalian orders are the flying bats, the aquatic whales and dolphins, the meat eaters, the insect eaters, the pouched marsupials, and a group of large-brained tree dwellers called the primates. This last group is our own, and our physical and behavioral features can only be understood as expressions of the basic primate adaptive pattern.

The Primates

The essential primate environment is the trees; primates are arboreal, or tree-dwelling. The fact that the human species is obviously built for locomotion on the ground—and clearly not for moving around in the trees—should not be misinterpreted. Among the primates, we humans are exceptional for our mode of locomotion. The vast majority of primates spend their time in the trees and, indeed, our own bodies and behaviors still reflect that arboreal theme.

There are, of course, many other arboreal creatures. Squirrels, birds, many insects, and even a few snakes all have adaptations for a tree-dwelling way of life. Primates don't have a monopoly on that environment, but they do adapt to it in a way none of these others do. It has obviously been a successful adaptation. For even now, with all the changes and disruptions to the natural environment brought about by the human primate, there are still about 200 species of primates spread pretty much worldwide—in Central and South America, Africa, Asia (including northern Japan), and Europe (on Gibraltar).

To examine the characteristics that make possible this arboreal adaptation, we'll use categories that reflect an organism's relation to its environment: the senses, locomotion, reproduction, intelligence, and behavior patterns.

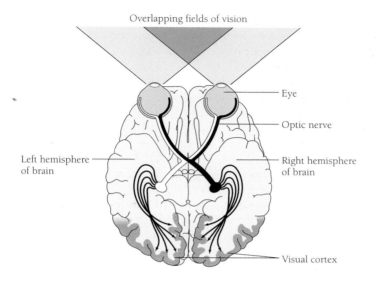

Overlapping fields of vision

Eye

Optic nerve

Left hemisphere of brain

Right hemisphere of brain

Visual cortex

FIGURE 5.1   Stereoscopic vision. The fields of vision overlap, and the optic nerve from each eye travels to both hemispheres of the brain. The result is true depth perception.

The Senses

The world in which an organism lives is to a great extent determined by its senses. All the information a creature takes in about its environment comes through the sense organs, which send signals to the brain for interpretation and (if possible) storage. The predominance of one sense over the others can make an enormous difference. Sound rules the sensory world of a dolphin or a bat; smell predominates for dogs. The primate's world is a visual one.

Unlike most mammals, the majority of primates see in color. Primate eyes face forward instead of out to the sides, so that each eye sees just about the same scene from slightly different angles. When the signals from such eyes are interpreted by the brain, the result is a world of three dimensions. Primates are said to have true depth perception, or **stereoscopic vision** (Figure 5.1). To protect their delicate muscles and nerves, primate eyes are enclosed in a bony socket.

This emphasis on the visual sense in primates seems connected to a reduction in the sensitivity of the other senses, at least as compared with many other mammals. Primates have neither the olfactory (smell) nor auditory (hearing) acuity of such familiar animals as dogs, cats, cattle, and horses. The areas of the primate brain that interpret these data are reduced in comparison with those of other mammals, and primates tend to have flat faces, reducing the olfactory receptor area within the nose. But no living creature, except possibly birds of prey, sees as well as we primates do.

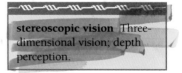

stereoscopic vision Three-dimensional vision; depth perception.

FIGURE 5.2 An orangutan and its trainer holding hands demonstrates the prehensile grasp of the primates, both human and nonhuman. *(Courtesy Marine World/Africa USA and Darryl W. Bush)*

Locomotion

Most mammals are **quadrupedal;** they walk on all fours. With the notable exception of humans, so do primates, but how they use their four limbs differs from other mammals. Whereas the limbs and feet of mammals in general are built for firm, solid contact with the ground (via hooves or paws with pads), primate limbs are highly flexible; the hands and, in many primates, the feet have the ability to grasp objects. Such hands and feet are said to be **prehensile** (Figure 5.2). Moreover, the hands of most primates have some degree of **opposability**—the ability to touch the other fingers with the thumb, enabling them to pick up small objects. Finally, most primates have flat nails instead of claws on the ends of their fingers and toes. Nails lend support to the sensitive tactile receptors of the fingertips, and they don't get in the way as claws would when the hand is closed.

Reproduction

In contrast to many other mammals, which bear litters, or to fish and reptiles, which may produce dozens of offspring at a time, nearly all primates have only a single offspring at a time. A small number of primate species normally give birth to twins or triplets. As mammals, the primates take direct care of their young, protecting, nursing, showing affection, and (even if indirectly) teaching. Particularly because of their large, complex brains, primates take a long time to mature. This time is related to size, so a

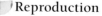

quadrupedal The ability to walk on four legs.

prehensile The ability to grasp.

opposability The ability to touch the thumb to the tips of other digits.

mouse lemur (which you could hold in the palm of your hand) grows up faster than a gorilla or a human. Relative to size, however, the primates have the longest period of **postnatal dependency** of all mammals.

Intelligence

Intelligence means the relative ability of an organism's brain to acquire, store, and process information. To a great extent, these abilities are related to brain size. A bigger brain simply has more room for the neural connections that make it all work. (This is not the case *within* a species, however. For humans, there has been no correlation established between brain size and intelligence, even though some people have brains twice the size of others.) But intelligence is also related to the complexity of the brain—how many parts it has—and to its size relative to the organism's body. No primate has a brain the size of a whale's or an elephant's; compared to body size, however, primates have the largest and most complex brains of all mammals.

The relatively large and absolutely more complex brains of primates allow them to take in, store, and process more information in more complicated ways than other mammals. Primates are smart.

Behavior Patterns

Primates are social creatures. Most live in social groups, but even solitary primates interact with other species members in ways far more complex than would be found among, say, a herd of antelope. The difference is that primates recognize individuals, and individuals each hold a certain status within a primate group. Some primates—baboons, for example—exhibit a form of **dominance hierarchy** in which individuals have differential social power and influence, and, perhaps, access to mates. Nearly all primates recognize a special status for females with infants. Chimpanzees have varying attitudes about members of their group that can only be described by our human term *friendship*.

Much of the reason for this social structure stems from the long dependency period of the young. Born helpless and with much to learn about their world, using large brains that take a long time to grow, primate babies need protection. The close bond between mother and infant common to all primates supplies most of this. But especially in dangerous areas like the open plains of Africa, the presence of a group adds greatly to the chance of successfully rearing offspring to become functioning members of the species' next generation. Care of offspring thus becomes another distinguishing feature of the primate behavior pattern.

Primate social systems are maintained through communication. Although only humans have a complex symbolic language, most primates do have a large repertoire of signs and signals with specific meanings. These take the form of facial expressions, body movements, and vocalizations.

postnatal dependency The period, after birth, of dependency on adults.

intelligence The relative ability to take in, store, access, and use information.

dominance hierarchy Individual differences in power, influence, and access to resources and mating.

FIGURE 5.3   A mother chimpanzee being groomed by another adult female. Grooming serves not only to rid the chimps of dirt and parasites but also helps maintain group unity and harmony. (© *Steve Turner/Oxford Scientific Films/Animals Animals*)

Touch, usually through mutual **grooming** to remove dirt and parasites, is another form of communication common to most primates and seems to serve as a source of reassurance to maintain group harmony and unity (Figure 5.3).

Given this set of mutually reinforcing traits, the primates may be generally defined as arboreal mammals with well-developed visual senses who, by virtue of a large, complex brain, complex social organization, and a long period of infant dependency with extensive and direct care of the young, adapt to life in the trees. They learn about, move with agility through, and manipulate this environment, with the last two abilities made possible by grasping and dexterous hands and feet.

grooming Cleaning the fur of another animal, a behavior that promotes social cohesion.

A Primate Portfolio

For groups with numerous species and a variety of geographical locations and environmental niches, it is necessary to add to the basic seven Linnaean taxonomic categories.

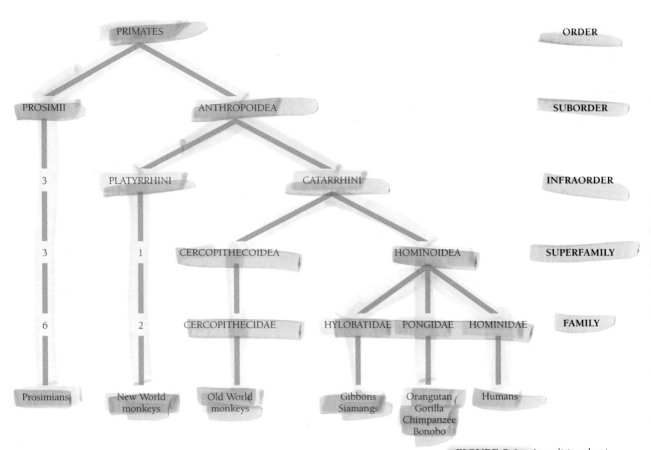

FIGURE 5.4 A traditional primate taxonomy. Numbers refer to living groups in that category. Alternative taxonomies exist. They will be discussed in the Chapter 8 Contemporary Issue.

The order **Primates** (Figure 5.4) is divided into two major groups, suborders **Prosimii** and **Anthropoidea**. Prosimians represent the most primitive primates. Biologically, the term *primitive* implies no value judgment but merely refers to age. Thus, prosimians are said to be primitive because they most closely resemble the earliest primates. As newer, more adaptively flexible primates evolved, the early prosimians were pushed into isolated, protected areas. Prosimians now live in such areas on mainland Africa and India and on the isolated islands of Southeast Asia but most inhabit the island of Madagascar (Figure 5.5, p. 100).

As a group, prosimians show some differences from the general primate pattern outlined in the last section (Figure 5.6, p. 101). About half of the prosimians are nocturnal. As nocturnal creatures, prosimians have a better sense of smell than most primates. To aid this sense, they have a protruding snout with a large olfactory receptor area and a moist, naked nose (like a dog or cat) to help pick up molecules that provide the olfactory signal.

Like nocturnal creatures everywhere, prosimians have large eyes to gather more light, but they have virtually no color vision because it's not useful at night. They do, however, have stereoscopic vision because, like

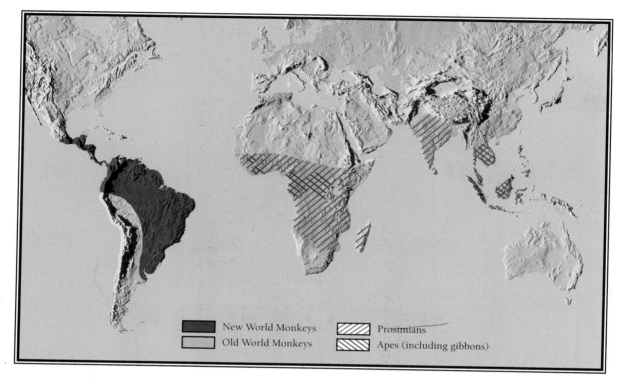

New World Monkeys   Prosimians
Old World Monkeys   Apes (including gibbons)

FIGURE 5.5   Distribution of the living primates.

all primates, they need to judge distances in bushes and trees. Many use this ability to catch insect prey.

Prosimians have prehensile hands and feet, but their opposability is different from the other primates. Rather than being able to touch the thumb to the other fingers individually, the four other digits of prosimians (or three, as some prosimians lack an index finger) move together. In addition, some prosimians have claws on a couple of fingers or toes. These *grooming claws* are used for cleaning fur.

Prosimians spend most of their time in the trees or, if they are small, in bushes. Their form of locomotion depends, of course, on their ability to grasp with hands and feet the trunks and branches on which they are moving. The characteristic way many move about has been called "vertical clinging and leaping" because they jump from branch to branch in an upright position, pushing off with their legs and landing with both arms and legs. This trait differs from the behavior of other primates, who "walk" one limb at a time through the trees, or **brachiate**, swinging arm over arm (see Figure 5.11).

A few of the Madagascar primates, the lemurs (see Figure 3.10), give birth to twins or even triplets on a regular basis. Transporting them seems

brachiate The ability to swing through the trees using arms and hands.

FIGURE 5.6   A prosimian, the slow loris of Southeast Asia. Notice the large eyes; the moist, naked nose; and the grooming claw on one toe of the prehensile foot. (© *Frank R. Sladek/Animals Animals*)

to pose no problem because a male or older sibling often helps the mother take care of the babies. Some species also build nests in which offspring may be kept.

A particularly interesting prosimian is the tarsier (Figure 5.7) of Southeast Asia, a small (4 or 5 ounces) primate noted for its powerful hindlimbs for leaping, enlarged fingertips and toetips for friction, ability to turn its head 180 degrees like an owl, and for its almost exclusively insect diet. Although classed as a prosimian, some authorities think it may be evolutionarily more closely related to anthropoids.

The suborder Anthropoidea (meaning "humanlike") includes the monkeys, the apes, and the humans. It is divided into two infraorders, **Platyrrhini** and **Catarrhini.** This division is based on a geographical separation, a result of continental drift, that split the primates into a Western Hemisphere, or New World, group and an Eastern Hemisphere, or Old World, group. All the New World, or platyrrhine, primates are monkeys. They have several physical characteristics that distinguish them from the Old World, or catarrhine, primates (Figure 5.8).

FIGURE 5.7   The tarsier of Southeast Asia. Note the enlarged fingertips and toetips and powerful hindlimb. (© *The Zoological Society of San Diego*)

FIGURE 5.8 The woolly spider monkey, or *muriqui,* of Brazil. Note the prehensile tail. (© *Andrew L. Young/Archipelago Films)*

One distinguishing feature is the nose. Platyrrhine means "flat nose," and the noses of the New World monkeys have widely spaced nostrils separated by a broad septum. Compare this with your own catarrhine nose. (We are considered Old World primates because that is where humans first evolved.) In addition, platyrrhine primates have more teeth than the catarrhines—twelve premolars or bicuspids compared to the Old World primates' eight. Because most New World monkeys are almost completely arboreal, they have evolved long limbs and long curved clawlike nails; a few even have prehensile tails capable of grasping things and supporting their weight. No Old World primate has this kind of tail. Finally, one group of platyrrhines, the marmosets, normally gives birth to twins.

Referring to Figure 5.4, we see that the Old World primates are divided into two superfamilies. The monkeys of Europe, Africa, and Asia make up superfamily **Cercopithecoidea** and family **Cercopithecidae.** The apes and humans comprise superfamily **Hominoidea.**

Within the cercopithecids are two subfamilies and about a dozen genera with numerous individual species. These monkeys have the nasal shape and tooth number of Old World primates, and most have tails, though none are prehensile. Males tend to be larger than females, unlike the New World species, which show little sexual dimorphism. The cercopithecids have fully opposable thumbs (also unlike the platyrrhines). In general, the monkeys of the Eastern Hemisphere seem more adaptively

FIGURE 5.9 Japanese macaques, the "snow monkey," are well adapted to life in cold, mountainous areas, even to the point of warming themselves in volcanic hot springs. (© *Steven Kaufman/Peter Arnold, Inc.*)

flexible. One large genus, **Macaca**, has representative species all the way from North Africa to India to the mountains of northern Japan, where they are called "snow monkeys" (Figure 5.9).

Another genus, **Papio**, is of particular interest to us because it contains most of the baboons, the large, long-snouted monkeys of the African savannas (Figure 5.10, p. 104). This is the environment in which our lineage developed. The savannas are nearly the same today as when the first humans lived on them. By observing the adaptations of another primate to the same environment, we may get some idea of how our ancestors survived. We'll discuss this topic in detail in Chapter 6.

Superfamily Hominoidea, the large, tailless primates, is made up of three families. Family **Hylobatidae** includes the gibbons and siamangs of

FIGURE 5.10   A family of olive baboons, related females, and their offspring. (© *Stefan Meyers/Animals Animals*)

Southeast Asia and Malaysia, sometimes referred to as the "lesser apes." These species are especially noted for their form of locomotion, called brachiation—arm-over-arm swinging from branch to branch (Figure 5.11). To aid in this movement, the arms of gibbons and siamangs are much longer and more powerful than their legs and end in hands with short thumbs and long, hooklike fingers. The hylobatids have, for the primates, an unusual social group: A male and female are monogamous and their offspring stay together and establish and defend a territory.

Family **Pongidae** are the "great apes," of which there are four living species: the orangutan of Southeast Asia (genus *Pongo*), the chimpanzee and the bonobo or pygmy chimpanzee (genus *Pan*), and the gorilla (genus *Gorilla*) of Africa (Figure 5.12). These are the most robust primates, heavy-boned with large, powerful jaws and chewing muscles they use in eating a wide range of fruits and vegetables and, in the case of the genus *Pan*, meat. The apes are essentially quadrupeds. Chimps and gorillas spend a large portion of their time on the ground, whereas the orangutan spends almost all of its time in the trees. In fact, the orangutan is so well adapted to arboreal locomotion that its feet look and function like two additional hands.

FIGURE 5.11   A gibbon brachiating. (*K. L. Feder*)

All the great apes are built like brachiators with large and powerful shoulders and arms, but they are too large to do much traveling in this fashion. Though predominantly quadrupedal, the apes can and do walk upright on occasion, usually when they want to look around or carry something.

Orangutans are solitary, but chimps, bonobos, and gorillas live in social units marked by a changing group membership, loose organization, and some degree of dominance recognition. Because the apes don't live in areas that present the dangers faced by savanna primates, dominance and its recognition may be even looser and more flexible than among baboons.

Apes have large brains, some having been measured at about half the size of the smallest modern human brains. Many features of the anatomy of pongid brains are also similar to those of humans. Apes are intelligent. They have, for example, a vast knowledge of a great number of food sources. Because many of these foods are fruits, they need to be aware of seasonal changes so they can be at the right place when the fruits ripen, a cognitive behavior found also in some monkeys.

Chimpanzees can even make simple tools. Their most well known are the "fishing sticks" they make from twigs and blades of grass. They stick

FIGURE 5.12   The great apes (clockwise from top left): orangutan of Southeast Asia; gorilla, bonobo, and chimpanzee of Africa. (*orangutan and bonobo, © Ron Garrison/The Zoological Society of San Diego; gorilla, M. A. Park; chimpanzee, © Steve Turner/Animals Animals/Earth Scenes*)

FIGURE 5.13   Chimps using tools they have made to extract termites from a mound. *(Jane Goodall, courtesy National Geographic Society)*

these down termite holes, wiggle them around, and draw out a meal of termites that have attacked the "invader" by clinging to it with their powerful pinchers (Figure 5.13). This is a cultural behavior: It is learned. It also involves abstract concepts; the chimps must visualize the tool within the bush or grass as well as the behavior of the unseen termites. It involves an artifact—a natural object specifically modified for a specific purpose. This tool-using behavior also differs from individual to individual and from group to group, with each chimp having a raw material that is her favorite (usually only females perform this activity). Most chimp troops don't do it at all, a sure sign that the behavior is learned rather than genetic. Humans are clearly not the sole possessors of culture.

Chimps are also known to hunt small mammals, including young baboons. Often just one chimp, nearly always a male, does the hunting and killing, but at times it is a cooperative venture appearing to have some sort of group strategy. The meat acquired is the one food that chimps share with one another. Bonobos also hunt and eat meat, although less often.

Like all primates, apes use vocalizations, facial expressions, and body language to communicate. They have nothing like a human language, but they do have brains capable of learning the rudiments of human language. Chimps, gorillas, and orangutans have been taught to use various symbolic representations of language, most notably American Sign Language for the hearing impaired (AMESLAN), because these species lack the vocal apparatus to make the full range of human sounds. Some researchers claim that these apes can communicate at about the level of a 4- or 5-year-old human, linking words in grammatically correct ways. Others refute this, saying the apes are only mimicking their trainers. This research remains controversial, although most evidence seems to be on the side of some elementary linguistic ability on the part of our closest relatives.

The other family within the hominoids, **Hominidae,** includes living humans, all of whom belong to the same genus and species, *Homo sapiens.* Humans of the past, when at times several genera and species existed, also belong to family Hominidae, the hominids.

The Human Primate

It should now be clear that humans are primates. We share with some 200 other species a common set of basic physical and behavioral traits. Each primate species, though, has its own unique expression of the primate adaptation. Humans are no exception. In fact, our expression of the primate adaptation involves not being arboreal at all. Let's review the five categories discussed earlier and see how we compare.

1. *The senses.* Our sensory organs are basically the same as those of the anthropoid monkeys and apes. Sense of smell seems exactly the same. Monkeys can hear higher sound frequencies than we can, but we are more sensitive to changes in pitch and intensity. Color vision is the same in humans, apes, and monkeys, except that humans may be more sensitive to slight differences in colors than monkeys. It is possible, though, that this may be because we have assigned cultural names to slightly different shades of color and so recognize them because we have learned them. It has also been suggested that we can distinguish many colors because we can concentrate harder on such tasks (Passingham 1982). In general, humans, apes, and monkeys perceive the same world.

2. *Locomotion.* The most striking physical difference between us and the other primates is the way we move about. We are the only primate that is habitually bipedal, walking on two feet. The bones of our back, pelvis, legs, and feet are all structured to balance us and hold us erect. Our musculature has evolved to serve the same purpose. Even the rather spherical shape of our head, as opposed to the more elongated heads of other primates, may have evolved in part to be more balanced atop a vertical spine. Because our legs are the limbs of locomotion, they are longer and more muscular than our arms—just the opposite of apes. Completely freed from locomotor functions, our hands have become organs of manipulation. We have the most precise opposability of the primates, facilitated by the longest and relatively strongest primate thumb.

3. *Reproduction.* Like nearly all primates, we normally have one offspring at a time. Though we are not the largest primate (gorillas are), we have the longest period of dependency and maturation. Chimps, for example, reach sexual maturity in about nine years and physical maturity in about twelve years. For us, the averages are thirteen years and twenty-one

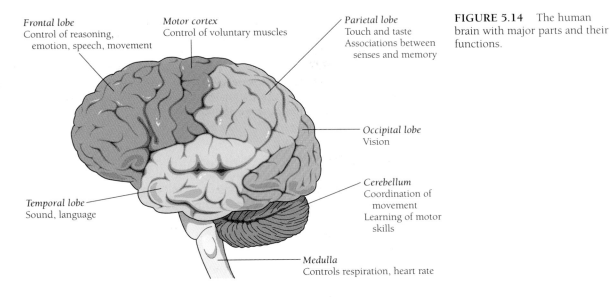

Frontal lobe
Control of reasoning,
emotion, speech, movement

Motor cortex
Control of voluntary muscles

Parietal lobe
Touch and taste
Associations between
senses and memory

Occipital lobe
Vision

Cerebellum
Coordination of
movement
Learning of motor
skills

Temporal lobe
Sound, language

Medulla
Controls respiration, heart rate

FIGURE 5.14   The human brain with major parts and their functions.

years. Not only do we grow up more slowly, we are born relatively more immature and helpless than other primates, so we get off to a late start.

4. *Intelligence.* We are clearly the most intelligent primate because we can store and process more information in more complex ways than the others. Our cultural behavior—our languages, societies, abstract belief systems, scientific knowledge—attests to these abilities. Our intellect is made possible by our big brain, the result of and reason for the extended period of growth after our immature births. Otherwise, our brains are built on the basic primate pattern, with the same proportions of various parts as most primates. In fact, some primates have larger brains, relative to body size, than ours. In absolute terms, however, our brains are larger and more complex. Especially large is our **neocortex,** the outer layer of the brain where abstract thought, problem solving, and attentiveness take place (Figure 5.14).

5. *Behavior patterns.* Like most primates, humans live in social groups. The difference is that our groups are structured and maintained by cultural values—ideas, rules, and behavioral norms we have created and share through complex communication systems. Moreover, we respond not only to a social system in its entirety but also to individual people within the society. A human social system is the result of the collective conscious responses of a group of individuals.

This is not to say that the social systems of nonhuman primates are entirely based on instinctive behaviors. The other primates can be quite flexible, adapting their actions to the specific situation at hand. But other primates' basic models of social organization are less flexible and more stable than ours.

neocortex The part of the brain responsible for memory and thought.

Our big brains have allowed us to move well beyond purely biological evolutionary processes. Certainly, natural selection brought about the evolution of our big brains in the first place, but the way in which this organ functioned permitted us to think up answers to the problems of our survival. As human societies moved around and encountered varying environmental situations and other human groups, these answers became so complex that strikingly different social systems evolved. In a sense, culture *became* our environment, to which we responded with still newer cultural ideas, systems, and artifacts.

Chimps may exhibit some cultural behaviors, may be able to learn to use the basic features of human language, and may differ from us genetically by only about 1 percent of their genes, but our behavior—the extent to which we use and indeed rely on culture—is very different from that of the other primates.

Genetics and Primate Relationships

Physical features are controlled by a complex interaction of genetic loci, evolutionary processes, and environmental factors. Trying to examine evolutionary relationships based solely on physical traits can lead us astray. A trait may look the same in two organisms, but the expressions of the trait may be based on very different genetic and developmental processes, and the traits themselves may differ in their adaptive significance. A famous example (Gould 1980) is the "thumb" of the panda, a bear. It looks very much like the thumb of many primates, but its use is specialized—it enables the panda to handle and strip the leaves off bamboo stalks. And it's not a finger at all but an elongated wrist bone.

Some investigators ask, then, would it not be more informative to look at the genes themselves—or at least at the immediate products of the genes? Two organisms with similar genes must certainly be closely related evolutionarily.

In the 1960s, Vincent Sarich and Allan Wilson of the University of California at Berkeley pioneered research along just such lines (Sarich 1971). They compared the blood proteins of a number of organisms, with the goal of quantifying similarities and differences. Blood proteins such as albumin are large, easy to work with, and are made up of amino acids, which are the immediate products of the genetic loci.

Sarich and Wilson indicated the degree of similarity between proteins by an "index" number. The proteins of an organism compared with themselves are represented by a figure of 1 unit since they are identical. Human protein compared with that of a cow gives a figure of 20 units; with an Old World monkey, a figure of 2.38. Human protein with chimpanzee protein gives the startlingly low figure of 1.17 units. The blood proteins of our two species are almost identical.

There was an even more startling inference from this research. Sarich and Wilson wondered if their figures might provide a relative idea not only of evolutionary distance but also of the timing of the evolutionary break. Because evolution involves the accumulation of mutations, the differences between two species in a genetic product like albumin might act as a "clock" if the mutations causing those differences take place at a fairly constant rate and if we can then figure out how many of those mutations take place over a certain period of time.

Comparing species whose time of divergence was well established from the fossil record, Sarich and Wilson concluded that the 1.17-unit difference between chimps and humans corresponded to an evolutionary separation of only 5 million years. At the time, the accepted date stood between 12 and 15 million. Based on the "protein clock," Sarich said that no primate that old could be a hominid no matter what it looked like. He was right.

But the protein clock theory was not universally accepted, largely because of two limitations. First, the mutations used must be neutral. If they are adaptively important, natural selection will bring about either their accumulation through generations (if they are beneficial) or their disappearance (if they are not adaptive). The genetic differences that actually appear between two species will thus reflect not simply how many mutations occurred but also how selectively advantageous they were.

Second, different species have different generation times. The more frequently a species reproduces, the more chances mutations have to pass to a succeeding generation. Thus, even if mutations occur at a standard rate—an idea that is still open to question—they may differ in their rate of accumulation depending on the generation time of the species in question.

Even so, the protein clock idea does seem to agree with the fossil evidence on the divergence time of some species, including chimps and humans. At the very least, the clock provides us with a rough estimate. In addition, four other types of genetic tests support a recent date of divergence for our two species.

One of those types of genetic evidence comes from comparison of the amino acid sequences in certain proteins, especially some of the shorter proteins like hemoglobin and other blood system components. Amino acids, you recall, are the direct products of the genetic code. The results of amino acid sequence comparisons between primates match remarkably well with the blood protein tests. Humans and Old World monkeys show a difference of 3.9 percent for amino acid sequences in the proteins examined. A 2.8 percent difference was found between humans and orangutans, and the amazingly low figures of 0.6 percent for humans compared with gorillas and 0.3 percent for humans compared with chimpanzees. Based on this evidence, not much time elapsed since our evolutionary branch diverged from that of the African apes.

Another method, called DNA hybridization, is very important because it compares actual genetic material. The strands of the DNA double helix,

FIGURE 5.15   Human chromosomes, on the left in each pair, compared to those of chimpanzees. The similarities in banding pattern are clear. In the far lefthand pair, the pattern of human chromosome 2 is similar to that of two chimp chromosomes. The far righthand pair are virtually identical. This is one piece of evidence for the 99 percent genetic similarity between our two species.

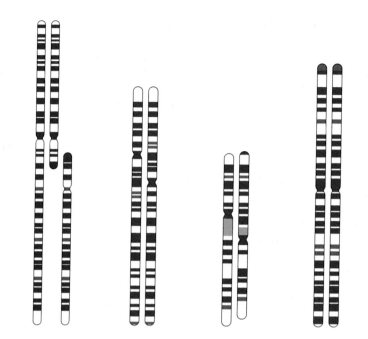

with their pairs of loci, can be broken apart with heat. Because the loci are paired, the strands will attempt to bond again. A measure of species similarity can be made by seeing how well a strand from one species will bond with a strand from another. The tightness of the new bond is determined by measuring how much heat is necessary to break it. Again, the results coincide with those of the other genetic tests. The difference between humans and Old World monkeys is expressed as 9; between humans and orangutans, 4.5; humans and gorillas, 2.5; and humans and chimps, 2.4. The derivation of the numbers is complicated, but, simply put, the lower the number, the more heat is needed, thus the tighter the bond and more similar the species.

Another method involves comparison of the patterns of bands appearing on chromosomes treated with certain dyes (Figure 5.15). The exact meaning of the patterns is unclear, but the patterns are unique for each chromosome within a species. There is evidence that when species are compared, similar banding patterns are an indication that the chromosomes carry similar genetic loci. There is approximately 98 percent similarity in the 500 bands observed in humans, chimps, gorillas, and orangutans. Twelve chromosomes of humans and chimps have virtually identical patterns. For certain specific regions on some chromosomes, humans show a greater affinity with gorillas.

The chromosome-banding studies show something else interesting. A major difference in the chromosomes of humans and the great apes is the fact that apes have more—48 as opposed to our 46. But when banding patterns are observed, it appears that one of our chromosomes may have been derived from two of the apes'. The difference in chromosome number may not indicate all that much difference in evolutionary relationship.

A final method of genetic comparison uses mitochondrial DNA, found not in the nucleus of the cell but in organelles outside the nucleus. This topic will be described in detail in Chapter 12. For now, suffice it to say that this test, too, indicates a close relationship among humans and the African great apes.

Taken together, this genetic evidence points to the chimpanzee as our closest living relative, but some specific tests within these four types give somewhat ambiguous results regarding the precise relationship among chimps, humans, and gorillas. Some indicate we have a closer affinity with gorillas; others seem to show that our three species are equally related. The exact nature of our evolutionary kinship is, according to one authority, "a close call" (Marks 1991). We are left, however, with the undeniable conclusion that we diverged from our closest relatives, the African apes, in the recent past, maybe as recently as 5 million years ago (mya).

The Evolution of the Primates

To say that the fossil record of the early primates is confusing is to understate the case. There are a large number of fossil specimens of primates, but, as one authority notes, 65 percent of extinct primate species are based on fossils that are "extremely fragmentary," mostly pieces of jaw or sometimes just teeth (Martin 1990:39). Although one extinct species may be represented by many specimens, fossils of its contemporaries are lacking, giving us no basis for comparison. For certain periods of primate evolution, all fossils are found in one or two locations. Still, we have been able to piece together the basic picture of the primate evolutionary story (Figure 5.16, p. 116).

Very little exists to tell us about the beginnings of the primates. A few primatelike teeth from Montana dated at 65 mya and some bones from Wyoming, from 60 mya show primatelike anatomical features related to climbing. There is a whole group of species from North America and Europe, the plesiadapiforms, once thought to have linked the very early primates to more modern forms. New evidence, however, suggests they are actually related to the Southeast Asian colugo, a gliding mammal.

It is not until about 55 mya that undisputed primates are found. They are often referred to as "primates of modern aspect" and are classed as prosimians. The fossils seem to come in two groups, both from North America and Europe, still connected at the time. One group, the lemurlike

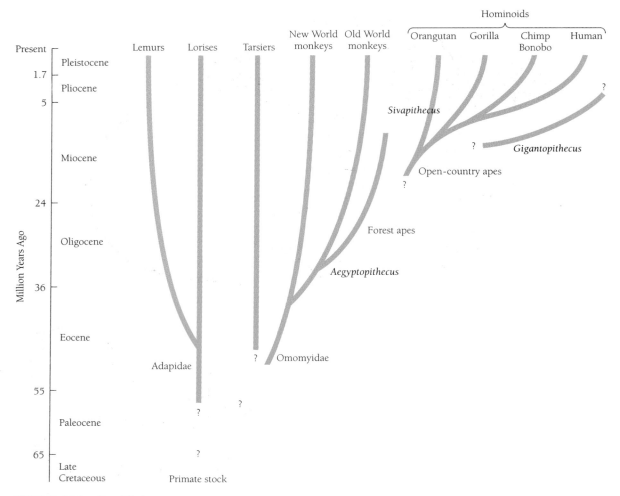

FIGURE 5.16   Simplified evolutionary tree for the primates, with major geological periods and dates. Question marks indicate insufficient data to establish evolutionary relationships.

Adapidae (Figure 5.17), is thought to be ancestral to modern lemurs and lorises. The other group, the tarsierlike **Omomyidae**, which may date back to 60 mya, gave rise to modern tarsiers (Figure 5.18, p. 118). It is thought either to have given rise to the anthropoids or to represent the tarsierlike primates that just split from the ancestors of the anthropoids.

By the time the omomyids were moving into Asia, the Eastern and Western Hemispheres were separate. The New World has so far offered virtually no fossil evidence to tell us what happened next. It may be that the prosimian forms that ended up in the New World moved into South America once it joined North America and evolved into the present-day platyrrhine monkeys. A second view is that prosimian evolution got no farther in the Western Hemisphere and that early monkeys from the Old World "rafted" over to South America, floating on logs and branches, or

FIGURE 5.17   Skeleton and reconstruction of early lemuroid *Smilodectes*. Note the resemblance to the lemur in Figure 3.10. (*Rudolf Freund from "The Early Relatives of Man" by Elwyn Simons*, Scientific American, *July 1964, p. 57*)

crossed over on a chain of volcanic islands when South America and Africa were still fairly close together. The degree of physical similarity among all modern anthropoids suggests a single origin and so argues for the second scenario, as does a new fossil from Chile of a 20-million-year-old monkey that is strikingly similar to older monkey fossils from Africa.

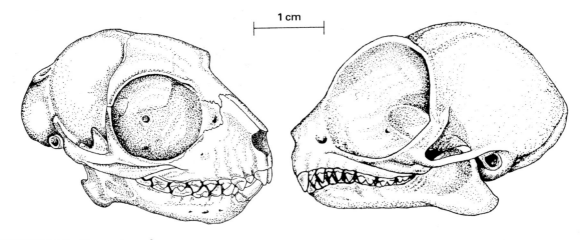

1 cm

FIGURE 5.18   Comparison of fossil omomyid *Necrolemur* (left) with modern tarsier. (*From R. D. Martin*, Primate Origins, *Chapman and Hall, 1990, p. 61*)

The early evolutionary history of the Old World monkeys themselves is known largely from a single site, though it has yielded a large number of fossils. This site is a desert depression, the remains of an ancient lake, southwest of Cairo, Egypt, called the Fayum.

From the Fayum come a number of monkeylike forms dated 40 to 25 mya, perhaps the most important of which is **Aegyptopithecus** (Figure 5.19) dated at 33 mya. From its postcranial skeletal remains, this anthropoid of about 10 pounds seems to have been an arboreal quadruped. It shows a number of features of the teeth, brain, and skull that resemble those of the later hominoids, the apes and humans. *Aegyptopithecus* may be an early ancestor of the hominoids, although it is still primitive enough to be ancestral to the modern Old World monkeys as well.

Definite apes appeared beginning about 23 mya and became more numerous over the next 10 to 15 million years. We refer to these as "dental apes" because their teeth have the characteristics of modern apes. Their bodies, though, are distinctly different. Do not get the impression that modern-looking chimpanzees were running around in these very ancient times. The early apes seem to come in two groups: an arboreal forest-dwelling form from Africa and Europe and a later, open-country, more ground-living form from Eurasia. The classification of these primates as apes is based on a number of physical features, the most important of which is a trait of the molar teeth found only in modern hominoids and no other primate—the Y-5 cusp pattern (Figure 5.20).

The forest-dwellers show a great deal of physical variation and wide geographical distribution, but all seem to be arboreal and fruit-eating. Although classed as apes, none shows a great resemblance to any of the modern ape species. The fossil record of these forms ends about 9.5 mya. A recent find from Spain dated from that period—a nearly complete skeleton of a form called **Dryopithecus**—shows traits that could be ancestral to all later apes and hominids, however.

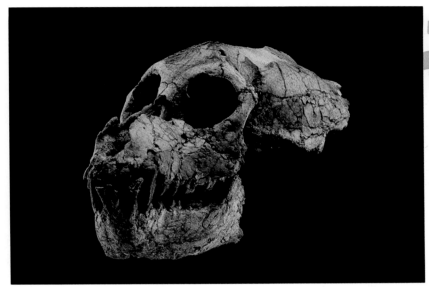

FIGURE 5.19 Skull of *Aegyptopithecus* from the Fayum in Egypt, considered an early monkeylike form that may be ancestral to later Old World monkeys and apes. (© David L. Brill 1985/Brill Atlanta)

The fossils of the ground-dwelling apes have been found in Africa, India, Pakistan, Turkey, China, Hungary, and Greece. The earliest specimens were teeth and partial jaws. On the strength of one interpretation of these remains, they were claimed to be the earliest hominids, the first members of the human lineage. This conjecture coincided nicely with what was then thought to be the 12- to 15-million-year separation of humans from apes.

In the 1960s, however, the new chemical and genetic techniques described above showed that humans and the African apes were much more closely related than had previously been thought. The implication for evolution is that we could not possibly have been evolving along separate lines for 12 million years. The new evidence pointed to a divergence of our lineages only 5 or 6 mya.

Additional and more complete fossils have supported this idea. The fossils are clearly still apes. In fact, the form from India, Pakistan, and Turkey, called **Sivapithecus** (Figure 5.21, p. 120), is, according to anthropologist David Pilbeam, an ancestor of the orangutan. *Sivapithecus* and the modern orangutan share detailed features of the face and teeth as well as a similar relative size and structure of the arms.

Another form, **Ouranopithecus,** so far found in Greece and dated at between 9 and 10 mya, shares some detailed features with hominids. Though clearly an ape, about the size of a female gorilla, it is thought by some to be a good candidate for a member of the ape line that led eventually to the hominids (De Bonis and Koufos 1994).

Yet another interesting fossil form in this general group is a giant ape from China, Viet Nam, and northern India called **Gigantopithecus.** So far,

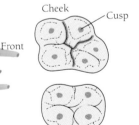

Cheek

Cusp

Front

FIGURE 5.20 Y-5 cusp pattern found only in hominoids *(top),* and the four-cusp pattern found in all anthropoids. The chewing surface is shown. A look in the mirror will probably give you a first-hand glimpse of a Y-5 tooth.

FIGURE 5.21   Skull of *Sivapithecus (left)* compared to modern orangutan. They are essentially identical. *(From Dr. Ian Tattersall, American Museum of Natural History, The Human Odyssey, 1993)*

only its massive jaws and teeth have been found, but estimates from these indicate that it may have been 10 to 12 feet tall when standing upright and weighed from 700 to 1200 pounds. Evidence from its teeth indicates that, like the gorilla, it was a vegetarian. Certain features of the teeth link it to the sivapithecid group.

Taking into account physical features and dates for the half-dozen or so forms of ground-dwelling fossil apes, Pilbeam (1986) suggests the following sequence: The large apes evolved in Africa about 20 mya and split from there into a number of distinct evolutionary lines. Gradually, though, these decreased, leaving relatively few forms to evolve into modern hominoids. One of these is the Asian *Sivapithecus*–orangutan line. A form remaining in Africa gave rise to gorillas and then, about 5 or 6 mya, split into two further lineages that would become chimpanzees and humans.

There is virtually no fossil evidence in Africa that shows us exactly where, when, and how this branching took place. The record stops about 8 mya with sivapithecid apes and picks up at about 4.5 mya with a group of bipedal hominids. For now, we can only take the fossil evidence at both ends of that gap, add to it what we know about climatic changes and ecological conditions as well as the differences between us and the modern apes, and make some informed guesses about what happened to start our evolutionary line. That is the subject of Chapter 8.

Summary

One important tool for learning about the past is to understand the results of all events that made up the past. By determining our place in nature and our relationships with other primates, we can see what the present-day

Contemporary Issue

Why Save the Primates?

Two days after Christmas 1985, American biologist Dian Fossey was murdered—hacked to death with machetes—at her camp in the mountains of Rwanda in central Africa. Fossey had spent the previous eighteen years studying and trying to save from extinction the endangered mountain gorilla, a subspecies of gorilla. (There are now only a few hundred mountain gorillas left in the wild. The other group, the lowland gorilla, is more numerous, but not by much.) Fossey allegedly was killed because of her campaign against poachers, who regularly murder gorillas for their hands and heads, which bring high prices as "souvenirs," and because the park in which she was working is wanted for farmland.

It is clear that the answer to the question "Why save the primates?" cannot be "because they are so similar to us"—look at what we can do to members of our own species. Rather, the answer must come from broader scientific and ethical considerations.

The problem is severe. Besides the gorilla, over 60 species of primates are classed as endangered (on the verge of extinction), vulnerable, or rare. These include the golden lion tamarin, the uakari, and the woolly monkey of South America and the proboscis monkey, pileated gibbon, and most lemurs of the Old World.

The endangered status of these primates, and of many other animals and plants, is largely the result of human actions—destroying natural habitats, hunting (usually for trophies rather than for food), and capturing for zoos and various medical experiments and tests, many of questionable value.

The world changes, and as it does species become extinct. That has been the normal trend of evolution. By accelerating the extinction rate, however, humans could be doing irreparable damage. We are really just beginning to appreciate the great complexity of ecological relationships. It is known that sometimes the loss of one species can bring about change in those species with which it had some ecological connection. Take away a source of food, for example, and the creatures that depend on that food might disappear as well. Destroy the world's rain forests by cutting them down or the ocean's plankton by pollution, and the result is a decrease in the amount of breathable oxygen produced by those plants.

In addition, by speeding the extinction of so many species, we are losing valuable knowledge about the world and—especially in the case of the primates—about ourselves. As we have seen, new scientific techniques and ideas arise all the time, but without the raw data from nature they remain abstract and unproven.

There are also ethical reasons for saving species. Ethical precepts are, of course, belief systems, and therefore not scientific. Yet what has been learned about the world through science, we believe, can support certain ethical ideas on this crucial matter. No matter how different the human species is from other organisms, we still arose and evolved through the actions of the very same processes that bring about the evolution of all living things. We are variations on the theme called life, sharing with every other living creature the same genetic code, amino acid building blocks, and metabolic processes. The very cells that make up our bodies evolved billions of years ago from the joining of different simple organisms that worked together in what is called a symbiotic relationship.

When the matter is seen in this light, one must ask whether we have any right to tamper with the welfare of other species. That the random changes of evolution have endowed us with big brains and thus with the ability to manipulate the environment hardly makes humans any better than our fellow creatures. Indeed, we think it gives us a *responsibility* to use these evolutionary gifts for the betterment of the world—not, as has been the case so often, for its selfish destruction.

Primates are smart, cute, and a lot like us. The argument to preserve life is often convincing when applied to them. But what good are less humanlike creatures such as the California condor, the spotted owl, or other species that are facing extinction? Well, what good was that little insect-eating mammal who, some 65 mya, started clambering about in the trees?

products are of the 65 million years of primate evolution. This gives us a road map for journeying into the past and looking at the other tool, the fossil record.

Humans are among some 200 species of living primates. In many ways we are typical of this group—with three-dimensional color vision; prehensile, opposable hands; emphasis on social groups; a long period of dependency shown by single-birth offspring; and the intelligence and flexibility of our brains in dealing with our world.

In other ways, however, we are atypical primates. We are not arboreal. Our feet are not prehensile but are built to support the entire weight of our upright locomotion. We have especially dexterous hands with long, strong opposable thumbs. We take the longest time of any primate to mature, and we have the largest, most complex brains. Finally, we rely for our very survival on one of the products of those brains: our culture.

The primate fossil record is a complex one that may stretch back to the time of the last dinosaurs. Much remains to be explained, especially about the early stages of primate evolution. Clearly, though, our group, the hominids, is a late arrival on the primate scene, splitting off from the African apes a mere 5 or 6 mya.

Study Questions

1. What is our place in nature; that is, where do we humans fit—from a scientific point of view—in the world of living things? How does taxonomy help us describe our place in nature?
2. What are the characteristics of the members of the primate order?
3. What are the different groups of primates? What are their characteristics, basic behaviors, and geographical distribution?
4. In what ways are humans like the other primates? In what ways are we unique?
5. What is the genetic evidence for our relationship with the other primates?
6. What is the basic story of primate evolution?

Key Terms

taxonomy	postnatal	brachiate
notochord	dependency	neocortex
stereoscopic vision	intelligence	
quadrupedal	dominance	
prehensile	hierarchy	
opposability	grooming	

For More Information

An excellent book that examines humans as an animal species is Richard Passingham's *The Human Primate*. Perhaps the major reference work on the nonhuman primates is *The Natural History of the Primates* by J. R. and P. H. Napier. The National Geographic Society has a beautifully illustrated book on the great apes, *The Great Apes: Between Two Worlds,* by Nichols, Goodall, Schaller, and Smith, that discusses not only the four species of apes but also talks about the scientific studies conducted on them in the wild as well as the dangers they now face from their closest primate relative.

On the evolution of the primates up to the hominids, see Frederick S. Szalay and Eric Delson, *Evolutionary History of the Primates,* and R. D. Martin, *Primate Origins and Evolution.*

It is no accident that this bonobo, or pygmy chimpanzee, strikes us as so humanlike; our behaviors, including upright walking, have the same evolutionary origin. What can we learn about the evolution of human behavior by examining our close relatives? (© *Frans Lanting, Minden Pictures*)

6

Learning About the Past
Behavioral Models for Human Evolution

CHAPTER CONTENTS

In reconstructing the human past, our focus is the concrete evidence from the fossil and archaeological records. Neither fossil bones nor artifacts alone, however, tell us what our ancestors were like in the most profound biological sense—in terms of how they were adapted to their environments, how they lived, in short, *how they behaved.*

Were the early hominids social? If so, how were their societies organized? Were group members social equals, or were there leaders and followers? How did they communicate? What did they eat, and how did they acquire their food? Were there family units within the group? Did they care for the sick or the aged? Did they share food? Were they individually self-sufficient, or did they divide their labors? Did groups recognize a territory, and did they defend it?

Fossils and artifacts alone cannot normally be used to answer these questions directly, although inferences can be made. Another source of information is living animals who serve as models for prehistoric hominid behavior. The rationale for such studies is that, although living animals do not represent "fossils" of ancient human behavior, they can provide insight into the behavior of those ancient humans, who are known only from their bones and their material artifacts.

Behavior, Adaptation, and Evolution

The idea of using behavioral models is based on the same premise as in using physical comparisons with other primates: We share a common heritage with the other primates and so have inherited our shared features from the same source, a common ancestor. It is not a coincidence, for example, that all primates have prehensile hands. Our common prehensile ability comes from the same ancient ancestor and serves the same basic function. Such traits, shared by multiple species through inheritance from a common ancestor, are called **homologies.** Thus, we can gain some perspective on our prehensile hands by fully examining the prehensile appendages of species with whom we share an ancestor from whom we all derived the trait.

Homologous traits need not share a common function. Your arms and the wings of a bat, although they are used for different things, are homologues. They are similar by virtue of having evolved from the same source, an early mammal.

On the other hand, the wings of a bat and the wings of an insect, although they share a similar function, have evolved independently and are not at all similar in structure. These functional but evolutionarily unrelated similarities are known as **analogies.** We can certainly learn something about the physics of flight by comparing these wings; however, we can get only a limited amount of information about the wings of *bats* by studying the wings of *insects* because they evolved quite separately from one another to facilitate very different adaptive systems.

Just as organisms pass on anatomical and physiological features in their genes, they also pass on behavioral characteristics. In some groups—ants, for example—complex behavioral repertoires are inherited. Ants completely rely on built-in instinct; they don't really think or, in fact, have much of anything to think *with.* So, even though ants live in highly complex societies and act in elaborate ways, all their behaviors are coded for in their genes, to be triggered by outside stimuli but with little or no flexibility or variation in the response (Figure 6.1).

Other organisms, with larger and more complex brains, can vary their behavior as needed to cope with specific situations. They have behavioral potentials or themes carried in their genetic codes. They respond to their

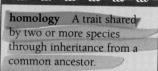

homology   A trait shared by two or more species through inheritance from a common ancestor.

analogy   A trait shared by two or more species that is similar in function but unrelated evolutionarily.

FIGURE 6.1   Weaver ants build nests by pulling edges of leaves together. While some of the ants hold the leaves in this position, others gently carry larvae along the "seam," stimulating them to excrete silk, which "sews" the leaves together. (© *Mantis Wildlife Films/Oxford Scientific Films/Animals Animals*)

environments by building onto these potentials—taking in information from the outside, remembering it, and using stored information in appropriate circumstances. In other words, they think.

The nature of the in-born behavioral potentials in complex organisms is still a matter of debate, especially when humans are the topic. Some argue that we are born as blank slates, or, in a more modern image, as computers with internal hardware but no programming. Others hold the extreme opposite view: Our brains come equipped with *specific* behaviors that are only modified to a degree by outside stimuli—like a computer with some basic programs already in the system.

The truth is no doubt somewhere in the middle. Certainly, we come into this world with some basic, built-in behavioral responses. Facial expressions like smiling, nursing behavior among infants, the bond between a mother and her offspring, and the drives to walk upright and learn language are all recognized as universal in our species and as being preprogrammed in our biology. But just as certainly we are not programmed for particular ways of expressing behaviors. Consider the highly complex structures of our brains and the great variability in our psychologies, intellects, personal behavior, and cultural systems. Language ability, for example, may be instinctive, but there are thousands of languages and the one you speak is learned within your specific cultural context.

At any rate, if it is the case that at least behavioral themes can be inherited, then we can shed light on our behaviors by looking into the behaviors of other creatures. In doing so, however, we need to take into account the concepts of homology and analogy. In comparing the behav-

FIGURE 6.2   A wolf cub begs for food from its mother. She will shortly regurgitate a partly digested meal for the cub. (© *Jim Brandenburg/Minden Pictures*)

iors of humans and chimpanzees, it is highly likely that a behavior is shared because it is the *same* behavior, derived by both species from our common ancestor of 5 or 6 million years ago. Understanding the nature and function of that behavior in chimpanzees is likely to provide insight into the origin of the behavior in humans because the behavior in question is *homologous*. A behavior similar in humans and baboons is more likely to be *analogous*. Our two species have evolved independently for about 36 million years, so there is a greater chance that the behaviors evolved separately, under separate environmental circumstances, for different adaptive reasons. Still, they may be variations on some general behavior pattern common to the primates and inherited from an early common ancestor.

The likelihood that two similar behaviors are analogous increases as the species being compared become less closely related. Some investigators have compared the behavior of humans with that of social carnivores like lions, wolves, and African wild dogs. There are strikingly "human" behaviors in these species. All three hunt cooperatively. Wolves and wild dogs have complex social relationships, use vocal and gestural signs to maintain them, and actively feed their young (Figure 6.2). Wolves are territorial.

These collections of similarities, however, are probably not derived from a common ancestor but have, at most, evolved independently from some general mammalian traits of social interaction, care for young, and relatively large complex brains allowing for flexibility of behavior. What we do learn from the **ethology** of such species is that one possible route to adaptive success for mammals is through complex social behavior and that it is common in species that include meat in their diet, especially meat from large animals. But it is only one route; other carnivores—the fox and the leopard, for example—are solitary hunters. Lions, although they hunt cooperatively, never share food with their young.

Comparing analogous behaviors, then, can be informative and can point out possible clusters of adaptive traits. But analogies must be used with the understanding that the more evolutionarily distant the species, the less useful the comparison. Ants live in highly complex societies to which investigators often apply human names (slave, caste, queen, nurse, soldier), but studying the social behavior of ants probably tells us nothing directly about our own societies.

With this understanding of the benefits and pitfalls of species comparison, we can now look at the behavior of some other species that have, to varying degrees, been used as models for the origin and evolution of human behavior. For years, nearly all our information about other species came from studies of their behavior in the artificial environments of zoos and laboratories. Only when the science of ethology started to study creatures in the wild, under natural conditions, could we see how they were *really* adapted. And only then did we begin to learn some of the truly remarkable adaptations that our fellow species possess.

Baboons

The five species of genus *Papio* have long been of interest to anthropologists because of the obvious complexity of the baboon's social organization and because baboon habitats include the savannas of East and South Africa—the very habitat of our early hominid ancestors.

The common notion of baboon behavior, handed down since the 1950s, once provided what seemed like a reasonable model for the behavior of our hominid ancestors, for baboon societies appeared to share a number of features seen as characteristic of human social systems. Baboon troops were seen as centered on and held together by a dominance hierarchy. Male baboons, often twice as large as females and equipped with long, sharp canine teeth, were thought to vie with one another from youth for social position. The largest, strongest, most aggressive, and smartest baboon became the dominant member, a position recognized and acknowledged by the whole troop. The dominant male was the leader and decision maker. He had first rights to food and females. He produced the most offspring, perpetuating those traits that made him dominant.

ethology   The study of the natural behavior of organisms under natural conditions.

FIGURE 6.3   A baboon in estrus. The skin around her genital area is swollen, a clear visual sign that she is fertile and sexually receptive. *(M. A. Park)*

According to this view, female baboons had a loose hierarchy among themselves but always ranked below males within the troop. A female's social position was often determined by that of the male she mated with during her **estrus** (fertile) period (Figure 6.3). The female's main function was thus to bear and raise offspring, and her identity was essentially based on this function.

Such a system, the thinking ran, was an obvious aid to surviving the rigors of savanna life. The vulnerable troop members—females and young—were an undifferentiated group found in the middle of the troop and surrounded by males, who held individually defined and recognized positions in the hierarchy. The males were thought to be organized in an almost military fashion to protect and defend the females and to pass on their genes through them.

The short duration of early studies, combined with the expectations of some (almost always male) researchers to observe a hierarchical, male-oriented society, led to an overemphasis on the aggressive, decision-making, mate-choosing role of the males. This perception made it hard, in turn, to see the females as possessing differentiated identities and roles. The logical conclusion was the prime importance of males and their competition for dominance.

This interpretation of baboon social organization has recently been questioned, if not put to rest (Fedigan and Fedigan 1988; Smuts 1985; Strum 1987). Studies over the last decade have verified that male baboons do have individual identities and differential social power and influence and that they do protect and defend the troop from members of other

estrus   The period during which a female is fertile; the signals indicating this condition.

FIGURE 6.4   A male baboon shows his long canine teeth and flashes his white eyelids in a "threat gesture," probably directed toward a less dominant male. (© *Irven DeVore/Anthro-Photo*)

troops and from predators (Figure 6.4). But a formal, tightly structured dominance hierarchy among males does not exist. Rather, the structure of the troop is based on "a network of social alliances" (Fedigan and Fedigan 1988:14), including friendships between females and between females and males (see Figure 5.10). These friendships may be so strong that a male will aid his female friend's infants even though he is not their father. Such friendships, rather than the social position of the males, may be what determines who mates with whom.

Differential social positions exist, but they are based not on those "masculine" traits listed before, but on an individual's (male or female) "experience, skill, and . . . ability to manipulate others [and] mobilize allies" (Fedigan and Fedigan 1988:15). If any subgroup is central to a troop and ties generations together, it is that of related females, the males being a more mobile and less stable part of the troop than was previously supposed. In fact, the competition that may be most important to the troop is not that among males but among females competing with one another "over access to the resources necessary to sustain them and their offspring" (Fedigan and Fedigan 1988:5). Finally, it appears that mate choice is more a female prerogative. Males make overtures toward females, but it is the females who decide with whom they mate.

The earlier version of baboon social organization indicated that to survive on the savannas a primate needed a tightly organized, male-oriented and -dominated, almost militaristic society (the use of the term *troop* is not arbitrary). The obvious conclusion (then) was that the early hominid savanna dwellers probably had a similar set of behaviors and that our modern social systems are, to one extent or another, variations on this theme. Many found this a satisfying idea.

But, again, we must remember that we can share with baboons only the most general primate homologous traits. Similarities between us and baboons exist because behaviors derive from the same behavioral themes. The specific expressions of those themes in the two species, however, are the results of separate and independent evolutionary histories.

Those separate histories, however, have produced results that are similar in baboons, humans, and, as we will see, chimpanzees: *the adaptive focus of a social structure built around a family unit, friendships, mutual aid within the group, defense of the group, and recognition of individuals.* This at least tells us that such a focus is one possible adaptive path among primates. It is thus conceivable to propose that something like it was the key to the survival of the early hominids. Given that our closest relative, the chimpanzee, exhibits this cluster of traits, it seems an even more reasonable proposition.

Chimpanzees

Some of the most remarkable results of ethological observations have come from three landmark studies of the great apes, all initiated by paleo-anthropologist Louis Leakey: Jane Goodall's study of the chimpanzee, Dian Fossey's study of the gorilla, and Biruté Galdikas's study of the orangutan. Each of these studies is interesting in its own right and tells us something of the variations possible on the basic primate pattern of social organization. The species most relevant to our present subject, however, is the chimpanzee.

The orangutan is an Asian ape and, as we have seen, is separated from us by 12 million years or more. The gorilla, although according to some as close to us genetically as the chimp and although exhibiting many of the same basic social behaviors, is a rather specialized ape. Unlike the chimpanzee, the gorilla spends nearly all its time on the ground and its almost exclusively vegetarian diet is largely of ground plants. It makes its sleeping nests on the ground. It is not known to make or use tools. The gorilla's huge size (males in the wild average 400 pounds) means that it has no enemies (except humans), and this, along with its easily obtained plant diet, makes its life fairly laid-back. Gorilla groups are headed by a dominant male, but on the whole the groups are unified and peaceful (Figure 6.5), without the tension over social position that is more characteristic of baboon and chimp societies. As zoologist and writer David Attenborough puts it, the gorilla has "no need [to] be particularly nimble in either body or mind" (1979:291). Although perhaps overstated—gorillas, like chimps, can be taught to communicate through sign language, for example—this statement seems an accurate impression of the nature of gorilla adaptation.

FIGURE 6.5   A group of mountain gorillas peacefully resting on a sunny slope. Note the silver fur on the back of the large male in the center. These "silverbacks" are usually the group leaders. *(© Michael A. Nichols/Magnum Photos Inc.)*

In contrast, the chimpanzee is "both agile and inquisitive" (Attenborough 1979:291). Much of what we know of the ethology of the chimp comes from the more than thirty years of research at Gombe Stream National Park in Tanzania led by Jane Goodall (1971, 1986, 1990). Goodall's studies have shown that, besides physical and physiological traits, we share with chimps a number of behavioral characteristics centered on aspects of social interaction. This commonality is instructive for our understanding of our own behavior (Figure 6.6, p. 134).

A herd of antelopes on the savannas of Africa is a social group, but the group itself is the focus. Antelopes interact with one another but less as individuals (except at mating time) than as members of the herd. Chimpanzees, however, live in groups, and the members interact with one another as *individuals*. The chimp group is the sum of all the relationships among the individuals that make it up at any given time. It is also defined by the relationships between its members and members of other groups. Although there are "norms" of social behavior in chimps, these are highly flexible and vary depending on the specific individuals and the specific situation.

FIGURE 6.6   A chimpanzee mother and infant. The bond between them is strong and will last a lifetime.   *(© Nancy Nicolson/ Anthro-Photo)*

The bond between mother and infant is strong in chimps, as it is in most mammals. These apes, though, have large, complex brains and have much to learn about their world before they can become functioning adults. Thus, the mother–infant bond is particularly long-lived and important, and the nature of that interaction can have a lasting effect on the rest of a chimp's life. Poor treatment by its mother, for example, often makes a chimp a poor mother herself when she bears young. Chimps have been seen to help their mothers with younger siblings, and siblings often remain close into adulthood. Chimps, in other words, don't just give birth to an offspring and then cast it out on its own. Chimps *raise* their young, and the family bonds that result may last a lifetime.

The chimps in a group are arranged in a dominance hierarchy. Males are generally dominant over all females, but within females a loose hierarchy exists. Males actually compete with one another in an attempt to achieve the highest position possible. The rewards are access to feeding places and females. Social position, although attained in males through violent but seldom injurious actions, is maintained via a series of expressions, gestures, and vocalizations. One of the most important is grooming (see Figure 5.3), which maintains social cohesion and on occasion is a sign of dominance when a subordinate male grooms his superior. Other expressions of social interaction include kissing, hugging, bowing, extending the hand, sexual gestures, grinning, and various vocalizations (Figure 6.7); we can freely use these terms because the meanings of these actions in chimp society seem to be precisely what they are in human society.

FIGURE 6.7   A chimpanzee exhibiting a low open grin, indicating he is moderately frightened or excited. (© *Joe McDonald/ Animals Animals*)

But a chimp society is in no way some sort of dictatorship. Instead, it is marked by cooperation and mutual concern. This is seen mostly within the family unit of mother and offspring (because chimps are sexually promiscuous, the father is unknown). Throughout their lives, members of this family unit protect and care for one another, especially during illness and injury. Males have even been known to help brothers in their competition for dominance.

But care also extends outside the family unit. When chimps hunt, for example, portions of the kill are often shared, sometimes proportionately depending on the degree of friendship between the hunter and the chimp begging for food. Offspring are important to the group as a whole, and unrelated adults come to the aid or protection of a youngster threatened with some harm, even risking their own welfare. Once, an adolescent male adopted an unrelated youngster who had been orphaned (Goodall 1990:202).

Group membership is somewhat fluid. Chimps, for various reasons, leave a group, and outsiders occasionally enter it. Despite this, there is a sense of group identity and territory. Small bands of males sometimes patrol the boundaries of their group's range; when members of other groups are encountered, they are reacted to and treated differently. In one chilling series of events, males from Goodall's main study group attacked and killed a female and all the males of a group that had broken away to establish its own territory. Goodall thinks the motivation may have been to reclaim the area.

Among the chimpanzee's wide range of food sources is meat. Chimps from some groups, including those studied by Goodall and associates, are hunters (Stanford 1995). Males, and occasionally females, will hunt and kill small pigs, antelopes, and monkeys, including young baboons. The Gombe chimps, sometimes hunting in cooperative groups, kill over 100 red colobus monkeys a year, nearly a fifth of that species within the chimps' range. Meat is the one food that chimps share, and male chimps are more likely to share with friends. They even withhold meat from rivals. There is evidence, too, that males hunt in order to get meat as an offering to an estrus female.

The vast majority of our information about this species comes from Goodall's research, but work on other chimp groups amply bears out her observations and conclusions and lends support to the idea that chimp behavior is flexible, adaptable, and the result of a degree of intelligence and reasoning. For example, a chimp group in the forests on the west coast of Africa uses hammerstones to crack open nuts, something the Goodall chimps never did. They also have different hunting techniques, relying more on cooperation between hunting males than did the Gombe chimps (Boesch and Boesch-Achermann 1991).

Recently, even more intriguing information has come to light about the other species of chimpanzee: the pygmy chimpanzee, or bonobo (Kano

FIGURE 6.8   A bonobo walking bipedally. Note that she is doing so because she is carrying something in her hands. (© *Frans Lanting/Minden Pictures*)

1990). The bonobo lives in the lowland forests of Zaire and has been estimated by molecular studies to have been separate from the common chimp for 1.5 million years. Not really pygmies, these chimps are as large as the common chimps, although more slender with smaller heads and shoulders. They walk upright more often than the common chimps (Figure 6.8). But there are more striking differences.

The bonobos are more peaceful and gregarious than the common chimps. They have a hierarchy, but it is looser than that of the common chimp and much less male-oriented. They more readily share food with one another, and the food shared is not limited to luxury items like meat. They have never been observed to kill another of their kind, and they appear to bind their group together with sex.

Bonobos, especially when feeding, constantly posture toward one another, rubbing rumps or "presenting" themselves as if initiating sexual activity. When sex does follow, it is usually face-to-face, a position common in humans but notably uncommon in nonhuman primates. Sexual activity is not limited to opposite-sex partners. Females commonly rub genitalia with other females, and males mount each other.

Moreover, the signs of fertility, the estrus signals (or "heat" in popular terminology), seem nearly always present in bonobo females. In all chimps, the female's fertile and therefore sexual period is marked by a swelling and coloration of the skin of the genital area. This stimulates sexual interest on the part of the males. In common chimps, the swelling only occurs when the female has ovulated and is fertile. In bonobos, however, there is some swelling almost all the time, and, indeed, bonobos seem almost constantly sexually receptive. Sexual activity in this species has become separate from purely reproductive activity. The motivation for sex may be as much psychological and social as it is reproductive.

The function of all this seems to be the same as some of the expressions and gestures among the common chimp: to prevent violence; to ease tension, especially while feeding; to offer a greeting, a sign of reconciliation, or a sign for reassurance. Sex or some form of sexual activity, heterosexual or homosexual, has even been seen to precede food sharing.

While on the subject of bonobos, Kanzi, a teenage male bonobo at the Language Research Center at Georgia State University, should be mentioned. Kanzi is one of the most successful apes at communicating through a language with the characteristics of human communication. He uses symbols on a computer keyboard, and he can even recognize, and respond to on his computer, a large number of spoken English words. In addition to his linguistic skills, he has been taught to make and use simple stone tools. Although not resembling even the earliest known hominid stone tools (see Chapter 9), Kanzi's tools are, nonetheless, true artifacts, and so may show us what the *very* earliest stone tools of our lineage might have looked like. Neither of these behaviors—using a humanlike language and stone toolmaking—are seen among wild bonobos, but they do give us an idea as to the cognitive potentials of the brains of these apes.

Now, if chimp behaviors sound more than vaguely human, the reason may be simple. We share certain behavioral patterns because we inherited them from a common ancestor. To be sure, our line and that of the chimps have been going their separate and independent ways for 5 or 6 million years, and even shared features have had the chance to become modified by all the processes of evolution—to be changed, eliminated, enhanced, and differently adapted to our species' different niches. Chimps are not "living fossils," stuck in some 5-million-year-old rut while our ancestors continued to evolve. But the fact that our common ancestor is relatively recent and the striking similarity of our bodies and behaviors argue for our shared behaviors being homologous.

This does not mean that we humans have specific genes for friendship, food sharing, territoriality, or continual sexuality. These are complex behaviors, and chimps and humans are complex species. The lesson is that, like that of the chimps, the focus of the human adaptation—what adapted our earliest hominid ancestors and has been the adaptive theme of our line—is social interaction based on individual recognition, a strong bond centered around family relationships (generally, mothers and their offspring), long-term friendships, sexual consciousness, mutual care within the group, and recognition and defense of the group. These are some of the possible answers to the questions listed at the beginning of the chapter. It seems reasonable to propose that our hominid ancestors—represented by the fossils to be discussed in Chapters 8 through 12—behaved in similar ways. As Goodall says,

> The concept of early humans poking for insects with twigs and wiping themselves with leaves seems entirely sensible. The thought of those ancestors greeting and reassuring one another with kisses or embraces, cooperating in protecting their territory or in hunting, and sharing food with each other, is appealing. The idea of close affectionate ties within the Stone Age family, of brothers helping one another, of teenage sons hastening to the protection of their old mothers, and of teenage daughters minding the babies, for me brings the fossilized relics of their physical selves dramatically to life. (1990:207)

Ethnographic Analogy

One more area of behavior has been used to try to open a window into our behavioral past. Modern human societies vary greatly in their cultural systems, including their degree of technological complexity and the extent to which they manipulate their environments to extract needed resources. Perhaps by examining the least technologically complex societies, those that live close to the land, we can see ways of life that may parallel in some aspects the lives of our ancestors. Such groups are collectively called **hunter-gatherers,** or **foragers.**

Such studies, however, must be made with caution. It is important to remember that modern foraging peoples are just that—modern. Though "primitive" perhaps by the **ethnocentric** standards of the industrial world, they are decidedly *not* humans arrested at some previous stage of evolution. They possess fully modern human intellectual capabilities, and these have given them cultural assets unknown to any humans until recently.

hunter-gatherer   A human society that relies on naturally occurring sources of food.

forager   A synonym for hunter-gatherer.

ethnocentric   Judging another society's values in terms of one's own social values.

Many, for example, use the bow and arrow, which is only about 20,000 years old.

In addition, evidence indicates that modern foraging groups, however isolated, are not as untouched by outside influences as we had thought or hoped. The most infamous example is the Tasaday, discovered in the jungles of the Philippines in 1971. This group of twenty-five people were thought to be hunter-gatherers (if catching frogs can be considered hunting) who used very simple stone tools and had been completely isolated for 2000 years. This was a glimpse into the past if ever there was one! But it turns out that at the very least the Tasaday were part of or had traded with a larger agricultural group. There is even some evidence that they were a publicity hoax, a small group of farming people paid to act like "a stone age tribe" (Berreman 1991). Indeed, it can fairly be said that all societies today have been influenced and changed by contact with other groups and so probably none accurately represents our species' previous way of life.

Moreover, like all humans, foraging peoples are culture-bearing. They consciously create and modify cultural systems to fit their environments and the basic ways they cope with those environments. So, rather than reflecting some lifestyle directly inherited from our ancient past, the social systems of foragers must be seen as the collective cultural responses of groups of people to the world they know and have to deal with. Now, however, with these cautions in mind, we may look at the lifestyles of foraging people to see if they shed some light on the human past.

Foragers are peoples who rely on naturally occurring resources for their subsistence. They *collect* food rather than *produce* it, by hunting wild animals and gathering wild plants. They don't farm, and they don't have domesticated animals (except for dogs). This is how all our ancestors lived until only about 12,000 years ago (see Chapter 14). Thus, by observing modern foragers, we are observing the real human condition, the lifestyle of most humans throughout most of human history.

It is probably safe to say that no true foragers are left in the world. But until recently, there have been groups whose adaptive focus was on this pattern of subsistence, and they have been observed and studied. Examples include a number of Native American cultures, most notably the Inuit (Eskimo), the native populations of Australia, some societies from the Philippines, and, perhaps the most studied, the !Kung San from the Kalahari Desert of southern Africa, sometimes referred to as Bushmen (Figure 6.9). (The ! represents a click sound in the !Kung language.) The !Kung have always seemed the best model because they inhabit dry, open areas of Africa, environments with much the same potential sources of plant and animal food available to early hominids.

The specific cultural systems of foraging peoples show a great deal of variation, but we can make some generalizations. Foraging bands are usually small collections of related family units, each known as a **nuclear fam-**

FIGURE 6.9   The !Kung San from the Kalahari Desert in Namibia, Botswana, and South Africa are, of course, fully modern humans. Yet their way of life, until recently that of hunters and gatherers, can give us a window into the lives of our ancestors before the invention of farming and animal domestication. Here, members of a !Kung family are on the move, carrying with them their children, tools, weapons, and other possessions. The lives of the !Kung have been changed forever by political and military events in southern Africa.
(© *Irven DeVore/Anthro-Photo*)

ily—a mother, her offspring, and, unlike the chimps and baboons, a father. Band sizes vary according to particular environmental circumstances, but the average number supported by this form of subsistence seems to be around twenty-five people. Foragers often have a home range within which they are mobile as they follow the travels of the animals they hunt and the seasonal cycles of the plants they gather.

Foraging societies tend to be **egalitarian**—that is, they don't have formalized social or economic hierarchies. Not everyone, of course, can do an equal amount of labor or fend completely for themselves. Thus, sharing is an important feature of such groups, to ensure that everyone benefits equally from the labors of the group as a whole. There is no division of labor as we think of it—no occupations. But tasks do tend to be associated with one gender or the other. Generally, men hunt, and women gather. This, of course, makes practical sense in that hunting is more strenuous, more dangerous, and more time-consuming and often takes hunters far from home. Participating in hunting is probably seen as normally too much of a burden on the gender that produces, nurtures, and socializes the society's future generations.

When women gather, they may do so in groups, but each woman normally works by and for herself and her immediate family. Plants, which may comprise up to 75 percent of a foraging group's food intake, are usually a more reliable source than meat. Hunting, on the other hand, especially if large game is the target, requires cooperation among the men; the

nuclear family   The family unit made up of parents and their offspring.

egalitarian   A type of society that does not recognize differences in social position or wealth.

meat acquired, usually much more scarce and less dependable than plant foods, is shared, sometimes via elaborate, ritualized exchanges to symbolize group unity.

Although foraging societies are egalitarian with regard to politics and economics, the people themselves still have differential relationships with one another. As in any group, there are friends of varying degrees and individuals who are not so friendly. Indeed, irreconcilable conflicts are one of the things that contribute to the flexibility of foraging-band membership. People come and go in these groups for various reasons—from personal choice to economic necessity, as when a scarcity of resources causes a band to split apart.

Despite the cautions we noted before, the behavioral themes running through this discussion can hardly be ignored. Striking similarities exist between many of the general traits of foraging societies and the societies of chimpanzees and baboons—particularly the importance of the mother–infant bond, the presence of a home range, differential relationships within the group, the flexibility of group membership, and, most notably, the focus on the group itself and the vital role of cooperation. Because we humans have been foragers for most of our time on earth, it seems a reasonable proposition that a similar set of behavioral features characterized the earliest humans.

What the foraging cultures may show us is that, despite our cultural ability to vary our specific behaviors over an incredible range, this variation may be based on certain general patterns of behavior established in our prehominid past. And so, when we look at baboons or, especially, chimpanzees, we are not necessarily seeing ourselves in the past, but we are seeing the patterns of behavior from which ours has evolved.

Summary

As noted in Chapter 5, one way to guide us as we look into our past is to understand the results of the events that made up that past. This approach works for behavior as well as for physical adaptations. We can compare the behavior of various modern human groups to that of species with whom we share general traits or environmental conditions. We search for trends or tendencies that may indicate how our ancestors might have adapted to similar circumstances. The importance of a well-defined organization among social African carnivores like the lion and wild dog and in another savanna primate, the baboon, is a good hint that an analogous behavior was a key to the survival of early savanna hominids.

More useful is the behavior of close evolutionary relatives, especially the chimpanzee. Chimp behavior differs in specifics from ours and has been evolving separately from ours for 5 or 6 million years, helping that species adapt to its particular niche. The basic patterns for the behavior of our two species, however, are homologous. They are the same because we inherited them from a common ancestor. It is highly likely, then, that our remote hominid ancestors also manifested these patterns.

Such studies indicate that the early hominids of the plains of Africa may very well have been highly social creatures and that their social organization was built around differing interpersonal relationships, a family unit, conscious sexuality, recognition of group membership and territory, and mutual care at both the individual and the group level.

Study Questions

1. What ideas must we consider in trying to explain the behavior of a living creature, especially one as complex as our species?
2. What are some of the basic behaviors of our close relatives? What light do they shed on the evolution of our own behaviors?
3. How may the study of living humans contribute to our understanding of human behavioral evolution? What limits must we recognize in conducting such studies?

Key Terms

homology	estrus	ethnocentric
analogy	hunter-gatherer	nuclear family
ethology	forager	egalitarian

For More Information

The latest thinking on baboon behavior can be found in Shirley Strum's *Almost Human* and in Barbara Smuts's *Sex and Friendship in Baboons.* Dian Fossey recounts her study of gorillas in *Gorillas in the Mist;* her own story in turn, including her murder, is told by Farley Mowat in *Woman in the Mists* and in the 1988 movie *Gorillas in the Mist.* Biruté Galdikas tells about orangutans in *Reflection of Eden: My Years with the Orangutans of Borneo.* Jane Goodall's latest work on the chimps and her experiences studying them is *Through a Window: My Thirty Years with the Chimpanzees of Gombe.* See also the article about her work in the December 1995 *National Geographic.* Bonobos are described in the March 1995 issue of *Scientific American* in an article by Frans B. M. de Waal called "Bonobo Sex and Society." For more on the amazing Kanzi, see *Kanzi: The Ape at the Brink of the Human Mind* by Sue Savage-Rumbaugh and Roger Lewin.

Some basic information about foragers can be found in *Man the Hunter,* by Richard Lee and Irven DeVore, and *Woman the Gatherer,* edited by F. Dahlberg.

Built nearly 800 years ago in a protected niche in a cliff, Square Tower House in Mesa Verde, Colorado, is symbolic of the often hidden nature of the data of human antiquity. Physical anthropologists and archaeologists have developed many methods for finding and analyzing evidence of the human past. How can scientists know what happened in the ancient past? How can we reveal the human story? *(K. L. Feder)*

7

Learning About the Past

The Material Record

—m—

This book focuses on the human past, but how do we learn about the past? How do we collect and analyze data about the ancient past of our species?

In this book our approach to understanding the human past will be through the field of anthropology, defined previously as the study of humanity. If you think about it, though, nearly all the courses you're now taking deal in some fashion with people or their works. What makes anthropology different?

The Anthropology of the Past:
Archaeology and Physical Anthropology

Many people have some very strange ideas about what archaeology and physical (or biological) anthropology are and what scientists in these fields do. Some people think archaeologists study dinosaurs. (They have seen too many episodes of "The Flintstones.") In reality, the dinosaurs became extinct more than 60 million years before even our earliest human ancestors appeared on the scene. Thanks, at least in part, to such movies as the *Indiana Jones* series, many think that archaeologists are tough, globe-trotting vagabonds who loot sites for treasure. Physical anthropologists are often stereotyped as those who identify the skeletal remains of dead people. The most common question we get, even from university colleagues, is, "Dig up any interesting bones lately?"

Actually, archaeology is simply that branch of anthropology focusing on the human cultural past. Whereas other anthropologists may study a people by actually living among them, archaeologists must study a people through analysis of what they left behind—yes, including bones. Archaeology is necessary because the only way we can learn *directly* about people in the past, especially those who lived before the invention of writing, is by studying the things they made and used. So archaeologists have, as their primary data, the material consequences of human behavior—the tools, edifices, art, and even garbage a society leaves behind. From potsherds to pyramids, from arrowheads to Stonehenge, these are the archaeologist's raw materials.

Because the materials archaeologists deal with—pyramids, cave paintings, pots, and the like—can be so interesting in and of themselves, it is easy to lose track of why we are studying them. Just remember that archaeologists are anthropologists; they are interested in the same sorts of things that all anthropologists are. They aim to understand how ancient people lived, not simply to collect interesting antiques.

Similarly, whereas some physical anthropologists collect data from living individuals, paleoanthropologists deal with the skeletal remains of people, and even then usually not with the complete skeleton. Nevertheless, they also seek to learn about the biology of the people who made the tools and pots and paintings. What did they look like? What diseases did they suffer from, and what sorts of injuries caused their deaths? What were the sex ratios and average ages of their populations? Moreover, paleoanthropologists are interested in how and why human biology changed over the more than 4 million years we and our upright-walking ancestors have been around. In other words, how do the processes of evolution apply to our species? Biological anthropologists also address these matters. The answers to such questions round out the understanding of ancient people.

The goals of the study of the past can be broken down into a series of general questions anthropologists wish to ask of the data:

1. *Where* did people live?
2. *What* materials did they leave behind?
3. *When* was an area occupied, and when did certain human activities occur?
4. *How* did people in a given region or time period live?
5. *Who* were the people, biologically?
6. *Why* did they live the life they did?

It is through asking and attempting to answer these questions that anthropologists illuminate the story of human physical and cultural evolution. In the rest of this chapter, we will briefly describe how the anthropologists who study the past go about this task.

Where? The Process of Finding Sites

To know where prehistoric people settled, where they lived out their lives, and where they died, it is necessary to find the material traces of their existence. These are archaeological **sites**—locations where humans once lived or worked and where their traces, in the form of **artifacts**—objects made by people, such as spear points or clay pots—and **features**—nonportable remains reflecting human activity, such as hearths, trash piles, or burials— were left behind and have been preserved. For nonarchaeologists, this ability to find sites may seem almost magical. It would probably not be giving away any trade secrets to tell you that, in reality, the discovery of archaeological sites does not depend on intuition, "psychic power," or magic. Instead, they are discovered through a scientific process demanding hard work and, often, a bit of luck.

Archaeological site survey, the actual process of finding sites, includes a set of basic, common-sense techniques, among them: (1) reference to previous research conducted in an area, (2) examination of local history for stories of discoveries made by inhabitants, and (3) contacting local artifact collectors (a popular pastime in many parts of the world). In addition, even people who do not go out consciously looking for artifacts or sites sometimes have valuable information for archaeologists. Farmers plowing their fields, homeowners building an addition to their house, workers constructing a highway, and gardeners planting their tomatoes all disturb the soil and as a result may encounter the remains of buried artifacts. Many of the important archaeological sites mentioned in this book were found accidentally by people engaged in nonarchaeological pursuits.

Another important approach to site survey involves a consideration of environmental variables. Whether they are prehistoric hunters, primitive farmers, or twentieth-century Americans, all people depend, ultimately, on nature's bounty. Archaeologists use that fact to help find archaeological sites. For example, all people need a source of fresh water, and no one is likely to live too far from one. Hunters tend to concentrate their settle-

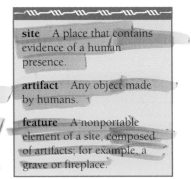

site A place that contains evidence of a human presence.

artifact Any object made by humans.

feature A nonportable element of a site, composed of artifacts; for example, a grave or fireplace.

FIGURE 7.1 Where preservation is high and where people built structures in durable materials, archaeologists can find sites simply by walking across an area. Hovenweep National Monument, in the American Southwest, is one such area. Remnants of ancient stone towers built by the ancestors of the modern Hopi Indians still stand at the site. *(K. L. Feder)*

ments in areas where animals are likely to be found. Farmers may prefer extensive areas of fertile flatland to make a living. People with hostile neighbors may choose to settle in protected areas. Pottery-making people may want to live close to a source of clay. The archaeologist must consider a constellation of environmental variables to isolate the kinds of areas where sites are most likely to be found.

This background research paves the way for the **field survey**, which includes both a surface and a subsurface investigation of an area. Before using procedures in which the soil is actually turned over in search of archaeological evidence, archaeologists can apply techniques of **remote sensing**. Such methods are non-invasive, like a medical CAT scan. Photographs taken from an airplane or satellite, radar images, analysis of magnetic anomalies in the ground, and variations in subsurface resistance to an electrical current can provide the archaeologist with data concerning the potential presence of archaeological materials unavailable by simple inspection and without having to dig holes in the ground. The results of remote-sensing procedures cannot ordinarily replace excavation, but they certainly are valuable in helping the archaeologist decide where to use surface inspection and subsurface investigation to investigate further.

Where prehistoric people have left above-ground structures of relatively resilient material (as in the case of the ancient Egyptians or the Pueblo Indians of the American Southwest), an above-ground investigation can locate sites (Figure 7.1). In densely settled parts of the world, most sites visible on the surface have probably been inventoried, but the discovery of unknown surface sites in less populated areas is still common.

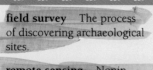

field survey   The process of discovering archaeological sites.

remote sensing   Noninvasive examination of sites where no soil is removed.

An above-ground inspection is also valuable when nature itself has conducted its own kind of excavation through erosion. A river eroding its bank or a gulley being cut by a flash flood may expose previously unknown archaeological material. In many instances, the fossil remains of human ancestors have been found in places where ancient soil levels have been exposed by natural processes. Olduvai Gorge, in Africa, is a famous example of this effect. Searching for and surveying areas where such ancient deposits have been exposed by natural erosion is an important part of the search for the vestiges of prehistoric humanity (Figure 7.2).

Most prehistoric archaeological sites, however, have been buried by natural processes of deposition. Rivers deposit soil when they flood, sand gets blown about by winds, volcanoes erupt and spew out lava and ash, mountains erode, and cave roofs collapse. All these processes can result in the burial of the remains of a town, camp, or cemetery. To find sites subjected to thousands and even millions of years of these natural processes of deposition, we must dig.

A research area may be enormous, and generally the archaeologist cannot turn over every square meter of soil to determine the presence or

FIGURE 7.2 In some areas, natural processes of erosion have exposed ancient soil layers. Here at Hadar, in Ethiopia, paleoanthropologists walk on these exposed layers searching for the fossil remains of human ancestors who lived when those layers were the surface of the earth. (© *Enrico Feroreli, 1996, National Geographic*)

149

FIGURE 7.3   Excavators digging a line of test pits along the floodplain of the Farmington River in Avon, Connecticut (*left*). Test pits are dug with shovels, and all soil is passed through ⅛-inch mesh hardware cloth (*right*). Systematic subsurface sampling is an important component of archaeological field survey. (*K. L. Feder*)

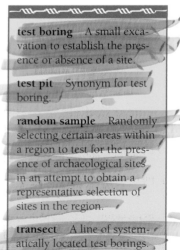

test boring   A small excavation to establish the presence or absence of a site.

test pit   Synonym for test boring.

random sample   Randomly selecting certain areas within a region to test for the presence of archaeological sites in an attempt to obtain a representative selection of sites in the region.

transect   A line of systematically located test borings.

absence of sites. Instead, the archaeologist may sample an area by excavating **test borings,** soundings, or **test pits**—soil corings, shovel-dug holes, and even test trenches excavated with mechanized equipment like backhoes.

Researchers may appraise the archaeological potential of a region and select specific areas to test based on local history, the reports of amateur archaeologists, and an assessment of the local environment. In some cases, archaeologists select a place to dig based simply on the desire to cover a given area—for example, if the area is to be destroyed as a result of development. In many cases, areas are identified through **random sampling.** Here, there are no preconceptions or biases about the best places to test or where sites will most likely be found—and, therefore, no self-fulfilling prophecies about where sites will be located. For example, if only areas adjacent to rivers are tested, then all sites found will be adjacent to rivers. By random sampling, the sites detected should be representative of all the sites in a region, not just those located in places where archaeologists expect them to be.

Within an area to be analyzed, test pits are placed according to a number of different sampling strategies. They may be placed at regular intervals, for example, every 10 meters, along a straight line or **transect** (Figure 7.3). They may be placed in a square grid or checkerboard pattern. Thousands of these shovel-dug holes may be excavated without finding much of anything. It may seem like looking for the proverbial needle in a haystack—and it is. There are no shortcuts to finding archaeological remains. If the archaeologist has done his or her homework, however, the most likely areas are isolated before test pits are excavated, and there is a good chance of finding something.

What? Recovering Archaeological Data

All scientists are faced with the problem of data collection. Astronomers need telescopes and microbiologists need microscopes. Archaeologists are faced with the problem that what they are interested in is the stuff people made and used. Most of it ends up in the ground and, through the processes mentioned, gets buried. Once sites have been discovered through site survey, the main tools of data collection are those that remove the soil from around the artifacts.

Not everybody recognizes the difficulty in retrieving the artifacts while still preserving the *information* that a site contains. For example, a local developer uncovered some 10,000-year-old woolly mammoth bones and invited one of the authors to take a look and dig them up; perhaps the mammoth had been killed by prehistoric people. We arrived with our dental picks and trowels, ready to spend days or even weeks removing the handful of bones from the ground. The developer, however, assured us that he could accomplish the same task with his backhoe in a few minutes, swearing he would be "real careful"!

The materials that archaeologists ordinarily study have been lying in the ground for hundreds, thousands, or even millions of years. It would be a terrible irony if, in attempting to recover these objects, we were to destroy them instead. Consequently, archaeologists need to be meticulous and exacting in excavation. Using small hand tools, including masons' trowels for careful scraping of the soil, dental picks, artists' brushes, and whisk brooms, archaeologists remove the soil from around the pieces discovered.

Not only do we want to preserve the items themselves, but we also want to preserve their **spatial contexts.** Knowing *where* an arrow was left or placed thousands of years ago can reveal as much about what it was used for as the arrow itself. An arrow found in an isolated spot with no other objects nearby might be a weapon lost during a hunt. One found with a cluster of arrows inside the remains of a hut could be part of a hunter's storage area. An arrow found in a fireplace may have fallen out of the animal it killed. One discovered in a human grave could be a tool to accompany the deceased to the afterlife. In each case, the tool itself would look exactly the same. But where it was found (its **provenience**) and what was found with it (its **associations**) tell us quite a bit about what the people who used it were doing (Figure 7.4, p. 152). A backhoe would make short work of this wealth of valuable evidence associated with the artifact itself. Spatial contexts provide crucial information about the behavior of ancient people. Without spatial context—which is absent with spear points, pottery, or carvings for sale by tomb looters—we can learn little about the behavior of the people who used these objects.

Archaeological sites are excavated in an extremely orderly and logical fashion (Figure 7.5, p. 153). Ordinarily, a site is segmented into grids or squares, usually 1 or 2 meters on a side, although this practice varies. The

spatial context   Where and with what an artifact is found in a site.

provenience   The precise location of an artifact.

association   The spatial relationships of artifacts, one to another.

(a)

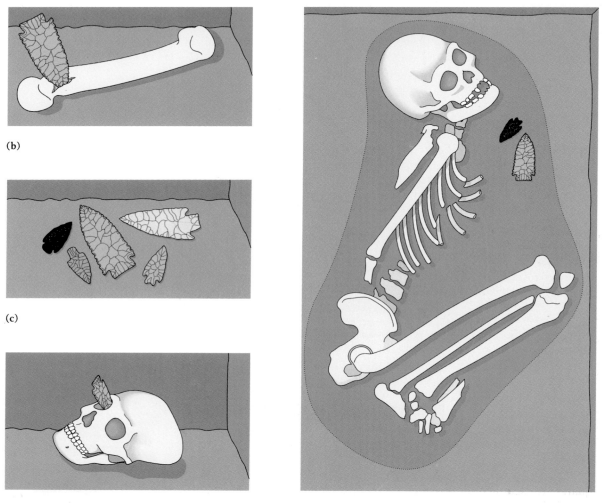

(b)

(c)

(d)

(e)

FIGURE 7.4   To understand the significance of archaeological material, context is crucial. Archaeologists must identify where each object was found and what it was found with—in other words, its associations. Here, a spear point (a), is shown in four different hypothetical contexts: (b) piercing the bone of an animal, (c) in a "cache" or hidden reserve of stone tools, (d) in the skull of a person, and (e) as a grave offering to a deceased hunter. In each case, the artifact is exactly the same, but its context—and, therefore, its inferred use—is different.

FIGURE 7.5   Excavation grid at the 5000-year-old Alsop Meadow Site in Avon, Connecticut (*top*). Sites are excavated in a regular, orderly fashion to preserve the spatial contexts of the material uncovered. Half a world away, the archaeological site at Non Nok Tha in Thailand shows the application of the same procedures (*bottom*). (*Alsop Meadow: K. L. Feder; Non Nok Tha: courtesy William G. Solheim II*)

squares are excavated individually or in clusters. Individual soil layers, distinguishable by color and texture may, in turn, be scraped back very carefully. In instances where distinct layers are not apparent or else quite thick, the soil may be scraped down instead in regular increments, only a few centimeters at a time. The soil is then sifted through screens with ¼-inch, ⅛-inch, or even smaller mesh to catch anything that may have escaped the watchful eye of the archaeologist.

FIGURE 7.6   By leaving each of the blades at the Glazier Blade Cache site in place as they were encountered in excavation, archaeologists were able to expose the entire archaeological feature exactly as it was left by the ancient inhabitants of north-central Connecticut.   *(K. L. Feder)*

When possible, artifacts encountered in excavation are left in place (**in situ**) so they can be viewed in their spatial contexts, as they were placed and last seen by the inhabitants of the site (Figure 7.6). Maps are made and photographs taken in an attempt to create a permanent record of the spatial contexts. In digging a site and taking to the laboratory or museum the materials found, of course, archaeologists do destroy the site. They do so systematically, however, to be able to study it. The careful recording of all information is crucial to maintain any hope of reconstructing what took place at the site from the often meager remains left behind.

When? Dating the Past

How old is a site? When were specific cultural advances made in human prehistory? When did people begin walking on two feet? When was agriculture invented? How old is a given artifact or the pieces of a skeleton? When did certain environmental changes occur? There are a number of techniques for answering these questions related to time. We will describe the most important ones here.

in situ   In place. An artifact or feature that remains in its exact place of discovery is said to be *in situ*.

stratigraphy   The arrangement of soil and rock in layers.

Stratigraphy   The term applied to the layering of the earth's soil is **stratigraphy.** You saw in Chapter 2 how recognizing this layering was an important step in the development of uniformitarianism and the modern concept of biological evolution.

Geologists recognize that the history of the earth is written in its rock. Rock and soil (rock and mineral particles mixed with organic material) are deposited by the wind, flooding rivers, eroding mountains, and erupting volcanoes—the same processes that bury archaeological sites. Soil is often deposited in distinguishable layers or may develop such layers later. The layering may result from different sources, or **parent materials**. For example, in the same spot one layer of soil may be from a river flood, another from a dust storm, and another still from a rock slide. Layering may also result from different conditions of deposition. For example, some layers may have been deposited underwater, others under dry conditions. Different climatic conditions after deposition may cause layering because soil texture is altered by temperature. Plants growing on the soil may also have an impact; layering develops as a result of the specific chemical and biological action of various plants extracting nutrients from the soil.

Whatever the cause of the layering, soil layers are superimposed, one on top of another, over time. Thus, barring disturbance, successively older layers are encountered as you dig deeper. Archaeologists, paleoanthropologists, and geologists use this **law of superposition** to help them place their sites in what is known as a **relative chronological sequence.**

Many of the objects people make and use eventually become incorporated into the soil beneath their feet through a number of cultural processes—loss, discard, storage, and abandonment (Schiffer 1978). After the people are gone, soil may be deposited over their artifacts. Sometime later, another group may move in and their objects become a part of the stratigraphic record—at a level *above* that of the previous group (Figure 7.7).

Imagine that many years later you have a picnic on the very spot where these prehistoric people lived. Some change falls out of your pocket, and you leave, unaware of your loss. Next spring a nearby river floods, depositing a fine layer of silt over your artifacts. Now your personal detritus has been incorporated into the stratigraphic record of this site. Not only is the history of the earth written in the soil, so too is the history of humanity.

Absolute Techniques   Stratigraphy can provide only a relative chronology. It reveals the order in which a series of different cultures inhabited a spot but not *when* those cultures existed—archaeologists cannot determine an age in years simply from the layering of soil. They do, however, have techniques that enable them to derive actual dates from material. These procedures are called **chronometric** or **absolute dating** techniques. Absolute dating techniques are not necessarily correct or precise. They are simply capable of providing a year or range of years to archaeological material.

Absolute dates can be expressed in a number of ways: B.C.E. (before the common era) or B.C. (before the birth of Christ), or A.D. (*anno Domini or* after the birth of Christ), or B.P. (before present). (For B.P., the "present" is fixed at 1950. Virtually all sites we will be discussing are far too old and the dating techniques too imprecise for it to make a difference; but techni-

parent material   The source material for a particular soil.

law of superposition   The principle of stratigraphy that, barring disturbances, more recent layers are superimposed over older ones.

relative chronological sequence   A sequence arranged in an older-to-younger relationship without the assignment of specific dates.

chronometric dating   A dating technique in which an actual age or range of years can be applied to archaeological objects or sites.

absolute dating   A dating technique assigning a specific age.

FIGURE 7.7   This stratigraphic section from the Old Farms Brook Site in Avon, Connecticut, shows a sequence of three prehistoric occupations and one historic occupation of the same location.

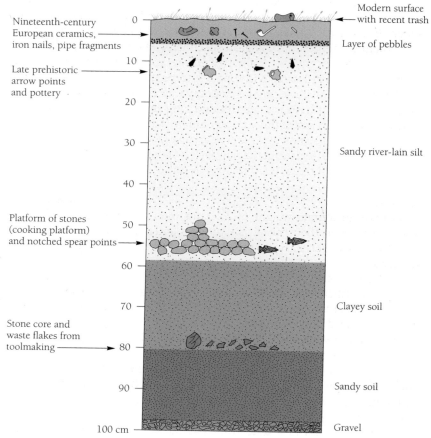

Modern surface with recent trash

Nineteenth-century European ceramics, iron nails, pipe fragments

Layer of pebbles

Late prehistoric arrow points and pottery

Sandy river-lain silt

Platform of stones (cooking platform) and notched spear points

Clayey soil

Stone core and waste flakes from toolmaking

Sandy soil

Gravel

cally, if the "present" were not set at some fixed point, all dates expressed in this way would need to be changed each year.)

One set of absolute methods is called **radiometric dating**. This means that the dating procedure is based on the decay of a **radioactive isotope** (unstable variety) of a particular element. Radioactive isotopes decay by a variety of natural processes. Scientists can measure the rate of decay of most radioactive isotopes—that is, how fast they change from an unstable to a stable form. They can also measure how much of the radioactive isotope is left in a given archaeological, biological, or geological specimen. By first estimating how much of the isotope must have been present initially, archaeologists can determine how old the object is—how long it must have taken for the initial quantity of the radioactive isotope to decrease to whatever the level is today.

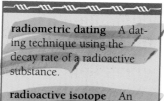

radiometric dating   A dating technique using the decay rate of a radioactive substance.

radioactive isotope   An unstable form of an element that decays to a stable form by giving off radiation.

There are many radioactive isotopes in nature, all with measurable decay rates. Most are useless to archaeologists and paleoanthropologists, though, because the elements are so rare that it would be unlikely to find any of them in cultural or biological specimens. Many are useless because their decay rates are so fast that even fairly recent specimens are unlikely to have any of the radioactive isotope left to be measured. Other radioactive elements have such slow rates of decay that even the oldest of anthropological specimens have not been around long enough for any measurable decay to have taken place; thus, no age can be derived.

A few elements, however, are abundant and have decay rates that make them useful for the dating of sites. Radioactive carbon is one of those. It provides the raw material for the **radiocarbon dating** technique.

Carbon is found in the atmosphere, linked to oxygen, in the form of carbon dioxide (CO_2) and it is found in all living things. Most carbon atoms have an atomic weight of 12 (and thus are labeled ^{12}C) for the twelve particles in their nuclei (six protons and six neutrons). Some carbon atoms, however, have two additional neutrons in their nuclei. These are called ^{14}C.

Carbon 14 is a radioactive isotope of carbon. As such it is inherently unstable; in other words, it changes into a nonradioactive element over time. The rate at which ^{14}C changes or "decays" is a constant called a **half-life**, measuring about 5730 years. In that amount of time, about half of the ^{14}C in a dead organism decays to nitrogen. In another 5730 years, half of what was left after the first half-life has then decayed, leaving one-quarter of what was there initially, and so on. By knowing the rate of decay, how much ^{14}C was present initially, and how much is left now, we can tell how old the item is. It's like knowing how much sand there is in an hourglass, how fast it flows to the bottom, and how much has flowed out of the top. From that, you know how much time has elapsed since the hourglass was overturned. From the measure of ^{14}C, we can know how many years have elapsed since the death of a living thing.

This technique has a few constraints. If something is only a few hundred years old, not enough decay has taken place to allow for its age to be determined reliably. Further, although new procedures have extended the upper range of carbon dating, if something is much more than 50,000 years old, not enough ^{14}C is ordinarily left for the technique to work. Also, the ratio of ^{12}C to ^{14}C in the atmosphere has changed during the last several thousand years, which creates a built-in error factor. Nevertheless, if an organic remain was part of an archaeological site that is more than a few hundred and less than about 50,000 years old, archaeologists often can obtain a fairly good idea of how old the site is using the radiocarbon technique. This range is more than enough to cover the entire period of human settlement in the Americas and Australia (see Chapter 13), but cannot be applied to the far older early hominid sites in Africa, Asia, and Europe (Chapters 8–12).

radiocarbon dating   A radiometric technique using the decay rate of a radioactive isotope of carbon found in organic remains.

half-life   The amount of time needed for half of a radioactive isotope to decay to a stable one.

Another important radiometric technique is **potassium/argon**, or **K/Ar, dating**. Many fossil human sites have been dated with this technique, which measures the age of volcanic rocks. The presence of the element argon in volcanic rock is primarily the result of the decay of a radioactive isotope of potassium (^{40}K). A measurement is made of the amount of argon gas that has built up in the rock. Because the half-life of ^{40}K is known (1.31 billion years), how old the rock is—when it last solidified—can be determined by measuring how much argon has accumulated. Because of the very long half-life, there is virtually no upper limit to the technique—nothing is too old to be dated. On the other hand, although it is technically feasible to date rock that is only 10,000 years old, the long half-life generally renders the technique inaccurate for anything less than a hundred thousand years old.

Potassium/argon dating reveals the age of the rock, how long ago it came out of a volcano. It is not, therefore, a direct measure of the date of a site. Archaeologists can, however, combine K/Ar dating with stratigraphic analysis. For example, if artifacts or bones are found in a stratigraphic layer *above* a volcanic flow that is dated to 3.8 mya (million years ago) and *below* a subsequent flow dated to 3.2 mya, then they are reasonably certain that the occupation of the site is not more than 3.8 million and not less than 3.2 million years old (Figure 7.8).

Still another series of radiometric techniques is based on calibrations of the decay rate of uranium isotopes to their various daughter isotopes and elements. For example, ^{234}U decays to thorium, and ^{235}U decays to protactinium. Rather than disappearing entirely, these isotopes decay at a known rate to an equilibrium level with their "daughter" isotopes. When a carbonate or phosphate has been deposited at the time of site occupation, typically as in a cave deposit called travertine, the site can be dated. Encrustations found on bones have also been dated using this technique. The decay to thorium is extremely useful because the half-life of ^{234}U is about 250,000 years and that of thorium, 75,000 years. As a result, sites too old to date with radiocarbon but too young to apply K/Ar dating to can sometimes be dated by means of uranium series.

Electron spin resonance, or **ESR**, dating is based on measurement of the cumulative "damage" produced on a paleoanthropological specimen (typically a tooth) by radioactive decay in the specimen itself as well as in the soil in which it was deposited (Grün 1993; Grün and Stringer 1991). Once the background radiation rate and susceptibility of the specimen to radiation damage are accounted for, the amount of damage present can be used to determine the age of the specimen. ESR dating is applicable to teeth that are several thousand years or older. The upper limit for ESR is estimated at somewhere between 10 and 100 million years (Grün and Stringer 1991:165).

Dendrochronology, or tree-ring dating, is an extremely accurate biological dating technique. It is very limited in its application, however, and depends on four conditions:

potassium/argon (K/Ar) dating A radiometric technique using the decay rate of radioactive potassium, found in volcanic rock, into stable argon.

electron spin resonance (ESR) dating A dating technique based on measuring the buildup of electrons in crystalline materials.

dendrochronology A dating technique using tree-ring sequences.

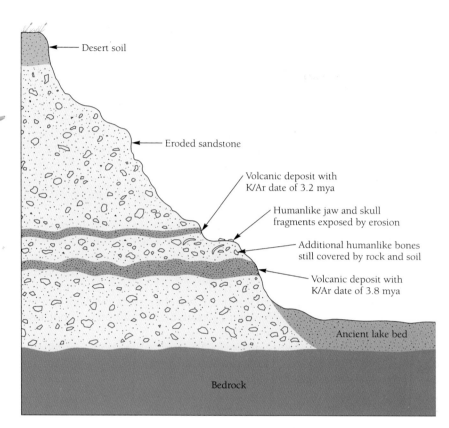

Desert soil

Eroded sandstone

Volcanic deposit with
K/Ar date of 3.2 mya

Humanlike jaw and skull
fragments exposed by erosion

Additional humanlike bones
still covered by rock and soil

Volcanic deposit with
K/Ar date of 3.8 mya

Ancient lake bed

Bedrock

FIGURE 7.8   Hypothetical geological profile showing human remains between two layers of volcanic rock. The archaeological material must be younger than the volcanic deposit below it (3.8 mya) and older than the volcanic deposit above it (3.2 mya).

1.   Trees add one growth ring for each year they are alive.
2.   The size of a ring in a given year varies according to some environmental condition or set of conditions like rainfall or temperature.
3.   Any sequence of varying tree-ring widths over a long period of time will be unique.
4.   All trees in a given area reflect the same changes in tree-ring width.

By overlapping ring sequences of living trees with those of old dead trees, a master sequence of tree-ring width variation over many years can be developed. A sequence of over 2000 years has been produced for the American Southwest. When an archaeological site is located that contains wood or even entire logs, the unique sequence of thick and thin rings in the ancient specimens can be compared to the master sequence (Figure 7.9, p. 160). In this way, the exact year a tree was cut down can be determined. This may or may not coincide with the date of house construction because an old log may have been reused in the building or a new beam may have replaced an original long after initial construction.

FIGURE 7.9   Cross section of tree rings from a living tree (a) overlaps the ring sequence from an archaeological sample (b) which, in turn, overlaps part of the sequence of another archaeological sample (c). The overlapping of many samples allows for the construction of a "master sequence" of tree-ring patterns shown at the bottom. (Archaeology: Discovering Our Past, *2d ed., Sharer and Ashmore, 1993:320, Mayfield Publishing*)

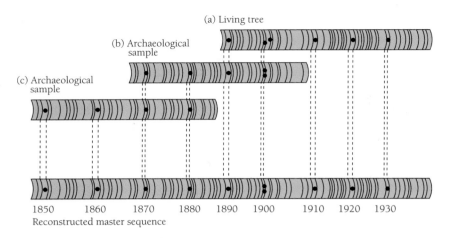

Reconstructed master sequence

Cultural Techniques   The final techniques to discuss are perhaps not the most accurate but are valuable nonetheless. These are known as **cultural techniques.**

Imagine that you are walking down the street and a car drives by. It is large with sharp tailfins and built low to the ground. You can tell almost immediately that this car is a 1950s model. Suppose I hand you a photograph of a young woman with a pony tail who is wearing saddle shoes, knee socks, a frilly blouse, and a pleated skirt with a picture of a poodle sewn onto it. Again, the time period is the 1950s. But how do you know this? You know because you are aware of certain style changes that have taken place in our own culture (Figure 7.10).

Archaeologists perform a similar kind of identification when they determine the age of a site based on the style of the architecture or artifacts found there. Archaeologists can pick up a piece of pottery or a stone tool and provide an estimate for its age because they are familiar with style changes in the ancient past. They can apply actual dates to these items if identical styles have been found at other sites where absolute dates have been obtained.

Archaeologists also measure the rates of change and gauge how quickly styles replace each other by a process called **seriation.** This technique assumes that styles of certain artifacts, like pottery, change in fairly regular patterns. When a new way of doing something—making arrowheads, designing gravestones, opening soft drink cans—is introduced in a culture, it starts off slowly, gains in acceptance until it reaches a peak, and then is slowly replaced by another, newer way of doing the same thing (Figure 7.11). The predictable pattern of this process is used as a relative dating technique by placing sites in the most logical chronological order based on these changes in style.

cultural technique   A dating technique using cultural comparisons.

seriation   Establishing a relative chronological sequence using the pattern of replacement of artifact styles.

1900

1910

1920

.1930

1940

1950

1960

1970

1980

1990

FIGURE 7.10 Styles of artifacts change over time as technology and taste change. Automobiles are one example. (*Archaeology: Discovering Our Past, 2d ed., Sharer and Ashmore, 1993: 307, Mayfield Publishing*)

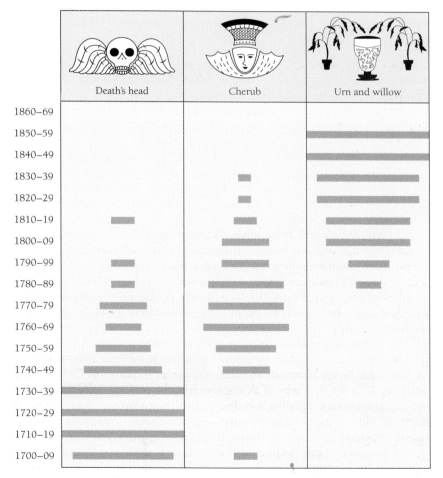

= 10% of the stones in a ten-year period

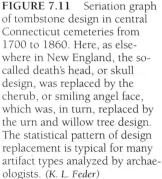

FIGURE 7.11 Seriation graph of tombstone design in central Connecticut cemeteries from 1700 to 1860. Here, as elsewhere in New England, the so-called death's head, or skull design, was replaced by the cherub, or smiling angel face, which was, in turn, replaced by the urn and willow tree design. The statistical pattern of design replacement is typical for many artifact types analyzed by archaeologists. (*K. L. Feder*)

TABLE 7.1   Other Dating Methods

Dating Method	Age Range	Material Dated	Basis
Thermoluminescence	No effective limits	Fired clay, pottery, bricks, burned rock	Measure of amount of energy captured in material from decay of radioactive elements in surrounding soil; amount of energy captured is proportional to age
Paleomagnetism	2000 B.P.– present	Material with magnetic minerals	Movement of earth's magnetic poles and known dates of the position of the poles
Amino (aspartic) acid racemization	1,000,000– 2000 B.P.	Bone	Shift in polarity of amino acids
Obsidian hydration	800,000 B.P.– present	Obsidian (volcanic glass)	Regular buildup of "hydration layer" caused by chemical reaction of obsidian with water over time
Fission track dating	1,000,000– 100,000 B.P.	Volcanic rock	Radioactive decay leaves microscopic damage "tracks" in rock at regular rate

Overview of time range, application, and basis of dating methods not discussed in the text.

Many other dating techniques are available to the archaeologist. Table 7.1 presents a list and some details of their applicability.

How? Reconstructing Past Lifeways

How did the people at a given archaeological site get by? What did they eat, how did they make their tools, how did they bury their dead? How did agriculture develop? How did the first cities evolve? A major problem in answering these questions is, of course, that the people being studied are dead. They cannot be asked about their relations with their neighbors. Their religious ceremonies cannot be observed. They cannot be interviewed about their reasons for adopting agriculture.

One way around this is through **ethnoarchaeology**. With this approach, archaeologists examine living groups in the same manner as ethnographers, but they focus on how human behavior becomes translated into the archaeological record. This is an important approach when analyzing the general processes by which sites are produced. But when it comes to attempting to reconstruct a particular culture, generally, all that archaeologists have are physical remains, the hardware left behind, the stuff made and used. Much methodology, then, concerns itself with this

ethnoarchaeology Observing living peoples to understand how archaeological records are produced.

task: How can a bunch of broken pots, pieces of bone, arrowheads, and ruins be transformed into a picture of a once vibrant, now past culture? Anthropologists who live with a people to understand their way of life are performing what we call **ethnography** (literally, "cultural description"). Archaeologists trying to understand an ancient way of life can be said to perform **paleoethnography.**

Paleoethnography includes a series of general categories of cultural inquiry: technology, environment, diet, social systems, trade, and ideology. Certainly, society's activities could be categorized other ways, but these should encompass many of the major questions an anthropologist might ask.

Technology   The study of prehistoric technology involves figuring out how the people made the things they used and how they used them. This can include everything from a simple stone spear point to an enormous pyramid. Technology is one of the areas of ancient life an archaeologist can study most directly. After all, most of what we find are physical objects, the direct products of a given technology. Archaeologists can use information from a number of sources to give them clues about how the things dug up were actually made by prehistoric people.

The historical record is one source of data. For example, the early Spanish settlers in Mexico described in writing how the Aztecs manufactured artifacts of silver and gold. We know how the longhouses of the Iroquois Indians of New York State were made because the early Jesuit missionaries wrote extensively about Iroquois lifestyles. The archaeologist simply attempts to extend the historical record back into the prehistoric past.

Another way to study prehistoric technology is by experimentation. The archaeologist attempts, through a process of trial and error, to replicate objects that have been recovered (Figure 7.12). If you wish to know how a certain variety of prehistoric stone tool was made, you try to make one exactly like it—same raw material, same size, same proportions.

To determine how a tool was used, experiments can be performed to identify the **wear patterns** that result from particular modes of use. In one such experiment, a series of sharp-edged stone tools were made by an experimental archaeologist (Keeley 1980). They were then used for different functions (cutting, scraping, chopping, engraving, piercing) on different raw materials (bone, wood, meat, leather, antler). The resulting wear patterns were different for each kind of use and included polishing, chipping, scratching, and dulling the edge used (Figure 7.13, p. 164).

Another researcher in this experiment was not told how the experimental tools were used or on what raw materials. Nevertheless, he was able to deduce the tools' uses very accurately. Because wear patterns come in many varieties and are often diagnostic of specific uses, archaeologists feel some degree of confidence in their ability to examine a prehistoric tool and suggest how it was most probably used.

FIGURE 7.12   Experimental archaeologist Terry del Bene produces replicas of stone tools with stone and antler hammers. By replicating stone tools, the archaeologist can gain some insight into how prehistoric specimens were made and used. (*Courtesy Terry del Bene*)

ethnography   The intensive study and description of a particular culture.

paleoethnography   Reconstructing a past cultural system through archaeological remains.

wear pattern   A mark indicative of certain uses, left on a tool.

FIGURE 7.13   Microphotograph of characteristic scratches (*area in circle*) on a prehistoric gouge. Wear pattern analysis can provide information concerning how a particular tool was used. (*K. L. Feder*)

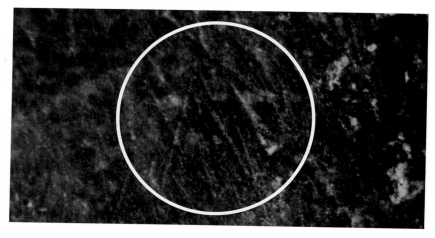

Archaeological experiments can try to replicate anything from a single artifact type—say, prehistoric axes from France—to an entire way of life. A recent ambitious experiment concerned Egyptian pyramid building and involved archaeologists, professional stone masons, and modern laborers ("Nova" 1993). Through historical research, archaeological analysis, and more than a little trial and error, they were able to quarry the stone, move it to the construction site and build a small replica of a pyramid using techniques available to ancient Egyptians (Figure 7.14). Another experiment was carried out in Denmark by a group of people who lived for about four months in a dwelling patterned on the remains of Danish **Bronze Age** structures. They worked and slept in the house in an isolated part of Denmark. They grew their own food, kept animals, and made tools. They immersed themselves in what is thought life was like in the Bronze Age based on archaeological findings. By actually attempting to live according to the reconstructions of the past, archaeologists can get a pretty good idea of where they are right—and wrong.

Environment   A number of techniques are available for ancient environmental reconstruction. For example, dendrochronology, mentioned previously for dating, can be used to reconstruct general rainfall patterns in some areas; the width of tree rings are proportional to the amount of rain that falls in a given year—the more rain, the thicker the ring.

More broadly, changes in worldwide climate can be recognized through an analysis of the ratio of two isotopes of oxygen, ^{16}O and ^{18}O, in seawater. This ratio varies through time as a function of changes in the earth's climate. Simply stated, water bearing ^{16}O, the lighter isotope, evaporates more readily than does water containing ^{18}O. In generally warm periods, this has little impact on the ^{16}O:^{18}O ratio in the ocean because most of the seawater that evaporates falls as rain and returns to the sea. When

Bronze Age   The period of European history when bronze toolmaking began.

FIGURE 7.14   In this archaeological experiment, an archaeologist, an experienced stone mason, and a small group of Egyptian stone workers tested various hypotheses regarding the construction of the ancient Egyptian pyramids by actually attempting to put suggested techniques into practice. Notice the ancient pyramid in the background. (*Courtesy Mark Lehner*)

the planet as a whole is colder, however, large quantities of seawater evaporate, fall as snow in northern latitudes and high elevations, and do not melt off. This effectively depletes the ocean of some of its ^{16}O, changing the ratio of the two isotopes.

How can the $^{16}O:^{18}O$ ratio in ancient seawater be measured? It can't be—directly. Fortunately, however, the ratio can be measured in the ancient skeletons of small marine organisms called **foraminifera**. These organisms incorporate oxygen into their skeletons, reflecting the $^{16}O:^{18}O$ ratio in the surrounding seawater.

Stratigraphic columns of suboceanic deposits have been dated by assuming a constant rate of deposition and by reference to a 180-degree shift in the earth's magnetic field dated by K/Ar to 780,000 years ago (Montastersky 1992). A chronological sequence of changes in the $^{16}O:^{18}O$ ratio has been constructed by Nicholas Shackleton and Neil Opdyke (1973; see Figure 10.3). Currently, the $^{16}O:^{18}O$ ratio is also being analyzed a bit more directly in ancient ice brought up in cores taken from deep in the Greenland ice sheet. It is hoped that the cores will cover 200,000 years of weather history (Montastersky 1991).

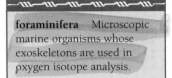

foraminifera   Microscopic marine organisms whose exoskeletons are used in oxygen isotope analysis.

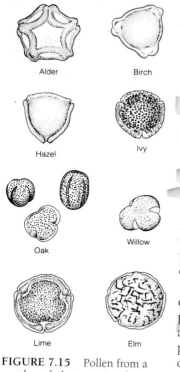

Alder   Birch

Hazel   Ivy

Oak   Willow

Lime   Elm

FIGURE 7.15   Pollen from a number of plant species, drawn to scale. (The grains are magnified about 5000 times actual size.) Palynology, the study of pollen, can provide information about the plant communities growing in an area. This, in turn, can be used to reconstruct the environment.

palynology   The identification of plants through their preserved pollen remains.

midden   A pile of trash produced by the inhabitants of a settlement.

flotation   A technique in which soil matrix and archaeological material is separated by the use of water.

A widely applicable procedure for environmental reconstruction is **palynology**—the study of pollen. The pollen from each species of plant is unique in its appearance (Figure 7.15). Every year great quantities of pollen are produced, and much of it ends up in the soil, where it preserves quite well under the right conditions. Palynologists can recover prehistoric pollen, identify the species represented, and date the pollen by reference to stratigraphy or by carbon-dating organic remains associated with it. (Usually pollen itself is not dated because there is too little of it by weight.) Because individual plant communities thrive under varying environmental conditions, knowing which plants grew in an area in given periods provides insight into what the climate was like. Knowing what grew there, and when, gives an idea of what the people who lived in that area may have eaten.

Diet   One of the most important pieces of information about a prehistoric people is the nature of their diet. This is especially true when trying to answer questions related to the origins of agriculture. Archaeologists can approach diet in a number of ways.

Diet can be studied indirectly by figuring out what people might have eaten based on what was available in their natural environment. For example, deer, moose, raccoon, duck, turkey, and fish are known to have been available in New England for about 7000 years. A hunting and gathering people in this area are likely to have used such resources at one time or another. The modern environment, however, may be quite different from the prehistoric one.

On the other hand, archaeologists can approach the question of diet more directly if there has been good preservation. In many instances, the food remains themselves are still present in archaeological sites. Archaeologists can study the fireplaces, hearths, and garbage heaps, or **middens**, of the people who lived at a site (Figure 7.16). From these we may recover food material if it has been preserved.

Such remains as bone, seeds, or nuts are often fragile and fragmentary, however, making it difficult to get them out of the ground and back to the lab for identification and analysis. In many cases, an archaeologist takes the entire feature, including all soil, back to the laboratory, instead of attempting to separate the dry soil matrix from the fragile archaeological remains in the field. In the lab, through a number of different procedures collectively called **flotation**, the archaeologist takes advantage of the fact that soil and rock will not float in some liquids, whereas organic remains will (Pearsall 1989). Liquid, then, does the delicate job of separation.

The next task in the reconstruction of a prehistoric diet is the precise identification of the species of plant or animal represented by the remains. This task can be difficult because of the fragmentary nature of such remains. In some cases, no precise identification can be made—the piece of bone is too small or the seed too broken up to tell with any degree of con-

FIGURE 7.16   The excavation of features allows archaeologists to recover the remnants of a discrete behavior at a particular time. A hearth, like this one, can tell us about prehistoric diet. Features also include burials, stone-working areas, pottery kilns, and structural remains. (*K. L. Feder*)

fidence. But by using a **comparative collection**—a sort of "library" of bones, nuts, and seeds—archaeologists can often identify many of the dietary remains found at a site (Figure 7.17, p. 168).

Examining the animal remains found at a site is called **faunal analysis.** Here the species represented, their sex, ages at death, health, and physical characteristics are identified. Knowing the species of the remains as well as their age, sex, and health status can provide insight into the hunting practices of prehistoric people. Were the people hunting large numbers of herd animals in group hunts, or were their prey solitary creatures that could be hunted by individual hunters? Were the ancient people

comparative collection   A "library" of animal bones used for comparison with archaeological specimens.

faunal analysis   An examination of animal remains from archaeological sites.

FIGURE 7.17   Even quite small bones recovered at a 2000-year-old archaeological site can be identified by matching them to known, modern bones from an osteological comparative collection or "bone library." The archaeological specimens (the two bones on the bottom) match the form of the two foot bones of a white tail deer from our comparative collection (top).   *(K. L. Feder)*

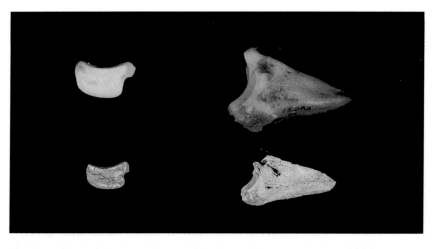

able to kill large animals in their prime, or only the very young, very old, or sick? Also, because many animals give birth to their young during restricted periods, knowing the age of death of a juvenile helps determine the season of the hunt. For example, the North American white-tailed deer usually bears its young in May or June. If the bones of a deer found at an archaeological site indicate an age of 9 months, the animals must have been killed, and the site was most probably occupied, in February or March.

An important factor that must be taken into account in using faunal analysis to reconstruct prehistoric diet is taphonomy. **Taphonomy** involves the analysis of how bones (animal or human) become part of the archaeological or paleontological record. How did the animal die? Was it killed by animals or by people? What happened to the bones of the animal after its death? Was it scavenged or immediately buried, say, in a flood? How were the bones deposited? Were they moved from the kill site by scavengers or some other process?

Taphonomy is a crucial consideration when trying to generate and test hypotheses concerning the behavior of an ancient people. Were they the hunters—or the hunted? Did they engage in organized communal hunts, or did they merely scavenge the remains of creatures killed by carnivorous animals? Were they ritualistic cannibals, or were their bones simply picked over by scavengers?

Imprecision in taphonomic details has led in the past to what Lewis Binford calls "modern myths" about the ancient past (1981:1). Before concluding that an animal was hunted, killed, and eaten by humans, archaeologists must distinguish between the marks left on animal bones by stone tools and the traces left by animal teeth. Before making inferences about hunting practices from a pile of bones in a cave, they must distin-

taphonomy   The study of how organisms become part of the archaeological or paleontological records.

guish between an assemblage of bones left by people and one left by carnivorous animals. Detailed analyses of how carnivores and scavengers kill, dismember, and deposit bones (Binford 1978, 1981; Read-Martin and Read 1975) and microscopic analysis of cut and tooth marks on bones (Shipman and Rose 1983) are contributing to the understanding of taphonomy and, ultimately, to the nature of the diet of our prehistoric ancestors.

General information about diet can sometimes be gathered from skeletal remains. For example, in mammals the nature of the dentition is a clue to overall food sources. Carnivores like dogs or cats, for example, have slicing teeth adapted to meat eating. Humans have a more generalized dentition, built for chewing a varied diet. Certain wear patterns on the teeth, examined microscopically, can reveal whether the diet was made up of soft foods like fruits or more abrasive, gritty foods like roots and tubers. The chemical content of ancient bones can be examined for their proportion of strontium and calcium to determine whether plants or meat made up the bulk of the diet of certain populations. An inadequate diet leaves its mark on the human skeleton too. For example, nutritional deficiencies may show up in porous bones or abnormal bone growth. Two specific deficiencies, those of vitamin D (rickets) and vitamin C (scurvy), leave characteristic signs on the skeleton.

Carbon isotopes can be used to identify diet patterns in some cases. Along with ^{12}C, the most abundant isotope of carbon, there is another stable variety of carbon, ^{13}C. About 1 in 100 carbon atoms are ^{13}C. It turns out that different varieties of plants use the ^{12}C and ^{13}C isotopes differentially in photosynthesis. The differences in ^{12}C and ^{13}C absorption is detectable not only in the plants themselves but also in the tissues of the animals that eat them. Thus, under certain circumstances, human bones can be analyzed for their $^{12}C:^{13}C$ ratio and the kinds of plants that were abundant in the diet can be determined. This approach has been applied in the examination of the domestication of maize (corn), which uses a photosynthesis process different from most of the wild plants that grow in the same area in Central America (Farnsworth et al. 1985; and see Chapter 14).

Another important method used in dietary reconstruction is usually applicable only in very dry areas of the world where the level of organic preservation is high. This technique is based on the simple fact that most animals, including human beings, do not completely digest everything they eat. In other words, some of what goes in very often comes out in recognizable form. The data in question are the preserved remains of prehistoric feces, or **paleofeces**. Paleofeces contain undigested particles of food that survived an organism's digestive system. Though not one of the more romantic activities in archaeology and paleoanthropology, there are few better ways of reconstructing an ancient person's last meal than by examining what passed through his or her system. Because many caves were used

paleofeces   Preserved fecal remains.

repeatedly, a large sample of paleofeces may be present and provide a broad view of the diet of an ancient group—at least during the time they used the cave.

A new line of research indicates that blood traces might be preserved on the edges of stone tools used to kill animals or process animal products. When this occurs, the blood can be analyzed, and the animal species identified. For example, using standard forensic procedures to identify blood at crime scenes, Australian archaeologist Tom Loy has identified blood residues on a stone artifact recovered at a 9000-year-old archaeological site in Turkey as belonging to sheep, humans, and an extinct form of cattle (Bower 1989a). Archaeologists Noreen Tuross and Tom Dillehay (1995) report the identification of mastodon blood on a 13,000-year-old stone tool found in Chile. There are a series of ongoing debates about the accuracy of such identifications (Kaiser 1995), but all agree that blood residue analysis is a procedure that deserves consideration.

Social Systems   Studying prehistoric technology and diet may be difficult tasks, but at least tools and food remains are often preserved, allowing archaeologists to study these aspects of culture directly. Social systems, or the interrelationships of people, leave little in the way of material remains, however. Whom do people marry, and with whom do they live? Whom do they consider to be family, and who not? To whom do they owe their allegiance, and on whom do they depend in time of trouble? All these ties are crucial to human survival, but direct remains are few.

Nevertheless, reconstruction of social systems is possible because the objects that people make and use—the material remains found at archaeological sites—were made, used, and discarded within a *social context*. The very careful analysis of sometimes minute details of artifact manufacture and design can provide information about the social system of the people being studied. Social information is *encoded* into the things that people make.

A good example of this phenomenon is found in archaeologist James Deetz's classic study of Arikara Indian ceramics (Deetz 1965). According to the historical record, the Arikara, who lived in Nebraska, were a **matrilocal** society. That is, after marriage a young woman stays in her home village and her husband, usually someone from another village, moves in with her. At any given time, therefore, a village is composed of grandmothers, daughters, and granddaughters who grew up in the same village and their husbands, who have moved in from different villages. Deetz was able to show that in these matrilocal Arikara villages, the pottery, which was made by the women, was homogeneous. In other words, because all the women were related and learned their craft from women who were related, their styles were highly similar. Different villages, then, each had their unique style.

matrilocal   A type of society in which a married couple lives with the wife's family.

When the matrilocal pattern broke down after European contact, however, women no longer stayed in one place as the postmarital residence pattern became **patrilocal.** The pottery in any one village was now heterogeneous, having been made by women from different villages with their different styles. Deetz could trace these changes in pottery styles as the social system changed through time. The material objects—the pots—reflected changes in the social context in which they were made.

In another example, at the 11,000-year-old Lindenmeier site in Colorado, there were two major concentrations of artifacts of a particular kind of spear point used in killing big-game animals (Wilmsen 1974). Careful analysis of the points in the two concentrations showed subtle differences in the style of the points, which led researcher Edwin Wilmsen to conclude that two separate bands of hunters had inhabited Lindenmeier at the same time. The points were probably made by men living in two different patrilocal bands. In Wilmsen's view, like the Arikara women making pottery in their matrilocal groups, men learned spear making from their fathers and brothers, all of whom stayed in the band when they got married. Thus, each patrilocal band developed a unique style of point making.

Trade: The Movement of Materials and People   Archaeologists are also interested in the relationships among the inhabitants of different ancient societies. Many prehistoric people, even those living at great distances from one another, engaged in trade. Obsidian (natural volcanic glass) from Turkey is found at sites in Syria, hundreds of miles from its source. Copper from Michigan is found in New York state. Turquoise from the American Southwest is found in Mexico. Shells from the Pacific Ocean are found in highland New Guinea. Once the source of raw materials can be ascertained, maps showing the movement of such materials can be drawn.

We can sometimes determine the precise sources of raw materials by *macroscopic* (naked eye) inspection. Often, however, it is not so easy, and much more sophisticated techniques are needed. In **petrographic analysis,** a thin slice can be cut from a stone artifact and examined microscopically. The "fabric" of the rock from which an artifact was made can then be compared to the fabric of various possible natural outcrops in order to associate the artifact's raw material with its particular source. Another procedure is called **trace element analysis.** This technique measures the quantities of so-called trace elements in materials. For example, whereas obsidian, wherever it comes from, is made up largely of silica, there are also tiny amounts (traces) of other elements—impurities like arsenic and copper. The precise proportions of these trace elements are generally unique to the area where the raw material originated and thus can serve as a sort of fingerprint for a raw-material source. Archaeologists can determine the trace elements in the raw material of an artifact and then match up that "fingerprint" to a source with the same trace element chemistry.

patrilocal   A type of society in which a married couple lives with the husband's family.

petrographic analysis   Examination of the morphology of a lithic source by the analysis of thin slices of rock.

trace element analysis   Determining the source of a material by identifying small (trace) amounts of impurities.

In the Lindenmeier example just discussed, Wilmsen performed trace element analysis on the obsidian tools from the two different concentrations. One showed obsidian from northeastern Wyoming and the other obsidian from central New Mexico. The hypothesis of two separate hunting bands was supported. Two distinct bands, making tools in their own styles and traveling in different territories, came together at Lindenmeier. That we can know this 11,000 years after the fact is a testament to anthropology of the past.

Ideology   It might not seem that ideology, philosophy, or religion are topics an archaeologist could readily deal with. After all, archaeologists study physical or material remains. Ideology, by its very nature, is a nonmaterial, abstract aspect of human existence. The same argument applies here that did regarding the archaeologist's ability to reconstruct social systems. Because everything we do takes place within the context of a specific social system, what we make bears some imprint of that system. Similarly, what we do also takes place within the context of an ideological system. In a general sense, all our artifacts are made within the context of an ideology and should reflect certain aspects of that ideology.

It is also necessary to point out that, although culture can be divided into categories such as social systems and ideology, human beings do not compartmentalize their lives. Culture is not simply a bundle of vaguely connected parts; it is an integrated approach to survival. Very often artifacts or features simultaneously reflect several of the separate aspects that make up a culture. One example of this expression of multiple cultural features is burials.

The manner in which a human being is buried, for example, reflects a number of abstract concepts. Think in terms of our own culture. Our tombstones—and tombstones are certainly very important "artifacts"—often record the accomplishments of individuals and their family lives as well as reflecting their religious beliefs (Figure 7.18). If some future archaeologist were to walk into a twentieth-century graveyard, he or she would almost certainly be provided with some insight into our perspective on life, society, religion, and, of course, death.

Prehistoric archaeology and paleoanthropology do not reveal tombstones to read. In burying their dead, however, prehistoric people made as much of a statement about their ideological beliefs as we do. Instead of using a written language, these people wrote their epitaphs in the language of artifacts. Tools and food were often placed in graves to accompany the deceased to the afterlife. Sometimes animals, or even other people, were killed and buried, apparently to serve the needs of the departed. Precious objects manufactured from valuable raw materials were placed in some graves; other burials contain no artifacts. In some instances, huge pyramids were raised over the remains of the dead; other bodies were thrown away in the trash heap. Information about social status, trade, religion, and even economics is contained in burials. (An economic system with

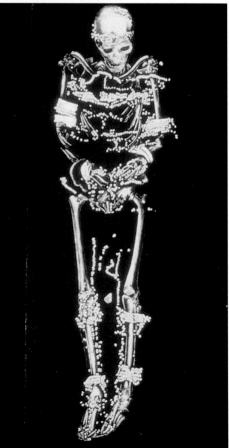

FIGURE 7.18   Artifacts associated with death and burial—such as the 300-year-old tombstone from colonial America (*top*), the 1300-year-old sarcophagus lid (*bottom left*) from the Maya site of Palenque in Mexico, and the ivory beads in the 25,000-year-old Sungir' burial site (*bottom right*) near Moscow in Russia—reflect the religious, social, economic, and political systems of the people who produced them.   (*Tombstone: K. L. Feder; sarcophagus lid: © Merle Greene Robertson, 1976; burial site: © O. Bader/Musée de l'Homme*)

FIGURE 7.19   The famous "Ice Man" (*left*), preserved for over 5000 years in the Italian Alps, was naturally mummified by cold and wind. He was discovered by hikers in 1991. His excellent state of preservation has allowed anthropologists to discover his age, health status, diet, time of death, genetic affiliations, and even, through artistic reconstruction, his facial features. The "Tollund Man" (*right*), preserved for 2000 years in a Danish peat bog, was probably a sacrificial victim—the rope noose was still around his neck. He was well enough preserved that the remains of his last meal (barley and linseed gruel) were still in his stomach. (*Ice Man: © Gerha Hinterleitner/Gamma Liaison; Tollund Man: © Ira Block 1986*)

many "extra" people is needed to build a pyramid every time a ruler dies.) This is why archaeologists are often so anxious to excavate grave sites: They provide valuable data not otherwise available. In addition, of course, the physical remains of the people themselves provide a great deal of information about just who they were.

Who? Identifying the Remains of Humans and Human Ancestors

We are all aware, from newspaper accounts, television, and movies, just how much information can be derived from examining the remains, through autopsies, of recently deceased humans. On rare occasions, anthropologists can examine well-preserved ancient remains such as the Ice Man from the Alps and the bodies preserved in peat bogs from northern Europe (Fig. 7.19).

But such finds are exceptional. Even though anthropologists studying the past cannot usually gather these kinds of data about an individual, they are nevertheless interested in the study of the deceased to learn, in a general sense, who the people were whose lifestyle is being studied. Moreover, anthropologists are interested in humans as a biological species, and the study of human remains addresses certain biological and evolutionary questions. Finally, they are also concerned with issues such as cause of death, which reveal something important about the lives of the subjects.

The problem paleoanthropologists face is that the remains they study are almost always in the form of bones. The further back in time one goes, the more fragmentary those skeletal remains become. So just what can one hope to discover from this biological data?

Species Identification and Definition   When skeletal remains are unearthed, often in connection with an archaeological excavation, perhaps the most basic task is identifying the species to which the bones belong. How do anthropologists know if the bones are human? A survey of **comparative osteology** (the study of bones of different species) is far beyond the scope of this book. Suffice it to say, though, that the anthropologist interested in this area of study is intimately familiar with the 206 bones of the adult human and is generally able to identify a recovered bone (Figure 7.20, p. 176). To help in this endeavor, most universities maintain comparative bone collections so that a bone that cannot be readily identified can be compared with similar ones from many species until a match is found.

The identification process gets more complicated when the bones belong to species that no longer exist. Throughout this book, however, we will be designating the species of ancient fossil remains. How is this done?

Using the system formalized by Linnaeus (see Chapter 5), scientists classify living animals on the basis of morphology and behavior. Animals that look very similar and share a common behavioral pattern are thought to belong to the same species when—and this is the key—they are interfertile. A species is defined as a group of animals in which fertile males and females can mate and produce fertile offspring.

For example, brown bears (genus *Ursus,* species *arctos*) from Eurasia, Alaska, Canada, and the western United States (called grizzly bears in the Western Hemisphere) are all placed in the same species because they look very similar, share the same general environmental niches, and can interbreed to produce offspring who can, in turn, produce offspring of their own. But brown bears are quite different in size, color, and behavior from black bears (*Ursus americanus,* the common bear from eastern North America). Both varieties are still recognizable as bears, but they are different in form and behavior and they cannot mate and produce fertile offspring; they belong to separate species.

You can readily see the problem species definition poses for paleoanthropology. Fossil bones are not found stamped with a species designation; paleoanthropologists name and define species. Further, fossil species are all extinct and are represented only by their bones—which often are quite

comparative osteology
Comparing bones of different species.

FIGURE 7.20   The human skeleton with the major bones identified. Adults have a total of 206 bones, many of which are the results of fusing of the nearly 270 bones present at birth. Each bone has features that characterize it as belonging to a member of our species.

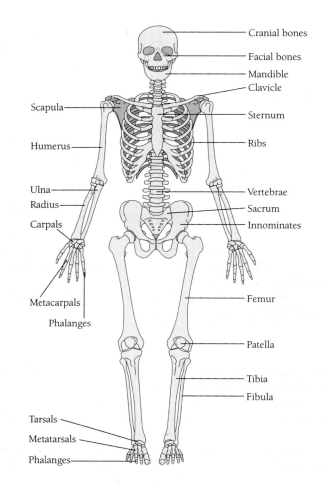

fragmentary. As a result, two fundamental sources of data concerning species are not directly available: behavior and the ability to mate and produce fertile offspring. In assessing species designations, paleoanthropologists can directly analyze and compare only the skeletal morphology of different specimens.

How, then, do paleoanthropologists know if two skulls or two thigh bones—or one skull and one thigh bone—from different locations, or even the same site, belonged to members of the same species? They base their conclusions on the degree of similarity or difference between the individual specimens: If they are very similar and, especially, if they share specific anatomical traits not seen in other specimens, they place them in the same species and distinguish them from other species.

How similar do two specimens have to be before paleoanthropologists conclude that they belong in the same species and how different before they are placed in two separate species? To answer this question, consider the degree of morphological variability present within living species. Some living creatures—for example, the domestic dog—include a great deal of physical and behavioral variation among animals that can, nevertheless, interbreed and therefore belong to the same species (see Figure 14.3). Even within our own species, we see a tremendous amount of variation (see Chapter 12). If humanity were extinct and extraterrestrial physical anthropologists had only the incomplete and fragmentary skeletal remains of an Inuit (Eskimo), a native Australian, a Scandinavian, and a Masai, they might not place them all within a single species, though we know that they all are demonstrably *Homo sapiens.*

Naming fossil species and assigning specimens to a species, then, are difficult and imperfect. Labeling specimens can often be controversial. Some researchers accept more variation within a single group and lump many different specimens together. Others, the "splitters," allow for less variation and, therefore, create more fossil species with fewer specimens assigned to each. Unless and until DNA can be extracted from ancient fossil bone and we can compare the actual genetic blueprints of different individuals, there will always be a certain amount of subjectivity to the process—with plenty of room for disagreement. We will see this quite clearly when we discuss the fossils belonging to the family Hominidae (Chapters 8–11), which are lumped or split differently by different researchers.

Sex   Once a skeleton or, more usually, a portion of one is identified as a human or a human ancestor, the next detail to be discerned is usually its sex. This is fairly easy to determine: A skull alone can be "sexed" with over 90 percent accuracy; a skull and pelvis together provide about 98 percent accuracy.

The general rule is that males on the average are larger and more heavily muscled than females. In fact, this generalization applies to many of the primates, especially our closest relatives, the great apes. Thus, researchers look at a skull for overall size and for the size and presence of certain features on the bones related to muscle attachment: The bigger the muscles, the more prominent the attachment area.

Similarly, the pelvis of a male tends to be larger and more rugged than that of a female. But the human female pelvis must be adapted to the process of giving birth to very large-headed babies. So the pelvises of females are generally wider in their openings and angles than those of males. Where the sex of a skull may be ambiguous, the pelvis is usually a dead giveaway (Figure 7.21, p. 178).

Other bones of the body can also aid in sexing. The same criteria of size and muscle attachment features can be used with the long bones of the arms and legs.

These rules, of course, represent *averages.* Averages can vary from group to group; similarly, an individual may not conform to the average and can be misidentified. For this reason, it is preferable, as in any kind of skeletal analysis, to deal with a large sample of skeletons, which allows

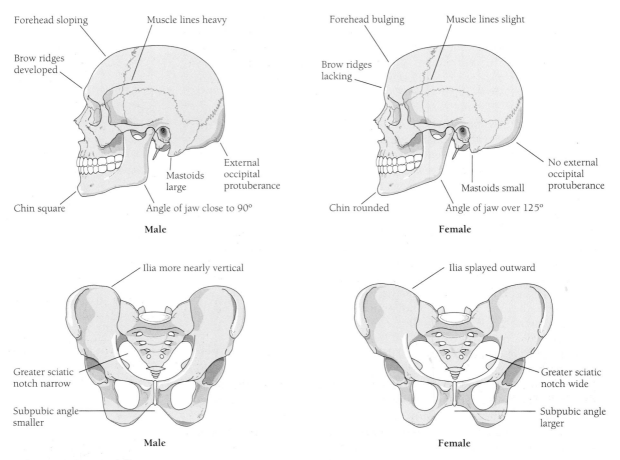

FIGURE 7.21   Sex differences in the skull and pelvis.

comparisons to be made. In the case of sex identification, many females are larger than the average male, and many males are smaller than the average female. No absolute criteria can be applied to sexing a skeleton or, for that matter, most other forms of skeletal analysis. It is a skill that takes practice and a great deal of observation of bones of known sex. With all this, though, experienced anthropologists can sex most human skeletal remains with acceptable accuracy.

But what about the remains of premodern humans? What happens with a skeleton from 30,000, or 300,000, or 3 million years ago? Anthropologists really have little choice but to begin with the assumption that the same criteria apply. After all, these are members of the same basic evolutionary line, and they are primates. One of the earliest sets of human remains, from 3.18 mya, was determined to be that of a female, using just such reasoning. (She is called "Lucy," and we'll tell you about her in Chapter 8.)

This approach, though, has its limitations because anthropologists don't know for sure if the degree of **sexual dimorphism**—the differences in appearance between the two sexes—was always the same in the past. In Lucy's case, more representatives of her stage of evolution were found, and the assessments of sex were substantiated. In other words, researchers had not just an individual, but a sample of a population.

Age   What about a person's age at death? The body goes through many physical changes as it develops, matures, and grows old. Many of these changes are reflected in the skeleton and take place at certain times in a human's life. By determining which changes have already occurred and which have yet to occur in a given set of remains, researchers can approximate a person's age at death.

Perhaps the best known method for "aging" a skeleton is the use of dental eruption dates (Figure 7.22). Like many mammals, humans have two sets of teeth: deciduous, or "baby," teeth, and adult teeth. Each tooth in both sets erupts through the gum line at a certain average age. Dental remains (among the most common because the outer layer of the teeth, the enamel, is the hardest substance the body produces) can reveal which tooth was the last to erupt and which unerupted tooth would have erupted next. The dates of eruption of those two teeth determine the minimum and maximum probable age at which that person died. Once all the adult teeth have erupted, of course, this method is no longer applicable.

Another aging technique makes use of the skull. A baby's head has *fontanelles,* or "soft spots," which are actually spaces between the bones of the skull. The bones develop separately, in part to allow some flexibility in our large heads during the birth process. Shortly after birth, the bones grow and fit together like a jigsaw puzzle. Later still, additional bone is added to the lines of attachment, called **sutures**, eventually forming a single cranial bone late in life. Because the sutures close at a fairly regular rate, a range may be derived for age at death from the last closure that has occurred and the next closure that would have occurred (Figure 7.23, p. 180). This method, which can be used from about ages 18 to 50 and even beyond, is now seen as fairly unreliable. It may, however, be the only method available if just a skull is recovered.

A third popular aging technique makes use of the bones of the arms, legs, hands, and feet. These bones all grow in three sections: a shaft, or **diaphysis**, and two caps, or **epiphyses**. When growth is complete, the cartilagenous disks between caps and shaft become ossified (turn to bone), and a single arm, leg, finger, or toe bone is produced. Since ages for **epiphyseal union** are known, the same logic outlined before is used to determine age at death (Figure 7.24, p. 181).

The final aging method uses the inner surface of the area where the two halves of the pelvis meet in front. This is called the *pubic symphysis.* Between the ages of 18 and 50+, the appearance of this surface undergoes

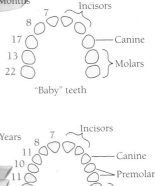

AGES OF TOOTH ERUPTION

FIGURE 7.22   Average ages of eruption of the deciduous (baby or milk) teeth (*top*) in months and of permanent teeth (*bottom*) in years. Individuals may deviate from these dates for some teeth, but most people display this basic pattern.

sexual dimorphism   The anatomical features that distinguish the sexes of a species.

suture   A line of contact between the bones of the skull.

diaphysis   The shaft of a long bone.

epiphysis   The end, or cap, of a long bone.

epiphyseal union   The fusion of the ends of long bones with the shafts.

FIGURE 7.23 Patterns of cranial suture closure. A great deal of individual variation is seen in the shapes of the sutures and in their closure dates. Once a popular technique, this method of determining age is no longer considered particularly useful.

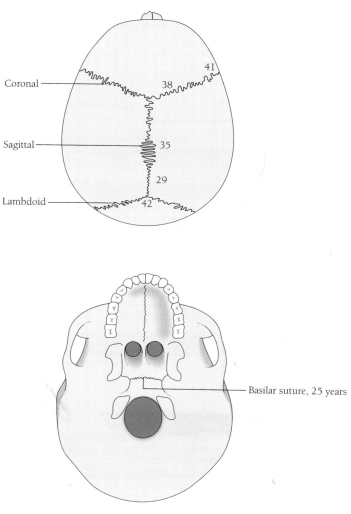

AVERAGE DATES FOR CRANIAL SUTURE CLOSURE (YEARS)

characteristic changes. By assessing the phase to which a specimen belongs, approximate age at death may be determined.

As with sexing, methods for aging rely on averages. No two humans are identical, and not everyone's growth pattern and rate follow the rules. Thus, the more data one can gather from a skeleton, the more accurate the determination will be. As with sexing, anthropologists must assume similar growth patterns and rates for our early ancestors, at least until they have a large enough number of fossils to establish separate criteria for different stages of human evolution.

AGES OF EPIPHYSEAL UNION

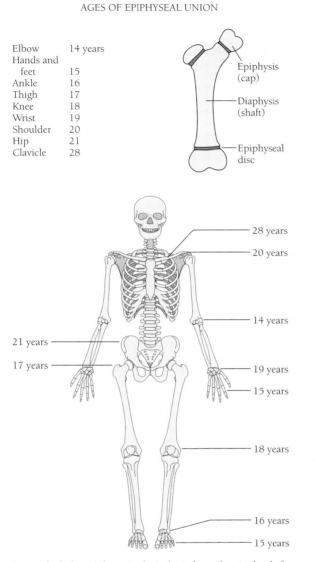

Elbow	14 years
Hands and feet	15
Ankle	16
Thigh	17
Knee	18
Wrist	19
Shoulder	20
Hip	21
Clavicle	28

Epiphysis (cap)

Diaphysis (shaft)

Epiphyseal disc

FIGURE 7.24   Pattern of epiphyseal union, one of the most reliable indications of skeletal age.

28 years
20 years
14 years
21 years
17 years
19 years
15 years
18 years
16 years
15 years

Age at which the epiphyses in the indicated area fuse to the shafts.

Researchers are now beginning to go beyond appearance to study certain chemical characteristics of ancient bone. Presently, for some bones preserved under the right conditions, blood type in the ABO system can be determined. This not only reveals something about an individual, but also—if a large enough sample of skeletal material is found at one site— may provide some genetic information about an entire population.

FIGURE 7.25   The effects of syphilis on the human skeleton. Note the extensive lesions on the skull and at the ends of the humeri and tibias. (Identification of Pathological Conditions in Human Skeletal Remains, *Ortner and Putschar, 1985:195, Smithsonian Institution Press*)

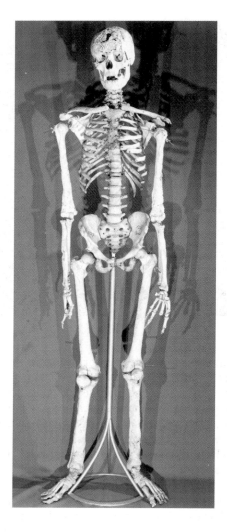

Health   The anthropologist of the past, like a medical examiner, plays detective and tries, where possible, to determine the presence of illness and injury as well as cause of death. This area of study is called **paleopathology.** What people suffer and die from can tell a great deal about the nature of their environments, their diets, and their relations with other humans. Many diseases leave characteristic marks on the human skeleton. These include such ailments as certain forms of arthritis, tumors and other cancers, tuberculosis, leprosy, some anemias, syphilis, osteoporosis, and various infections such as dental abscesses (Figure 7.25). Any developmental anomalies, such as curvature of the spine or other deformations, will, of course, be clearly evident on the bones.

paleopathology   The study of ancient disease.

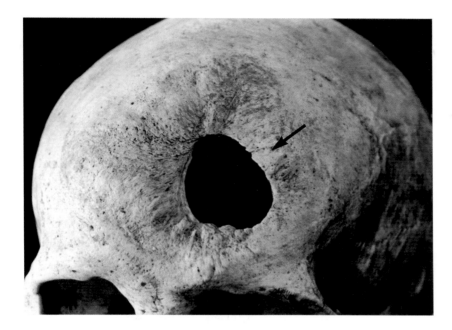

FIGURE 7.26   A trephined skull from Peru. The arrow shows the outer margin of the wound. The edge of the hole indicates that healing has taken place. (Identification of Pathological Conditions in Human Skeletal Remains, *Ortner and Putschar, 1985:98, Smithsonian Institution Press*)

People also die from wounds and accidents. Bones have revealed that people of the past suffered from fractures, dislocations, and accidental amputations. Deaths from arrow, spear, knife, and gunshot wounds have also been seen. Scalping (usually done after death) shows up as a characteristic set of cut marks on top of the skull. Large holes cut into the skull show that **trephining**, a form of prehistoric skull surgery, was not always successful, although healing around some holes indicates that many obviously survived the operation (Figure 7.26).

Appearance   The skeleton acts as a framework for the body as a whole; thus the size and shape of the bones can reveal something of the appearance of the entire living person. For example, the sheer size and ruggedness of their bones shows that the Neandertals, humans from ancient Europe (see Chapter 11), were big, brawny, and extremely strong. Anthropologists can obtain a more exact idea of size, especially stature, by using a series of mathematical formulas. By measuring, say, a femur, they can calculate the height of the individual who once owned it.

There is a direct relationship between bone and muscle because muscles attach to bones. This relationship has led a number of investigators to attempt to reconstruct the faces of our ancestors from the shapes of their skulls and facial skeletons. Using their knowledge of human anatomy, they artistically add missing bones, eyes, fatty tissue, cartilage, muscle, and skin to ancient skulls, literally "fleshing out" the picture of early humans. As be-

trephining   Cutting a hole in the skull to treat an illness.

fore, of course, these reconstructions assume that present anatomical relationships also held true in the past. Researchers have yet to find an entire ancient face preserved as a fossil. (The same procedure is used also in law enforcement to try to identify skeletal remains and match them with missing persons.)

The relationship between bone and soft tissue also provides a basis for determining geographical location or origin. In living humans, a number of physical and chemical characteristics show variation on a geographical scale. Such traits as skin color, eye shape, nose shape, hair color and texture, blood type, and other genetic features are all variable in our species, and all show some geographical regularity.

Similarly, some skulls look as if they come from a certain place or belong to a certain general population (we will discuss this phenomenon in more detail in Chapter 12). Such analysis, to be sure, can be rather subjective, but with enough examples and enough practice, anthropologists can make an accurate identification of the general population from which a skull came. Some numerical generalizations can also accomplish the same task. Average head length, relative length of arms and legs, and other measurements tend to differ geographically. Last, some very specific traits can be found most often in certain populations. "Shovel-shaped incisors"—upper front teeth with an appearance rather like a shovel—are not exclusive to, but are very common among, Asian groups. This trait can help distinguish Native American skeletal remains from those of Europeans since Native Americans are of Asian origin.

Behavior   Finally, the skeleton can be a source of information about behavior. In evolutionary perspective, the first distinguishing feature of human anatomy was upright posture and locomotion. Anthropologists know when this feature first evolved because the skeleton directly reflects it: The nature of the bones of the pelvis and the femur along with the position of the hole in the base of the skull are clear indications of locomotor posture. It is obvious from such evidence that humans have walked upright for over 4 million years.

Sometimes skulls are found deformed in uniform ways, although the individuals themselves seem otherwise normal. Such artificial deformation was sometimes performed to reflect standards of beauty. Historic records—from ancient Egypt, for example—can substantiate the practice. The famous Queen Nefertiti had a cranial deformation of this sort. Sometimes, however, the deformation was accidental, caused by pressure from a cradleboard, a device used in many parts of the world to hold an infant's head (and thus the infant itself) steady and secure while the parents were otherwise occupied (Figure 7.27).

Methods from engineering have been applied to the assessment of strength from cross-sections of human bones (Bridges 1996). Some interesting relationships between arm and leg strength and subsistence pattern

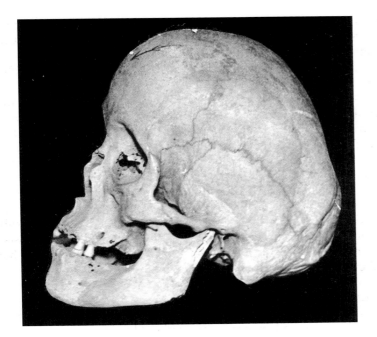

FIGURE 7.27   An example of cradleboarding from ancient Illinois. The board flattened the forehead and, especially, the back of the skull, but probably had no ill effects. *(Illinois State Museum, reproduction by written permission only)*

have been proposed. For example, one study indicates that arm and leg strength declined among males when Native American populations along the Georgia coast moved from hunting and gathering to maize agriculture. Another study shows a decrease in right arm strength among males in the American Midwest during the Late Woodland period when the atlatl (spear thrower) was replaced by the bow and arrow around A.D. 900.

Finally, evidence of wounds from arrows, spears, and guns indicates another kind of human behavior (Figure 7.28, p. 186). Such evidence tells something about the relations of a group of people with its neighbors.

While studying these remains, however, anthropologists must keep in mind an ethical consideration. In the case of recent remains, these data are the bodies of people whose living descendants belong to an identified group. This is true for many Native American populations, whose ancestral burial areas have long been sources of human skeletal remains for the anthropologist. The scientific value of such studies cannot be denied and is certainly valid. But the rights and values of the people involved should also be respected. Remains ought not to be treated as curiosities.

Why? Explaining the Past

Over 4 mya, the first humans stood upright. Why? At least 80,000 years ago (ya), our human ancestors began the practice of burying their dead. Why? About 32,000 ya, the Neandertals disappeared. Why? Soon after

FIGURE 7.28   The small arrow point embedded in the base of the skull of this ancient Illinois Indian no doubt caused this individual's death.   *(Illinois State Museum, reproduction by written permission only)*

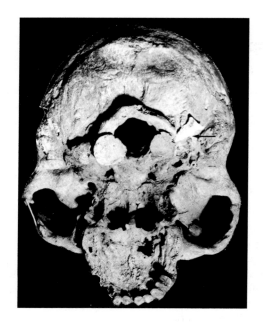

11,000 ya, in Southeast Asia and the Middle East, we find evidence that human beings were raising their own crops and domesticating animals, instead of simply hunting and gathering what nature provided. Why? About 5000 ya, in the Middle East, and soon after in India, China, Mesoamerica, and South America, people began to live in cities and build enormous monumental works like pyramids and temples. Why?

Why, indeed! The final question that anthropologists studying the past confront is perhaps the most difficult of all. They can locate sites, figure out how old they are, describe the people themselves, and to a large extent reconstruct what went on. But answering the many "whys" poses the greatest challenge.

It is indeed difficult to suggest why a given people 3 million, 10,000, or even 500 ya made a certain decision or changed their culture in a certain way. As difficult as it is, however, the answers to certain crucial "why" questions about humanity in general can only be pursued by the application of anthropological data. Many of the important questions that people want to answer have roots extending far back into the mists of antiquity. Anthropologists can only penetrate these puzzles if they apply the types of biological and cultural analysis described here.

Imagine a book 400 pages long. Imagine that each page represents a period of time in the development of humanity. The very first sentence on the first page represents the first time a human ancestor stood upright on the African savanna. The very last sentence on page 400 is today. The amount of space in the book devoted to certain time periods is proportion-

Contemporary Issue

Preserving the Past

We have tried to impart here the importance of anthropological research in our quest to understand human physical and cultural evolution. Unfortunately, however, the raw data of archaeology and paleoanthropology are in great danger. Many agricultural practices, mining techniques, and construction projects, along with general greed and indifference, contribute to the destruction of important sites all over the world each year. Farmers in some countries practice land-leveling techniques that destroy buried sites. Strip mining in some places causes terrific destruction of archaeological resources. In developed and developing nations alike, the construction of roads and water projects contributes to the destruction of the fragile prehistoric record. In some countries, including our own, sites are looted for their more aesthetically pleasing artifacts, which are then sold to the highest bidder.

No more ancient sites are being made. They are, in a sense, nonrenewable resources like coal and oil. Some nations have recognized the importance of protecting these fragile remnants of the past. A series of federal, state, and even town laws in this country afford at least some protection to archaeological sites. Other countries have patrimony laws that make it illegal to export the artifacts of their ancestors—which are usually sold to the wealthy of other nations for their amusement. Many countries and some states have laws against the disturbance of ancient human burials.

Laws are very important, but people's attitudes are perhaps most important of all. If people would only recognize the importance of understanding the past, site destruction would become unthinkable. Ancient sites would be preserved for future study, money would be made available for archaeological research, and the market for antiquities would dry up. It would be a terrible tragedy and irony indeed if, just as our study of the past is becoming a sophisticated scientific enterprise, the raw data of the past were to become as extinct as the cultures we are attempting to understand.

Looters dug more than 450 holes in this Kentucky field in search of Native American artifacts. (*Steve Wall*)

Construction-related development often poses the greatest threat to archaeological resources. Here an archaeological excavation is conducted in the shadow of highway expansion in Southbury, Connecticut.(*K. L. Feder*)

al to their actual length. There's just one hitch; we can only read that part of the book corresponding to the period after human beings invented writing some 6000 ya. The pages before the invention of writing are blank.

Can you guess where the writing would begin? On the last half of the final page! Imagine reading a 400-page book with writing only on the last half of the last page and then being asked to explain what happened. If the book were a detective novel, you might know that "the butler did it," but it is unlikely you would know what he did, when, to whom, or, most importantly, why.

So the first 399½ pages of the book about our human story are blank, at least as far as writing is concerned—for they are filled not with words but with spears and pots, burials and monuments, bones and seeds. In the story of our species, the first 99.99 percent of our existence on this planet is prehistoric and therefore the purview of archaeologists and paleoanthropologists. To ask who we are and why we are is to be almost by definition an anthropologist studying the past.

Summary

The study of human antiquity includes the methodologies of the archaeologist and the biological anthropologist. This research attempts to answer these general questions: where, what, when, how, who, and why. Investigating the human past begins by determining *where* the physical evidence of ancient people can be found. Various techniques are used to locate and recover the physical remains of these people—*what* they left behind, the artifacts and features clustered in the sites where they once lived. Techniques from various disciplines are applied to determine the age of these remains, establishing *when* the people lived. Acting as ethnographers, anthropologists analyze the remains of the human past to establish *how* these people survived—how they made their tools, what their physical environment was like, and what diet, social systems, trading networks, and ideology comprised their culture. Studying the physical remains of the people themselves—their bones—helps us understand *who* they were as individuals and as populations. Finally, anthropologists attempt to discern and reveal *why* they lived the lives they did. Through the application of the procedures outlined in this chapter, anthropologists studying the human past attempt through science to illuminate the story of our species.

Study Questions

1. List and describe the general "questions" archaeologists and paleoanthropologists ask about the human past.
2. How are archaeological and paleoanthropological sites discovered? How is evidence of a past people's way of life recovered from such sites?

3. How can the behavior of ancient people be analyzed? How can we reconstruct the ancient environment, a people's diet, social system, trading patterns, technology, and belief system?
4. How can archaeologists and paleoanthropologists determine the age of specimens?
5. What information can be gathered from the skeletal remains of humans and human ancestors?

Key Terms

site
artifact
feature
field survey
remote sensing
test boring
test pit
random sample
transect
spatial context
provenience
association
in situ
stratigraphy
parent material
law of superposition
relative chronological
   sequence
chronometric dating

absolute dating
radiometric dating
radioactive isotope
radiocarbon dating
half-life
potassium/argon
   (K/Ar) dating
electron spin reso-
   nance (ESR) dating
dendrochronology
cultural technique
seriation
ethnoarchaeology
ethnography
paleoethnography
wear pattern
Bronze Age
foraminifera
palynology

midden
flotation
comparative collection
faunal analysis
taphonomy
paleofeces
matrilocal
patrilocal
petrographic analysis
trace element analysis
comparative osteology
sexual dimorphism
suture
diaphysis
epiphysis
epiphyseal union
paleopathology
trephining

For More Information

Although we have been able to devote only a chapter to the techniques of learning about the human past, many fine texts deal with the methodology of archaeology and physical anthropology. A few of the best are *Archaeology: Discovering Our Past*, Second Edition, by Robert Sharer and Wendy Ashmore; *In the Beginning: An Introduction to Archaeology*, by Brian Fagan; and *Archaeology*, Second Edition, by David Hurst Thomas.

For more detailed discussions of analysis of the human skeleton, see the excellent books *Human Osteology: A Laboratory and Field Manual of the Human Skeleton*, by William Bass, and *Handbook of Forensic Archaeology and Anthropology*, by Dan Morse, Jack Duncan, and James Stoutamire. Especially noteworthy for its beautiful photographs is *Human Osteology* by Tim White and Pieter Folkens.

Ancient Disease in the Midwest, by Dan Morse, is a good source for information on paleopathology.

The 3000-mile-long Rift Valley in East Africa is thought to be intimately connected to the beginnings of hominid evolution. What happened in Africa 5 or 6 million years ago that began the human story? *(Emory Kristof/National Geographic Society Image Collection)*

8

The Emergence of the Human Lineage

CHAPTER CONTENTS

In 1912, amateur scientist Charles Dawson announced the recovery, from a gravel pit in Piltdown, England, of perhaps the most famous and controversial bones in the history of anthropology. The find consisted of a mandible and several cranial bones in association with some primitive stone tools. The cranial bones were clearly those of a large-brained human, but the mandible was indistinguishable from that of an ape. This combination of traits was precisely what many scientists of the time expected of the evolutionary "missing link" between ape and human. Unfortunately, the find was a fraud.

FIGURE 8.1 Reconstruction of the skull of the Piltdown fraud. This modern human braincase was planted in the same site with an orangutan jaw and claimed by the discoverers to belong together. The result was exactly what science at the time expected of the earliest human. *(Courtesy Department of Library Services, American Museum of Natural History, neg. no. 36240A, photo: A. E. Anderson)*

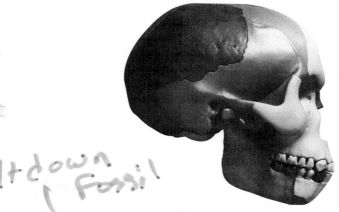

Piltdown Fossil

The remains were named ***Eoanthropus,*** the "dawn man" (Figure 8.1). For nearly forty years, many scientists, especially in Britain, accepted "Piltdown Man" as the earliest human. In other countries, however, opinion ranged from withheld judgment to downright skepticism. Many felt the combination of the apelike jaw and human brain case was too good to be true. Furthermore, during those forty years no similar fossils were found that could provide supporting evidence for *Eoanthropus.*

The skeptics were proved correct. In the early 1950s, in a classic example of the self-correcting nature of science, Piltdown was unmasked as a fake—it was *literally* the cranium of a modern human and the jaw of a modern orangutan, filed, stained, and otherwise modified to appear ancient. With that revelation, other early remains suddenly took their rightful place in human evolution.

To this day, incidentally, no one knows who perpetrated the fraud. Piltdown remains one of the great mysteries of science. For accounts of the story, see Weiner (1955), Gould (1983), Blinderman (1986), Spencer (1990), and Feder (1996).

Despite a great deal of skepticism, the Piltdown find appeared in many books on human evolution during those forty years. What accounts, then, for the popularity and acceptance of so obvious a fake as Piltdown for so long a time? The answer, in part, is nationalism. No important fossil human had yet been found on British soil, so the possibility that the "dawn man" might be British had obvious appeal. More important, however, Piltdown fulfilled expectations of what the earliest human *should* look like. At that time, the most important difference between human and ape was believed to be humans' big brain. The "missing link" should therefore be essentially an ape with a big head.

In this expectation, scientists were committing a classic error in the study of evolution, thinking that a modern situation represents the original situation—in this case, that the most characteristic feature of modern humans would also have been the first feature of our lineage. This mistaken idea is part of the reason why the evolutionary position of the australo-pithecines, whose remains had first come to light in 1925, remained enigmatic for so long. Their bipedal posture but ape-sized brains did not fit expectations of what the earliest humans should look like.

It is now clear, as it has been for nearly forty years, that the large brains of humans appeared relatively late in hominid evolution. Our brains achieved their modern size 400,000 years ago at the earliest, whereas the feature that first distinguished us from the apes—our bipedalism—is over 4 million years old. So the first question in our discussion of the emergence of the human lineage is not how and why humans evolved big brains—but how and why humans stood up and walked around on two legs.

The Bipedal Primate: Fossil Evidence

First Find

The first evidence from the dawn of hominid evolution came in 1925. South African anatomist Raymond Dart was given a fossil found in a limestone quarry at a site called Taung ("place of the lion"). It took Dart 73 days to separate the fossil from its limestone matrix. When freed, it revealed the face and braincase of a young apelike primate (Figure 8.2), but with two important differences. First, the canine teeth, long and large in apes with gaps to accommodate them when the jaws are shut, were no bigger than those of a human child. Second was the position of the **foramen magnum.** This is the hole in the base of the skull through which the spinal cord extends from the brain, and around the outside of which the top vertebra articulates. In the Taung specimen, this hole was well underneath the skull rather than toward the back, as in apes, indicating an upright, bipedal posture rather than a quadrupedal one. Dart hypothesized that the "Taung Baby," as it came to be known, was an intermediate between apes and hominids. Nevertheless, he named it *Australopithecus africanus,* the "southern ape of Africa"; because of its many apelike traits, he wasn't ready to classify it in the human family.

Further finds in Africa substantiated Dart's assessment of the anatomy of his fossil and his opinion that it represented a new type of primate. They also made it clear that *Australopithecus,* rather than being an intermediary, was, in fact, a hominid, a bipedal primate. (The rules of scientific nomenclature, or taxonomic names, however, require that first-used names stick even if they later prove to be descriptively inaccurate. Thus, these hominids are still named "southern apes.")

The story of the discoveries and various interpretations of the fossil hominids from the first years of hominid evolution is fascinating in itself. Several of the books listed at the end of the chapter tell that story. Here, we'll look at the story as it stands today. There is still no general agreement on exactly how this part of our evolutionary tree looks, but anthropolo-

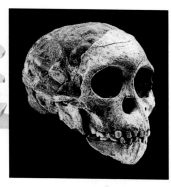

FIGURE 8.2   The "Taung Baby," the first specimen of *Australopithecus.* Note the naturally formed cast of the brain (see also Figure 9.11).   (*© David L. Brill 1985/Brill Atlanta*)

foramen magnum The hole in the base of the skull through which the spinal cord emerges and around the outside of which the top vertebra articulates.

TABLE 8.1   List of Early Fossil Hominid Species*

	A. anamensis	A. afarensis	A. africanus	P. robustus	P. boisei	H. habilis
Dates	4.2–3.9 mya	4–3 mya	3–2.3 mya	2.2–1.5 mya (?)	2.2–1 mya (excludes Black Skull)	2.2–1.6 mya
Sites	Lake Turkana	Hadar Omo Laetoli	Taung Sterkfontein Makapansgat Lake Turkana (?) Omo (?)	Kromdraai Swartkrans	Olduvai Lake Turkana Omo	Olduvai Lake Turkana Omo Sterkfontein (?) Swartkrans (?)
Cranial capacity (in ml)	(no data)	380–500 $\bar{x} = 440$	435–530 $\bar{x} = 450$	520 (based on one specimen)	500–530 $\bar{x} = 515$	500–800 $\bar{x} = 680$
Size (average, in lb.)	114	110	100	105	101	89
Skull	Canines large, but hominidlike canine roots More apelike chin than *afarensis* Tooth rows parallel as in apes	Very prognathous Receding chin Large teeth Pointed canine with gap Shape of tooth row between ape and human Hint of crest	Less prognathous than *afarensis* Jaw more rounded Large back teeth Canines smaller than *robustus,* larger than *afarensis* No crest	Heavy jaws Small canines and front teeth Large back teeth Definite crest	Very large jaws Very large back teeth Large crest	Flatter face Less sloping forehead Teeth similar to *africanus* No crest
Postcranial skeleton	Bipedal knee and ankle joints Fibula intermediate between ape and hominid	Long arms Short thumb Curved fingers and toes Bipedal	Similar to *A. afarensis*	Hands and feet more like modern humans Retention of long arms	Similar to *P. robustus*	Limited evidence Retention of long arms Maybe retention of primitive features of hand and foot

*Excludes *Ardipithecus ramidus,* which is still under study.

gists have found fossils with well-established dates (Table 8.1) and locations (Figure 8.3).

The Fossil Record

First, a general orientation. All the fossils discussed here belong to Family Hominidae. Within that family anthropologists now recognize four de-

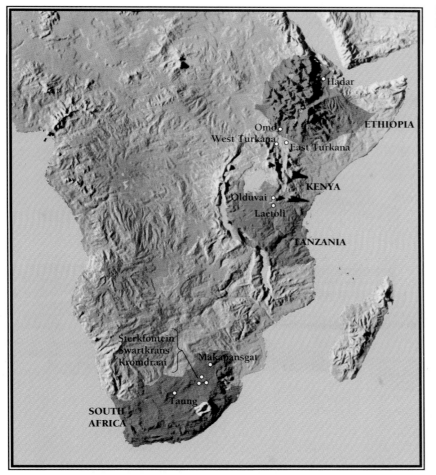

FIGURE 8.3   Map of early hominid fossil sites.

fined genera, *Ardipithecus, Australopithecus, Paranthropus,* and *Homo.* Only the last genus still exists; the other three are extinct. These groups may be distinguished by the following definitions, on which we'll elaborate:

Family Hominidae: the bipedal primates

Genus *Ardipithecus:* the most apelike hominid

Genus *Australopithecus:* small-brained, gracile hominids with a mixed vegetable diet

Genus *Paranthropus:* the small-brained, robust hominids with a grassland vegetable diet

Genus *Homo:* the large-brained, omnivorous hominid

Authorities seem about evenly divided on the issue of whether the fossils called *Paranthropus* belong to a separate genus or are part of *Australopithecus*. We differentiate them here in part because we think the data warrant it and in part because using a different genus name makes understanding the trends of hominid evolution a little easier.

The oldest hominid fossils so far are among those most recently found. First discovered in Ethiopia in 1992 and 1993, the finds consisted of seventeen fossil fragments including some arm bones, two skull bases, a child's mandible, and some teeth (Figure 8.4). The fossils were different enough from any found previously to warrant creating a new hominid genus, and they have been named *Ardipithecus ramidus* (the genus name means "ground ape" and the species name means "root" in the local language). The fossils are dated at 4.4 mya.

In 1994, more fossil bones were recovered close to the first site. These consisted of 90 fragments representing about 45 percent of a skeleton, including the telltale pelvis, leg, ankle, foot. These new finds, however, are still being analyzed and, as yet, the results have not been published.

Ardipithecus ramidus is considered a hominid because the foramen magnum is more forward than in apes, and because of some detailed features of the elbow joint and the teeth. At the same time, it is "the most apelike hominid ancestor known" (White et al. 1994). Among other things, the canine teeth are larger, compared to the other teeth, than in later hominids. It seems, then, that *ramidus* is very close to the time when the hominids and the apes split; it may be, as the name implies, the "root" hominid species.

These fossils, though, remain somewhat enigmatic for the moment. Although the evidence from the foramen magnum indicates that these creatures were bipedal, a detailed examination of the legs, pelvis, and feet is needed before reaching a definitive conclusion. Furthermore, along with the fossils of *ramidus* were those of many forest mammals as well as fossilized seeds and wood. It appears that *ramidus* lived in the forests and not on the open plains or savannas, where most early hominids lived. As you'll see, all interpretations of early hominid evolution have been linked to a savanna environment. We'll address this potential interpretive problem later.

In August 1995, the newest hominid species was announced (Leakey et al. 1995). Called *Australopithecus anamensis,* it consists, so far, of twenty-one specimens from the Lake Turkana region of Kenya (*anam* means "lake"), including jaws, teeth, a skull fragment, a tibia, and a humerus (Figure 8.5). The specimens are dated at 4.2 to 3.9 mya. Although they exhibit apelike features such as large canine teeth, the root of the canine is vertical as in other hominids rather than angled as in apes, and the tooth enamel is thicker than in apes or in *Ardipithecus ramidus*—more like other hominids. Most notably, the leg bones are clearly those of a biped. These finds are new, but there appears to be some consensus that they may represent the ancestor of all hominids, with *Ardipithecus ramidus* representing a side-branch of the hominid family.

FIGURE 8.4   Fossil tooth and a portion of jaw from *Ardipithecus ramidus*. (© *1994 Tim D. White/Brill Atlanta*)

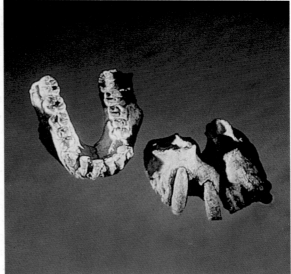

FIGURE 8.5   A mandible (*left*) and maxilla of *Australopithecus anamensis*. The chinless jaw is apelike, but the vertical root of the canine is clearly a hominid trait (the canine roots of apes are angled). (© *Kenneth Garrett/National Geographic Society Image Collection*)

The next species, by contrast, is well established and its nature more generally agreed upon. This is **Australopithecus afarensis** (named for the Afar region in Ethiopia), and its first and most famous specimen is the 3.18-million-year-old skeleton, also from Ethiopia, known as Lucy (Figure 8.6, p. 198), found in 1974 by Donald Johanson and his team. Lucy is remarkable because, as old as she is, nearly 40 percent of her skeleton was preserved and all parts of her body were well represented—except the cranium, whose remains are fragmentary. Based on modern criteria, she was a female who stood about 3'8" and weighed about 65 pounds. Although there is some disagreement about details, there is no doubt that Lucy was a biped.

Other fragmentary specimens, including a portion of a skull dated at 3.9 mya, were unearthed in Ethiopia and Tanzania and assigned to this species. Based on this evidence, a reconstruction of the head of *A. afarensis* was attempted, but a single complete fossil skull was not found until 1992. In February of that year, Donald Johanson and his team discovered 200 skull fragments, again from Ethiopia. Once reconstructed, the skull closely resembled the previously discovered fragments, except that it was large and rugged, probably the skull of a male. It was dated at about 3 mya (Figure 8.7, p. 198).

FIGURE 8.6 The skeleton of "Lucy," the first specimen of *Australopithecus afarensis.* (© *John Reader/Science Photo Library/ Photo Researchers, Inc.*)

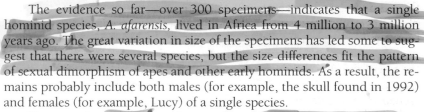

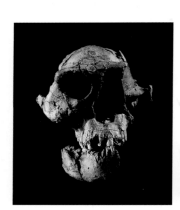

FIGURE 8.7 Reconstructed by paleoanthropologists Bill Kimbel and Yoel Rak, this skull shows us the face of *Australopithecus afarensis.* This individual was a large male whose worn teeth indicate he was probably fairly old. He was notably larger than Lucy, showing that this early hominid species exhibited sexual dimorphism. (© *Enrico Ferorelli*)

The evidence so far—over 300 specimens—indicates that a single hominid species, *A. afarensis,* lived in Africa from 4 million to 3 million years ago. The great variation in size of the specimens has led some to suggest that there were several species, but the size differences fit the pattern of sexual dimorphism of apes and other early hominids. As a result, the remains probably include both males (for example, the skull found in 1992) and females (for example, Lucy) of a single species.

However, in 1995 a French team found the remains of a partial hominid jaw in Chad, in north-central Africa, dated at 3 to 3.5 mya. The team recently announced that this find represents a second species of hominid living during that time (Simons 1996). The species has been named ***Australopithecus bahrelghazalia*** (based on an Arab name for a nearby riverbed), and it suggests that early hominids were more widely spread on the continent than previously thought. Full acceptance of this classification, and the implications of the fossil, await further study.

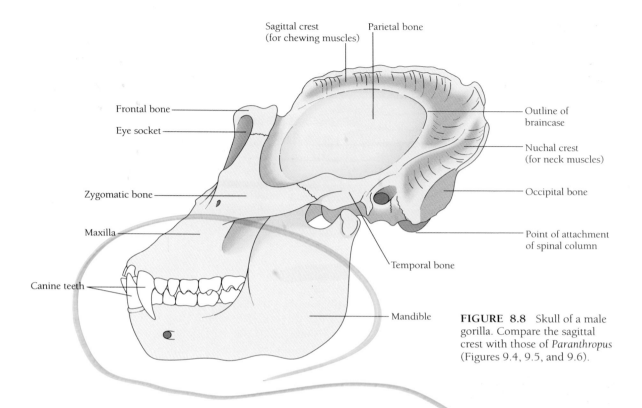

Sagittal crest
(for chewing muscles)

Parietal bone

Frontal bone

Eye socket

Zygomatic bone

Maxilla

Canine teeth

Outline of
braincase

Nuchal crest
(for neck muscles)

Occipital bone

Point of attachment
of spinal column

Temporal bone

Mandible

FIGURE 8.8 Skull of a male gorilla. Compare the sagittal crest with those of *Paranthropus* (Figures 9.4, 9.5, and 9.6).

What did Lucy and her kin look like? They might be described as "bipedal apes." Their average brain size was about 440 ml (a milliliter is about one-twenty-eighth of a fluid ounce), close to the average for chimpanzees and with the same maximum size of about 500 ml (about one-third the modern human mean). They have the **prognathism** (projection of the lower face and jaws), and the pointy canine teeth and gaps in the tooth rows characteristic of apes, though these last two are not as pronounced as in apes. There is a hint of a sagittal crest, a ridge of bone along the top of the skull for the attachment of major chewing muscles. Gorillas have these crests (Figure 8.8). In modern humans, these muscles are attached on the side of the head. (Put your hand on your head, about 2 inches above your ears, and clench your teeth. You'll feel the muscle.)

The arms of *A. afarensis* are about in the same proportion to the body as those of modern humans, but the legs are relatively shorter, making the arms functionally longer. The hands and feet were relatively longer and showed some curvature of the bones. The shoulder and arm bones show evidence of heavy musculature. These individuals, though adapted for bipedal walking on the ground, may still have been fairly good tree climbers.

prognathism Protrusion of the lower portion of the face.

At first, there was some disagreement as to just how bipedal *A. afarensis* was, especially considering the apelike nature of much of the rest of its anatomy. All the interpretations, after all, were based on fossilized bones; no one, obviously, had ever actually seen one walk. But in 1976, Mary Leakey recovered the next best thing at a site in Tanzania called Laetoli—a set of footprints made in a fresh layer of volcanic ash that quickly hardened and preserved for us a striking picture of an event that took place 3.7 million years ago. Two hominids, one large, one small, had walked side-by-side through the ash shortly after a volcanic eruption. Their footprints show an anatomy and stride no different from ours today (Figure 8.9).

Clearly, then, bipedalism was the very first hominid trait to evolve. It is, essentially, the only hominid trait in the otherwise apelike australopithecines. Therefore, bipedalism may be seen as the adaptation that began our family of primates.

Why We Walk Upright

What is the benefit of walking upright, an adaptation that involved major realignments of much of the body (Figure 8.10, p. 202). Under what circumstances was it selected for in our earliest ancestors? Not many creatures use this form of locomotion. Kangaroos do and many dinosaurs did, but they also use their tails for balance and support. Birds are bipedal, but their feet are able to grasp; they can even sleep perched on a branch. Human bipedalism, although it obviously works quite well and involves a large number of individual physical features and remarkable acts of coordination, may at first glance seem a rather odd way of getting around. Humans attempt to balance their bodies vertically on two small points of contact with the ground. When we walk, we throw ourselves off balance, swing one leg forward, and catch ourselves before falling flat on our faces. We can't run particularly fast, and we aren't very stable on rough or slippery surfaces. To try to understand why this adaptation occurred, let's work through an explanation using the scientific approach of posing questions, suggesting answers, and then testing the logic of those answers.

Remembering that natural selection does not create new traits, but selects from variation already present, we can look again to our close relatives for clues about the beginnings of hominid's characteristic posture and locomotion. Most primates can, in fact, walk bipedally on occasion. The best occasional bipeds are, not surprisingly, the chimpanzees and bonobos, and one of the most common motivations for these quadrupeds to walk upright is to use the arms and hands for something other than locomotion—usually to carry something (Figure 8.11, p. 202). Assuming that this behavior was true of apes' and humans' common ancestor, bipedalism may have been selected for among some group of apes because it conferred an adaptive and reproductive advantage in their particular environment.

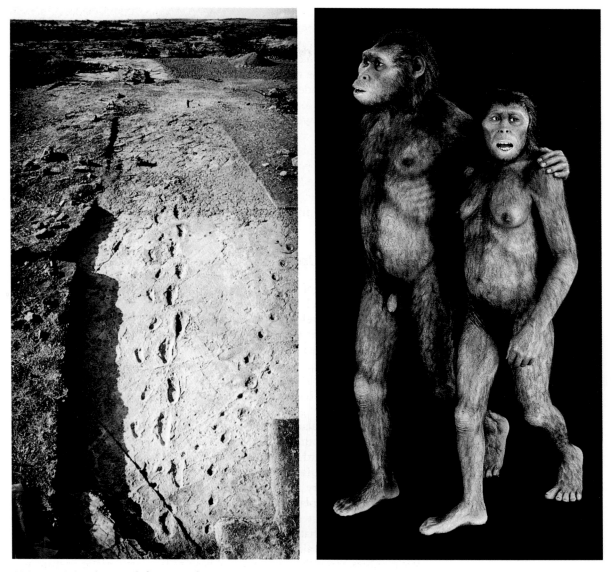

FIGURE 8.9   The Laetoli footprints from Tanzania, and the reconstruction of the hominids that probably produced them, from the American Museum of Natural History in New York City.   *(Laetoli footprints: © John Reader/Science Photo Library/Photo Researchers, Inc.; reconstruction: Negative # 4744(5). Photo by D. Finnin/C. Chesek. Courtesy Department of Library Services, American Museum of Natural History)*

FIGURE 8.10   The skeletons of a gorilla (*left*) and a modern human. Note especially the differences in the shape and orientation of the pelvis, the relative lengths of the arms and legs, and the shape of the feet. The size and shape of the muscles of posture and locomotion would also reflect the difference between quadrupedalism and bipedalism. (*From "The Antiquity of Human Walking" by John Napier. Copyright © 1967 by Scientific American, Inc. All rights reserved*)

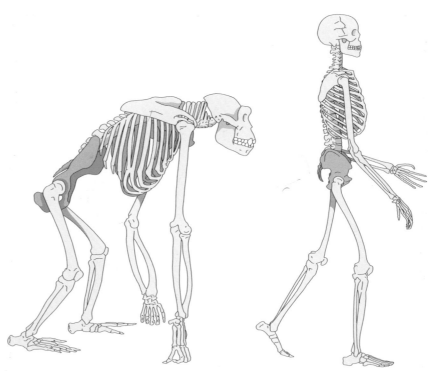

FIGURE 8.11   Chimpanzee walking bipedally while carrying bananas. Carrying may have been one of the functions that promoted the evolution of bipedalism in early hominids. (*A. Kortlandt*)

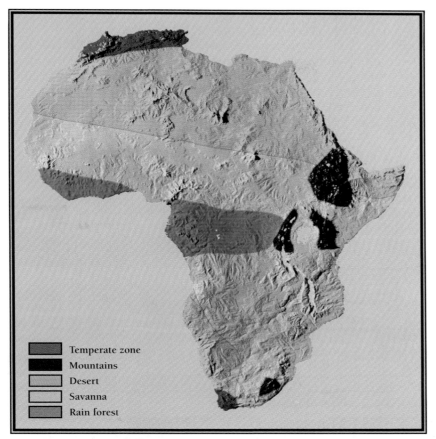

FIGURE 8.12   The climatic zones of Africa today. Except for the large deserts in the north and south, the zones are much the same as when our evolutionary story began some 6 mya. *(Redrawn with permission from: Bernard Campbell,* Human Ecology *[New York: Aldine de Gruyter] © 1983 by Bernard Campbell)*

Temperate zone
Mountains
Desert
Savanna
Rain forest

Except for the recently discovered fossils named *Ardipithecus ramidus,* nearly all specimens of hominids from Africa between 4 and 1 million years ago were thought to have been found in areas that are, or were at the time, savannas—the great open grasslands that characterize much of eastern and southern Africa today (Figure 8.12; see also Figure 3.11). The savannas were even more extensive during the period in question, as the great deserts of North Africa are fairly recent. Some event, or series of events, it was thought, caused our ancestors to move from the forests of Africa out onto the plains. Just how could bipedalism be related to a savanna environment?

To a primate, savannas present a very different set of problems than do forests. Primates are basically vegetable eaters. Although there are plenty of plants on the savannas, there are not as many that can be utilized by the digestive systems of most primates. Most primates cannot digest cellulose as can the ungulates, grazing animals such as the African antelopes. Edible plants or plants with edible parts are not as concentrated on the open plains, and so primates living on the savanna have to travel over a wider area to find food. The savannas are more affected by seasonal change than are the forests, and so there may be greater variation between the wet and dry seasons. Finally, there is more danger involved in acquiring these widely dispersed foods on the savannas. Lions, leopards, cheetahs, wild dogs, hyenas, and other predators of the savanna are more than happy to make a meal out of a small primate. (The leopard is the only major forest predator.)

There are, of course, sources of meat on the savannas. Chimpanzees are known to hunt, kill, and eat other mammals. They are even known to **scavenge** the kills of leopards found hanging in trees (Byrne and Byrne 1988; Cavallo 1990). It is unlikely, though, that our earliest savanna ancestors hunted, and there is no physical evidence that they did. There is evidence that they scavenged kills, which we will cover later. While scavenging provided access to meat, it was dangerous. The animals had to be taken away and kept away from other predators or scavenged after the predators had finished.

Bipedalism, however, could have allowed our early ancestors to accomplish some of these activities in greater safety and with greater efficiency. Freeing the arms and hands from a role in locomotion means that food could be transported from open areas to safer locations such as a grove of trees or a rock shelter. This would have been especially important if the food were part of an animal carcass, since other meat eaters would also find it attractive. Children could be carried while mothers walked in search of food. Perhaps sticks and rocks were carried and thrown to scare predators and scavengers away from a kill. (Chimps will occasionally hurl rocks and sticks, though not particularly accurately).

It has also been proposed that bipedalism, by elevating the head, provides better views of potential sources of food and danger. The vertical orientation, according to another view, helps cool the body by presenting a smaller target to the intense equatorial rays of the sun and by placing more of the body above the ground to catch what cooling air currents there may be. The savannas can be hot, and the heat built up by hours of steady walking in search of food needs to be dissipated. (This factor may be the adaptive significance of the relatively hairless bodies of modern hominids. Having no hair allows sweat to evaporate more quickly and cool the body more efficiently.)

Finally, data indicate that although bipedalism is an energy inefficient way of *running* compared to quadrupeds, it is more efficient for walking. Long periods of steady walking in search of food would seem to require less energy if done upright. The importance of this has, however, been called into question (Steudel 1996). Remember that the first hominids did not walk bipedally quite like later members of our family and may not have been any more efficient at walking upright than are chimpanzees. Moreover, it is not certain that

scavenge To eat the flesh of an animal that has died of natural causes or that has been killed by another creature.

what makes our walking more efficient is simply our upright stance. Body mass is related as well. It may be that bipedalism had, initially, all the other advantages listed above and that, once it was established, further changes made it more energy efficient.

At least some of these hypotheses can be offered as reasonable explanations why bipeds were better adapted to life on the savannas. They could search for and find food, and transport it to safety with less heat build-up, less danger, and, perhaps, greater energy efficiency. But does this explain why bipedalism would have made some individuals more reproductively successful? Remember that reproductive success is the measure of natural selection. Simple survival and longevity are only part of it.

Once again, we may get a clue from our close relatives, the chimpanzees and bonobos. Although chimps normally have no need to share resources, they do share meat from a hunt, possibly because it is—in some chimp way—considered a luxury item.

The bonobos, on the other hand, share even foods that are plentiful. This serves to avoid conflict and to establish and maintain peaceful coexistence within the group. Food sharing is, in a sense, a symbol of group peace and unity. In times of need, of course, food sharing might have practical consequences.

Moreover, as you recall from Chapter 6, the bonobos use sex—in various combinations and with a variety of techniques—to strengthen and maintain group unity and to defuse tension. Sex for them is separate from purely reproductive activity. It has social and psychological meaning as well.

Perhaps, then, our early ancestors survived by the enhancement of adaptations that focus on peaceful cooperation and group unity, including the sharing of resources. The acquisition of these resources was made easier and safer by the ability to walk habitually upright.

Such a set of adaptations would certainly have been one way of surviving on the savannas. But two more questions come up. First, what about baboons, another successful savanna primate that survives in that environment *without* bipedalism and food sharing, and whose sexual activity is limited to the estrus periods of the females?

Second, what about *Ardipithecus ramidus*? It is not certain at this point that they were fully bipedal. If they were, however, the question is *why*. Remember that—unlike other early hominids—they appear to have lived in the dense forests.

The first problem can be answered by remembering that adaptations are relative to a particular species at a specific point in time and in response to a specific environment. Just as the primate adaptations are not the *only* successful way of living in the trees, neither are the hominid adaptations the only way to survive on the savannas. The different responses of the baboons and the hominids simply show that there is more than one way to adapt to the same environment—even within the same general group of organisms. Even so, despite the important differences, both types of primates still focus on social organization in adapting to the savannas.

The answer to the second question is that perhaps bipedalism was actually first selected for not on the savannas but in the forests. Bipedal walking is common among the bonobos, as is food sharing and sex with social meaning, and yet the bonobos live in denser forests than do the chimpanzees. In fact, it has been suggested that the bonobos have undergone less evolutionary change than humans or chimpanzees and so may most closely resemble the common ancestor of all three of these species (de Waal 1995). These adaptations, then, may have been the particular manner in which our ancestors responded to a forest environment. Later, in response to some change that required life on the savannas, those adaptations proved to work well in that environment too.

Indeed, there is continuing debate as to just what sort of environmental change may explain the evolution of the hominds. One view (Vrba 1993), suggests that a decrease in global temperature between 5 and 6 mya made Africa drier, shrinking the forests and producing savannas, isolating some populations of our ancestors in that environment and selecting for the traits that would become the hallmarks of our family. A further consequence of this drying trend would be an increased reliance on scavenged meat, a resource that would have been available year-round in contrast to seasonal plant food.

A second scenario (Coppens 1994) claims that the ancestors of the hominids and modern apes were isolated from one another not by a drastic climatic change but by a geological one—the formation of the Rift Valley in East Africa starting about 8 million years ago (Figure 8.13). Tectonic movements caused the valley to sink and a line of mountains to rise on its western rim. In this view, the result was a localized climatic change resulting in the area west of the valley remaining moist and forested, and the area to the east turning drier and becoming savanna. Today, chimpanzees and bonobos are found only to the west, most hominid fossils only to the east.

Yet another view says that, at least at one site in Kenya, there is no evidence of an abrupt change, but rather indications that East Africa at the time was a "heterogeneous mosaic" of environments from forests to open plains (Kingston et al. 1994:958). The early hominids may not have been forced out of the forests but may, in some more complex reaction, have taken advantage of new opportunities and less competition (at least from other homonoids) on the savannas. There, their bonobolike forest adaptations proved equally useful and, over time, were enhanced by natural selection.

Finally, some recent studies have supported the idea that bipedalism was originally a forest, not a savanna, adaptation. Reassessment of the environments of some important early hominid sites have shown them to be more forested than previously thought (see Shreeve 1996c for a summary). The Lake Turkana site where *Australopithecus anamensis* was found, for ex-

FIGURE 8.13 A portion of the Great Rift Valley in southern Kenya. The Rift, formed some 8 million years ago, stretches 3500 miles from Mozambique to the Red Sea and is, in places, over 2000 feet deep. Many lakes, such as Little Magadi in the picture, lie in the valley. (*Emory Kristof/National Geographic Society Image Collection*)

ample, may have been in an arid area, but the lake itself was surrounded by forest. Lucy, the first specimen of *A. afarensis*, probably lived in a mixed forest and bushland area, as did some of the other members of this genus from South Africa (discussed in Chapter 9). *A. bahrelghazalia,* the new find from Chad, is thought to have inhabited forests with grassy patches.

The details about the early evolution of our hominid family and its characteristic traits are still being debated. Clearly, however, the hominid line had emerged by 4 million years ago, perhaps associated with a savanna environment. Clearly, too, the major adaptation of the hominids—the trait that distinguishes them from the other primates—is bipedalism. Accompanying upright locomotion, perhaps, was an emphasis on group unity and survival facilitated by food sharing and perhaps by sexual activity separated from purely reproductive functions and linked to emotional, social, and personal relationships.

Whatever happened, it was successful. At least one hominid species was well ensconced in East Africa by 3 million years ago. From there our family began to branch out. This is the topic of the next chapter.

How We Emerged

Because we now differ from our closest relations, chimps and bonobos, by only about 1 percent of our genetic material, it seems obvious that a relatively small number of mutations must have taken place to bring about the divergence of our evolutionary line from theirs. Given, however, the distinct morphological differences between our two species, it also seems reasonable that these mutations were macromutations—mutations of genes that code for important processes or that have extensive phenotypic effects.

Mutations of genes for developmental rates are important examples of macromutations, for even a slight change in the timing of the development of certain features can make a great difference in an organism's final appearance and physiology. There can be, after all, an incredible distinction between forms of organisms at different stages of their life cycles. Consider tadpoles and frogs, for instance, or caterpillars and butterflies. The different stages could easily be mistaken for separate species. It seems possible, then, that the overall difference between humans and chimpanzees might be related to the rate at which certain important traits develop.

A theory exists to support this idea. Called **neoteny** (literally, "holding youth"), it refers to the fact that adult members of some species possess characteristics of young, even fetal members of related species. Such a phenomenon could be the result of a mutation of one or more developmental genes that slow or retard the development of those features. Among the many examples in nature, perhaps the most famous is the Mexican axolotl. The axolotl is a salamander that never grows up. Even when a reproducing adult, it retains the totally aquatic life of a salamander larva, including the larva's external gills. This occurs because the axolotl fails to secrete a growth hormone, a condition controlled by a single genetic locus. Could a similar phenomenon account for the evolution of our species from that of the African apes?

In the 1920s Dutch anatomist Louis Bolk noted that some of the most notable features of adult humans are possessed by the fetal or newborn stages of other mammals (see Gould 1977). Chimpanzees are a striking example (Figure 8.14). These features include:

1. *Lack of body hair.* Actually, we have body hair, but it hasn't developed into the thick fur of the apes.
2. *Rounded cranium and flat face.* Newborn chimps have heads remarkably like ours and only later develop a protruding face, heavy jaws, and sloping forehead.
3. *Position of the foramen magnum underneath the skull.* As the chimp grows, the position of this feature shifts toward the rear of the skull, a characteristic of quadrupeds.
4. *Nonopposable big toe.* The infant's big toe is not widely separated from the other toes. The grasping foot of the chimp develops later.
5. *Retention of open cranial sutures.* By the time a chimp is born, the sutures have fused to form a single bone; in humans they remain separate for about a year and don't fully fuse for decades. Ossification occurs more slowly at other sites in humans than it does in apes as well.

neoteny The retention, in adults of one species, of the juvenile features of a related species.

6. *Period of brain growth.* The brains of apes grow very rapidly shortly before and just after birth. The brain of a chimp is 40 percent fully developed at birth and 70 percent by 1 year. Our brains, on the other hand, have retained the growth period for a longer time. At birth our brains are only 25 percent complete, and they don't achieve 70 percent until 3 years. Full size is not reached in humans until about 10 years, compared to 5 years in chimps. This growth rate, as well as the fact that our brains are larger than a chimp's at birth, accounts for the prolonged suture closure.

Could neoteny, then, help account for our two most distinguishing features? The shift to habitual bipedalism required a great many anatomical and neurological changes (see Figure 8.10). Though the orientation of the head and spine of newborn chimps, as well as the shape of their heads and their big toes, may be like ours, their pelvises and legs are certainly not those of a biped (Gould 1980). Bipedal locomotion itself is not a neotenous trait. It is not present in newborn apes, so it is not something that could be evolutionarily retained. But a retention of the skull-to-spine orientation of newborn apes along with the rounded crania (for balance) and nonopposable big toe may have given a head start toward bipedalism by endowing more neotenous individuals with an adaptive advantage pronounced enough for selection to act on.

Our big brains, on the other hand, seem very nicely accounted for by a mutation that caused our ancestors to retain the period of rapid brain growth characteristic of newborn chimps. Human babies for the first year of life maintain the rapid brain growth rate of fetal chimps. Although the difference between quadrupedalism and bipedalism is profound, the difference between the brain of a chimp and that of a human may not be so profound. Certainly, the human brain is capable of more complex functions than that of a chimp, but the basic structure does not seem fundamentally different. Our brains are larger, more complex versions of chimpanzee brains. This difference can be compared to two computers: One may be bigger and capable of performing functions the other can't, but the only structural difference between them is in size and complexity of the same basic parts. Our big brains might actually be less of an evolutionary accomplishment than our upright posture.

FIGURE 8.14   Young chimpanzee compared to adult, showing the striking resemblance of the young chimp to a modern human, an example of neoteny.

This hypothesis has been criticized (B. T. Shea 1989; Godfrey and Sutherland 1996). The arguments are quite complicated, but essentially, say that without knowing the precise genetic and developmental bases for the features shared by infant chimps and adult humans, these supposed neotenous features may simply be superficial similarities caused by processes other than the retention of fetal or newborn characteristics.

In addition, of course, the same phenomenon is being posited for influencing two changes—bipedalism and an increase in brain size—that took place several million years apart. We were bipedal over 4 mya, but

Contemporary Issue
Our Cousin, the Chimp?

It is clear that humans and chimps are members of different species: We are reproductively isolated from each other. At the very least, this is because the chromosome numbers are different—chimps have 48, we have 46—so that at fertilization the chromosome pairs can't match up. But it is also clear that we are very closely related species. How close *are* we compared with other primates? Are we distant cousins? First cousins? Siblings?

The classic way of answering this question is to place species into taxonomic relationships based on their degrees of similarity and difference. This was the approach adopted by Linnaeus (see Chapter 5). By this method, although we are genetically closer to chimps, bonobos, and gorillas than to orangutans, humans are classed in a different taxonomic family (Hominidae) from those other four species (Pongidae). *They* are all apes because of features they share with one another that they do not share with us.

There is, however, another way of looking at evolutionary relationships, called the cladistic or "branching," method. It uses the pattern of evolutionary branching to determine classification. If two or more species are derived from a common ancestor, those species are said to be a *sister group* regardless of how similar or different they look today. Phrased another way, species that share a homologous trait or traits derived from a common ancestor, and found in no other lineage, are classed together.

Viewed this way, our traditional taxonomic categories would no longer be valid. For example, a traditional primate taxonomy (see Chapter 5) groups tarsiers with the prosimian suborder based on overall physical similarities. A cladistic taxonomy, however, notes that all the prosimians *except* the tarsier have a moist nose used to enhance the sense of smell. The tarsier's nose is dry, like those of all anthropoids—monkeys, apes, and hominids. Under the assumption that all dry noses in primates were derived from a common ancestor, some authorities divide the primates into moist noses (suborder Strepsirhini) and dry noses (suborder Haplorhini) and so include the tarsiers in a large sister group with monkeys, apes, and us.

Applied to our section of the primate family tree, the cladistic method shows that the latest evolutionary divergence among the hominoids is between the common chimp and the bonobo. These two species share a great deal of genetic similarity and a great many homologous traits with relatively minor differences. They form a sister group. Going backward in time, the hominid line, according to anatomical, behavioral, and genetic evidence, was the next to branch. Thus, hominids, chimps, and bonobos form the next, larger sister group. Then comes the sister group that includes hominids, chimps, bonobos, and gorillas, and so on.

Under the cladistic scheme, then, there is no such thing as an "ape" (traditional family Pongidae) because there is no sister group that *includes* the four great apes and *excludes* the hominids. Adherents to cladistics have thus proposed new taxonomies to reflect this idea. One places only the orangutan in family Pongidae and lumps the gorilla, chimp, bonobo,

hominid brain size did not increase over the brain size of apes until about 2.5 mya. Even then, the evolution of hominid brain size took place gradually, not reaching modern size until less than half a million years ago.

The exact causes of bipedalism and the increase in brain size have still to be determined. Nevertheless, the list of juvenile ape features possessed

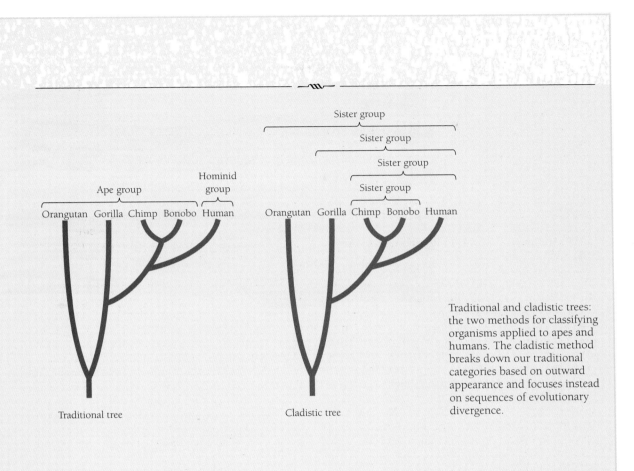

Ape group

Hominid group

Orangutan Gorilla Chimp Bonobo Human

Sister group

Sister group

Sister group

Sister group

Orangutan Gorilla Chimp Bonobo Human

Traditional tree

Cladistic tree

Traditional and cladistic trees: the two methods for classifying organisms applied to apes and humans. The cladistic method breaks down our traditional categories based on outward appearance and focuses instead on sequences of evolutionary divergence.

and humans under family Hominidae (Richard 1985). Humans and chimps are indeed "first cousins."

Now add that thought to the other evidence—the overall genetic similarity, the similarities in behavior, the phenotypic differences based, perhaps, on different developmental rates, and the mental po-

tentials apes show for such things as language learning and toolmaking—and remember that all of this is the result of a simple twist of genetic fate. Suddenly, those cute creatures we put in cages to stare at, in circuses to laugh at, and in labs to experiment on don't look quite the same to us anymore.

by adult humans does support the general idea that our traits are variations of those of our nearest evolutionary relatives—variations that became selectively important sometime around 5 million years ago and that gave rise to the basic adaptive responses selected for and enhanced during our evolution.

Summary

To understand the place of our species in the broad evolutionary scheme of things requires understanding the adaptive significance of bipedalism—the first of the characteristic hominid traits to appear. The evidence from the fossil record shows that habitual bipedalism was already established over 4 mya. Genetic comparisons with our cousins indicate that the African great apes and hominids split only shortly earlier. It's clear, then, that bipedalism was the initial hominid trait and that it was relatively rapidly selected for within a population of the common ancestor of us and the chimpanzees.

Analysis of the fossil record and of the ethology of modern chimps and bonobos allows us to imagine the situation in which bipedalism might have been adaptively advantageous. The picture that emerges is of small groups living in forests and/or open areas; getting food by gathering, perhaps scavenging, and maybe even hunting small animals; organized around some sort of family unit and with interpersonal bonds supported by conscious sexuality, sharing of important resources, and defending the group members and territory.

Study Questions

1. What is the fossil evidence for the beginnings of hominid evolution? How do these fossils support the idea that bipedalism was the first hominid trait?
2. Why was bipedalism adaptively important to the early hominids? When, and under what circumstances did it evolve?
3. What is neoteny, and how may it help account for the evolutionary changes seen in hominid evolution?
4. What is another way in which living organisms may be classified taxonomically? What implications does this method have for the taxonomy of hominids?

Key Terms

foramen magnum
prognathism
scavenge
neoteny

For More Information

For more on the Piltdown controversy, see Kenneth Feder, *Frauds, Myth, and Mysteries: Science and Pseudoscience in Archaeology,* Second Edition.

See Donald Johanson and Maitland Edey's *Lucy: The Beginnings of Humankind* for the story of the early hominid fossils with many good pictures and diagrams. The story of Johanson's work continues in *Lucy's Child* by Johanson and James Shreeve and in *Ancestors: In Search of Human Origins* by Johanson, Johanson, and Edgar. For a lively recounting of the personalities involved in the major fossil finds, see Roger Lewin's *Bones of Contention: Controversies in the Search for Human Origins.* The entire human evolutionary story is the topic of two books by Ian Tattersall of the American Museum of Natural History—*The Human Odyssey: Four Million Years of Evolution* and *The Fossil Trail: How We Know What We Think We Know About Human Evolution.* For great pictures and diagrams, though it is now a bit out-of-date, try the November 1985 issue of *National Geographic.* The new fossils of *A. anamensis* are covered in the September 1995 issue.

See Stephen Jay Gould's *Ever Since Darwin* and *The Panda's Thumb* for more on neoteny and, in the latter, an article titled "The Telltale Wishbone" about the cladistic method.

These natural casts of the brains of early hominids compel us to wonder what our ancestors were like. How did they look and behave? Why did some continue to evolve while
others became extinct? (© *John Reader/Science Photo Library/Photo Researchers, Inc.*)

9

The Human Lineage Established

―――――――――――――――――― ⚏ ――――――――――――――――――

In 1999, according to current projections, the 6 billionth living human will be born. Six *billion* of us, in various shapes, sizes, colors, and cultures. And yet we all belong to the same species. Our ability to produce fertile offspring, no matter how different the parents' biological and cultural backgrounds, proves it.

The present-day biological unity of humankind makes it hard to imagine that a single hominid species inhabiting the earth was not always the case. Yet, for a large part of hominid history—perhaps as much as half—at least two major branches of the hominid family tree lived. Clearly, only one survived to the present, but we must not think that this line was somehow *destined* to survive or that the line that became extinct was a failed side branch.

Evolution, even human evolution, is not a simple ladder or even a mighty tree trunk with smaller branches extending from it. It is not the record of uninterrupted progress toward perfection. Rather, evolution is, to use Stephen Jay Gould's metaphor (1987a,b,c), a bush, with countless, endlessly branching twigs representing individual species—evolution's experiments.

In fact, Gould says it is "life's little joke" that the oversimplified view of evolution as a ladder of progress can be forced on the data only when there is just one living species to represent a family of organisms—in other words, when the lineage has, as a whole, been relatively unsuccessful. Only our twig remains on the bush of hominid evolution, so we can easily get the impression that evolution has been leading toward us all along.

Indeed, primate evolution as a whole is typical of the bush model. It is, as Gould (1987a:25) puts it, "a formerly luxuriant bush" now reduced to a relatively few surviving twigs. And the human primate is "a fragile little twig of recent origin" (1987c:19). Keep this perspective on humankind in mind as we continue exploring the story of human evolution.

The Hominids Evolve

Hominid evolution is a complex story. At least a half-dozen different family trees have been proposed to show hypothesized relationships among the hominids from about 4 to 1 million years ago (Boaz 1988; Grine 1988a; Kimbel et al. 1988), each with evidence in its support as well as arguments against it. The differences are often based on technical data—measurements of anatomical details, for example. For our purposes here, detailing these arguments is, as paleoanthropologist David Pilbeam (1984, 1986) puts it, like "peering" too closely at a pointillist painting or a newspaper photo; the details become a bunch of "meaningless dots."

We will indicate some of the more important disagreements over these fossils, but we will basically, as Pilbeam advises, view the hominids of this period "from a distance," trying to see the dots come together to present a general picture. We still, however, need to express that general picture so we have some basis for our discussion. For the moment, then, we think the model depicted in Figure 9.1 is a reasonable, and fairly simple, interpretation of existing data.

Somewhere around 3 million years ago, *Australopithecus afarensis* branched into at least two lineages, one leading to an extinct form of hominid and the other to the line that would eventually lead to modern humans (refer also to Figure 8.3 and Table 8.1).

The initial set of hominid features, as represented by Lucy and her kin, continued after the split for another three-quarters of a million years. With some changes from *A. afarensis*, the fossils representing this period are called by their original name, *Australopithecus africanus* (Dart's "south-

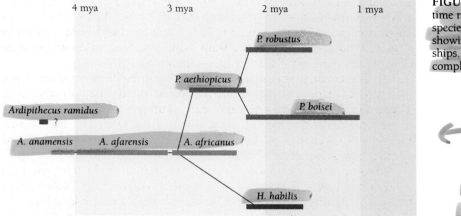

FIGURE 9.1   Approximate time ranges of the early hominid species discussed in the text, showing hypothesized relationships. This family bush will be completed in Figure 12.15.

ern ape of Africa"). The remains of this species have been found mostly in South Africa, but there are some possible fossils from Kenya and Ethiopia as well. They have the same body and brain size as *A. afarensis*. Their faces are a bit less prognathous and they lack a sagittal crest, however. Their canine teeth are smaller, there are no gaps in the tooth row, and the tooth row is more rounded, like a human and unlike an ape (Figure 9.2, p. 218). Recent studies suggest that the arm and leg proportions of *A. africanus* may have been more apelike than in *A. afarensis* and that they may have had more arboreal ability (Shreeve 1996b).

The relative sizes and shapes of the teeth of both *A. afarensis* and *A. africanus,* although on the whole larger than those of modern humans, indicate a mostly mixed vegetable diet of fruits and leaves. This is confirmed by taphonomic analysis of microscopic scratches and wear patterns on the teeth (Figure 9.3, p. 218). Though there is no direct evidence of meat eating, they probably ate some small creatures.

The essential similarity of *A. afarensis* and *A. africanus* suggests a plausible and simple interpretation. We may consider *A. africanus* as a continuation of *A. afarensis*, more widely distributed in East and South Africa, and showing some evolutionary changes, including, perhaps, a return to a more tree-dwelling way of life and more apelike limb proportions.

Between 2 and 3 million years ago, two distinctly different types of hominid show up. One type retains the chimpanzee-sized brains and small bodies of *Australopithecus*, but has evolved a notable robusticity in the areas of the skull involved with chewing. This is genus *Paranthropus*. As we noted in Chapter 8, some researchers place fossils of this group in the genus *Australopithecus*, but many recent interpretations consider them a separate genus.

FIGURE 9.2   Skull of *Australopithecus africanus* (female?) from Sterkfontein, South Africa. Note the general similarity to *A. afarensis*. *(Transvaal Museum, D. C. Panagos)*

FIGURE 9.3   Scanning electron microscope pictures of the surfaces of early hominid teeth. The enamel of the teeth of *Australopithecus africanus* (*left*) is polished and scratched, while that of *Paranthropus* (*right*) is pitted and very rough. This is evidence of the hard, tough, gritty foods eaten by the latter. *(Micrographs courtesy of Dr. Frederick E. Grine, SUNY, Stony Brook. Photographed by Chester Tarka)*

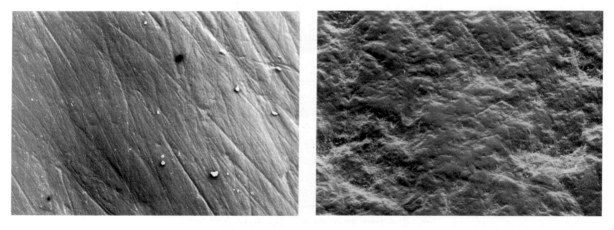

The fossils representing the beginning of this genus are a single skull from Lake Turkana, Kenya—dubbed the "Black Skull" because of its dark color, the result of minerals in the ground (Figure 9.4)—and some fragmentary fossils from Ethiopia. These fossils are grouped into a separate species, **Paranthropus aethiopicus**, and are dated at between 2.8 and 2.2 mya.

The Black Skull is striking for several reasons. First, at only 410 ml, it has the smallest adult hominid brain ever found. On the other hand, it has the largest sagittal crest of any hominid, the most prognathous face, and an

FIGURE 9.4   The Black Skull, *Paranthropus aethiopicus*, a possible ancestor of *P. robustus* and *P. boisei*, showing a great degree of prognathism and the largest hominid sagittal crest.   (*Alan Walker, © 1986 National Geographic Society*)

extremely large area in the back of the mouth for the molar teeth, although no actual teeth were found. It appears that its molars were four or five times the size of a modern human's.

The Black Skull, then, represents the beginning of a second major type of hominid, sometimes referred to as "robust" hominids. Although pretty much the same as *Australopithecus* in body size, the members of genus *Paranthropus* were considerably more robust in all those features involved with chewing. The sagittal crests; broad, dished-out faces; large cheekbones; huge mandibles; and back teeth much larger relative to the front teeth—all point to a diet of large amounts of vegetable matter with an emphasis on hard, tough, gritty items like seeds, nuts, hard fruits, and tubers. This is clearly shown by microscopic wear pattern analysis (see Figure 9.3).

A few hundred thousand years later, two types of robust hominids appear. We may, tentatively, consider them two species that branched from the first robust form, *P. aethiopicus*. One species, **Paranthropus robustus,** is found in South Africa and dates between 2.2 and 1.5 mya (Figure 9.5, p. 220). It retains the body size of *Australopithecus*, but there is a slight increase in average brain capacity to about 520 ml. The jaws are heavy, the back teeth are large, and there is a sagittal crest—all indications of a tough vegetable diet. The crania, though, are obviously not as robust as *P. aethiopicus*.

The second robust species continues the extreme ruggedness of *P. aethiopicus,* though not quite as pronounced (Figure 9.6, p. 220). Found in Tanzania, Kenya, and Ethiopia and dating from 2.2 to 1 mya, **Paranthro-**

FIGURE 9.5   Skull of *Paranthropus robustus* from Swartkrans, South Africa. Note the remnant of a sagittal crest. (*Transvaal Museum, D. C. Panagos*)

FIGURE 9.6   *Paranthropus boisei*, the "Zinjanthropus" specimen. Note the extremely large teeth and the remnants of what was a very large sagittal crest. (*© Bob Campbell*)

pus boisei shows features that, along with those of *aethiopicus*, are sometimes referred to as "hyperrobust." The specimen that defined the species was found by Mary and Louis Leakey in 1959 at Olduvai Gorge. First placed in a new genus, *Zinjanthropus*, and dubbed "Nutcracker Man" because of its extremely large jaws, back teeth, and sagittal crest, it was later lumped in with the other robust hominids of *Paranthropus*. It shares the brain and body size of *P. robustus*.

The second new hominid genus that appeared about 2.2 mya is *Homo*, the one to which modern humans belong. We will discuss the first species of our genus in the next section. For now, however, we need to account for the overall shape of the early hominid family "bush" (see again Figure 9.1). What might have caused the branching that founded the new genera of *Paranthropus* and *Homo?* What caused the extinction, around the same time, of *Australopithecus?* Finally, what might have caused the extinction of the *Paranthropus* species about a million years ago?

We can't answer these questions with certainty, but there is evidence (Vrba 1993) that there were further drying trends, accompanied by a decline of forests and expansion of savannas, at about 2.8 mya and again at about 900,000 years ago. The first change may have selected for the robust hominids, increasingly adapted to a diet of the tough vegetables found on the open plains, and for the genus *Homo*, with (as we shall see) its increased brain size and ability to make stone tools. Both these sets of adaptations would prove useful on the savannas. The remaining populations of *Australopithecus* may not have been able to cope with these further changes and may, at the same time, have been outcompeted by the new hominid lines.

Although it is intriguing to picture some sort of direct and violent confrontation that caused the extinction of the first hominid genus, and, subsequently, of *Paranthropus*, such a scenario is not necessary. When the niches of several similar species overlap to too great an extent, those species find themselves in ecological competition with one another and, often, all but one are pushed out, sometimes to the point of extinction. This mechanism is called **competitive exclusion.** With the third climatic and vegetational change 900,000 years ago, this competition probably accounts for the fact that genus *Homo*, from that point on, was the only surviving type of hominid.

The Beginning of the Genus *Homo*

When the Leakeys found *P. boisei* in Olduvai Gorge in 1959, they found some simple stone tools at the same level. At first, they thought *P. boisei* had made the tools, but they began to feel that *boisei* was too primitive to have made something so sophisticated.

These tools, called *Oldowan* after Olduvai Gorge, at first seem very simple to us. Some, called *pebble tools*, are nothing more than water-smoothed cobbles up to 3 or 4 inches across, modified by striking off a few flakes from one or two faces to make a sharp edge. These are termed **core tools.** More investigation has suggested, however, that the stone tools reflect sophisticated mental abilities.

Originally, it was thought that the Oldowan tools were all core tools and that the flakes were the waste products of their manufacture. Recently, however (Toth 1985; Schick and Toth 1993), it has been shown that, though some flaked cores may have been used as tools, the majority were the raw materials for the manufacture of **flake tools** (Figure 9.7, p. 221) used for a variety of tasks such as cutting meat and plant material, scraping meat off a bone, and sawing wood or bone. Under microscopic analysis, the edges of these flakes show a polish that is characteristic of these activities.

It also appears that the makers of the Oldowan tools may have traveled some distance to find a source of stone known to be superior for the production of sharp, durable tools. The cores themselves were probably carried around to wherever flakes were needed; it is common to find flakes at a site but not the cores from which they were struck. All this shows a high level of planning (Schick and Toth 1993).

Moreover, unlike the termite sticks of the chimpanzees, there is nothing in the raw material of the Oldowan tools—the stone—that immediately suggests the tools that can be made from it or the method of manufacture. Making even a simple Oldowan tool is a far more complex technological feat than stripping the leaves off a branch to make a stick narrow enough to

competitive exclusion
When one species outcompetes others for the resources of an area.

core tool Tool made by taking flakes off a stone nucleus.

flake tool Tool made from the flakes removed from a core.

FIGURE 9.7 The process by which flakes were removed from a stone core in the Oldowan tradition: A hard stone was struck with another stone in just the right locations to allow for the removal of sharp, thin flakes. *(From "The First Technology" by Nicholas Toth. Copyright © 1987 by Scientific American, Inc. All rights reserved)*

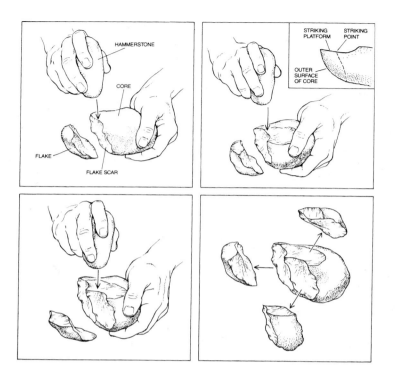

fit down the hole of a termite mound. (We can attest to the difficulty). A stone tool also requires the maker to be able to imagine within the stone the tool he or she wants to make and to mentally picture the process needed to make it. This leap of the imagination and increase in technological skill are what make the first evidence of stone tool manufacture so important.

Because there was no accepted evidence that any of the previously identified fossil hominids made stone tools, it appeared that *Zinjanthropus* was not a good candidate for the maker of the pebble tools. Then, in 1961, the Leakeys found a second hominid from the same time period. Actually, they had found fragmentary fossils of this form in the same year as *P. boisei,* but they had not recognized these fossils as something different. They named the new form ***Homo habilis,*** "handy man" (Figure 9.8).

The reasons for including these fossils in genus *Homo* are two-fold. First, there is a notable increase in brain size, from the average of about 480 ml for *Australopithecus* and *Paranthropus,* to an average of 680 ml with a possible maximum of 800 ml in *H. habilis.* Second, the presence of the stone tools indicated that those larger brains were capable of a complexity of thought not seen in the record of the other two hominid genera. Thus, *H. habilis* seems to mark the beginning of a new trend in hominid evolution toward bigger brains and greater intelligence. Fossils of *habilis* have

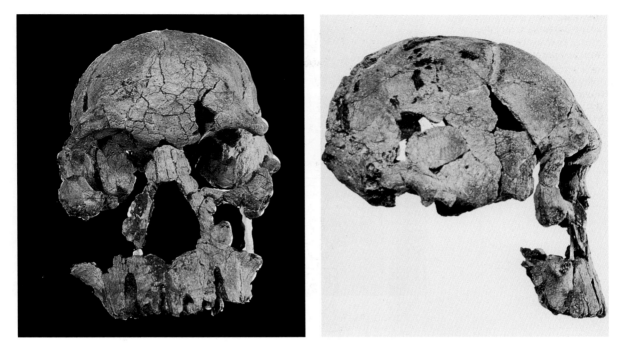

FIGURE 9.8   Front and side views of *Homo habilis* from Lake Turkana, Kenya. Note the flat face, smooth contours, lack of sagittal crest, and rounded braincase. (© *National Museums of Kenya*)

now been found in Tanzania, Kenya, and Ethiopia, and perhaps from southern Africa, and have been dated at between 2.4 and 1.5 mya. It should be noted that some authorities claim certain of the fossils labeled *H. habilis* might represent yet another species of our genus, **H. rudolfensis.** (One such fossil, in fact, is the one pictured in Figure 9.8.) We will treat all these fossils as a single species, the majority viewpoint at the moment.

Other than the larger braincase, *H. habilis* still resembles the other two hominids in many respects. The face is a bit less prognathous, but the back teeth are still relatively large, the arms proportionately long, and the bodies small. In fact, a partial skeleton of *H. habilis* from Olduvai may be the smallest adult hominid fossil known.

Lifestyles of the Short and Prognathous

Why might the Oldowan stone tools have given *Homo habilis* an edge? Paleoanthropologist Richard Leakey, the son of Louis and Mary, suggests that sharp stone tools allowed these hominids to more quickly cut meat and bones off a carcass, making the addition of meat to the diet through scavenging safer and more efficient. There is evidence for this suggestion. Ten sites at Olduvai that date from the *Homo habilis* period contain Oldowan

FIGURE 9.9   This micrograph of a fossil bone from Olduvai Gorge shows tool marks (the horizontal lines and the diagonal line beginning at the top of the photo) and a carnivore tooth mark (beginning on the right side and angled toward the center). The tooth mark overlies the tool mark, indicating that the hominids sliced meat off this part of the bone before a scavenger began eating.   *(Photo by Pat Shipman)*

core and flake tools and animal bones. Once thought to be some sort of "home base," it has been suggested that these areas are "stone cache" sites (Potts 1984), where hominids left supplies of stones and to which they took recently scavenged animal remains for quick and safe processing and eating. Analysis indicates that these sites were used repeatedly for short periods—what one would expect of such places.

Archaeologist Lewis Binford (1985) has analyzed the animal bones from these sites and has found that they are mostly the lower leg bones of antelopes. These bones carry little meat and, along with the skull, are about the only parts left after a large carnivore has finished eating. Such bones are, however, rich in marrow, so a major activity at the sites in question may have been to cut off what little meat remained on these bones and then to break them open for the nutritious marrow inside.

Finally, Pat Shipman has studied the taphonomy of these and other bones with a scanning electron microscope (1984, 1986). She found that stone tool cut marks were usually on the shafts of the bones as if pieces of meat were cut off, not near the joints as if an entire carcass had been butchered. Sometimes, the hominid tool marks overlie carnivore tooth marks, showing that the carnivores got there first. Sometimes it's the other way around (Figure 9.9).

We may envision *Homo habilis*, then, in small cooperative groups, maybe family groups, foraging on the savannas for plant foods and always on the lookout for a carnivore kill by watching for a group of scavengers gathered on the ground or a flock of vultures circling overhead. Their big brains allowed them to better understand their environment and to manipulate it, making imaginative and technologically advanced tools from stone. With these they cut apart the carcasses they found and then took the pieces back to a safe place, perhaps where they had stored more tools. There they cut the remaining meat off the bones and, probably using large cores, smashed open the bones for marrow. It was no doubt a harsh life, but it was successful. The adaptive themes of large brains, and the social organization and tool technology they made possible, set the stage for the rest of hominid evolution.

The Question of Language

The chimpanzees described in Chapter 6 support their lifestyle with a fairly complex communication system made up of a large number of calls, facial expressions, and body gestures. It is legitimate to ask whether our hominid ancestors had an even more complex communication system to support a more complex lifestyle with its inclusion of scavenging and the manufacture and use of stone tools. Modern humans communicate with symbolic languages made up of individual sounds that are strung together to produce units of meaning. These meanings are arbitrary; that is, words have meaning because we agree they do, not because they sound like the thing or idea being expressed. How far back in human evolution did such a system first appear?

This is a difficult question to answer. After all, a communication system is not like stone tools or animal bones. It is ephemeral; once used, it is gone, leaving no material evidence of its existence, at least until the invention of writing about 6000 years ago. Moreover, virtually all anatomical features of an organism that relate to the ability to communicate orally are soft parts that are not preserved in the paleontological record.

So it would seem that we are only able to speculate on the origin and evolution of this basic, definitive human ability. Luckily, however, this is not quite the case. Soft anatomical parts related to the human ability to speak—most notably the pharynx and larynx—are connected to hard parts that are preserved (Figure 9.10, p. 226). The most important of these are the bones of the base of the skull, the **basicranium**. The form and positioning of the basicranium enable us to reconstruct, to a degree, the form and positioning of the soft parts. This, in turn, provides an indirect indication of whether a particular hominid species possessed the ability to speak as a modern human does and so, by inference, its ability to use a complex symbolic language that such speech makes possible.

The question of the origin and evolution of human speech has been the focus of several scientists (Crelin 1987; Laitman and Heimbach 1984; Leiberman 1984). Although they argue over details, all agree on a number of fundamental points. Virtually all land mammals exhibit a flat skull base. Such a base accommodates a straight pharynx and a larynx positioned

basicranium The bones of the base of the skull.

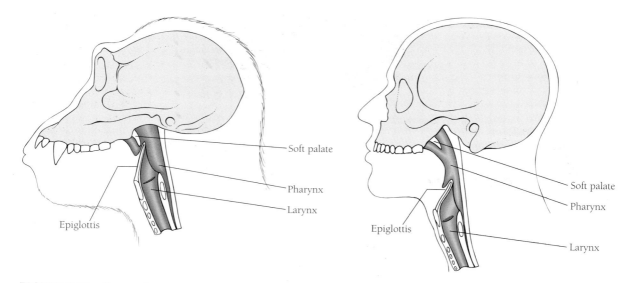

FIGURE 9.10   The vocal apparatus of a chimp (*left*) compared to a modern human's. The chimp's pharynx is straight and it and the larynx are positioned high in the throat, limiting the ability to produce a wide range of sounds. The human pharynx is bent and, along with the larynx, is lower in the throat. This allows a broader range of sounds. (*Redrawn and reprinted by permission of the Smithsonian Institution Press from Roger Lewin,* In the Age of Mankind: A Smithsonian Book of Human Evolution, *1989:181, Smithsonian Institution Press*)

endocasts Natural- or human-made casts of the inside of a skull.

high up in the throat. This positioning allows animals to breathe and swallow at the same time, greatly diminishing the possibility of choking to death while eating or drinking. Human infants up to about 18 months of age possess this configuration and the attendant ability to nurse and breathe simultaneously. This positioning of the pharynx and larynx also diminishes the ability to produce sounds, however.

In the modern human adult, the basicranium is uniquely flexed. The rear of the skull base is, in comparison to a chimpanzee, for example, bent forward, in, and down. This produces a bend in the pharynx and pushes the larynx farther down in the throat. Computer models show that this anatomical conformation enables the broad range of sounds and great speed that characterize human speech and are required for spoken language (Leiberman 1984).

Unfortunately, not enough remains of the basicrania of *Homo habilis* specimens to allow for vocal tract reconstruction. The fossil evidence for *Australopithecus*, however, is clear in this regard. The cranial bases of australopithecine fossils are quite flat—indistinguishable, in fact, from the cranial bases of apes. This seems to indicate that *Australopithecus* could communicate through sound, but the sounds were probably more similar to the hoots and howls of chimps than to the spoken language of human beings.

On the other hand, some evidence suggests that *H. habilis* possessed the capacity for spoken human language, if not the ability to produce all the sounds of modern languages. According to Phillip Tobias (1987), **endocasts** of *H. habilis* skulls show impressions of certain features of the brain that have, in modern humans, been associated with language pro-

FIGURE 9.11   Natural endo-casts from South African aus-tralopithecines showing the degree of detail possible. Notice the blood vessels that show, especially in the upper right cast. Such casts can be made artifi-cially as well, allowing compari-son of the brains of our ancestors with those of modern humans. (© *John Reader/Science Photo Library/Photo Researchers, Inc.*)

duction and comprehension (Figure 9.11). Selection in *H. habilis* for the beginnings of language of a modern type may have been underway as a re-sponse to that species' more complex adaptive behavior. (We will return to the topic of language evolution in the following chapters.)

Homo habilis fossils indicate that this species was around for less than a million years. Before *H. habilis* disappears from the fossil record, however, a new hominid species appears on the scene—one that continues and en-hances the trends of big brains and tool technology, adaptations that would soon carry it all over the Old World.

Summary

The changing environment of Africa, where the hominid branch first arose, nurtured a number of different hominid twigs during the first three-quarters of our evolutionary history. These twigs can be divided into three general types. The australopithecines were small, bipedal primates who retained the brain size and, perhaps, some of the arboreal abilities of our apelike ancestors. They represent the common ancestor of all later hominids including the paranthropines, specialized savanna vegetarians characterized by robust crania and teeth. The australopithecines were extinct by about 2.5 mya, the paranthropines by 1 mya.

The third type was also small and, at first, also retained the long arms of the apes and early australopithecines. But this twig, the genus *Homo*, is defined by a new adaptive trend—an increase in brain size, which, as it turns out, afforded it an advantage in the ever-changing environs of the African plains. Although the first members of our genus still had brains only about half the size of the average modern human's, they were large and complex enough to allow their possessors, *Homo habilis*, to manufacture stone tools, an imaginative and technological leap in adaptive behavior. This set the stage for the next million years.

Study Questions

1. What do we know about the evolution of the now-extinct early hominid lineages?
2. How and when did the genus *Homo* first evolve? Why are the first fossils of our genus placed in that taxonomic category? What do we know about their behavior?
3. What can we say about the evolution of human language? What sorts of evidence may we use in this investigation?

Key Terms

competitive exclusion
core tool
flake tool
basicranium
endocasts

For More Information

All the sources listed in Chapter 8 apply to the topic of this chapter as well. For more on bushes versus ladders as the metaphor for evolution, see "Bushes and Ladders in Human Evolution" in Stephen Jay Gould's *Ever Since Darwin* and Gould's columns in the April, May, and June 1987 issues of *Natural History.* On the evolution of language, see John McCrone's *The Ape That Spoke: Language and the Evolution of the Human Mind.*

This finely crafted hand axe is emblematic of the species *Homo erectus*. When did *Homo erectus* expand beyond Africa? What cultural adaptations enabled its survival in climates very different from those of its evolutionary ancestor?

(© Lee Boltin Picture Library)

10

The Human Lineage Evolves

A swirling white powder cascaded past the streetlights as a heavy snowfall began to blanket the campus. School and business closings scrolled across television screens, airlines cancelled flights, and those huddled at home braced for the two to three feet of snow predicted by local meteorologists. Even with all of the technological sophistication of the late twentieth century, the "blizzard of 1996" paralyzed communities and frightened even long-time residents of the Northeast.

As cold as it got and as much snow as fell, however, we could all rest easy in the knowledge that it would end. Spring would come and with it a thaw and a halt to the snow and cold—at least until next winter. It hasn't always been this way for much of the Northern Hemisphere, however. For long periods of time—sometimes lasting thousands of years—spring didn't come. We call this "deep-freeze" the Pleistocene.

The Coming of Ice

For reasons that are still debated, world-wide temperature began a long period of decline about 3.2 million years ago (Shackleton and Opdyke 1976). An additional, steeper temperature drop occurred about 2.4 million years ago (Shackleton et al. 1984; Stipp, Chappell, and McDougall 1967).

This cooling of the earth may have resulted from a decrease in the heat generated by the sun. It may have been precipitated by interplanetary dust blocking out a portion of the sun's radiation. It may have been caused by a substantial increase in volcanic activity here on earth, with material spewed out by volcanoes blocking the warming rays of the sun. It may have been initiated by a deviation in the geometry of the earth's orbit, resulting not in a change in the total amount of solar heat reaching our planet but merely in its distribution. The reasons have yet to be determined.

The initial drop in worldwide temperature occurred during the **Pliocene Epoch** (see Chapter 3). The temperature decline was at its most severe and the spread of ice most extensive after about 1.6 mya in what is called the **Pleistocene Epoch.**

Though initially regarded as an "Ice Age," the Pleistocene was actually a climatologically complex period with several lengthy, extremely cold episodes separated by a number of phases with mean temperatures as warm as—and occasionally even warmer than—today's. Geologists and **paleoclimatologists** have established that eight or nine distinct cold periods separated by warmer spells occurred during the last 780,000 years of the Pleistocene (Shackleton et al. 1984; Shackleton and Opdyke 1973, 1976). Another ten cold phases separated by warmer periods may have characterized world climate between 780,000 ya and 1.6 mya (Bowen 1979).

During these cold phases, some of which lasted tens of thousands of years, worldwide temperature dropped and ice and snow accumulated in higher elevations and northern latitudes. As these ice fields grew in size—hundreds of meters to several kilometers in thickness—internal pressures forced the ice to move in frozen rivers and great ice sheets called **glaciers** (Figure 10.1). These glaciers covered many higher elevations in the world, much of Canada and the northern United States, Europe, and part of Asia (Bradley 1985; Flint 1971) (Figure 10.2). Nonglaciated parts of the world, the tropics and subtropics, also underwent climate changes, experiencing generally cooler summers along with wetter winters in some regions and drier conditions elsewhere. The coasts of the continents were redrawn as sea level dropped as much as 125 meters (400 feet), a result of so much of the planet's water being locked in land-based glaciers.

The periods during which world ice cover expanded are called **glacials** or **glacial periods.** The times between the glacials, when the glaciers temporarily receded and temperature warmed up, are called **interglacials.** The glacials themselves were made up of shorter, colder intervals

Pliocene Epoch Geological epoch that dates from 5 million to 1.6 million years ago. This is the epoch during which the first hominids appeared in Africa.

Pleistocene Epoch The geological time period from 1.6 mya to 10,000 ya characterized by a series of glacial advances and retreats.

paleoclimatologist A specialist in ancient climate conditions.

glacier A massive body of ice that can move and expand.

glacials Synonym for glacial periods.

glacial periods Phases of Pleistocene glacial expansion.

interglacial A period between glacial advances.

FIGURE 10.1   A veritable river of ice, the Moreno Glacier is located in Patagonia, a region of Argentina. (© *Geoffrey Clifford/ Woodfin Camp and Associates*)

stadial A short period of rapid glacial advance and extreme cold.

interstadial A short period of glacial retreat during a longer phase of glacial advance.

Holocene Epoch The modern epoch that began 10,000 ya with the retreat of glacial ice and a worldwide warming.

called **stadials** and relatively warmer periods called **interstadials**. Some paleoclimatologists contend that the cycle of glacials and interglacials, stadials and interstadials ended about 10,000 ya with the beginning of the **Holocene Epoch**. This is the modern epoch in which we live, the beginning of which is defined by the inception of warmer temperatures worldwide and the regression of much of the glacial ice of the Pleistocene

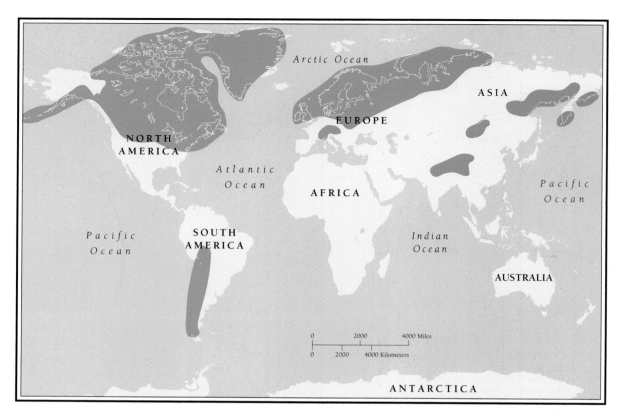

FIGURE 10.2   Maximum worldwide glacial expansion during the Pleistocene. The Antarctic ice cover, not shown here, also expanded during this epoch.   *(Data compiled from Bowen 1978; Bradley 1985; and Flint 1971)*

10,000 years ago. Other scientists believe that we are merely in an inter-glacial remission, with another glacial period certain to follow. Most previous interglacials lasted about 10,000 to 20,000 years and the warmer temperatures of the Holocene began about 10,000 years ago, presenting some interesting scenarios for life in the twenty-first century and beyond (Shackleton and Opdyke 1976).

Reconstructing Paleoclimate

Worldwide temperature trends might seem impossible to reconstruct millions of years after the fact. The nature of glaciers makes the problem even more difficult. Though glaciers leave traces of their presence in the form of geological deposits and diagnostic patterns of erosion, the precise sequence of glacials and interglacials is difficult to study on land because ice advances are discontinuous events. Each subsequent movement of ice obliterates much, if not all, of the evidence of previous glacial expansions.

The stratigraphy of the ocean floor, however, provides a more or less continuous column of sediment for the entire Pleistocene and even for some time before. We may not be able to study ancient temperatures di-

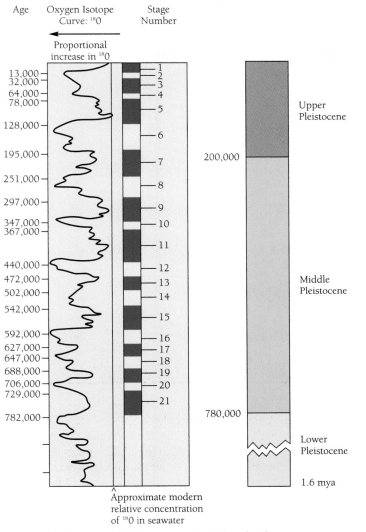

Age   Oxygen Isotope   Stage
      Curve: ¹⁸0   Number

Proportional
increase in ¹⁸0

FIGURE 10.3   Pleistocene glacial chronology based on the oxygen isotope ratio in seawater as derived from foraminifera. *(Data compiled from Shackleton and Opdyke 1973)*

Approximate modern relative concentration of ¹⁸0 in seawater

Odd-numbered stages (in blue) = warmer periods, less glacial ice cover
Even-numbered stages = colder periods, more glacial ice cover

rectly, but we can examine an indirect effect of temperature and the attendant expansion and meltoff of ice in the ratio of two isotopes of oxygen, ^{16}O and ^{18}O, in seawater. The oxygen isotope curve derived by Nicholas Shackleton and Neil Opdyke (1973, 1976) and discussed in Chapter 7 gives a fairly detailed picture of climate change during at least the last 780,000 years of the Pleistocene (Figure 10.3).

The Pleistocene is commonly divided into three sections. The beginning of the Pleistocene, about 1.6 mya to 780,000 ya, when the earth's

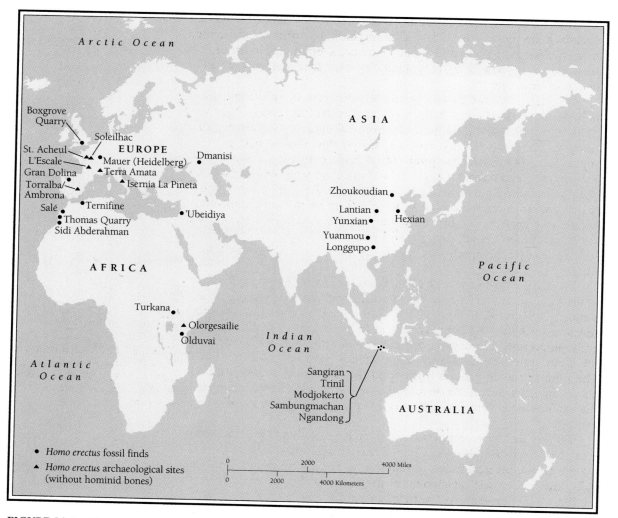

FIGURE 10.4 *Homo erectus* fossil localities and archaeological sites.

magnetic field shifted, is called the **Lower Pleistocene** (Montastersky 1992); 780,000 to 200,000 ya is the **Middle Pleistocene**; and 200,000 to 10,000 ya is the **Upper Pleistocene**.

Hominids of the Pleistocene

Hominid fossils with larger brains and a generally more modern appearance than *Homo habilis* have been dated to a little before the beginning of the Pleistocene Epoch. They date from almost the same period in Africa

Lower Pleistocene Part of the Pleistocene from 1.6 mya to 780,000 ya.

Middle Pleistocene Part of the Pleistocene from 780,000 ya to 200,000 ya.

and Asia and quite a bit later in Europe (Figure 10.4). Because the African specimens are among the oldest and because more primitive hominids (more apelike and with smaller brains) have been found only in Africa, it is believed that this new group of hominids evolved there and then spread to the rest of the world.

Although there are many continuities between *H. habilis* and these more recent fossils (Figure 10.5), there are distinct differences (Rightmire 1990; Wood 1984). The crania dating from 1.8 million years ago to as recently as 250,000 years ago tend to be long and low, with large brow ridges, a sharply angled **occipital** with a marked **torus,** a robust, prognathous face, and a sagittal keel—a long ridge running the length of the top of the skull from front to back. At a shade under 1000 ml (two-thirds of the modern human mean of 1450 ml), their mean cranial capacity is significantly greater than that of *H. habilis,* calculated at 680 ml. Indeed, the range of their cranial capacity falls between 750 and 1250 ml (Table 10.1), putting larger specimens within the lower limit of modern human crania.

These crania belonged to a creature larger than *habilis,* and at least part of the increase in skull size—and therefore brain size—can be attributed simply to an increase in body size. However, these more recent crania represent more than just a larger version of *H. habilis.* These skulls are differently proportioned, reflecting the differential growth of specific parts of the brain, especially the frontal and posterior portions (Wolpoff 1980a). The front of the cranium is higher and the back more rounded than in *habilis.* In other words, the brain of this new hominid was more similar to the modern form. The implication is that their intelligence was also more evolved.

Differences in the architecture of these new skulls when compared to that of *H. habilis* are also significant. These changes may represent the response to selective pressures resulting from behavioral changes. Specifically, areas of muscle attachment at the base and back (occiput) of the skull are significantly larger with a bone ridge (the nuchal torus) being prominent. These changes imply a great increase in neck muscle size and strength over that of *habilis.* This development has been attributed to selection for stronger necks and jaws as a result of increased use of the mouth as a "third hand" in tool use (Wolpoff 1980a:178).

Even the nose, as indicated by the preserved nasal bones, was more modern in appearance than that of *H. habilis.* These new creatures were our first hominid ancestor with the typically human projecting nose, an adaptation, apparently, to conserve moisture in arid environments (Franciscus and Trinkaus 1988).

Below the neck, the skeletons of these new creatures are, in many ways, quite modern in appearance. The bones of the arms, legs, pelvis, vertebrae, hands, and feet are similar to those of modern humans. There are some differences; for example, their femurs have quite thick shaft walls

FIGURE 10.5 Comparison of cranial features of *Australopithecus* (*top*) with *Homo habilis* (*middle*) and *Homo erectus* (*bottom*).

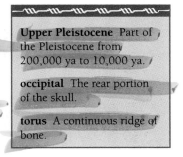

Upper Pleistocene Part of the Pleistocene from 200,000 ya to 10,000 ya.

occipital The rear portion of the skull.

torus A continuous ridge of bone.

TABLE 10.1   Overview of _Homo erectus_ Fossils

Country	Locality	Fossils	Crania	Age (million years)	Brain Size (ml)
Algeria	Ternifine	Three mandibles and a skull	—	0.5–0.7	—
China	Hexian (Lontandong)	Partial skull	"Hexian Man"	0.25–0.5	1000
	Lantian (Gongwangling)	Cranial fragments, mandible	"Lantian Man"	>1	800
	Longgupo	Mandible fragments	—	1.8	—
	Yunxian	Two crania	—	>0.35	—
	Zhoukoudian	Cranial and postcranial remains of 40 individuals	II	<0.46	1030
			III	<0.46	915
			VI	<0.46	850
			X	<0.46	1225
			XI	<0.46	1015
			XII	<0.46	1030
			Locality 13	0.7	—
England	Boxgrove Quarry	Tibia	—	0.515	—
Georgia	Dmanisi	Mandible fragment, 16 teeth	—	1.6	—
Germany	Heidelberg	Mandible	—	0.5	—
Israel	'Ubeidiya	Fragments	—	>1	—
Java	Modjokerto	Child's cranium	—	1.8(?)	—
	Ngandong	Cranial and postcranial fragments from >12 individuals	N-1	<1	1170
			N-6	<1	1250
			N-11	<1	1230
			N-12	<1	1090
	Sambungmachan	Large cranial fragment	Sambung-machan	<1	1000
	Sangiran	Cranial and post-cranial fragments	S-2	0.7–1.6	800
			S-4	0.7–1.6	900

Country	Locality	Fossils	Crania	Age (million years)	Brain Size (ml)
Java	Sangiran	from ~40 individuals	S-10	0.7–1.6	850
			S-12	0.7–1.6	1050
			S-17	0.7–1.6	1000
			1993 cranium	1.1–1.4	856
	Trinil	Skull cap, femur	"Java Man"	<1	940
Kenya	East Turkana	Cranial and post-cranial fragments including mandibles and pelvis and long bone fragments	KNM-ER 3733	1.78	850
			KNM-ER 3883	1.57	800
	West Turkana	Nearly complete juvenile individual	KNM-WT 15000	1.6	880
Morocco	Salé	Cranium	Salé	0.4(?)	880
	Sidi Abderrahman	Two mandible fragments	—	—	—
	Thomas Quarry	Mandible and skull fragments	—	0.5	—
Spain	Gran Dolina	Remains of at least 4 individuals	—	0.78–1	—
Tanzania	Olduvai	Cranial and post-cranial fragments including mandibles and pelvis and long bone fragments	OH9	1.25	1060
			OH12	0.6–0.8	700–800

Mean   971.96

Standard deviation   138.05

Data from Feibel et al. (1989); Holloway (1980, 1981); Rightmire (1990); and Walker and Leakey (1993).

and are flattened, characteristics that indicate muscularity and great strength. Despite the differences, however, we can infer that their ability to walk upright and manipulate objects with their hands was virtually indistinguishable from that of modern humans.

Naming the Fossils

As we will see, the geographic extent of these fossils is enormous and they span a vast period of time—from the later Pliocene through the Lower and Middle Pleistocene. Nevertheless, some scientists place all of these fossils in a single species: *Homo erectus* (Rightmire 1990). For example, paleoanthropologist G. Philip Rightmire (1990:190) maintains that all the crania in question, from 1.8 million years ago to 250,000 years ago, from east Africa to eastern Java, "are built on a common plan," and he places the many specimens to be discussed in this chapter in the single species *erectus*. Supporting this view is the analysis by paleoanthropologist Andrew Kramer (1993) that shows no greater variability among these fossils than that seen among modern human beings.

Remember our discussion (Chapter 7) concerning the difficulties in naming and defining fossil species and resulting problems in placing individual specimens into those separate species. Especially as a result of a series of new discoveries and analysis of specific differences among the fossils found in different regions, a growing number of researchers now divide these Lower and Middle Pleistocene hominids into at least two different species (Wood 1992). Though the African and Asian specimens are broadly similar in form, the African fossils possess a higher cranial vault, have smaller facial bones, and are more lightly constructed with thinner bones (Tattersall 1993). These characteristics give the African fossils a more modern appearance than the Asian fossils. As a result of these differences, some paleoanthropologists (most notably Bernard Wood [1992] and Ian Tattersall [1993, 1995]) label the African fossils *Homo ergaster* (the species name comes from the Latin word for work, reflecting the species' ability to work stone to make tools). In this view, only the East Asian specimens retain the species name *Homo erectus*.

Adding to the complexity, specimens from Europe are called by some *Homo heidelbergensis* (named for the German city of Heidelberg where an important early specimen—the so-called Mauer Mandible—was discovered). Figure 10.12 contrasts two views proposed to explain the evolutionary relationships of the fossils discussed in this chapter. We will label all the specimens as *Homo erectus*, recognizing that views concerning this point are currently in a state of flux. (See the discussion later in this chapter).

The Fossils of *Homo erectus* in Africa

The oldest known *Homo erectus* fossil from Africa is a nearly complete cranium found by Richard Leakey in 1975 on the east shore of Lake Turkana

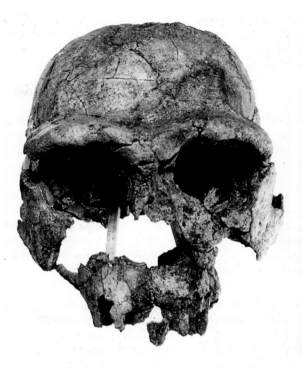
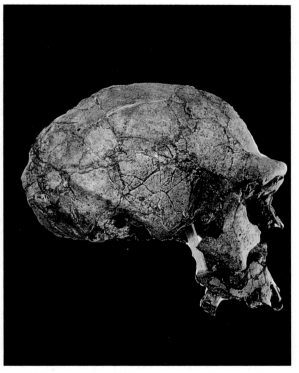

FIGURE 10.6 The skull of fossil KNM-ER 3733 from the area around Lake Turkana, Kenya, appears to be that of a female. Its cranial capacity is estimated to have been about 850 ml. (© *The National Museums of Kenya*)

in Kenya (Leakey and Walker 1985a) (Figure 10.6). The skull, designated KNM-ER 3733, with its jutting brow ridges, distinct sagittal keel, small face, and 850-ml cranial volume, is now estimated to be 1.78 million years old (Feibel et al. 1989). A similar but less complete skull (KNM-ER 3883), dating to 1.57 mya, was also found by the Leakey team on the east shore of the lake. Although its cranial capacity is slightly smaller than that of KNM-ER 3733, it appears to be more ruggedly constructed. It has been suggested that 3883 is a male and 3733 is a female.

Several other cranial fragments that reflect the morphology of *H. erectus* have been found on the east shore of the lake. Also found here and dating to the same period have been a few fragmentary mandibles and bits of leg and pelvic bones (Day 1971).

On the west side of Lake Turkana, the Leakey team found a remarkably complete specimen (KNM-WT 15000) (Figure 10.7, p. 242) that included most of the skull, the jaw, some ribs, most of the vertebrae, the right shoulder blade and forearm, the complete pelvis, almost all of the left arm, and elements of both legs (Leakey and Walker 1985b; Walker and Leakey 1993). The skeleton was found on a volcanic deposit dated 1.6 mya; it is believed that this fossil is probably also about that old.

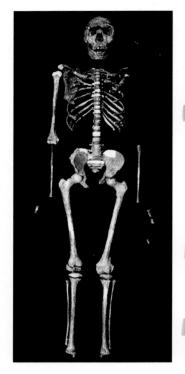

FIGURE 10.7 The skeleton of the 12-year-old boy from the west shore of Lake Turkana in Kenya (fossil KNM-WT 15000) is the most complete specimen of *Homo erectus* yet discovered. (© *The National Museums of Kenya*)

The fossil is that of a 12-year-old boy, as determined by tooth eruption and the shape of the pelvis. All of the boy's second or "twelve-year" molars are in place and his permanent canine on the upper right side, which ordinarily erupts at age eleven, was just in the process of erupting (Brown et al. 1985:789; B. H. Smith 1993). The skeleton is essentially modern in appearance from the neck down, but the proportions of the upper part of the femur, or thigh bone, are slightly unlike that of either modern or more ancient hominids. The exact significance of this difference is unclear, although it seems not to imply any major difference between his ability to walk and that of modern humans (Lewin 1984).

Although we commonly picture previous hominid species as smaller than modern humans, this boy was already close to 5½ feet tall and might have attained a height of 6 feet had he survived to adulthood. Although we cannot be certain of the growth curve for *H. erectus*, the appearance of the skeleton is that of a physically immature, still-growing individual: Neither his epiphyses nor his cranial sutures had yet fused and his teeth were those of a modern human 12 year old (Brown et al. 1985). He was, in fact, a boy.

The fact that this individual was about 12 years old and still growing has significant evolutionary implications. Humans begin life outside the womb at a rather immature stage of fetal development. This may result from the evolution of our larger brains and anatomical changes in the shape of the pelvis necessitated by the evolution of upright walking. If we were born at the more advanced level of development of some other primates, our heads would be too large to pass through our mothers' birth canals, which are restricted in size as a result of bipedalism. It is estimated that, in a sense, we are born three months "prematurely" when compared with the level of development of the great apes (Trinkaus 1983a). As we discussed in Chapter 8, a chimpanzee's brain size at birth is 40 percent what it will be when it reaches adulthood; a human's is only about 25 percent what it will be at maturity. Compared to chimps, a far greater percentage of the physical development of our brain happens after birth, outside of the womb. This results in the need for a tremendous investment of time and energy in raising human children; they are born helpless and remain nearly so for a much longer time than do other primates.

A detailed analysis of the pelvis of the Lake Turkana boy supports this directly (Walker and Ruff 1993). Assuming about the same amount of sexual dimorphism in *Homo erectus* and *Homo sapiens*, Walker and Ruff determined birth canal size in *Homo erectus*. They concluded that for a *Homo erectus* newborn to be able to pass through the mother's narrow birth canal, the baby's head had to be small relative to its adult brain size. Thus, *Homo erectus* babies, like modern human ones, were born more immature, more helpless, and more dependent on adults than is the case for other primates.

FIGURE 10.8 The OH 9 cranium, thought to be more than 1.25 million years old, is similar in appearance to KNM-ER 3733 but has a larger cranial capacity (1060 ml). (© *Courtesy G. P. Rightmire*)

In addition, we develop slowly after birth. In most other animal species, a 12-year-old individual would be a fully grown, physically mature adult. Yet this is certainly not the case for modern humans, and it seems not to have been true of *H. erectus*, either.

Why do we have such a long period of immaturity, and what are the implications of a similarly long developmental phase for *H. erectus*? Although it is difficult to point to any one cause for this phenomenon, it is clear that a long maturation period provides more time for young individuals to learn what they need to know to become successful adults. Remember, the major adaptational strategies of our species are cultural, which must be learned. The more complex the knowledge that needs to be mastered, the longer the period needed for such learning. The physical immaturity of KNM-WT 15000 may be evidence of selection for a longer period of development to allow for the mastery of sophisticated cultural skills. Moreover, a longer period of dependence contributes to a stronger social bond between offspring and their parents than that seen in other species. *H. erectus* may have shared this characteristic with modern humans.

A few more recent *H. erectus* fossils have been found in Olduvai Gorge in Tanzania (Rightmire 1979a). Dating to about 1.25 mya, OH 9 is a partially preserved brain case with an estimated cranial capacity of more than 1000 ml (Figure 10.8). OH 9, although larger, is similar in its anatomical details to KNM-ER 3733. OH 12, found nearby and estimated to be between 600,000 and 800,000 years old, consists of several cranial fragments. Although quite small and less complete, it is clear that OH 12 is another *erectus*, with an estimated cranial capacity of between 700 and 800 ml. OH 28 consists of a pelvic fragment and part of a femur. Although slightly different from the modern human configuration, together they reinforce the notion that *erectus* was completely bipedal (Day 1988).

Even more recent are the skull fragments and three mandibles from Ternifine, Algeria, and the mandible and skull fragments from Thomas Quarry, the two mandible fragments from Sidi Abderrahman, and the braincase from Salé, all from Morocco. The Ternifine material is dated to more than 500,000 ya and as much as 700,000 ya. The fossils from Thomas Quarry are probably a bit younger. The fossils from Salé and Sidi Abderrahman have not been reliably dated.

Out of Africa: Hominid Radiation

All the fossil hominids discussed up to this point were discovered in Africa, for an obvious reason: Africa was home to the species that gave rise to the hominid line. Apparently, for a few million years after the ape–hominid split, our ancestors did not expand beyond that continent. The first hominids and the species from whom they developed were adapted to life in the warm climate of Africa. The first evolutionary steps of our hominid ancestors were taken in Africa. The evolution of upright walking, the initial expansion of the braincase, and the beginnings of stone tool use and manufacture all took place on that continent. All the australopithecines and paranthropines as well as *Homo habilis* were African species.

Remember, however, that humans are culture-bearing animals. As hominids evolved and their cultures became more complex, their ability to adapt to new environments and circumstances also grew. The species descended from *Homo habilis*, for the first time in the history of hominid evolution, were able to expand beyond Africa to populate Europe and Asia. Whether a result of population increase, climate change, or merely the search for food, this geographic expansion is called the **hominid radiation**.

West Asia   The most reasonable route by which African hominids could spread into Asia leads north and east, through the Middle East. Unfortunately, the paleoanthropological record for the period between 2 million and 1 million years ago in that region is not ample. A single site, 'Ubeidiya, in Israel, has been dated to more than 1 million and perhaps as much as 1.4 million years ago. Just a few hominid fossils have been found there, along with stone choppers, picks, and bifaces that are similar to tools found in Africa of a similar age (Belfer-Cohen and Goren-Inbar 1994).

To the north, east of the Black Sea, a well-preserved lower jaw and sixteen teeth have been dated to more than 1.6 million years ago at Dmanisi, Georgia (Bower 1995a). The mandible shares much with the African fossils and was probably from a member of the same species. Together, these west Asian sites may represent some of the earliest (though not *the* earliest) hominid migrants out of Africa.

Java   The first recognized discovery of what we now call *Homo erectus* was made outside of Africa by a Dutch physician, Eugene Dubois. Serving

hominid radiation The expansion of the hominids out of Africa, beginning more than 1.5 mya—and perhaps close to 2 mya.

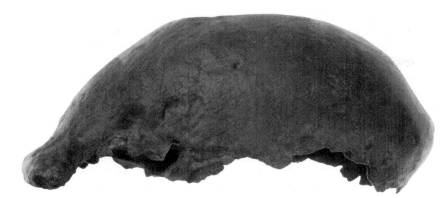

FIGURE 10.9   The "Java Man" skullcap was the first known specimen of what we now call *Homo erectus*. It was discovered by a Dutch physician, Eugene Dubois, near the town of Trinil on the island of Java. *(Rijks Museum of Natural History, Leiden)*

in the military in the Dutch colony of Java, Dubois thought that he might unearth important evidence there related to human evolution. Because all of humanity's nearest evolutionary relations, the apes, lived in the tropics, Dubois reasoned that ancient fossils of human ancestors might be found on Java, a tropical island. In 1891, along the Solo River near the village of Trinil, workers found the top of a skull at a depth of close to 50 feet. The skull was small by modern standards, flat, with large brow ridges (Figure 10.9). Some distance away, a completely modern-looking diseased human femur was found. Dubois felt certain that the skull and femur belonged together and represented a link in evolution between apes and humans. He called the specimen ***Pithecanthropus erectus***—the upright ape-man. That designation is no longer used. *Pithecanthropus* is considered to be a member of the species *Homo erectus.*

The skull from Trinil has an estimated cranial capacity of about 940 ml and shows the array of typical *H. erectus* features. The femur allegedly belonging to "Java Man" has had its association with the skull disputed, although at this point such a connection is not crucial because we have femurs of other *erectus* fossils, and they are largely modern in appearance. Absolute dating of volcanic material from the area has been confusing. At this point, it is probably safe to say only that the Trinil fossil is less than 1 million years old (Rightmire 1990:14).

Since 1937 a number of *H. erectus* fossils have been recovered 40 miles west of Trinil. The site at Sangiran has yielded the cranial remains of about forty individuals. Those crania that can be reconstructed with some degree of confidence clearly belong to *erectus* (Holloway 1981). The most complete skull, Sangiran 17, has thick, arching brow ridges; a sharply angled occiput; a distinct sagittal keel; and a long, low vault (Figure 10.10, p. 246). In most characteristics, Sangiran 17 and the others are similar to the African and other Asian specimens. Their cranial capacities range from about 800 to 1050 ml.

The Sangiran fossils were long thought to date to between 700,000 to 800,000 years ago based on the geological layer in which they were found.

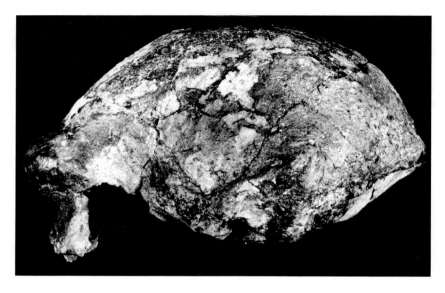

However, more recent dating of volcanic rock in which two new specimens were discovered in 1974, has produced a much older date of about 1.65 million years ago (Swisher et al. 1994). Also on Java and east of Sangiran, at the site of Perning, the deposit in which the top of a child's skull (the so-called Modjokerto child) was found in the 1930s has now been dated to 1.8 million years ago, about the age of the oldest African specimens. These dates confuse the evolutionary picture and will be discussed in more detail later in this chapter.

Northeast of Trinil, on the Solo River, is the locality of Ngandong, where the crania of about a dozen individuals were found in the 1930s. With a mean of about 1185 ml, their cranial volumes fall at the upper range for *H. erectus,* leading some to suggest that they might represent a later hominid line (Wolpoff et al. 1984). However, dating the material excavated more than sixty years ago has been a problem (Bartstra et al. 1988). Nevertheless, cranial endocasts (Holloway 1980) and a recent, detailed analysis (Rightmire 1990) show that, despite their great size, the proportions as well as the anatomical details of the Ngandong crania place them firmly in the species *erectus.*

China   A recent discovery in China places members of the genus *Homo* in Asia between 1.78 and 1.96 million years ago (Larick and Ciochon 1996). Excavated at a site called Longgupo (Dragon Bone Cave), researchers recovered thousands of animal bones, two simple stone tools (cobbles with evidence of battering) and a small fragment of a hominid mandible along with an isolated hominid tooth (Ciochon 1995; Larick and Ciochon 1996). The two teeth found in the jaw and the isolated tooth are similar to

Homo habilis and later fossils found in Africa, but are unlike those found in later *Homo erectus* specimens from China. Though the fossil and artifactual remains are meager, they seem to reflect a very early migration out of Africa, similar in time to the oldest dates cited above for Java. The excavators of the site suggest that the hominid represented here may be a previously unidentified species that later gave rise to *Homo erectus* in Asia.

Beginning in the 1920s, a large sample of *Homo erectus* fossils representing as many as forty individuals was unearthed in a cave at Zhoukoudian, outside of Beijing (Shapiro 1974). Interestingly, the cave was seen initially as a good place to verify the discovery at Piltdown, and some of the scientists involved in the excavation and analysis of the Piltdown material were also involved in these excavations.

Sadly, this spectacular collection of fossils, called "Peking Man" by the media, was lost during World War II when U.S. Marines, attempting to take them out of China, were captured by Japanese troops. The fossils may very well have been destroyed, although stories have occasionally surfaced that some or all of them are in the possession of the Japanese government, museums on Taiwan, or even the widows of the captured marines. A long, sustained effort to track down the fossils, including the offer of a substantial reward and the promise of immunity from prosecution, has resulted in a few interesting leads but little of substance (Shapiro 1974).

Although the fossils themselves were lost, they were in the possession of scientists long enough for most important measurements to be taken and casts to have been made. The fossil assemblage consisted of 15 fragmentary skulls, 6 more complete crania, 13 fragmentary mandibles, 3 upper jaws, 157 teeth, and some postcranial bones including pieces of femur, upper arms, toes, and a single vertebra (Jia and Huang 1990:161–162; Wu and Lin 1983).

Although the number of postcranial bones was small, we can summarize that *H. erectus* at Zhoukoudian was short and stockily built, with males averaging just over 5 feet in height and females a few inches shorter. Their arms were relatively longer than in modern humans, and their shoulders were broad. The average capacity of the Zhoukoudian crania is just under 1100 ml. Their faces were broad, their brow ridges thick, and their skulls displayed the sagittal keeling so common in their species (Figure 10.11, p. 248). Recent uranium series dating of the fossil-bearing strata in the cave indicates that it was first occupied by *erectus* 460,000 ya, with subsequent use of the cave until about 230,000 ya (Wu and Lin 1983).

Just as with some of the *Homo habilis* sites in Africa, the Zhoukoudian site was interpreted for many years as a home-base habitation for wandering hunters. It was even suggested that these hominids practiced ritual cannibalism as the bases and faces of most of the skulls recovered there were broken as if shattered to provide access to the brains.

This view has been questioned (Binford and Chuan 1985; Binford and Stone 1986). The skulls of these specimens were indeed broken into, but

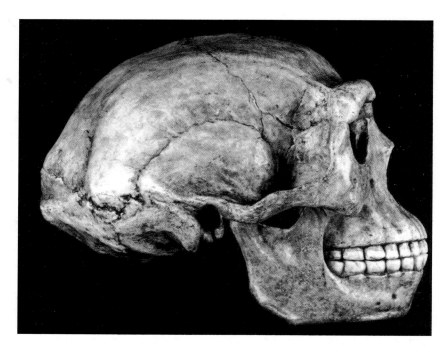

in a manner now understood to be typical of carnivorous animals. Closer examination of the faunal assemblage shows tool marks on relatively few of the animal bones and plenty of evidence of carnivore tooth marks on both the animal and hominid remains. One of the species showing the greatest proportion of tool cuts was the horse, but only 11 percent of the horse bones show evidence of butchering with stone tools (Binford and Stone 1986:468). Many of the horse mandibles show tool cut-marks, which seems to be best explained as the scavenging by hominids of undesirable anatomical parts left by carnivores. In a very small sample of animal bones (four), tool marks overlay teeth marks, clearly indicating that meat-eating animals got at the meat first.

The presence of stone tools is indisputable evidence that *H. erectus* used the cave at Zhoukoudian. It is likely, however, that most of the hominid and animal remains were brought into the cave by carnivores returning to their lairs with prey. Those bones that display hominid activity indicate scavenging, not hunting. Although Zhoukoudian should still be considered an enormously significant hominid fossil locality, it appears not to represent a long-term Middle Pleistocene village site. Hominids probably inhabited the cave only intermittently.

The sites of Lantian (Gongwangling) and Hexian (Lontandong) have also yielded significant remains of *H. erectus* in China. The Lantian specimen consists of the top of a skull, including the brow ridges, and fragments of the upper and lower jaw. The cranial capacity has been estimated at 800 ml. The fossil has recently been dated to more than 1 million years ago (Chen and Zhang 1991). The Hexian fossils (at least two individuals are represented) are probably younger, perhaps 250,000 to 500,000 years old and therefore generally contemporary with the Zhoukoudian fossils. The skulls, as with all other *erectus* crania, are low-vaulted, flat, angled to the rear, and possessed of enormous brow ridges. Cranial capacity has been estimated at 1000 ml (Wu 1985).

Europe   Until fairly recently, few if any indisputable *H. erectus* fossil remains were known outside of Africa and Asia. The discovery of a hominid tibia at Boxgrove Quarry, in England, dated to about 515,000 years ago, was quickly touted as the oldest human ancestor found in Europe (Bahn 1994). Of similar age was the so-called Mauer Mandible, found in Heidelberg, Germany, in 1907. It has been less firmly dated to about 500,000 years ago—and it provides the species name, *Homo heidelbergensis*, that some apply to the Middle Pleistocene European fossils mentioned earlier and discussed in the next chapter.

There were also at least a few Middle Pleistocene sites in Europe where artifacts—but no hominid bones—had been found. One of the oldest is Isernia La Pineta in central Italy. Here a stone tool industry of limestone choppers and unmodified flint flakes was found in association with the remains of bison, deer, elephant, rhinoceros, and hippopotamus (Coltorti et al. 1982). The site was found under a volcanic deposit K/Ar-dated to 730,000 ya. At Soleilhac in France, artifacts and faunal remains have been dated to 800,000 ya (K. Weaver 1985).

Spectacular confirmation of an ancient human presence in Europe more than 500,000 years ago has been found at the site of Gran Dolina in the Atapuerca Mountains in Spain (Carbonell et al. 1995). We now know that humans were present in western Europe before the magnetic reversal of 780,000 years ago (see Chapter 7) and perhaps as much as 1 million years ago (Parés and Pérez-González 1995).

The Gran Dolina hominid fossils include the fragmentary remains of at least four individuals including two adults, one teenager, and one small child. The researchers maintain that a detailed analysis of the bones shows substantial differences between them and those of *Homo erectus*. They tentatively assign them to *Homo heidelbergensis*, or at least an early, primitive version of that species.

The Timing of Geographical Expansion

Paleoanthropologists are probably on firm ground in maintaining that the human lineage evolved in Africa and spread from there; there simply is no fossil evidence of this occurring anywhere else. So the first evolutionary descendants of *Homo habilis* almost necessarily evolved in Africa because it is only in Africa that *Homo habilis* has been found. In this book, the imme-

FIGURE 10.12 Two competing models for the number of species, evolution, and spread of hominids after 2 million years ago. In the more traditional model (*left*), *Homo habilis* gave rise to *Homo erectus* in Africa sometime after 2 mya; from there *Homo erectus* populations quickly spread into Asia and later Europe. In the competing model (*right*), *Homo habilis* gave rise to *Homo ergaster* in Africa sometime after 2 mya. *Homo habilis* or a descendant spread into Asia also soon after 2 mya, where it evolved into *Homo erectus*. *Homo ergaster* may have spread into Europe, where it gave rise to yet another hominid species, *Homo heidelbergensis*.

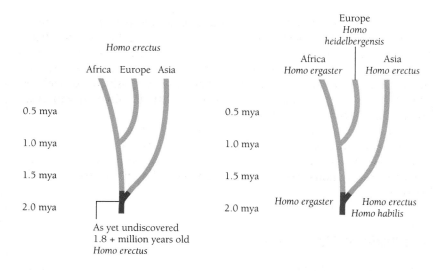

diate evolutionary offspring of *Homo habilis* has been called *Homo erectus,* though some label these African fossils *Homo ergaster* based on their somewhat more modern-looking crania. As stated, the oldest African specimen dates to about 1.78 million years ago.

The date of the Dmanisi mandible in west Asia—1.6 million years ago—is difficult enough to incorporate into this common view of human evolution and geographical expansion; it does not provide very much time for *Homo erectus* to expand from Africa into west Asia. That being said, the new dating of some of the Javanese fossils and the discovery of the *habilis*-like mandible fragment at Longgupo in China dated to about the same time has stunned many paleoanthropologists because it places hominids in Java and China at about 1.8 million years ago, the same time—and maybe even a little before—they had evolved in Africa!

Of course, if *Homo erectus* did evolve in Africa, that is impossible—some time must have passed between their evolution in Africa and their spread throughout the rest of the Old World. If the fossils discussed in this chapter all belong to *Homo erectus,* there must be older *erectus* specimens yet to be found in Africa, predating the east and west Asian specimens by a time period sufficient to allow for their expansion to those areas (Figure 10.12). Alternatively, although there is no evidence as yet outside of Africa for *Homo habilis* or any other older hominid, a species older than *Homo erectus* might have begun expanding out of Africa closer to 2 million years ago or even a little before. Perhaps in Africa, this hominid evolved into the species *Homo ergaster* (this would include the African fossils we are here calling *Homo erectus*); in Asia, it developed into *Homo erectus;* and in Europe, *Homo heidelbergensis* (see Figure 10.12).

Until more fossils are discovered and analyzed, the precise nature of the evolutionary relationship among the various post–*Homo habilis* fossils in Africa, Asia, and Europe will remain enigmatic. A consensus may be building to separate *Homo erectus* into three named species (*Homo ergaster* in Africa, *Homo erectus* in Asia, and *Homo heidelbergensis* in Europe), but until that consensus is reached, we will continue to place all within the species *Homo erectus*.

Finally, we should not despair over this problem. Though the evolutionary relationships among the hominid inhabitants of Africa, Asia, and Europe are unclear, quite a bit is known about the ancestral humans who lived in these regions. We will focus on what is known in the rest of this chapter.

The Brain of *Homo erectus*

Although the brains of ancient hominids have not been preserved, the containers that held them sometimes have. The inside surfaces of skulls often bear evidence of the external appearance of the brains they housed. The skull is not a dead, inert vessel but a living part of an organism. It is made of living bone that reacts with the material it is in contact with, whether muscle, arteries, or brain tissue.

Endocasts of some fossil crania have been created naturally when fine sediments filled in the skull as the brain decayed. These sediments then fossilized, leaving a model in stone of the prehistoric brain. Where natural endocasts did not form, they can be made artificially by pouring or painting liquid latex into the interior of the skull to make an impression of the inside surface and therefore produce a model of at least the major features of the exterior surface of the ancient brain.

Ralph Holloway (1980, 1981) has produced a series of endocasts for the Ngandong and Sangiran *Homo erectus* fossil skulls from Java and compared them with endocasts made from the skulls of gorillas, chimpanzees, orangutans, and forty ancient hominid fossil crania, including australopithecines and *Homo habilis, erectus,* and *sapiens* (Figure 10.13). Holloway notes some interesting similarities between the *H. erectus* and modern *H. sapiens* endocasts. The *erectus* endocasts show that the brains of this species were asymmetrical. This asymmetry is caused by the hemispheric specialization of our brains; because the two halves perform different functions, they look a bit different. For example, in general the left hemisphere houses abilities for language and symbol use, whereas the right hemisphere controls spatial-visual manipulation, as in hand–eye coordination.

As Alan Walker (1993) points out, cerebral asymmetry is also present to a certain degree in some Old World monkeys and in chimpanzees. Interestingly, their larger left hemispheres house the areas of their brains em-

FIGURE 10.13   Drawing of an artificial cranial endocast made on the Sangiran 17 cranium by anthropologist Ralph Holloway. *(Redrawn from R. C. Holloway 1981)*

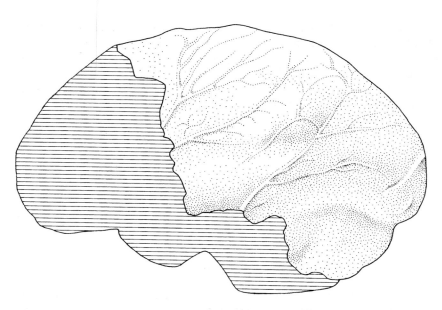

ployed in recognizing vocalizations used in communication. Perhaps the enlargement of the left brain of the hominids is related to communication.

A similar kind and degree of asymmetry of the brain seen in modern humans and visible in endocasts made from modern human skulls appears in the endocasts made from the Sangiran and Ngandong crania as well as the African skulls KNM-ER 3733, KNM-ER 3883, and OH 9. From this evidence, we can infer that *H. erectus* possessed a level of hemispheric specialization similar to that of modern humans. The fascinating inference that Holloway draws is that more than 1.7 million years ago, *Homo erectus* possessed linguistic skills and the ability to manipulate symbols, along with a level of hand–eye coordination similar to, or at least approaching, that of modern humans. Although the scientific jury is still out on this suggestion, Holloway's is an extremely interesting approach that will probably make a major contribution to our understanding of the intellectual abilities of extinct hominids. At the least, we can be certain that the brain of *erectus* resembled ours in some very specific ways.

The cranial anatomy of *erectus* lends further support for Holloway's interesting hypothesis. As mentioned previously (Chapter 9), basicranial anatomy can be used to reconstruct the vocal tracts of prehistoric hominids. Australopithecine basicrania, as mentioned, are quite similar in their architecture to those of modern apes, and, therefore, they probably could not speak. The fossil record indicates that *erectus* basicranial anatomy, on the other hand, was quite different, far more like the modern form (Laitman and Heimbach 1984). Researcher Jeffrey Laitman (as quoted in Bower 1989c:25) compares *erectus* basicrania—and, by inference, their vocal tract anatomy and their ability to produce humanlike speech—to that of a 6-year-old human child. Anyone who has listened to a group of first-graders knows the range—as well as the volume and rapidity—of the speech they can produce. Although some of the details of their vocal tract anatomy certainly were different, *erectus* may have been capable of some level of humanlike speech as well.

Clearly, reconstruction of the evolution of language is extremely difficult. Alan Walker (1993), in his analysis of the 12-year-old *Homo erectus* boy from Lake Turkana, is quite critical of all the evidence presented to support the hypothesis that *Homo erectus* could speak, arguing that cranial asymmetry and basicranial form do not prove the existence of speech capabilities. The origins of the crucial human ability to speak, thus, are still unclear. Additional research is needed to provide further insights into this skill, which so defines us.

Behavioral Innovations of *Homo erectus*

The greater intellect of *Homo erectus* certainly allowed for the elaboration of culture and innovations in behavior. There is a good deal of debate, however, on how this is reflected in the archaeological record. We will look at four important areas of such possible innovation: tool manufacture, the controlled use of fire, construction of dwellings, and cooperative hunting.

Stone Tools

The essentials of the stone tool tradition practiced by the precursors of *Homo erectus* were continued by them. Simple chopping tools created by the removal of a relatively small number of flakes from a stone cobble are present at many *H. erectus* sites. A new, more sophisticated toolmaking tradition, however, was developed by *erectus*. Called **Acheulian** after the site of St. Acheul in France where it was first identified (though the tradition is actually older in Africa), it involved an elaboration upon the removal of a few flakes. The end result is called a **hand axe**: a symmetrical, edged, pointed tool, flaked on both sides or faces (Figure 10.14, p. 254). Hand axes were probably all-purpose tools for piercing animal flesh, butchering, hide scraping, wood cutting, root digging—a sort of Swiss Army rock of the Middle Pleistocene. They may even have served as projectiles if thrown like a discus (O'Brien 1984).

Experimental archaeologist Mark Newcomer (1971) has made replicas of Acheulian hand axes in an attempt to understand how they were made. In one attempt, he produced a hand axe weighing 230 grams from a stone nodule of around 3 kilograms. In producing this one hand axe, he also generated 51 large and potentially usable flakes and more than 4500 smaller waste pieces.

Acheulian The toolmaking tradition of *Homo erectus*, including hand axes, cleavers, and flake tools.

hand axe A bifacial, symmetrical all-purpose tool first produced by *H. erectus*.

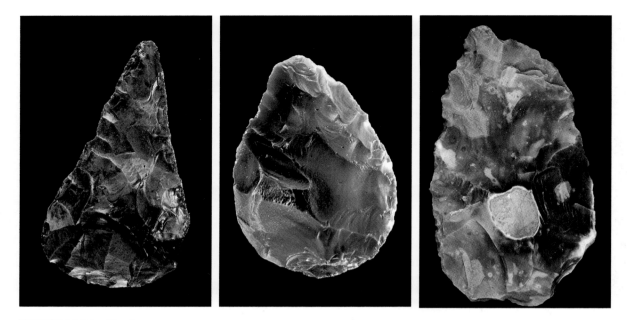

FIGURE 10.14   Hand axes symmetrically flaked on both sides produced by *Homo erectus* beginning 1.4 mya, represent an advance in stone tool technology over the Oldowan tradition. This popular tool has been found in a variety of sizes and varying degrees of quality *(left, center: © Lee Boltin Picture Library; right: K. L. Feder)*

From this and other experiments, Newcomer concluded that the manufacture of a hand axe probably progressed in three stages: First, a rough form was produced from a nodule of stone by striking the nodule directly with a stone hammer. Next, that rough blank was thinned and shaped by percussion with a softer tool, perhaps an antler. Finally, the tool would have been finished, again with a soft hammer, straightening the edge of the axe and producing the final, symmetrical shape.

The hand axe certainly shows more forethought, greater skill, and more utility in its design and manufacture than Oldowan tools. It is a more sophisticated tool and represents a great technological advance over the ability of previous hominids. That the Acheulian tradition of toolmaking evolved from the Oldowan, however, seems clear. Oldowan choppers from Sterkfontein in Africa were well enough made to resemble crude hand axes.

Homo erectus also made cleavers with a straight, sharp edge. (The hand axe, in contrast, had a point.) Along with these core tools—both hand axes and cleavers were shaped from cores of stone—*erectus* also used flake tools (Figure 10.15). Stone flakes removed from a core in the process of making hand axes or cleavers were often used, without further modification, for cutting, scraping, or piercing animal flesh as well as for cutting or scraping plant material, including wood. Some flakes were themselves worked to produce a desired shape or cutting edge.

The hand axe tradition began in Africa about 1.4 mya and continued through the Middle Pleistocene, lasting even into the Upper Pleistocene. It spread into Europe after its invention in Africa.

FIGURE 10.15   Flake tools and a chopper associated with *Homo erectus* from the cave at Zhoukoudian.   (*Drawings by Patricia J. Wynne from Wu Rukang and Lin Shenglong, "Peking Man"* Scientific American, *June, 1983:92*)

Burin

Points

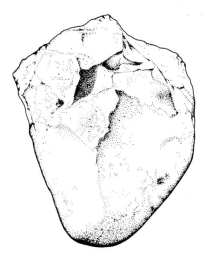

Scrapers

Chopper

Though hand axes are commonly found in Africa and Europe, they are extremely rare or entirely absent from *H. erectus* sites in Asia east of India. There is such a clear geographic dividing line between the makers of hand axes in the west and those who made simple chopping tools from stone nodules in the east, a name is applied to this division: the **Movius Line,** named for the researcher (Hallam Movius) who first articulated it. The existence of the Movius Line may be explained by the fact that hominids left Africa and arrived in East Asia long before the hand axe was developed back in Africa. The persistence of this break—the fact that hand axe man-

Movius Line   A geographic break between the manufacture of hand axes and that of simple stone chopping tools. Hand axes appear to the west of this line—located in eastern India—but not east of it.

ufacturing did not spread into East Asia after its invention in Africa—is interpreted by some paleoanthropologists as supporting the view that the east Asian hominids that date to this period were a different species (*Homo erectus*) than those who invented and perfected the technology (*Homo ergaster*) in Africa.

Quest for Fire

The ability to control fire is extremely significant. Fire provides heat, which may have helped our tropically adapted ancestors to survive in the inhospitably cold climate of Pleistocene Europe and Asia. Fire can provide protection from animals, and it can be used in cooking, which makes more of the nutrition present in meat available to our digestive systems.

Perhaps just as significantly, says science writer John Pfeiffer (1969), fire extends the day. We are—and our ancestors were—a visually oriented species. *Homo erectus*, like us, depended on vision for most sensory input; like us, it did not see well in the dark. The light produced by the fires of *H. erectus* allowed for an increase in the number of hours during which they could interact and create.

Although there is some possible evidence for the controlled use of fire by *H. erectus* perhaps as much as 1.5 mya in Africa (James 1989; Sillen and Brain 1990) and 750,000 ya at the French cave of L'Escale, the earliest confirmation of the control of fire comes from Zhoukoudian in China and is dated to after 500,000 B.P. (Binford and Chuan 1985; Binford and Stone 1986).

Residues of million- or half-million-year-old fireplaces, however, are not so easy to distinguish from other, natural phenomena. Even the evidence for fire at Zhoukoudian, long thought to be definitive, has been questioned at least in part by Lewis Binford and Kun Ho Chuan (1985) and Binford and Nancy Stone (1986), who remind researchers that indisputable hearths have not been found in the cave. Instead, large deposits of supposed ash have been interpreted as the result of hominid-controlled fires. Binford and Chuan point out, however, that these so-called ash deposits are not generally found in the same strata as the tools and hominid remains. Some of the animal bones found in the ash deposits appear to have been mineralized, not burned. Finally, they have reidentified much of the so-called ash as more likely to have been owl (or other bird) droppings. Though Binford and Stone agree that fire belonged in the cultural repertoire of *H. erectus*, they maintain that the evidence, at least in Zhoukoudian, occurs late in the sequence.

We can only conclude that *H. erectus* almost certainly used fire as part of an adaptation to the colder regions of the earth, but that more research needs to be conducted to determine with any certainty how long ago and where this occurred.

Construction of Dwellings

The geology of Terra Amata in southern France indicates that the site was occupied perhaps as much as 400,000 and certainly before 200,000 ya. Here, it is asserted, a population of hominids built what are some of the oldest known shelters in the world (de Lumley 1969, 1975).

Based on the presence of a few fireplaces, what are assumed to be decayed wooden posts, and the distribution of artifacts and organic debris, it was suggested by the excavator Henri de Lumley that the *Homo erectus* inhabitants of Terra Amata built oval structures measuring between 7 to 15 meters long by 4 to 6 meters wide. De Lumley suggested that a number of saplings or branches a few inches in diameter were driven into the ground, bent together on top, and somehow connected. In this reconstruction, stones were placed around these stakes to help support the walls and larger wooden poles were erected inside, probably to serve as roof supports.

On the floors of all of the supposed huts discovered at Terra Amata were the remains of hearths with stone windscreens around them. Littering the floors of the huts were tools, stone flakes resulting from the manufacture of tools, and the bones of the animals perhaps eaten by the inhabitants, including those of an extinct species of elephant, wild boar, stag, ibex, wild ox, and rhinoceros. Although meat was apparently a significant part of the diet of the inhabitants of the site, they also collected shellfish and fish in the nearby Mediterranean. Again, we have the image of a home-base village where people returned again and again.

This scenario, however, depends on the archaeological integrity of the site. The assumption is that natural processes have not acted to disturb the spatial contexts of the archaeological material over a period of more than 200,000 years and perhaps twice that long. Research by archaeologist Paola Villa (1982), however, calls into question how intact the site really was and thus casts doubt on the interpretation.

Villa shows that there has been substantial postdepositional movement of artifacts at Terra Amata. Fragments of stone that could be put together again, particularly cores and the flakes from those cores, were recovered from what were defined by the excavators as different stratigraphic layers. In fact, 40 percent of the pieces that could be joined back together were found in different levels. In one case, four flakes and the core they all were derived from had been vertically separated by as much as 40 centimeters. On this basis, Villa characterizes detailed reconstruction of prehistoric life at Terra Amata as being "largely speculative" (1982:285). The presence of huts at Terra Amata is therefore questionable.

Hunters or Scavengers?

The sites of Torralba and Ambrona in Spain, Olorgesailie in Kenya, and Olduvai BK II in Tanzania, dating perhaps to at least 400,000 ya, all associated with the artifacts of *Homo erectus*, have been interpreted by some as seasonal camps where groups of related individuals came together perhaps on a yearly basis to hunt, socialize, and exchange information. At these sites, according to some, we see the earliest evidence of cooperative hunting by our hominid ancestors.

Torralba and Ambrona are two hills flanking a major pass in the Guadarama Mountains of Spain, a natural migration route for people and animals. The remains of at least fifty prehistoric elephants, twenty-six horses, twenty-five deer, ten wild cattle, and six rhinoceros have been excavated. It has been suggested that they represent perhaps as many as ten separate cooperative *H. erectus* hunts (Butzer 1971, 1982; Howell 1966). The animals may have been stampeded into swampy, boggy traps where they would become mired and then be killed and butchered by *erectus* hunters. Some researchers suggested that the animals were stampeded and directed to the wetlands by the use of fire.

At the BK II locality at Olduvai Gorge, groups of wild cattle were also thought to have been driven into a swamp, where they were then killed and butchered by *H. erectus*.

Olorgesailie, in Kenya, is a site where a *H. erectus* population living west of a large lake is said to have cooperatively hunted baboons (Isaac 1977). Recent K/Ar dating indicates that the site may be from 700,000 to 900,000 years old (Bower 1987b). More than sixty individuals of a now-extinct baboon species have been discovered. All around the bones were large, unmodified, round cobbles that Isaac believes were used as weapons thrown by the hominids. Other stone tools, used in butchering the animals, were also found. In Isaac's reconstruction, the hominids surrounded the baboons in their tree roosts, forced them to flee by throwing rocks at them, and clubbed them to death as they attempted to escape. Next, the animals would have been butchered and their bones cracked open to extract the nutrient-rich marrow inside. A more recent excavation at the same site has revealed possible evidence of an elephant kill. The bones of a now-extinct elephant species were discovered surrounded by hand axes, and there appear to be tool marks on some of the bones (Bower 1987a).

If this interpretation of hunting is correct, we can infer a high level of knowledge, cooperation, and coordination among hominids living several hundred thousand years ago. The *H. erectus* hunters of the Middle Pleistocene would have had to possess a sophisticated understanding of animal behavior, including migration and herding schedules and patterns and different animal reactions to a threat. The level of cooperation and coordination necessary for such hunts implies an ability to communicate, delegate responsibilities, divide labor, and possibly even distribute results of a successful hunt.

Based on our discussion of the possible similarity of the brain of *H. erectus* to ours, such a reconstruction, though remarkable, is certainly not out of the question. Recent careful investigation of the taphonomy of these alleged *H. erectus* kill sites, however, has called the cooperative hunting scenario into serious question (Binford 1981; Shipman and Rose 1983). In the case of Torralba and Ambrona, for example, the animal bones were found in an area where carnivorous animals were likely to have been active. Very few indisputable tools were found in association with the bones.

One way of determining human activity at these sites involves the search for cut marks on animal bones. Are there marks made by stone tools present on animal bones found at these sites? In an analysis of approximately 3000 bones from Torralba and Ambrona, Pat Shipman and Jennie Rose (1983) determined that over 95 percent of the specimens were so heavily damaged they could not be used in the search for cut marks. In fact, they maintain that the great majority of marks on the Torralba and Ambrona bones previously identified as cut marks are merely the scratches left by soil abrasion and root growth. Of the fifty-five specimens intact enough for analysis, a scanning electron microscope revealed only sixteen stone tool cut marks on fourteen bones (1983:467), and these show no pattern that could be interpreted as systematic butchering (Figure 10.16). Shipman and Rose also found very little evidence of animal tooth marks, indicating that carnivores, including scavengers, cannot be shown to have played a major role in producing the assemblage either.

Given that it is impossible to determine whether the rest of the bones had been cut with stone tools, the most that can be said is that *H. erectus* was present at Torralba and Ambrona and cut some meat off some animal carcasses there. The site, however, cannot be used to support a hypothesis of big-game hunting for *H. erectus*.

Our understanding of the cultural capabilities and achievements of *H. erectus* is in flux. As with *Homo habilis,* projecting modern hunter–gatherer analogues into the past to explain *H. erectus* settlement and subsistence, though once popular, now seems to be unwarranted. The evidence can no longer be interpreted as supporting the idea that *erectus* constructed dwellings at home bases or hunted cooperatively—though it should also be said that the evidence does not necessarily *disprove* that this group of hominids possessed these adaptations, either. They almost certainly scavenged animal meat where they could. They may have hunted, although probably not big game and not habitually. They probably gathered wild plant foods where they could. They used fire, and they may have built shelters.

Whatever the case, *H. erectus* was an enormously successful hominid. The fact that the species was able to expand into Asia and Europe shows great ability. They lasted as a species for more than 1 million years. That their adaptations do not mirror those of modern humans is to be expected. Only more research will enable us to understand the nature of those adaptations more completely.

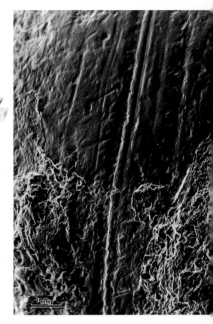

FIGURE 10.16   Scanning electron microscope photograph of cut marks on an elephant bone recovered at Ambrona, Spain. These longitudinal marks made by stone tools 400,000 ya are some of the few bits of evidence that indicate the butchering of animals by *Homo erectus* at this site. (*Courtesy Pat Shipman*)

Continuity and Change in *Homo erectus*

Although it would be an exaggeration to say that if you've seen one *Homo erectus* you've seen them all, there is, nevertheless, a fair degree of homogeneity in these fossils across both space and time. Though some researchers see enough variation to place specimens in separate species, the fossils in Africa, Asia, and Europe, though certainly exhibiting some degree of regional variation, are generally quite similar. As G. Philip Rightmire (1990) shows, comparisons of *erectus* specimens widely separate in time and space—for example, OH 9 from Tanzania and Sangiran 17 from Java, or KNM-ER 3733 from Kenya and Sangiran 2 from Java—show a great degree of similarity. Beyond this, the oldest specimens from Africa dating to close to 1.8 mya do not look so different from Asian examples dated to 1.4 million years later.

Regular anatomical change through time appears to be relatively minor in *H. erectus*. The posterior teeth decrease in size, and there is a similar decrease in the size of the structures of the face and lower jaw, which supported the muscles needed to use those back teeth (Wolpoff 1980b). At the same time, the incisors of *erectus* increase in size through time. Many other features, such as bone thickness in the skull and limbs, remain constant, however, and the size, position, and proportions of the sagittal keel, nuchal torus, and supraorbital torus as well as the size and proportions of the limbs remain fairly constant through time—or at least show no consistent pattern of change.

Even as important a feature as brain size seems to exhibit relative stability over time. Rightmire (1985) has shown that there is a measurable but surprisingly weak pattern of increase in *H. erectus* brain size from the species' initial appearance in the Lower Pleistocene throughout the Middle Pleistocene (Figure 10.17). He estimates this weak pattern of growth at about 180 ml per 1 million years (1990:196). As Rightmire quickly points out, however, the sample size in this analysis is quite small—just twenty-six crania—and in some cases the precise dating of crania is uncertain. For example, the very large Ngandong crania confound this analysis because they cannot be firmly dated. If you eliminate these five crania, the overall cranial growth rate drops substantially to only about 120 ml per 1 million years, a figure that is not statistically significant. If the Ngandong specimens are quite recent—younger than 500,000 years—they indeed serve to verify a general and significant trend of increasing brain size through time. If they are relatively ancient—closer to 1 million years old—they support a deduction of no pattern of brain increase throughout the tenure of *erectus*. Other researchers, in particular Milford Wolpoff (1980b, 1984), J. E. Cronin et al. (1981), and Steven Leigh (1992) argue for the former, Rightmire for the latter.

It is not yet possible to come to a definitive conclusion on this very important point, but the technical argument concerning "statistical signifi-

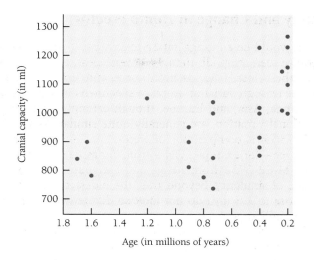

FIGURE 10.17   Graph showing the relative stability of *Homo erectus* brain size from 1.75 mya to 400,000 ya. Note the more rapid increase after 400,000 ya. This may represent an evolutionary jump—a punctuation—to *Homo sapiens*. (*Data from Rightmire 1990*)

cance" is, perhaps, not the crucial issue for us here. However the data are manipulated, even if this increase in brain size was an authentic trend and not just an artifact of incomplete data, its tempo, certainly, was quite slow. After all, a 180-ml increase over a 1-million-year time span is not very much (an 18 percent increment). The increase from the *Homo habilis* to the *Homo erectus* mean capacity was about 300 ml—a 44 percent increase that occurred in less than half the time.

The *H. erectus* toolkit also seems to be largely stable over time. Hand axes vary little over the course of more than 1 million years, as do flake tools. In their reexamination of the Zhoukoudian material, Binford and Chuan see little change over more than 200,000 years of use of the cave. In fact, they state: "We can see no evidence that the form and composition of the tool assemblage is changing at any greater rate than the anatomy of the hominids themselves" (1985:429).

On the other hand, the toolkit is not entirely static. Hand axes become more symmetrical and their edges straighter in later specimens. Similarly, there appear to be a greater number of distinct flake tool forms at later *H. erectus* sites. Still, although change clearly took place, the overall impression is one of stability.

In contrast, as Rightmire points out, beginning about or shortly after 400,000 ya, fossil hominids in Africa and Europe exhibit a noticeable increase in cranial capacity. This brain size expansion might be interpreted as a punctuation in hominid evolution after a long period of equilibrium. Again, however, the sample size is quite small.

Such a hypothesis would be supported if features other than brain size exhibited this same jump toward a more modern appearance. The fossil hominid record is rarely simple, however. As we will see, other anatomical characteristics of these new hominids—such as cranial bone thickness, brow ridge size, occipital form, postcranial robustness, and even the shape of their skulls—are highly variable, and many show no great leap toward modern forms. Some characteristics of some of the skulls seem no more modern than those of many *H. erectus* specimens, others seem to be intermediate in form, and still others seem even to be more primitive—that is, less modern—than the same features in *erectus*. Such complexities, though frustrating, make the story all the more intriguing.

Regardless of other features found in the hominids that followed *H. erectus,* the apparently rapid increase in cranial capacity, based on our admittedly small sample of fossil crania that date to this period, has led to the hypothesis that at least some of the post–400,000-year-old fossil hominids represent a new species. At least in terms of their brain size, they are so much closer to us than *Homo erectus* that we call them by our species name, *Homo sapiens.*

Summary

In Africa, beginning sometime before 1.8 mya, a hominid appeared with a more modern cranial architecture than *Homo habilis* and a cranial capacity about 44 percent larger; at a bit under 1000 ml, it approaches two-thirds of the modern human mean brain size (1450 ml). The species exhibiting this rapid increase in cranial capacity is called *Homo erectus.*

From East Africa, a number of well-preserved crania and the nearly complete skeleton of a young boy all date between 1.78 and 1.57 mya. The skeleton of the boy shows that he was physically immature at his death at around 12 years of age. This is evidence for the beginning of the typically human pattern of delayed maturation of children, beginning with the birth of large-brained, relatively undeveloped babies, and providing for the time necessary for imparting cultural adaptation.

H. erectus was the first of our ancestors to have expanded its range beyond Africa. Fossils exhibiting typical *erectus* forms have been found in west Asia from as much as 1.6 million years ago, in Java from as much as 1.8 mya, and in China from about the same time.

The famous site of Zhoukoudian, located near the modern city of Beijing, dates to after 500,000 ya. Forty or more individuals were found in the cave, located in an area with a climate very different from the tropical and subtropical home of the species. Evidence at Zhoukoudian and elsewhere indicates that it was culture—including the use of fire, at least toward the end of its existence—that enabled *erectus* to survive in areas with cold climates.

Over its tenure of more than 1 million years, *H. erectus* seems to have been a remarkably stable species with only a very weak pattern of cranial capacity increase. Other features of *erectus* anatomy are also quite stable, exhibiting a very modern human appearance from their first occurrence in the archaeological record about 1.8 mya. It is not until about 400,000 ya that brain size appears to surge again, and *erectus* is replaced by a more modern-appearing fossil form: archaic *Homo sapiens*.

Study Questions

1. Briefly describe the Pleistocene Epoch.
2. How does the cranial anatomy of *Homo erectus* differ from that of *Homo habilis*?
3. What does it mean for our understanding of *Homo erectus* behavior that the Nariokotome boy (KNM-WT 15000) was, at twelve years of age, still a child?
4. Discuss the behavioral innovations of *Homo erectus*. Which of their innovations allowed them to expand beyond their African homeland?
5. During its existence for nearly 1.5 million years, was *Homo erectus* a stable or slowly changing species? How do we know?

Key Terms

Pliocene Epoch	stadial	torus
Pleistocene Epoch	interstadial	hominid radiation
paleoclimatologist	Holocene Epoch	endocast
glacier	Lower Pleistocene	basicranial
glacials	Middle Pleistocene	Acheulian
glacial periods	Upper Pleistocene	hand axe
interglacial	occipital	Movius line

For More Information

The November 1985 issue of *National Geographic* provides information on some *Homo erectus* discoveries (K. Weaver 1985). An informative although somewhat dated presentation of the *H. erectus* evidence is provided in the volume *The First Men* in the Time-Life series, *The Emergence of Man;* the artwork is appealing (The Editors of Time-Life 1973). The most thorough and recent synthesis of *erectus* can be found in G. Philip Rightmire's *The Evolution of Homo erectus: Comparative Anatomical Studies of an Extinct Human Species*. The discussion is detailed and enormously informative. See recent articles in *Archaeology Magazine* by Jean-Jacques Hublin (1996) and Roy Larick and by Russell Ciochon (1996) for a discussion of the oldest hominids in Europe and eastern Asia.

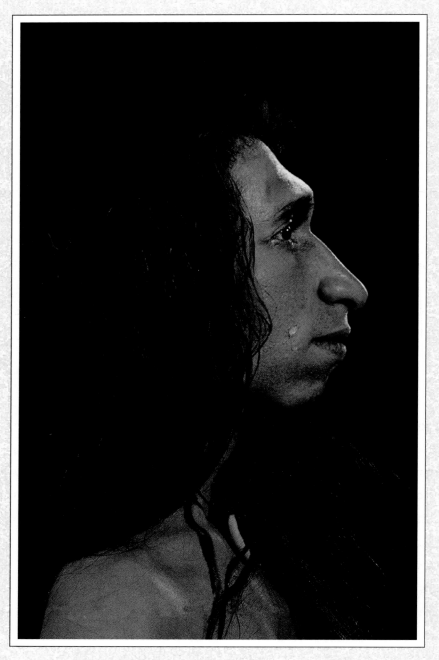

Neandertals, probably looking very much like this computer-generated photograph, were only one variety of archaic *Homo sapiens*. How are the various premodern forms of humans related to anatomically modern humans? What happened to the Neandertals? *(Kenneth Garrett/© National Geographic Society Image Collection)*

11

On the Origin of Our Species

CHAPTER CONTENTS

We have journeyed a great distance in our story of human antiquity. Beginning with a creature that appears to have been little more than an ape that walked on two feet (*Australopithecus*), we have traced the human saga through a species with an expanded braincase and the ability to make and manipulate stone tools (*Homo habilis*). These creatures were not apes, but they certainly were not *us* either. We then continued the tale with a creature (*Homo erectus*) with a braincase expanded to two-thirds of the modern human mean and whose reliance on culture, a product of its increased intelligence, allowed it to expand beyond Africa for the first time. We can easily recognize, in its appearance as well as its abilities, the developing humanity of *Homo erectus*. Yet here too, its "otherness"—its alienness—is apparent. *Homo erectus*, like *Homo habilis* before it, is familiar to us, but, again, it is not us.

Now we will confront the "person in the mirror." To be sure, it is not an exact match, for we do not see our precise image. Nevertheless, the face looking back at us is so familiar we can call this creature by the human name: genus *Homo*, species *sapiens*.

"Archaic" *Homo sapiens*

In one view, the evolutionary bush in the Lower Pleistocene had been pruned from at least four highly variable twigs—*Australopithecus africanus, Australopithecus boisei, Paranthropus robustus,* and *Homo habilis*—to a single, rather homogeneous species, *Homo erectus.* About 400,000 years ago (ya), however, our evolutionary bush branched again. The fossils who made up this twig on the evolutionary bush are called *Homo sapiens* (Figure 11.1). Although they are classified as belonging to the same species as

FIGURE 11.1 Fossil localities of archaic *Homo sapiens* (excluding Neandertals).

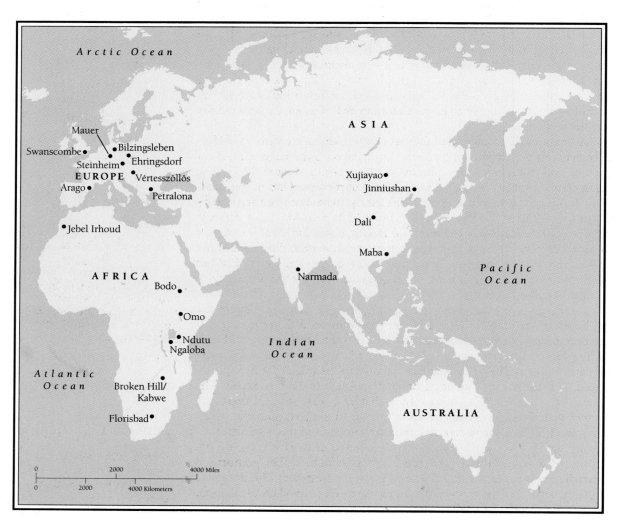

all modern human beings, they were not exactly like us. To distinguish them from anatomically modern humans, many experts characterize them as **archaic *Homo sapiens;*** whereas some researchers assign them to various nonmodern subspecies. One of the populations of these archaic humans, the Neandertals, is probably the best known and has generated the greatest amount of controversy.

Remember the discussion of biological nomenclature in Chapters 5 and 7: Calling a fossil species *Homo sapiens* is not an arbitrary act. It means that the species was so similar to us that it shares almost all our biological designations—it lived, in other words, at practically the same evolutionary address as we do. Technically, modern people are *Homo sapiens sapiens*—the second *sapiens* designating our subspecies. Subspecies designations are based on even finer distinctions than the species label. There is only one recognized human subspecies today and, as we will see in Chapter 13, all people belong in it. The archaics, on the other hand, are thought to represent an ancient and extinct subspecies—or several subspecies—of the human species. According to the rules of biological nomenclature, all the different groups of people alive today, no matter how different their appearance, are more similar to each other than any of us are to these extinct members of our species.

As mentioned at the end of the last chapter, the one consistent difference between the archaics and *H. erectus* in general is the larger cranial capacities and, therefore, bigger brains of the archaics (Figure 11.2). The mean cranial capacity of a small sample (ten) of preserved braincases of archaic *H. sapiens* (not including the Neandertals, to be discussed separately) is just over 1250 ml (Rightmire 1985; Table 11.1, p. 268). This represents a 25 percent increase over the mean for *erectus,* about 1000 ml. As we saw in comparing the skulls of *H. habilis* and *erectus,* however, the brains of the archaic *sapiens* were not just larger than those of previous hominids, but they appear to reflect a different arrangement, with greater similarity to modern humans.

Continuing the same trend seen in comparing *H. habilis* and *H. erectus,* the brains of the archaics were differently proportioned than those of earlier hominids, with a greater emphasis on the front or forebrain, and a resulting higher forehead, although the latter is not nearly as steep as in modern humans. The size of the face, relative to the rest of the head, is reduced; and the overall degree of prognathism is less than in *erectus.* The bones that make up the skulls of the archaics, at least some of them, are thinner than in older fossils and more similar to modern humans, which are quite thin. In some specimens, the brow ridges, although still spectacular by modern standards and as clearly defined as in *H. erectus,* do not dominate the face to the degree seen in earlier hominids. The **postorbital constriction**, so prominent in *erectus,* is greatly diminished. This is a result of the expansion of the front of the braincase to accommodate the increasing size of the frontal part of the brain (see Figure 11.2).

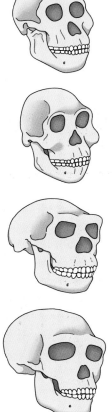

FIGURE 11.2   Comparison of cranial features of *Australopithecus (top)* with *Homo habilis, Homo erectus,* and archaic *Homo sapiens (bottom).*

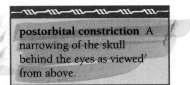

postorbital constriction A narrowing of the skull behind the eyes as viewed from above.

TABLE 11.1   Archaic *Homo sapiens* in the Late Middle Pleistocene

Country	Locality	Fossils	Age	Brain Size (ml)
Ethiopia	Bodo	Cranium	200,000–400,000	—
South Africa	Elandsfontein	Cranium	—	—
Tanzania	Ndutu (Olduvai)	Cranium	200,000	1100
Zambia	Kabwe (Broken Hill)	Cranium, additional cranial and postcranial remains of several individuals	>125,000	1280
China	Dali	Cranium	200,000	1120
	Jinniushan	Nearly complete skeleton	200,000	1350
	Maba	Cranium	130,000–170,000	—
	Xujiayao	Fragments of 11 individuals	100,000–125,000	—
India	Nardama	Cranium	150,000?	1300
England	Swanscombe	Occipital cranium and parietals	276,000–426,000	1325
France	Arago	Cranium and fragmentary remains of 7 individuals	250,000	1200
Germany	Bilzingsleben	Cranial fragments and tooth	228,000	—
	Ehringsdorf	Cranial fragment	225,000	—
	Mauer	Mandible	500,000	—
	Steinheim	Cranium	200,000–240,000	1200
Greece	Petralona	Cranium	160,000–240,000	1200
Hungary	Vértesszölös	Occipital fragment	250,000–475,000	1250

Mean 1252.50

Standard deviation 78.50

Data from Day (1986); Pope (1992); and Rightmire (1990).

FIGURE 11.3 The Kabwe (formerly called Broken Hill) specimen is one of the best-known examples of a premodern or archaic *Homo sapiens* from Africa. Note the extremely large brow ridges on this skull, which has a cranial capacity of 1280 ml, quite close to the modern mean. *(The Natural History Museum, London)*

The archaic members of our species are a varied lot. They share a brain larger than that of *H. erectus*—one within the normal human range. Beyond that, they seem to show quite a bit more variation than that seen in *erectus*. Several fossils show these contrasts clearly.

Africa

A number of fossils found in Africa, based on their general cranial form as well as their possession of cranial capacities larger than *Homo erectus* and overlapping the modern human range, are placed in the taxonomic category *Homo sapiens,* but of an archaic variety. The Broken Hill, or Kabwe, site in Zambia produced such an ancient skull (Figure 11.3). It has brow ridges larger than many of the *Homo erectus* specimens, but its cranial capacity (1280 ml) and the roundness of the skull are similar to archaic *H. sapiens.* Unfortunately, dating the fossil has been a problem; estimates ranging from 250,000 to 40,000 years have been suggested. It is probably about 125,000 years old.

In East Africa, the Ndutu skull from Tanzania has a cranial capacity of over 1100 ml and is more rounded in profile than in *H. erectus.* Also from East Africa, the Bodo fossil probably fits into the archaic human category. Ndutu and Bodo are both likely to be more than 200,000 years old; the latter may be as much as 400,000 years old. Interestingly, it has been suggested that the Bodo cranium shows evidence of defleshing (removal of

FIGURE 11.4   The nearly intact cranium of an archaic *Homo sapiens* from Steinheim, Germany. Note the more rounded appearance of the skull and the higher forehead than in *Homo erectus*. However, also note the large brow ridges. *(State Museum for Nature, Stuttgart, Germany)*

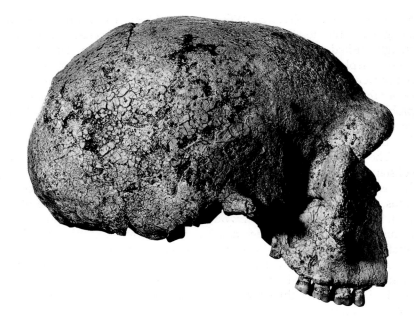

skin) for some unknown purpose. Paleoanthropologist Tim White (1986) identified thirteen areas on the skull where scanning electron microphotographs show clusters of what appear to be cut marks made by stone tools.

A number of more modern-looking specimens from Africa probably date to about 200,000 years ago (Brauer 1984; Rightmire 1984). Among these we can include the fossils from Jebel Irhoud in Morocco (although the dating is uncertain), Florisbad in southern Africa (now dated to 259,000 ya [Grün et al. 1996]), and Ngaloba from Tanzania.

Also in Africa, two skulls found about 1 kilometer apart near the Omo River in Ethiopia are important. The layer in which the Omo 1 skull was recovered has been radiometrically dated to about 130,000 B.P. Omo 2, found some distance away, may be from the same stratigraphic level, but it cannot be dated with certainty. The Omo skulls have cranial capacities of about 1400 ml but are quite different in appearance. Omo 2 exhibits a mixture of primitive and modern characteristics. Omo 1, which is surprisingly modern-looking, is discussed in Chapter 12.

Europe

In 1933 the cranium of an archaic *Homo sapiens* was found in a gravel pit adjacent to the Murr River, in the town of Steinheim, just north of

Stuttgart, Germany (Howell 1960) (Figure 11.4). The skull was found along with the fossil remains of several extinct species, including a straight-tusked elephant, wild ox, cave bear, and cave lion. The straight-tusked elephant was adapted to life in woodlands, suggesting that these bones were deposited during an interglacial or relatively mild early glacial rather than a full-blown glacial period. Although dating the skull has been problematic, an electron spin resonance date indicates that it is probably between 200,000 and 240,000 years old (Ikeya 1982). No artifacts were found with the hominid remains.

The skull is long and relatively narrow. Although the brow ridges are substantial, they are smaller than in most *Homo erectus* specimens. The face is flat and rather small, as in modern humans. There is no occipital torus, giving the rear of the skull a modern appearance. The bone of the skull is thinner than in *H. erectus* but thicker than in modern humans. The cranial capacity has been estimated at just below 1200 ml, toward the small end of the modern human range but large for *erectus*.

Another probable example of archaic *Homo sapiens* was found in Swanscombe, England, in 1935 (Howell 1960; Ovey 1964). The Swanscombe find includes three major skull fragments: the back (*occipital*) and both sides (**parietals**). Remarkably, the three fragments, which fit together perfectly, were found over a period of more than twenty years and were located as much as 50 feet away from each other.

The face was missing, so it is difficult, if not impossible, to judge brow ridge size or the degree of prognathism. The skull is nevertheless informative. The bone itself is quite thick, as in older specimens. Additionally, in a detailed analysis of seventeen cranial measurements (Weiner and Campbell 1964), it was concluded that in many respects the skull is quite similar to *Homo erectus*. A few characteristics of the Swanscombe skull, though, are more modern. As in Steinheim, the occiput shows little sign of a torus. Beyond this, the skull is quite large, with an estimated cranial capacity of over 1300 ml. This places the brain size of this fossil well within the modern human range, though, it must be said, its general appearance is a mosaic of ancestral and modern traits.

The skull fragments were found in a gravel deposit along with the fossilized remains of wolf, lion, straight-tusked elephant, horse, ox, deer, and rhinoceros. A radiometric date (uranium series) for this associated material was calculated at 326,000 B.P. (Szabo and Collins 1975). The margin of error for this date, however, is large, and the skull could be 100,000 years older or 50,000 years younger. Flint tools, including hand axes and flakes, were found in the same deposit.

A cavern at Petralona, southeast of Thessalonika, Greece, was investigated in 1959. Initially, only fossilized animal bones were discovered, but in 1960 an ancient-looking and very well-preserved hominid skull was found in a stalagmite deposit (Poulianos 1971–72). The Petralona skull

parietals The bones of the sides and top of the skull.

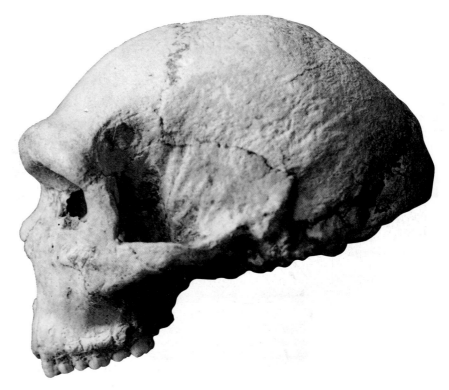

FIGURE 11.5 The Petralona skull from Greece is clearly that of an archaic *Homo sapiens*. The skull was discovered in a cave near Thessalonika, the rest of the skeleton apparently was lost. (*Christopher B. Stringer*)

possesses very large brow ridges, but it is rounder and the face is flatter than in *Homo erectus* (Figure 11.5). The cranial capacity is judged to have surpassed 1200 ml.

Although its cranial vault is similar to that of the later Neandertals, some of its cranial measurements are reminiscent of the Zhoukoudian *Homo erectus*. Christopher Stringer (1974) concluded that Petralona represents an early form of *Homo sapiens*, even though it possesses a mixture of traits.

Animal bones found in the cave included cave bear, cave lion, several kinds of deer, wolf, and rhinoceros. The mix of animals indicates a possible contemporaneity with the Steinheim skull, suggesting an interglacial date corresponding to stage 7 on the oxygen isotope curve (see Figure 10.3). The skull, however, could be much older or much younger—it may have washed into the cave from somewhere else. Electron spin resonance performed on an encrustation on the skull resulted in a date between 160,000 and 240,000 ya (Henning et al. 1981).

Several other examples of archaic *Homo sapiens* have come from Eu-

FIGURE 11.6   The Arago skull from France, deformed after deposition, shows the typical array of archaic characteristics. Note the very large brow ridges. (*The Institute of Human Paleontology, Paris. H. de Lumley*)

rope. Material associated with a small occipital fragment found in Vértesszöllös, Hungary, has produced a uranium series date of between 250,000 and 475,000 ya (Gamble 1986). The bone is rather thick, and there is an indication of an occipital torus, but the extrapolated cranial capacity is larger than in *Homo erectus*. At Arago, near the village of Tautavel, France, the fragmentary remains of at least four adult and three juvenile hominids were found (Cook et al. 1982). The best preserved of these is a distorted face with large, thick brow ridges (Figure 11.6). The Arago fossils appear to represent archaic *H. sapiens* dating to more than 250,000 ya (Gamble 1986).

In Germany, the Bilzingsleben site produced two occipitals, two frontal bones, and a molar. These were found together with about 60,000 flint flakes reflecting a range of scraping tools, awls, points, and chopping tools (Gamble 1986). A minimum age of 228,000 B.P. has been calculated (Harmon et al. 1980). An adult skull fragment was also found in Ehringsdorf, Germany, and dated to 225,000 B.P. (Cook et al. 1982). Bifacially worked points and scrapers were also found at this site.

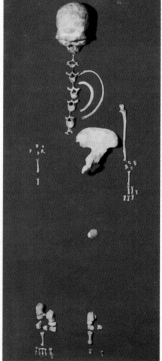

FIGURE 11.7   This specimen from Yingkou in the Jinniushan Mountains is one of the most complete archaic human fossils outside of Europe. Dating to about 200,000 years ago, it possesses a cranial capacity between 1330 and 1390 ml. A sizeable proportion of the postcranial skeleton also was recovered. (*China Pictorial Photo Service*)

Asia

The Dali cranium with a cranial capacity of 1120 ml and an estimated age of 200,000 years and the nearly complete skeleton found at Yingkou, called "Jinniushan Man" (Lu 1987; Pope 1988) represent Asian examples of archaic *H. sapiens*. The nearly complete cranium of Jinniushan Man presents a cranial capacity of between 1330 and 1390 ml, far larger than *Homo erectus* and well within the modern human range (Figure 11.7) (Chen et al. 1994). Electron spin resonance and uranium series dating procedures suggest that Jinnuishan is nearly 200,000 years old. In southern China, the Maba specimen, a partial skullcap, is reminiscent of the European Neandertals to be discussed later in this chapter. It has been dated to between 130,000 and 170,000 years ago. Xujiayao in Shanxi Province has produced a series of hominid remains that seem to belong in the general category of archaic *Homo sapiens*. Dating from about 100,000 to 125,000 years ago, the eleven individuals exhibit a form midway between that of Chinese *Homo erectus* specimens from Zhoukoudian and modern *Homo sapiens* (Pope 1992).

The Narmada cranium found in central India is another early representative of our species. The dating of the specimen is not entirely clear, and its analysts recognize some affinities with the Ngandong crania (Kennedy et al. 1991:492). Nevertheless, its estimated cranial capacity of about 1300 ml and a range of anatomical traits comparable to those seen in the fossils from Petralona, Bilzingsleben, Kabwe, Dali, Steinheim, and Swanscombe supports its identification as an early *Homo sapiens* (Kennedy et al. 1991).

The Culture of Archaic Humans

Having introduced you to a sample of archaic *Homo sapiens*, it must be admitted that, beyond knowing what they looked like, researchers are certain about little else. Several of the discoveries were accidental and made by nonscientists with no training in proper techniques of excavation. Nor is there much in the way of habitation remains dating to the period 400,000 to 100,000 ya that could reveal something about their culture.

One aspect of their culture, however, is fairly well represented: stone tool technology. Many aspects of earlier Middle Pleistocene technology continued among these hominids. They continued making Acheulian hand axes and using the larger flakes that resulted from the hand axe–manufacturing process.

About 200,000 ya, however, these archaic *H. sapiens* made a great advance in stone toolmaking. They invented a technique of preparing cores according to a regular pattern that ensured a certain degree of consistency in the stone flakes removed. In other words, they did not simply rely on

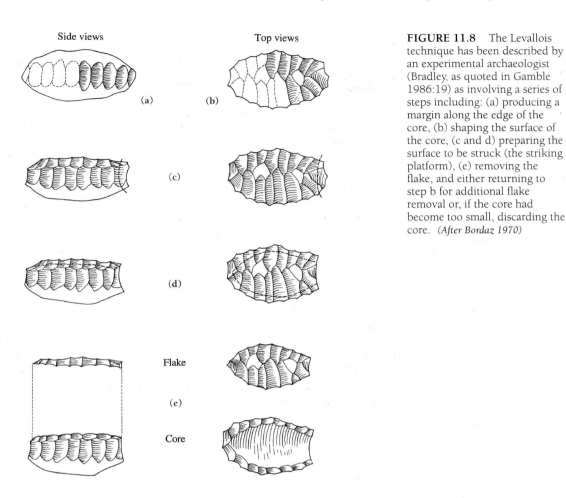

Side views   Top views

(a)   (b)

(c)

(d)

Flake

(e)

Core

FIGURE 11.8   The Levallois technique has been described by an experimental archaeologist (Bradley, as quoted in Gamble 1986:19) as involving a series of steps including: (a) producing a margin along the edge of the core, (b) shaping the surface of the core, (c and d) preparing the surface to be struck (the striking platform), (e) removing the flake, and either returning to step b for additional flake removal or, if the core had become too small, discarding the core. (*After Bordaz 1970*)

accidentally well-shaped flakes to make tools but developed a technique for controlling the shape of the flakes. The new technique is called **Levallois** after the Paris suburb where it initially was recognized.

Before Levallois, stone tools were either core tools like the Oldowan choppers of *Homo habilis* or the Acheulian hand axes of *Homo erectus* or else they were made from flakes that came off cores and happened to meet the needs of the toolmaker; undoubtedly, a certain amount of luck was involved in this process. With Levallois, in contrast, we see a great deal of forethought in the preparation of the stone core to ensure that a number of flakes of the desired shape would ultimately be produced; this "predetermination" of flake shape through careful preparation of the core from which the flakes are removed is a key feature of the Levallois technique (Van Peer 1992) (Figure 11.8). The core reduction process involves more

Levallois A tool technology involving striking flakes from a prepared core.

work in the beginning but results in better flake "blanks," which can then be made into specific cutting, scraping, or piercing tools. The technique was also more efficient, getting more sharp edge for the amount of stone started with.

In an experiment designed to analyze the Levallois technique, Bradley (1977, cited in Gamble 1986) produced twenty Levallois cores from flint blocks. He found that he could usually strike off four or five similarly shaped flakes from a core before it became too small to use. Preshaping the core was the key to controlling and standardizing the shape of the flakes. The Levallois technique was clearly a more complex way of producing flake blanks and also more effective and efficient than any previous method.

Beyond their stone tool technology, the archaics showed little else in the way of cultural innovation. This is perplexing considering the increase in their brain size compared to *H. erectus*. But perhaps something else can be suggested about these earliest members of our species. In Europe, they managed to survive during a period of great climate change—the ending of an interglacial (isotope stage 7) and the beginning of a glacial (isotope stage 6). In all likelihood, glacial periods came on slowly relative to the length of a human generation. The ability of a *culture* to change over several generations, however, reflects a flexibility that suggests modern humanity.

Archaic humans were faced with substantial changes in their environment. Animal species on which they relied became extinct or migrated. Plants on which they depended for food, fuel, and construction materials changed in response to the fluctuations in climate as well. Seasonal duration and intensity shifted, with longer, deeper winters and shorter, cooler springs and summers. Subsistence activities must have changed to meet the demands of nature's shift in seasons. Whereas other species, biologically adapted to specific environments, were forced to move or die, archaic humans—with their *cultural* adaptations—were able to remain and thrive by changing their way of life. This flexibility allowed for their continued existence under new, drastically different circumstances.

The Neandertals: A Special Case

Neandertal. The name itself has entered our language as an insult. People use the term to describe someone who is stupid, violent, brutish. The first artistic reconstruction of a Neandertal based on an actual skeleton appeared in the French magazine *L'Illustration* in 1909 (Figure 11.9). The image is a grotesque caricature of a hairy, ape-human beast. We now know that the Neandertals and their culture bore little similarity to this caricature.

FIGURE 11.9   The first artist's conception of a Neandertal as it appeared in the popular press, first in the French magazine *L'Illustration* and soon thereafter in the *Illustrated London News* (March 6, 1909). This reconstruction set the precedent for subsequent depictions of the Neandertals as apelike, primitive beasts. (Illustrated London News, *March 6, 1909. Artist: Kupka*)

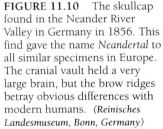

FIGURE 11.10   The skullcap found in the Neander River Valley in Germany in 1856. This find gave the name *Neandertal* to all similar specimens in Europe. The cranial vault held a very large brain, but the brow ridges betray obvious differences with modern humans. (*Reinisches Landesmuseum, Bonn, Germany*)

The Concept of "Neandertal"

The fossil that gives us the name was discovered by workers in the Neander Valley in the Rhine Province of Germany in 1856 (Figure 11.10). Only the top of the skull was recovered, but this fragment was enough to make the Neandertal fossil an enigma. It was a relatively large skull, with a cranial capacity apparently larger than the modern mean, but with a flattened forehead and enormous, thick brow ridges. These characteristics gave the skull an apelike look, not at all what people in the nineteenth century expected a human ancestor to look like. People were just getting used to the general notion of biological evolution and its specific application to our own species. The Neandertal skull simply looked too apelike for most to accord it a place in the human lineage.

Those who accepted the notion of human evolution had expected the discovery of a "missing link," a creature part-ape, part-human. (This assumption explains the reception of the Piltdown hoax decades later.) As mentioned in Chapter 8, because what most clearly distinguishes us from other animals is our intelligence, the assumption was that the brain had evolved first. Those looking for a missing link expected it to be primitive from the neck down but to have an advanced, almost modern head. The Neandertal skull did not meet that expectation.

Though a few similar-looking skulls had already been discovered in Europe, these had not generated great interest, but the find in the Neander Valley produced a large amount of publicity and public attention (Kennedy 1975; Trinkaus and Shipman 1993). Scientists pondered the significance of the skull in terms of human evolution. Many decided that it could not have been a human ancestor but was, instead, a pathological oddity—a relatively recent, deformed individual. One well-known anatomist, Rudolf Virchow, even suggested that the large brow ridges were the result of blows to the head.

As more Neandertals were found, however, it became impossible to ignore their evolutionary significance. Many specimens were discovered, especially in caves. Nevertheless, even with general acceptance of this group as an ancient, primitive variety of human, biases and preconceptions (and, as it turns out, misconceptions) have colored scientific interpretations of Neandertal's place in the human family (Trinkaus and Shipman 1993; Stringer and Gamble 1993).

In 1913 the French anthropologist Marcellin Boule produced one of the most important and influential reconstructions of Neandertal (Boule and Vallois 1923) (Figure 11.11). Unfortunately, his model was riddled with errors. Most of the mistakes stemmed from Boule's preconception that Neandertals did not fit into the human evolutionary mainstream. Having already decided that they were very primitive, he exaggerated their differences from modern humans and ignored their similarities. His reconstruction had the Neandertals barely upright with their heads so far forward they could hardly stand, shoulders hunched, and knees bent. He even gave them an opposable big toe similar to that of the apes.

It has been thought that Boule's reconstruction of a stooped-over individual resulted from the fact that the skeleton he used, from the French cave of La Chapelle-aux-Saints, was actually an aged man crippled by arthritis. We now know that this was not the case (Trinkaus 1985). Al-

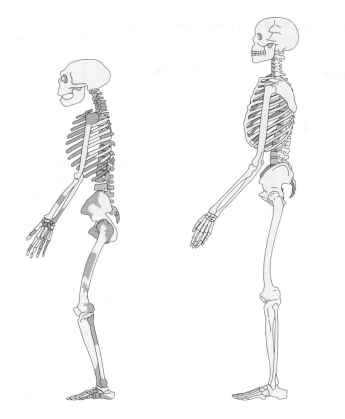

FIGURE 11.11 Marcellin Boule's reconstruction of the skeleton of the so-called Old Man of La Chapelle-aux-Saints *(left)* compared to that of a modern human. Boule, who regarded the Neandertals as primitive, reconstructed the skeleton in a way that made it appear apelike with bowed legs and head thrust forward. *(From Fossil Men by Marcellin Boule and Henri Vallois, Dryden Press [CBS Educational and Professional Publishing])*

though the individual did suffer from degenerative bone disease, those areas of the skeleton most directly involved would not have affected his ability to walk to any great degree. Beyond this, Boule had two other perfectly normal Neandertal specimens (La Ferrassie 1 and 2) in his lab at the time and also used them in his reconstruction. More likely, Boule simply reconstructed the "typical" Neandertal as apelike because that is how he expected it to look. After Boule, even reconstructions of facial characteristics emphasized the primitive; in most, Neandertal was given a vacuous and rather stupid expression—an open mouth and dazed look contribute to this impression. Certainly these characteristics were not indicated by the actual fossil skulls.

Neandertals: Not Brutes, but Not Us

When examining the evolution of the Neandertals, we cannot help but consider the evolution of thinking about them. Since Boule's time, researchers have revised their opinions of the Neandertals so greatly that recently these archaics were considered quite advanced and virtually

FIGURE 11.12 A recent display at the Neandertal Museum in Erkrath, Germany, posing a clean-shaven, chicly coiffed Neandertal in a business suit. He would hardly be noticed in any world city. *(Kenneth Garrett/© National Geographic Society Image Collection)*

modern in appearance and behavior (see Figure 11.12 and *The Neandertals* [Constable 1973] in the Time-Life series, *The Emergence of Man*). Their physical appearance was reassessed, and reconstructions of the face became much more human. Often, merely choosing to depict the Neandertal face as shaven and clean did wonders for its appearance (see, for example, the artwork in the article by Boyce Rensberger in the October issue of *Science 81*). Opinion had shifted so far that until recently the Neandertals have been considered by just about all researchers to be an archaic subspecies of *Homo sapiens,* specifically, *Homo sapiens neanderthalensis.* In fact, by 1957, W. L. Straus and A. J. E. Cave could generate little disagreement when they said: "If he could be reincarnated and placed in a New York subway—provided that he were bathed, shaved, and dressed in modern clothing—it is doubtful whether he would attract any more attention than some of its other denizens" (1957:359). In an article published in *Newsweek* in 1989, Sharon Begley and Fiona Gleizes maintain, "With a decent shave he would be hard to distinguish from the linebacker at the next table" (1989:70).

Just as Boule and other researchers at the turn of the century exaggerated alleged primitive features of the Neandertals, however, more recent scientists and writers have exaggerated the degree of similarity these archaics show to modern humans. Although they were by no means primitive brutes, Neandertals did differ in some important ways from modern humans in their cranial as well as postcranial characteristics (Trinkaus

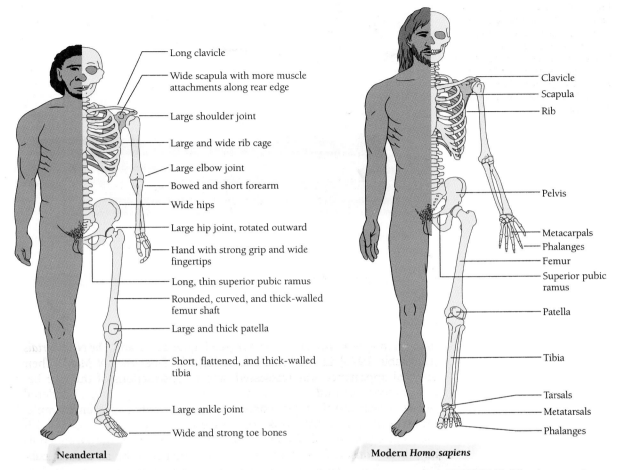

Long clavicle

Wide scapula with more muscle attachments along rear edge

Large shoulder joint

Large and wide rib cage

Large elbow joint

Bowed and short forearm

Wide hips

Large hip joint, rotated outward

Hand with strong grip and wide fingertips

Long, thin superior pubic ramus

Rounded, curved, and thick-walled femur shaft

Large and thick patella

Short, flattened, and thick-walled tibia

Large ankle joint

Wide and strong toe bones

Clavicle
Scapula
Rib

Pelvis

Metacarpals
Phalanges
Femur
Superior pubic ramus

Patella

Tibia

Tarsals
Metatarsals
Phalanges

Neandertal

Modern *Homo sapiens*

FIGURE 11.13   A comparison of the skeletons of a modern human and a Neandertal. Though previous reconstructions of the Neandertals as apelike are no longer accepted, the "musculo-skeletal hypertrophy" of the Neandertals is readily apparent. (*From* **In Search of the Neanderthals** *by Christopher Stringer and Clive Gamble. Published with permission of the publisher, Thames and Hudson Ltd.)*

1988). As Erik Trinkaus and Pat Shipman put it, they were not "simply funny looking humans" (1993:385), but different in significant ways (Figure 11.13).

For example, Neandertal skulls are immediately recognizable as different from those of modern humans. Although their cranial capacity ranged from about 1300 ml to 1640 ml, well within the modern span, the front part of their skulls was rather flat. The back of their skulls was broad, and the sides were bulging. Their brow ridges were not straight, as in earlier *H. sapiens,* but were rounded over each eye orbit. The ridges were thick, long, and protruding, although not as large as in some of the earlier archaics. The Neandertal face was large and prognathous, with broad cheeks, a wide nose, and widely set eyes. The mandible showed little development of a chin, unique to modern humans. These characteristics, which readily dis-

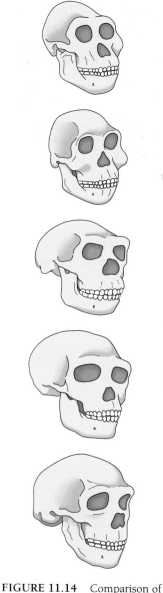

FIGURE 11.14 Comparison of cranial features of *Australopithecus (top)* with *Homo habilis, Homo erectus,* archaic *Homo sapiens,* and Neandertal.

tinguish Neandertals from modern humans, can be seen even in their infants. The recently excavated 10-month-old Neandertal baby from Amud Cave in Israel lacks a chin and exhibits areas for muscle attachment on the interior of the jaw much larger than in modern human babies (Hovers, Rak, and Kimbell 1996) (Figure 11.14 and Figure 11.15).

Below the neck, Neandertals exhibit consistent, significant differences from modern humans as well. Certainly, they were fully bipedal, and we need not resurrect Boule's image of awkward balance. We now recognize that Neandertal traits previously misinterpreted as primitive or apelike are really just physical adaptations for great strength, part of an overall adaptation for life in Europe during some of the glacial maxima of the later Pleistocene. On close inspection, almost all Neandertal bones show a robustness and enlargement of the areas of muscle attachment that are either at the limit or beyond the range of modern human variation (Trinkaus 1983a). Paleoanthropologist Fred Smith put it most succinctly when summarizing these data: "Neandertals seem to represent the high-water mark for the genus *Homo* in favoring the brawn approach to environmental adaptation" (1991:225).

For example, their ribs display a thickness and heaviness that reflect great size and strength in shoulder and back muscles. Neandertal shoulder blades (**scapulae,** singular *scapula*) similarly display the enormous power of Neandertal musculature in comparison with modern humans (Churchill and Trinkaus 1990). In comparing Neandertal upper-arm bones (**humeri,** singular *humerus*) with fossil and recent modern humans, researchers found a clear pattern of greater strength and weight in the Neandertal specimens (Ben-Itzhak et al. 1988).

Neandertal leg bones show this same pattern of size and strength. When C. Owen Lovejoy and Erik Trinkaus (1980) subjected three Neandertal tibia and a sample of modern American Indian and European tibia to a test of twisting and bending strength, they found the Neandertal bones to be twice as strong as the modern human examples. Neandertal stamina for walking must have been impressive.

Even in the hands, Neandertal bones display evidence of enormous strength and power. In an extremely detailed comparative analysis of the finger bones (**phalanges**) of Neandertals and modern human beings, Eric Trinkaus and Isabelle Villemeur (1991) have shown that the relative proportions of the bones in the Neandertal thumb provided them with a grip far more powerful than that exhibited by modern human beings. Neandertal stone toolmakers may have been able to perform actions that both earlier and subsequent hominids could not.

The pattern is clear and consistent; when Neandertal bones are compared with their counterparts in anatomically modern human beings, both fossil and contemporary, the Neandertals almost always come out on top when it comes to features of strength and power. Simply put, Neandertals were strong, powerful creatures, exhibiting anatomical features of the skeleton related to muscle size, power, and strength that fall beyond the

FIGURE 11.15 Modern computer technology was used to combine a photograph of a modern human being and a series of photographs of Neandertal crania, creating this remarkable image of a Neandertal profile. This "virtual" Neandertal is as close as we can come to seeing a living, breathing Neandertal. *(Kenneth Garrett/© National Geographic Society Image Collection)*

range of modern human beings. While some experts seem to have believed that all Neandertal needed was a shower and a shave to pass muster on the cover of *Gentlemen's Quarterly,* scientist and writer Jared Diamond is closer to the truth when he states, "While a Neandertal in a business suit would attract your attention, one in shorts or a bikini would be even more startling" (1989:54).

Some researchers argue that the postcranial differences between Neandertals and modern humans are genetically based rather than simply the result of a more active lifestyle by the Neandertals (Ben-Itzhak et al. 1988:241). The differences are so extreme, they maintain, they must be the result of biological adaptation. Beyond this, these differences are seen not only between the Neandertals and present-day humans (with our relatively easy lifestyle), but also between Neandertals and ancient modern humans, who lived lives that must have been not all that different from the Neandertals.

Physical anthropologist Patricia Bridges (1996) has questioned this interpretation. She agrees that in most measurements, Neandertal skeletons are more robust and, therefore, probably exhibited greater strength than most modern humans. Interestingly, though, she points out that the one group of modern humans who approach the Neandertals in terms of their

scapula (plural *scapulae*)
The shoulder blade.

humerus (plural *humeri*)
The bone of the upper arm.

phalange (plural *phalanges*)
A finger or toe bone.

level of upper arm bone robusticity (and therefore, strength) and degree of asymmetry (with one arm much stronger than the other) is professional tennis players. The great strength of one arm over the other in tennis players is the result of their behavior, not determined by genetics. As Bridges points out, the same could be true for the Neandertals.

Neandertal bodily proportions, with relatively short distal limb segments (that is, the lower arms and lower legs) and a broad torso, also differ from modern humans. These proportions were probably adaptive (Trinkaus 1983a). Such a configuration is common in cold-adapted mammals because body heat loss increases with the surface area of the organism, and limbs expose a proportionally large amount of surface to the elements. Among modern people, those living nearest the Arctic have proportionally the shortest lower limbs, and those living nearest the equator have the longest. As anthropologist Christopher Ruff (1993) points out, the form of the Neandertal body is similar to that of the modern Inuit (Eskimo).

Recent analysis of Neandertal pelvises also shows significant differences from modern humans. A nearly complete 60,000-year-old Neandertal pelvis was excavated in Kebara Cave on Mt. Carmel, Israel, by Yoel Rak and Baruch Arensberg (1987; Rak 1990). They identified this specimen as belonging to a male. These researchers maintain that the pelvic outlet in this specimen was differently shaped but not larger than it is in modern humans.

Rak (1990) compared the Neandertal Kebara pelvis to the fossil pelvis of an anatomically modern human being found just 35 kilometers away (from the site of Qafzeh; see Chapter 12). His study reinforces the assertion that the configuration of the Neandertal pelvis was significantly different from the modern human one. The Neandertal pubic bone is long, thin, and flat when compared to a modern human's. This difference, Rak maintains, reflects differences of posture and locomotion. If Rak and Arensberg are correct, Neandertals and modern humans differ significantly in the biomechanics of their locomotion.

M. C. Dean, Christopher Stringer, and T. G. Bromage (1986) analyzed the cranial remains of a Neandertal child from Gibraltar. They concluded that the child died at age 3 and that his cranial development was advanced when compared to a modern human's of the same age. They believe that Neandertal children were probably more developed at birth than are modern humans and that Neandertals developed more quickly after birth.

It should be apparent that the Neandertals and modern humans were, in some important ways, physically quite different from each other. Reconstruction of Neandertals as virtually identical to modern humans is almost as much a caricature as Boule's image of the primitive brute. As a result of the now-recognized differences between the Neandertals and modern humans (and other extinct archaics), the idea has been resurrected that the Neandertals do not belong in the species *sapiens* at all, but deserve the status of a separate species, *Homo neanderthalensis* (Gould 1988). The irony here is that this is what Boule suggested more than seventy years ago. Al-

FIGURE 11.16 Cranium of one of the more complete pre-Neandertal specimens from Sima de los Huesos (the "Pit of the Bones") in the Atapuerca Mountains, Spain. The Sima de los Huesos hominids have been dated to about 300,000 years ago and have been shown to possess many of the anatomical features of the later Neandertals. (© *Javier Trueba/Madrid Scientific Films*)

though for the wrong reasons, he may have been right about Neandertal's place in human evolution after all.

The Neandertal Fossils

The Neandertals are now recognized as having very deep roots in Europe. In one of the more spectacular finds, more than 1600 bones representing remains of at least thirty-two and as many as fifty individuals have thus far been recovered from a spectacular site in a cave called Sima de los Huesos ("Pit of the Bones") in the Atapuerca Mountains of northern Spain (Figure 11.16) (Bahn 1996; Arsuaga et al. 1993). Remarkably, this site is located only a few hundred meters from the Gran Dolina site that has produced the oldest hominids in Europe (see Chapter 10).

The bones have been recovered from beneath a layer in the cave that has been dated to more than 300,000 years in age. The researchers characterize the crania of the two adults and one child thus far recovered as Neandertal-like and as anticipating the Neandertal cranial form (Arsuaga et al. 1993:535). Cranial capacities have been measured at 1125 and 1390 ml for the two adults and 1100 ml for the juvenile. Preliminary analysis by paleoanthropologist Chris Stringer indicates that of fifteen typical Neandertal cranial and postcranial characteristics, the Atapuerca hominids exhibit ten, or two-thirds (Stringer 1993). These fossils have less in common with either *Homo erectus* or modern *Homo sapiens*.

These very early Neandertals—or pre-Neandertals—from northern Spain share some features with the archaic *Homo sapiens* from Europe already discussed. Stringer (1993) proposes that the Atapuerca fossils and most if not all of the other European archaics represent a single, variable group of hominids, whose differences are the result of geographic distance and time. In this view, the Atapuerca fossils imply a gradual evolution of Neandertal in Europe through time.

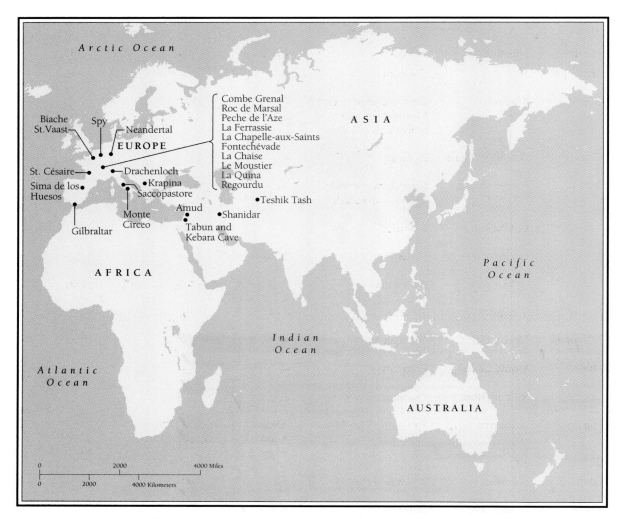

FIGURE 11.17 Neandertal fossil localities. This distribution shows quite clearly that the Neandertals were essentially a European and Southwest Asian population.

In the rest of Europe, Neandertal remains date to more recent periods. Two fragmentary Neandertal crania have been recovered in France at the site of Biache Saint-Vaast; these are now dated to 230,000 years ago. But the majority of Neandertal sites—where the remains of more than 400 individuals have been recovered—date to a period after the juncture of isotope stages 5 and 6 (see Figure 10.3) of the Upper Pleistocene, about 130,000 ya (Figure 11.17 and Table 11.2). For example, the Krapina finds in Croatia consist of the fragmentary remains of at least 45 and as many as 65 individuals (Trinkaus and Thompson 1987). Although very broken up, they appear to have large brow ridges and fairly rugged occiputs; cranial capacity estimates range from 1200 ml to 1450 ml. They are dated to about 130,000 years ago.

TABLE 11.2   Major Neandertal Specimens

Country	Locality	Fossils	Cranium	Age	Brain Size (ml)
Belgium	Spy	Cranium	—	—	—
Croatia	Krapina	Cranial and postcranial fragments of >45 individuals	—	130,000	1200–1450
France	Biache St. Vaast	2 crania	—	230,000	—
	Fontechévade	Cranial fragments of several individuals	—	100,000	1500
	La Chaise	Cranium	—	126,000	—
	La Chappelle	Skeleton	"Old Man"	—	1620
	La Ferrassie	8 skeletons	LF-1	>38,000	1680
	St. Césaire	Skeleton	—	36,000	—
Germany	Neandertal	Skullcap	—	—	>1250
Italy	Monte Circeo	Cranium	—	—	—
	Saccopastore	Cranium	—	—	—
Spain	Atapuerca	Remains of 32–50 individuals	Adult	>300,000	1125
			Adult	>300,000	1390
			Juvenile	>300,000	1100
Iraq	Shanidar	9 partial skeletons	S-1	70,000	1600
Israel	Amud Cave	Skeleton	A-1	70,000	1740
	Kebara Cave	Postcranial skeleton	—	60,000	—
	Tabun	Skeleton, mandible, postcranial fragments	T-1	60,000	1270

With Atapuerca: Mean	1410.42
Standard deviation	181.32
Without Atapuerca: Mean	1478.89
Standard deviation	165.68

Data from Day (1986) and Arsuaga et al. (1993).

FIGURE 11.18 A Neandertal skull from La Ferrassie, France, exhibits many of the typical Neandertal features. The skull also shows the degree of variation among Neandertals because it is relatively rounded, with a high forehead. (*Museum of Man, Paris*)

The Fontechévade skull fragments also are possible early Neandertals dating to this period. Found in a cave in France, they were recovered under a stalagmite layer and may be more than 100,000 years old (Gamble 1986). Although the remains are fragmentary, cranial capacity has been estimated at just under 1500 ml.

It was isotope stage 4, however, that witnessed an apparent flowering of Neandertal population and culture in Europe and Southwest Asia (Trinkaus 1986). Neandertal sites dating to between 80,000 and 40,000 ya are abundant in these areas. Sites include Le Moustier, La Chapelle-aux-Saints, La Quina, Regourdu, La Ferrassie, Pech de l'Aze, Roc de Marsal, and Combe Grenal, all in France; Monte Circeo and Saccopastore in Italy; Spy in Belgium; Gibraltar on the southern tip of the Iberian Peninsula; and the Neandertal Valley in Germany (Figure 11.18). Outside Europe, examples of fossils similar to the European or "Classic" Neandertals have been recovered in Shanidar in Iraq, Teshik Tash in Uzbekistan, and Amud and Tabun in Israel (Figure 11.19). An additional group of even more modern-looking fossils that still exhibit some Neandertal traits is known from the Middle East. This last group will be discussed in more detail in Chapter 12.

Neandertal Culture

Just as the reconstruction of the physical appearance of the Neandertals has drastically changed, so too have ideas about their behavior. Here again, the initial verdict of brutishness and savagery was replaced by the other extreme, seeing them as kind and gentle souls. Neither of these views accurately describes Neandertal behavior.

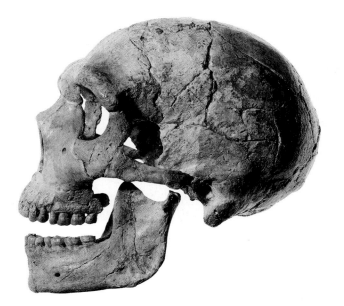

FIGURE 11.19   The Amud Neandertal cranium from Israel is quite similar to those from Europe, indicating, at least in part, the geographic range of this variety of archaic *Homo sapiens.* (© *Israel Antiquities Authority*)

The European Neandertals were certainly highly intelligent and adaptive hominids who faced the extreme climate of a glacial maximum. During such extended cold periods, large portions of the forested land of central Europe were transformed into arcticlike **tundra**—virtually treeless expanses covered by ground-hugging bushes, mosses, and lichens. Those trees that survived in this climate were all cold-loving conifers, grouped in bunches, few and far between. Into this environment moved great numbers of woolly rhinoceros and mammoth, bison, horse, reindeer, and musk ox (Kurtén 1968).

The Neandertals flourished in this seemingly forbidding climate. They became adapted to life on the windswept tundra, scavenging and perhaps hunting large game animals, collecting what vegetable foods they could in season, and controlling fire. Although these Neandertals may have possessed a physical adaptation to the cold, it was their culture that enabled them to survive in the freezing world of Europe during the last glacial period.

Tool Technology

The Neandertals continued the Levallois technique of flake removal observed in earlier archaics and elaborated on it. The stone tool tradition of the Neandertals, called **Mousterian** after the French site of Le Moustier, is technically characterized as a retouched flake technology. This means that the Neandertals removed from cores the flakes that they then proceeded to

tundra A treeless expanse with low-growing vegetation and permanently frozen ground.

Mousterian The flake tool culture associated with European and southwest Asian Neandertals.

sharpen or shape by precise additional flaking, usually on a single face or side of the flake but occasionally on both faces. Using this method, the Neandertals produced cutting, scraping, and piercing tools (Figure 11.20). They also continued the tradition of making bifacially flaked hand axes in some areas.

The Mousterian industry exhibits a much greater level of variation than did the earlier Acheulian. One of Europe's preeminent prehistorians, François Bordes, identified sixty-three tool types and twenty-one hand-axe forms in a detailed analysis of the Mousterian (Bordes 1972). He notes that these different tool categories do not all appear at all sites. Instead, Bordes maintains, at least five different groupings of the sixty-three categories can be recognized in Europe. He interprets these as representing the toolmaking traditions of five and possibly more distinct Mousterian cultures that "co-existed in the same territory but influenced each other very little" (1972:146).

Lewis and Sally Binford offer a contrasting view (Binford and Binford 1966; S. Binford 1968). Using a statistical approach called factor analysis, they found that there were indeed five discernible groupings of the sixty-three artifact types, but that these could be explained on functional grounds. They suggest that the groupings do not reflect the different traditions of coexisting, noninteracting Mousterian people but that these clusters reflect different toolkits used for different functions—such as hunting, making tools of bone and antler, and plant processing—by the same people in different places.

Archaeologist Harold Dibble (1987) has suggested a third possibility for one tool category: The different types of scraping tools defined by Bordes reflect different stages in the use histories of these tools. According to Dibble, single-edged, double-edged, and converging-edged scrapers do not reflect different styles of separate groups of people, nor do they represent different functions. When scrapers with a single edge got dull, he proposes, the users sharpened a second edge; as more edge was sharpened, the edges converged.

A recent analysis of Neandertal tool function was conducted by archaeologist John Shea (1989). Focusing on wear patterns (see Chapter 7) of tools recovered from Kebara Cave, Shea noted patterns that suggested various activities: animal butchering, woodworking, bone and antler carving, and hideworking. Among the 448 artifacts on which he found wear, Shea identified fifty triangular flaked points with wear on their bases; this wear was of the sort typically produced by the friction of a stone spear point in its wooden shaft. These fifty flakes also exhibited small breaks on their pointed tips. Shea suggests that such breaks may have been made when the points were thrust into the bodies of hunted animals. If so, Neandertals were hunting game animals, at least at this site dated to between 50,000 and 100,000 ya. The recent discovery at a site in Syria of a Mousterian scraper and flake with bitumen, a derivative of coal or petroleum, still adhering to their surfaces, may show that by about 40,000 years ago, ancient humans were affixing their stone tools to handles with an adhesive (Boëda, et al. 1996). An adhesive would make stone points far more secure on their wooden shafts.

Subsistence

The precise meaning of the different Mousterian tool types is still a point of contention among European prehistorians. In any event, with such tools the Neandertals developed a way of life dependent on the animals that flourished in Europe during the height of the final glacial stage, including reindeer, ibex, horse, woolly rhinoceros, bison, bear, and elk.

There is no question that Neandertal existence was largely dependent upon animal resources; Europe during glacial maxima offered little else. But were the Neandertals great hunters, as is sometimes suggested? Archaeologist Lewis Binford examined the faunal assemblages of a number of Neandertal sites and concluded that there is little evidence to support such a claim. Binford conducted an ethnoarchaeological study among the Nunamiut Eskimo of Alaska, focusing on their hunting, butchering, and disposal practices (1978). He compared his findings among these living people with archaeological evidence from the French Mousterian site of Combe Grenal (Binford 1981). Binford found a patterned distribution of cut marks on the bones from France that were similar in some ways to those he saw among the Nunamiut. For example, characteristic marks on aurochs (wild ox), horse, and reindeer mandibles from Combe Grenal matched those the Nunamiut made on caribou jaws in order to extract the animals' tongues. There were also cut marks on the joints of the long bones found at Combe Grenal indicating butchering. Cut marks Binford noticed on the antler bases of the Combe Grenal reindeer skulls matched those the Nunamiut made on young caribou when they were skinning the animals for winter clothing.

Cut marks that would reflect butchery of the choice cuts of meat were not abundant, however. The cut marks on mandible and leg bones may represent scavenging, not hunting. In this view, cut marks are abundant at Neandertal sites on mandibles and legs because that is where the meat was left on animal carcasses after the carnivores were through with them.

Most human groups are good at planning during times of plenty to ensure food during harder times. Binford suggests that the record at Combe Grenal and other sites shows that Neandertals were not very good at such planning ahead (Binford 1981; and see Fischman 1992). There is no evidence, Binford maintains, for the kind of laying in of food stores commonly practiced by modern people during times when food is abundant. As Binford points out, salmon was abundant in the surrounding rivers when Combe Grenal was occupied. Modern people commonly take advantage of the abundance of salmon during the fish's annual spawning run by catching them in large numbers and storing the meat for later use. At Combe Grenal, there is no evidence that the inhabitants did anything of the kind. They probably caught salmon and ate it, Binford asserts, but it was all quite fortuitous, and there was little forethought or planning to take advantage of this cyclically abundant resource. To Binford, this suggests that Neandertals were unable to think beyond their immediate needs for food and to plan for the future—a fundamental difference between Neandertals and modern humans.

Altruism: Were the Neandertals Their Brothers' Keepers?

That the Neandertals were capable of producing effective tools and of surviving in a rigorous climate is undeniable and reflects their great intelligence and ability. Some researchers have also suggested that in other spheres of behavior they were indistinguishable from modern human beings. Neandertals are said to have been altruistic, engaged in burial ceremonialism, and practiced the first religion. Let us consider these cultural activities in turn.

Commonly, the fossil of the "Old Man of La Chapelle-aux-Saints" and the Shanidar I skeleton are cited as evidence that Neandertals possessed the human quality of altruism by caring for their sick and aged (Constable et al. 1973; Straus and Cave 1957).

The La Chapelle remains are said to be those of an old man who probably suffered from arthritis. This would imply that he could not have contributed much to the subsistence of the group—he was presumed to be long past the point where he could have hunted or gathered much in the way of food. He also was missing most of his teeth and thus, it is often said, may even have needed some help chewing.

A reexamination of the "Old Man" has shown this interpretation to be wrong (Tappen 1985). Much of the tooth loss in this individual occurred after death, not before. Toward the end of his life, he still had five matching upper and five lower teeth on the left side; he also might have had teeth on the upper right. The only teeth certainly missing were those on the right side of the mandible, where a tumorous growth destroyed the bone, leading to tooth loss. But even this event probably occurred close to the end of his life. In all likelihood, the "Old Man" was perfectly capable of chewing his own food.

Beyond this, it is not certain how bad his arthritis really was. As stated before, Erik Trinkaus and D. D. Thompson (1987) maintain that the locations of the disease were not those that would have significantly affected locomotion. Characterizing this person as a helpless "cripple" who survived to old age only because of the selfless assistance of his comrades is also wrong.

Finally, it is ironic to note that the so-called "Old Man" was probably less than 40 when he died (Trinkaus and Thompson 1987), based on tooth wear and cranial suture closure. Does the evidence here support the scenario of altruistic Neandertals caring for the aged? Is the image of a society very much like our own, where the elderly are nurtured and where they can share the knowledge of their experience with the group, supported by the Neandertal data? Trinkaus and Thompson say no.

In most animal species, they point out, survival beyond the years of reproduction is rare. From an evolutionary perspective, there is little selective pressure for survival beyond the reproductive years for noncultural animals. In humans, with cultural adaptations, however, there are advantages to having older individuals survive. Their greater knowledge, expertise, and experience can greatly improve the chances of group survival and more than make up for whatever burden they might impose if they become physically hampered. It is therefore significant that in a sample of 246 individual Neandertals, Trinkaus and Thompson found that nearly 40 percent died before reaching adulthood (1987:126). Of the 152 adult Neandertals in the sample, only 8.6 percent appear to have been 40 years or older (1987:127). For the Neandertals, death in their twenties was common; in their thirties, it was the rule.

The Shanidar I remains, on the other hand, do appear to show compelling evidence of altruism on the part of Neandertals. The skeleton is of an individual who survived severe injuries that resulted in blindness and the probable paralysis of his right arm (Trinkaus 1983b). It seems likely, at least in this case, that other members of his group cared for this individual during his recuperation, otherwise he would not have survived.

Although the image of compassionate Neandertals caring for their wounded comrade may be compelling, the survival of a wounded individual, as K. A. Dettwyler (1991) maintains, may not mean that much. There is, he points out, an implicit bias in the assumption that simply because an individual was "disabled," he or she was helpless and could survive only through the compassion of others in the group. Simply because the Shanidar example had some significant disabilities does not mean that he could not contribute to the survival of the group. As Dettwyler points out, although he may no longer have been able to hunt, he still could have collected plants, processed food, or performed some other useful function. The archaeological record, although suggestive, does not support an image of compassionate, purely altruistic Neandertals caring for the sick, the aged, and the disabled. The survival of such individuals probably was a result of their own self-determination as well as the help of their comrades and partly due to the fact that they could still make significant contributions to the survival of the group.

Burial Ceremonialism

The reconstructed scenes are certainly evocative. At Teshik Tash, in Uzbekistan, a young Neandertal boy, dead in the flower of his youth, was carefully laid out in a shallow grave around which were placed six pairs of Siberian mountain goat horns as a memorial (Movius 1953). At La Chapelle-aux-Saints in France, the Old Man was placed in a shallow trench, surrounded by tools, and even accompanied by a bison leg—perhaps as food thought necessary for use in the afterlife (Bouyssonie et al. 1908). In the Shanidar cave in Iraq, pollen analysis has been used to construct a scenario of a recently deceased young man placed on a bed of pine boughs and then covered with wildflowers: bachelor's buttons, hollyhock, and grape hyacinth (Solecki 1971). At La Ferrassie in France, six Neandertal burials occur together. A man, a woman, two children, and two infants had been placed in trenches. Five were laid out east to west. The woman was placed in a flexed position (Figure 11.21); the man had a flat stone slab placed over his chest (Heim 1968). The infant found in Amud Cave had been placed in a small niche in the north wall of the cave, the lower jaw of a red deer placed on the child's body (Hovers, Rak, and Kimbell 1996).

It seems undeniable that Neandertals buried their dead—although, even on this point, there are some skeptics (Gargett 1989). But detailed scenarios are often difficult to assess, and the precise meaning of the burials is even harder to evaluate. Many of the burials were excavated in the late nineteenth and early twentieth centuries. Because archaeological methodology was not as advanced then as it is today, much information was lost and the taphonomy of many of the claimed burial sites is impossible to resolve.

Was the bison leg at La Chapelle-aux-Saints intended to be food for the next life, or were the Neandertal and bison bones merely dragged into the cave by carnivores? Is the site at Teshik Tash evidence of Neandertal ceremonialism or simply carnivore activity? (Only the skull lay within the

FIGURE 11.21 An undisputed Neandertal burial from La Ferrassie, France. Here, the individual was interred in the flexed position with knees drawn up to the chest. (*Museum of Man, Paris, M. Lucas, photographer*)

circle of goat horns; the rest of the bones were dispersed.) Were the flowers at Shanidar intended as symbols of life, were they used for their medicinal qualities, or was the pollen brought in later by rodents or simply blown in? To some, the meaning of these apparent burials is clear: evidence of the origins of belief in an afterlife. That may well be, but the specific meaning is lost to us.

Anthropologist Frank Harrold (1980) has analyzed a sample of presumed Neandertal interments and found thirty-six where the evidence strongly indicates intentional burial. In these, there was clear evidence of the digging of a grave, special positioning of the body (as in, for example, a fetal position), or the presence of indisputable grave offerings. These burials had ages of between 75,000 and 35,000 years. When they were compared with ninety-six burials of anatomically modern humans dating from 35,000 to 10,000 B.P., some obvious differences became apparent. In those cases where the data could be used, almost 90 percent of the modern human burials contained grave goods, including such objects as stone and bone artifacts, mollusc shells, coloring materials, and items of personal adornment such as necklaces (1980:205). On the other hand, only about 40 percent of the Neandertal burials contained grave goods, and these were restricted to objects like stone tools and animal bones.

It seems that the Neandertals indeed buried their dead, although such burials are generally not as elaborate as those of later periods involving anatomically modern humans. Whether Neandertal burials were intended to ensure that the deceased had the necessities for life in the hereafter or were simply part of ceremonies to comfort his or her companions left behind is impossible to determine, although ultimately, perhaps, not so important. Whatever their actual intent, these burials show that the Neandertals treated the dead and death in a ceremonial way, and that is a uniquely human trait. They were conscious of their own mortality and treated death in a way that reflected that recognition.

Cave Bears

Neandertals are commonly credited with the worship of a now-extinct species of bear that inhabited the caves of Europe (Figure 11.22). A closer look at the data, however, does not support the dramatic picture of a prehistoric cave bear cult.

We know that the European Neandertals used caves. We also know that they competed for such natural shelters with bears that were up to 30 percent larger than the largest living bears, the Alaskan Kodiak. When a Kodiak stands on its back legs, it can be as much as 9 feet tall. When a cave bear stood up, it could surpass 12 feet. Needless to say, people have been fascinated by the suggestion that Neandertals killed such enormous animals and then paid special attention to the remains.

At a cave in Drachenloch, Switzerland, Neandertals are alleged to have made chests of stones more than 3 feet on a side inside of which were several cave bear skulls. Deeper in the cave, six more cave bear skulls had been placed in niches in the cave wall. Other caves supposedly show similar treatment of cave bear remains. For example, Regourdu in France has twenty cached skulls housed in a cubicle topped with a huge stone slab.

Did Neandertals worship the cave bears? Did they collect their skulls as a part of that worship? Did Neandertal hunters collect the heads of slain

FIGURE 11.22   In the last few decades, reconstructions of Neandertal physical features and cultural practices have emphasized similarities to modern humans. Here, a painting by Rudolph Zallinger depicts Neandertals conducting a ceremony, much in the same manner as modern human hunters. *(Courtesy of R. F. Zallinger and Life Magazine)*

bears and keep them in stone chests, much as modern trophy hunters collect the heads of animals they have killed and then mount them on their walls? These are all thought-provoking possibilities, but they are unsupported by the data.

Anthropologists Philip Chase and Harold Dibble (1987) have reassessed Neandertal ceremonialism, pointing out that the excavations at Drachenloch and Regourdu were not as carefully conducted as would be hoped. When original field notes were examined, their descriptions did not always correspond to later, far more dramatic, reconstructions. For example, the so-called stone chests at Drachenloch were far less well defined than most people realize; they appear instead to be natural clusters of rock. Beyond this, no butchering marks have been found on the bear bones. One would expect cut marks of some kind if Neandertals had really killed the animals and then removed the bears' heads. The stone slab covering the so-called cubicle at Regourdu weighs 850 kilograms and was far more likely the result of a cave-in than any intentional construction by Neandertals or anyone else.

As understanding of cave taphonomy has become more sophisticated, researchers recognize that the bones of animals may accumulate by many natural processes. It seems, at least at present, that the accumulation of cave bear bones in European caves was the result of such processes. They do not show that Neandertals worshipped cave bears.

Could Neandertals Talk?

As we saw earlier, *Australopithecus* possessed a cranial base comparable to the apes, whereas that of *Homo erectus* was more similar although not identical to modern humans. This implies that while *Australopithecus* probably could not produce human speech, *H. erectus* may have been at least partially adept at spoken language.

In examining the basicrania of archaic *Homo sapiens*, Jeffrey Laitman and R. C. Heimbuch (1984) concluded that specimens like Petralona, Steinheim, and Kabwe (Broken Hill) are essentially modern in form. This implies that the vocal tract anatomy of these fossils dating to more than 250,000 ya was just like ours, and their ability to speak was the same as our own.

However, when we come to the basicrania of the Neandertals, the nice, neat progression of vocal tract anatomical evolution appears to have been interrupted or deflected. The base of the Neandertal skull shows a greater degree of flexion than *H. erectus,* but less than that of older archaic *H. sapiens.* It has been suggested that the differences between human and Neandertal vocal tract anatomy, the latter as reconstructed from analysis of the basicranium, indicate that Neandertals could not articulate some of the sounds that we can, notably the vowels *a, i,* and *u.* Laitman and Heimbuch, along with Philip Leiberman (1984) and Edmund Crelin (1987) are quick to point out that this still would leave the Neandertals capable of making a wide range of sounds and developing and speaking a complex language. This language may simply have been more restricted than that of modern human beings.

Not all researchers agree with the conclusions reached by these scientists. For example, the form of the recently discovered **hyoid** bone at the Neandertal site of Kebara in Israel has been interpreted by the researchers as being fully modern in appearance (Arensburg et al. 1990). The hyoid bone's location in the throat and its relationship to the larynx, pharynx, basicranium, and mandible indicates to these scientists that Neandertals were capable of fully modern speech.

The question of Neandertal speech capability, then, remains up in the air. Certainly, they could speak, but it is still unclear if they could produce the full range of sounds found in modern human languages.

hyoid The horseshoe-shaped bone in front of throat. Its form and position may provide insights into the ability of members of a species to speak.

Contemporary Issue

Suppose Neandertal Survived

Today there is a single living species of hominid—indeed, as we will show, a single living subspecies: **Homo sapiens sapiens.** But as we saw in Chapter 9, a single hominid species has not always been the case. In fact, throughout much of hominid history, there have been multiple contemporary species. *Paranthropus robustus, Paranthropus boisei,* and *Homo habilis* shared the evolutionary stage, overlapping in time and perhaps even territory. As we will show in Chapter 12, the Neandertals, with differences from anatomically modern human beings and classified in a different subspecies or even a different species, overlapped in time and space with early modern humans.

It is clear that hominid evolution has not been a steady, unbroken progression from the first upright primates to the modern peoples of today. Rather, hominid evolution—like evolution in general—has been a bush with many twigs. It is simply a twist of evolutionary fate that all but one of the hominid twigs are extinct. It needn't have turned out that way.

Evolution follows the principle of historical contingency. The specific nature of each event in evolutionary history is contingent upon—that is, conditional upon—the precise sequence of events that led up to it. If one of those events had been different, all the events that followed would have been different. So complex is this series of contingent events, we are not able to predict from knowledge of one event what effects it will have on the future.

Had Adolf Hitler, a sickly youth, died at a young age, world history would certainly not have turned out as it did. But we have no way of knowing *how* it would be different.

The same holds true for biological evolution, even the evolution of the hominids. This brings up an interesting and thought-provoking possibility. There are no Neandertals around today. But imagine, along with Stephen Jay Gould, what it would be like if the specific events of hominid history had been different, and the Neandertals had survived into the present. What would their place be in our world? Would we exploit their great strength, viewing them as expendable draft animals? Would we use them to perform dangerous tasks? "Would we," Gould asks, "have built zoos, established reserves, promoted slavery, committed genocide, or perhaps even practiced kindness?" (1985a:198).

We will, of course, never know what our modern world would have been like had other hominid twigs survived. The prospects of such a scenario, however, are certainly unsettling, considering how poorly we often treat members of our own species and subspecies. Not having been able to work out the difficulties that differences *within* our species present us, we seem hardly prepared to cope with the presence of another type of hominid. Perhaps, with this in mind, the Neandertals are better off having become extinct.

The Place of the Archaics

We ended Chapter 10 by saying that the appearance of archaic *Homo sapiens* may have been a punctuational event, a sudden surge in evolution. In this chapter, we have shown that the data present a complicated picture. Apart from their brain size, the archaics, including the Neandertals, are a varied lot indeed. Some of the crania look highly advanced, more similar to the modern form than to *Homo erectus.* Others possess a mosaic of traits, some primitive, some modern. The most recent of the archaics and the one about which we possess the most information, the Neandertals, differ in some very significant ways from modern humans.

The false abstraction of evolutionary ladders has not helped our understanding of the place in the human lineage of the Neandertals and the other archaic *H. sapiens*. The "ladder" model of development causes us to interpret fossil species as distinct points on an evolutionary continuum heading in a given direction. But the archaics do not fit neatly on any particular rung of an evolutionary ladder.

The Neandertals, although more recent than the other specimens of archaic *H. sapiens* discussed in this chapter, appear more primitive in some cranial characteristics, particularly in the size of the face and brow ridges. Their brain size, on the other hand, indicates a great degree of modernity—yet again, it fits no neat continuum because in some cases brain size surpasses that of some modern humans.

The Neandertals and most of the other archaics should be viewed not as rungs on a ladder but as twigs on the human evolutionary bush, parallel to our own. The Neandertals appear more significant than they actually are to human evolution in general because we have the bones of so many of them. But they are so abundant in the archaeological record simply because they lived in caves and buried their dead.

Summary

By about 400,000 ya, a new hominid appeared on the evolutionary stage. Called *Homo sapiens,* the creature was so like us that it was given the same biological designation as modern humans. Recognizing that there are physical differences between them and us, however, most scientists designate them as archaic *H. sapiens,* or they identify them as a subspecies different from modern human beings.

The archaics are represented in Europe by fossils like Swanscombe, Steinheim, and Petralona; in Africa by the Kabwe, Ndutu, and Bodo skulls; and in Asia by the remains found at Narmada (India) and Dali and Jinniushan (China). Mean cranial capacity for these archaics was about 1220 ml, close to 85 percent of the modern human mean cranial volume.

The best known subset of the archaics were the Neandertals, whose immediate ancestors first appeared in Europe about 300,000 ya. The so-called classic Neandertals, bearing the full complement of physical features enumerated in the chapter, appear in Europe at about 130,000 years ago, and disappear a little more than 30,000 ya. Neandertals are best known in Europe but also have been found in Southwest Asia. The Neandertals possessed large, flat skulls, often exceeding modern human cranial volume, with enormous brow ridges and steeply angled foreheads.

Below their crania, Neandertal bones exhibit features of muscle attachment indicative of great strength, often measurably beyond the modern human range of variation. Although once considered to be subhuman in intellect, the Neandertals were not brutes, but neither were they exactly like us. They probably were not altruistic people who cared for their sick and aged, buried their dead in elaborate ceremonies, and worshipped cave bears, as was once thought. They were, however, intelligent beings whose role in the evolution of modern humans is still being debated and will be addressed in Chapter 12.

Study Questions

1. How does the cranial anatomy of archaic *Homo sapiens* differ from that of *Homo erectus?*
2. Discuss the behavioral innovations of archaic *Homo sapiens.* How is Levallois stone tool technology "superior" to Acheulean?
3. Who were the Neandertals? In an evolutionary sense, how are they related to anatomically modern *Homo sapiens?*
4. How can the postcranial anatomy of the Neandertals be explained? How was their "robustness" adaptively advantageous where and when they lived?
5. In which of their behaviors do the Neandertals reflect essential elements of modern human behavior?

Key Terms

postorbital constriction	scapula	tundra
parietals	humerus	Mousterian
Levallois	phalange	hyoid

For More Information

For capsule descriptions of many of the fossils discussed in this chapter, see Clark Spencer Larsen and Robert M. Matter's *Human Origins: The Fossil Record* and, especially, Michael H. Day's *Guide to Fossil Man.* Kenneth A. R. Kennedy's *Neanderthal Man* (1975) provides a discussion of the history of scientific thought on the Neandertals. The book by Erik Trinkaus and Pat Shipman (1993), *The Neandertals: Changing Images of Mankind,* is an informative and very well-written history of the discovery and interpretation of the Neandertals. Paleoanthropologist Christopher Stringer and archaeologist Clive Gamble (1993) have written a terrific book detailing modern arguments and agreements about the Neandertals and their place in the evolution of anatomically modern people. The February 1992 issue of *Discover* magazine has an informative piece on current thinking about the Neandertals. *National Geographic* (Gore 1996) has published an up-to-date summary of our understanding of the Neandertals.

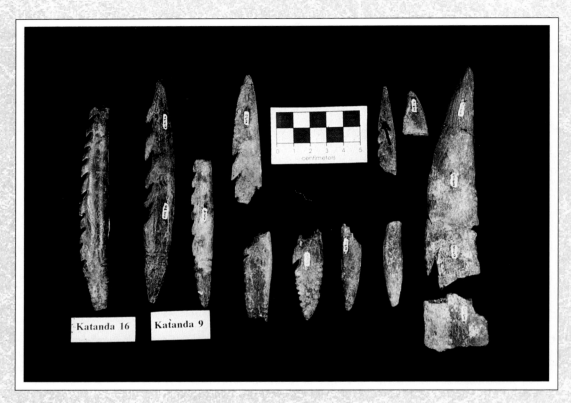

Katanda 16   Katanda 9

These bone tools from Zaire are more than 90,000 years old and represent some of the earliest evidence of increased sophistication in toolmaking on the part of our anatomically modern ancestors. How did anatomically modern humans evolve? Where and when did this happen? How does modern human biological variation reflect a point along an evolutionary continuum? *(Allison Brooks, George Washington University)*

12

The Evolution of Modern Humanity

---・m・---

CHAPTER CONTENTS

Where Do We Come From? An Evolutionary Enigma • Testing the Models of Human Evolution •
The Shape of the Human Evolutionary Tree • Biological Diversity in Modern Humans •
Contemporary Issue: The "Eve" Hypothesis • Summary • Study Questions • Key Terms • For More Information

In the short story "The Reigate Squires," Sir Arthur Conan Doyle's great detective Sherlock Holmes characterizes the key to successful police work:

> It is of the highest importance in the art of detection to be able to recognize, out of a number of facts, which are incidental and which vital. Otherwise your energy and attention must be dissipated instead of being concentrated. (1981:275)

It is much the same in science. This explains, at least in part, one of the great ironies of scientific investigation: In the journey toward understanding a complex issue, scientists sometimes become *more* confused as they know more about a subject. In a way that is both maddeningly frustrating and intellectually exhilarating, this irony characterizes the understanding of the origin and evolution of anatomically modern human beings.

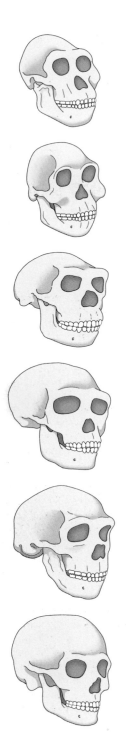

Where Do We Come From? An Evolutionary Enigma

One would have hoped—and expected—that the nearer the present and the more abundant the data, the greater the certainty of the scenarios about the evolution of humankind. This, unfortunately, is not the case. To be sure, the "number of facts," as Holmes puts it, increases dramatically, but scientists are not yet in a position to apply Holmes's advice; they cannot yet distinguish the "incidental" from the "vital." Perhaps even more lamentably, their attention has too often been dissipated in acrimonious debate over competing hypotheses.

We cannot provide here a simple, comprehensive solution to the controversial questions surrounding the origin of *anatomically modern Homo sapiens,* officially named *Homo sapiens sapiens* (Figure 12.1). What we can attempt is a synopsis of the evidence presented by the champions of the different explanations.

Two basic models and a middle ground have been proposed to explain the evolution of anatomically modern humans from the archaics: the in-place, or **multiregional hypothesis;** the **population replacement hypothesis;** and the **genetic replacement hypothesis,** which combines elements of both (Figure 12.2).

These competing models have their own cadres of supporters. Most active in advocating the multiregional model has been Milford Wolpoff of the University of Michigan (Frayer et al. 1993; Thorne and Wolpoff 1992; Wolpoff 1988, 1989; Wolpoff et al. 1984; Wolpoff et al. 1994); while speaking most vociferously in favor of the population replacement model has been Christopher Stringer of the Natural History Museum in London (Stringer 1989, 1990, 1992a, 1992b, 1994; Stringer and Andrews 1988). Different versions of the genetic replacement model (Park 1996) have among their chief supporters paleoanthropologists Fred H. Smith (1992) and Günter Bräuer (1992).

Each model also has its own suite of deductive implications—those things that should be true if the hypothesis is true (see Chapter 1 for a brief discussion of the scientific method of reasoning). These predictions, presented in Figure 12.3, can be used to test the models, at least tentatively.

Multiregional Evolution

Multiregional evolution posits the gradual, in-place evolution of regional populations of ancient hominids into modern humanity (see Figure 12.2). In this view, archaic populations throughout the world—the European Neandertals as well as the archaic humans of Africa and Asia—each evolved, more or less separately, into the modern form at about the same

FIGURE 12.1 Comparison of cranial features of *Australopithecus (top), Homo habilis, Homo erectus,* archaic *Homo sapiens,* Neandertal, and anatomically modern *Homo sapiens.*

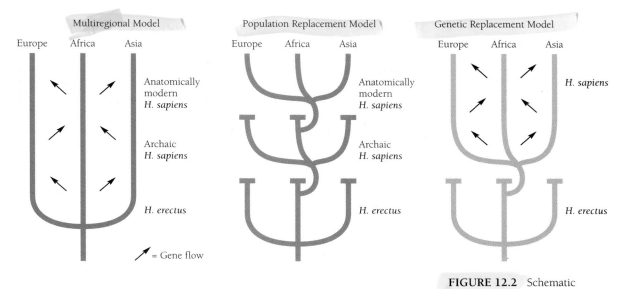

FIGURE 12.2 Schematic depiction of competing models of the evolution of anatomically modern *Homo sapiens*.

time. As Fred Smith et al. (1989) point out, this explanation presumes that long-term, gradual trends produced modern humans from archaic ones in several areas through the resorting of genetic material and natural selection.

If the multiregional model is correct, the paleontological records of Asia, Africa, and Europe should show parallel changes more or less simultaneously. Within each region, archaic populations would have gradually evolved into moderns, with distinctive regional traits maintained through time within different geographic populations.

In other words, regional anatomical traits seen in modern human populations in particular geographic areas today—the so-called racial traits discussed later in this chapter—should be traceable through time to the archaic *Homo sapiens* and even earlier *Homo erectus* groups in those same areas. In the multiregional model, the human anatomical variation seen today began 1 million years ago or even more. This lengthy period of at least partly separate development should be reflected in substantial genetic differences between geographically distinct populations of modern humans.

One of the earliest advocates of a multiregional model, Carleton Coon (1962), suggested that anatomically modern human beings had developed from earlier hominids entirely independently—and at different times—in Europe, Africa, Asia, and Australia, with today's modern "races" representing the endpoints of these separate evolutions. Such a scenario is highly unlikely and has virtually no supporters today.

To hold such an idea one would have to argue that the same evolutionary changes occurred among separate groups of archaic humans, under conditions of very similar selective pressure but in areas of the

multiregional hypothesis The idea that anatomically modern humans evolved independently in a number of different geographic areas.

population replacement hypothesis The idea that anatomically modern humans evolved in a limited geographic area and migrated from there, physically replacing indigenous groups of archaic *Homo sapiens*.

genetic replacement hypothesis The idea that anatomically modern humans evolved in a limited geographic area, migrated from there, and mated with indigenous archaic humans. In this way, modern genes replaced archaic ones.

	Multiregional Model	Population Replacement Model	Genetic Replacement Model
Paleontological evidence necessary	1. Transitional forms widespread 2. Simultaneous worldwide appearance of modern traits 3. Regional traits traceable from modern back through ancient forms	1. Transitional fossils in one or limited areas 2. Anatomically modern fossils appear earliest in single region, later elsewhere 3. Temporal overlap and contemporaneity of archaic and modern forms outside source area	1. Transitional forms widespread (hybrid) 2. Anatomically modern fossils appear earliest in single region, later elsewhere 3. Temporal overlap between anatomically modern and archaic forms within each region
Genetic evidence necessary	1. High genetic diversity among modern human populations 2. Same amount of diversity within each human group	1. Low genetic diversity among human groups 2. Highest genetic diversity among modern humans within source region (where moderns first appeared)	1. High genetic diversity among human groups 2. Highest genetic diversity among modern humans within source area (where moderns first appeared)

FIGURE 12.3 Paleontological and genetic evidence needed to support the multiregional, population replacement, and genetic replacement models of the evolution of anatomically modern *Homo sapiens*. (*Adapted from Stringer and Andrews 1988*)

world with strikingly different environments, while still resulting in inter-fertile groups of anatomically modern people. Because of the problems presented by this scenario, today's supporters of the multiregional theory generally maintain that sufficient gene flow (see Chapter 4) occurred across all, or at least most, of the world, biologically linking archaic human groups (Kramer 1991; Wolpoff et al. 1984). Thus, new and highly adaptive biological traits appearing in one corner of the globe would have rapidly moved across the face of the earth through the interbreeding of various archaic human groups. At the same time, the amount of interbreeding had to be below that necessary to eliminate geographically localized variation.

Evolution by Population Replacement

The population replacement hypothesis (see Figure 12.2) proposes that anatomically modern human beings evolved from archaic humans in a single or limited geographic location. These newly evolved modern humans then migrated out from this place of origin, expanding their populations into areas where only archaic humans had previously lived (Figure 12.4). Therefore, archaic and anatomically modern humans were, at least for a time, contemporaries, and in some cases close neighbors and competitors for the same territory and resources. As a result of their more highly adaptive traits—perhaps greater intelligence, better ability to communicate, superior hunting abilities, better technology—modern humans replaced

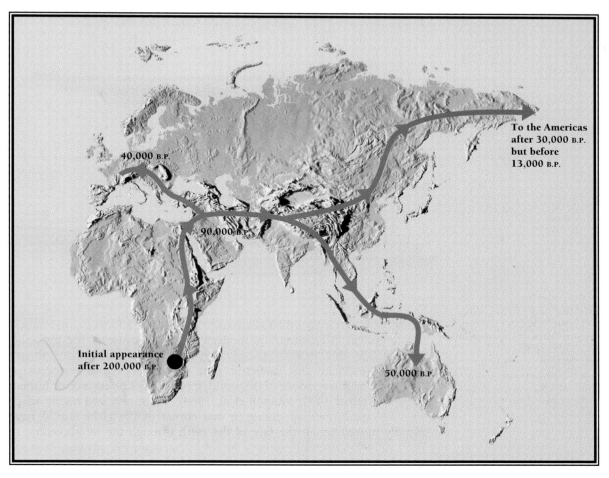

FIGURE 12.4 Timing of the appearance of anatomically modern *Homo sapiens* in Africa and expansion throughout the world according to the population replacement model.

archaic populations wherever they came into contact. They developed better adaptations and simply outcompeted the archaics in this evolutionary struggle, an example of competitive exclusion.

If this model is correct, then we can deduce that fossils transitional between archaic and modern humans should occur only in the single region where moderns evolved. Elsewhere, there should be evidence of archaics and moderns coexisting in the same regions, once the latter spread out from their initial source area—their "Eden," as opponents of the replacement model disparagingly characterize it (Smith et al. 1989; Wolpoff 1989). Eventually, the archaic human forms would have become extinct, unable to compete with their anatomically modern cousins. Modern genetic diversity should be small because, in this model, *all* living human groups have descended from a relatively recent ancestral group. Anatomical differences visible today among modern humans thus evolved only since the first moderns replaced the archaic forms. Archaic forms in areas outside the source area contributed little or nothing to modern human genes. Genetic diversity should be greatest where modern humans first appeared because we have obviously been there the longest.

A Middle Ground: Genetic Replacement

The population replacement and multiregional views have been tempered by scholars who have attempted a middle ground in this debate. Günter Bräuer (1992), for example, agrees with Stringer that Africa was the source of modern humanity at a fairly late date, but does not accept the notion that the archaics were completely replaced by migrating moderns. He believes that as the first anatomically modern human beings spread from Africa, they did not replace the archaics they encountered but mated with them, producing hybrid populations. With continued interbreeding, modern traits would have been selected for because, for example, the greater intelligence and resulting cultural sophistication they conferred gave their possessors a substantial selective advantage. Through this evolutionary process, all *Homo sapiens* were ultimately pulled along to the modern form.

Also falling somewhere in between is Fred Smith (1992), who leans toward the notion that modern human traits developed in a single population (perhaps in Africa, perhaps someplace else) and then spread into archaic groups. In Smith's model, however, the traits spread not through migration of populations so much as through gene flow, as neighboring populations mated and exchanged genes. In other words, the genes "migrated," even if the people themselves did not.

The deductive implications of the genetic replacement model fall between those of the multiregional and population replacement models. As in the population replacement model, modern humans should appear first in a single area. If Bräuer is correct, outside that source area, the newly arrived moderns and the indigenous archaics should overlap in time, as in the population replacement model. But, unlike that model, and like the multiregional model, the genetic replacement view expects to see some continuity of regionally restricted traits in each area, as the genes of modern and archaic humans combine in hybrid populations.

Testing the Models of Human Evolution

To assess the validity of these models, we must first examine the paleontological records of Africa, Asia, and Europe (Figure 12.5). We will then go on to assess the evidence supplied by modern human genetics and culture.

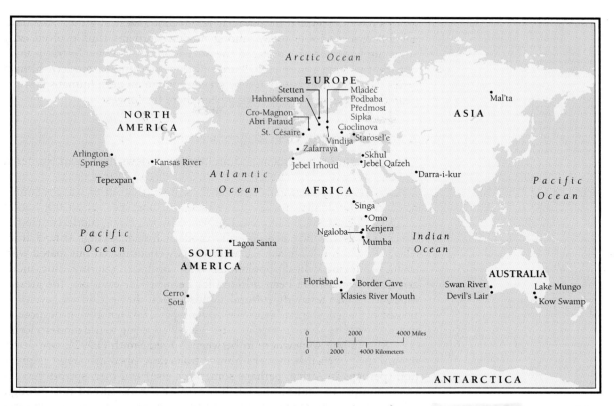

FIGURE 12.5 Locations of the sites of late Neandertals, some late premodern human skeletal remains, and early anatomically modern humans.

The Paleontological Record

Fossil evidence provides us with a set of data with which we can assess the validity of these competing models of the evolution of anatomically modern human beings.

Africa Several fossil sites in the southern and eastern parts of Africa support the population replacement model and the hypothesis that, as it was the rootstock of the first hominids, Africa was also the source of anatomically modern human beings—at a surprisingly early date (Bräuer 1984; Rightmire 1984; Stringer 1989, 1990, 1994; Stringer and Andrews 1988).

Klasies River Mouth (KRM), Border Cave, Omo (the Omo 1 skull), Kanjera, Mumba, and Singa are all sites in Africa at which the fossils of anatomically modern human beings have been discovered at early levels (Singer and Wymer 1982). For instance, recent electron spin resonance dating of animal teeth found in the same layer as the fragmentary hominid fossils at Klasies River Mouth places the age of the specimens at about

FIGURE 12.6 A mandible from Klasies River Mouth (KRM) in southern Africa. Lightly built and possessing a chin, this quite modern lower jaw dates to about 90,000 years ago. The preponderance of skeletal evidence from this date at KRM indicates that the cave was occupied by an early population of anatomically modern *Homo sapiens.* (*From* The Middle Stone Age at Klasies River Mouth, South Africa, *by Ronald Singer and John Wymer, University of Chicago Press*)

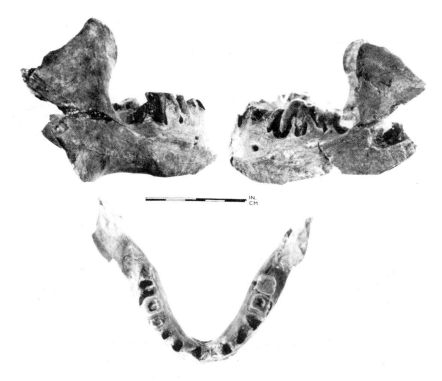

90,000 years (Grün et al. 1990). The presence of a chin on one of the better preserved mandibles at KRM is a distinctly modern human trait (Figure 12.6; see also Chapter 7). Detailed analysis of the upper jaws discovered at KRM indicates that they also are quite modern (Bräuer, Deacon, and Zipfel 1992). Recent statistical analysis of the KRM fossils further confirms the modern aspects of the fragmentary skeletal material (Deacon and Shuurman 1992; Rightmire and Deacon 1991).

The Border Cave hominid remains are more complete than those at KRM. They consist of a nearly complete cranium with a partial mandible, a mandible from a different individual, and a partial infant skeleton (Beaumont et al. 1978; Rightmire 1979b) (Figure 12.7). Recent electron spin resonance dates on animal teeth found in the cave suggest that the cranium and partial mandible are probably more than 70,000 and less than 90,000 years old, the complete mandible is 50,000 to 65,000 years old, and the infant skeleton 70,000 to 80,000 years old (Grün et al. 1990). Unfortunately, the materials were not excavated professionally and it is not certain precisely where they came from in the cave; therefore the association between the dates and the remains is questionable. The Omo 1 fossil appears to be pretty firmly dated to 130,000 years, and the Mumba re-

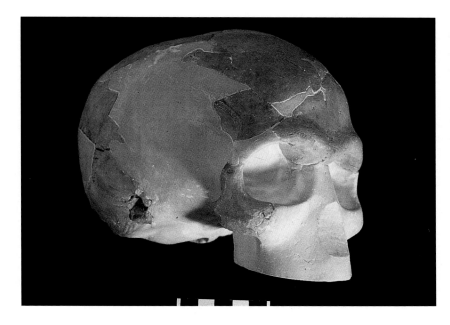

FIGURE 12.7   The Border Cave skull from South Africa may date to more than 100,000 ya. Entirely modern in appearance, it is one of several from sub-Saharan Africa that seem to support the replacement model and point to Africa as the source for modern humanity. *(Courtesy P. V. Tobias, University of the Witwatersrand, Johannesburg, South Africa)*

mains (mostly teeth, entirely modern in their appearance) are at least 110,000 years old. Singa and Kanjera appear to be of similar antiquity.

As luck would have it, the more firmly dated examples like KRM tend to be the more fragmentary, so precise identification is a problem. The more complete Border Cave specimen, clearly anatomically modern, is not as firmly dated. Nevertheless, these African fossils represent a growing group of anatomically modern human remains dating to about 100,000 years ago.

Significantly, at least some hominid fossils found in Africa appear to represent forms intermediate between archaic and modern humans. For example, the somewhat older fossils from Florisbad, Jebel Irhoud, Omo (Omo 2), and Ngaloba (Laetoli Hominid 18) all exhibit a mixture of archaic and modern traits (Figure 12.8, p. 312). Smith et al. (1989) label these the "African Transitional Group." These crania are larger, more rounded, and have higher foreheads and smaller brow ridges than older African archaic humans such as those from Kabwe, Bodo, or Lake Ndutu (see Chapter 11). At the same time, they are not as modern looking as the KRM, Border Cave, and other fossils listed earlier.

This intermediate group of fossils may be the key. They seem to present physical evidence for the evolution in Africa of modern human beings from archaic ones. The next question is whether such intermediate forms are found elsewhere in the world, as the multiregional and genetic replacement models require, or are restricted to only one region, as required by the population replacement model.

FIGURE 12.8 The cranium from Jebel Irhoud in Morocco possesses anatomical characteristics intermediate between those of archaic and anatomically modern *Homo sapiens*. Like the Florisbad, Ngaloba, and Omo 2 specimens, it lends support to the hypothesis of evolution of modern human forms in Africa. (*Museum of Man, Paris*)

Europe The famous Cro-Magnon fossils of France, discovered in 1868 (Figure 12.9), are still the oldest examples of anatomically modern humans from western Europe. Although varied, the five individuals found were all clearly modern in appearance, with long, large skulls; broad, short faces; and narrow noses. Their cranial capacities were quite large (upward of 1600 ml), and their brains were housed in very modern looking skulls with high foreheads, rounded profiles, and small brow ridges. The site dates to less than 30,000 years ago (Stringer et al. 1984). The site at Abri Pataud, also in France, provides the remains of several more individuals with modern crania and dates to more than 27,000 ya (Stringer et al. 1984). The crania of these first anatomically modern human beings in western Europe look nothing at all like the Neandertals (Chapter 11) who inhabited the same territory before them.

The postcranial skeletons of the earliest anatomically modern human fossils from western Europe also show many fundamental differences from the Neandertals. Indeed, it is potentially quite significant that even though the Neandertals were physically adapted to life in the cold, the earliest European moderns were proportioned more like tropically adapted humans (Trinkaus 1983a). This fact would seem to indicate that they evolved in a warmer climate and had only recently moved into colder regions.

In western Europe at least, there are *no* fossils that can be interpreted as intermediate in form between Neandertal and these early modern human beings (Smith 1984; Smith et al. 1989). There seems to be a genuine anatomical gap between the local archaic humans—the Neandertals—and the earliest moderns. The Cro-Magnons appear to have come

FIGURE 12.9 One of the famous skulls of anatomically modern humans from the cave at Cro-Magnon, France. All the anatomical features of this skull are entirely modern. (*Museum of Man, Paris*)

into Europe from somewhere else, which supports the population replacement model.

Some European sites farther east also seem to support population replacement. Stetten, Germany, with a radiocarbon date of 36,000 B.P. (Smith 1984); Cioclinova in Romania; and Podbaba and Predmost in the Czech Republic are only a few examples. All share an entirely modern cranial morphology. None can be interpreted as an intermediate or evolving human. They are all fully modern.

Recent discoveries in western Europe of Neandertals dating to a time *after* the initial appearance of modern humans there seem to further support the population replacement hypothesis. At Saint-Césaire, France, a fossil that is clearly Neandertal has been found in a level dated to about 36,000 ya (Mercier et al. 1991; Stringer and Grün 1991). At Hahnöfersand in Germany, a cranial fragment with clear affinities to Neandertal has been dated to 35,000 B.P. (Bräuer 1984). At Zafarraya, in Spain, a fully Neandertal mandible has been dated to after 34,000 B.P. (Rose 1995) and a 34,000 year old Neandertal temporal bone has been recovered at the French site of Arcy-sur-Cure (Hublin et al. 1996). It is unlikely that the Neandertals were ancestral to modern humans in western Europe if they survived for so long after the appearance of anatomically modern humanity in eastern Europe (Stringer and Gamble 1993).

The European evidence at this point would seem to support a scenario in which anatomically modern human beings who had originated someplace else—probably someplace tropical such as Africa, considering their body proportions—entered western Europe, first coexisting with and then replacing Neandertals. So far, so good, for the population replacement model.

The evidence in central, southern, or eastern Europe differs, however. For example, several robust crania were recovered from the site of Mladeč in the Czech Republic (Smith 1984). Among the fossils recovered here were the remains of a 3-year-old child. The skull is different in appearance from that of the 5-year-old Neandertal from Teshik Tash, the 3-year-old from Gibraltar, or the ten-month-old infant from Amud Cave, Israel, all mentioned in Chapter 11. On the other hand, the Mladeč child does not look modern either; it simply is too robust. Some interpret this robustness as representing a transitional form between Neandertals and modern humans (Smith et al. 1989).

A partial cranium found on Crete has a uranium series date of 51,000 years ago (Facchinni and Guisberti 1990). While appearing modern, it also exhibits anatomical features reminiscent of Neandertals. Of even greater interest are the eastern European sites of Vindija, Kůlna, and Sipka. These sites, dated to between 38,000 and 45,000 ya, have produced fossils interpreted by some experts as transitional between older Neandertals and anatomically modern human beings. In particular, their brow ridges are intermediate in size between Neandertals and moderns, and they also seem to be transitional in other aspects of their cranial and facial anatomy (Smith et al. 1989). As Fred Smith states, the remains are "clearly still Neandertals, [but] it is difficult not to recognize Vindija as a transitional sample between most Neandertals and early modern Europeans" (1994:232).

On the other hand, as Erik Trinkaus (1983a) points out, postcranially there is little evidence of Neandertals slowly evolving into the modern form anywhere in Europe. In their bones below the head, even the so-called transitional European forms retain the standard robust Neandertal features.

So we are left without a clear consensus. In western Europe, modern humans seem to have replaced Neandertals, but in eastern (and, possibly, central and southern) Europe, there is some evidence supporting continuity, perhaps through interbreeding, as suggested by the genetic replacement hypothesis.

Southwest Asia   A number of Neandertals excavated in Southwest Asia date to early in the last glacial (Amud, Shanidar, Kebara, Tabun, and Teshik Tash—see Chapter 11). All are fairly typically Neandertal.

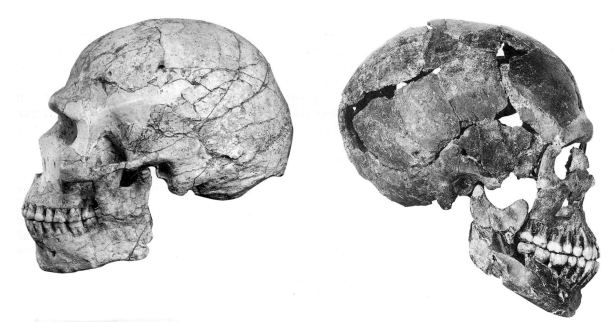

FIGURE 12.10   The skulls from Skhul (*left*) and Jebel Qafzeh (*right*) from Israel are examples of robust but otherwise anatomically modern crania. Both date to more than 90,000 ya. (*Skhul V: Peabody Museum, Harvard University, photograph by Hillel Burger. Jebel Qafzeh: Laboratory of Vertebrate and Human Paleontology, Paris. B. Vandermeersch*)

In the same region, however, several specimens that are clearly not Neandertals have been excavated in Skhul and Jebel Qafzeh in Israel (Figure 12.10). Skhul is located only about 100 meters away from the Neandertal cave of Tabun, and Qafzeh is only about 30 kilometers east of these caves. Like modern skulls, the Skhul and Qafzeh crania are more rounded than those of the Neandertals, with higher foreheads and smaller faces. Where mandibles have been recovered, it is clear that these individuals had chins, a trait exhibited by modern humans but not Neandertals. Nevertheless, these skulls are ruggedly constructed and exhibit, by modern standards, relatively large, distinct brow ridges.

With their modernlike rounded skulls and their archaiclike large brow ridges and somewhat prognathous profiles, the Skhul and Qafzeh crania could be transitional between the indigenous, classical Neandertal hominids from Amud, Tabun, and Shanidar on the one hand and anatomically modern human beings on the other. But for the Skhul and Qafzeh crania to represent transitional forms—a Southwest Asian version of the African Transitional Group—they would have to be intermediate in age as well as morphology—younger than the Neandertals from whom they evolved and older than the anatomically modern humans whom they became.

Dating does not support such a scenario. Skhul and Qafzeh, in fact, are much *older* than most Neandertal specimens known from the area. Burned flint artifacts associated with the Qafzeh skull have been dated by thermoluminescence to 92,000 B.P. (Valladas et al. 1988), and an electron spin resonance date on the Qafzeh materials further verifies a probable age in excess of 90,000 years (Stringer 1988). Skhul specimens have been associated with an electron spin resonance date of between 81,000 to 101,000 years ago (Stringer et al. 1989) and have been dated to about 80,000 years ago by uranium series (McDermott et al. 1993). However, Neandertal sites like Amud (60,000 B.P.) and Kebara (70,000 B.P.) are substantially younger, whereas Tabun (100,000 B.P.) is about as old as the early modern sites. This shows that some rugged but otherwise anatomically modern human beings predated some Neandertals in Southwest Asia by as many as 40,000 years and would have coexisted with them for as many as 60,000 years. This date also means modern humans existed in the area about 60,000 years before they appeared in Europe.

Based on the dating of the Neandertal sites and the dates from Skhul and Qafzeh, it seems clear that anatomically modern humans turn up in Southwest Asia about the same time or even sometime *before* the appearance there of the Neandertals. It seems possible that the Neandertals may have migrated into the Middle East from Europe, where they are substantially older and where their evolutionary antecedents have been firmly dated (see Chapter 11). In this view, they shared Southwest Asia, perhaps intermittently, with modern human beings for 60,000 years, but eventually were replaced by anatomically modern human beings.

Considering the degree of anatomical difference and the chronological gap, the Neandertals from Southwest Asia do not seem to have been ancestral to modern humans in that region—they are too different and overlap in time. As Yoel Rak maintains, for example, in an evolutionary sense you simply can't readily get from the Kebara pelvis to the modern pelvis—they are too different. For Southwest Asia, the multiregional model cannot be upheld, and the population replacement model seems to better fit the data.

East Asia   One piece of evidence used by the supporters of the multiregional hypothesis is the apparent continuity through time of specific, regionally distributed physical traits, particularly in Asia. *Homo erectus,* archaic *Homo sapiens,* and modern humans in the Far East share certain skeletal characteristics, it is claimed, that are either rare or absent in modern populations in Africa and Europe (Wolpoff et al. 1984). These include shovel-shaped lateral incisor teeth, extra cranial sutures, and a ridge inside the lower jaw. This evidence is used to support the notion that in the evolution of anatomically modern humans, local populations did not become extinct nor were they replaced by groups from elsewhere. Instead, local groups of archaic humans each evolved into modern humans more or less independently (but always with some amount of gene flow), with local "racial" traits preserved over hundreds of thousands of years.

In a recent, detailed analysis of the Sangiran *H. erectus* specimens (see Chapter 10), Andrew Kramer (1991) compared their lower jaws to those of anatomically modern human beings from Africa and Australia. Kramer deduced that, had the East Asian *erectus* population been replaced by an expanding population of anatomically modern human beings from somewhere else, then the modern mandibles from Australia should not look like those from the *erectus* specimens from Java. The Sangiran and other Javanese hominids would have, in this scenario, contributed nothing to modern human evolution. In fact, however, Kramer found that the modern Australian jaws did share many common anatomical features with the Sangiran mandibles, suggesting to him genetic continuity supporting the multiregional model.

As Kramer (1991) points out, Australia poses a problem for the population replacement hypothesis, as even the strongest proponents (Stringer and Andrews 1988) of that model admit. The earliest settlement of Australia dates to more than 50,000 ya, well after local (to East Asia) *H. erectus* or archaic *H. sapiens* would have been replaced by anatomically modern *H. sapiens* who had come from somewhere else. However, some of the early Australian fossil crania—most notably Willandra Lakes Hominid 50—are remarkably robust. Looking quite archaic, they share many features with older, indigenous East Asian premodern hominids. Do such specimens reflect regional continuity with older, local forms, or did fully modern humans enter Australia as part of a general wave of replacement of archaics in East Asia, evolving a more robust form later on? This crucial question simply cannot be answered because the dating of the most important crania is uncertain (Habgood 1989; Jones 1989). If the oldest crania in Australia turn out to be the modern, lighter variety, then the population replacement model is upheld. If, on the other hand, the more robust form turns out to be older, the multiregional model is supported (see Chapter 13).

Colin Groves (1989) and Phillip Habgood (1992) have provided detailed analyses of the claim of morphological continuity from *Homo erectus* to modern Asians. In their view, many of the features that show continuity in Asia are also seen in many ancient hominids in Africa and Europe. These features, they maintain, simply have been maintained to a higher degree in modern Asians. For example, the presumably regionally restricted Asian trait of shovel-shaped incisors turns out not to be so diagnostic after all, at least, not in the ancient past. Habgood (1992:279) provides a list of European and African fossils (including australopithecines, *Homo erectus*, Neandertal, and early and relatively late anatomically modern humans) exhibiting shovel-shaped incisors.

If these supposedly diagnostic Asian traits are not really geographically restricted but were once widespread, the case for regional continuity in Asia is weakened. It would be entirely possible for those traits supposed to be regionally restricted to have been present in the earliest anatomically modern African migrants to Asia and Europe. These traits simply were maintained to a higher degree in subsequent Asian populations, and lost in Africa and Europe. The case for regional continuity of traits, therefore, seems only weakly supported by the Asian evidence.

The Paleontological Verdict   We began this chapter by warning that there was no easy answer to the question, "How did modern humanity evolve?" We presume that you now agree. Nevertheless, although a definitive answer based on the paleontological evidence is yet out of reach, there are some tentative conclusions we can reach. Consider the deductive framework established at the beginning of this chapter and summarized in Figure 12.3. The paleontological evidence needed to support the multiregional and the genetic replacement hypothesis included the existence of forms intermediate between archaic and modern humans throughout the world. Parallel changes from archaic to modern forms should have been taking place everywhere more or less simultaneously, either more or less independently or as the result of interbreeding. The evidence presented does not universally support such a scenario.

On the other hand, the population replacement model demands that paleontological evidence for modern humans appears in a restricted region at a date preceding their appearance elsewhere. The existence of intermediate forms should similarly be restricted to the source region. Archaic and modern humans should have coexisted for a time outside the source as the moderns spread to other areas. The paleontological evidence seems to provide stronger support for this view and points to sub-Saharan Africa as the probable source for all modern human populations.

However, proponents of the population replacement model have to be able to explain the presence of apparently intermediate forms elsewhere, particularly in eastern Europe. It is conceivable that when modern human beings coexisted with archaics, there was some interbreeding between the two groups, as the genetic replacement model suggests. Thus, what appear to some to represent morphologically and chronologically transitional forms are, in reality, the result of the interfertility of the anatomically modern humans and archaics, with offspring exhibiting a mixture of traits.

Although it appears that the paleontological evidence tips the scales a bit toward the population replacement hypothesis, such a conclusion certainly cannot be characterized as definitive. Recent advances in genetic research—a sort of archaeology of our genes—seem, however, to lend support to a replacement hypothesis.

The Genetic Evidence

We mentioned genetic evidence in Chapter 5 regarding the relationship between humans and the nonhuman primates. Genetic data can also be used to compare living human populations and examine the question of modern human origins. Most genetic lines of inquiry support a replacement model and point to an African source for modern humanity.

The multiregional model implies the existence of more genetic variation among different human groups than does the population replacement model because they evolved more or less separately from archaic to modern forms. Human beings, however, although showing variation in appearance, actually exhibit little genetic variation—in fact, less than that seen within ape species (Stringer and Andrews 1988:1264). This suggests a relatively recent, common source for all living humans, which is consistent with the population replacement hypothesis.

Although genetic variation is low in modern human beings, when some very detailed genetic instructions coded by the DNA in the nuclei of our cells (**nuclear DNA**) are compared across geographic populations, the world's peoples tend to cluster into two groups: those from sub-Saharan Africa and those from everywhere else (Stringer and Andrews 1988:1265). This evidence also supports the population replacement model and an African origin of modern humanity—if people have been evolving in Africa longer than elsewhere, the African population should be distinct from those of Europe and Asia.

Another approach in genetic analysis is shedding additional light on the question of the origin of anatomically modern *Homo sapiens*. This research involves the analysis of **mitochondrial DNA** (mtDNA). Mitochondria are the energy factories within the cells of plants and animals. They possess their own distinct DNA, which, in complex interaction with the nuclear DNA, codes for the mitochondria's function of producing the biological fuel that provides energy for the cell. Each human cell contains thousands of mitochondria.

At some point in early cellular evolution, the ancestors of mitochondria were separate organisms. Through what may be the first example of **symbiosis,** they became functional elements within larger cells, maintaining their own genetic code. This code is particularly useful for some genetic studies because mtDNA accumulates mutations at a rate five to ten times faster than nuclear DNA, and there is evidence that the mutation rate is fairly constant.

Molecular biologists Allan Wilson, Rebecca Cann, and Mark Stoneking used mtDNA in an attempt to answer questions concerning human evolution (Cann et al. 1987; Lewin 1987a, 1987b, 1991; Stoneking and Cann 1989; Wilson and Cann 1992). Their initial study analyzed the mtDNA of 147 modern human females from New Guinea, Australia, Asia, Europe, and Africa. They chose females because mtDNA is inherited in the female line; although both human eggs and sperm contain mitochondria, sperm do not pass theirs on at fertilization.

If human populations had been geographically separate for a long time and had evolved separately into modern humans—as the multiregional model suggests—the mtDNA in each geographic sample should be quite distinct. Different mutations would have been accumulating in the separate populations during that time.

When the mtDNA of the sample groups was compared, however, the researchers found that it was all quite similar. Compared to chimpanzees, for example, the mtDNA of human beings is extremely homogeneous. In

nuclear DNA The genetic material in the nucleus of a cell.

mitochondrial DNA DNA from the mitochondria of cells rather than the nucleus.

symbiosis A long-term relationship between members of two species that may or may not be beneficial to both.

fact, chimp mtDNA commonly exhibits ten times the amount of variation as does human mtDNA (Wilson and Cann 1992:71). From this, the researchers inferred that the different geographic groups in the sample could not have evolved separately over a long period, which stands in apparent contradiction to the multiregional model of evolution. The mtDNA of women around the world seems to show that their populations all came from the same source at a relatively recent date.

The one geographic group that stood out was the women of sub-Saharan Africa. As with nuclear DNA, their mtDNA was relatively distinct from that of the other groups (Figure 12.11). The mtDNA in Africa was also the most internally heterogeneous. Together, these two pieces of evidence suggest that the African mtDNA is older than that of the other groups—it has been independently accumulating mutations longer and therefore has more variation. If the African mtDNA is older, then it would most logically be the source for the mtDNA in the rest of the world's populations. This, in turn, would seem to support the notion that modern human beings evolved first in Africa (and so have been there longer than anywhere else) and that other human populations must be ultimately derived from that source, as with the population replacement hypothesis.

Beyond this, the researchers were able to suggest a rate for mtDNA mutation accumulation and from this projection construct an mtDNA clock. They used the New Guinea subsample because they could measure two variables in the equation. First, they could measure the amount of mtDNA variation within the New Guinea subsample. Because the aboriginal population of New Guinea probably derives from a small group of original settlers, all the modern mtDNA variation has come about since the initial settlement of the island. Second, the date when that settlement occurred is known; archaeological evidence indicates that human beings first came to New Guinea about 40,000 ya (see Chapter 13). Thus, they could calculate how much variation has developed in mtDNA as a result of accumulated mutations over approximately 40,000 years. That enables the calculation of a general rate of mtDNA mutation through time.

The researchers applied this equation to the African subsample. They concluded that the variation of the mtDNA within the African group would have taken five times as long to develop as the variation within New Guinea. In other words, mtDNA in humans has been accumulating mutations in Africa for approximately $5 \times 40,000$ or 200,000 years. This result seems to be in line with the inference drawn from the anatomically modern human fossils found in Africa and dated to more than 100,000 ya. This idea is popularly referred to as the Eve hypothesis (see the "Contemporary Issue" feature).

Parts of this interpretation have now been called into question, even by some of its proponents (Barinaga 1992; Hedges et al. 1992). It turns out there are far more computer-generated family trees, like the one depicted in Figure 12.11, than previously thought. There may be literally millions of trees that reasonably account for the complex genetic data that

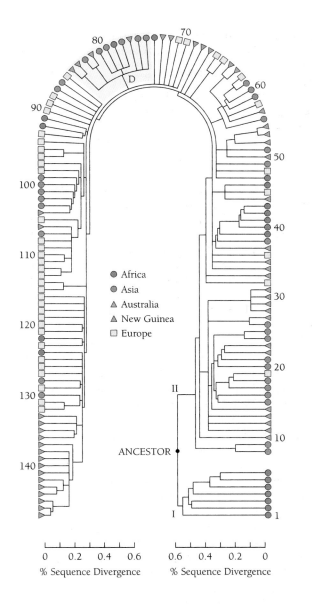

FIGURE 12.11 Computer-generated tree showing the lines of descent of the 147 women sampled in the mtDNA study described. Note the cluster of women of African descent at lower right and the proposed ancestor based on the genetic distinctions between African and non-African women. As explained in the text, recent mtDNA studies have generated trees showing very different relationships. *(Allan Wilson, University of California, Berkeley)*

are used. Altogether, these genetic trees differ in terms of the exact relationships of the human groups sampled. They even vary in which group—African or non-African—is shown to be the ancestral population of modern humans. Indeed, a group of researchers that includes Stoneking, one of the originators of the Eve idea, now states that the data, in light of the latest computer analyses, are insufficient to resolve the issue of the ancestral population. They do, however, still propose that the data suggest an African origin (Hedges et al. 1992:739).

Rebecca Cann and others have recognized some of the mistakes made in the original research and have gone on to conduct additional work on the mtDNA of living humans, using a combined sample of more than 5000 women. Their research seems to lend some, though admittedly not extremely strong support, for an African source for modern human beings (Cann 1992; Cann et al. 1994; J. Long et al. 1990; Stoneking 1993; Vigilant et al. 1991). It must be concluded, then, that the various mtDNA arguments are still being sorted out (Hedges et al. 1992).

In re-analyzing the same data, however, biologist Alan Templeton (1993, 1996) comes to conclusions opposite to those of Cann, Wilson, and Stoneking. He views the mtDNA *as well as the nuclear DNA* of modern humans as showing "no evidence that supports the hypothesis of an African–non-African population split . . ." (1996:1363). Rather, the data show "recurrent gene flow" within a "single evolutionary lineage," with restrictions in that flow giving rise to limited regional genetic differentiation. Thus, Templeton's interpretation supports either a multiregional model or a genetic replacement model, although which of these models is correct, he says, can only be discerned through the fossil data.

Some recent studies on nuclear DNA, however, have lent further support to the replacement model. Geneticist David Goldstein and his team (Bower 1995b) compared segments of nuclear DNA called microsatellites from 148 individuals representing 14 native populations from around the world. Based on similarities and differences at the microsatellite sites, and on rates of change at those genetic locations, the researchers suggest that all modern humans originated in Africa and then spread from there at about 150,000 years ago.

A recent study using a section of the Y (male) chromosome concluded that the most recent common ancestral male lived about 270,000 years ago (Dorit et al. 1995). No geographic conclusions were reached. This study, however, has been questioned, with several reinterpretations giving dates of half the original or even more recent (Fu and Li 1996; Donnelly et al. 1996; Weiss and von Heasler 1996; and Rogers et al. 1996).

More recently, a team coordinated by Ken Kidd at Yale (Tishkoff et al. 1996) compared more than 1600 people from 42 populations for two segments of DNA on chromosome 12. Sub-Saharan Africans showed a relatively great variety of genetic patterns for these segments, northeast Africans showed fewer varieties, and the populations from the rest of the world all shared a similar pattern. The suggestion is, again, an African origin for all modern humans. The team's calculations of the variation of one of the DNA segments points to a date of origin of around 100,000 ya.

In a somewhat different interpretation, it has also been hypothesized that population dynamics, rather than evolutionary branching, could account for some of the genetic data. As anthropologist John Relethford (1995) suggests, a large long-term population size in Africa could account for the greater genetic diversity found in modern populations there. Moreover, if some sort of population bottleneck (a drastic reduction in population size) took place at a recent point in time, and non-African populations have descended from a relatively small number of individuals (an example of the founder effect), the result would be the reduced genetic diversity seen in the rest of the world. The modern human species could *appear* young and evolutionarily distinct genetically, but in fact be much older.

An intriguing proposal has been made that infectious diseases (viruses like the well-known Ebola virus being likely candidates) might have been important agents of selection contributing to that bottleneck. Then, subsequent migrations of carriers of those pathogens might have brought them into contact with archaic populations who lacked immunity. This could help explain the replacement of archaics by moderns in some areas (Linda Van Blerkom, personal communication, 1996).

The great antiquity and anatomical modernity of some of the African fossils, the existence of fossils intermediate in appearance between archaic and modern, and the mtDNA and nuclear DNA research, if supported by further study, may solve the question posed at the beginning of this chapter: Where do we come from? Just as Africa served as the cradle of hominid evolution 5 million ya, it may also have served as the crucible in which modern humanity was forged perhaps as recently as 100,000 ya.

Clearly, however, the origin of modern humans is confusing. To return to Sherlock Holmes, we cannot yet distinguish the incidental from the vital. Existing evidence supports, if only in part, replacement over continuity, with modern *H. sapiens* appearing first in Africa and then expanding across the globe (Figure 12.12; see Figure 12.4). As is always the case in science, however, new data may support or refute the accepted model.

The Cultural Evidence

There is, of course, another source of data that we may use to assess the two models of modern human origins. If archaic *Homo sapiens* evolved into modern *Homo sapiens* only in Africa, as suggested by paleontological and genetic lines of evidence, then there should be an attendant jump in the sophistication of material culture—more elaborate tools—first in Africa, marking the greater intelligence of anatomically modern human beings.

Africa   The artifacts recovered at a number of early modern human sites in Africa do show a more sophisticated technology than contemporary tool assemblages in Europe and Asia associated with archaic humans. Anthropologist Sally McBrearty has discovered the world's oldest blade tools in Kenya (Gutin 1995). The tools were recovered at a site near Lake Baringo and dated to about 240,000 ya. The form of the blades indicates that their makers carefully prepared the stone cores from which they were struck to ensure the tools' precision and consistency (Figure 12.13, right). As McBrearty indicates, this kind of core preparation implies a high level of abstraction and planning on the part of the toolmakers. These stone blades offer a tantalizing first glimpse of the intellectual advance of hominids in Africa during a period of transition from archaic to modern *Homo sapiens*.

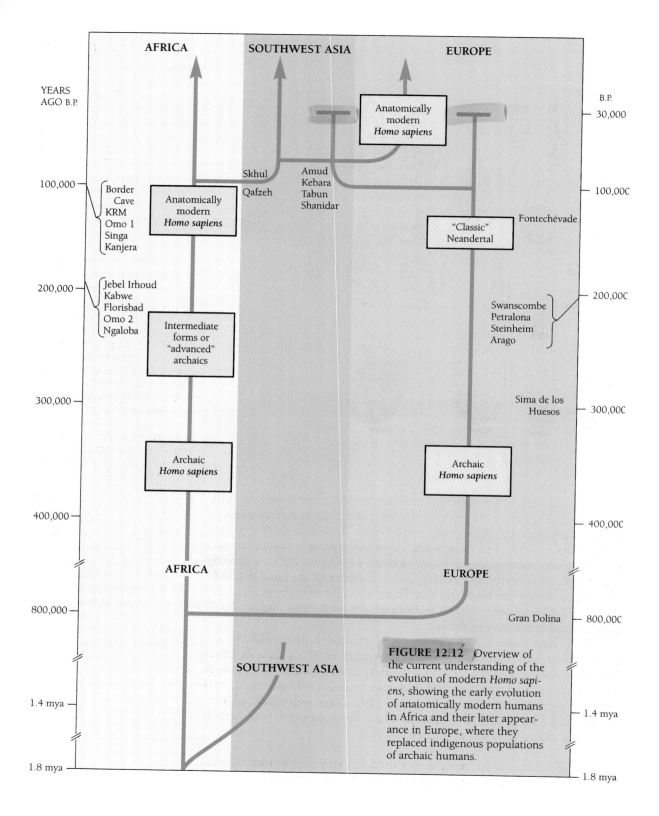

FIGURE 12.12 Overview of the current understanding of the evolution of modern *Homo sapiens*, showing the early evolution of anatomically modern humans in Africa and their later appearance in Europe, where they replaced indigenous populations of archaic humans.

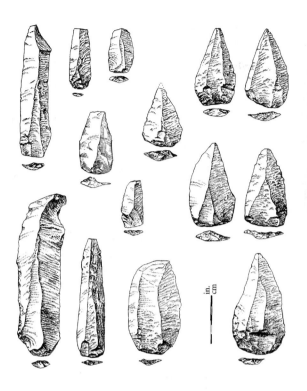

FIGURE 12.13   The precisely worked blade tools *(left)* were recovered from Klasies River Mouth in association with the skeletal remains of early anatomically modern human beings dating to about 100,000 ya. The stone blades *(right)* found near Lake Baringo in Kenya date to about 240,000 ya. These tools were produced after carefully preparing the stone core from which they were struck, implying a high level of planning on the part of the toolmakers. Both sets of tools are evidence of great technological sophistication on the part of anatomically modern human beings in Africa at an early date.   *(Left, from* The Middle Stone Age at Klasies River Mouth, South Africa, *by Ronald Singer and John Wymer, University of Chicago Press; right, Sally McBrearty)*

At Klasies River Mouth (KRM) in southern Africa there are long, bifacially worked spear points made on stone blades detached from cores by means of a punch technique (Singer and Wymer 1982). In this technique, long blades are removed from stone cores by striking a punch, usually made of antler, with a hammerstone, instead of striking the core directly with the stone hammer. The punch directs the force of the blow precisely, resulting in longer, narrower, thinner flakes of predictable shape and form (Figure 12.13, bottom). Such a technique, although more highly developed, occurs much later in Europe.

Three sites located in Katanda, Zaire, provide further evidence for more sophisticated toolmaking appearing earlier in Africa than in either Europe or Asia (Yellen et al. 1995). The sites, dated to about 90,000 years ago, have produced rather remarkable bone tools including barbed, harpoonlike piercing tools (Figure 12.14, p. 326). These well-made tools required quite a bit of skill to produce. Archaic *Homo sapiens* are not known to have produced anything at this level of skill.

Outside of Africa   If the replacement model is correct, the more intelligent moderns should have brought their more sophisticated tools with

FIGURE 12.14 Barbed bone artifacts found in Katanda, Zaire. These sophisticated implements date to more than 90,000 years ago and may reflect the greater intelligence and technological sophistication of the first anatomically modern *Homo sapiens* when compared to archaic members of our species. (*Allison Brooks, George Washington University*)

them as they expanded out of their African homeland. These new, advanced tools should show up in the archaeological record along with the skeletons of these first anatomically modern human beings.

The artifactual evidence is interesting, although not clearly supportive of this model. The stone tool assemblage of the earlier Neandertals of Europe and Southwest Asia simply does not look very different from the toolkits of the early moderns of Africa and Southwest Asia (Wolpoff 1989). Whatever advantage anatomically modern human beings may have had, outside of Africa it does not seem to have been in a more sophisticated material culture. As Alan Thorne and Milford Wolpoff (1992) point out, for example, the artifacts associated with the anatomically modern crania from Skhul and Qafzeh are virtually identical to those recovered from nearby, contemporaneous sites associated with typically Neandertal crania. There are striking similarities at 100,000 ya and even later, and it is not until fairly recently that the Upper Paleolithic modern human inhabitants of Europe produced the far more sophisticated tools of the Aurignacian tradition, to be discussed in Chapter 13.

On the other hand, some scientists see elements of replacement in the archaeological sequence. Archaeologist Frank Harrold (1989), for example, studied the older Mousterian industry associated with the European Neandertals (see Chapter 11) and a later industry, the **Châtelperronian**, also associated with the later Neandertals; it is the tool industry seen at the Neandertal sites of Saint-Césaire (36,000 B.P.) and Arcy-sur-Cure (34,000 B.P.). He compared Mousterian and Châtelperronian with the **Aurignacian** tool industry of Europe's first anatomically modern humans (see Chapter

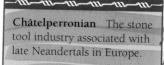

Châtelperronian The stone tool industry associated with late Neandertals in Europe.

Aurignacian The toolmaking tradition of anatomically modern *Homo sapiens* of the European Upper Paleolithic.

13). Aurignacian tools at Istallöskö in Hungary and Bacho Kiro Cave in Bulgaria (Straus 1989) dated to 43,000 years ago and in the El Castillo and L'Arbreda sites in Spain, have been dated to 38,000 years ago (Bischoff et al. 1989; Valdes and Bischoff 1989). Harrold found that the Châtelperronian possesses more sophisticated tools than the Mousterian, and the Aurignacian, in turn, is more sophisticated than the Châtelperronian. But there is no evidence of a transition from a Mousterian to an Aurignacian tradition, no sign of an evolution of the simpler Mousterian tradition of the Neandertals to the more sophisticated Aurignacian tradition of the first anatomically modern humans in Europe.

Harrold suggests, instead, that Mousterian-wielding Neandertals in Europe developed the more advanced Châtelperronian after coming into contact with and borrowing some ideas from Aurignacian-wielding modern humans who had entered Europe probably from Southwest Asia. Although the Aurignacian and Châtelperronian share many elements, Harrold suggests that the modern toolkit was slightly better and provided an advantage to the modern humans who used it. So, the artifactual evidence seems to support the replacement hypothesis. But it must be admitted that there is no good evidence in most areas for the wholesale replacement of a primitive tool technology practiced by archaic humans by an advanced technology practiced by modern humans.

The Shape of the Human Evolutionary Tree

We have brought you from the first bipedal steps of our hominid ancestors to the evolution of modern humanity. Let's now return to a topic first addressed in Chapter 4 and ask, What is the shape of our section of life's family tree? Is it made up of just a few fairly long branches with marked evolutionary change along some? Or is it more like a dense bush, with numerous, relatively short twigs—the individual hominid species?

At the moment, no one knows. Ian Tattersall (1993, 1995) and Bernard Wood (1992), probably the most extreme "splitters," recognize thirteen different hominid species in three genera. Others list fewer, in a bewildering array of combinations. For example, as we noted, some researchers lump *Paranthropus* with *Australopithecus;* others consider the Neandertals as *Homo sapiens* rather than a distinct species.

But the fact that a group of hominids is given a new name does not necessarily mean that the group was a whole new species. The differences upon which species names are given could be the result of evolutionary change within a single evolving lineage or of a considerable degree of phenotypic variation within a species. So the answer to these questions hinges on whether a new group is really different on a species level from other groups, regardless of what it is called for the sake of categorization. As you recall from Chapter 7, however, the ultimate test of a species—reproductive isolation—cannot be applied to fossil bones. The best that can be

FIGURE 12.15 Summary of the evolutionary chronology of the hominids from *Australopithecus* to anatomically modern humans.

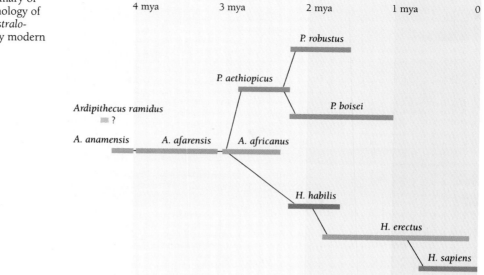

done is to compare variation in fossil groups to variation exhibited by living species. In this case, there are only a few living species—us and the African apes—to use as comparisons.

We would like to offer the diagram shown in Figure 12.15 as a reasonable working model for the evolutionary relationships among the well-acknowledged groups of hominids. We have already discussed *Australopithecus, Paranthropus,* and *Homo habilis* in Chapter 9. It seems clear that *Homo erectus* is a separate species (although some divide this group into several species), and the most logical guess at the moment is that it evolved from *Homo habilis* (although, again, some divide this species into multiple groups). Though there are strong arguments that archaic *Homo sapiens,* including the Neandertals, and anatomically modern *Homo sapiens* are different species, until there is better evidence the simplest view (and one for which there is support) is to consider these groups a single species, *Homo sapiens,* that displays considerable evolutionary change over time and across geographic space.

A new fossil find tomorrow, however, could change our minds. Such is the self-testing, self-correcting, self-critical nature of science.

Biological Diversity in Modern Humans

Anatomically modern *Homo sapiens* inhabits a wide geographic range. Indigenous populations of our species are found on all the continents but Antarctica. From our appearance in Africa perhaps sometime around 200,000 years ago, we quickly spread throughout the Old World and

JEMAAT GKI ZOLNER
Walley

moved into the New World about 15,000 years ago. We live in environments ranging from frigid Arctic tundra to hot, dry deserts; from low-lying, humid tropical rainforests to the cold, thin air of mountains thousands of feet high. One would certainly expect evolution to have acted on us over these many years and in these many environments to bring about a great deal of biological variation.

In addition, such widespread populations must have a degree of isolation from one another. It is unlikely, for example, that indigenous populations of Central Africa exchange genes either directly with peoples in the North American Arctic or even in a series of steps through intermediate populations. Moreover, humans add to their reproductive isolation through cultural rules of **endogamy**, which, for purposes of maintaining cultural, religious, or ethnic identity, require people to find mates only within their group. As a result, even human populations living side by side may not exchange genes on a regular basis.

Our wide geographic spread coupled with this cultural isolation make it no surprise that modern humans display a large number of **polymorphisms** and that certain clusters of these polymorphisms are characteristic of particular geographic areas (Figure 12.16). Nor can there be any doubt that the explanation for human polymorphisms lies in the processes of evolution acting on populations as they spread out into their incredible variety of environments.

FIGURE 12.16 A European American photographer with a group of Yali people from the highlands of Irian Jaya (the western half of New Guinea). There is little doubt as to who is who, nor that members of our species can display a striking degree of phenotypic variation. The major question then becomes: Does this degree of variation mean that there are distinguishable human races? (*© George Steinmetz/National Geographic*)

endogamy Marriage restricted to those within the same social group. Exogamy is marriage restricted to those outside the social group.

polymorphism A trait showing variation within a species as a result of genetic variation.

At issue are two concerns: first, the nature and extent of the role of natural selection and the other evolutionary processes in producing our variation, and second, whether our variation is such that we are divisible into identifiable biological races.

Natural Selection and Human Variation

To determine the role of natural selection in bringing about the variable expressions of a trait, one must first try to link those expressions to particular environmental circumstances. This is a difficult task with humans. For one thing, we have always been a mobile species, and, with modern modes of transportation and motives for travel, we are becoming more so. As a result, urban centers contain a wide cross section of human biological variation. Nearly every corner of the world must be represented by the inhabitants of New York City, for example. We must try, then, to make generalizations about the distributions of our polymorphisms, usually by using only indigenous groups—groups that we can assume represent populations that have been in certain areas for long periods of time with a minimum of genetic exchange.

In addition, as we have shown in previous chapters, culture allows us to adapt to new environmental conditions much more quickly than natural selection can evolve adaptations. Thus, one of our most notable biological traits, our big brain, has actually allowed us, via culture, to buffer ourselves increasingly against some of the action of natural selection. Traits that may have been selectively disadvantageous may now, in the context of our *cultural* adaptations, be neutral. Biological fitness is relative to the environment in which a trait is found. Where a society can correct physical impairments, these are no longer a barrier to reproductive success. If they have a genetic basis, they may then be passed on to future generations. Similarly, if some infectious disease is cured, then any genes it selected for or against may now vary at random through genetic drift. As a result, it can be difficult to tell just how important natural selection is in determining the existence and distribution of a human polymorphism.

For instance, the variation in blood type for the ABO system, a trait controlled by a single gene with three alleles, remained a mystery for some time—and is still not entirely solved. All people have one of four phenotypes: A, B, AB, or O (as do chimps and gorillas, by the way). These types appear in markedly different frequencies around the world (Figure 12.17). Type A, for example, is totally absent among some native South American groups but is found in frequencies of over 50 percent in parts of Europe, native Australia, and among a few native North American groups (although in North America it is still generally found among less than a quarter of the population). Type O, the most common worldwide, still ranges from 40 percent in parts of Asia to 100 percent among some native South Americans.

Studies have indicated that persons with particular blood types have greater susceptibility to such disorders as duodenal ulcer, stomach cancer,

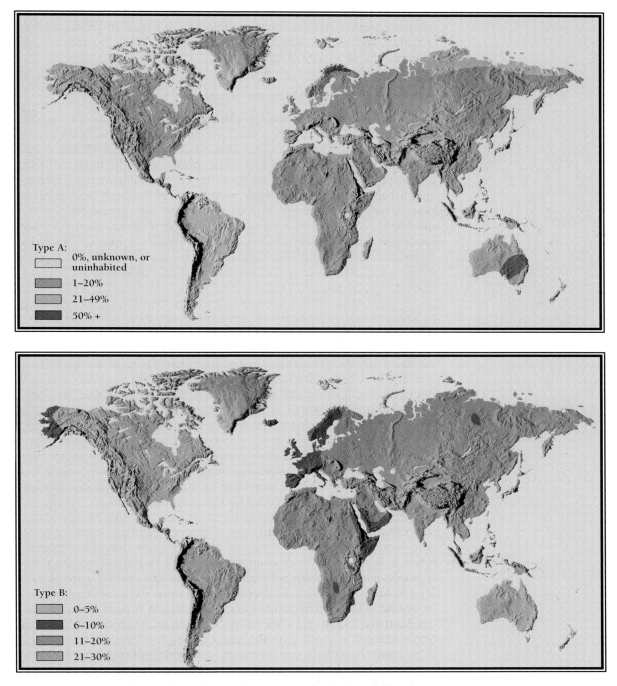

FIGURE 12.17   Approximate frequency distributions of type A and type B blood, demonstrating the lack of a pattern in the distribution of this polymorphism.

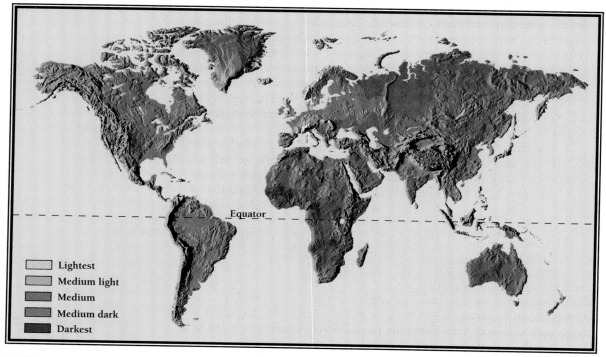

FIGURE 12.18 Skin color distribution. Darker skin is concentrated in equatorial regions. Compare the distribution of this polymorphism with the blood groups from Figure 12.17.

Legend:
Lightest
Medium light
Medium
Medium dark
Darkest

Equator

forms of anemia, bronchial pneumonia, smallpox, bubonic plague, and typhoid. Type O persons seem more attractive to mosquitoes, which, as we saw in the discussion of sickle cell anemia, can be disease carriers. But the completion of such studies is hindered by two obstacles. First, because humans have gained a good deal of control over many of these diseases, it is difficult to gather data about their links to blood type on a worldwide scale. We are forced to look into the past, before such control was gained, and thus make inferences based on historical records—data that are less than ideal. Second, we have yet to establish a cause-and-effect connection: What is it *about* certain blood types that makes the people who have them more or less susceptible to a disease or to the bite of an insect?

Perhaps phenotypic traits more directly and obviously affected by outside environmental conditions would be easier to explain adaptively. The human polymorphism of skin color is the classic example. Skin color is determined largely by the amount of the pigment melanin produced in the lowest layer of skin and distributed in the upper layers. This is a genetically controlled trait, though the exact genetic mechanism is still unknown.

Looking at indigenous populations, we see that darker skin is generally found closer to the Equator, and skin color gets lighter north and south of that line (Figure 12.18). Sunlight is more intense and less affected by seasonal fluctuations at the Equator, and too much ultraviolet (UV) radiation from the sun can cause sunburn, with accompanying cell destruction, infection, and heat exhaustion. Excessive exposure to the sun has also been shown to cause skin cancer. On the other hand, ultraviolet light is necessary for the synthesis of vitamin D, important for proper bone growth. Because human evolution began in the tropics (some early hominid fossils are found right on the Equator), our distant ancestors probably had dark skin. Populations that stayed in tropical regions retained this dark skin; those that moved away from the tropics underwent selection for lighter skin pigmentation.

It was thought that, in such populations, those with darker skin could not manufacture sufficient vitamin D for normal bone growth and maintenance. Those with lighter skin, therefore, had an adaptive advantage. Over time, lighter skin became the normal, inherited condition in such groups. Skin color was thus seen as a balancing act—dark enough to protect the skin from UV but light enough to allow UV's beneficial effects.

The vitamin D story has been questioned (Robins 1991). Rickets—abnormal bone growth caused by a deficiency of vitamin D—is associated largely with recent urban populations (in narrow city streets, children get little direct sun) and is seldom found in rural areas. There is little evidence for it in the human fossil record. The implication is that vitamin D production was not an important selective factor in the remote past. Moreover, although dark skin does slow down the production of vitamin D, it can still allow for sufficient synthesis of that chemical to maintain healthy levels at just about any latitude. The explanation for the evolution of light skin in humans remains a question.

There are, however, some human polymorphisms for which selective explanations, of varying strengths, exist. We discussed sickle cell anemia in Chapter 4. Another example is body build, which tends to be linear in hot climates to promote heat loss and, as with the Neandertals, stockier in cold climates to preserve heat (Figure 12.19, p. 334). Noses are long and narrow in cold or dry areas to help warm and moisten the air taken into the lungs. Short and broad noses are more common in places where air is already warm and moist.

Of course, some phenotypic variation may result not from natural selection to particular environmental circumstances but from one of the random processes of evolution—gene flow and genetic drift (see Chapter 4). This especially may be the case because human groups tend to be temporarily genetically isolated through geography or culture but are generally mobile and prone to genetic exchange. Groups have also, for most of human history, been relatively small. These are, as you recall, the conditions under which gene flow and genetic drift work best. For example, the high incidence of blood type A among the Blackfeet Indians might be attributed to the founder effect—the population being originally founded by a small group that, by chance, was uncharacteristically high in type A. Or, in a small ancestral Blackfeet population, allele frequencies may have drifted toward a high percentage of type A.

FIGURE 12.19 Body build is in part selected for conservation of heat, as in the Inuit (*left*) or promotion of heat loss, as in the Masai cattle herder from Kenya (*right*). (*Inuit: Courtesy Department of Library Services. American Museum of Natural History. Photo by D. B. MacMillan, July 1916; Masai: Bruce Dale, © 1969 National Geographic Society*)

If natural selection is not actively selecting for or against the frequencies of a set of alleles, these random processes are free to operate. Because not all variation is adaptively important all the time—and some variation may not be important at all—gene flow and genetic drift can have major effects on the distribution of alleles. For example, one of us (Park 1979, 1996) found a significant degree of variation in inherited features of fingerprints among populations and between generations of the Hutterites, a religious isolate from the western United States and Canada. Because these variables in fingerprints are of no known adaptive significance, this variation could only be the result of gene flow, founder effect, and gamete sampling.

In addition, variation results from environmental effects operating on the genotype–phenotype relationship. Although not clearly understood,

there is clearly some nongenetic influence on certain aspects of human fingerprints. Skin color is certainly affected by nongenetic factors. So some of
the variation in certain phenotypic traits may be caused by complex direct
environmental action. For blood type, however, there are no direct environmental influences, so all the variation must be genetic.

Modern humans display numerous variable traits. Some can be explained as the result of natural selection to certain environmental contexts.
Others are accounted for by flow and drift. Many show regularity in terms
of their geographic distribution. Does this mean that our species consists
of identifiable subspecies, semispecies, or races?

The Question of Human Races

Recall from Chapter 4 the discussion of speciation. Three conditions are
required for the evolution of subspecies or semispecies that may give rise
to a new species: (1) population isolation; (2) environments different
enough to promote adaptive selection in different directions, or a macromutation making a subpopulation genetically different; and (3) enough
time.

If either of the two replacement hypotheses is correct, then modern
humans have been around for somewhere between 100,000 and 200,000
years. One could argue about whether this is enough time for subspecies of
humans to have evolved. Since anatomically modern humans arose, however, and while we have been spreading and moving about, no human population has been isolated long enough or completely enough to allow
absolutely separate and independent genetic changes to take place. During
all that time, humans have in fact become increasingly mobile, and it seems
fair to say that we exchange genes at most opportunities.

To be sure, rules of endogamy do exist, and they tend to isolate certain
populations genetically at certain times. But such rules are not always fully
upheld and sometimes they are changed. Also, the populations defined by
the rules change through time. Endogamy is a temporary condition. Geographic isolation is temporary. Gene flow is the real rule.

Then there is the matter of culture—our major adaptive mechanism.
Even where natural selection had an effect on certain characteristics, such
as skin color, these adaptive differences were minor compared to the major
adaptation of culture. The cultural adaptation was well developed and part
of our hominid line long before modern humans arose. Our big brains—
the basis of our cultural potential—are shared by all modern humans and
are so important and basic that they are unlikely to show much major variation. Further, the products of the cultural ability—social systems, beliefs,
technology—act as a buffer against much of the effect of natural selection.

Finally, as recent genetic studies have shown, we are a very genetically
homogeneous species. About 75 percent of all human genes are
monomorphic; that is, all humans are identical for 75 percent of the

human genome (Lewontin 1982:120). The genetic variation that does exist is relatively evenly distributed. Richard Lewontin (1982:123) calculates that if some great cataclysm left only Africans alive, that remnant of the human species would still retain 93 percent of the total genetic variation of the former world population.

Our variation, then, is part of ongoing dynamic processes: the editing by natural selection of traits within a widespread, highly mobile, generalized, and fairly recent species combined with the operation of the other processes of evolution on our temporarily isolated but generally highly mobile individual populations. Such a situation doesn't allow for the kinds of conditions necessary to produce distinguishable subspecies or semispecies. Although some human traits or trait clusters tend to be geographically localized (see Figure 12.16), nearly all our features are spread across many populations and geographic areas. Dark skin, for example, is an *equatorial* trait, not only an African one, as many are inclined to consider it.

Further, no real boundaries exist between trait expressions. Although we divided skin color expression into five categories for the sake of diagramming the distribution of this trait (see Figure 12.18), skin color doesn't change abruptly as the map may imply. It changes *gradually* in populations closer to or farther from the Equator. Such a distribution, called a **cline,** simply cannot be divided into discrete units because its expressions don't come in neat packages with clear geographic boundaries.

Finally, when we compare the distributions of human polymorphisms, we see incongruities. The distribution of one trait seldom matches the distribution of any other. Some sort of subspecific division based on one trait will invariably differ from that based on another. Compare the maps (Figures 12.17 and 12.18) for blood type and skin color, for instance. The variations of these traits are very different in their distributions. Subspecies based on the distribution of one would be very different from those based on the other. It would be hard to force either of these traits—or nearly any human trait—into biologically meaningful units. At the phenotypic level, human variation exists, but human races don't.

Does this mean, however, that the modern human species is one gigantic stew of people, with no discernible groups and thus no way to trace the history of populations? Whereas phenotypic traits only serve to confuse the matter, increasing knowledge of genetics does permit precise comparisons of living indigenous populations to one another and the beginning of a family tree determining where populations originated and how they spread.

Some of the genetic studies noted earlier with regard to the origin of modern *Homo sapiens* have allowed researchers to produce trees indicating the relationships among populations from which the DNA samples were drawn (see Figure 12.11, for example). One early study by L. L. Cavalli-Sforza and colleagues (Cavalli-Sforza 1991) was interpreted to show a series of major migrations by which our species populated the planet (see

cline A geographic continuum in the variation of a specific phenotype.

Genetic Groups	Living Populations	Linguistic Groups
African	San	Khoisan
	Masai	Nilo-Saharan
	Mbuti	Niger-Congo
	Ethiopian	Afro-Asiatic
Caucasoid	Southwestern Asian	
	Mediterranean	Indo-European
	Northern European	
	Indian	
American	North American	Amerind
	Central American	
	South American	
Arctic	Eskimo	Eskimo-Aleut
	Siberian	Altaic
Northeast Asian	Japanese	
	Korean	
	Tibetan	Sino-Tibetan
Mainland Island Southeast Asian	Southern Chinese	
	Indonesian	
	Philippine	Austronesian
	Polynesian	
Pacific Islands	Melanesian	Indo-Pacific
	New Guinean	Australian
	Australian	

FIGURE 12.20   The correlation between genetic and language groups within modern humans. The living populations listed are a representative sample. Note that where populations live close to one another under similar conditions, as is the case for Ethiopians and Southwest Asians, they may speak languages of the same group even though they are genetically different. *(Data from Cavalli-Sforza 1991)*

Figure 12.4). Moreover, it was found that the distribution of genes coincided to a great degree with the distribution of languages. Languages and genetic populations can be correlated because as human populations split and separate, "each fragment evolves linguistic and genetic patterns that bear marks of shared branching points" (Cavalli-Sforza 1991:109). In addition, "linguistic differences [and the cultural differences they reflect] may generate or reinforce genetic barriers between populations. Hence, some correlation is inevitable" (1991:109). Figure 12.20 is a simplified diagram of this correlation.

Contemporary Issue

The "Eve" Hypothesis

Using mitochondrial DNA differences in modern populations to work backward toward establishing the origin of modern *Homo sapiens* has led to a rather confusing issue. Because mtDNA is only inherited maternally, these studies are actually tracing descent through females. The fact that our species, according to these studies, began fairly recently plus the fact that no modern population differs from any other by even as much as 1 percent of their mtDNA, has led some investigators to conclude that *all* modern mtDNA is derived from a single female who lived in Africa around 200,000 ya. Naturally, it was tempting to dub her "Eve," a metaphorical reference to the creation story in Genesis.

Obviously, this mitochondrial Eve is *not* the Eve of the Bible. None of the scientific account of evolution is refuted by the mtDNA studies. It was, perhaps, just a poor choice of names, confounded by some very sketchy, sensationalized, and confusing early reports in the media.

The second area of misunderstanding is more technical. Some took the Eve idea to mean that our *entire species* began with one African female. First of all, there clearly has to be at least one male involved. (Yes, some media accounts called him "Adam.") But no species (at least no complex, multicellular, sexually reproducing species) begins with a single couple. Anatomically modern *H. sapiens* began with an interbreeding population, genetically different and isolated from its ancestral archaic population.

What the Eve hypothesis says is that all *modern mtDNA* is inherited from a single female. Although our species began with a number of "Eves," the mitochondrial lines of all but one died out. An analogous phenomenon occurs with family names (Lewin 1991:52–53). Begin with ten couples, each with a different surname. Assume that the surnames are passed down through the males and each couple has two children. After twenty generations, the chances are very good that only one surname will remain. Why? In each generation one-quarter of the couples on average will have two boys who will pass on the name. But one-half will have a boy and a girl, so one of the children will not pass on the name, and one-quarter will have two girls, so the name will die out.

The same thing happens with mtDNA, except, of course, that it is inherited through the females, and there is the added factor of different numbers of children born to different women, including, of course, the fact that some women have *no* children.

So, if the replacement model is correct, all of us living now are descended with nuclear DNA from an African population of archaic *H. sapiens* that, for reasons not yet understood, diverged and evolved along its own lines. That we may have all inherited our mtDNA from one female simply serves to indicate that the divergence was localized rather than the widespread event proposed by the multiregional hypothesis.

Our species doesn't sort itself into the clear-cut, ancient, and profoundly different racial groups assumed by earlier generations. We are too new, too mobile, too genetically homogeneous, and too culturally adapted for that. But the richness of our genetic, ethnic, and cultural variety is not lost within some worldwide melting pot. And to say that there *are* human populations, identified by several correlated factors, is not to say that such groups are in any way so different as to warrant differential social treatment. We have far more similarities than we do differences. Still, racism and bigotry—often based on a misreading of the biological facts—remain one of our most vexing problems.

Summary

Although the evidence is far more substantial for the most recent 200,000 years of hominid evolution, the origin and development of anatomically modern human beings are still points of contention and controversy for paleoanthropologists. None of the three major competing models—multiregional, population replacement, or genetic replacement—can be proven absolutely at this time. Nevertheless, the paleontological, genetic, and archaeological evidence currently available seems to point toward the population replacement model. In this view, anatomically modern human beings evolved in a single place—probably Africa, south of the Sahara—from a local population of archaic *Homo sapiens,* sometime after 200,000 and before 100,000 ya. From their place of origin, these modern humans spread across the globe, coming into contact with local, indigenous archaics (the Neandertals) in Europe and Southwest Asia and with other archaics and, possibly, even remnant groups of *Homo erectus* in East Asia. Everywhere the moderns came into contact with the archaics, they replaced them as a result of some adaptive advantage.

The current state of our species includes a striking degree of phenotypic variation. Our polymorphic traits, some showing geographical regularity in distribution, may be explained as the result of the processes of evolution acting on a widespread, populous, mobile, and culture-bearing species. These traits, however, do not sort themselves into clear-cut, discrete categories that would constitute subspecies, semispecies, or races.

Study Questions

1. Contrast the multiregional, population replacement, and genetic replacement models of the evolution of anatomically modern *Homo sapiens.*
2. How, and in what ways, does the fossil hominid record support or refute each of the three models presented to explain the evolution of anatomically modern *Homo sapiens:* the multiregional, population replacement, and genetic replacement models?
3. How, and in what ways, does modern human genetics support or refute each of the three models presented to explain the evolution of anatomically modern *Homo sapiens?*

4. How, and in what ways, does material culture—the artifacts recovered by archaeologists—support or refute each of the three models presented to explain the evolution of anatomically modern *Homo sapiens?*
5. What can we say about the overall shape of the hominid section of life's family tree? How many branches of hominids have there been, and how and when have they diverged from one another?
6. What is the nature of the biological diversity within the human species? What processes account for variable phenotypes?
7. Based upon this knowledge, what can we say—on a biological level—about the existence of human races?

Key Terms

multiregional hypothesis	nuclear DNA	polymorphism
population replacement hypothesis	mitochondrial DNA	cline
genetic replacement hypothesis	symbiosis	
	Châtelperronian	
	Aurignacian	
	endogamy	

For More Information

For brief descriptions of many of the fossils discussed here, see Michael Day's (1988) *Guide to Fossil Man.* Also see Smith (1984), Trinkaus (1984), and Smith and Spencer (1984).

For presentations of the multiregional hypothesis, see Milford Wolpoff's (1988, 1989) articles in *The Emergence of Modern Humans: Biocultural Adaptations in the Later Pleistocene* and *The Human Revolution: Behavioral and Biological Perspectives in the Origins of Modern Humans.* For a defense of the replacement hypothesis, see Christopher Stringer's (1990) article "The Emergence of Modern Humans," in *Scientific American. Discover* magazine has published a number of articles on this debate; see Jared Diamond's article in the May 1989 issue, James Shreve's article of August 1990, and Joshua Fischman's article of February 1992. For technical summaries of the debate over modern human origins from the perspective of the multiregionalists, see Volume 95, Number 1 of *American Anthropologist* for articles by Frayer et al. (1993) and Templeton (1993) as well as a replacement-oriented position in an article by Leslie Aiello (1993). Another nice summary favoring replacement is an article by Richard Klein (1992) in the journal *Evolutionary Anthropology.* And, of course, see any of the articles by Christopher Stringer, especially his 1994 summary, "Out of Africa: A Personal History," for a strong presentation of the replacement model. Also find a strong defense of the replacement model in a new book co-authored by Christopher Stringer and Robin McKie (1996) titled *African Exodus: The Origins of Modern Humanity.*

On the issue of human biological diversity, we recommend Stephen Molnar's *Human Variation: Races, Types, and Ethnic Groups;* Richard Lewontin's *Human Diversity* (1982), and Jonathan Marks's *Human Biodiversity: Genes, Race, and History* (1995). For a collection of articles on the nonexistence of human biological races, see *The Concept of Race* edited by Ashley Montagu (1964), and for a nice treatment of the history of race studies, try Kenneth A. R. Kennedy's *Human Variation in Space and Time* (1976).

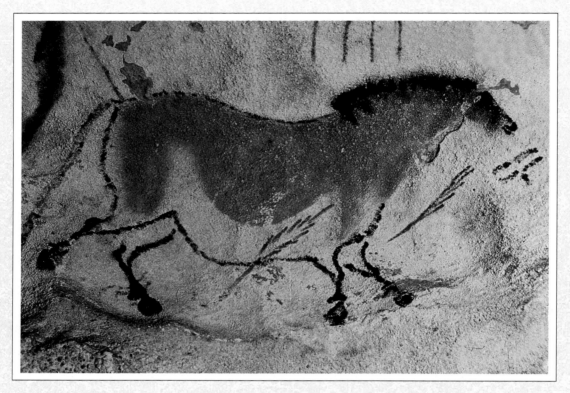

The cave paintings of the upper Paleolithic are recognizable as modern human behavior; they are, in fact, art. What is the significance of the apparent intellectual leap forward that characterizes this period? How and when did the Upper Paleolithic inhabitants of the Old World expand into Australia and North and South America? *(© Art Resource, NY)*

13

New Ideas, New Worlds
Life in the Upper Paleolithic

—◊◊—

CHAPTER CONTENTS

Comparing the Middle and Upper Paleolithic • Art in the European Upper Paleolithic •
Brave New Worlds • Summary • Study Questions • Key Terms • For More Information

Anatomically modern *Homo sapiens,* people who looked just like us, can be traced in the fossil record to at least 100,000 years ago. With brains the size of ours and with proportions indistinguishable from ours, these first anatomically modern humans are assumed to have been intellectually modern as well, in the sense that they possessed the same level of intelligence as us. Certainly, their cultures differed from ours, but the consensus is that their intellectual capabilities were identical; if an anatomically modern human being from 100,000 years ago could be transported to the present and given your education, he or she could read this book and understand it as well as you.

Therein lies a great apparent mystery. There are some hints of intellectual sophistication by 240,000 years ago in the blade tools found near Lake Baringo in Kenya and later, a bit after 100,000 years ago in the toolmaking technologies of the anatomically modern humans at Klasies River Mouth and in the bone industry at the Katanda sites (see Chapter 12). Still, the material culture—the artifacts—of the earliest anatomically modern human beings is by and large not all that different from that of the archaic humans who shared their world. In fact, a great jump in the sophistication of material culture does not occur until long after the initial appearance of anatomically modern humans. It is not until after 50,000 years ago, and in some spheres of culture after 40,000 and even 30,000 years ago, that we begin to see the material remains of behaviors reflecting recognizably modern capabilities on the part of ancient people.

We do not yet understand why recognizably modern human culture lags behind the appearance of anatomically modern humans. Archaeologist Richard Klein (1989, 1994) has proposed that the so-called anatomically modern humans of 100,000 years ago were only superficially modern, retaining a fundamentally archaic brain. In other words, their modern-looking skulls continued to house archaic brains that were intellectually incapable of producing a modern material culture. Klein suggests that what amounts to a rewiring of the human brain occurred sometime between 40,000 and 50,000 years ago, allowing for a great leap to modern intelligence.

Whatever the case—and there is no general consensus on this issue—most scientists agree with archaeologist Anthony Marks (1990:56), who characterizes what happens after 50,000 years ago as "a profound and fundamental change in both behavior and human potential." The period of this fundamental change—the Upper Paleolithic or Late Stone Age—is the focus of this chapter.

Comparing the Middle and Upper Paleolithic

Paleoanthropologist Randall White, both alone (1982) and together with Heidi Knecht and Anne Pike-Tay (Knecht et al. 1993), has examined some of the major differences between cultures of the European Middle and Upper Paleolithic, identifying several significant cultural innovations:

1. Stone tool technologies based on the production of elongated blades rather than flakes.
2. Broadening of the subsistence base to include big-game hunting, small-mammal trapping, fishing, and catching birds.
3. Increased use of bone, ivory, and antler for making tools.
4. Manufacture of nonutilitarian objects, particularly items of personal adornment.
5. Larger, perhaps more sedentary, settlements.

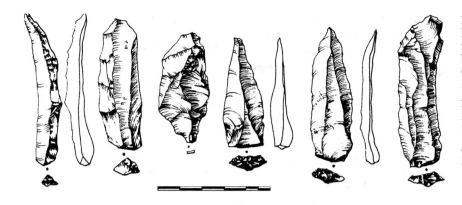

FIGURE 13.1   Upper Paleolithic stone tool technologies marked by elongated blades can be seen at Ksar Akil, in Lebanon (examples shown here) dated to 52,000 years ago.   *(Reprinted from Paul Mellars, ed.:* The Emergence of Modern Humans: An Archaeological Perspective. *Copyright © Edinburgh University Press. Used by permission of the publisher, Cornell University Press)*

6. The movement of raw materials across long distances, implying greater social integration of distant and diverse groups.
7. Elaborate burials including personal items to accompany the deceased.
8. Production of the first recognizable works of art in the form of paintings and sculpture.

1. Stone tool technologies based on the production of elongated blades rather than flakes. Blades are commonly defined as a special variety of flakes at least twice as long as they are wide (Figure 13.1). More than five times the amount of usable edge can be produced from the same quantity of stone than when regular flakes were being produced. Blade tools are now dated back as much as 240,000 ya in central Africa and constitute a significant part of the artifact assemblage at Klasies River Mouth in southern Africa at about 100,000 ya (see Chapter 12). In Southwest Asia, a broader shift from a Levallois prepared core and flake technology (see Chapter 11) to a stone tool technology based on the production of blades has been dated to perhaps as early as 52,000 ya at Ksar Akil in Lebanon, 45,000 B.P. at Boker Tachtit in Israel (A. Marks 1993), a bit before 40,000 B.P. in central and southeastern Europe (Svoboda 1993), and 40,000 B.P. at Haua Fteah Cave in Africa (Van Peer and Vermeersch 1990).

A blade-based stone tool technology developed in western Europe by about 35,000 B.P. (Allsworth-Jones 1990). The earliest such tools, belonging to the so-called Aurignacian culture, date to between 34,000 and 27,000 years ago (Figure 13.2). The Aurignacian includes long, sharp cutting tools; engraving tools called burins; and stone scrapers. The Aurignacian is followed by the **Gravettian** tradition (27,000 to 21,000 B.P.) with its emphasis on smaller blades and denticulate knives—cutting tools with numerous small, pointed projections along their cutting edges. The **Solutrean** tradition, dated from 21,000 to 16,000 years ago, includes the production of exquisite, bifacially flaked, symmetrical, leaf-shaped projec-

Gravettian Upper Paleolithic toolmaking tradition, characterized by the production of small and denticulate knives. Dated from 27,000 to 21,000 B.P.

Solutrean Stone toolmaking tradition of the European Upper Paleolithic, dating from 21,000 to 16,000 B.P.

FIGURE 13.2 Aurignacian flint blades from France. This Upper Paleolithic industry made use of a core and blade technology in which long, thin, extremely sharp stone blades were struck from stone nodules. (*K. L. Feder*)

tile points (Figure 13.3). The Solutrean was followed by the **Magdelanian** from 16,000 to 11,000 B.P., where very small **microblades** were made. The Magdelanian is best known for the manufacture of bone and antler tools.

2. Broadening of the subsistence base to include big-game hunting, small-mammal trapping, fishing, and catching birds. Leslie Freeman (1973) has compared faunal assemblages from seventy-seven levels at twenty Middle and Upper Paleolithic cave sites in northern Spain. He found that the older assemblages showed that a small number of animal species were exploited and few members of each species were represented. He concludes that the Middle Paleolithic inhabitants of this area were opportunistic hunters, killing what they could when they could.

In the Upper Paleolithic levels, however, Freeman identified a consistent increase through time in the number of prey species represented, indicating, perhaps, more efficient hunting strategies. The evidence seems to indicate that the anatomically modern inhabitants of these caves were habitual hunters.

At Dolni Vestonice I in the Czech Republic, the remains of more than 100 mammoths slaughtered and butchered by the inhabitants have been identified (Soffer 1993). At this same site, butchering marks have been located on the remains of horse and reindeer as well. Subsistence at Mal'ta, in south-central Russia near the modern city of Irkutsk (Chard 1974), clearly was based on the hunting of the big-game animals that migrated across the tundra in a yearly pattern, especially woolly rhinoceros, woolly mammoth, and reindeer. They almost certainly used the hides from these animals for clothing. They also trapped foxes and other small mammals for their pelts. Interestingly, they buried the remains of the skinned foxes.

Magdelanian Late Upper Paleolithic culture in Europe dating from 16,000–11,000 B.P. Includes finely made barbed harpoons, carved decorative objects, and cave paintings.

microblades Small, usually extremely sharp, stone blades. Microblades were set into handles of bone, wood, antler, and so forth.

FIGURE 13.3   Bifacially flaked Solutrean spear points of the European Upper Paleolithic are examples of some of the finest stonework the world has ever seen. (*K. L. Feder*)

3. Increased use of bone, ivory, and antler for making tools. The Upper Paleolithic is the period when our human ancestors perfected technologies that previously they had only experimented with, employing raw materials other than stone, including bone, ivory, and antler. These tools include sewing equipment like awls, punches, and eyed-needles, as well as hunting equipment like projectile points. Barbed bone harpoons; antler hammers; and wrenchlike, bone "shaft-straighteners" all have been found in Upper Paleolithic sites from Western Europe to East Asia. The technology hinted at by the Katanda sites (Chapter 12) flowers during the Upper Paleolithic.

People living in the harsh glacial climate at the site of Mal'ta would have needed shelter for protection from the cold conditions of the Pleistocene. During its occupation, however, the site was located in tundra, so trees would have been largely unavailable for construction purposes. The people at Mal'ta developed an ingenious solution to this problem. They used the leg and rib bones of large animals such as the woolly mammoth for the structural framework of their dwellings. On the roof, where the weight of such bones would have been too great, they used lighter elements like reindeer antlers. On this bone–antler frame, they attached animal hides, held in place on the ground with large boulders (Figure 13.4).

4. Manufacture of nonutilitarian objects, particularly items of personal adornment. At the 13,000-year-old site of Rocher de la Peine in France, an Upper Paleolithic jewelry maker produced a beautiful necklace made of dentalium shell beads, three large bear teeth and one tooth of a European

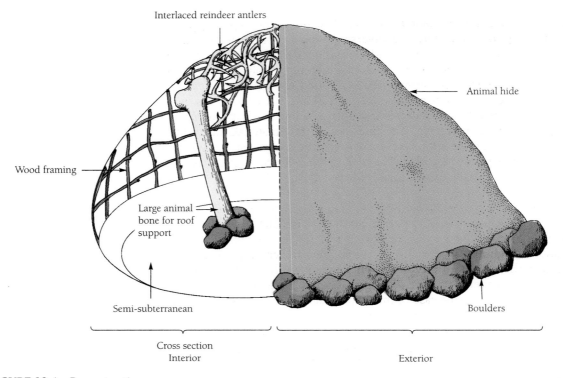

Interlaced reindeer antlers

Animal hide

Wood framing

Large animal
bone for roof
support

Semi-subterranean

Boulders

Cross section
Interior

Exterior

FIGURE 13.4 Reconstruction of a hut at the 18,000-year-old site of Mal'ta in south-central Russia. Because wood was not available on the tundra, the bones of woolly mammoth and the antlers of reindeer were used as construction materials.

lion (Dennell 1986). The shell came from the coast, located about 100 miles away from the site. At Mal'ta we see a tradition of carved artwork, perhaps as part of a religious pattern. These three-dimensional bone and ivory carvings included human female figurines and waterfowl as well as jewelry. These people also incised on antler and bone intricate two-dimensional, abstract designs of curved lines and occasional realistic animals like the woolly mammoth.

As Randall White (1982) points out, the appearance of well-made items of personal adornment, often manufactured from exotic material that must have been difficult to obtain is diagnostic of the Upper Paleolithic. In White's view, items of personal adornment imply a growing awareness and significance of the individual in Upper Paleolithic society.

5. Larger, perhaps more sedentary, settlements. Some Upper Paleolithic sites are much larger than Middle Paleolithic habitations and the artifact scatter is far denser. The site of Mal'ta, in Siberia, for example, covers an area of some six hundred square meters (about 7,500 square feet) (Chard 1974:20), with the remains of numerous dwellings similar to those described earlier. Randall White (1982) interprets these as places of aggregation, sites that people repeatedly visited at times of the year when resources in the area may have been particularly abundant.

6. The movement of raw materials across long distances, implying greater social integration of distant and diverse groups. In south-central Europe, tools made of flint have been found more than 100 kilometers (65 miles) from their source (Oliva 1993:52). Apparently highly valued material like obsidian (volcanic glass) from Hungary is found in Paleolithic sites up to 500 kilometers (325 miles) away (Oliva 1993:52). Even in cases where quite serviceable stone was locally available, often material obtainable only at great distances was used. The discovery of raw materials many miles from their sources may indicate the existence of an extensive network of trade in the Upper Paleolithic. The ability to trade across great distances implies geographically broad social connections.

7. Elaborate burials including personal items to accompany the deceased. We saw in Chapter 11 that the Neandertals were the first hominids to bury the dead and include grave goods in their interments. As Frank Harrold's analysis shows (1980), Neandertal burials were rather simple when compared to those of anatomically modern humans in the Upper Paleolithic. Compare Neandertal burials with their handful of stone tools or animal bones with the extreme case of the Upper Paleolithic burials at the site of Sungir' located about 150 kilometers (100 miles) northeast of Moscow (R. White 1993). Dating to at least 25,000 to 30,000 years ago, five burials (an older male, an adult female, a young girl, a teenage boy, and an individual whose sex has not been determined) have been excavated at the site.

The Sungir' graves are filled with objects, primarily items of adornment. Nearly 3000 finely worked ivory beads, some apparently part of a beaded cap, were found with the body of the old man. On his arms were twenty-five finely carved bracelets made from woolly mammoth ivory. The young boy's body was surrounded with more than 4900 ivory beads and he wore a decorated belt with 250 polar fox teeth; there was an ivory pin at his throat, an ivory lance and carved ivory disk at his side, and an ivory sculpture of a woolly mammoth under his shoulder (all data on the Sungir' graves taken from White 1993:287–96). The Sungir' burial goods obviously represent an enormous investment in time and energy. They also seem poignantly to reflect the care and love provided to the dead by their living comrades. In this respect, perhaps especially, the humanity of these people is clearly recognizable.

8. Production of the first recognizable works of art in the form of paintings and sculpture. Beginning as early as 35,000 ya and continuing until about 10,000 ya, human groups in Europe, Africa, and Australia produced some of the world's first art.

In a 25,000-year period that, as Margaret Conkey (1983) points out, constitutes the first two-thirds of human art history, Upper Paleolithic people produced a remarkable variety of artwork in numerous media and styles. They carved stone, bone, antler, and ivory; produced bas-reliefs;

made ceramic figurines; engraved objects with both natural figures and abstract designs; and painted fantastic friezes on cave walls. Their artwork was rendered in styles ranging from representational to abstract.

At Panaramitee North in Australia, a curvilinear petroglyph (a design scratched into the rock) has been dated to 43,000 B.P. (Bednarik 1993:6). At the nearby site of Wharton Hill, an oval shape was etched into a rock face more than 36,000 years ago (Bednarik 1993:5). These dates, if correct, render the Australian petroglyphs the earliest evidence of art in the world.

The first African art has been dated to about 28,000 years ago (Phillipson 1993). Stone slabs with painted and engraved images of animals have been excavated from deposits dating to this time at the Apollo 11 Cave site in southern Namibia (Wendt 1976). The animals are natural renderings of the fauna of southern Africa at the time. The oldest cave art in the New World probably dates to between 10,000 and 11,200 years ago in the Caverna da Pedra Pintada in Brazil (Roosevelt et al. 1996). Red pigment images in that cave and in other caves in the region include concentric circles, human handprints, and spirit beings (see the discussion of the site later in this chapter).

Art in the European Upper Paleolithic

It is largely the European Upper Paleolithic cave paintings and engravings, however, that so capture the imagination; a few hundred caves with paintings are known, most of them clustered in southwest France and northern Spain, the region called Franco-Cantabria (Figure 13.5). In often naturalistic works, the ancient artists painted bison, oxen, horses, deer, mammoth, ibex, rhinoceros, lion, and bear. Though there is a great deal of variation, many of the animals are by no means simplistically or childishly rendered. They are sophisticated, fluid, and natural, and they were painted on cave walls from 30,000 to 10,000 years ago (Bahn and Vertut 1988).

The artwork is striking indeed, moving even the most objective of scientists to speak in superlatives. In anthropologist Pat Shipman's words, "I had looked at photographs of Lascaux [one of the best known caves], of course, so I knew that the paintings were beautiful; but what I did not know was that they would reach across 17,000 years to grab my soul" (1990:62).

Natural pigments were produced by grinding into powder ochre for orange, yellow, and red; iron oxides for brown; and manganese dioxide for black. The powder was then mixed with a binding agent like grease, marrow, or blood. Using fingers, wooden spatulas, and brushes made of twigs or even animal hair, the artists applied the paint to their prehistoric canvases—the cave walls of Lascaux, Roc de Sers, Trois Fréres, Niaux, and the recently discovered Chauvet in France, Altamira and Casares in Spain, and many others.

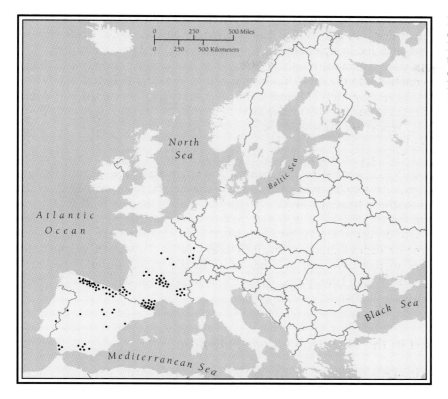

FIGURE 13.5   Geographical distribution of Upper Paleolithic European cave paintings. Most of the sites are clustered in the area of Franco-Cantabria in southern France and northern Spain. *(After Jochim 1983)*

The painted figures of these caves are not static or two-dimensional. They seem to move across the cave walls with muscles rippling, sinews straining (Figure 13.6, p. 352). A herd of woolly mammoths, extinct for more than 10,000 years, lives again as they march single file across the cave wall at Rouffignac. An extinct bison with tail upraised, poised to flee, is frozen in time in Altamira. Another bison stands motionless, mortally wounded by spears, on the rock face in Niaux. A cluster of rhinoceros stand guard on the wall at Chauvet Cave (see Figure 13.7, p. 353). Such paintings offer us a rare glimpse into an ancient world. They are a wonderful legacy left by the ancient peoples of Europe.

These Upper Paleolithic artists also produced three-dimensional works. For example, carved in limestone or ivory and even made of baked clay, the so-called **Venus figurines** largely are faceless women, many with exaggerated secondary sexual characteristics (large breasts and buttocks) and often swollen stomachs (Figure 13.8, p. 354). Beginning about 28,000 years ago and produced over as much as a 10,000 year timespan, the Venus figurines are geographically more widespread than the cave paintings, with examples found in sites nearly 5000 kilometers (3000 miles) apart (Soffer 1988) (Figure 13.9, p. 355).

Venus figurines Sculptures of women, sometimes with exaggerated secondary sexual characteristics, dating to as many as 32,000 ya.

FIGURE 13.6 The so-called Chinese horse (*left*), depicted in mid-gallop on the cave wall of Lascaux, France. The Great Black Aurochs (*right*)—a species of wild cattle—also from Lascaux. Painted more than 17,000 years ago, the images at Lascaux exemplify the truly artistic character of the Upper Paleolithic cave paintings. (*Both photos: © Art Resource, NY*)

What Did the Venus Figurines Mean?

It seems unlikely that cave paintings, engravings, or sculptures were simply decoration; many of the cave sites where paintings have been found were not occupied by humans. The Venus figurines have long been thought to represent a mother goddess or to reflect an Upper Paleolithic ceremonialism regarding fertility. And, indeed, some of the figurines do appear to be of pregnant women. However, the situation is not at all clear. Patricia Rice (1981) looked at a group of 188 Venus figurines and found their shape, size, and form to be quite varied. There were depictions of thin and fat women, women with large breasts and women with small breasts, pregnant and not pregnant women, and women who were, by Rice's careful estimation, old, middle-aged, and young.

FIGURE 13.7 The Upper Paleolithic paintings at Chauvet Cave in France are among ▶ the most spectacular ever found. In caves found previously, the extinct rhinoceros species that inhabited late Pleistocene Europe was rarely depicted. At Chauvet, however, the artists portrayed about fifty of them. (*AP/Wide World Photos*)

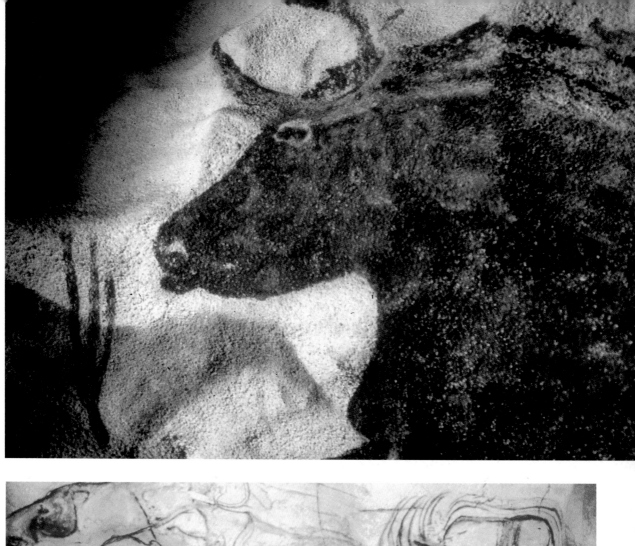

FIGURE 13.8 The precise meaning of the so-called Venus figurines is unknown. Only some possess the stereotypical exaggerated secondary sexual features and pregnant appearance. The famous "Venus of Willendorf" *(left);* a cast of the Venus from Dolni Vestonice, the Czech Republic. *(Left: © Naturhistorisches Museum Wien, Neg. #9057F; right: Courtesy Department of Library Services. American Museum of Natural History. Neg. #2169(2).)*

Rice (1981:408) suggests that the apparent age spread of the women depicted in her sample of figurines was similar to the actual age distribution in historical hunter-gatherer populations. Rice deduces that the Venus figurines are renderings of women of all ages and states of fertility. In her view, the figurines can't be used to support a hypothesis of a fertility cult.

In another approach, Clive Gamble (1982, 1983, 1986) has attempted to explain the social significance of the Venus figurines, if not their actual meaning to the makers. He states that these portable artworks peaked during a glacial maximum. Outside Franco-Cantabria, resources would have been dispersed, and people would have needed to disperse to exploit them. The social problem that resulted was one of maintaining mating networks within cultural systems of low population density. According to Gamble, a common art style associated with ritual would have functioned to keep such a widespread system intact.

What Do the Cave Paintings Mean?

Several hypotheses have been advanced to explain the meaning of the cave paintings in particular and Paleolithic art in general. As summarized by Conkey (1983), cave paintings have been explained as:

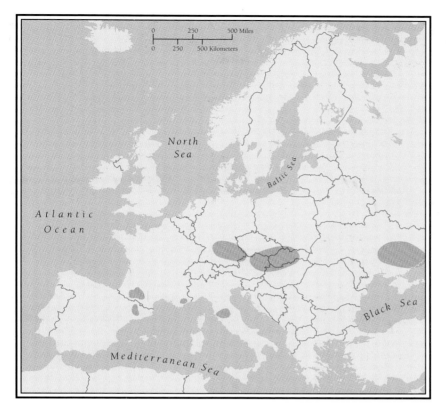

FIGURE 13.9   Geographical distribution of Venus figurines, which cluster outside Franco-Cantabria. (*After Gamble 1983*)

1.   The hunter's sympathetic magic
2.   Trophyism
3.   Expressions of sexual symbolism
4.   Components of information or communication systems

Perhaps the early artists were performing sympathetic magic based on the belief that if you can "capture" an animal by painting it, you ensure its literal capture in the hunt (Breuil 1952). This might explain the apparent avoidance of realistic depictions of people—maybe painting a person captures his or her spirit, soul, or essence.

Certainly, the animal species represented in the cave paintings were not randomly selected by the artists. Anthropologist Patricia Rice and sociologist Ann Paterson have applied statistical analysis to the cave paintings of the Dordogne–Garonne drainage of west-central France (1985) and the Cantabrian region of northern Spain (1986). These researchers found a pattern to how often individual animal species turned up in the paintings. The Paleolithic artists depicted smaller animals like red deer and reindeer in direct proportion to the abundance of their bones in local archaeological sites of the same period. Larger animals that would individually have provided a lot of meat, especially horses and bison, were depicted more frequently in the caves than might have been expected from a simple count of their bones at the same sites. Rice and Paterson conclude that species frequency in the cave art largely was a function of the economic significance of the animal. Small animals hunted with great regularity and large animals that provided a large amount of meat even though hunted less frequently, were the cave artists' favorite subjects. At the same time, animals only rarely or never seen in faunal assemblages, but impressive, dangerous, and productive of large quantities of meat when they were successfully procured were also commonly selected for inclusion in the artwork. Overall, Rice and Paterson conclude that the cave art can be explained as "fertility magic, hunting magic, hunting education, and story-telling about hunting" (1985:98).

Animals of no consequence in subsistence, but impressive and dangerous, were depicted by the artists as well. For example, at the most recently discovered cave painting site, Chauvet Cave near Avignon, France, there are depictions of about fifty woolly rhinoceroses, a large, probably aggressive animal not known to have been hunted by Upper Paleolithic people (see Figure 13.7) (Chauvet 1996; Clottes 1995).

The placement of individual animals in the cave paintings is not random. André Leroi-Gourhan (1982) has identified a pattern to the appearance of the animals in the caves. Bison, oxen, and horses generally were accorded a central position within caves as well as within individual groups of paintings. Deer, ibex, and mammoth tend to be peripheral. Rhinoceros, bear, and lion are usually far away, often deep in the recesses of caves, as much as a kilometer down narrow, winding, rock-strewn passageways.

The hypothesis of trophyism explains the cave paintings as virtual historical records of successful individual hunts (Eaton 1978a,b as cited in Conkey 1983:217). The paintings are trophies much in the way a modern hunter may mount an animal head on a wall. This seems unlikely based on the previous discussion; there are many cave paintings of animals for which there is no archaeological evidence of their having been hunted by people in the Upper Paleolithic.

The idea that the cave paintings reflect sexual symbolism is essentially a psychological explanation and difficult, if not impossible, to test scientifically. Leroi-Gourhan (1968) bases this hypothesis on an analysis of abstract designs on cave walls that he interprets as symbols of masculinity and femininity. In this vein, the Venus figurines may be fertility symbols.

More recent researchers have interpreted what Conkey (1978:74) calls the "explosion of symbolic behavior" in the Upper Paleolithic as an attempt to transmit information in symbolic ways (Conkey 1980; Gamble 1982, 1983, 1986; Hammond 1974; Jochim 1983). All these researchers propose that as human ecological circumstances changed during the late Pleistocene, social systems changed as well. Art, these writers suggest, served the purpose of transmitting socially important information within cultural systems stressed by changes in their ecology.

For example, Michael Jochim (1983) notes that most of the art can be dated from the period 25,000 to 10,000 B.P., which corresponds to a glacial maximum. He maintains that parts of Europe became uninhabitable during this period. The Franco-Cantabrian area, where the cave paintings are clustered, would not have been as severely affected, however. Jochim suggests that this would have resulted in population shifts into this area, creating the social problems attendant with different peoples coming into increased contact. He sees art as a way of marking territory, of ritually reinforcing group identity and solidarity.

Human Depictions

Interestingly, the Paleolithic cave painters were not so adept at self-portraits (Figure 13.10). Cave paintings of human subjects are relatively rare and not nearly as naturalistic as the paintings of animals. Here too, however, such portrayals provide us with a remarkable, if clouded, glimpse into the lives of people who lived more than 15,000 ya. Rice and Paterson (1988) analyzed some thirty-two caves in western Europe where there were a total of 116 human images. Of those images where gender could be identified, 78 percent were male and only 22 percent female.

The males tended to be portrayed conducting some specific activity; all running, walking, or dancing figures were males. There were even three paintings of people who appear to have been speared—all males as well. Females were always represented as simply standing or lying down, usually in groups with other females. They were never portrayed in an active mode. Although we cannot be certain of the precise meaning of these paintings and patterns, certainly they reflect aspects of the differences between the lives of males and females in the Upper Paleolithic.

Engraved Bones

Conkey (1980) examined 1200 abstractly engraved bones and antlers from twenty-seven sites in the Cantabrian area in Spain (Figure 13.11). She identified 264 design elements that were engraved according to three structural principles. She then compared the bone and antler assemblages at five cave sites and found that one, Altamira (which also has spectacularly painted walls), was the most diverse. This, she argues, indicates that Altamira was an aggregation spot for Paleolithic populations. Bruce Dickson (1990:215) has gone so far as to state that the larger caves were "ceremonial centers," the art serving as a focal point for ceremonies that took place during such aggregations.

Conkey believes that artifacts like engraved bone and antler contained information that identified and differentiated groups of people living in

FIGURE 13.10   Interestingly, though they were accomplished artists and rendered animals with great accuracy, only occasionally did Upper Paleolithic cave painters depict human beings, and these portrayals are often vague and indistinct. It is unclear why, but it seems to have been intentional. This human image is from the Le Portel cave site in France.

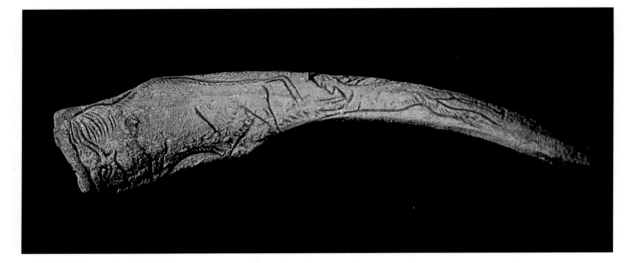

FIGURE 13.11 Along with cave paintings and sculptures, Upper Paleolithic artists also etched their designs into bone, ivory, and antler. Here, an artist rendered a bison on a piece of antler. *(Courtesy Department of Library Services. American Museum of Natural History. Neg. #606)*

different areas. These people needed to come together on occasion to exchange environmental information, to trade, and to find mates. Groups congregating at Altamira brought with them their engraved objects, each in their own style. Thus, the assemblage at Altamira is the most diverse because it reflects the styles of a number of different groups.

Lunar Observations?

The people who produced these spectacular works of art may also have been making simple, though remarkable, advances in science. A more than 30,000-year-old fragment of antler found in a French cave bears a succession of some sixty-nine incised marks. After examining it under a microscope, science writer Alexander Marshack (1972a,b) noted that the marks were made with a number of different tools and that they resembled the succession of lunar phases, the correct order and number for more than two months (Figure 13.12). Marshack believes that this and other artifacts indicate that not only did these people produce the first true art, but they also made the first calendars.

Geometric Signs

Among the most difficult elements of ancient artwork to attempt to interpret are simple geometric patterns. How are we to ascribe Upper Paleolithic paintings of wavy lines, zigzags, spirals, parallel lines, parallel and perpendicular crossing lines, and so on? Were these meaningless scrawl-

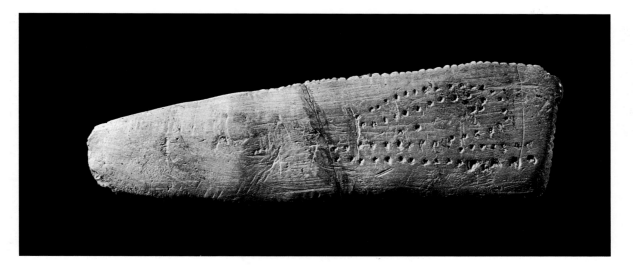

FIGURE 13.12   A 32,000-year-old engraved antler plaque from Abri Blanchard, France, which Alexander Marshack interprets as a calendar based on the phases of the moon. (© *Alexander Marshack*)

ings—the equivalent of our doodling? Were these designs part of an ancient code that we may never decipher?

A fascinating suggestion to explain these designs has been offered by researchers J. D. Lewis-Williams and T. A. Dowson (1988). They explain these images as being derived from visual artifacts of the nervous systems of the artists brought on during altered states of consciousness. The authors refer to visions that result from stimulation of the optic system during these altered states as **entoptic phenomena.** These images are not culturally controlled but result from the structure of the optic system itself and are therefore universal. This may explain why the kinds of geometric designs seen in the Upper Paleolithic art are found throughout the world at different times. Perhaps through sleep deprivation, staring at a flickering fire, or the ingestion of drugs, shaman or priests induced these images in their own optic systems. They then translated these images to cave walls as part of religious rituals.

The Implications of Upper Paleolithic Artwork

Did people in the Upper Paleolithic practice sympathetic magic, worship a fertility goddess, mark their ritual sites with paintings, engrave antlers with symbols that reflected their membership in distinct hunting bands, make calendars based on their observation of the sequence of lunar phases and paint visions seen during altered states of consciousness? We cannot be certain. As John Halverson (1987) points out, there are great problems posed in testing any of these hypotheses. He suggests that the art may have

entoptic phenomena Visual images that result from stimulation of the optic system during altered states of consciousness.

had no meaning at all in the sense that no special, and now indecipherable, code was ever attached to it. Maybe, as the title of his article suggests, it was simply "art for art's sake." In his view, Paleolithic painters and sculptors depicted the world around them and produced abstract symbols simply out of a sense of "delight in appearance" (Halverson 1987:68).

It is impossible at present to fully explain the art of the Upper Paleolithic, although the work of Jochim, Conkey, Gamble, and Rice and Paterson has provided great insight into its possible meaning. What is clear is that in viewing the world around them and in translating that reality through a prism of human understanding and belief into engravings, sculptures, and paintings, the people of the European Upper Paleolithic were exhibiting the depth of their intelligence and the degree of their humanity. Whichever hypothesis provides the best explanation for the art of the Upper Paleolithic (and they need not all be mutually exclusive), one thing is clear: In painting cave walls, carving figurines, and engraving bone, ivory, and antler, the people of the Upper Paleolithic in Europe left us an impressive artistic legacy.

Brave New Worlds

Not surprisingly, anatomically modern humans were able to survive in all the environments their archaic predecessors had inhabited before them. But modern humans were also able to thrive under conditions that had previously proved insurmountable and to migrate into areas that were previously unreachable.

Australia

Prehistoric migration into Australia poses an interesting problem. Australia has been separate from the Asian landmass for over 30 million years. During glacial maxima, Java, Sumatra, Bali, and Borneo were connected to each other in a single landmass called **Sunda,** while Australia, New Guinea, and Tasmania were joined into a single landmass called **Sahul** or **Greater Australia** (Figure 13.13). The Wallace Trench, which separated Sunda and Sahul, was so deep that even when worldwide sea level was at its lowest during the Pleistocene these landmasses were separated by ocean waters.

Sunda The combined landmass of the modern islands of Java, Sumatra, Bali, and Borneo.

Sahul The combined landmass of New Guinea, Tasmania, and Australia.

Greater Australia Another name for *Sahul.*

Coming to Australia Any population movement into Greater Australia necessarily involved the use of watercraft of some kind. Today this would entail a sea voyage of 1500 kilometers (with a few possible stops in between). At the time of presumed initial migration, sea level was lower and more of the continental shelves of Asia and Australia were exposed, making the voyage substantially shorter. Anthropologist Joseph Birdsell (1977)

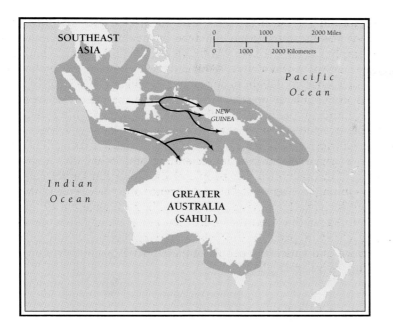

FIGURE 13.13   When sea level was lowered during the Pleistocene, the islands of Southeast Asia were joined to the continent in a landmass called Sunda. At the same time, New Guinea, Australia, and Tasmania were joined into a single landmass called Sahul or Greater Australia. Even during glacial maxima, Sunda and Sahul were separated by water so migrants from the former to the latter must have come by boat, probably island-hopping along one or more of the routes depicted.

has suggested a series of possible routes from Sunda to Sahul during these periods of lowered sea level (see Figure 13.13). One route starts on the eastern shore of what is today Borneo, continues east through the island of Sulawesi, and includes several island hops to northwest New Guinea. The longest gap between islands would have been about 70 kilometers (43 miles); the mean length of the eight gaps in this route is only about 28 kilometers (17 miles) (Birdsell 1977:127). Another possible route begins in Java, crosses the Indonesian archipelago, continues south to Timor and then south to Australia proper. This route also contains eight ocean crossings with a maximum of 87 kilometers (54 miles) and a mean of a little more than 19 km (12 miles) between landfalls (Birdsell 1977:127).

The Archaeology of the First Australians   The oldest archaeological sites in Greater Australia are located around the perimeter of the continent. As archaeologist Sandra Bowdler (1977, 1990) points out, people entered Australia from the north, and then spread along the coast, inhabiting areas with tropical coastal environments similar to the places from which they migrated. They moved inland along major rivers, shifting their subsistence focus from marine to riverine resources.

The oldest human sites in Australia indeed are located along the coast or in interior areas once drained by rivers or dotted with lakes (Figure 13.14, p. 362). Archaeological evidence on Australia and New Guinea shows that the earliest settlement by human beings occurred at least

FIGURE 13.14 Map showing the location of some of the earliest archaeological sites yet discovered in Sunda and Greater Australia.

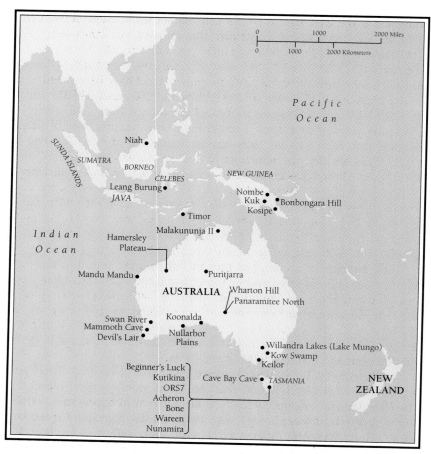

50,000 years ago, and possibly 10,000 years before this. Archaeologists Richard Roberts, Rhys Jones, and M. A. Smith (1990) have excavated at the Malakunanja II site in Arnhem Land in northern Australia, recovering more than 1500 artifacts including stone flakes, a grindstone, and pieces of ground hematite and ochre used to produce yellow and red pigments for paints. Thermoluminescence dates of 61,000, 52,000, and 45,000 were obtained from the deposit in which the artifacts were found (Roberts et al. 1990:154).

The earliest known settlement of New Guinea is located at Bobongara Hill, on the north coast on an ancient, exposed coral reef. The site has been dated to 40,000 B.P. by thermoluminescence (Groube et al. 1986).

In southwestern Australia is Swan River (the Upper Swan Bridge site). About 200 artifacts—including stone chips, worked flakes, and flakes with edges exhibiting wear—have been found there. The site has been dated to between 35,000 and 40,000 years ago (Jones 1992). Also in southwest

Australia is the cave site of Devil's Lair. Radiocarbon dates derived from a series of hearths that contained the remains of kangaroos killed, butchered, and eaten by the cave's human inhabitants place occupation of the cave at 32,000 to 38,000 years ago (Jones 1992). At Mammoth Cave, burned bones, possible stone artifacts, and charcoal have been dated to between 31,000 and 37,000 years ago (White and O'Connell 1982).

The Willandra Lakes region located in western New South Wales in the southeastern section of the country has been a treasure trove of archaeological data related to the early human settlement of Australia. The so-called lakes are dry, the remnants of ancient, Pleistocene lakes. One of them, Lake Mungo, has evidence of occupation dating back to as early as 32,750 years ago (Barbetti and Allen 1972). Fireplaces, some stone cores and flakes, steep-edged scraping tools, an earth oven, and the burned eggs of emu (a large, flightless bird indigenous to Australia) have been found. Charcoal from the fireplaces produced radiocarbon dates ranging from 24,020 to 32,750 years (Barbetti and Allen 1972:48).

The remains of a cremated human female were found at one Lake Mungo site. She was anatomically modern and rather gracile in her physiology, lacking the large brow ridges or heavy buttressing bone typical of modern Australian natives. She has been dated to 26,000 years ago (Bowler et al. 1970). Another skeleton from the same area, Mungo III, looks quite similar to Mungo I and has been dated to between 28,000 to 30,000 years ago (White and O'Connell 1982:37).

A skeleton (W.L. 50) was recovered just north of Lake Mungo. Dating to between 20,000 and 30,000 years ago (thus, possibly more recent than the Lake Mungo remains), W.L. 50 is far different in appearance, exhibiting a very robust morphology with thick cranial bones and quite large brow ridges. The great differences between these robust and gracile Australian crania have led some to suggest that two separate populations migrated into Australia more than 30,000 years ago (Jones 1992). Others (White and O'Connell 1982) believe that such variability is to be expected in a large continent with a broad range of environmental conditions.

Australia's Dry Interior   Between 20,000 and 25,000 years ago, human groups moved into the dry interior of central Australia. The Puritjarra rockshelter in the Cleveland Hills of central Australia was occupied by 22,000 years ago (M. A. Smith 1987). Other interior rockshelter sites on the Hamersley Plateau in western Australia date to 21,000 and 26,000 B.P. (Jones 1987).

Conditions in the interior were entirely different from those at the humid coast. The ability of the first Australians to migrate into a formerly unknown territory, to expand across thousands of miles and to adapt to entirely new and alien environmental conditions and resources is a testament to their resourcefulness. Such resourcefulness and inventiveness is what makes us human.

FIGURE 13.15 When the sea level dropped during the Pleistocene, the Bering Land Bridge was exposed. This 1500-km-wide platform connected northeast Asia and northwest North America, allowing Asian populations to migrate into and populate the New World.

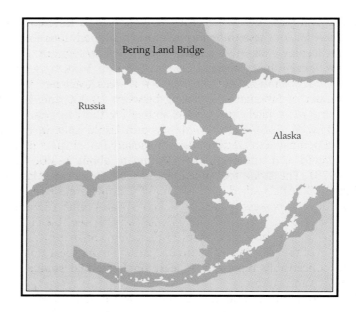

The Americas

Asia was the source of the human population of Greater Australia. It was also the source for the people who moved into the New World.

The Bering Land Bridge   Unlike the situation in Australia, the trip to the Americas could have been made entirely by land. Several times during the Pleistocene when a substantial amount of the earth's water was locked up in glaciers, sea level was reduced 125 meters or more, sufficient to expose a wide platform of land some 1500 kilometers across that connected northeast Asia—Siberia—with northwest North America (Figure 13.15). What is now the Bering Sea and Bering Straits, today separating eastern Russia from Alaska by only about 150 kilometers, was then the Bering Land Bridge, across which animals and people moved. The precise chronology of the exposure and flooding of the land bridge is unknown, but we can be fairly certain that it was intermittently available for human movement between 75,000 and 35,000 ya (Hopkins 1982). We know it was exposed continuously from about 35,000 to 11,000 years ago (Elias et al. 1996).

From Siberia to Alaska   The movement of people across the Bering Land Bridge was not an intentional migration. Groups of migratory hunters and gatherers living in northeast Asia probably followed the movement of large game animals onto the newly exposed territory of the land bridge and eventually into the Americas. This journey thrust these people, unintentionally, into the role of pioneers with a new world to explore and settle. The question is, when did this happen?

Siberia is a place deserving of its reputation for a miserable climate. Partly as a result of these difficult environmental conditions for the conduct of archaeology, Siberia is poorly known archaeologically. There was not a substantial human occupation much before 30,000 B.P., however, and even evidence much before 20,000 B.P. is weak (Meltzer 1993a:161).

A number of Siberian sites dating between 18,000 and 14,000 B.P. represent the most likely population source for the American migrants (Figure 13.16, p. 366). For example, around Ushki Lake in the central Kamchatka peninsula in eastern Russia, bifacially flaked spear points have been recovered at a number of sites dating to about 14,000 years ago (Dikov 1978). The stone tool assemblages at a number of Alaskan sites (see Figure 13.16) classified as the **Nenana Complex** and dating to soon after 12,000 B.P. possess bifacially flaked spear points (Figure 13.17, p. 367) (Powers and Hoffecker 1989). As we will see, bifacially flaked spear points are a major component of the toolkit of at least some of the early settlers of the New World south of Alaska. So the spear point makers of Ushki conceivably represent at least one potential source for New World people and culture.

Dating to about 18,000 B.P., Dyuktai Cave is located on the Aldan River in central Siberia (Yi and Clark 1985). Though much more distant from the New World than the Ushki sites, Dyuktai is significant for the form of the stone tools found there. There are some striking similarities between the small **wedge-shaped cores** and microblades made at Dyuktai (and a number of sites in central Siberia of similar age) and tools found in Alaska several thousand years later, which are part of the **Denali Complex.** Denali Complex sites date to after 10,700 B.P. In one view (Powers and Hoffecker 1989), people with wedge-shaped core technology constitute a second, somewhat later migration from Siberia to Alaska (see Figure 13.17).

How Old Are the Oldest New World Sites?   The question of when people living in northeast Asia first crossed the Bering Land Bridge is still an open one (Meltzer 1989, 1993a, 1993b; Owen 1984). A number of sites in the Old Crow River basin of the Canadian Yukon have produced some interesting material initially presumed to be bone artifacts with radiocarbon dates of approximately 30,000 B.P. (Irving 1978; Morlan 1978). Questions have been raised about whether most of the specimens are indeed artifacts, however. Features of the bone splinters initially thought to reveal human activity are now known also to be caused by animals chewing. Beyond this, some of the artifacts could have been made on bones that were already old—the ^{14}C date only shows the age of the bone, not the date that someone picked it up and made something out of it. Finally, the specific ^{14}C technique applied to the Old Crow specimens is now known to frequently produce overly old dates.

Another site with possible evidence of an early human presence in the New World is Bluefish Caves, about 65 kilometers (40 miles) southwest of

Nenana Complex Stone tool complex in Alaska, dating from 11,800 to 11,000 B.P. Nenana includes bifacially flaked spear points similar to tools made in eastern Russia about 14,000 years ago.

wedge-shaped cores Cores shaped like wedges from which blades are struck.

Denali Complex Stone tool technology seen in the American Arctic consisting of wedge-shaped cores, microblades, bifacial knives, and burins. Dates to about 10,000 years ago.

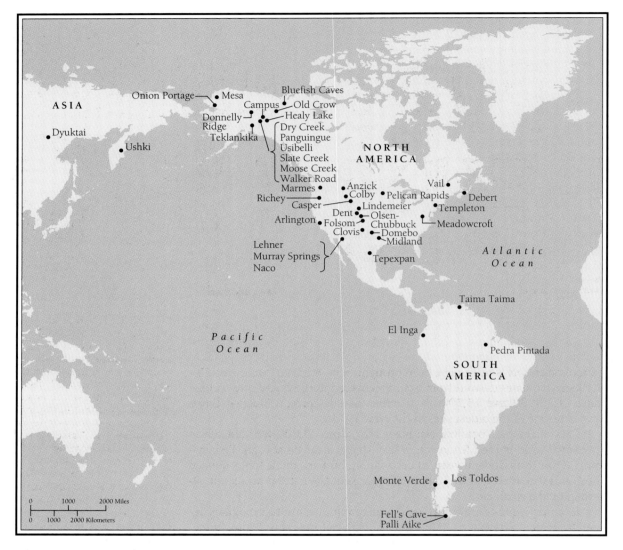

FIGURE 13.16 Map showing the location of some of the oldest archaeological sites known in the New World and sites in Siberia representing possible source populations for these first settlers of the Americas.

Old Crow (Cinque-Mars 1978). A wide variety of animal bones has been found at the site, including those of woolly mammoth, horse, caribou, bison, and sheep. Many of the bones show evidence of butchering with stone tools which also have been recovered at the site. The tools found there include sharp-cutting flakes, burins for engraving bone, and stone hammers for making the stone tools. The chert from which the tools were made is not native to the limestone ridge in which the caves are situated, indicating that either the raw material for making the tools or the complet-

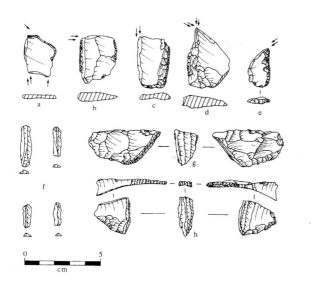

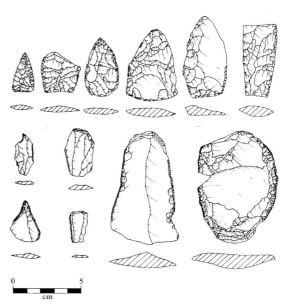

FIGURE 13.17   Stone tools from the Nenana (*right*) and Denali (*left*) cultures of Alaska. Dating to as much as 11,800 years ago, the Nenana stone tool assemblage, with bifacially flaked blades, is similar to that seen in some sites in eastern Russia and also similar to later industries in America south of Alaska. Dating to about 10,000 years ago, Denali tools also resemble artifacts found in Siberia, possibly evidence of a second, later wave of Asian migrants to the New World in the Late Pleistocene. (*Nenana and Denali tools courtesy William Powers*)

ed tools themselves must have been brought in by humans (Morlan 1983). Radiocarbon dates derived from bones recovered in the caves have yielded dates of 12,900 and 15,500 B.P. If either date is correct, Bluefish Caves would be one of the oldest sites in the New World.

One of the best possible candidates for a pre-15,000-year-old site in the New World is the Meadowcroft Rockshelter near Pittsburgh, Pennsylvania. Over thousands of years of occupation, humans made tools, cooked food, and threw away trash, taking advantage of the natural protection afforded by the small cave.

In a meticulous excavation, part of an ambitious, multidisciplinary research project, a deeply stratified deposit with cultural material was excavated. At the base of the sequence brought to light by these researchers may be material with the oldest radiocarbon dates associated with human-made material in the New World. Sealed beneath a rock fall were more than 400 stone tools including blades, knives with retouched edges, and an unfluted, bifacial projectile point, all dated to 12,000 B.P. (Figure 13.18). Six dates in excess of 12,800 B.P. have been associated with stone tools found near the base of the Meadowcroft sequence.

Unfortunately, the rockshelter is in an area where there is naturally occurring coal. Coal comes from very ancient trees that contain dead carbon—carbon in which all of the ^{14}C has already decayed away. Water dissolving this coal could have contaminated more recent cultural mate-

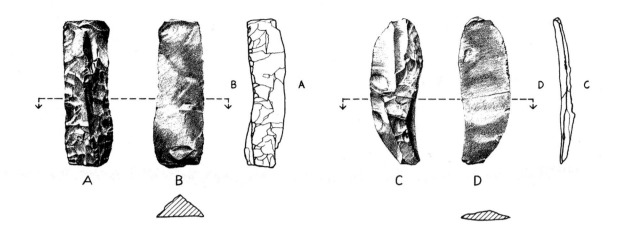

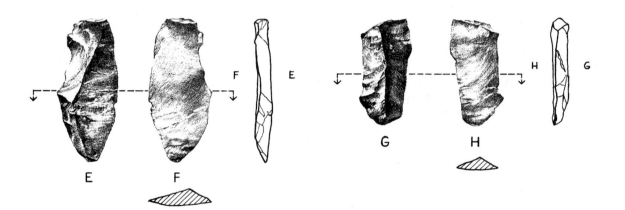

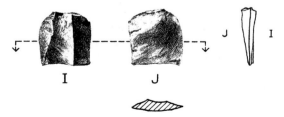

FIGURE 13.18 A series of blade tools recovered from the oldest cultural level at Meadowcroft Rockshelter in western Pennsylvania. These blades and a handful of bifacial knives and one spear point have been dated to approximately 12,800 years ago. *(Courtesy J. M. Adovasio, Mercyhurst College)*

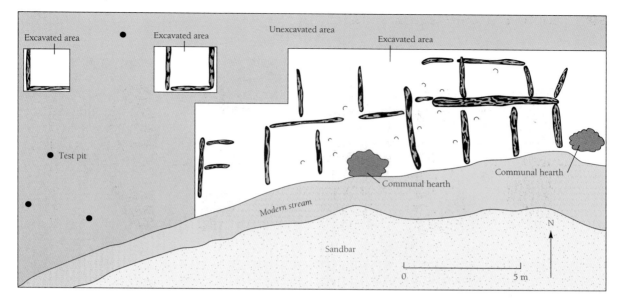

Excavated area

Excavated area

Unexcavated area

Excavated area

Test pit

Communal hearth

Communal hearth

Modern stream

Sandbar

N

0   5 m

rial, resulting in an incorrectly old ^{14}C date. Meadowcroft researchers have provided some good arguments in response to this criticism (Adovasio et al. 1983), but the jury is still out on the antiquity of the lower levels of the site.

Also important is Monte Verde, in Chile (Dillehay 1987, 1989; Dillehay and Collins 1988). The major cultural level at the site has produced bifacial spear points and a number of other stone tools. Organic preservation is remarkable at the site with pieces of mastodon meat, wooden hut foundations, and plant remains recovered in the excavation (Figure 13.19). Nine of the ^{14}C dates for the main occupation range from about 11,800 and 13,500 B.P.

FIGURE 13.19 The remarkable level of preservation apparent at Monte Verde, in Chile, belies the great antiquity of the site's occupation. Dating to about 13,000 years ago, Monte Verde, though more than 16,000 kilometers from the Bering Land Bridge, is nevertheless one of the oldest sites known in the Americas.

Paleo-Indians: If Not the First, the First Successful   Though much disagreement exists about these possible older sites, there is little disagreement about the human population explosion that occurred in the New World after 12,000 ya. We call these peoples the **Paleo-Indians.** Whether they were new arrivals or people descended from earlier migrants, they had a hunting-gathering economy with a seasonal emphasis on the big game that flourished in North America at the tail end of the Pleistocene. Using large-bladed spear points called **Clovis** points, with chipped channels or flutes on the faces to facilitate attachment to a shaft, Paleo-Indians hunted woolly mammoth, now extinct bison, horse, caribou, and other large game animals (Figure 13.20, p. 370). At sites like Olsen-Chubbuck, Colorado (Wheat 1972) and Casper, Wyoming (Frison 1974), there is evidence for bison drives where hundreds of animals were driven over cliffs or into sandy traps in communal hunts. Doubtless these peoples also collected roots, seeds, nuts, and berries when in season.

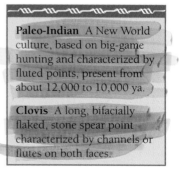

Paleo-Indian A New World culture, based on big-game hunting and characterized by fluted points, present from about 12,000 to 10,000 ya.

Clovis A long, bifacially flaked, stone spear point characterized by channels or flutes on both faces.

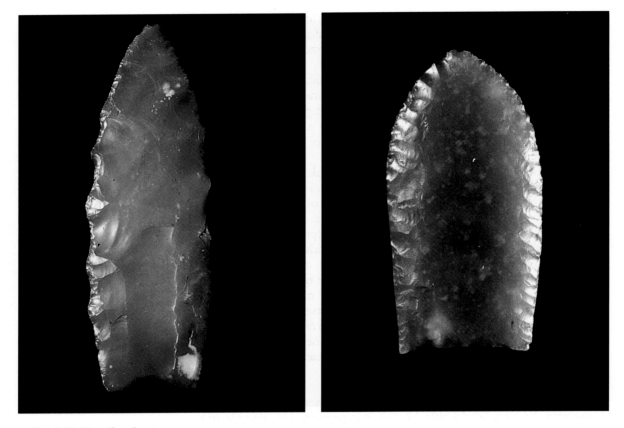

FIGURE 13.20   Fluted points of the Paleo-Indian settlers of North America: the earlier Clovis point, dated to 11,700–11,000 B.P. from the Richey Clovis Cache *(left)* and the later Folsom, a variant on the fluted point technique, dated to after 11,000 B.P. With such weapons, these first inhabitants of the Americas hunted the large game animals that flourished at the end of the Pleistocene. *(Both photos courtesy of R. M. Gramly, Great Lakes Artifact Repository; right, artifact courtesy of Dr. Douglas Sirkin)*

These people were enormously successful and quickly spread throughout the entire New World (see Figure 13.16). After their initial appearance perhaps 13,000 or 14,000 ya in Alaska, we find sites throughout the American Midwest by 11,500 ya. By 11,000 ya they had reached as far east as Maine, and by 9500 ya we find traces of their presence at the southern tip of South America.

Paleo-Indians were not just plains-dwelling hunters of Pleistocene big game. They lived in many diverse habitats, including the tropical rainforest to the south and the tundra of the north. An early South American site displaying the great range of Paleo-Indian adaptation has been excavated recently by a team of researchers led by archaeologist Anna C. Roosevelt (Roosevelt et al. 1996). The Caverna da Pedra Pintada site is located in the Amazon basin in Brazil. The researchers recovered more than 30,000 stone flakes and 24 formal tools including triangular, stemmed, bifacial points from a layer in the cave that has been radiocarbon dated to between 10,000 and 11,200 years ago. Paleoenvironmental evidence recovered at the cave—particularly preserved remains of plants and animals used by the Paleo-Indian inhabitants—shows quite clearly that when the site was occupied the area was, as it is today, a tropical rainforest. Abundant remnants of tree fruits, fish, mollusks, birds, and small and large game attest to the broad food base of the cave's occupants.

Also found in the same layer as the Paleo-Indian artifacts of this site were hundreds of lumps and drops of red pigment and two spalls of painted cave wall. The chemistry of the drops of red pigment match that of painted images found on the cave wall, implying a similar age for the paintings. The Pedra Pintada paintings, therefore, may be the oldest known examples of cave art in the New World.

The Paleo-Indians may have been too successful. It has been suggested that their population grew so quickly and their skill as hunters was so remarkable that they contributed to the extinction of many large animals already strained by the change in climate at the end of the Pleistocene (P. Martin 1982). The horse, woolly mammoth, mastodon, bison, and ground sloth, all likely hunted extensively by the Paleo-Indians, became extinct sometime after these people arrived on the scene.

Others believe that environmental change at the end of the Pleistocene played a more important role in the extinctions of many species of large game animals. Biologist R. Dale Guthrie (1990) suggests that the Pleistocene/Holocene boundary was unlike previous periods of warming, producing far more drastic consequences for large herbivores hunted by humans and also for small rodents and other species not part of Clovis subsistence.

Was Clovis First?   The abundance of their indisputable cultural remains throughout the New World after 12,000 ya is presumed by some to indicate that the Paelo-Indians were, indeed, the first Americans. At the very least, it is an indication that if any people made it to the New World before them, they were unsuccessful at conquering this hemisphere.

In an interesting approach to this question of when the first people arrived in the New World, Joseph Greenberg, Christy Turner, and Steven Zegura (1986) used linguistic, dental, and genetic data to calculate how long Native Americans have been separated from their Asian counterparts. Their analysis was based on the rate of linguistic change through time from a particular source, the degree of change seen in human teeth once a group of migrants has become isolated from its source population, and the rate at which genetic change builds up in a migrant population isolated from its source. They conclude that the first migrants arrived about 14,000 years ago, supporting the Clovis-first model.

However, concerning Monte Verde and other sites that are nearly as old in South America, researchers David Whitley and Ronald Dorn (1993) have constructed an interesting argument that suggests an earlier migration to the New World. The accepted dates for Clovis sites in the North American Southwest are too recent, Whitley and Dorn maintain, to get the

Clovis people to ancient South American sites like Monte Verde by their accepted dates. Even with rather rapid rates of population growth and geographic expansion, if the ancestors of the Clovis hunters entered the New World at about 13,000 ya, they still would have arrived at the oldest sites in South America *after* carbon dates indicate that these sites were settled. Whitley and Dorn maintain that these South American sites must have been populated by a people who inhabited North America *before* the people who made the Clovis points, part of a pre-Clovis migration into the New World.

Because Monte Verde is about 16,000 kilometers (about 10,000 miles) away from the Bering Land Bridge, there should be a trail of successively older archaeological sites leading from Chile back to that bridge. To date, virtually all researchers would agree, the better part of such a trail is apparent for the Clovis Paleo-Indians, but not for any pre-Clovis migration. Future research may yet find such a trail. Then again, it may not.

Skeletons of the First Americans   The oldest human skeletons yet found in the New World date to the Paleo-Indian period. The female skeleton from Midland, Texas (originally called "Midland Man" but now known to have been a female), has been dated by uranium series to 11,600 years ago (Hoppe 1992). From Mexico comes Tepexpan Man (probably a female) with a date of 11,000 B.P. A small group of other human remains have been dated to between 11,500 and 10,500 years ago: There is the Pelican Rapids find (known as "Minnesota Man," another mis-identified female), the Marmes skull from Washington state, "Arlington Man" from Santa Rosa Island in California (Owen 1984), Wilsall (also called Anzick) in Montana, and the Mostin site in northern California (Taylor 1991). Cerro Sota 2 from Chile is about 11,000 years old. Several individuals from Lagoa Santa in Brazil are probably 10,000 years old. A recent electron spin resonance analysis performed on human bone found along the Kansas River in Kansas has produced a date of 15,400 B.P. (Bower 1987c). If the date is accurate, this fossil would be the oldest human remain in the New World.

All these fossils are anatomically modern and all resemble modern American Indians. All share a series of skeletal traits possessed by Asian people as well, further supporting an Asian source for New World populations.

The Arctic

The final "brave new world" we will briefly touch upon is not a previously uninhabited continent, but a region not previously exploited by human beings: the Arctic. Archaic *Homo sapiens,* especially the Neandertals, had evolved a highly successful adaptation for life on the tundra. As just shown, modern human beings also occupied some very cold, harsh territory as they expanded into the tundra and eventually across the Bering

Land Bridge into the North American tundra. But even the cold-adapted Neandertals did not penetrate into the ice-covered region of the Arctic and anatomically modern humans did not enter this region until fairly late in prehistory. The oldest archaeological evidence for occupation of the Arctic dates to only about 4500 years ago.

Life is difficult for humans in the Arctic. Even fresh water, the most basic necessity of life, is largely unavailable in liquid form for most of the year, and must be processed by heating ice. The Arctic is severely cold much of the year, yet wood is not widely available as a fuel because trees cannot grow under these conditions. Human settlement of the Arctic, therefore, required an extremely sophisticated material culture with tailored clothing and well-insulated shelters to protect people from the cold, and a highly specialized toolkit to exploit the resouces available in such an environment. As anthropologist Moreau Maxwell (1993:209) points out, when the Arctic was finally settled by human beings it was the last of the "habitable lands" to be mastered by our species.

In the New World, the spread of people throughout the Arctic is signaled by the appearance of a series of stone artifacts of the **Arctic Small Tool Tradition.** This tradition includes small blades barely 2.5 cm long used in cutting and carving, equally small burins for engraving bone and antler in the production of harpoons and sewing needles, small blades inset into bone and antler arrow and spear points, and even smaller microblades about 1 cm long set into handles and used for various tasks, for example, butchering and skinning animals and manufacturing watertight clothing from their skins (Maxwell 1993).

In the American Arctic, these small tools spread remarkably quickly across the north, appearing first in Alaska about 4500 years ago and turning up all the way east in Greenland about 4000 years ago. The modern descendants of the people bearing this culture are the Inuit (commonly known as Eskimo), whose lifeway is emblematic of our species' remarkable ability to adapt to even the most extreme of environmental circumstances.

Summary

Sometime after 50,000 years ago, a remarkable transformation occurred that resulted in cultures all over the world with a decidedly modern cast. The cultures of the period are characterized by the production of blade tools; a broadening of the subsistence base; an increase in the size of some sites implying the practice of temporary population aggregation; the use of bone, antler, ivory, and shell in toolmaking; the manufacture of nonutilitarian items, some of which served as items of personal adornment; the extensive use of nonlocal, exotic raw materials; the regular placement of elaborate grave goods in burials, including items of personal adornment; and the first appearance of artwork in the form of naturalistic paintings, fanciful sculptures, and engraved bone and antler.

Arctic Small Tool Tradition
A stone tool tradition dating to about 4500 B.P. in the Arctic, that involved the production of small blades used in cutting and carving, small burins, and even smaller microblades.

In the Late Pleistocene, human populations migrated into three previously uninhabited continents: Australia and North and South America. Greater Australia (Australia, New Guinea, and Tasmania) was populated by coastally adapted Southeast Asians who arrived by boat. The New World was settled by northeast Asians who walked across a vast land bridge connecting the Old and New Worlds during glacial maxima. This occurred by at least 12,000 years ago. Some of these early settlers moved south, perhaps through an ice-free corridor into the American west, where they invented a new projectile point technology. Their fluted points allowed them to expand across two continents. These Clovis people may not have been the first arrivals; some sites in both North and South America may be older. But Clovis certainly represents the first broadly successful occupation of the New World.

Study Questions

1. In what ways does the culture of the Upper Paleolithic represent a great behavioral leap beyond that of the Middle Paleolithic? Why are the behaviors recognized for the Upper Paleolithic considered to be essentially modern?
2. How can the sophisticated artwork of the Upper Paleolithic be explained? Why did people of the Upper Paleolithic paint on cave walls, carve figurines, and scratch geometric designs on bone, antler, and ivory?
3. When and how were Australia and New Guinea peopled? What technology must these first settlers have possessed to accomplish this?
4. When and how was the New World peopled? How is the migration of these people related to glacial advance and retreat?
5. Was Clovis first? Consider the evidence for a pre-Clovis migration to the New World.

Key Terms

Gravettian	Sunda	Paleo-Indian
Solutrean	Sahul	Clovis
Magdelanian	Greater Australia	Arctic Small Tool
microblades	Nenana Complex	Tradition
Venus figurines	wedge-shaped cores	
entoptic phenomena	Denali Complex	

For More Information

For technical articles concerning the Middle to Upper Paleolithic cultural transition, see the articles contributed to *The Emergence of Modern Humans:*

An Archaeological Perspective (Mellars 1990). For wonderful photographs of the paintings in the cave of Lascaux, see Mario Ruspoli's (1986) *The Cave of Lascaux: The Final Photographs.* For thoughtful discussions of the meaning of Upper Paleolithic artwork, there are no better places to start than John Pfeiffer's (1982) *The Creative Explosion: An Inquiry into the Origins of Art and Religion* and Paul Bahn and Jean Vertut's (1988) *Images of the Ice Age.* For a more recent and more technical book-length treatment, see the thought-provoking *The Dawn of Belief: Religion in the Upper Paleolithic of Southwestern Europe* by Bruce Dickson (1990). For a more popularly oriented, article-length piece, one of the best and most succinct is archaeologist Pat Shipman's (1990) "Old Masters" in the magazine *Discover.* For another popularly oriented article, this time by one of the most thoughtful researchers in the field of Paleolithic art, see Margaret Conkey's (1981) article "A century of Paleolithic cave art" in *Archaeology* magazine. Also, see the recently published book describing the discovery and characteristics of the artwork of Chauvet Cave by its discoverer, Jean-Marie Chauvet.

J. Peter White and James F. O'Connell's (1982) *A Prehistory of Australia, New Guinea and Sahul* is still an excellent synthesis of the archaeology of Greater Australia. A more recent and thorough work on the archaeology of Australia is Josephine Flood's (1990) *Archaeology of the Dreamtime: The Story of Prehistoric Australia and Its People.* For a helpful discussion of the controversy over the earliest settlement of the Americas, read David Meltzer's (1993a) article, "Pleistocene peopling of the Americas," in the journal *Evolutionary Anthropology.* A recent popular book by the same author (1993b), *Search for the First Americans,* provides a very helpful summary of the current consensus and arguments over the earliest settlement of the New World. A very interesting, popular treatment of the controversy surrounding the timing of the peopling of the Americas—with personal anecdotes of the author's experiences researching the topic—can be found in E. James Dixon's (1993) *Quest for the Origins of the First Americans.* For detailed information about the Paleo-Indian adaptation to the Americas, see the numerous articles in *Clovis: Origins and Adaptations* edited by Rob Bonnichsen and K. L. Turnmire (1991).

Beginning after 12,000 years ago, much of humanity experienced a fundamental revolution in subsistence; they began planting crops (like the wheat shown here) and domesticating animals. Why did this revolution take place? How did this revolution set the stage for the development of the modern world? *(Food and Agriculture Organization, United Nations; F. Botts)*

14

The Origins of Agriculture

So far in this book, we have recounted the story of human antiquity as it is now understood. The human ancestors we have discussed, whether they belonged to a species different from our own or were entirely modern, were all hunter-gatherers, relying on nature's bounty for their survival. In fact, for more than 99 percent of hominid history, our ancestors fed themselves by foraging—gathering wild plant foods and hunting and scavenging wild animals. It is difficult to imagine that the subsistence mode that feeds virtually all people on this planet today, which we so take for granted, developed only in the very recent days of our evolutionary calendar. We are talking about the fundamental subsistence shift from food gathering to food *producing*.

Life at the End of the Pleistocene

The end of the Pleistocene and the beginning of the Holocene—the modern epoch that began 10,000 years ago—brought the last recession of the glaciers and a general warming of the world's climate. Sites throughout the world show people adapting to the changing conditions. The cultural developments that characterize the human response to the changing climate of the end of the Pleistocene include the following:

1. People changed their subsistence focus as the animals and plants on which they previously had relied became extinct or unavailable.
2. Different human groups responded differently to the new environmental conditions, resulting in a far higher level of cultural diversity even within relatively small regions than had been seen across broad areas during the Pleistocene.
3. In many areas, this subsistence shift included exploiting a broader range of resources such as small game, fish, shellfish, and birds. For some, the warming afforded an opportunity to add plant foods unavailable during glacial periods.
4. In other regions, the subsistence shift involved an intensification of exploitation of some uniquely productive element or elements in the food quest.
5. Finally, in some places, the focus on certain abundant resources encouraged a shift from a nomadic existence to a more sedentary one. In some particularly rich regions, intensification of the food quest and the shift to a **sedentary** way of life set the stage for a revolutionary change in the relationship between people and food, a shift from food collecting to food production, the focus of this chapter.

Mesolithic and Archaic Cultures of the Early Holocene

As archaeologist T. Douglas Price (1991) points out, the key characteristic of the environment of Holocene Europe is its vast array of plants and animals available for exploitation by the human groups living there. This diversity of resources allowed for a diversity of cultural adaptations by **Mesolithic** people.

For example, the inhabitants at Star Carr in England hunted red and roe deer, elk, ox, pig, fox, wolf, badger, beaver, and hare (G. Clark 1971). They also ate birds; the bones of duck, mergansers, grebes, and cranes were recovered. At the Danish coastal site of Meilgaard, there is evidence of a heavy reliance upon shellfish (Bailey 1978). At Mesolithic sites in southern France, a wide array of plant food remains have been recovered, including vetch, lentils, and chick peas (Price 1987). In coastal contexts, fishing played a major role in subsistence; the remains of pike, cod, ling, perch, breem, eel, and haddock have been found at Mesolithic sites (Clark 1980). Marine mammals including ringed, harp, and grey seal were hunted and beached whales and porpoises were utilized.

sedentary A settlement pattern in which people mostly stay in one place.

Mesolithic Name given cultures in Europe at the end of the Pleistocene and before the Agricultural Revolution.

In North America, the waning stages of the Pleistocene brought with it extinction of many tundra-adapted large-game species and their replacement with more modern fauna. The **Archaic** period cultures in North America represent the beginning of regionalization, as cultures settled into different post–Pleistocene environments. Strategies for survival in the northeastern woodlands, Southwest desert, Northwest coast, and elsewhere were established. For example, piñon nuts became a major component of the diet throughout much of the desert west. In the east, cultures evolved with specific adaptations to the coast, to the area around the Great Lakes, and to the forested interior. Groups pursued different characteristic combinations of hunting, fishing, shellfish collection and the exploitation of local seed plants and nut foods.

The Koster site in Illinois provides a wealth of information on Archaic lifeways (Struever and Holton 1979). Beginning about 7,000 years ago, the residents of the site hunted deer, small mammals, and migratory fowl including ducks and geese. The carbonized seeds of the wild plants smartweed, sunflower, goosefoot, pigweed, and marsh elder—plants that later were part of an indigenous agricultural revolution—were major components of the diet. Fish and freshwater shellfish were collected in the river, and hickory nuts, hazelnuts, and acorns were harvested from the forests in the fall. Other plant foods like ground nuts, wild duck potatoes, cattail shoots, pecans, pawpaws, persimmon, and sassafras root round out the broad subsistence base at Koster.

In East Asia, we see a similar process of post-Pleistocene subsistence shifts and regionalization. For example, in Thailand, Spirit Cave was occupied more than 7500 years ago. The Khong stream at the base of the cave's cliff face provided fish and freshwater crab to the human inhabitants. Otter, bamboo rat, badger, porcupine, sambar, and pig deer were caught and eaten by cave inhabitants (Gorman 1972). The remains of twenty-two genera of plants have also been recovered in the cave including bamboo, butternut, and tropical fruits (Higham 1989).

In the early Holocene of Africa and the Middle East we see a number of sites where subsistence emphasis seems to have shifted to plant resources sometime after 18,000 ya. Along the Nile, gazelle, hippopotamus, wild cattle, wart hog, and buffalo were still hunted, but fishing had also become important. At some of the Nile sites, microliths—small stone flakes set in groups into bone, wood, and antler handles—exhibit a wear pattern that indicates their use in sickles for harvesting plant food (Butzer 1982). The abundance of grinding stones used for processing seeds also points to a focus on plants for food. Finally, the presence of carbonized grains of wild barley, wheat, rye, and oats bears direct witness to the growing importance of plant foods in the diet.

This shift in subsistence at the end of the Pleistocene and beginning of the modern, or Holocene, period led in some places to a radical change in the relationship between people and their environment. The rest of this chapter chronicles this revolution.

Archaic Time period in the New World that follows the Paleo-Indian period.

The Food-Producing Revolution

The focus of this chapter is the **Food-Producing Revolution**, or **Agricultural Revolution**. Although the impact of this change on human life certainly was revolutionary—in the sense that it was momentous—there was no abrupt change in how people fed themselves. The shift to food production was a process that transpired over the course of several millennia in a number of different world areas and then spread out from these initial hearths (Figures 14.1 and 14.2) (B. Smith 1995).

Archaeologists have another name for the period when agriculture first became the dominant subsistence mode for some human groups—the **Neolithic.** Neolithic simply means "new stone" and specifically refers to the production, during this period, of a new stone tool type made of polished or ground stone, unlike the chipped tools of the "old stone" age, or Paleolithic. Although this shift in tool type is no longer viewed as the defining element of the period, the name has stuck.

It is not an exaggeration to say that the kind of life most of the world's people now lead was made possible by this change in subsistence that began only some 12,000 years ago. The shift to food production marks a major break in how people related to their environment. Whereas before they could exploit only what nature already provided, now they could take at least some control over the production of food. The Neolithic marks a point in time when people began to **domesticate** those plants and animals they previously had relied on for food only in their wild or undomesticated state.

The Domestication of Plants and Animals

Domestication uses **artificial selection** to change the character of a plant or animal species according to a people's own needs or purposes. Artificial selection is analogous to natural selection as Charles Darwin defined it (see Chapter 2). Darwin's hobby as a pigeon breeder, in fact, provided him with crucial insights into how natural selection might work.

In natural selection, the plants or animals that survive and reproduce are those with the characteristics best adapted for survival in a specific environment. In artificial selection the individual members of plant or animals species are *allowed to survive* because they possess certain characteristics deemed desirable by humans. Those with other, less desirable traits are killed off or simply not allowed to reproduce. In essence then, artificial selection is managed evolution, and the managers are people. In comparing artificial selection to natural selection, Charles Darwin (1898:47) said, "One of the most remarkable features in our domesticated races is that we see in them adaptations, not indeed to the animal's or plant's own good, but to man's use or fancy."

The social consequences of this shift to food producing were enormous. Ultimately, the ability to ensure a constant, reliable, and expanded

---

Food-Producing Revolution The shift from foraging to food production through domestication, beginning after 12,000 ya.

Agricultural Revolution Another name for the **Food-Producing Revolution.**

Neolithic Literally "New Stone Age." Now refers to period of the beginning of agriculture.

domesticate To change, through artificial selection, the wild form of a plant or animal to a form more useful to humans; also used for the end product of this process.

artificial selection The process where humans choose the plant or animal that will live and reproduce, based on its useful characteristics.

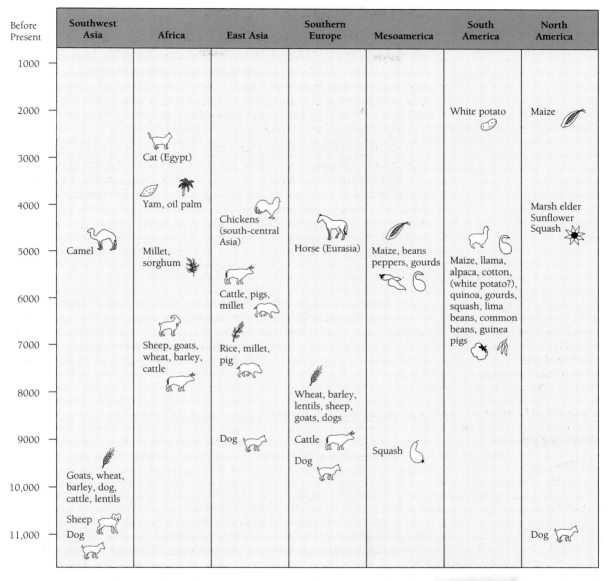

Before Present	Southwest Asia	Africa	East Asia	Southern Europe	Mesoamerica	South America	North America
1000							
2000						White potato	Maize
3000		Cat (Egypt)					
4000		Yam, oil palm	Chickens (south-central Asia)				Marsh elder Sunflower Squash
5000	Camel	Millet, sorghum		Horse (Eurasia)	Maize, beans peppers, gourds	Maize, llama, alpaca, cotton, (white potato?), quinoa, gourds, squash, lima beans, common beans, guinea pigs	
6000			Cattle, pigs, millet				
7000		Sheep, goats, wheat, barley, cattle	Rice, millet, pig				
8000				Wheat, barley, lentils, sheep, goats, dogs			
9000			Dog	Cattle Dog	Squash		
10,000	Goats, wheat, barley, dog, cattle, lentils						
11,000	Sheep Dog						Dog

FIGURE 14.1   A chronology of domestication.

food supply allowed for an increase in sedentism and population growth, along with the development of new social structures needed to maintain order in these larger settlements. The kinds of social hierarchies made possible by—and sometimes made necessary by—the consequences of food production led to the developments that are the focus of Chapter 15.

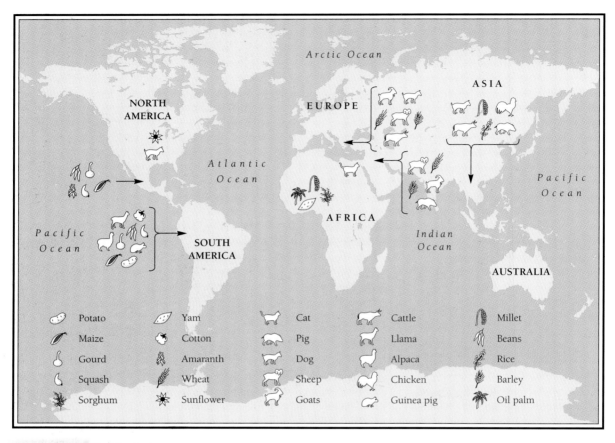

FIGURE 14.2 Worldwide distribution of apparent hearths of domesticated plants and animals.

From Wolf to Dog

Although generally not a food species, the dog provides a good example of the process of domestication. Many of us have dogs, and we are all at least passingly familiar with some modern breeds. Although the characteristics selected for were quite different than for those of a food species, the process of selection is essentially the same.

All domesticated dogs are members of the species *Canis familiaris.* Beagles and spaniels, German shepherds and chihuahuas, St. Bernards and retrievers, toy poodles and dobermans are all members of the same species. And all are ultimately descended from a single wild species, *Canis lupus*— the wolf (Figure 14.3). Now, as we all know, wolves are pretty fierce creatures, and it is not obvious how a wolf can be bred into a Pekingese. It is, however, just a matter of artificial selection, genetic accidents, and time.

FIGURE 14.3   The many breeds of dogs are all members of the species *Canis familiaris* and are all descended from the wolf, *Canis lupus*—including *(upper left)* the wolflike German sheperd, *(upper right)* the Labrador retriever, *(lower left)* the Irish wolfhound, and *(lower right)* the decidedly nonwolflike West Highland white terrier.   *(German sheperd: J. M. Beatty; Labrador retriever and Irish wolfhound: M. A. Park; West Highland white terrier: K. L. Feder)*

We know that the wolf was one of the first species domesticated by people—though probably not as a source of food. In a scenario suggested by osteologist Stanley Olsen (1985), orphaned wolf pups may have been picked up by local people and brought back to their village as a curiosity. If orphaned early enough in life, they would bond with the people raising them, who in turn would tolerate the pups because they were little trouble and very entertaining. As they grew, however, most became dangerous. Because they perceived the people around them as part of their "pack," these wolves would attempt to assert themselves as in the wild. People would be bitten, children might be seriously hurt, and the wolves would more than likely be killed.

There is, however, inherent variation in a wolf population. Although some wolves grow to be quite large, with enormous teeth and aggressive dispositions, others are smaller and more timid. In nature those wolves may be killed by larger wolves or, more likely, simply have a lower status in wolf society, where their characteristics put them at a disadvantage: They eat only after the more dominant wolves get their fill; if they are males, they may not have much opportunity to mate. Within a human society, however, smaller, timid wolves might be at a tremendous *advantage*. Although their larger, aggressive siblings might be killed, the smaller, more compliant wolves might be allowed to live. This would be especially true if they performed valuable services for the humans. Because wolves are social animals that cooperate in nature, it is possible they would do the same when raised by people. They might help in hunting and then, being less aggressive and assertive, would wait to eat what they were given by their human masters. They might also help in protecting the village from animals and even other people.

By killing off some wolves with dangerous characteristics and by allowing only those wolves with attractive (from a human standpoint) characteristics to survive, humans *select* which animals will live to reproduce. The qualities of small size and nonaggressiveness would tend to be passed down to the next generation, and the selection process would continue, refining the animals to human standards.

As genetic accidents—mutations—occurred, people found even more variation from which to select various desired characteristics, such as attractive fur color or extremely small size. Eventually, the wild animal became so changed according to a human blueprint that it is no longer considered the same species.

The same general process of selection is applicable for a plant or animal food species. For example, those individuals of a plant species that possess desired characteristics—they produced bigger seeds or were hardier and easier to harvest—would be allowed to survive, reproduce, and pass down those characteristics. Those with undesirable features would be eliminated. Thus, without knowing anything about genetics, humans have genetically sculpted animal and plant species in the process of domestication via artificial selection, using the raw material provided by the inherent variation in wild species.

Why Food Production?

Agriculture began just a little after 12,000 ya. By 2000 ya most of the world's people relied on food production for their subsistence. As anthropologist Mark Cohen (1977) has pointed out, 10,000 years is a very brief time in the 4-million-year evolutionary history of our lineage. That in this short period several different cultures independently developed an agricultural way of life, and that many of those who didn't quickly borrowed the idea from their neighbors, shows how powerful the forces were that led to this revolution. The goal of the prehistorian is to identify and describe these forces. Doing so explains the Agricultural Revolution.

Hypotheses

> The ancient people ate meat of animals and birds. At the time of Shen Nung, there were so many people that the animals and birds became inadequate for people's wants, and therefore Shen Nung taught the people to cultivate.

—from an early Chinese legend about a culture
hero, Shen Nung (Chang 1968:79)

It might seem self-evident to us that an agricultural way of life is superior to hunting and gathering, but this is not necessarily the case. Studies have shown that a hunting and gathering way of life can be very productive, providing a great deal of security and a lot of free time (Lee 1979). Under most circumstances, an agricultural way of life is, in fact, much harder, requiring a good deal more work and quite a bit more risk. If the hunting is bad, after all, it might be relatively easy to pack up and move to where it is better. Agriculture, however, represents a tremendous investment in time and energy devoted to a specific location: to clear fields; prepare the soil for planting; plant, weed, protect the crops from animals; and harvest. If, after all that work, the harvest fails, the consequences can be dire. It is also true that although agriculture has the potential of producing enormous quantities of food, reliance on one or a few crops can actually result in nutrition levels lower than those of hunter-gatherers (see the discussion later in this chapter). Why, then, did different groups of prehistoric people, during a relatively short time span, independently begin the process of domestication and move away from a hunting and gathering way of life?

Numerous explanations have been proposed. Some cultures, it was suggested, domesticated plants and animals simply because their people were inherently smarter. This sort of nonsense deserves little attention; all human groups have equal intellectual capacities.

It was also once common to explain the beginnings of agricultural life as the result of **diffusion.** According to this school of thought, cultures became agricultural when domestication was introduced to them by other groups—in other words, the process "diffused." This is, in reality, a nonexplanation. Of course, ideas and techniques do move from area to area, but this doesn't explain how they got started in the first place or why some groups might accept them when others will not.

We will focus briefly on a number of the more reasonable hypotheses for the origin of agriculture. Then we will present data on the major sequences of prehistoric domestication that archaeologists have developed. Finally, we will assess the hypothesis or hypotheses that best explain the

diffusion The geographic movement and sharing of cultural traits or ideas.

TABLE 14.1   Summary of Hypotheses Proposed to Explain the Origins of Agriculture

Hypothesis	Proponent	Summary
Oasis	V. Gordon Childe	Post-Pleistocene drying of the environment led to the concentration of people, animals, and plants at permanent water sources, or oases. There, people in close proximity to wild plants and animals studied them, tended them, and eventually domesticated them.
Sedentary	Carl Sauer	People living in areas with naturally abundant food would experiment with methods of increasing the abundance of nonfood plants. Eventually, they would apply what they learned through this experimentation to plant foods.
Readiness	Robert Braidwood	People had, by the end of the Pleistocene, accumulated knowledge about wild plants and animals in their regions. When people were intellectually ready, they domesticated those plants and animals that were amenable to domestication.
Dump heap	Edgar Anderson	Human beings disturb the habitat around their settlements as a matter of course. Certain wild plant species grow abundantly in these disturbed habitats. People soon realized that by intentionally disturbing areas they could encourage the growth of such plants, which they then began to tend and eventually domesticate.
Coevolution	David Rindos	Domestication was not achieved intentionally or in response to a challenge or a need. Humans and the plants and animals on which they subsisted developed a symbiotic relationship in which the evolutionary fitness of both was enhanced. Humans selected the best individuals (from their standpoint) within species and tended and encouraged them, to the exclusion of others. Human groups

data now at hand. Because each of the hypotheses was introduced and championed by individual scholars, we will present them by researcher. (These hypotheses are summarized in Table 14.1.)

The Oasis Hypothesis

> Food-production—the deliberate cultivation of food-plants, especially cereals, and the taming, breeding, and selection of animals—was an economic revolution—the greatest in human history after the mastery of fire. (Childe 1953:23)

Prehistorian V. Gordon Childe (1942, 1951, 1953) proposed the oasis hypothesis in the 1920s. Believing that there must have been some reason why agriculture began when and where it did, Childe suggests that certain areas of the world became drier at the end of the Pleistocene. As the Euro-

Hypothesis	Proponent	Summary
		evolved a dependence on certain species as these same species evolved a reliance on human encouragement. Domestication and an agricultural economy was the natural result.
Demographic	Ester Boserup	People had long recognized their ability to manipulate plants and animals through artificial selection. Because of the greatly increased amount of work this entails, however, they did not apply their knowledge of the processes of domestication until population increase and the need to produce more food necessitated it.
Marginal habitat	Lewis Binford Kent Flannery David Harris	As population grew at the end of the Pleistocene, human groups expanded into less than optimal habitats. They brought with them wild plants and animals from their source areas. These plants and animals could survive in the new areas only through the care and attention of people. People began to select only those individuals among the displaced plants and animals that thrived in the new habitat, thus leading to domestication.
Sedentism and population growth	Donald O. Henry	Some groups of nomadic foragers became more sedentary at the end of the Pleistocene, focusing on particularly productive, locally abundant wild foods. A sedentary existence encouraged population growth as infant mortality declined, life span increased, and female fertility increased. The response in some areas was to artificially raise the resource ceiling by encouraging certain plants and animals. This led to artificial selection of those plants and animals with the most beneficial characteristics, mutual dependence, and, ultimately, domestication.

pean glaciers melted off, weather patterns and attendant storm tracks shifted, and less rain fell in Southwest Asia, which had previously been much wetter. Plant life became concentrated in areas watered by underground springs—oases (Figure 14.4, p. 388). As plant life concentrated in these limited areas, animals too were drawn to the oases, both for the water they contained and the lush stands of plants they supported. Finally, Childe contends, people congregated in such areas to take advantage of the water and food concentrated there.

A previously nomadic people would now have no reason to migrate and, in fact, good reason to stay put—to become sedentary. Their concentration in oases resulted in attempts to expand food resources by sowing seeds, weeding, and irrigating. These efforts resulted in artificial selection of seed plants and led to domestication. Animals previously hunted tended to live near the humans who hunted them, for the stubble from the fields

FIGURE 14.4 Childe's Oasis hypothesis argues that the prehistoric inhabitants of Southwest Asia congregated in oases like this one in Jericho as a result of a drying trend at the end of the Pleistocene, thus setting the stage for the Agricultural Revolution. *(M. H. Feder)*

of planted crops attracted them to human settlements. Such close proximity caused humans to become familiar with these animals, perhaps even tending them, and eventually domesticating them through artificial selection. Thus, the shift to food production had an environmental cause in the Oasis hypothesis.

The Sedentary Hypothesis

> It took man so very long to get around to the invention of agriculture that we may well doubt that the idea came easily or that it came from hunger, as is often supposed. (Sauer 1969:19)

Carl Sauer (1969), a well-known geographer, does not believe that people who were short of food had the time or inclination to experiment actively with domestication. Too much effort devoted to an experiment with an uncertain outcome could result in starvation.

Sauer believes instead that the first agriculturalists were well-fed, sedentary people. Nomadic people would not suddenly give up established practices of migration; a migratory people, moreover, are not in one place long enough to make domestication successful. Therefore, domestication began in relatively rich areas where failed experiments in food production would have resulted in nothing more than wasted time and where people could stay in one place long enough to see a crop through from planting to harvesting. Such rich areas, in Sauer's view, also offered these prehistoric experimenters lots of raw material to experiment with. Plant and animal diversity were high, with many different species and abundant variation within those species.

Sauer also thinks that the earliest agriculturalists would not be found along rivers because of the problems of water control, primarily flooding. He believed that woodlands, perhaps in hilly areas, were most amenable to early cultivation, even suggesting that the first domesticates might not be food but rather poisons—used in hunting and fishing—and fibers. The area of the world that best met his criteria for early domestication, says Sauer, was Southeast Asia.

The Readiness Hypothesis

> In my opinion there is no need to complicate the story with extraneous "causes." The food producing revolution seems to have occurred as the culmination of the ever increasing cultural differentiation and specialization of human communities. (Braidwood 1960:94)

Robert Braidwood (1960, 1975) is a well-known American prehistorian who has done quite a bit of work on the question of domestication. He does not believe that specific environmental conditions caused domestication to take place. Braidwood ascribes the beginnings of agriculture to purely cultural or historical factors. According to Braidwood, people began to domesticate plants as a result of accumulating knowledge of the plants and animals that lived in their territories. As various groups began specializing in this process, they became expert in the characteristics of particular plant or animal species, a familiarity that resulted first in domestication and then agriculture. In Braidwood's view, agriculture began where it did because these were areas where the wild ancestors of plants and animals amenable to artificial selection were found.

The Dump Heap Hypothesis

> It is now becoming increasingly clear that the domestication of weeds and cultivated plants is usually a process rather than an event. (Anderson 1956:766)

Edgar Anderson (1952, 1956) was an eminent plant biologist interested in the beginnings of cultivation. In his dump heap hypothesis, Anderson suggests that certain plant species he called "camp followers" establish themselves in the kind of disturbed habitat that humans produce in and around their villages. Such plants flourish where people dig up the ground, set fires, discard their organic refuse, and so on. As people began to notice the concentrations of these plants around their villages, they began to exploit them. They realized rather quickly that they could further encourage the growth of these plants by purposely creating the disturbances that had previously and accidentally attracted the plants. Because these plants were tended, unconscious artificial selection would have eventually resulted in domestication. Here domestication is viewed as an inevitable byproduct of how people alter the landscape.

The Coevolution Hypothesis

> Man selects, but his selection is similar to nature's—he selects the best, the most useful, the most desirable, the most vigorous, the most successful (in other words, the most "fit") plant present in the immediate environment at a given time. (Rindos 1984:4)

Anthropologist David Rindos questions all hypotheses proposed to explain agriculture that are based on intentionality. He does not believe that humans consciously or deliberately became agricultural. He views agriculture as merely a point along a continuum of human-plant relationships.

In this view, we cannot speak of agriculture as an invention developed to respond to a problem or even as an accidental discovery that then became important in human subsistence. Instead, in Rindos's view, humans and the plants and animals on which they subsisted became mutually dependent. In Rindos's terminology, humans and these species "coevolved." During such coevolution, selection took place not through conscious experimentation to "improve" a plant or animal species, but simply as a byproduct of how people collected and used those plants and animals. Artificial selection simply occurred as economically sensible decisions were made concerning which individuals within a plant or animal species to eliminate, harvest, hunt, tend, or encourage. In turn, human groups evolved a dependence for their subsistence on certain plant and animal species, and cultural practices (scheduled seasonal movement, dispersing seeds, tending wild plants, differential hunting) evolved to maximize food output.

In Rindos's view, we can no more say that people intentionally selected certain plants to domesticate than we can say that certain plants or animals selected humans to tend them. Instead, plants, animals, and people and their cultures evolved together in what amounts to a symbiotic relationship. Human groups increased their evolutionary fitness by ensuring and expanding their food base, and the evolutionary fitness of certain species of plants and animals was increased as humans protected, watered, weeded, fenced in, and in general, tended to them. Rindos maintains that domestication was a natural result of this mutual dependence. Agriculture was the ultimate result.

The Demographic Hypothesis

> It is more sensible to regard the process of agricultural change in primitive communities as an adaptation to gradually increasing population densities, brought about by changes in the rates of natural population growth or by immigration. (Boserup 1965:117–18)

Ester Boserup (1965) is an agricultural economist. Technically, her hypothesis concerns the evolution of complex agricultural systems, not the origins of domestication. Her explanation, however, can certainly be expanded to cover the Agricultural Revolution as well, and has been used by prehistorians in this way.

Agriculture demands a tremendous investment in terms of time and labor. People would not make such an investment, Boserup contends, unless they had to, unless it was necessary for their survival. Boserup believes that population increases forced people to adopt more intensive strategies of subsistence in order to feed a greater number of mouths. New techniques of agriculture are not so difficult to develop, but ordinarily they are not used because they require more work than older, less-intensive techniques. Thus, the Agricultural Revolution was triggered by demographics.

The Marginal Habitat Hypothesis

> Change in the demographic structure of a region which brings about the impingement of one group on the territory of another would also upset an established equilibrium system and might serve to increase the population density of a region beyond the carrying capacity of the natural environment. Under these conditions, manipulation of the natural environment in order to increase its productivity would be highly advantageous. (Binford 1968:328)

Lewis Binford (1968), an American archaeologist whose work we have previously discussed, presents a hypothesis that also argues for the beginnings of domestication driven by population increase. In Binford's view, as in Boserup's, agriculture is not so difficult to invent, but it is not terribly attractive because it requires so much work. Because most societies have strategies for maintaining their population below the **carrying capacity** of the natural environment, they remain in equilibrium. In other words, most societies keep their population below the maximum that can be fed in a given environment, and everything goes smoothly.

When climate changed at the end of the Pleistocene, however, certain areas became extremely rich in food resources, leading to increased sedentism and, perhaps, marked population growth. Eventually, in Binford's view, some cultures overshot the carrying capacity of their local environment and were forced to expand into less attractive or marginal areas that had lower carrying capacities. Competition with people already living in these areas led to pressure to apply more intensive strategies of subsistence. This led to tending plants and animals, artificial selection, and, ultimately, domestication.

Kent Flannery (1965, 1968, 1973), another American archaeologist, added to Binford's scenario. He suggests that when groups expand into neighboring, less productive areas as a result of population growth, they might bring along with them some of the plant or animal species that were native to their richer home areas in a conscious attempt to increase the productivity of their new homes. Because these species were not naturally

carrying capacity The number of organisms a given habitat can support.

adapted to these marginal habitats, however, the only way they would survive was with human assistance. Animals might be sheltered and tended and plants planted, weeded, watered, and protected. New selectional pressures, both natural and artificial, would result, and domestication would follow.

Flannery (1968) views this as a process of **deviation amplification.** Once a small change occurs in the relationship of people to their food resources, greater changes result. The need to expand the food base by investing increasing amounts of time in tending wild resources can only be satisfied by a greater degree of sedentism. This sedentism produces a greater reliance on tended species—there is no longer as much time to hunt and gather wild foods. Population may increase as a result of greater sedentism through, for example, lower infant mortality. This in turn requires the production of even more food to feed more mouths, which is made possible by an increased investment of time, and so on.

Also following Binford, David Harris (1977) suggests that a hunter–gatherer society in equilibrium with its environment could be shifted toward food production as a result of a reduction in the availability of a staple food resource. Such a reduction, he suggests, can lead to an intensification and specialization of the food quest; other food resources, in other words, would be more intensively exploited. Where these alternative food resources were available at fixed points, Harris contends, group mobility would be reduced, and local population would increase. This would lead to a need to further intensify the food quest to feed more mouths, which might result in tending and artificial selection to increase productivity.

The Sedentism and Population Growth Hypothesis Archaeologist Donald O. Henry (1989) has proposed another explanation for the origins of food production. His hypothesis includes several elements of the explanations described above including an environmental shift, an attendant shift in subsistence, and population increase. Henry suggests that at the end of the Pleistocene, as a result of a changing environment, some groups abandoned foraging for an extensive number of wild foods and adopted a strategy of increased sedentism, focusing on a smaller number of particularly productive, locally abundant wild foods. This produced an inherently unstable subsistence system: When nomadic foragers are faced with a food shortage, they can simply move to where food is more abundant. On the other hand, sedentary peoples may not wish to displace their entire society and adopt a new settlement pattern. Instead, they can, under the right circumstances and with the right kinds of plants, artificially raise the "resource ceiling" (Henry 1989:4) of their territory by tending and encouraging economically important wild crops—by planting seed beds, corralling animals, or fencing in plots.

In Flannery's sense, this may further disturb the equilibrium of the system. Henry suggests that in some regions, sedentism and human inter-

deviation amplification
The process by which a small change in one part of a cultural system results in larger changes in the rest of the culture, which, in turn, cause the original change to become increased.

vention in encouraging certain crops or animals led to a dramatic increase in human populations for a number of reasons. For example, a sedentary existence would have resulted in a decrease in infant mortality and increased longevity among the aged, both of whom could survive more easily than in nomadic existence with its greater potential risk for mishaps.

Beyond this, in some regions (Henry points to the Middle East; see the discussion later in this chapter), the shift to a more sedentary existence would have contributed to higher fertility levels overall. A diet higher in wild cereal foods produces proportionally more body fat, leading to higher fertility among women. Also, cereals are easily digested foods that would have supplemented and then replaced mother's milk as a primary food for older infants. Since lactation inhibits fertility, earlier weaning would have resulted in closer spacing of births and the potential for a greater number of live births for each woman.

Domestication: How Can You Tell?

Before we test these hypotheses by reference to site data, we need to explain how the early stages of domestication can be recognized archaeologically. Certainly, full-scale agricultural villages look very different from hunter–gatherer villages, and we can recognize this difference in the ground. But what about the transition, when **settlement patterns** really hadn't yet changed much? Here we have to look at the remains of the plants and animals being exploited to see if human selection has caused any alteration from the wild state. Even this identification is not terribly easy during early stages of domestication. The changes can be extremely subtle; the vagaries of preservation being what they are, moreover, it is virtually impossible to distinguish absolutely between ancient wild plants and animals and early domesticated species. But a number of features can be examined.

Recognizing Domesticated Plants

For plant species, domestication alters at least four reasonably recognizable characteristics.

Seed Size   When seeds or fruits are the part of the plant eaten, people will artificially select for those individuals of a species that produce larger seeds. This selection may result from an attempt to extract a greater amount of food from each plant. It also may come about as an accident of what archaeologist Bruce Smith (1992a) calls "seed bed selection." In this view, ancient people intentionally planted the seeds of wild plants in seed beds to increase the number of economically valuable wild crops growing in the vicinity of a settlement. Like all gardeners, they planted more seeds

settlement pattern The distribution of archaeological sites and the analysis of their functions in relation to each other and to features of the environment.

than can be accommodated in the seed bed. Because plants that germinate slowly or later than others are likely to get weeded out of the seed bed and because larger seeds germinate more quickly, they were selected for in this human controlled environment. After several generations of plantings, seed size of plants will be bigger and also more homogeneous as large seeds are regularly selected for (Figure 14.5).

Seed Coat Thickness   In the wild, seed-coat thickness is a crucial variable in determining whether the plant that grows from that seed will survive. A thicker seed coat may forestall germination until the last killing frost of early spring. In a human controlled seed bed, however, a thicker seed coat that delays germination confers a significant disadvantage because early sprouting and vigorous growth is selected for. Since seeds with a thicker seed coat sprout later than thin-coated seeds, they are likely to be culled. In this way, thinner seed coats, sometimes disadvantageous in nature, are selected for by people. A comparison of the seed coats of archaeological specimens and their modern wild counterparts can sometimes aid in distinguishing early domesticates from wild plants; the domesticates have thinner seed coats (B. Smith 1992a).

Seed-dispersal Mechanisms and Terminal Clusters   In nature, plants evolve mechanisms for dispersing seeds to produce the next generation of their species. Seeds tend to be dispersed throughout the plant; that way, if any part of the plant becomes damaged, seeds from the undamaged parts can still survive. Beyond this, when ripe, some seeds fall to the ground as a result of wind. Some may be knocked off by passing animals, or they may attach themselves to the fur of animals. Others may be eaten but undigested by animals or birds, to be excreted and, in a sense, planted elsewhere. For any of these mechanisms to work, the seeds have to become readily detachable from the plant at the appropriate time.

Easily detached seeds, however, pose a problem in human exploitation. If most of the seeds fall to the ground, harvesting is a very inefficient and time-consuming process. In the process of domestication, then, humans select for those individuals of a plant species that are at a disadvantage in nature because their seeds tend not to fall off when handled roughly. As Bruce Smith (1995) further points out, seeds that are located in tight clusters at the end of plant stalks rather than dispersed singly throughout the plant are similarly more conveniently harvested by humans. Seeds likely to pass down this characteristic are more likely to be selected by humans simply because they are easier to harvest. Early evidence for plant domestication includes an alteration in the area of attachment of seeds or fruits to the plant. In domestication such areas lose their naturally brittle character and allow for greater adhesion of the seed to the plant and the seeds tend to be more clustered at the ends of stalks (Figure 14.6).

FIGURE 14.5   Larger seeds produce faster germinating and quicker-growing plants; these plants have an advantage under the culturally controlled environment of the seed bed. Smaller, slower germinating seeds are selected against. Through this artificial selection, people produce crops that produce larger seeds that, in turn, produce more food. Compare these wild marsh elder, sunflower, and squash seeds (*top to bottom, left*) with domesticated examples (*top to bottom, right*). (© *Chip Clark 1995*)

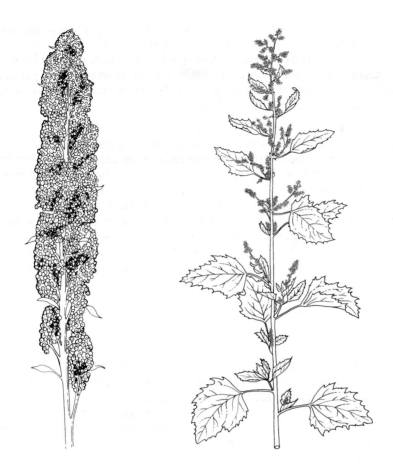

FIGURE 14.6 In the wild, many seed-producing plants have seeds in numerous small clusters throughout the plant, rendering harvest difficult. Humans tend to select for those individual plants that produce more easily harvested, large numbers of seeds in compact clusters. Compare wild lamb's quarter on the right with its domesticated variety on the left. *(Left, reprinted by permission from "The Emergence of Agriculture," by Bruce D. Smith, copyright 1995, The New York Botanical Garden; right, courtesy Bruce D. Smith)*

Geographic Distribution   As Flannery (1965) proposes, when humans expand their territory, perhaps as a result of population growth and attendant dispersion, they often take food resources with them. In this way, wild plants may be introduced into areas where they do not grow naturally. Another early sign of domestication, then, is the appearance of a plant species in an area where its wild ancestors are not found.

Recognizing Domesticated Animals

Several characteristics of early animal domestication can be seen in the archaeological record.

Size Selection   As with seed plants, humans may select animals on the basis of size. With the domestication of the wolf, for example, smaller individuals were preferred and selected for. This preference shows up very nicely in the archaeological record of the earliest domesticated dogs, which had smaller jaws but large, wolflike teeth (Olsen 1985). In the process of domesticating cattle, smaller size also was selected for, again probably for the reason of safety. Wild horses, on the other hand, were selected for larger size because their function was to carry loads, pull carts, and transport people. Any sort of ordered change in the size of a species through time, either larger or smaller, may indicate the beginning of domestication.

Geographic Distribution   As with plants, one indication of the domestication of animals is their transport by people into habitats where they are not found naturally. As people moved into new territories, they may have brought formerly wild animals with them. Different selection pressures, both natural and artificial, on the species in the new habitat may have resulted in their further alteration.

Population Characteristics   There is a great deal of chance involved in the hunting of wild animals. Animals killed may be male or female, very young, very old, or in the prime of life. Certainly, hunting is not entirely random and hunters may focus their attention on particular animals, but they may not exercise much control over which animal they finally kill. On the other hand, humans have virtually absolute control over domestic animals. The animals are penned or herded together. Most people who keep animals avoid killing females for the obvious reason that they produce more animals; very few males are necessary to maintain a herd, so herders often kill and eat young males and let females survive to an old age. In the case of tended and domesticated animals, the population statistics of the animals killed should show a recognizable difference from the statistics for hunted animals.

Osteological Changes   Changes occur in the bones of animals if they are penned and prevented from engaging in their normal activity. Such changes are not genetic; they occur as a result of the difference in lifestyle. The bones of wild animals tend to be denser and stronger to allow the animals to withstand the rigors of life in the wild. In contrast, penned animals not allowed to roam freely and not forced to escape predators do not develop this denser microscopic architecture. Such osteological changes do not necessarily indicate domestication; they may occur even in wild zoo animals. Such alterations, however, do imply a change in the relationship between people and the animals on which they subsist, probably indicating at the very least the initial stages of animal domestication.

Hearths of Domestication

We are now in a position to discuss in some detail archaeological data relevant to the question of the invention of agriculture. We will focus on those

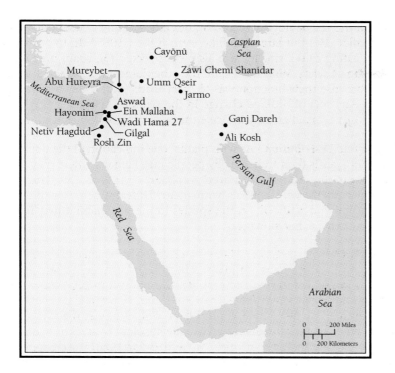

FIGURE 14.7   Map showing the locations of Middle East archaeological sites mentioned in the text where evidence of domestication has been recovered.

areas of the world where domestication seems to have occurred, at least in part, independently. These areas are Southwest Asia, Africa, East Asia, southern Europe, Mesoamerica, western South America, and North America (see Figure 14.2).

Southwest Asia

A series of archaeological sites are known from the area called the Levant, a stretch of uplands across modern Israel, Lebanon, and Syria. The sites all date to the period 13,000–9800 B.P. and the culture is known as **Natufian** (Figure 14.7).

The Natufian   Natufian sites are mostly in caves, although some open-air camps have been located. The Natufian sites are all nonagricultural; there is no evidence that domestication of any plant or animal species had yet taken place, but they were reliant on wild crops that were to become the world's first domesticates (Figure 14.8). For example, kernels and stalks of wild wheat and barley have been found at many Natufian sites. At Mureybet and Abu Hureyra, in Syria, wild einkorn wheat and vetch (a **legume**— plants that produce pods with seeds), have been found in roasting pits

Natufian Late Paleolithic– Early Neolithic culture of Southwest Asia, dated from 13,000 to 9800 ya.

legume A family of flowering plants that produce pods containing seeds.

FIGURE 14.8 Domesticated early in the Neolithic of Southwest Asia, wheat remains one of the world's most important food crops. *(© FWP/FAD; Food and Agricultural Organization, United Nations; F. Mattioli)*

dated to more than 11,000 years ago. Carbonized kernels of wild barley as well as lentils, chick peas, and field peas have been recovered at Wadi Hama 27 in Jordan, dated to 12,000 B.P.

Artifacts recovered at Natufian sites, as well as archaeological features reflecting practices of food storage and preparation, also indicate Natufian reliance on locally abundant wild cereal grains: grinding stones or mortars, food storage pits, pits for roasting plant foods, and microblades of flint.

The stone mortars certainly could have been used for grinding plant material, but the evidence from the microliths is even more compelling. These tiny, very sharp stone blades inset into bone, wood, and antler handles were used much in the way of modern sickles to harvest wild grains—most probably wheat, barley, and oats. The stone blades exhibit a sheen or polish that has been shown through replicative experiment to be the result of cutting cereal plant stalks like those of wheat and barley (Unger-Hamilton 1989).

Archaeologist Ramona Unger-Hamilton (1989) has conducted an experiment focusing on the tools that may have been used to harvest the wild and early domesticated cereal crops of the Levant. After making 295 stone blades and then using them to harvest a number of locally available wild and domesticated plant species, she compared the wear patterns (see Chapter 7) on these experimental tools with those she found on 761 prehistoric blades from sites in Israel dating from 12,000 to 8000 ya. She found that one-quarter of the blades from Natufian sites and three-quarters of the more recent tools had striations, or scratches, that were just like those she experimentally produced when harvesting cereal crops from tilled soil. In her experiment, when harvesting grains from tilled soil, the sickle handle in which the blades were inset invariably would scrape the ground, giving the blades these characteristic scratch marks. Unger-Hamilton interpreted this evidence to indicate that tilling the soil and harvesting the cereals that grew there began with the Natufian culture.

Harvesting and storing abundant, dependable, and nutritious wild cereals, legumes, and nut foods supported a more sedentary way of life by the Natufian people. Natufian sites reflect this developing sedentism in a sophisticated architectural pattern of permanent villages. At Ein Mallaha, Hayonim Cave, and Rosh Zin in Israel archaeologists have excavated house remains with stone foundations ranging from 2 to 9 meters (about 6 to 28 feet in diameter (Henry 1989). The work invested in the construction of these homes is a clear indication that they were intended for long-term use.

Karim Shahir   Our focus now shifts to the Zagros Mountains of northeastern Iraq, where sites of the Karim Shahir culture have been excavated. One of the most important of these sites is Zawi Chemi Shanidar (see Figure 14.7), which dates to 10,600 B.P. (Wright 1971). The site is characterized by round hut floors within a cave. Artifacts include some microliths, grinding and milling stones, beads, rings, pendants, and axes. Most important were the faunal remains, almost exclusively the bones of sheep. The bones themselves were not so different from the bones of ordinary wild mountain sheep. What is striking about the assemblage at this site is the population distribution of the animals. Almost all the bones from Zawi Chemi Shanidar are from young animals. As discussed, that kind of consistency almost certainly implies that the people were in control of the population of animals they were feeding on. Such control implies tending, if not incipient domestication.

The First Food Producers   Sometime around 11,000 years ago, Natufians and Karim Shahirians appear to have produced the first domesticated plants (Henry 1989; Maisels 1990; N. Miller 1992). At Netiv Hagdud and Gilgal in Israel and at Ganj Dareh in Iran, recovered barley kernels have been identified as an early domesticated version of that cereal. The size and form of the kernels is distinct from wild barley, showing features present in the domesticated grain. At Aswad in Syria and Çayönü in Turkey, domesticated wheats known as **emmer** and **einkorn** have been dated to more than 10,000 B.P. At both of these sites lentils may also have been cul-

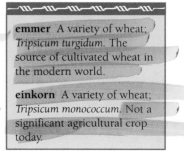

emmer A variety of wheat; *Tripsicum turgidum*. The source of cultivated wheat in the modern world.

einkorn A variety of wheat; *Tripsicum monococcum*. Not a significant agricultural crop today.

FIGURE 14.9 Excavation of the Bus Mordeh occupation of Tepe Ali Kosh. *(Frank Hole)*

tivated: at Aswad, 55 percent of the seeds of food plants recovered were from cultivated peas and lentils (Miller 1992:48).

Ali Kosh   In the early to mid-1960s, a multidisciplinary project was undertaken, in the Deh Luran Plain of southwestern Iran. The project was directed by archaeologists Frank Hole, Kent Flannery, and James Neely (1969). Their objective was to investigate the nature of early domestication and the development of settled village life in Southwest Asia. Among the sites located in their research were two, Tepe Ali Kosh and Tepe Sabz, that provided data bearing directly on this question.

At Ali Kosh, for the period 9450 to 8700 B.P., the investigators defined the Bus Mordeh Phase of occupation (Figure 14.9). The site was relatively small, as were the individual structures, made from local red clay. The Bus Mordeh people depended for their subsistence, at least in part, on the hunting of wild animals like gazelle, wild ox, boar, and ass. They also fished, as evidenced by the remains of carp and catfish in their trash pits.

The Bus Mordeh people were also pretty clearly at an early stage in the domestication of goats. Just as at Zawi Chemi Shanidar, the bones differ very little from wild ones, but the population distribution of the animals can best be interpreted as indicating tending and an early stage in the process of domestication. Most of the animals killed at Ali Kosh during the Bus Mordeh Phase were young males. Females, it seems, were protected for breeding (Hole et al. 1969:344).

The Bus Mordeh phase also provides evidence for domestication of plants, but as in Tehuacán (see later in the chapter) domesticates seem to have played a minor role in the diet during this early stage. Thousands of seeds were recovered in the Bus Mordeh levels at Ali Kosh. Most represented wild alfalfa, vetch, goosefoot, and other wild grasses and legumes. The domesticated versions of emmer wheat and two-row barley were also found at this level, but they represent less than 10 percent of the seeds recovered, indicating a very small contribution to the diet (Hole et al. 1969:343).

The period of 8700 to 7950 B.P. at Tepe Ali Kosh is called the Ali Kosh Phase. It is unknown whether the site grew larger, but certainly individual structures were larger and more substantial. Here we can see again the rather slow development of a reliance on food production. By this time, Ali Kosh was an agricultural and herding village, but much of the diet still consisted of wild animals and plants as well as fish. In this phase, the osteological evidence shows quite clearly that the goats were no longer wild but domesticated. About 40 percent of the seeds recovered in these levels were from domesticated versions of emmer wheat and two-row barley (Hole et al. 1969:347). Not surprisingly, many small flint blades (for harvesting) as well as grinding stones (for processing) were recovered.

From 7950 to 7550 B.P., the Mohammad Jaffar Phase, the people at Ali Kosh were building larger and more substantial houses. They still hunted gazelle and other animals and collected wild plants for part of their subsistence. They also planted wheat and barley and herded both goats and increasing numbers of domesticated sheep.

At the Tepe Sabz site, in the period 7450 to 6950 B.P., two significant shifts in food-production strategies occurred. First, there was a change of emphasis from goats to sheep. Second, at least beginning in this phase, these people started to use irrigation to expand the area available to them for agriculture.

After this period, the population of the Deh Luran Plain exploded. There was a greater number of villages, which grew larger and more stable. At first, domesticates were a minor part of the diet. Population was still low, but increased effort in food production resulted in large increases in the amount of food produced, which allowed for increased population, which in turn led to a demand for more agriculture. Eventually, this effect led to the necessity of artificially increasing the amount of cultivatable land through irrigation. Irrigation resulted in an even higher output of food, which then allowed for increased population.

Domesticating Wheat   The emmer and einkorn wheat that grew wild in the hilly areas of Southwest Asia at the end of the Pleistocene was used

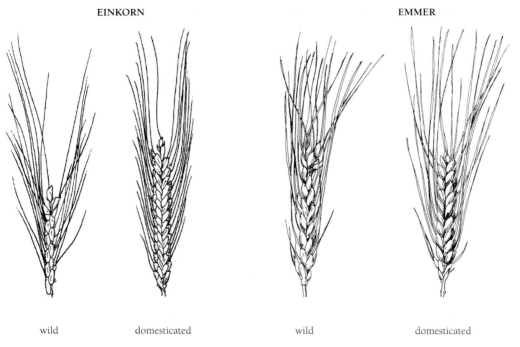

FIGURE 14.10 A comparison of the seed head of wild and domesticated wheat. The brittle rachis (where the seeds are attached) of wild wheat allows for the dispersion of seeds; the nonbrittle rachis selected for in domestication allows for ease in human harvesting.

rachis The area of attachment between seeds and other seeds or between seeds and other parts of the plant.

glume Seed case in which an individual cereal grain is enclosed on the plant.

by local hunter-gatherers. Modern experiments have shown that large amounts of these wild grains can be harvested (Harlan et al. 1966). These wild wheat kernels are also higher in protein than modern domesticated wheat.

There are, however, a number of problems. The **rachis** of wild wheat—the point of attachment of the seeds to the plant—becomes quite brittle when the kernels are ripe. In fact, it has been noted that wild emmer wheat and barley growing near some of the older archaeological sites in the region can be harvested only during a very short period because they ripen quickly, their rachis become quite brittle, and the strong winds common to the region can blow the individual grains off the plant and onto the ground (Bower 1989b). This renders harvesting wild wheat problematic and provides a rationale for human selection of only those plants with a nonbrittle rachis. Also, each kernel of wild wheat is encased in a tough rind, or **glume.** The wheat still needs a good deal of processing to remove the edible kernels from the inedible glumes.

But wild wheat stands have mutants that possess tough, nonbrittle rachis and naked glumes. Only a very few genes are involved in determining these characteristics. Under natural conditions, neither a tough rachis nor naked glumes is advantageous. It appears, however, that people who were collecting wild wheat in Southwest Asia at the end of the Pleistocene were artificially selecting for those very characteristics (Figure 14.10).

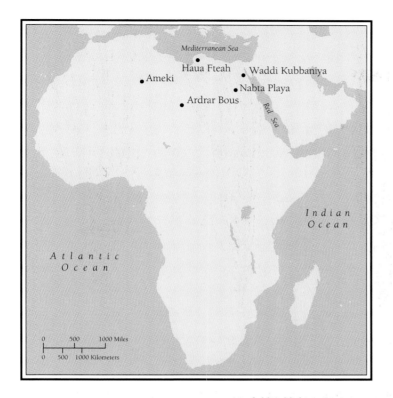

FIGURE 14.11   Map showing sites in Africa mentioned in the text where evidence of domestication has been recovered.

Additional evidence of early steps in domestication in Southwest Asia comes from the 8600-year-old site of Mureybet in northern Syria, where researchers have found the remains of wild wheat and barley. These crops were not native to the region and probably came from a source some 160 kilometers to the north in the Zagros Mountains of Turkey. This is good evidence for human intervention. People, likely from the Zagros Mountains, must have brought these crops with them as they expanded their territory into northern Syria where they planted and tended them.

Africa

The 8000-year-old site of Nabta Playa in the Sahara Desert of southern Egypt supplies evidence of an African culture just on the cusp of its own Food-Producing Revolution (Figure 14.11) (Wendorf et al. 1992).

Nabta Playa   Excavators found more than one hundred cooking features and were able to recover thousands of seeds representing some forty different species of wild plants. The most common seeds found at Nabta Playa were sorghum and a number of varieties of millet. Both are grass crops that produce edible grain. Though not well-known outside the semiarid trop-

FIGURE 14.12 Domesticated in the African Neolithic, sorghum is a primary source of protein in some modern African agricultural systems. *(Food and Agriculture Organization, United Nations; J. van Acker)*

ics, millet and sorghum are the primary sources of protein in some modern African agricultural systems (Figure 14.12).

The sorghum seeds found at Nabta Playa look like those of the wild plant. There is no evidence of selection for seeds larger or with thinner seed coats than in wild varieties. On the other hand, the chemistry of the fats contained in the preserved Nabta Playa seeds is more similar to the modern domesticate. Though the seeds are not believed to represent a domesticated variety of sorghum just on the basis of their chemistry, as the site researchers point out, it is a "short step" (Wendorf et al. 1992:724) from the intensive use of wild plants to their domestication.

Additional evidence for domestication in Africa comes from Egypt, where domesticated wheat, barley, sheep, goats, and cattle are present in sites along the Nile dating to more than 7000 ya. Also in North Africa,

Haua Fteah Cave in Libya shows early evidence of the use of domesticates. Here the bones of domesticated sheep and goats were found in a level dated to before 6800 B.P. (Clark 1976). Domesticated cattle are also known from sites of similar age. Recent mitochondrial DNA research on a sample of cattle from Europe, India, and Africa indicates that African cattle form a distinct group that separated from European wild cattle as early as 26,000 years ago, long before they were domesticated anywhere (Kaiser 1996). These wild African cattle, not more recent European or Asian imports, formed the breeding stock for domesticated cattle. This indicates native Africans domesticated African cattle independently of cattle domestication in Europe or Asia (Zimmer 1994).

Food Producers in Africa South of the Sahara The data are very sparse for southern Africa, but there appears to have been separate hearths of domestication south of the Sahara. Domesticated pearl millet has been found dating to as much as 6500 years ago at the Ameki site in Mali (Harlan 1992). At around 5000 B.P., we find evidence of sorghum and at least two other varieties of domesticated millet (finger and foxtail); these were not Asian or European plants, so it is probable that they were the result of purely local domestication. Each sorghum plant produces a number of stems with clusters of seeds that, in the wild condition, mature at different times. In the process of domestication, the plants selected for produced seeds maturing all at the same time for ease of harvest (Harlan et al. 1976). A host of other plants unknown in the rest of the Neolithic world were domesticated in sub-Saharan Africa as well, including tef (a cereal), fonio (a cereal), ground nuts (similar to peanuts), enset (a relative of the banana), and noog (which produces an edible oil).

Also in western Africa, a non-Asian variety of rice was domesticated. Yams were another important crop, but tubers are notoriously difficult to study archaeologically because they do not produce hard parts that might preserve. Sheep, goats, pigs, and cattle came into the area from the north and quickly became significant components in the subsistence of many sub-Saharan African agriculturalists. Recent palynological evidence suggests that the oil palm, an important domesticated tree that produces oil used in cooking, wood for construction, leaves for thatching, and fibers for cordage, was probably domesticated at about 2800 B.P. (Sowunmi 1985). It is at about this time that pollen analysis in Western Africa shows a decrease in the percentages of several wild tree species and a dramatic increase in the oil palm.

The Far East

At Spirit Cave in northwestern Thailand (Figure 14.13), excellent preservation has allowed researchers to reconstruct much of the diet (Gorman

FIGURE 14.13 Map showing the location of East Asian archaeological sites mentioned in the text where evidence of domestication has been recovered.

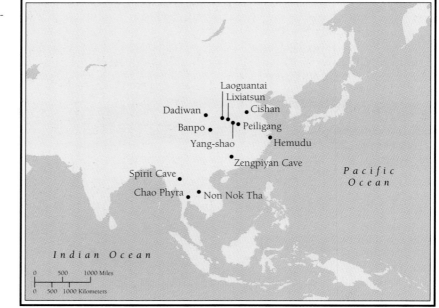

1969; Solheim 1972). As early as 12,000 ya, we can see the utilization of such species as water chestnut, bean, soybean, almond, and cucumber. These plants were probably not yet domesticated at this time. Just as in Iran, however, the data show an early post–Pleistocene adaptation that focused on the local wild antecedents of those species that were to be domesticated shortly afterward and were to become mainstays of local diet right up to the present time. The data are sparse for the period after this, but we do know that by 6000 B.P. fully agricultural villages had evolved. The site of Non Nok Tha in northeast Thailand, with domesticated rice, cattle, and pigs, is an example (Figure 14.14).

The earliest evidence of possible animal domestication in China dates to about 10,000 years ago at Zengpiyan Cave in Guilan in southeast China. A large proportion (85 percent) of the animal bones are those of young pigs, less than two years of age (Chang 1986:102–3). This age distribution implies that the animals were not being hunted in the wild but were kept and tended, with some animals held for breeding purposes and many of the surplus piglets killed for food. Also, the canine teeth in the Zengpiyan pigs are smaller than in a wild pig population, which may show the artificial selection of less dangerous animals with smaller teeth.

In the deciduous forest zone of northern China, the earliest food-producing culture yet encountered is called **Peiligang** and is seen at sites like Cishan, Peiligang, Laoguantai, Dadiwan, and Lixiatsun (Chang 1986). Dating to between 8500 and 7000 years ago, these Peiligang sites were well-established farming villages, though hunting, fishing, and gathering

Peiligang Earliest Neolithic culture in north China with well-established farming villages dated to 8500 to 7000 years ago.

FIGURE 14.14 The Non Nok Tha site in Thailand is an early agricultural site in Southeast Asia. *(Courtesy W. G. Solheim II)*

FIGURE 14.15 Today, rice is emblematic of East Asian agricultural systems. The earliest domesticated rice in China has been identified at the Hemudu site on the Yangtze River just south of Shanghai with a radiocarbon date of about 7000 B.P. *(Food and Agriculture Organization, United Nations; F. Mattioli)*

wild plants continued to be important in subsistence. Domesticated crops include foxtail millet, broomcorn millet, and Chinese cabbage. Domesticated animals include pig, dog, and chicken.

Yang-shao Preagricultural people in central China practiced a nomadic way of life, fishing and hunting deer, elephant, and bear. We also know that sometime after 8000 ya, sedentary villages of what is called the **Yang-shao** culture developed in the Huang-ho River valley in which the domesticated versions of foxtail millet, pigs, and dogs were eaten (Chang 1986). Only later did these people begin to raise chickens, sheep, horses, and cattle. As for the most significant East Asian domesticate, rice, little is known for certain other than it appears to have originated independently in China, Southeast Asia, and India (Ho 1977) (Figure 14.15). Though rice is

Yang-shao The early Neolithic culture of China dated to about 8000 ya.

FIGURE 14.16 Map showing the location of southern European archaeological sites mentioned in the text where evidence of domestication has been recovered.

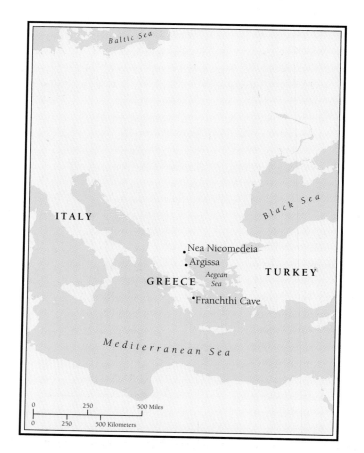

emblematic of East Asian agricultural systems, it appears relatively late in the sequence. The earliest domesticated rice in China has been identified at the Hemudu site on the Yangtze River just south of Shanghai with a radiocarbon date of about 7000 B.P. (G. Crawford 1991:25).

Here again, though the data are not nearly as detailed as for Southwest Asia, we do see the slow acceptance of domesticates, for wild plant foods remained important to the Yang-shao people long after they began using cultivated ones. Full-scale agricultural villages did not appear until the appearance of the **Lung-shan** culture a few thousand years later. Unfortunately, the time period that interests us most in terms of the actual development of domestication is still very poorly known for East Asia.

Lung-shan The first fully agricultural people in China, dated to about 6000 ya.

Europe

In southern Europe at the end of the Pleistocene (Figure 14.16), we see a pattern of big-game hunting with an emphasis on wild cattle, deer, ass, bison, and mountain goat (Milisauskas 1978; Whittle 1985). A typical site

is Franchthi Cave in Greece, where these animals were hunted about 11,000 ya (Figure 14.17). By 9500 B.P., we see a decrease in the size of the animal species being hunted and a marked increase in the presence of fish bones and other aquatic resources. This seems to indicate a shift to coastal resources as the coasts were beginning to stabilize after the sea-level rise that accompanied glacial meltoff. Although the data are unclear, the emphasis on coastal resources may indicate an increase in sedentism; commonly, coastal areas are rich enough to allow hunter-gatherers to abandon nomadism. Such a shift, however, may have resulted in a population increase or at least increased local population densities sufficient to force some groups to try to intensify the subsistence quest. Such an intensification may have resulted in the shift from food gathering to food production. At Franchthi Cave, we also see the exploitation of wild oats, barley, peas, and lentils between 13,000 and 11,000 B.P. (Hansen 1991), showing the use of wild crops that were soon to become important domesticates.

Europe's First Food Producers After 8000 B.P. in southern Europe, sites become larger and more permanent; evidence of domestication is clear. These early European sites, however, are not full-scale farming villages.

FIGURE 14.17 Franchthi Cave, in Greece, was occupied during the Late Pleistocene and early post-Pleistocene. Wild species of crops that would later be domesticated, such as oats, barley, peas, and lentils, were eaten by the inhabitants more than 11,000 ya. (*Thomas W. Jacobsen*)

Domesticated plants and animals appear to have been grafted onto an in-place hunting–gathering economy that continued even after domestication began. Domesticated plants and animals did not replace wild varieties; they supplemented them.

The domesticated plants that first turn up in Europe are traceable to Southwest Asia; with the possible exception of cattle, all domesticates that appeared in Europe at 8000 B.P. were domesticated by at least 1000 years earlier in Southwest Asia. It is rather easy to imagine contact between early agriculturalists living in the Levant and southern Europeans living along the Mediterranean coast. Almost certainly Southwest Asian domesticated plants and animals were introduced into Europe through this contact. Along with their proximity, the similarity in climate also enabled the movement of Southwest Asian domesticates into southern Europe. These crops thrived under the environmental conditions in parts of southern Europe and the established schedule of planting and harvesting could be maintained.

For example, at Franchthi Cave, domesticated emmer wheat appears without antecedents at about 8000 B.P. Two-rowed barley, another Southwest Asian domesticate, was important in the diet of the cave's inhabitants; they also relied on domesticated sheep and goats whose source, again, was probably Southwest Asia. At around the same time or soon after, early farming villages appear along the Mediterranean coast of Italy and France, where the Middle Eastern domesticates of wheat, barley, lentils, sheep, and goats contributed to the diet. It is important to point out that at the sites mentioned, wild plants continued to play an important role in subsistence. Many of the same species that contributed to subsistence before the introduction of domesticates—deer, wild pig, fish, and sea mammals—continued to do so.

An Agricultural Europe   Beginning about 7500 years ago, we see the first nearly completely agricultural economies in Europe, still based on a suite of Southwest Asian domesticates. For example, at the Nea Nicomedeia site on the Aegean coast of Greece, the hunting of wild animals such as deer, wild pig, and hare had become a minor part, along with fishing, of the subsistence quest; only about 10 percent of the animal bones found at the site were of wild species. Seventy percent of those bones were from domesticated sheep and goats, and pig and cattle made up the rest (Rodden 1965; B. Smith 1995). Wheat, barley and legumes were the primary agricultural crops at the site. After about 7200 years ago, fully agricultural economies based on the growing of wheat, barley, and lentils and the raising of sheep, goats, cattle, and pigs are seen throughout Greece and Italy.

The essentially Southwest Asian agricultural economy that had successfully transplanted to southern Europe could not penetrate north into the more temperate conditions of central Europe. As Bruce Smith (1995:102) points out, it took a shift in the scheduling of planting and

FIGURE 14.18 Maize was domesticated approximately 5000 years ago by the native people of Mesoamerica. It continues to be one of the world's most important food crops, the most significant of the many contributions Native Americans have made to the subsistence base of the modern world. *(Food and Agriculture Organization, United Nations; I. Velez)*

harvesting to allow for an agricultural economy to the north; in a schedule more familiar to North Americans, crops were planted in the spring and harvested in the fall, the opposite of the situation to the south. Emphasizing wheat, legumes, barley, and cattle, agriculture spread rapidly throughout central Europe after 6700 years ago.

Mesoamerica

In the late 1950s and early 1960s, American archaeologist Richard MacNeish (1964, 1967) began conducting archaeological surveys in highland Mexico. MacNeish was looking for early evidence of maize, what we commonly call corn (Figure 14.18). He focused on dry highlands because these regions would have better preservation of ancient organic material and because botanist Paul Mangelsdorf (1958), an expert on maize, had declared that it had originally been a highland grass species.

The Tehuacán Valley Project   Searching through several highland valleys with freshwater sources, MacNeish came upon the Tehuacán Valley (Figure 14.19). After scrambling through some thirty-eight caves where organic preservation would have been best, he was finally successful. A few test pits dug in Coxcatlan Cave produced six of the most primitive-looking maize cobs anyone had ever seen.

This initial find inspired the Tehuacán Valley Project, one of the largest and most ambitious archaeological expeditions ever undertaken. From

FIGURE 14.19 The Tehuacan Valley, looking past El Riego Cave on the left. Here Richard MacNeish discovered evidence for a sequence of New World agricultural development. *(R. S. Peabody Foundation for Archaeology, photo by R. S. MacNeish and Paul Manglesdorf)*

1961 to 1964, fifty experts in various fields converged on the valley. Major excavations were conducted on twelve valley sites and hundreds of others were tested (Figure 14.20). What resulted was a nearly continuous stratigraphic sequence of human occupation of the valley from 12,000 B.P. to A.D. 1500. By following this sequence, and through the application of accelerator-mass-spectrometry, a variety of radiocarbon dating applied directly to some of the maize cobs, we can construct a picture of human cultural evolution in the valley—an evolution that included the development of a food-producing economy.

Tehuacán Subsistence and Settlement Through Time Highland cultures in Tehuacán and probably other upland valleys at the end of the Pleistocene depended to a great degree on hunting (Flannery 1967). Of greatest importance at the lowest levels of Coxcatlan Cave were pronghorn antelope and jackrabbit. Such animals can be most easily hunted by groups. Pronghorn travel in herds, and jackrabbits live above ground and can be run into nets in large numbers. As climate changed at the end of the Pleistocene, both these animal species became extinct in the Mexican uplands. They were replaced by whitetail deer and cottontail rabbit, animals that can be hunted most efficiently by solitary hunters or small groups. Deer are solitary animals; cottontail rabbits live in burrows and cannot be netted in large numbers. It is likely, therefore, that people living in the valley at the end of the Pleistocene found it necessary to broaden their subsistence quest and to spread their numbers out over more territory to exploit

FIGURE 14.20   Map showing the locations of Mesoamerican archaeological sites mentioned in the text where evidence of domestication has been recovered.

these more spread out animal resources. It is possible that, as a result of this change in settlement pattern, the people also intensified their exploitation of plant species.

At many of the caves excavated in the project, human paleofeces had been preserved producing a total of 116 fecal deposits. The analysis of these deposits allowed an extremely detailed reconstruction of diet. For example, in the paleofeces from El Riego Cave, MacNeish's coprologist, E. O. Callen (1967), recovered undigested remains of wild beans, amaranth (a grain), chili peppers, and avocados. Also in the paleofeces were the remains of domesticated squash. The squash found here was *not* a primitive or incipient version of a domesticate; it was entirely different from its wild antecedent.

Using the paleofeces and other data, MacNeish (1967) has attempted to reconstruct the settlement pattern in the valley. During the initial period, winter occupations were small hunting camps. In the spring, populations coalesced into larger camps along the rivers. During the spring and summer, various wild seeds and cactus pods were important elements of the diet. Wild fruits were exploited when they ripened in the fall. Domesticates would have been incorporated into a still rather nomadic way of life, serving only as a minor element in the diet in the spring and summer.

Maize   Shifting back to Coxcatlan Cave, we begin to see another change in subsistence, again based on an analysis of the paleofeces. Most of the diet still consisted of wild game and wild plants, but domesticates including maize were found. Twelve of the Tehuacán maize samples have now been dated directly using accelerator-mass-spectrometry. The oldest maize has been directly dated using this method to about 4700 B.P., though some of the material may be a bit older (Fritz 1994; A. Long et al. 1989).

This oldest yet discovered maize is certainly not the corn with which we are familiar. Modern maize consists of some 300 different races or varieties, some with enormous ears 12 or more inches long, with many rows and hundreds of kernels. The maize found in this level at Coxcatlan Cave is barely 1 inch long with eight rows of six to nine kernels each (Figure 14.21). As humble as they appear, these remains nevertheless mark an incredibly important development in the evolution of agriculture. But even these oldest, tiny cobs from Tehuacán are clearly well down the path of domestication as their morphology is maladaptive for life in the wild. The kernels of this early maize were held in place by long glumes, a casing in which the individual kernel is enclosed. Like modern maize, the kernels of this ancient maize would not have fallen out on their own, and thus the crop could no longer have regenerated itself in the wild. A human had to remove the kernels from the glumes for eating or planting. Still to be discovered are samples of older, more primitive maize that show the first steps toward domestication.

A New World Agricultural Revolution   At another site in the valley, Abejas, we can see increasing reliance on domesticates. By the time this cave was occupied, the domesticates included maize, squash, and beans, the triumvirate that was to become the basis of subsistence for most of the agricultural peoples of the pre-Columbian New World.

The sites that date to this period in the valley after 4700 years ago exhibit a size and degree of sedentism previously unknown in the area. MacNeish (1967) has suggested that what had been temporary spring and summer camps along streams were now becoming permanent base camps at which at least some members of the population stayed year round. We are probably seeing the process of deviation amplification suggested by Flannery (1968), where a small, initial change or deviation in a traditional cultural practice related to subsistence has an enormous ripple effect across the culture, resulting in a fundamental change in a lifeway.

For agriculture to make a significant contribution to the diet, people need to become more sedentary. The more sedentary they become, however, the greater the need to produce food because they can no longer roam around as much in the food quest. At the same time, the very old and the very young can make significant contributions to the subsistence quest; they can weed, sort seeds, and perform other light work. In the period we are examining, this very labor in fact may have extended people's life spans and thus increased overall population, which, in turn, would have put pressure on the subsistence system to produce more food. Thus, the original deviation from the traditional subsistence practice became amplified, further necessitating a shift toward food production.

A cave site, Ajalpa, picks up the story and again exhibits what appears to be a still very slow evolution toward an agricultural way of life. Domesticates now made up a part of the diet, the rest still supplied by hunting wild animals and gathering wild plants. Finally, the Santa Maria site, exhibits an acceleration in the shift to food production.

Isotope analysis of human bones found in the Tehuacán Valley shows a clear jump in the reliance upon maize and related tropical grasses early in the Tehuacán sequence and then little change thereafter (Farnsworth et al. 1985). Based on the isotope analysis, the overall diet of these people did not change much for several millennia.

Combining MacNeish's reconstruction as well as the isotope data, it appears that the inhabitants of the valley went through a long period of increasing sedentism before adopting a fully agricultural way of life. This lengthy period of dietary reliance on tropical grasses—including, perhaps, the wild progenitor of maize—is similar to the situation seen in the Near East.

Teosinte: Wild Maize   Though the identification is still uncertain, many researchers believe that the highland grass **teosinte** is, in fact, wild maize (Beadle 1977) (Figure 14.22). Teosinte is a wild plant that looks rather similar to the maize plant; instead of cobs with kernels, however, it produces rows a few inches long with five to ten seeds (technically fruits) each (Figure 14.23). A single plant can produce thousands of seeds that fall to the ground when the rachis becomes brittle and is shattered by any slight movement.

We know that teosinte was used as a prehistoric food source, but quite a bit of work is involved in harvesting and preparing the seeds for eating. The brittleness of the rachis leads to loss of seeds, the individual seeds are very small, and the seed cases are extremely tough. There is variation, however, and mutations do occur. In fact, these characteristics are controlled by only a very few genes (Beadle 1977:626). It is likely that during the time teosinte was being exploited, there was selection for those plants with less brittle rachis and naked kernels or seeds. Recent research by botanist Jane Dorweiler shows that a single alteration in a small section of one of teosinte's chromosomes changes the ordinarily tightly encased seeds into soft, exposed, more maizelike kernels (Roush 1996). The cob in maize can be accounted for as a mutation of the seed spike in teosinte (see Figure 14.23). Thus, teosinte, called "God's corn" by the Aztecs, appears to have been modified through artificial selection to produce the small, relatively brittle cobbed corn of the Tehuacán Valley.

FIGURE 14.22   Teosinte may be the wild ancestor of maize. Pictured here is a modern variety (*Zea mays parviglumis*) from the Rio Balsas in Mexico that may be the form from which domesticated maize is descended. (*Courtesy of Dolores Piperno, Smithsonian Tropical Research Institute*)

▼ **FIGURE 14.23**   With its brittle rachis and tough glumes, teosinte (*left*), a wild Mexican grass called "God's corn" by the Aztecs is the most likely candidate for wild maize. It is here compared to maize (*right*). The fruitcase of teosinte can be converted to the cob and naked kernels of maize by changes in very few genes. (*From Beadle in Reed 1977*)

Teosinte spikelet (left) and seeds (right)

Teosinte plant

Maize plant

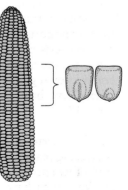

Maize cob (left) and kernels (right)

FIGURE 14.24 Map showing the location of South American archaeological sites mentioned in the text where evidence of domestication has been recovered.

South America

Although hypotheses have been proposed for the early cultivation of root crops such as manioc in South America, there is no solid evidence to support this notion. The earliest indisputable domesticates used in South America are common beans, lima beans, and chili peppers dating to 5000 years ago at Guitarrero Cave in highland Peru (Figure 14.24) (Kaplan et al. 1973; Lynch et al. 1985; Patterson 1973).

Some of the earliest evidence for the domestication of quinoa—an extremely important crop in the agriculture of South America (Figure 14.25, p. 418)—has been found at Panaulauca Cave in Peru. Quinoa plants produce nutritious seeds with a healthy mix of amino acids superior to the better known grains. Quinoa seeds with thinner seed coats than wild specimens have been dated there to between 4000 and 5000 B.P. (B. Smith 1995:173).

South American Root Crops Though far more difficult than seed-producing plants to trace archaeologically, root crops, especially the potato (but other species not so well-known to people outside of South America), are known to have been an important food source for much of upland South America (Vietmeyer 1992). Several different varieties of domesticated potatoes were developed by ancient South Americans by at least

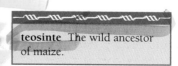

teosinte The wild ancestor of maize.

FIGURE 14.25   Quinoa plants produce nutritious seeds with a healthy mix of amino acids superior to the better known grains. Quinoa seeds with thinner seed coats than wild specimens have been dated to South American sites between 4000 and 5000 B.P. and continue to be an important source of protein on that continent. (*Courtesy John F. McCamant*)

4000 years ago and possibly much earlier. The potato was unknown in ancient Europe, though it became an important crop there in the sixteenth century A.D. after it was introduced by travelers to the New World. This South American crop became a dietary mainstay in parts of northern Europe. A terrible famine occurred in Europe—most severely in Ireland—when much of the potato crop was killed by a blight in the 1840s.

Other high-altitude roots were domesticated and relied on as sources of food in the South American uplands. For example, *oca*, second in importance only to the potato, produced nutritious tubers at altitudes up to 13,500 feet. Also, the root crops *yacon, ulluco, mashua, oca,* and *arracacha* and the legume *jícama* were important contributors to the diet (Figure 14.26). The turniplike *maca* was cultivated at elevations of 14,000 feet. The Inca civilization in western South America (see Chapter 15) relied more heavily on root crops than any of the world's ancient civilizations.

Cotton Domestication and Animal Husbandry   In South America, domestication included at least one significant nonfood crop: cotton. Evidence of its domestication can be traced back to about 5000 B.P.

South America also provides data for the most significant animal domestication in the New World (Kent 1987; Wing 1977). There are four types of camelids in South America: the wild guanaco and vicuña and the domesticated llama and alpaca. The precise relationships among these four types are still unknown—all four are interfertile. Some researchers suggest that the guanaco was domesticated to produce both the llama and the alpaca (Figure 14.27). In any event, the llama is primarily a beast of burden and the alpaca a source of wool; both are used for food. The llama and alpaca show signs of domestication before 5000 B.P., according to finds in Pikimachay Cave and Lauricocha Cave in Peru (Wing 1977).

FIGURE 14.26 Root crops were an important food source for the high-altitude civilizations of South America. Along with the potato, other high-altitude crops like *oca, ulluco* and *mashua* were contributors to the diet. (*Dr. Steven R. King*)

Maize in South America Though maize became a very significant element of South American subsistence, it appears rather late in the sequence. The oldest maize in South America dates to after 4000 B.P. at the Vegas site on the Ecuadorian coast. Most experts believe that domesticated maize diffused from Mesoamerica into South America, where it was adopted by cultures already practicing agriculture with their own, native crops, but that verdict is not unanimous (Bruhns 1994).

FIGURE 14.27 Llamas, probably the most important animal domesticated in the New World, were used as beasts of burden and as food. Here, a packtrain of llamas carries firewood in southern Peru. (© *Loren McIntyre*)

North America

Though most people think of maize, beans, and squash as being the chief agricultural crops of North American Indians, evidence now shows that squash was domesticated independently by North American natives as part of an indigenous and separate agricultural revolution that preceded the introduction of the two Mesoamerican domesticates of maize and beans (B. Smith 1989, 1992a, 1992b, 1995).

North American Squash   Long thought to have moved into North America from Mexico, archaeological evidence now indicates that native squash was independently domesticated in eastern North America. A variety of wild squash is known to grow in parts of the American mid-south, and it probably was domesticated soon after 5000 years ago. Squash seeds recovered at the Phillips Spring site in Missouri, dated to 4500–4300 B.P., are early domesticates with seeds significantly larger than their modern wild counterparts (B. Smith 1995).

North American Seed Crops   Other native crops now known to have been domesticated by the Indians of the eastern woodlands were sunflower, sumpweed (also known as marsh elder), pigweed (also called

FIGURE 14.28   The sunflower was one of a number of crops domesticated by Native Americans living north of Mexico. The many-headed sunflower show here is similar to some wild varieties. (*K. L. Feder*)

lamb's quarter), and goosefoot—all producers of starchy or oil-rich seeds (Figure 14.28). Sumpweed seeds recovered from a 4000-year-old archaeological deposit at Napoleon Hollow in Illinois (Figure 14.29), for example, are uniformly larger (by almost a third) than the seeds of wild sumpweed (Ford 1985). Domesticated sunflower with seeds substantially bigger than those of wild varieties has been dated to 4265 B.P. at the Hayes site in central Tennessee (B. Smith 1995). Dating to about 3400 B.P., goosefoot seeds from the Newt Kash Hollow and Cloudsplitter rockshelters in Kentucky have significantly thinner seed coats than those of wild plants, indicating selection for faster growing sprouts. At Salts Cave in Kentucky, 119 pre-

FIGURE 14.29 Map showing the locations of North American archaeological sites mentioned in the text where evidence of domestication has been recovered.

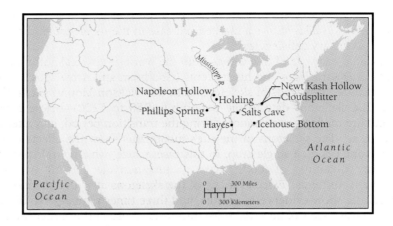

served fecal deposits associated with a radiocarbon date of 3450 B.P. (Yarnell 1977:864) contain an abundance of sunflower and sumpweed seeds, whose large size is indicative of domestication.

The Adoption of Maize   North America also saw the adoption of Mesoamerican domesticates, especially maize and later beans. Because the wild ancestors of these crops do not grow in North America, they must have been brought in from areas where they do grow. But the earliest evidence for the use of maize in North America postdates the appearance of the domesticated local foods by about 2000 years. The oldest evidence for use of maize in North America has been found at the Icehouse Bottom site in eastern Tennessee with a radiocarbon date of 1775 B.P. (Chapman and Crites 1987). The Holding site east of St. Louis also has produced maize and may be slightly older (B. Smith 1995:191).

As important as it was to become in the diets of many North American natives, for nearly 1000 years maize was only a minor supplement to their subsistence. Analysis of the carbon isotope chemistry of prehistoric human bones in North America (see Chapter 7) indicates that a shift away from local domesticates to a heavy reliance on maize did not occur until sometime between A.D. 900 and 1000. All of the wild and indigenously domesticated crops of eastern North America follow a different photosynthetic pathway than maize and possess a different concentration of ^{13}C than does maize. Human bones in North America show a big jump in ^{13}C concentration and, by inference, in maize consumption at about this time (B. Smith 1995:200).

The Nutritional Impact of Agriculture

Although a shift to agriculture almost always results in increased amounts of food, the diet of agriculturalists is not always nutritionally superior to that of hunter-gatherers. In fact, analysis of the skeletons of some prehistoric agriculturalists shows a marked increase in the incidence of diseases related to dietary deficiencies.

A good example of this comes from the work of physical anthropologist George Armelagos and his students (Goodman and Armelagos 1985), who analyzed hundreds of skeletons from the Dickson Mound site in Illinois. The skeletons date to the period A.D. 950 to 1200—before maize agriculture made its appearance, during the transition period, and after its acceptance. The skeletons of the site's inhabitants show the effects of dietary emphasis on a single crop, in this case, maize, which, while providing large quantities of food, led to an unvaried diet lacking in some important nutrients. Twice as many of the skeletons after the adoption of agriculture show evidence of anemia, and three times as many exhibit the osteological effects of bacterial infections as do those of the earlier hunter-gatherers. Beyond this, the bones of the children of the agriculturalists are narrower and shorter, showing a delayed growth rate in their early years. Among agriculturalists who rely on single crops or very few crops, there was higher infant mortality and a shortened average life span.

So, it may be, at least in some cases, that the varied diet of hunter-gatherers was more nutritionally complete than that of many agriculturalists. The health of people often suffered, therefore, in their attempt to produce a greater quantity of food when this resulted in a less varied diet. So, we may infer, there must have been a significant motivation to produce more food.

Can Agriculture Be Explained?

Earlier in this chapter, we presented some hypotheses for explaining the Food-Producing Revolution (Table 14.1). Then we presented data on the actual sequences of the evolution of food production in Mesoamerica, Southwest Asia, East Asia, Europe, South and North America, and Africa (see Figure 14.1 for a summary time chart). We are now left with the question of which hypothesis or hypotheses are borne out by the data. In truth, the data are too limited even for the most well-known sequences to give a definitive answer, but we can begin to attempt to isolate the useful aspects of each of the proposed explanations and—to use an appropriate metaphor—winnow out those aspects that do not bear up under scrutiny.

Childe's oasis hypothesis is probably not correct in positing a significant drying of the environment as a factor. Evidence now shows that this long-term climate effect did not occur. Beyond this, the key elements of his hypothesis are not borne out. The idea that only an oasis situation would allow people to become knowledgeable about plants and animals makes no sense. Hunters and gatherers the world over possess detailed knowledge about the plants and animals on which they subsist.

Sauer was correct at least in terms of proposing that a certain degree of sedentary life was a significant factor in the development of agriculture.

But other aspects of his hypothesis are not supported. Aside from the dog, early domesticates were, in fact, food sources. Also, although the data are meager, Southeast Asia was certainly no earlier and perhaps a bit later in developing an agricultural way of life than was Southwest Asia.

Braidwood may have been correct in assuming that people would not begin the process of domestication without having a great deal of knowledge about the species they were domesticating, but this really does not explain the timing of the Agricultural Revolution or the fact that it was so widespread. His explanation is really no explanation at all—saying, in essence, agriculture developed when people were ready to develop it. It leaves unanswered *why* they were ready.

Anderson's claim that domestication may have been accidentally encouraged by many of the practices of hunter-gatherers is certainly correct. But again, it really does not approach the question of why they would have gone through the extra bother of an agricultural way of life. This, too, is a nonexplanation.

The Rindos hypothesis of coevoution is intriguing. It is particularly valuable as a way of looking at the process of domestication, providing an evolutionary framework for how it may have come about. The Rindos hypothesis does not necessarily contradict hypotheses based on population growth. Rather, it is a valuable model for how the relationship between people and the plants and animals on which they depended might, in some cases, inevitably lead to a more productive subsistence system that would allow for a greater yield to feed an expanding population base.

The hypotheses of Boserup, Binford, Flannery, Harris, and Henry, which are really complementary and not competing, are perhaps the most attractive. Together, they take into account environmental, demographic, and cultural factors. The problem is that one key element of all their explanations—population growth impinging on the carrying capacity of local environments—cannot, at present, be shown to have occurred immediately prior to the beginning of domestication.

Nevertheless, following Binford's model, we can propose a tentative scenario: At the end of the Pleistocene, cultures were forced to adjust their adaptations in response to climatic changes wrought by the melting of the ice sheets. Some groups shifted their subsistence focus to habitats that allowed for a more sedentary existence—coasts, river banks, and so on. Such sedentism may have produced larger, or at least denser, populations. The rich food resources were localized, and group mobility decreased. The old and the lame could make significant contributions to the food quest. Where previously children had been a burden—just more mouths to feed—now they too could become active in the food quest when that quest focused on collecting objects like shellfish, bird eggs, or seeds. The birth rate may have increased as fertility increased and the proportion of surviving babies may have increased as well.

An increase in population, however, may have upset the previously evolved equilibrium between human populations and their environments,

Contemporary Issue

Our Worst Mistake?

The fabric of modern life depends absolutely on the subsistence mode called agriculture. Without a steady, reliable, predictable—not to mention enormous—food supply, modern life with its cities, universities, and, yes, anthropologists simply would not be possible. One might think it obvious, therefore, that agriculture—the invention that more than anything else has made modern life possible—was a good thing. But not everyone agrees. UCLA medical school scientist and writer Jared Diamond (1987) has provocatively characterized the Food-Producing Revolution as "the worst mistake in the history of the human race."

It is an interesting assertion. Diamond points out that hunter-gatherers, in many instances, led relatively easy lives. In response to the stereotype many of us hold of the short, hard lives and hand-to-mouth existence of hunter-gatherers, they often have it better than those who rely on agriculture. Their diets frequently are healthier, providing more protein and more variety than those of agriculturalists. And, even in those few, relatively poor areas where the last hunter-gatherers were pushed by expanding agriculturalists, they didn't need to work very long for the necessities of existence. Agriculture, with its clearing of land, tilling of soil, planting, weeding, watering, and harvesting, is exceedingly hard work, and farmers typically work far more hours than hunter-gatherers.

While most hunter-gatherers practice a broad-spectrum subsistence strategy that includes regularly collecting dozens of different kinds of foods, agriculturalists often devote all of their energies to a very small number of crops—generally rice, corn, or wheat. These high-carbohydrate crops are extremely productive and can feed many more people than hunting or gathering, but, because they are lacking in some essential amino acids, they can lead to a rather poor diet. Also, if a pestilence befalls a major crop, people will starve because they have little else to fall back on.

Beyond this, Diamond points out, it was the enormous output potential of agriculture that led to class societies. Where there is the potential for surplus food production, there is the potential for groups of haves who control the extra and have-nots who need that food in times of trouble. Eventually, Diamond asserts, this led to class societies where most are poor and work their lives away for those few wealthy individuals who control the food surplus.

Thus, in Diamond's accounting, people at the end of the Pleistocene had two choices: They could maintain their hunting and gathering way of life and invent new ways of keeping population down to ensure enough food for their small populations, or they could allow population to grow and intensify the food quest through plant and animal domestication. The irony, in Diamond's view, was that those who made the smart decision—the hunter-gatherers who opted to keep population down and maintain their traditional subsistence mode—were quickly overrun by those who allowed their populations to grow.

What are we to make of this? Diamond does have a point. Certainly, without agriculture there can be no wealth or classes—or wars to dispute who should have that wealth. Equally certainly, however, there could be no anthropologists or UCLA medical school professors. Indeed, agriculture brings with it good and bad. And ultimately, as with nearly all other cultural inventions, the results are up to us.

causing groups to overshoot the carrying capacity of their territories. This may have resulted in expansion into marginal or less attractive habitats and subsequent intensification and specialization of the food quest. Historical hunter-gatherers are known to broadcast the seeds of their wild food plants, so it is not difficult to believe that people at the end of the Pleistocene did the same out of necessity. We need only assume that in attempting to expand their wild food plants (or animals) into new habitats or to intensify their productivity within the same area, they would, as a matter of course, have selected for more productive, more easily harvested, more easily processed, or more tractable individuals of a species. These folks were not stupid. They depended on wild species for their survival. They knew how plants and animals propagated. It would have been a short step for them to assist in propagation and to make the end products more amenable to human use through artificial selection.

Whatever the specific case, such decisions made at the end of the Pleistocene forever altered human cultural evolution. They led to the far-reaching developments to be discussed in the next chapter of this book—and, indeed, to our current chapter in human history.

Summary

Beginning sometime after 12,000 ya, human groups in Southwest Asia, sub-Saharan Africa, Southeast Asia, southern Europe, Mesoamerica, coastal South America, and central North America—began to domesticate the plants and animals on which they depended for their subsistence. That is, they began to produce their own food rather than simply gather what nature provided.

Many hypotheses have been proposed for this fundamental change in how people fed themselves. It seems that the best explanation involves the necessity of feeding more mouths as human populations grew in the above-mentioned regions at the end of the Pleistocene. In Southwest Asia, wheat, barley, sheep, and goats were the primary domesticates, whereas in Africa it was yam, sorghum, millet, and oil palm; in Southeast Asia, rice, millet, cattle, and pigs; in southern Europe, sheep, goats, cattle, wheat, and barley; in Mesoamerica, maize, beans, and squash; in South America, maize, beans, potatoes, llamas, and alpacas; and in North America, sunflower, squash, and marsh elder.

In a relatively short time—something less than 10,000 years—the vast majority of the world's people had adopted an agricultural mode of subsistence. Agriculture allowed for larger, denser populations and necessitated new social structures for controlling and organizing the dense, sedentary settlements that resulted. Ultimately, in some regions, the shift to an agricultural way of life led to the development of cities, civilization, and eventually modern life.

Study Questions

1. What are the key characteristics of human adaptation to the post-Pleistocene world? What is the meaning of the diversity of archaeological remains dated to the Mesolithic in the Old World and the Archaic in the New World?
2. Describe artificial selection and compare it to natural selection. Explain what domestication is and how artificial selection leads to the domestication of plants and animals.
3. How have various scientists attempted to explain the Food-Producing Revolution?
4. What characteristics did people select for in wild plants and animals? Considering this, how can the archaeological remains of domesticated species be distinguished from those of wild ancestors?
5. When and where did people first domesticate plants and animals? What species were domesticated in these world areas?

Key Terms

sedentary	artificial selection	einkorn
Mesolithic	diffusion	rachis
Archaic	carrying capacity	glume
Food-Producing	deviation	Peiligang
Revolution	amplification	Yang-shao
Agricultural	settlement pattern	Lung-shan
Revolution	Natufian	teosinte
Neolithic	legume	
domesticate	emmer	

For More Information

If you are interested in the details of specific hypotheses on the origins of agriculture or if you would like to know more about the development of agriculture in a specific region, any of the works cited in this chapter would be a good place to start. A volume edited by C. Wesley Cowan and Patty Jo Watson (1992) titled *The Origins of Agriculture* has a number of excellent articles on the shift to food production in a number of world areas. Daniel Zohary and Maria Hopf (1994) have provided a virtual encyclopedia of Old World domesticated plants in *Domestication of Plants in the Old World*. Perhaps the best discussion of our current understanding of the Food-Producing Revolution throughout the Old and New Worlds can be found in Bruce Smith's (1995) splendid book, *The Emergence of Agriculture*. Finally, a monograph by Mark Cohen (1977), *The Food Crisis in Prehistory,* gives a detailed argument for demographically driven hypotheses of the origin of prehistoric agriculture.

Monumental construction works, such as the so-called Colossi of Memnon in Egypt, are the unique products of state societies. How did civilization evolve from a Neolithic base of egalitarian farming communities? Are civilizations destined to collapse? *(Food and Agriculture Organization, United Nations; F. Mattioli)*

15

The Evolution of Civilization

CHAPTER CONTENTS

The images are evocative indeed: The sun sets behind the great pyramid of the pharaoh Khufu (better known by his Greek name, Cheops) at Giza in Egypt; the dark, humid jungle frames the Temple of the Jaguars at the ancient Mesoamerican city of Tikal; the "skeleton" of urban sprawl that is the ancient Indus Valley city of Mohenjo-daro crawls upslope toward the citadel that marks the political center of the settlement. Although each is unique, these and other images reflect the culmination of what appears to have resulted from a single, unifying process of cultural evolution. For want of a better term, we characterize these great tombs, pyramids, and cities as evidence of civilization. They symbolize and demarcate a way of life far different from any that had preceded it.

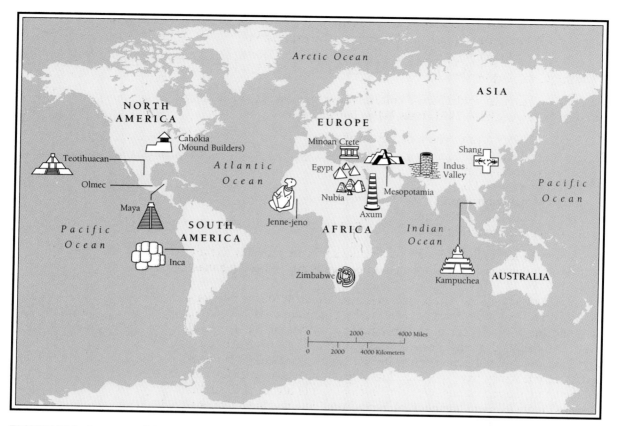

FIGURE 15.1 Locations of the world's earliest civilizations.

The Food-Producing Revolution set the stage for developments that were to characterize a number of world areas after about 6000 years ago. Beginning close to that time, perhaps as a consequence of the shift to agriculture with its potential for producing enormous surpluses of food—and the attendant potential for the accumulation of wealth and power—the Neolithic pattern of small, largely autonomous farming villages became radically altered in some world areas (Figure 15.1). Social and political systems were transformed beyond recognition. The kind of life people led was entirely different from what it had been. We call these developments **civilization.**

civilization Cultures with a food surplus, social stratification, labor specialization, rule by power, monumental construction projects, and a system of record keeping.

The Meaning of Civilization

What is civilization? Common usage usually implies a level of social sophistication or gentility. The dictionary definition ordinarily includes reference to a "high level of technological development," being in an "advanced stage in the arts and sciences," and the invention of writing. Confusion over the precise meaning has led some to abandon its use as a scientific term. We will use it here for lack of a better, inclusive expression.

Defining Civilization

To be categorized as civilizations, cultures must possess the following common features (Childe 1951; Haas 1982; Tainter 1988):

1. Food and labor surplus controlled by an elite
2. Social stratification
3. A formal government
4. Specialization of labor
5. Monumental public works
6. Densely populated settlements
7. A system of recordkeeping

As we will see, each of the early civilizations you are probably already familiar with possessed many, though not necessarily all, of these qualities.

Food and Labor Surplus   Food surplus is a requirement for the development of a civilization. In most societies in the beginning of the Neolithic, the great majority of people probably made contributions to the food quest. Because food output was still relatively low, it was necessary for a large proportion of the population to be directly involved in food production. A very few may have specialized in religious activities or leadership, but they were the exceptions. With the development of higher-yield strains of crops, more efficient methods of agriculture, and the use of animal power, however, the percentage of a given population required to work in the fields certainly dropped.

We can see such a process taking place even today. According to census statistics, in 1920 more than 30 percent of the U.S. population lived on farms. By 1950, that figure had dropped to just a little more than 15 percent, and by 1980 less than 3 percent lived on farms (Figure 15.2). Looked at another way, before 1920 each American farmer, on the average, supplied food products for about seven people. By the 1940s each American farmer produced enough food to feed almost eleven people. By 1970 that figure jumped to fifty people, and by 1980 the American farmer produced enough food to feed almost eighty people (Kranzberg 1984).

The reason you can be a student—and can go on to become a physician, engineer, social worker, or even an anthropologist—rests on the fact that you are not needed on the farm. For complex civilizations to develop, the same process must have occurred. All of the trappings of civilization—pyramids, temples, great art, science, canals, roads—are possible only when large numbers of people are freed from agricultural activity and available to spend much or even all of their time quarrying stone, building roads, serving in the army, and being priests, artisans, builders, merchants, scribes, and so on.

Percentage of U.S.
Population Living on Farms

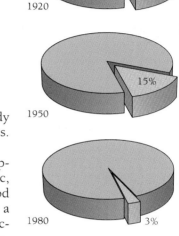

1920

1950

1980

Farm
Nonfarm

FIGURE 15.2   Drop in the percentage of U.S. population living on farms, 1920–1980.

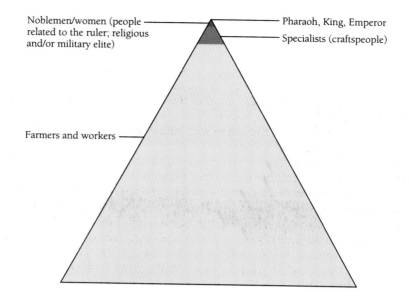

Noblemen/women (people related to the ruler; religious and/or military elite)

Pharaoh, King, Emperor

Specialists (craftspeople)

Farmers and workers

Social Stratification   In egalitarian societies like those of most hunter-gatherers, people within the same age and sex categories are essentially equal; they have the same rights and privileges, similar responsibilities, and about equal wealth. Most Paleolithic and many early Neolithic societies were probably egalitarian, or pretty close to being so. On the other hand, societies with **social stratification** have fixed layers of power, leadership, or wealth. People are born into social strata and remain there for their entire lives. Ordinarily there is a hierarchy with a ruler like a chief, king, pharaoh, or emperor on top, his or her family and religious rulers or military leaders next, special workers like craftspeople under them, and perhaps everyone else—farmers and soldiers, for example—below them. In other words, building a pyramid is made possible by a social system shaped like a pyramid (Figure 15.3).

Government   All civilizations, as we are using the term here, are **state** societies. Along with social stratification, a state possesses a true government, defined by archaeologist Joseph Tainter (1988:26) as a "specialized decision-making organization with a monopoly of force, and with the power to draft for work, levy and collect taxes, and decree and enforce laws." The leaders of this government belong to the upper social classes.

Nonstate or prestate societies certainly have leaders, people who make important decisions and whose instructions ordinarily are heeded. But leaders in nonstate societies rule through consensus and by their ability to persuade other people to follow their commands and to marshall the opin-

social stratification The presence of acknowledged differences in social status, political influence, and wealth.

state Class societies, often rigidly stratified into social levels, with a ruling class controlling the populace not by consensus but by coercion and force.

ion of the group. For example, in societies identified by anthropologists as having a tribal level of political organization, leaders, called headmen, don't have absolute power. They have no laws, police force, or army to force others to obey them. They do, however, have authority—they are good at organizing labor, keeping people happy, and conducting projects that people recognize are for the good of the group. Their leadership usually results from their accomplishments and abilities. It is this earned respect that convinces people to listen and follow. If people no longer wish to listen to a headman, they don't.

Some societies possess a level of political organization more complex than that of tribes. Anthropologists call these groups **chiefdoms.** Chiefs rule by more than simple authority; they have the ability to enforce certain types of decisions. Further, the power of a chief is legitimized on the basis of religious ideology and is supported and symbolized by the chief's greater access to wealth. However, a chief's power is neither absolute nor exclusive. There is no formal political apparatus, no government, that legitimizes the chief's rule or backs up the chief's authority. A chief does not possess a monopoly on the use of force and, as such, power may be widely distributed in a chiefdom among subchiefs.

The kings, pharaohs, or emperors of state societies have much more than authority, and they rule by more than simply the consensus of the populace. They have true power—the ability to make decisions, give commands, and then make sure that those commands are carried out. Jail, enforced labor, and execution await those who fail to heed the dictates of the ruler of a state society. And, unlike chiefs, the rulers of state societies sit atop a formal government that further concentrates, magnifies, and formalizes their power, and they have fixed laws and possess the ability to enforce those laws.

Labor Specialization   For great monuments to be constructed, spectacular works of art to be produced, or extensive networks of canals to be built, people who are not needed in subsistence activities must specialize. It is unlikely that part-time artists could have painted the Maya murals at Cacaxtla (Figure 15.4, p. 434); it stretches the imagination to believe that part-time sculptors could have produced the carvings at Abu Simbel in Egypt (Figure 15.5, p. 435). The ability of civilizations to produce great art, architecture, engineering, crafts, and science depends on specialization, and specialization can occur only when the farmers produce enough food to feed the people who are engaged in other pursuits.

Monumental Works   If the trappings of civilization require the development of specialization and social stratification, we are left wondering why such works as monumental architecture, great art, and even scientific achievements are always associated with civilization and the development of the state.

chiefdom A level of sociopolitical integration more complex than the tribe but less so than the state.

FIGURE 15.4 Great works of art, like these reconstructed murals at the Maya site of Cacaxtla, require the existence of full-time artists or craftspeople who specialize in their particular fields. Full-time specialists are provided for and required by state societies. *(Enrico Ferorelli; National Geographic)*

We can make some rather reasonable guesses. In the next section, we will approach hypotheses about why the civilized state developed in the first place. As for why it developed the *way* it did, however, we can suggest the following.

Civilization involves a tradeoff. In return for the protection and security such societies offer, most people end up working harder and giving up some of their freedom and independence. They give up living in an egalitarian society for a stratified system, and most people in a stratified society make up the bottom of the social pyramid; they work harder and have less control over their own destinies. Why would anyone consent to this? Great pyramids, burial chambers, spectacular works of art, great engineering projects, and mysterious astronomical knowledge are all symbols of the power held by the leaders of a given civilization. They are also part of a feedback system that serves to magnify the power of those leaders.

As archaeologist Joseph Tainter points out, rulers in such societies need constantly to reinforce the legitimacy of their leadership. They need, in essence, to continually convince the great mass of people that their position above the masses is reasonable and justifiable. As Tainter points out, along with an army and police force, which enable rulers to impose their

FIGURE 15.5 Monumental
architectural or engineering
works, such as Abu Simbel in
Egypt, are products of specialized classes of workers.
Specialization of labor is possible
only in civilized state societies.
(M. H. Feder)

will on people through physical coercion, "sacred legitimization provides a binding framework" (1988:28). Monumental works such as pyramids, great tombs, and palaces serve as this "sacred legitimization."

The strategy proceeds along the following lines: Pharaoh is the offspring of the gods, and therefore deserves our loyalty. Pharaoh decrees that 10,000 of us shall help construct a great pyramid to be his burial chamber. We obey because we believe him to be all-powerful. After a time, the pyramid is complete, and it is spectacular. Only someone with godlike powers could have accomplished such a feat. Any doubts that we might secretly have harbored are eliminated. The pharaoh's exalted position has been legitimized by his ability to produce a spectacular monument to himself.

In this light, the great achievements of civilization in the arts and sciences are made possible by the nature of civilization. At the same time, they contribute to the creation and further consolidation of such a society. In other words, such cultural achievements are both causes and effects of civilization. A pyramid, the accurate prediction of a solar eclipse, a great wall around a city are all real achievements as well as symbols of the abilities and power of a leader. Such achievements are not usually possible in egalitarian societies.

435

Dense Population   With the evolution of civilization usually, but not inevitably, comes the development of the city. Although no absolute line can be drawn between a large village and a small city, we mean the term *city* to indicate a settlement with a large, dense population.

Cities are usually features of civilized life. Dense populations can be more easily ruled than dispersed groups, and large groups of people are needed to support the running of the state.

A System of Recordkeeping   Finally, we come to the necessity of recordkeeping. We must be careful in this discussion not to equate recordkeeping with writing, because not all records need to be written down.

Recordkeeping is necessary for a number of reasons. Think of our own civilization. Our government can pay the bills for defense, social programs, and construction only by taxing its citizens. At one time, our nation sustained its military force through a draft, another sort of taxation. Imagine how well these would be carried out if there were no ways of keeping track in some kind of permanent form of how much wealth each citizen produces, how much tax was paid last year and this year, age, and the like. Without records, it would be virtually impossible to perform these functions.

The same was certainly true for early civilizations. Early civilized societies depended on a great mass of people providing at least some of their wealth in the form of labor, food, and children to support the existence of the elite and the specialists. There had to be some way of tracking each citizen's contribution in support of the state. There had to be records to make sure that each farmer provided a certain percentage of grain to feed those not involved in agriculture. There had to be some way of keeping track of the labor of the citizens as soldiers or monument builders. Without some sort of permanent storage of information, the state could not exist (Figure 15.6).

Explaining the Evolution of Civilization

We must now address this basic question: Why did civilized states develop at all? Interestingly, we see a situation similar to the beginning of domestication. The world's first civilizations appeared in several different areas at about the same time. Where they arose is no coincidence. Such cultures could have evolved only where there was a food surplus, and such a surplus is possible ordinarily only under conditions of intensive agriculture. Because the Food-Producing Revolution occurred almost simultaneously in a number of locations, it is not surprising that civilization later developed in many of these same areas. That it did indicates that under certain conditions civilization may have been almost an inevitable outcome of the Food-Producing Revolution, as Jared Diamond asserted (see the "Contemporary Issue" in Chapter 14). It also implies that there were identifiable reasons for these developments.

FIGURE 15.6 Examples of early systems of recordkeeping: *(top left)* cuneiform writing from Mesopotamia; *(top right)* Maya hieroglyphic writing; *(bottom left)* hieroglyphic writing from Egypt; and *(bottom right)* quipu, a nonwritten system of recordkeeping based on a series of knotted strings used by the Inca civilization of South America. A system of record-keeping—written or not—was crucial in the development of early civilizations. *(cuneiform: © Ashmolean Museum, Oxford. All rights reserved; Maya hieroglyphic writing: University of Pennsylvania Museum, Tikal Project, Neg. #58-4-1007; hieroglyphic writing from Egypt: M. H. Feder; quipu: Peabody Museum, Harvard University. Photo #N21754)*

Why Did Civilization Develop?

As we did for explanations of the Neolithic Revolution, we will now present some of the hypotheses proposed by various thinkers to explain the emergence of civilization. (See Table 15.1.)

The Explanation of Race   Some hypotheses suggested for the development of civilization in specific locations are racist. In the mid-nineteenth century, Gustav Klemm in Germany and Count J. A. de Gobineau in France both argued that race was the key factor in the development of civilization and that each civilization was unique because of biological factors (M. Harris 1968). Those people who had not attained a level of civilized existence were biologically unequipped to.

Very often such racist constructs could not admit that dark-skinned people had attained civilized status, even when the physical evidence argued for it. So Native American cultures such as the Maya, who clearly created a remarkable civilization, were either explained as the result of cultural borrowing or were denied the status of civilization. Human history and cultural evolution was reduced to an argument based on biology. These racist explanations are not supported by any data and need not concern us further.

Environmental Determinism

> Man can apparently live in any region where he can obtain food, but his physical and mental energy and his moral character reach their highest development only in a few strictly limited areas. (Huntington 1924)

Ellsworth Huntington was an early twentieth-century geographer who championed the notion of **environmental determinism,** an approach that actually first had found favor with the ancient Greeks. In attempting to explain cultural differences and the development of civilized life, Hippocrates had suggested that human behavior was the result of the interaction of four bodily "humours," or liquids: yellow bile, black bile, phlegm, and blood. Hippocrates suggested that climate was responsible for the balance of these liquids within the human body. Their proportion was in turn responsible for the development of the human intellect, health, and personality traits. Thus, climate was a determinant of cultural development. It is difficult to understand, but even into the nineteenth century some scholars seriously considered phlegm, bile, and blood as being responsible for culture.

Huntington, however, developed a much more complex and reasoned approach to environmental determinism. He felt that climate has a direct impact on human intelligence. In this view, environments that were too easy or too naturally productive hampered cultural development—if people did not *need* to invent things to survive, if they were not "challenged"

environmental determinism   The notion that the nature of the environment directly determines the technological level of a culture.

TABLE 15.1   Summary of Hypotheses Explaining the Evolution of Civilization

Hypothesis	Proponent	Type	Summary
Race	Various	Pseudoscience	A racist explanation that assumed that certain racial or ethnic groups were inherently superior and so evolved civilized societies.
Environmental determinism	Ellsworth Huntington	Deterministic	Human groups became more intelligent and progressed further where the environment was more challenging.
Unilinear evolution	Lewis Henry Morgan	Deterministic	Culture, in essence, drives itself forward as specific inventions are made: fire, bow and arrow, pottery, domestication, iron, writing. Without coming upon these successive inventions, cultures became stuck and did not progress.
Marxism	Karl Marx Frederich Engels	Internal conflict	The trappings of civilization developed after the invention of private property. Some individuals became wealthy and needed to protect their wealth. Social classes and specialization followed.
Hydraulic	Karl Wittfogel	Managerial Integrative	The need to control water for irrigation purposes led to the development of organizations to build and maintain waterworks. To accomplish this, there had to be leaders and followers, and institutions originated for this purpose evolved into the bureaucracy of the state.
Circumscription	Robert Carniero	External conflict	Societies that had effectively filled up their territory waged war against their neighbors to obtain their land. The losers in such battles became the lower class in an emerging stratified society that led to the civilized state.
Social integration	Jonathan Haas	Synthetic Conflict/ integrative	In different combinations, trade, warfare, and irrigation led to the formation of complex social and political structures. This led to social stratification with those at the top of society given differential access to resources. This, in turn, led to their accumulation of wealth and power and the need to symbolically reinforce the legitimacy of their wealth and power through the construction of monumental works.

by their environment, they would not be obliged to advance, and civilization would not develop. On the other hand, if the climate were too rigorous, people would be too caught up in the necessities of survival to progress beyond mere subsistence. Only those climates lying in between the too generous and the too rigorous would lead to the development of civilized life. Not coincidentally, Western European writers who supported this hypothesis viewed the climate of Europe, particularly Western Europe, as just right for such developments.

Environmental determinism began to fade in importance as a theory because it didn't work. If the European environment was so right for such developments, why did the earliest civilizations evolve elsewhere? Also, the environments in Mesopotamia, Egypt, India, China, lowland Mesoamerica, highland Mesoamerica, and South America were quite different from one another, yet each had early civilizations. Beyond this, even though the climates in these same regions had not changed since the evolution of their civilizations, the cultures had.

Unilinear Evolution

It is both a natural and proper desire to learn, if possible, how all these ages upon ages of past time have been expended by mankind; how savages, advancing by slow, almost imperceptible steps, attained the higher condition of barbarians; how barbarians, by similar progressive advancement, finally attained to civilization. (Morgan 1877:5)

Another approach to the question of why civilization developed avoided seeking causes in biology or climate or any factor of influence outside culture itself. This approach sought to explain cultural evolution through cultural explanations. The work of Lewis Henry Morgan (1877), a nineteenth-century lawyer and early anthropologist, is of great importance here. Morgan, whom we mentioned briefly in Chapter 2, believed that all cultures developed or evolved through similar phases: "The experience of mankind has run in nearly uniform channels" (1877:15), he wrote. These general phases Morgan labeled savagery, barbarism, and civilization. Savagery and barbarism could each be broken down into early, middle, and upper stages (Figure 15.7).

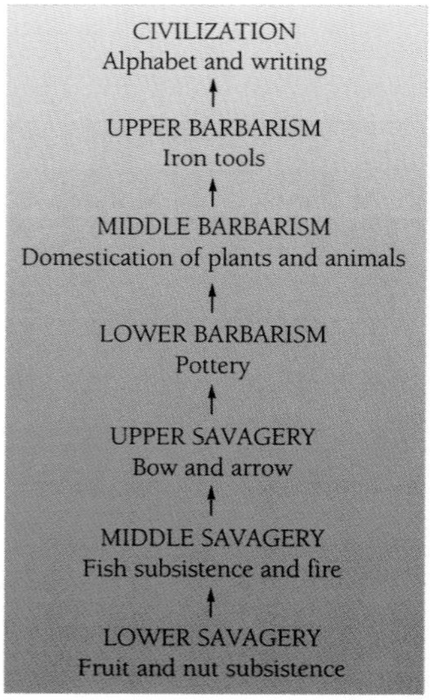

Morgan's view of the development of civilization as a product of cultural evolution was essentially *materialistic*: Culture evolved as successive levels of material achievement were attained. His view was also economically based; Morgan considered advance in subsistence technology to be the most significant aspect of cultural evolution driving people toward civilization. Development was contingent on certain specific inventions and followed a natural sequence. As Morgan put it, "The most advanced portions of the human race were halted, so to express it, at certain stages of progress, until some great invention or discovery, such as the domestication of animals or the smelting of iron ore, gave a new and powerful impulse forward" (1877:40).

CIVILIZATION
Alphabet and writing
↑
UPPER BARBARISM
Iron tools
↑
MIDDLE BARBARISM
Domestication of plants and animals
↑
LOWER BARBARISM
Pottery
↑
UPPER SAVAGERY
Bow and arrow
↑
MIDDLE SAVAGERY
Fish subsistence and fire
↑
LOWER SAVAGERY
Fruit and nut subsistence

FIGURE 15.7 The cultural evolutionary model of Lewis Henry Morgan, who believed that all cultures passed through these stages of development, although some became "stuck" in a stage.

Culture, in essence, drove itself forward toward civilized life. But notice that Morgan was circular in his argument while begging the question. Civilization, he said, develops because it does. If great inventions like iron smelting, domestication, and the alphabet were necessary to establish civilization, what caused them? Morgan had no answer to this question. He believed that inventions occurred through ingenuity and spread out from wherever they were invented. Such an approach simply cannot explain why civilization developed where it did and when it did. And these are precisely the questions we are asking.

Marxism

Civilization is . . . the stage of development in society at which the division of labor, the exchange between individuals arising from it, and the commodity production which combines them both come to their full growth and revolutionizes the whole of previous society. (Engels 1942:233)

Karl Marx and his benefactor and collaborator Frederich Engels developed a variation on Morgan's cultural evolutionary scheme. In a scenario laid out by Engels (1942), the domestication of animals led to specialization in animal herding. Animal domestication also allowed humans to produce far more food than was needed for subsistence. Thus, wealth—meat, milk, hides, and wool—became concentrated in the hands of those who possessed animals. There arose a need for regular exchange between the haves and the have-nots, and the excess wealth accumulated by the producers had to be defended from those who might want to take it for themselves.

As groups became larger and as the processes of exchange intensified, a class of specialists arose to conduct this new business. These were the first full-time merchants. For the first time, people not involved in subsistence or production were in charge of economic life, and they became rich and powerful at the expense of producers. In Marx's view, the key invention of civilization was the formal governmental structure that defines state societies. With a government in place that justifies, legitimizes, and protects the power of the emerging elite, the propertied class could better maintain its wealth and benefits. In this view, struggle between emerging classes results in the development of a formal government as a political structure that, on the one hand, mediates and dampens such conflict, and on the other, allows members of the upper class to validate their position over the lower classes and to justify their exploitation of them as peasants, soldiers, workers, and even slaves. A class society with rulers, workers, and slaves results. The trappings of civilization followed, Engels proposed, as the result of the need to formalize and solidify the unequal structure of society. Thus, civilization developed from a sort of economic determinism.

The Hydraulic Hypothesis

A large quantity of water can be channeled and kept within bounds only by the use of mass labor; and this mass labor must be coordinated, disciplined, and led. Thus a number of farmers eager to conquer arid lowlands and plains are forced to invoke organizational devices which—on the basis of premachine technology—offer the one chance of success; they must work in cooperation with their fellows and subordinate themselves to a directing authority. (Wittfogel 1957:18)

Karl Wittfogel (1957), a German historian, proposed the hydraulic hypothesis for the development of ancient civilization. He sees civilization as a logical, though not inevitable, consequence of the need to control water.

To feed an expanding population, people need to bring more land under cultivation. In some regions, they do so through the construction of waterworks, canals and aqueducts, which requires people working together and "subordinat[ing] themselves to a directing authority" (Wittfogel 1957:18). To organize and coordinate a large number of people, a centralized government may develop. There need to be canal designers, supervisors, and workers—thus, labor specialization occurs. Mathematics and a recording system can become necessary for planning and designing such projects.

The same social, economic, and political apparatus set in motion by constructing canals, Wittfogel suggests, can be used to build defensive works. Such works become necessary because territory in which so much labor has been expended becomes a tempting target for those who might wish to reap the benefits without investing the labor.

Similarly, the organization of labor can be used to construct temples, great palaces, and impressive tombs for those important people who are in charge. Real power and control, and thus wealth, now rest in their hands because they can deny access to water to those who do not follow their lead or heed their commands. The other trappings of civilization all follow from this concentration of power and serve to reinforce it. Thus, according to Wittfogel, the development of civilization is sparked by a need to increase agricultural production via development and control of water resources.

The Circumscription Hypothesis

A close examination of history indicates that only a coercive theory can account for the rise of the state. Force, and not enlightened self-interest, is the mechanism by which political evolution has led, step by step, from autonomous villages to the state. (Carneiro 1970:734)

In the scenario of Robert Carneiro (1970), an American anthropologist, civilization developed through coercion in areas where resources, especially agricultural lands, were circumscribed—in other words, limited and bounded. Where land is not limited and bounded, people can migrate into new territories when population grows. Where it is circumscribed, however, they cannot. Mountains, deserts, seas, or other geographic features confine some peoples to a limited area.

Within such a bounded area, only a small number of responses are possible if population grows: (1) Restrict population growth through sexual abstinence, contraception, abortion, or infanticide; (2) intensify agriculture through irrigation or other means; or (3) seize land through warfare against neighboring groups.

In this final option, the territory of the defeated becomes incorporated into the political unit of the victor. In some cases, the members of the defeated group are also integrated into the victorious group, usually as subordinates. Warfare between increasingly larger groups, Carneiro believes, led to larger and larger political entities with progressively larger territories. In his opinion, most of the world's early civilizations evolved under conditions of geographic circumscription and developed as a reaction to them.

Hearths of Civilization

As we have said, the world's first civilizations evolved in areas where agriculture had evolved. We will now examine the sequences in a number of these cases to assess the usefulness of these hypotheses for explaining the evolution of civilized life. In each instance, our primary question concerns how a pattern of small, sedentary, largely self-sufficient Neolithic farming villages was transformed into one of a dense, socially stratified, urban civilization. We will briefly discuss the prestate societies of west Asia and then move on to the ancient civilizations of Mesopotamia, Egypt, India and Pakistan, China, Mesoamerica, South America, southern Europe, Africa, North America, and Southeast Asia (see Figure 15.1). Each civilization's section begins with a brief description of the civilization at its peak and then assesses the origins and development of each culture, beginning with its roots in the Neolithic.

Civilization's Roots: Chiefdoms in West Asia

Jericho   The modern city of Jericho in Israel is the same town as that mentioned in the Bible, but the roots of Jericho go back even further. Excavated by archaeologist Kathleen Kenyon in the 1950s (Kenyon 1954), Jericho is now known to have been occupied more than 9000 ya. At this very early date, Jericho may have been inhabited by more than 3000 people in an area of about ten acres. The entire area was encompassed by what may have been the first example of a large-scale construction project anywhere in the world—an enormous wall (Figure 15.8). This wall ranged from more than 3.5 meters (11 feet) to 7 meters (22 feet) in height with ramparts more than 9 meters (30 feet) high. Built entirely of dry-laid stone (mortar was not used), it was 2 meters thick at its base.

Trade was an important factor in Jericho's economy. Raw materials from distant sources including obsidian from Turkey, turquoise from the

Sinai Peninsula, and cowrie shells from the Red Sea are found at early levels of the site.

The distribution of some of these exotic materials in burials implies the beginning of social stratification at the site. Most of the graves in the earliest levels at Jericho were situated in one area, and all were pretty much the

FIGURE 15.9   This artist's conception of Çatal Hüyük shows the architectural complexity of this 8000-year-old site. Note the number of rooms at the site labeled "shrine" on the basis of the artifact assemblages found within them.   (© *Times Books 1988. Reproduced with permission.*)

same. A cluster of burials, however, was different. Clay was molded over the faces of the deceased, with cowrie shells positioned over their eyes. The significance of this practice is unknown but suggests differences in social status. Without much more than this to differentiate social groups, Jericho cannot be labeled a state society. On the other hand, with the beginning of social differentiation and the construction of a monumental wall, we can reasonably suggest that Jericho was a chiefdom-level society.

Çatal Hüyük   Çatal Hüyük, in modern Turkey, postdates Jericho by perhaps 1000 years (Mellaart 1965; Todd 1976). The site covers more than thirty acres and consists of blocks of rooms made of mud brick. In these blocks, there are hundreds of individual rooms (Figure 15.9). Many were habitation areas, but a large proportion were religious shrines. In these shrines were sculptures of bull heads, bas-reliefs of leopards with female figures riding them, paintings of stylized birds chasing after headless people, and the outlines of human hands.

FIGURE 15.10 The ziggurat at Ur, built in stages over a lengthy period, is more than 4000 years old. It stands 22 meters high, with a temple originally on the top platform. *(© 1994 Comstock)*

The population at this site is estimated to have been between 5000 and 10,000. Such a large accumulation of people may have occurred here because of the settlement's location at the base of the Konya Mountains, a major source of obsidian—volcanic glass used for making sharp-edged tools. It is also located along a historical trade route between Europe and Southwest Asia, which perhaps was another important factor in its size and location. Again, there is no clear evidence of social classes and differential wealth and power, so we would not label Çatal Hüyük a state society. However, considering the monumental nature of the settlement itself, the large population, and the apparent specialization in ceremony and trade, it was at least a chiefdom-level society.

Mesopotamia

At the ancient city of Ur in Mesopotamia (literally "the land between the two rivers," the Tigris and the Euphrates), a massive structure consisting of superimposed platforms was constructed more than 4000 ya. Made of mud brick and faced with fired brick, this **ziggurat** stood 22 meters (70 feet) high and measured over 60 meters (200 feet) long by nearly 46 meters (150 feet) wide at its base (Figure 15.10). Steps led up to each successive platform; at the top was a small temple or shrine where priests conducted worship services (Lloyd 1978).

The cemetery at Ur contains more than 2000 graves, 16 of which were the interments of members of the elite class. These royal tombs were as much as 9 meters (30 feet) deep and 9 meters across. The burials were

ziggurat Large, mud brick structures in Mesopotamia.

FIGURE 15.11 This beautiful gold cup was just one of the many impressive artifacts found in the tomb of the Sumerian queen Pu-abi. The concentration of such wealth in the hands of an elite class of people is diagnostic of the stratified societies of even the world's oldest civilizations. (© *Lee Boltin Picture Library*)

placed in stone chambers with vaulted roofs—one even possessed a dome. One of the tombs, that of a queen called Pu-abi, is typical of the royal interments at Ur (her name appears in writing).

In death Pu-abi wore a headdress of gold and semiprecious stones. Around her were gold and silver containers, an intricately designed harp, a gaming table, and another 250 or so objects (Figure 15.11). Pu-abi did not have to pass on to the afterlife alone. As with the other royalty at Ur, she was accompanied by humans and animals sacrificed as part of the royal burial ceremony. In her burial chamber were two female attendants. Just outside the royal chamber were ten more women (one with a harp to provide musical accompaniment for the journey), five soldiers, and two oxen. Beneath Queen Pu-abi's chamber was another tomb—a man's, possibly her husband. He was accompanied by six soldiers, nineteen females wearing gold headpieces, six oxen, two chariots, a lyre, a gaming table, and an exquisite silver model of a boat.

Such were the death settings of Ur nobility. Their lives were lived in even greater splendor. But how did the Neolithic farming villages described in Chapter 14 give rise to the grandeur of Ur? How did the surplus and social stratification develop that made such monuments as the ziggurat and royal tombs of Ur possible? To answer these questions, we must look back into the Neolithic of Southwest Asia.

Mesopotamian Roots   From 8000 to 6500 B.P., we see the beginning of population movement away from the foothills of the Zagros Mountains, mentioned in our discussion of the Neolithic, onto the floodplain between

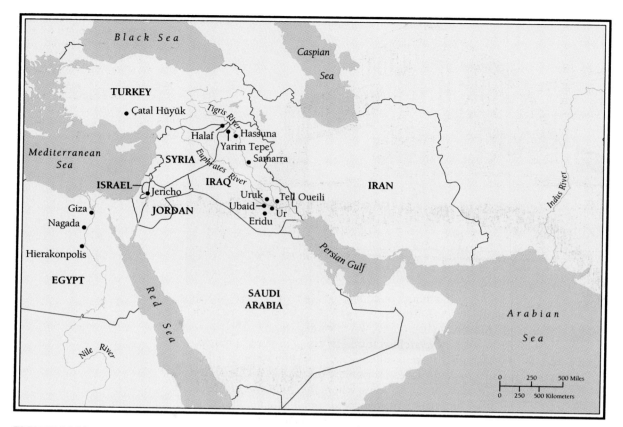

FIGURE 15.12 Location of Southwest Asian and Egyptian sites related to the development of civilization and mentioned in the text.

Hassunan Neolithic culture in Mesopotamia dated from 8000 to 7200 B.P.; characterized by small farming villages and some reliance on hunting.

Samarran Neolithic culture of southern Mesopotamia; sites are located on the floodplain of the Tigris and Euphrates Rivers and date to after 7500 years ago.

the two rivers (Figure 15.12). The sites of Hassuna, Samarra, and Halaf, each exhibiting distinctive pottery and architecture, have provided names to three distinctive Mesopotamian cultures with substantial temporal overlap: **Hassunan, Samarran,** and **Halafian.**

Dating from 8000 to 7200 B.P., Hassunan sites are small, typically about 100 to 200 meters (about 330 to 660 feet) in diameter, with populations estimated only in the hundreds (Lamberg-Karlovsky and Sabloff 1995:96). Though population is low, some Hassunan sites, such as Hassuna and Yarim Tepe, do provide evidence for large-scale construction. For example, the latter has multiroomed houses with interior and exterior courtyards.

Samarran sites also show evidence of increasing architectural complexity and size as well as increasing evidence of social differentiation. For example, the village of Tell es-Sawwan was surrounded by a monumental wall and a ditch. Samarra itself has a large fortification wall with buttresses. While most burials at Tell-es-Sawwan are rather plain, others are filled with alabaster, turquoise, copper, greenstone, obsidian, carnelian (a lustrous, reddish brown stone), and shell bead necklaces and bracelets,

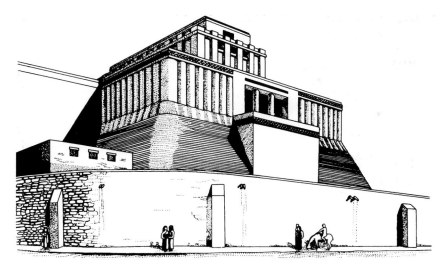

FIGURE 15.13 An artist's impression of the temple at the early Mesopotamian city of Eridu, dated to around 5000 B.P. *(From* Art of the Ancient Near East *by Seaton Lloyd, copyright ©1961, Thames and Hudson, page 259, Praeger Publishers, an imprint of Greenwood Publishing Group, Inc., Westport, CT. Reprinted with permission.)*

implying an increasing gulf among members of the society (Lamberg-Karlovsky and Sabloff 1995). Turquoise, carnelian, and obsidian are not locally available and must have been obtained through trade.

After about 7400 B.P. a new architectural feature is seen at Samarran sites: T-shaped buildings that were used to house the community's grain. The communal storage of grain suggests a pooling of labor in both farming as well as in the construction of the building where the grain was stored.

The site of Halaf, on the Syrian-Turkish border, shows what appear to be the earliest shrines in Mesopotamia. These are circular, beehive-shaped rooms that range from 5 to 10 meters (15 to 30 feet) in diameter at their base. The round buildings at some sites also contained human burials accompanied by ceremonial objects, leading some to suggest that they also served as the burial places for important people.

As archaeologists C. C. Lamberg-Karlovsky and Jeremy Sabloff (1995) suggest, after 8000 ya, economic, social, and political structures were beginning to form at Hassunan, Samarran, and Halafian sites, that would set the stage for later developments.

Ubaid   It is not until after about 6300 B.P., in the broad floodplain to the south, that a clearly great leap forward was taken by the early Mesopotamians. The culture of southern Mesopotamia during this period is called **Ubaid** and is reflected in Tell al-'Ubaid, Tell Oueili, Eridu, 'Usaila, and Ur. These sites are larger, with evidence of specialization in pottery and metallurgy. The population at Eridu, for example, is estimated to have exceeded 5000 (Lamberg-Karlovsky and Sabloff 1995:108) even at this early stage. The Ubaid sites show development of large temple structures that may indicate that these villages functioned as ceremonial centers as they were evolving into urban centers (Figure 15.13) (Wheatly 1971). Temples prob-

Halafian Neolithic culture in Mesopotamia dating from 7500 to 6700 B.P. Halafian sites generally are small farming villages.

Ubaid Site that lends its name to the culture of southern Mesopotamia at 6300 B.P.

ably served as granaries, administrative centers, and redistribution points for food.

The First Cities   By about 6000 B.P., Ubaid sites had spread throughout Mesopotamia. And, finally, by 5800 B.P. or so, one of these villages, **Uruk**, had grown to such a size and density that it can confidently be proclaimed as the world's first true city. Uruk was not isolated; it appears to have been interconnected in a settlement hierarchy that included, in descending size, smaller towns, villages, and hamlets (Crawford 1991). This pattern—large urban centers surrounded by three orders or levels of smaller settlements that owed their political, social, and economic allegiance to the city—was to be the rule for Mesopotamian **city-states**.

What Led to the Development of Civilization in Mesopotamia?   The push toward urbanization in Mesopotamia was probably encouraged by several factors. First came the need to intensify agriculture through the construction of irrigation networks as a result of population increase. By 5800 B.P., there were 17 villages, three large towns, and one city in Mesopotamia; by 4900 B.P., there were 124 villages, twenty towns, and twenty centers of urban populations (Adams and Nissen 1972:18). To expand agricultural production, irrigation was necessary, and canals up to 40 kilometers (almost 25 miles) long were eventually built (Lamberg-Karlovsky and Sabloff 1995). The requirement of organizing labor to build these canals would have fostered social differentiation, and differential access to irrigation water would have further served to segment and stratify society. Note how well this fits Wittfogel's hydraulic hypothesis discussed earlier.

As archaeologist Harriet Crawford (1991) suggests, the need to trade was another important impetus to urbanization. Southern Mesopotamia lacked most resources beyond fertile soil and water. Ores for the production of metals, wood for building and fuel, and stone had to be traded for, and such trade needs to be organized. The need to organize people to engage in trading networks may have contributed toward differentiating classes as well. Unequal access to trade goods would have served to further distinguish groups of people.

Another likely factor was the presence of nonagricultural, nomadic animal herders on the peripheries of Mesopotamia. From later documentary accounts, we know that settled villagers in Mesopotamia had hostile relations with neighboring nomads. As Lamberg-Karlovsky and Sabloff (1995) point out, however, such nomads probably provided urban dwellers with livestock and, as a result of their greater mobility, may also have assisted in trade and communication. The threat of potentially dangerous nomads, however, may have also forced people out of small, vulnerable outlying villages and into increasingly urban, protected settle-

Uruk The earliest city in Mesopotamia and, almost certainly, the world, dated to about 5800 ya.

city-state A large politically complex society with villages surrounding a dense central population.

ments. As wealth became concentrated in such dense settlements—effectively making it easier to steal—the need grew for protection from these nomads and from competing city-states. This may have led to the development of monumental works—not pyramids or tombs, but enormous defensive walls. Such projects require a social system unlike that of an egalitarian society.

The Role of the Temple   Early Neolithic cultures in Mesopotamia were probably egalitarian or **rank societies.** They likely had no existing social structure—no government or army—to fill the leadership roles demanded by large-scale construction or trade. There was, however, one institution where extraordinary powers resided even before social complexity increased: the temple. We have seen that shrines or temples date back to the time before the Ubaid period. Early prototypes for Mesopotamian temples are seen in Samarran sites, and, perhaps, in the sense of a functional prototype, in the Halafian round storage buildings. These early temples were not only places of religious worship, they also served as communal granaries.

In the view of archaeologists C. C. Lamberg-Karlovsky and Jeremy Sabloff (1995), when population grew and moved out onto the floodplain, irrigation works became a necessity. Such works necessitated a social and political institution that could organize the labor necessary to build and maintain them. In their view, an already powerful religious elite became the dominant political and social force in Mesopotamian society as well. In other words, priests first became chiefs and later kings. Control of the irrigation networks led to power, and with power came the ability to control the enormous food surplus that the evolving system produced. Together, these forces helped transform the village farming culture of Mesopotamia into what is recognized as the world's first civilization.

Egypt

The name Egypt alone is enough to conjure up potent images. Great pyramids, the Sphinx, the boy-king Tutankhamun, and all-powerful pharaohs are elements of Egyptian civilization that have fascinated people for centuries.

Just consider some of the remarkable accomplishments of the culture of ancient Egypt. For example, at Giza, north of the ancient capital city of Memphis and near modern Cairo, three pyramids rise out of the desert (Figure 15.14). Each one was constructed as the burial chamber and memorial for a different pharaoh; each is a spectacular achievement unto itself. Together they are one of the true wonders of the ancient world.

The two smaller pyramids were actually built later for the pharaohs Cephren and Mycernius (names given to these kings by later Greeks). It was the first and largest, however, built for the pharaoh Khufu (sometimes

rank societies Nonegalitarian societies with a few sociopolitical levels filled by a relatively small number of people.

FIGURE 15.14 The three great pyramids at Giza. Enormous monuments such as these testify to the power wielded by the rulers of the early Egyptian state. *(M. H. Feder)*

known by his Greek name, Cheops), that represents one of the largest structures *ever* built by human beings—before or since.

The Great Pyramid at Giza measures over 230 meters (750 feet) on each of the four sides of its base. Rising like an artificial mountain more than 145 meters (almost 500 feet) in height, it was constructed from nearly 2.5 million quarried stone blocks averaging 2270 kilograms (5000 pounds) each. Some of the larger blocks weigh more than 13,000 kilograms (30,000 pounds).

The pyramid itself was built at a level of accuracy rarely achieved even in modern construction. The smooth blocks making up the surface of the pyramid have joints a mere 0.5 millimeter (1/50 inch) in width. The pyramid is aligned to the cardinal compass directions; that this was intentional is clear from the writings of the ancient Egyptians. That alignment is almost perfect; the margin of error on the north–south sides of the pyramid is 0.09 percent, on the east–west sides 0.03 percent.

But the pyramid of Khufu is not just an enormous, accurately laid pile of limestone blocks. Within the pyramid is a maze of passageways, several connected chambers, and an arched vault that served as the final resting place for the pharaoh and the things intended for his use in the afterlife. It is, indeed, a spectacular achievement. Though the largest, the Great Pyramid is but one of almost 100 large pyramids built by the ancient Egyptians. And pyramids were just one aspect of Egyptian culture.

We are all awed by these spectacular achievements of ancient Egyptian civilization. But we want to go beyond fascination to understanding. How

FIGURE 15.15 This photograph of the Nile, taken by astronauts aboard the Space Shuttle, shows how the river literally demarcates the boundaries of life for the inhabitants of Egypt. *(Courtesy NASA)*

was the magnificence that was ancient Egypt achieved? Where did this civilization come from? How did it develop? To answer these questions, we need to go back to a time before pharaohs and pyramids. We need to examine the Egyptian Neolithic.

The Evolution of Egyptian Civilization   The Greek historian Herodotus called Egypt the "gift of the Nile." The Nile River is a narrow ribbon of life winding through a dry, lifeless desert (Figure 15.15). In Egypt a great civilization could have developed only along the banks of the Nile, so our attention must focus there.

Some Egyptologists believe that as a result of increasing competition for agricultural land, some towns became what geographers call **central places**—places viewed by the local populace as locations of great spiritual and social power. Two of these were Nagada and Hierakonpolis.

By 5500 B.P. at Nagada we see early evidence of social differentiation in the form of elaborate burials provided to a small proportion of the population. Nagada apparently controlled a vast surrounding territory.

Hierakonpolis   Excavations led by American archaeologist Michael Hoffman (1979, 1983) at Hierakonpolis have provided a more detailed picture of the early evolution of Egyptian civilization. This site is also significant because it is thought to have been the home of an important figure in Egyptian history, Narmer, who united Egypt for the first time under one ruler.

central place The geographic focus of a political entity.

Located on a bay adjacent to the Nile, Hierakonpolis consisted of about 100 inhabited acres some 5800 ya. Habitation areas consisting of houses of mud brick as well as wattle and daub (intertwined sticks covered with mud or clay) were surrounded by farmland, and at least 2500 and perhaps as many as 10,000 people lived there. The town seems to have prospered during the Neolithic on the basis of a booming pottery industry. Enormous kilns and millions of fragments of broken pots have been found here, and pottery manufactured at Hierakonpolis was probably traded to other towns along the Nile for inclusion in their fancy burials.

At Hierakonpolis during this period, the first evidence of impressive tombs appears. Although by no means comparable to the pyramids, these tombs may be the first step toward their development. The tombs were sometimes lined with mud brick; some were cut into bedrock. In a practice that was to characterize later Egyptian civilization, they were filled with items to accompany the dead: finely made pottery, baskets, leatherwork, woodwork, and flintwork. The tombs were covered by structures—not yet pyramids, but earth mounds and wood and reed buildings.

The largest and most sumptuous of the burials at Hierakonpolis and other sites dating to this period along the Nile were limited to a developing elite class. With increased population density along the Nile came the need to coordinate activity, to enforce rules and law. Although rule by simple authority—where there is consensus, not coercion—was possible in earlier, smaller towns, in a settlement of several thousand rule through power was probably beginning to replace the emphasis on authority. At Hierakonpolis a group of leaders may have evolved simply to maintain order. This elite was in charge of producing the pottery, they probably controlled trade, and excess wealth was becoming concentrated in their hands. With wealth came even more power. The production of fancy pottery and the interment of people in impressive tombs may have served as symbols reinforcing the legitimacy of that leadership.

Social and political change began to accelerate by 5500 ya in what is known as the Gerzean period. The local climate seems to have become drier, possibly because of deforestation that resulted from collecting firewood to feed the kilns. This challenge was met at Hierakonpolis and probably elsewhere by the construction of irrigation canals, which allowed for intensification of agriculture even while the local climate was becoming less agreeable for it. As archaeologist Hoffman has pointed out, the power that was already concentrated in the hands of the pottery barons probably allowed them to control the construction of irrigation canals. Once the local farmers began to rely on the canals for food production, the former pottery barons became even more powerful—they now controlled the water necessary for farming.

For a few hundred years, such developments continued at Hierakonpolis and elsewhere. By 5200 ya, however, local development and expansion began to impinge upon neighboring groups. Warfare among

FIGURE 15.16 Dating to 5100 B.P., the Narmer Palette was found in the Egyptian site of Hierakonpolis. The ruler Narmer is shown on the left, brandishing a weapon over a defeated enemy. On the right, Narmer (the tallest character on the left, top) is shown wearing the combined crowns of Upper and Lower Egypt. As the ruler of a unified Egypt, Narmer is generally thought to be the first pharaoh. *(left: © Werner Forman/Art Resource, NY; right: © Giraudon/Art Resource, NY)*

neighbors seems to have been the result. Elites in different towns began to compete among themselves for territory and for the loyalties of the people in these areas.

The Unification of Egypt There appear to have been earlier attempts to unify parts of northern and southern Egypt (see Bower 1990). (Northern Egypt is called Lower Egypt, as it is downriver; southern Egypt is Upper Egypt. The Nile runs south to north.) But it was not until about 5100 B.P. that a ruler of Hierakonpolis, Narmer (also known as Menes), was able to unite all villages up and down the Nile.

Narmer was, indeed, the first ruler of Egypt, if not the first actual pharaoh. On a carved piece of stone found by archaeologists in Hierakonpolis in 1898, Narmer is depicted as uniting the northern and southern halves of Egypt, becoming the ruler of all who dwelled along the Nile (Figure 15.16).

FIGURE 15.17 The stepped pyramid of King Djoser at Saqqara represented an important step in the evolution of the pyramid memorial that was to characterize the tombs of later Egyptian pharaohs. (*M. H. Feder*)

With the growth of villages and then cities along the Nile, the emergence of a powerful elite class, the production of sufficient food surplus to feed this class as well as a class of specialists like the pottery makers, we have all the prerequisites for the evolution of civilization. By 4700 ya, a successor to Narmer, King Djoser, exploited the power that had been concentrated in his hands and caused the construction of the first Egyptian pyramid at a place called Saqqara (Figure 15.17). As kings became pharaohs and as pharaohs became all-powerful, pyramids became larger, construction projects became more ambitious, and the army increased in size. Egyptian civilization flourished.

The Indus Valley

That a spectacular early civilization developed in ancient India and Pakistan comes as a surprise to most Americans. Yet a magnificent civilization with two of the ancient world's largest early cities did indeed develop and flourish on the Indian subcontinent some 4500 ya (Allchin and Allchin 1982; Fairservis 1975).

Mohenjo-daro was one of those cities. During its peak period—from approximately 4500 to 4000 ya—the religious and political life of the city's 35,000 inhabitants was centered in its citadel. There, on an enormous mud-brick mound some 450 meters (almost 1500 feet) long, 90 meters (almost 300 feet) wide, and 12 meters (40 feet) high, were built a temple, a granary, and a bath house (Figure 15.18). Within the great bath house was a bathing pool nearly 12 meters (40 feet) long, 6 meters (20 feet) wide, and 2.5 meters (8 feet) deep. The entire citadel was surrounded by a brick wall reaching 13 meters (over 40 feet) in height in some sections and marked by square towers and bastions.

To the east of the citadel lay the lower city. Here, spread across 240 acres, lived the vast majority of the residents of Mohenjo-daro. Their

FIGURE 15.18 The citadel of Mohenjo-daro, one of the Indus civilization's two great cities, which held a temple, a granary, and a bath house. Note the brick-covered sewer trench with connections to separate apartments, a testament to city planning some 4500 ya. (© *Dilip Mehta/Woodfin Camp and Associates, Inc.*)

streets were laid out in a well-planned fashion. Wide boulevards paralleled each other in a north-south orientation. Other smaller streets ran parallel to the boulevards. Still other streets were neatly perpendicular (Figure 15.19, p. 458).

Individual dwellings reflected the wide range in economic, social, and political status of the inhabitants. There were single-room apartments,

FIGURE 15.19 This map of a section of the planned city Mohenjo-daro shows its major avenues, parallel and perpendicular streets, and regularly sized buildings and rooms. *(From M. Wheeler. 1968. The Indus Civilization. New York: Cambridge University Press. Reprinted with permission of the publisher)*

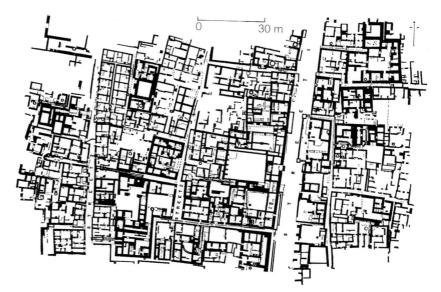

houses with many rooms and courtyards, and great houses with dozens of rooms and private wells. Almost all houses had private bathrooms connected by chutes to a citywide network of drains—probably the world's first engineered sewer system.

Mohenjo-daro, like its contemporary sister city on the Indus River, Harappa, was a spectacular achievement of this little-known civilization. But where did this Indus Valley culture come from? How did it develop?

The Evolution of the Indus Valley Civilization   We can trace the roots of this civilization back to a series of Neolithic sites in an area of western Pakistan called Baluchistan (Figure 15.20). Mehrgarh is located at the foothills of the Baluchistan Mountains. Dated to 7100 B.P., this site is an extensive settlement of mud brick structures including a number of domestic units—probably the homes of individual families—containing six and sometimes nine rooms. Some separate structures appear to have been public granaries. Subsistence was provided by domesticated wheat, barley, and dates, along with cattle and water buffalo. The inhabitants of Mehrgarh also participated in a wide-ranging trade network. Conch shell from some 500 kilometers (about 310 miles) away as well as lapis lazuli and turquoise from similar distances were found at the site.

Another typical site, Kili Ghul Mohammad, was a small agricultural settlement also located in the foothills of the Baluchistan Mountains. Dated to 6000 B.P., it has evidence of domesticated wheat, goats, sheep, and cattle.

Mehrgarh and Kili Ghul Mohammad grew larger through time, indicating a general population increase. By 5000 ya, settlement was spreading

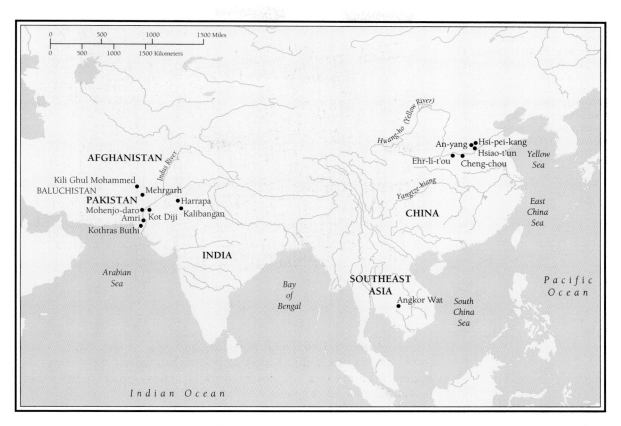

FIGURE 15.20 Location of South Asian and East Asian sites related to the development of civilization and mentioned in the text.

out of the mountain foothills southward along the streams that drained the mountaintops and fed the large Indus River to the southeast.

Where previous Neolithic sites in Baluchistan each exhibited its own artifact styles in pottery and items of adornment, a certain degree of uniformity appears as people began moving out onto the floodplain of the Indus, implying a greater level of cultural and perhaps political unification (Figure 15.21) (Allchin and Allchin 1982). For example, a common image of a horned buffalo head begins appearing on pottery throughout the area at many sites. Terra-cotta statues of women, that show a standardized style also appear at many sites from this period; some have dubbed these "mother goddesses," implying a degree of religious unification as well (Allchin and Allchin 1982:163).

Sites dating to after 5000 B.P. are included in what is called the Nal culture. Kohtras Buthi is a fairly typical Nal site. Much larger than Kili Ghul Mohammad, it covers some 15 acres. Significantly, at this site we see some of the earliest evidence in the area for water-control construction. The inhabitants built a wall surrounding one end of the village, apparently to protect themselves from intense flooding that characterizes this area in

FIGURE 15.21 The "cultural convergence" seen in the Indus Valley after 5500 B.P. can be seen in these artifacts. A consistency of design elements is found throughout the valley at this time, signifying a cultural unity that presages the political unification that was to come in the Mature Harappan phase of Indus Valley civilization. (© *Lee Boltin Picture Library*)

the spring. At other Nal culture sites, we see dams built across small streams for the accumulation of alluvial soils behind the dams, dams on small rivers to impound water that is then diverted to irrigate fields away from the rivers, and large dams forming reservoirs with impounded water drained away by irrigation canals.

Settlement Along the Indus   Apparently population kept growing and flood-control technology kept improving. By 4500 B.P., settlement expanded onto the floodplain of the Indus River itself. The Indus is a large, unpredictable river given to violent flooding. It is unlikely that an agricultural people could have survived on its banks without sophisticated flood-control construction. Two sites that typify this period are Kot Diji and Amri. The latter contains a large number of connected mud brick structures, and there is evidence of canal building.

It is at Kot Diji, however, that we see the earliest evidence for large-scale flood-control construction (Figure 15.22). This site is surrounded by a wall measuring up to 8 meters (26 feet) high and 1.5 meters (about 5 feet) thick. The base of the wall is constructed of cut limestone, and the top is made of mud brick. Such construction implies a certain amount of coordination of the population and may indicate the beginning of social differentiation.

FIGURE 15.22 The excavation at Kot Diji exposed a large village site, predating Mohenjo-daro and Harappa. (*Department of Archaeology and Museums, Karachi*)

Florescence of the Indus Valley Civilization   After 4500 B.P., Mohenjo-daro and Harappa developed into complex urban centers. Hundreds of small farming villages were aligned with each of these two cities, which together controlled more than 300,000 square miles of territory (Possehl 1980:2).

Indus Valley urban sites were planned out in virtually every detail. Mohenjo-Daro, Harappa and other, smaller urban centers like Kalibangan follow virtually identical plans (see Figure 15.19). A citadel was built up on a platform of mud brick on the western margin of Indus cities. Each citadel was surrounded by public bath houses and granaries, and this "upper city" was encompassed by a monumental wall. The residential areas of Indus Valley cities were spread out to the east of the citadel and, at Harappa and Mohenjo-daro, housed tens of thousands of people. The "lower city" likewise was surrounded by a great wall. Broad, parallel main roads were separated by secondary streets, which were connected by perpendicular avenues, which were, in turn, connected by narrow passageways that led to individual residences constructed with regularly-sized, clearly standardized, mud bricks.

Residences in the lower cities of Indus urban centers exhibit a range in size from single-room apartments to mansions with dozens of rooms and enclosed courtyards. This is a clear reflection of differences in the wealth and status of the individuals who lived in them. Neighborhoods of craft specialists have been identified at Mohenjo-daro and Harappa. Some parts of Indus Valley cities contained the workshops and residences of metal workers, potters, clothmakers, bakers, stone workers, and bead makers. Each craft neighborhood can be defined archaeologically; the tools of their various trades have been found restricted to their respective parts of the

FIGURE 15.23 The ancient city of Yin was the apparent center of the Shang culture of China. Exquisite bronzes have been found in elaborate burials of the royalty. *(Courtesy of the Freer Gallery of Art, Smithsonian Institution, Washington, D.C.—36.6 Chinese Bronze: Shang, late An-yang, 11th century B.C., ceremonial vessel/typehuo. 17.2 × 21.2 × 10.6 cm overall)*

cities. Other areas of the cities appear to have been the residences of scribes, priests, administrators, and traders (Allchin and Allchin 1982:185).

China

In northern Honan province of China, on the banks of the Huan River, near the modern city of An-yang, rests the ruins of the ancient city of Yin. Here, in what was the culmination of East Asia's earliest civilization, the Shang, a succession of twelve kings ruled for 273 years beginning about 2400 ya (Chang 1968; Gernet 1987).

In and around An-yang is a series of settlements articulated into what was the center of Shang culture. At Hsiao-t'un were the royal palaces—large structures with stamped-earth foundations, large stone support pillars, and platform altars. Around the palaces were smaller structures used to manufacture bronze, pottery, stone tools, and bone carvings (Figure 15.23).

Nearby Hsi-pei-kang had an extensive cemetery complex containing more than 1200 burials. Eleven large tombs were found, possibly the interments of all but the last of the historically recorded Shang rulers at Yin (the twelfth supposedly died and was consumed in a fire during the de-

FIGURE 15.24 The great rulers of the Shang civilization, China's first complex state society, were buried in splendor and accompanied on their journey to the afterlife by people sacrificed by beheading, as shown here. *(Courtesy of the Institute of History and Philology, Academia Sinica, Taiwan)*

struction of the city). These royal tombs were enormous construction projects with large grave pits up to 40 meters (130 feet) long and 30 meters (nearly 100 feet) wide. Ramps as long as 50 meters (more than 160 feet) led down into the burial pits where the king was interred in a log-lined tomb accompanied by elaborate objects manufactured of bronze, jade, antler, stone, bone, and shell. Hundreds of people were apparently sacrificed to accompany these kings into their afterlife; their decapitated remains surround the royal tombs (Figure 15.24).

The Evolution of Chinese Civilization   Although once presumed to result from outside developments, the Shang civilization is now recognized as having evolved from the Neolithic Lung-shan culture of China (see Chapter 14). The subsistence base of Shang civilization was essentially the same as that of local Neolithic cultures. Domesticated rice, millet, and wheat were the primary agricultural products. Pigs, sheep, cattle, and chickens were raised and eaten. Well into Shang times, this agricultural base was supplemented by hunting deer and bear and fishing.

Early manifestations of Shang civilization have been identified at the Erh-li-t'ou site on the Lo River in Honan province. Dated to around 3800 ya, the site is larger than anything seen previously in East Asia, covering an area of 2.5 kilometers (1.6 miles) by 1.5 kilometers (a little less than 1 mile). Bronze and jade artifacts are common. Some of the bronzes were tools including knives, chisels, axes, adzes, arrowheads, and other weapons. Many of the bronze artifacts at the site were ceremonial or ornamental, including disks, fancy drinking vessels, and musical instruments.

Evidence of social stratification is shown in differential burial patterns. Some human remains were rather casually interred in storage or refuse pits with no accompanying grave goods. Other burials were much more elaborate, with the deceased buried in lacquered coffins. Grave goods include jade carvings, turquoise and shell jewelry, finely made ceramics, and bronze. Finally, the presence of some headless human burials bears witness to human sacrifice.

A unique feature at Erh-li-t'ou are the remains of two palaces, far larger than any of the residences located at the site. One palace was about 100 meters (325 feet) on a side; the second was somewhat smaller. The walls of both palaces consisted of thick berms of stamped earth.

A later site was excavated nearby the modern city of Cheng-chou. The ancient remains at Cheng-chou are clearly urban in character with residential areas, industrial zones, elite areas, and a cemetery. Surrounding the central part of the site—which had large, upper-class houses and elite burials—was a monumental wall more than 7000 meters (more than 22,000 feet) in circumference. It encompasses an area of more than 3 square kilometers, stood close to 10 meters (32 feet) high, and was more than 35 meters (almost 115 feet) wide at its base. Archaeologist K. C. Chang quotes estimates that 10,000 workers must have toiled for almost two decades to construct the wall alone (1968:205). Outside the wall were residential and industrial sectors of the city, with bronze foundries, pottery manufactories, and bone workshops.

Although monumental works in the form of pyramids or ziggurats do not appear at Shang sites, Shang is certainly an early civilization. Large populations were concentrated in urban centers. Differential burials and variations in house size and construction show clear evidence of social stratification. There was specialization in various crafts, including bronze metallurgy, ceramics, bone carving, and stone sculpture. Finally, there was writing. More than 100,000 inscribed bones and tortoise shells have been recovered, mostly at Yin. The writing included some 5000 different characters, of which about 1500 have been interpreted (Gernet 1987:47). Translations indicate that most of the writing involved divination and predictions concerning social, political, military, and economic affairs.

Mesoamerica

The ancient Mexican city of Teotihuacan stands as mute testimony to the wondrous achievements of the prehistoric civilizations of Mesoamerica. From 1700 to 1300 ya, Teotihuacan was the most powerful political entity

FIGURE 15.25 The Pyramid of the Sun at the ancient city of Teotihuacan in central Mexico. Fifteen hundred years ago, Teotihuacan was a metropolis of 125,000 to 150,000 people. *(M. H. Feder)*

in the Western Hemisphere (Adams, 1991; Lamberg-Karlovsky and Sabloff 1995; Millon et al. 1973; Sabloff 1989; Sanders and Price 1968; Weaver 1972). At its peak, Teotihuacan was a teeming city covering 20 square kilometers (almost 8 square miles). Its population is estimated between 125,000 and 150,000 people who lived in more than 2000 apartment complexes situated along a patterned grid of streets and avenues (Millon et al. 1973). As many as 1 million people may have been part of what might be considered the nation of which Teotihuacan was the capital.

The center of the city was dominated by two large pyramids connected by a broad boulevard today called the Avenue of the Dead (Figure 15.25). The smaller Pyramid of the Moon sits at one end of the boulevard, overlooking a large plaza surrounded by several smaller pyramids and temple complexes. The avenue is lined with temples and palaces. On one side rests the spectacular Pyramid of the Sun, 210 meters (682 feet) along one side of its base and rising 64 meters (208 feet) high. Steps lead to its summit where a small temple once stood. Near the Pyramid of the Sun are compounds, temples, and palaces. Sculpted reliefs of skulls, snakes, birds, jaguars, and mythological creatures adorn walls and ceilings everywhere. When the city was inhabited, the architecture was awash in bright color, with walls and ceilings painted blue, brown, red, green, yellow, white, and black.

In the sixteenth century, when the Spanish *conquistadores* asked the Aztecs, the inhabitants of the area at that time, who had constructed Teotihuacan, the Aztecs, possessors of a remarkable civilization in their own right, responded that the gods must have built it.

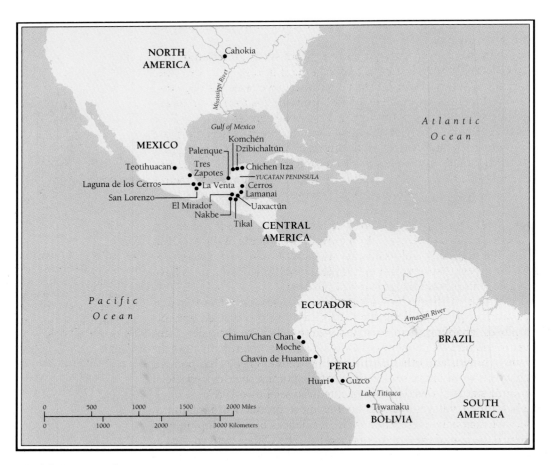

FIGURE 15.26 Location of New World sites related to the development of civilization and mentioned in the text.

The Evolution of Mesoamerican Civilization   Teotihuacan, of course, did not appear without antecedents (Figure 15.26). Beginning about 3200 B.P., the trajectory of cultural evolution in Mesoamerica changed significantly although there is no major change in subsistence technology or urbanization. In the uplands and lowlands, people were relying on maize, beans, and squash as their food base. In the lowlands, they practiced a form of agriculture called slash-and-burn. Typical in subtropical and tropical forest lowlands, slash-and-burn involves cutting trees, burning them to release their nutrients quickly into the soil, planting and harvesting, and then moving on to other areas, allowing the harvested area to return to forest.

After 3200 B.P., an interesting phenomenon, similar to that seen in the Indus Valley about 4500 B.P., appears—cultural convergence. In this case, a unique style of art permeates most of Mesoamerica. The style, called **Olmec**, appears to represent not just a single set of art motifs but a unified ideology. Archaeologists Linda Schele and David Freidel characterize the Olmec in this way: "They were the people who forged the template of

Olmec The artistic and iconographic style in Mesoamerica, starting about 3200 B.P.

world view and governance" that marked Mesoamerican civilization for more than two millennia (1990:38).

Along with this converging style and the belief system inferred from it appears a different kind of settlement concentrated in the lowlands of the Mexican states of Veracruz and Tabasco. Four sites have been discovered—La Venta, San Lorenzo, Tres Zapotes, and Laguna de los Cerros—that appear not to be villages or cities but rather ceremonial centers. There is little evidence of habitation, but for the first time in Mesoamerica there are pyramids—albeit constructed of earth and clay. At San Lorenzo, for instance, earth pyramids and flat plazas were built on top of an enormous, human-made earth platform. At La Venta, a single large pyramid 30 meters high was built with long mounds of earth flowing out from it.

Why Did Olmec Develop?   Population growth may be part of the reason that the Olmec pattern developed. In the tropical lowlands of the Mexican Gulf Coast, the richest agricultural lands are located on natural levees produced by the rivers that flow through it. These rich regions seem to have attracted a large portion of the growing population.

Archaeologist Michael Coe (1968) has proposed that families that used the productive lands along the Gulf Coast likely produced agricultural surpluses, enabling them to amass wealth. Their wealth gave them the power to mobilize regional populations to produce monumental works such as the pyramids and other earthworks. As Tainter (1988) has pointed out, such works would have served ritually to legitimize the elevated social and economic status of this developing elite (also see Lowe 1989).

Small farming villages located on the most productive agricultural lands became regionally significant as the residences of a developing elite class—hence the rise of the ceremonial centers. The Olmec pattern seen at these sites includes several common artistic and architectural elements: depictions of a half-human, half-jaguar god, the use of jade (Figure 15.27), iron ore mirrors, the construction of large earthen platforms, the construction of earthen pyramids, and the carving of huge basalt boulders into the form of human heads—perhaps actual depictions of some of the regional chiefs. The largest of these, standing 3 meters (10 feet) high and weighing more than 16,000 kilograms (18 tons), was found nearly 130 kilometers (80 miles) from the source of the stone (Figure 15.28, p. 468).

Certainly, we can see in the Olmec artifacts the beginning of the process of state formation in Mesoamerica, but the question remains why? Beyond the fact that the Olmec appears to be a unifying art style, we do not know what else it signified to the ancient people of Mesoamerica. William Sanders and Barbara Price (1968) suggest that "microgeographical zoning" led to competition among groups in areas that provided different sets of resources. Population grew with the advent of slash-and-burn agriculture in the natural richness of the lowland environment. A single ideology reflected in a panregional art style may have unified disparate groups who needed to trade with each other.

FIGURE 15.27   An Olmec ceremonial jade carving with a humanlike face. Jade was widely used in Olmec art and is believed to have been of great religious significance. (*Courtesy Department of Library Services. American Museum of Natural History. Neg. #K9850*)

FIGURE 15.28 An enormous head carved from a single block of basalt, a volcanic rock. Some of these Olmec heads weighed up to 18,000 kilograms (about 20 tons) each. The raw materials for these monolithic sculptures were transported to Olmec ceremonial centers located up to 130 kilometers (80 miles) from their source in the Tuxtla Mountains. (© 1959 Inge Morath/Magnum Photos Inc.)

The Maya   Various regional civilizations followed the Olmec in Mesoamerica. The Maya, located in the lowlands of Mexico, Honduras, Belize, and Guatemala, are one of the best known (Sabloff 1994).

The origins of the Maya can be traced back more than 2800 years. The earliest evidence of monumental public architecture is seen by about 2300 B.P., at villages like Nakbe, El Mirador, Lamanai, Cerros, and Tikal in the south and Dzibichaltún and Komchén in the north (Figure 15.29). Such structures were related to Maya religion, and these early ceremonial centers probably housed members of a religious elite and their attendants. Some settlements, such as Cerros, located on a bay by the mouth of a river, became trading centers (Freidel 1979). Here, raw materials such as obsid-

FIGURE 15.29   This large stone platform topped by a temple is located at Dzibichaltún in the northern Yucatán. Dated to about 2300 B.P., Dzibichaltún and a handful of sites from the same period exhibit evidence of some of the earliest public architecture in the Maya realm.   *(K. L. Feder)*

ian and jade, finely crafted goods from these raw materials, agricultural products such as cotton and cacao, and perhaps fine ceramics were distributed, contributing to the wealth and power of the developing religious elite (Sabloff 1994:115).

A highly productive agricultural system focusing on maize (see Chapter 14) provided subsistence for the Maya. Food surpluses allowed for population growth. As a result of this growth as well as the movement of people from the countryside to the population centers, some Maya villages developed into true cities with large, dense populations after 2300 years ago.

The energy and resources needed to support large, competing population centers and the growing elite class grew. This probably led to increased competition for resources—and even for people, on whose labor the economic, political, and social systems relied. There is evidence of defensive earth embankments at some Maya cities at this time, and there are numerous depictions in Maya art of military conflicts as cities fought against one another.

The Maya relied on a broad range of agricultural techniques to feed their growing population. One of their primary subsistence practices, slash-and-burn agriculture, requires quite a bit of land (perhaps twenty acres for each family) and quickly depletes the soil of its nutrients, requiring a long fallow period for the soil to regain its productivity. Shortening the fallow time to obtain a greater yield from a plot of land in the short term can deplete the soil of its nutrients and lower productivity in the long term.

The Maya added other, more intensive agricultural techniques including terracing hills, building raised fields in swamps, planting kitchen gardens, and tree-cropping (McKillop 1994). By mounding up fields in wetlands, as they did at the Pulltrouser Swamp site in Belize, the Maya were able to use areas previously too wet to farm and to farm the same plots every year (Turner and Harrison 1983).

FIGURE 15.30   The Temple of the Giant Jaguar at the classic Maya site of Tikal in Guatemala. At its peak, Tikal had a resident population of more than 40,000. (*M. A. Park*)

The Classic Maya civilization, with splendid ceremonial centers and cities such as Palenque, Tikal, and Uaxactún with their temples and pyramids, is dated to about 1650 B.P. (A.D. 300) (Sabloff 1994). By 1350 years ago Tikal, in Guatemala, had a resident population of at least 40,000 people and perhaps thousands more in the surrounding countryside (Figure 15.30). Tikal also has produced evidence of neighborhoods in the city where particular craftspeople lived and produced their goods: stone tools, ceramics, and wooden implements.

It has been through the remarkable and persistent work of many scholars that the Maya are beginning to speak to us in their own voice across the centuries (see Schele and Freidel's splendid book, *A Forest of Kings: The Untold Story of the Ancient Maya* for a discussion of the translation of Maya writing). Their writing tells of a fascinating culture of more than fifty independent city-states spread across some 100,000 square kilometers (almost 40,000 square miles) of Mesoamerica. The story of the Maya is one of great achievements in science and engineering, bloody and protracted wars, and an intriguing belief in the cyclicity of time and history. Deciphering the Maya written language has made enormous strides in recent years. Continued success will allow for more complete understanding of the Maya civilization.

Teotihuacan We began this section with a description of the Mesoamerican city of Teotihuacan at its peak. Like the Maya, this civilization had its roots deep in antiquity. In the early third millennium B.P., Teotihuacan was just one of many small farming villages in the basin of Mexico. Its location, however, offered its inhabitants several advantages over those of most of the other villages. Teotihuacan was located near an important source of obsidian, was adjacent to a major trade route, and was well-suited to irrigation-aided agriculture. When population growth in the area challenged the ability of simple agriculture to feed the increasing number of people living there, Teotihuacan flourished.

By 2100 B.P. there were a number of developing population centers, yet Teotihuacan outstripped them all in growth. The key to Teotihuacan's success was not only the advantages noted above but also a volcanic eruption that decimated its rivals. To take advantage of its obsidian resource, miners of the stone, makers of tools, and full-time traders were needed. A greater emphasis on irrigation allowed for the production of more food which, in turn, allowed a greater proportion of the population to engage in specialties related to the obsidian trade. Great power and wealth rested in the hands of the elite who controlled both trade and irrigation.

South America

The Romans of the New World, the Inca held their far-flung empire together by military might. First fully consolidated in A.D. 1476, and at their peak immediately before the Spanish conquest in A.D. 1534, they controlled 2000 miles and millions of people along the South American coast from northern Ecuador to southern Chile (Obo 1653; Patterson 1973).

The Inca did not achieve control by introducing a new subsistence technology or by imposing their religion. The Inca were, purely and simply, militarists who achieved domination through conquest. By using a professional standing army and constructing thousands of kilometers of

FIGURE 15.31 The fortress city of Machu Picchu is located high in the Andes Mountains. Enormous, complex construction projects like this are diagnostic of cultures labeled "civilizations." *(P. Nute)*

roads, they were able to control a huge territory (Figure 15.31). They forged bronze tools, making them widely available for the first time in the New World. They taxed all under their sway. To be a citizen of the Inca empire meant working for the state—in agriculture, the military, or public works.

Cleverly, the Inca did not depose local deities as they deposed local autonomous rulers. Instead, local gods were incorporated into the Inca pantheon. All people living under the Inca state, however, had to learn the language of the Inca, Quechua. Today, this language is still the primary tongue of the central Andes region.

Metallurgists in copper, bronze, silver, and gold, the Inca were also fine stonemasons, and their architecture is a major legacy of this culture. Using neither mortar nor cement, they constructed enormous walls of intricately carved blocks made of volcanic stone. The precision with which individual blocks were fitted together is impressive. Gold and silver adorned the walls and temples of the capital city of Cuzco.

The Evolution of South American Civilization   Cultural developments leading to the Inca were greatly affected by environmental features of the western coast of South America. Valleys, cut by streams draining the Andes, parallel each other and run westward onto the coastal plain. Resources are similar from valley to valley but differ depending on one's location within an individual valley. Archaeologist Thomas Patterson (1973) maintains that these valleys, each providing a complete mix of resources, appear to have been self-contained cultural units in early South American prehistory. Seasonal movements occurred within the confines of individual valleys, and there was little intervalley contact. By 4000 ya, this general isolation among the inhabitants of different valleys led to cultural differentiation.

At the same time, population was increasing within valleys as agriculture was replacing hunting and gathering. As elsewhere, agriculture led to a more sedentary settlement pattern. The patchy nature of resource availability led to differentiation within valleys. Where people could previously get whatever they needed simply by moving within a single valley, they now needed to trade to obtain resources available in other parts of the valley. Some villages, situated where resources were more abundant, became richer at the expense of others. Perhaps as validation of this differentiation, ceremonial centers begin to grow at this time.

As populations increased and approached the carrying capacities of the valleys, the need to trade and cooperate with people in neighboring valleys arose. Then, beginning about 3000 ya, there occurred what archaeologist Richard Burger calls "a decisive change in Central Andean prehistory" that resulted in a "radical restructuring of earlier Andean cultures" (1988:99). A common artistic and iconographic style called **Chavin** quickly spread along natural routes of communication and trade within and across the valleys. The style consisted of relief and full sculptures of jaguars, caimans (South American alligators), snakes, and eagles as well as humans with jaguarlike features (Figure 15.32). Along with these images came the spread of technological innovations in textiles and metallurgy, including new methods of manufacturing textiles, the widespread use of gold, methods of alloying gold and silver, soldering, sweat-welding, and the **repoussé** method of decorating gold objects (Burger 1992).

Chavin The artistic and iconographic style of Peru starting 3000 ya.

repoussé A method of decorating thin metal where the pattern is beaten up from the underside.

FIGURE 15.32 The religious art style—the iconography—of Chavin, like the Olmec in Mesoamerica, served to unify a geographically broad group of people, setting the stage for their political unification in a series of powerful, complex state societies. (*© Lee Boltin Picture Library*)

The style seems to have been centered at Chavin de Huantar in north-central Peru. Here, at about 3000 B.P., a pyramid and temple complex 13 meters (more than 40 feet) high and over 200 meters (650 feet) along one side was built. Within this complex are many relief sculptures in typical Chavin style and a 4-meter (13-foot) tall carved column of granite representing a standing man with jaguar fangs and snakes for hair.

Chavin may have served a function similar to that of the Olmec style in Mesoamerica—a facilitator of trade, communication, and cooperation among previously alien people. Sharing the same art style and, probably more significantly, the same religious belief system with the same gods would have made interaction that much easier. Burger suggests that the spread of this common style and ideology may have resulted from some sort of broad crisis among the people living in their separate Andean river valleys. Chavin, in this interpretation, may have started as a local cult that seemed to many to offer a mystical solution to the crisis.

Whatever the reason, Chavin did, for the first time, join the various valley cultures in a set of common cultural practices related to religion. It therefore set the stage for later political amalgamation of the various valley polities into larger, inclusive empires.

At about 1700 ya on the north coast of Peru, we see the Moche site with its 41-meter (more than 130 feet) high stepped Pyramid of the Sun made up of 130 million sun-dried bricks, the spread of its unique pottery style far beyond the confines of its own valley (Conklin and Moseley 1988), and the presence of spectacular burials of a class of warrior-priests.

The Moche were accomplished potters. They commonly painted quite

FIGURE 15.33 Warrior priests in pre-Inca western South America were buried in fabulous tombs surrounded by great amounts of wealth. This tomb in Sipán, Peru, was discovered by grave robbers and then excavated by archaeologists. (*Nathan Benn*)

naturalistic scenes on their pots, depicting everyday life, rituals, plants, and animals. Some of the pots were shaped into extremely realistic depictions of human faces and people engaged in various activities. These images represent a wonderful artistic legacy and also provide us with a detailed glimpse into Moche life and culture.

The royal cemetery of the Moche elite has been found about 150 kilometers (95 miles) north of the Pyramid of the Sun, in the village of Sípan (Alva and Donnan 1993, 1994). One tomb in the cemetery, dating to about 1660 years ago, contained the remains of a man in his late thirties or early forties (Figure 15.33) (Alva and Donnan 1994:29). The tomb was filled with turquoise, copper, silver, and gold jewelry. To his right lay a gold and silver scepter; on his left was a staff of cast silver. On his head was a feathered headdress; in death, he also wore nose ornaments and a beaded chest covering. Also accompanying this lord of the Moche were hundreds of pottery vessels, some quite elaborate and displaying human shapes; a number were in the form of warriors vanquishing their enemies. Two other men appear to have been sacrificed as part of the burial ceremony. The Moche lord was also accompanied by llamas, a dog, three women, and a child.

The clothing, ornamentation and headdresses of those buried at Sípan match artistic depictions of warriors from other Moche sites. In those depictions, victorious warriors are presented with the hands and feet of their enemies as trophies. Alva and Donnan discovered the remains of human hands and feet associated with the major burials at Sípan. On this basis, the Sípan burials are characterized as those of warrior-priests.

475

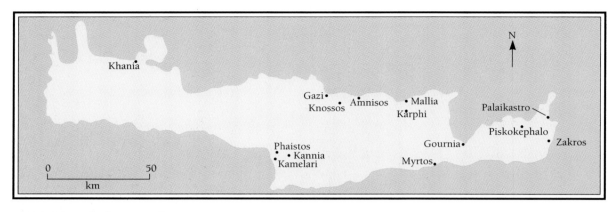

FIGURE 15.34 Major sites of the Minoan civilization on Crete. Knossos, with its large palace, is the largest and most complex of these sites.

By 1400 to 1200 ya, two separate civilized states, Tiwanaku and Huari, came into existence. Again, the respective capitals of these states are marked by monumental architecture, far-flung trading networks, differentiated burials, and a level of artistic skill implying specialization. Art and architectural styles, religious motifs, and burial patterns of the Tiwanaku and Huari civilizations spread over hundreds of square miles through expansion, friendly incorporation, and conquest. As archaeologists William Conklin and Michael Moseley (1988) point out, Tiwanaku and Huari represent the development of a kind of large-scale "national" Andean unity.

By about 1000 ya, another large state, the Chimu, evolved, with its 15-square-kilometer (6-square-mile) capital, Chanchan. The Chimu were an expansionist, militaristic empire. They followed the practice of split inheritance, in which the son of the king inherited only his title while others in a king's family inherited his wealth, property, and land—along with the right to collect the taxes—the proceeds of which they were obliged to use to maintain the king's burial. This fueled the military expansionism of the new king, who wanted to acquire new lands and subjects to support the state and his kingship. The Chimu were the precursors of the Inca, who also practiced a policy of split inheritance. The Inca ascended to supremacy when they defeated the Chimu in war.

Southern Europe

Knossos was the center of what certainly was Europe's first literate civilization (Cherry 1987; Warren 1987). Built on the island of Crete close to 4000 ya, it was the nucleus of the **Minoan** civilization whose influence was felt throughout the central Mediterranean (Warren 1975) (Figure 15.34). The social and political hub of Knossos was the Labyrinth, a palace built in 3880 B.P. that covered an enormous area of some 20,000 square meters (215,000 square feet) and may have contained 1000 separate rooms or chambers (Castleden 1990:8) (Figure 15.35). It is a remarkable structure made of mud brick, marked with numerous columns tapered

Minoan The earliest European civilization, centered on Crete and beginning about 4000 ya.

FIGURE 15.35   Looking down into one of the rooms of the palace at Knossos on Crete. The columns have been reconstructed and repainted, conveying only an impression of how beautiful it once had been. (*M. H. Feder*)

from top to bottom, and painted in earth-toned hues of browns and reds. Its interior walls were covered with paintings showing details of Minoan life and belief 3800 ya: Priestesses gaze at visitors across the millennia; an athlete-acrobat performs a handstand on the back of an enormous bull in a palace fresco; the images of two animals that appear to be a mythical mixture of dogs and birds flank what seems to be a throne; beautifully rendered dolphins frolic among a school of fish.

The palace at Knossos was the center of a civilization that stood at the center of a vast network of trade encompassing the Aegean region of the Mediterranean. This trade—focused on an agricultural product cultivated on Crete (olives, particularly valuable for their oil)—may have been one of the key factors contributing to the importance of the island, leading to the evolution of a complex political and economic entity.

The power of Knossos began to fade after about 3400 ya while the importance of the **Mycenaeans** on the Greek mainland grew at its expense. The Mycenaeans were accomplished traders, too, although their focus was not in olives but copper and tin. These two metals, when alloyed, produce bronze, a material far more durable and useful than either of the metals from which it was made. It may have been as a result of the need to keep

Mycenaean The civilization of Greece that followed the Minoans and preceded the Greek city-states.

FIGURE 15.36 Map of sites related to the development of African civilization south of Egypt and mentioned in the text.

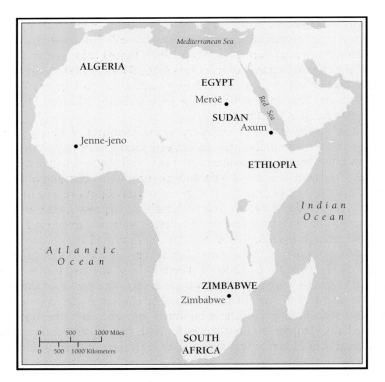

track of trade that the Mycenaeans expanded on the writing system first developed by the Minoans.

The Mycenaeans flourished until a bit after 3200 ya when invasions from the north sapped their strength, leading to the destruction of their civilization. The fall of the Mycenaeans paved the way for the ascendance of the Greek city-states that produced the great architecture, science, and philosophy that contributed so very greatly to the development of Western society.

Africa, South of Egypt

The evolution of civilization in Africa presents us with a long, complex, richly detailed story. Once thought to reflect only late reaction to developments in other regions, the city, the state, and civilization are now known to have been ancient in Africa south of the Sahara and, in some cases, independent from cultural evolution in other areas (Connah 1987) (Figure 15.36).

Perhaps the oldest African civilization south of pharaonic Egypt—in what the Egyptians called Kush and today we call Nubia—is the 3500-year-old civilization of Kerma (Connah 1987). Kerma is located on the east bank of the Nile in Sudan. Kerma covers 60,000 to 100,000 square meters (15 to 25 acres) and is surrounded by a monumental wall some 10 meters (33 feet) high. The wall includes huge towers nearly 20 meters (60 feet) high, constructed of mud brick.

East of Kerma is a large cemetery where members of Kerma's upper classes were buried. Individuals have been found here placed on finely made wooden beds, some encased in gold. Well-crafted items were entombed with them: bronze swords, bronze razors, fine clothing of leather, fans made of ostrich feathers, and large quantities of pottery. The most impressive grave in the cemetery, that of Tumulus X, represents the final resting place of an obviously important ruler of Kerma, surrounded by the sacrificed remains of close to 400 retainers (O'Connor 1993).

The best known of the ancient Nubian civilizations is that of Meroë, dated from about 2500 to 2200 ya. The city of Meroë covered an area of about 0.75 square kilometers (0.3 square miles). The center of the settlement consisted of a maze of monumental structures made of mud brick and faced with fired brick. These buildings appear to have been palaces, meeting halls, temples, and residences for both nobility and their workers. The central area of Meroë was surrounded by a monumental wall of mud brick.

A commoners' graveyard has been excavated to the east of the city where about 600 simple interments were found. In comparison, the North Cemetery is where Meroë's nobility were buried. Beautifully constructed small, stone pyramids capped their graves (Figure 15.37).

South of Nubia is the prehistoric city of Axum, in modern Ethiopia. Here the inhabitants built a four-towered "castle" some 2000 ya. In Axum and in surrounding towns that belonged to the same prehistoric state researchers have found enormous, narrow towers, each carved from single blocks of stone. The tower at Axum, for instance, is carved from a block of granite and stands 21 meters (69 feet) tall. False windows and doors have been carved into its four sides, making it look similar to a modern skyscraper.

Another ancient African civilization south of the Sahara is that of Jenne-jeno in Mali (McIntosh and McIntosh 1982). Jenne-jeno was a true city more than 1000 ya, with a population of between 10,000 and 20,000 people. It shows evidence of public works, particularly in the form of its 2-kilometer (1.2-mile) surrounding wall. Jenne-jeno probably developed before any substantial contact with Arabs living north of the Sahara, so it was truly an indigenous, independent prehistoric African kingdom. The city may have served as a trading center, bartering its rich agricultural products for salt, iron, and copper—the last obtained from sources 1000 kilometers (over 620 miles) distant (McIntosh and McIntosh 1982:414).

FIGURE 15.37 The pyramids of the rulers of Meroë, an African civilization located to the south of pharaonic Egypt and dated to between 2500 and 2200 B.P. (© *Mike Yamashita/Woodfin Camp*)

In southern Africa, the ruins of Zimbabwe consist of two main groups about a kilometer away from each other: the Hill Complex and the Great Enclosure (Figure 15.38). Between the two is an unbroken series of stone walls, enclosures, and foundations—in essence, the heart of an ancient city with an estimated population of about 18,000 (Connah 1987:184). The Temple is a large, dry-laid stone ruin surrounded by a huge wall more than 9 meters (30 feet) high enclosing an area of more than an acre. When the site was mined in the late nineteenth century, many artifacts of gold and iron were found. Unfortunately, it was not professionally investigated until the early twentieth century.

The area around Zimbabwe contains more than 300 additional sites that appear to have been inhabited by people bearing the same culture. Dating to the fourteenth and fifteenth centuries A.D., Zimbabwe was an indigenous African civilization.

North America

Cahokia was not a full-fledged city, but the argument can be made that it was on its way to becoming one. Some 200 earthen mounds, platforms, and pyramids were spread across its 18 square kilometers (7 square miles) (Figure 15.39). In the core of the settlement was Monk's Mound, the largest pyramid, covering more than 57,000 square meters (14 acres), containing over 50 million cubic meters (60 million cubic yards) of earth, and rising more than 30 meters (100 feet) over the river floodplain. In volume,

FIGURE 15.38 Ruins of the 1000-year-old stone enclosure at Great Zimbabwe in southern Africa. Great Zimbabwe was the central place of an indigenous southern African civilization. (© *Jason Laure/Woodfin Camp*)

FIGURE 15.39 Monk's Mound contains about 50 million cubic meters (60 million cubic yards) of earth, covers an area of about 69,000 square meters (740,000 square feet or about 14 acres), and rises to about 30 meters (100 feet) at its summit. It is the central earthwork in a Native American settlement containing more than 120 smaller mounds. At its peak at around A.D. 1200, Cahokia's population probably exceeded 5000. (*K. L. Feder*)

Monk's Mound rivals the size of the pyramids of Mesoamerica and of many of those built in Egypt. From its summit, one can still gaze out upon a large open plaza encompassed by large mounds: flat-topped pyramids, conical mounds, and low-lying earthworks.

Surrounding 200 acres of the main part of the settlement with its eighteen major mounds (including Monk's Mound), was a log wall or palisade with bastions and watch towers. That wall was constructed from an estimated 20,000 logs, and it was rebuilt three times. The wall was as monumental a feat as Monk's Mound itself, enclosing the central part of the settlement and protecting the homes of Cahokia's elite. At its peak, Cahokia was a settlement of 5000 or more inhabitants (some estimates range up to 20,000), including priests, artisans, merchants, farmers, and kings. Its rulers were buried in sumptuous splendor in log-lined tombs with precious artifacts of stone, shell, and copper. One ruler was laid out on a cape made of over 20,000 drilled and sewn shell beads. Also in his tomb were more than 1000 beautifully made arrow points, a copper tube, sheets of mica, and numerous shaped stones (called chunky stones). Around his grave were the remains of more than sixty other people, all killed to accompany the chief to the afterlife.

With its food surplus, specialists, stratification, and dense settlement and as the economic and political center of a geographically broad entity, Cahokia has the appearance of an early stage of a civilization (Paukatat 1994). But Cahokia is not in the Indus or Nile valleys. It is not in northern China or Mesoamerica. Cahokia is found on the Illinois side of the Mississippi River, just east of St. Louis. More than 500 ya, Cahokia was the center of an American Indian chiefdom.

Southeast Asia

In Kampuchea (Cambodia) in Southeast Asia lie the ruins of the spectacular Khmer civilization. There, between A.D. 800 and 1300, seventy-two temples and monuments were constructed of sandstone, laterite (a hard red soil), and brick. Each complex of temples represented the capital of the Khmer state during the reign of successive kings. Angkor Wat, built after A.D. 1100, is the largest and most impressive (P. T. White 1982) (Figure 15.40). The temple at Angkor Wat is surrounded by a rectangular outer gallery over 800 meters (0.5 mile) long. The walls of the gallery are covered with bas-relief sculptures depicting important events and personages in Hindu mythology. There are eight huge panels of reliefs, each close to 2 meters (6 feet) high and from 50 to 100 meters (160 to 300 feet) long. One panel depicts the Hindu creation myth; another contains the relief sculptures of 1700 spirit women. There also is an interior rectangular gallery with hallways connecting it to the outer gallery. At the center is the temple of Angkor Wat itself, a hauntingly beautiful building with five intricately carved domes.

Water control seems to have been the key to Khmer civilization. Through a series of enormous reservoirs called *barray* and miles of canals, the Khmer were able to produce two and sometimes three yearly harvests. The western barray is, in its way, as monumental and impressive as the temple complex. Constructed at ground level with dikes, this reservoir is 8 kilometers (5 miles) long and 2.25 kilometers (1.25 miles) wide.

Khmer civilization fell as a result of warfare with neighboring groups who had previously been under the sway of Khmer rule. Warfare today threatens the remains of this once great civilization.

Why Did It Happen?

The evolution of civilization is difficult to chronicle (Figure 15.41) and even more difficult to explain. There are numerous gaps in the archaeological record, which become gaps in our thinking.

As you read the brief descriptions here, you may have recognized some of the factors mentioned in the hypotheses about the emergence of civilization presented earlier (Table 15.1). As Lamberg-Karlovsky and Sabloff have pointed out, each civilization had its own unique character, but "some strikingly similar developmental patterns characterized the beginnings of agriculture and the later rise of civilizations in both the Old and New World localities" (1995:214). Irrigation certainly played an important role in almost all the societies discussed, but it cannot be shown to have occurred first and therefore cannot have been in all places a prime cause. It is certainly the case that circumscription of resources served as a catalyst in the emergence of the civilized state, but a catalyst is not necessarily a cause. Managing trade of highly desirable localized resources seems to have been an important factor in all the examples discussed. You see the problem: It becomes a chicken-and-egg argument. We cannot determine which, if any, of those characteristics used to define civilization were causes, which were effects, and which were both.

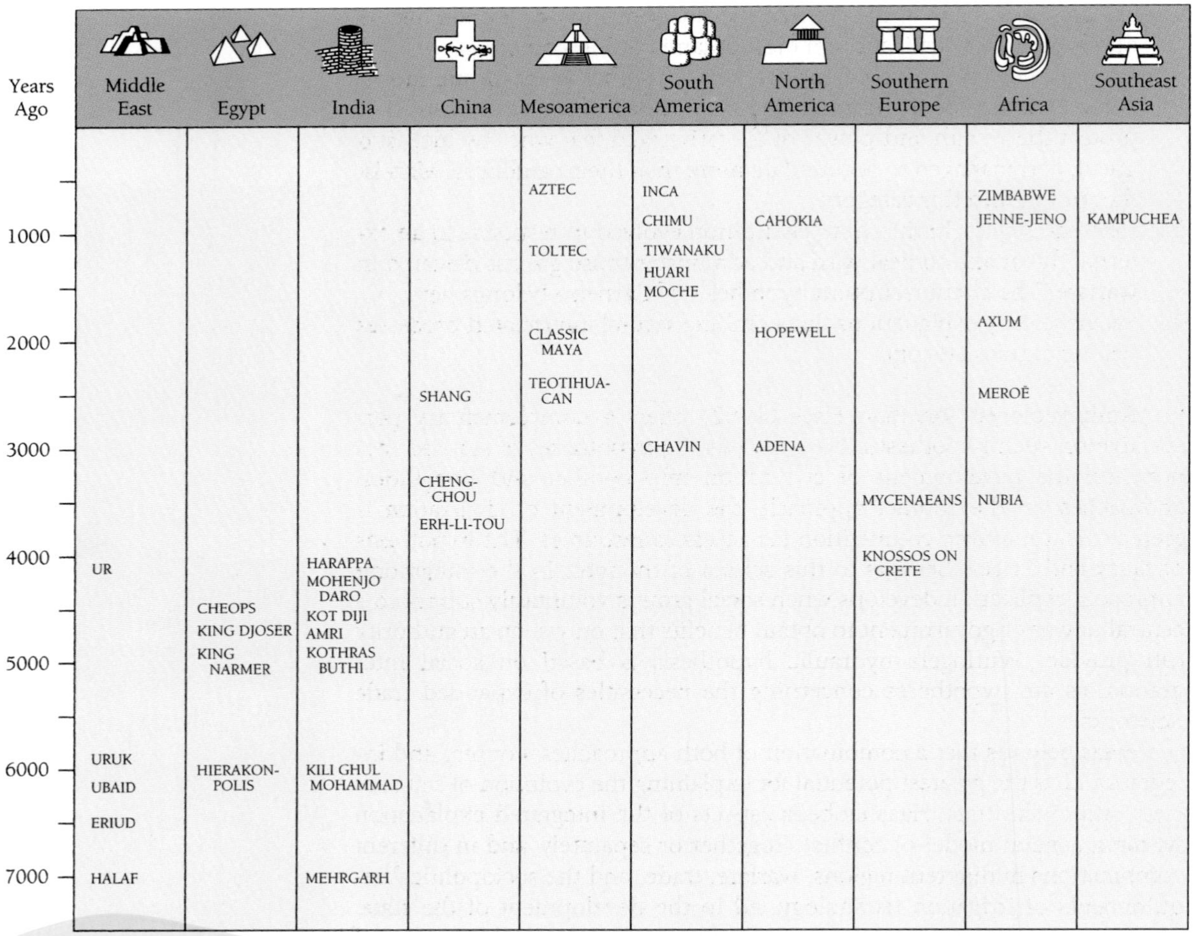

Years Ago	Middle East	Egypt	India	China	Mesoamerica	South America	North America	Southern Europe	Africa	Southeast Asia
1000					AZTEC	INCA / CHIMU	CAHOKIA		ZIMBABWE / JENNE-JENO	KAMPUCHEA
					TOLTEC	TIWANAKU / HUARI / MOCHE				
2000					CLASSIC MAYA		HOPEWELL		AXUM	
				SHANG	TEOTIHUA-CAN				MEROË	
3000						CHAVIN	ADENA			
				CHENG-CHOU				MYCENAEANS	NUBIA	
				ERH-LI-TOU						
4000	UR		HARAPPA / MOHENJO DARO					KNOSSOS ON CRETE		
		CHEOPS / KING DJOSER	KOT DIJI / AMRI							
5000		KING NARMER	KOTHRAS BUTHI							
6000	URUK / UBAID	HIERAKON-POLIS	KILI GHUL MOHAMMAD							
	ERIUD									
7000	HALAF		MEHRGARH							

FIGURE 15.41 Summary chart showing the chronology and geography of the world's ancient civilizations.

Archaeologist Joseph Tainter (1988:32) has provided a valuable taxonomy of the hypotheses proposed for the origin of civilization. He categorizes the scientifically based hypotheses we have discussed—and myriad others—as follows:

1. *Managerial.* Managerial hypotheses essentially maintain that civilization developed in response to a need for more complex forms of political integration. In other words, the need arose in some societies to accomplish some complex task such as the construction of irrigation canals or the management of trade for valuable items not locally available. Managerial hierarchies developed to oversee these new, complex tasks, which led to social stratification and the other trappings of civilization. Clearly, the hydraulic hypothesis of Wittfogel fits into this

category, as do any of the specific explanations involving trade for the development of civilization in Mesopotamia or Mesoamerica.

2. *Internal conflict.* In this perspective, class conflict is the prime mover behind the rise of civilization. The institutions of the state evolved to protect the wealth and power of the privileged few who, by luck and greed, had managed to accumulate more than their neighbors. Marxist theories fit into this category.

3. *External conflict.* In this view, civilization evolved in response to an external threat and to deal with and administer those groups defeated in warfare. The circumscription hypothesis of Carneiro belongs here.

4. *Synthetic.* Any explanations that combine several interrelated processes belong in this category.

Anthropologist Jonathan Haas (1982) offers a complementary perspective on such hypotheses. Haas divides the hypotheses of state formation and the development of civilization into conflict and integration approaches. In the conflict approach, the development of civilization is seen as resulting from competition for access to resources. The hypothesis of Marx and Engels belongs to this school of thought. In the integration approach, civilization develops when social groups voluntarily submit to a central power or government to obtain benefits that only such an authority can provide. Wittfogel's hydraulic hypothesis is based on social integration, as are hypotheses concerning the necessities of expanded trade networks.

Haas believes that a combination of both approaches, conflict and integration, has the greatest potential for explaining the evolution of state society and civilization. Haas embeds aspects of the integrated explanation within a general model of conflict. Together or separately, and in different combinations in different regions, warfare, trade, and the sociopolitical requirements of irrigation technology led to the development of the state. Processes of social integration are required to maximize the effectiveness of long-distance trade, warfare, or irrigation. Such integration leads to social stratification, with those on top of the social pyramid gaining differential access to and control over basic resources. This elite can then accumulate wealth in the form of land, water, or other precious resources that other people in the society need or desire. With differential access based on "control over the *production or procurement* of the resources in question" (Haas 1982:151), the elite also accumulates power, which can be used to coerce people to do whatever is required—to fight in wars, be taxed, build pyramids, and so on.

Following Haas's perspective, it probably serves little purpose to look for a single cause for the development of any one of the civilizations described, much less all of them. Instead, we can generalize that constellations of factors including population growth, warfare, and uneven distribution of resources were involved for all the cultures.

Looked at another way, we can say that post-Pleistocene agricultural societies were living in various states of equilibrium with their environments. Some of these states of equilibrium, however, were unstable. Archaeologist David Clarke identifies a state of unstable equilibrium as one in which a "small displacement from the equilibrium state gives rise to a cumulatively greater displacement from that specific state" (1978:48). Relatively minor perturbations from without or within—population growth, climate change, technological advance, outside threat—may have upset that delicately balanced equilibrium and changed the equation for survival. Decisions were made, challenges met, and strategies revised to respond to these changes. Canals may have been built, population density increased, agriculture intensified, or trading networks established. Under conditions of unstable equilibrium, these new approaches, though perhaps solving initial challenges, sometimes produced a ripple effect that greatly transformed other aspects of culture. Patterns of social integration had to change to make such activities possible. Power was invested in emerging elites to build canals or walls, completely altering established social systems. Wars of conquest were initiated, changing the political nature of a region. Certain groups of people obtained differential access to resources by controlling trade. Such changes in turn may have triggered a spiral of change as a new equilibrium was sought but not attained. Changes in subsistence or trade may have required more coordination of individuals, triggering changes in social structure. The maintenance of this new order may have required symbols in order to perpetuate and justify itself. Use of these symbols, in turn, put more power in the hands of the leaders of the new social order. This power would enable even greater accomplishments in architecture and science.

Thus, myriad factors impinging on agricultural groups in the Indus and Nile valleys, in Mesopotamia, highland and lowland Mesoamerica, China, South America, North America, southern Africa, southern Europe, and Southeast Asia may have set in motion forces whose ultimate impact on these societies was enormous. In the broadest sense, we are all living with the consequences of those changes.

Summary

Beginning sometime after 6000 ya, in several world areas, fundamental changes occurred in the social and political lives of human groups. The food surplus made possible by the Food-Producing Revolution allowed for a dramatic increase in cultural complexity that resulted in what we call civilization.

Characterized by densely populated settlements, specialization of labor, social stratification, monumental public works, a system of record-

Contemporary Issue

The Collapse of Civilization

—⁓—

Is the collapse of civilization inevitable? Perhaps so. Joseph Tainter, in his book *The Collapse of Complex Societies* (1988), discusses the case histories of all the civilizations mentioned here and many more. In his view, civilizations do not disintegrate because of random or unpredictable factors. He rejects single, serendipitous, fundamental causes like resource depletion, environmental catastrophes, or barbarian invasions. He also rejects claims that civilizations are inherently fragile entities or that the elite classes invariably mismanage things, leading to a revolt by the masses.

Instead, in Tainter's view, civilization and all of its trappings involve increasingly complex and costly investments of time and energy. The development of civilization is seen as an extreme case of a process of deviation amplification; civilization is a runaway train on a track leading to greater political and social complexity. Once the complex social and political structures of the state are established, an increasingly greater human investment in time and energy are demanded merely to keep things going. More and more people are needed to run the bureaucracies necessary for the complex social arrays that civilization fosters and depends upon. In essence, for civilizations to survive, the pyramids must continually get bigger, the armies larger, and the food surpluses greater. But eventually, as greater economic investment is made simply in running the political and social bureaucracies of the civilized state, the economic returns diminish dramatically. As Tainter puts it, "a society invests ever more heavily in a strategy that yields proportionately less" (1988:195).

In Tainter's view, the collapse of a civilization, however, is not a bad thing. In his opinion, it is a "rational, economizing process that may well benefit much of the population" (1988:198). While the elite may certainly lose out, the masses may actually see their lives improve as they no longer have to support burdensome, nonutilitarian institutions that had previously served only to maintain the economic, social, and political status quo and that had outlived their ability to effectively manage the society.

Finally, it is little more than conceit on our part to believe that our civilization is immune to the kinds of collapse that befell earlier civilizations.

One major difference is apparent, though. For the first time in human evolution, the collapse of a civilization may come as a result of destruction by our own hand. We can accomplish this through the madness of nuclear annihilation or, as is perhaps more likely, environmental destruction. And, unlike the geographically isolated collapses of the world's ancient civilizations, if we go down in a nuclear war or destroy the planetary ecosystem, we will almost certainly bring the rest of humanity with us.

OZYMANDIAS
I met a traveller from an antique land
Who said: Two vast and trunkless legs of stone
Stand in the desert . . . Near them, on the sand,
Half sunk, a shattered visage lies, whose frown,
And wrinkled lip, and sneer of cold command,
Tell that its sculptor well those passions read
Which yet survive, stamped on these lifeless things,
The hand that mocked them, and the heart that fed:
And on the pedestal these words appear:
"My name is Ozymandias, king of kings:
Look on my works, ye Mighty, and despair!"
Nothing beside remains. Round the decay
Of that colossal wreck, boundless and bare
The lone and level sands stretch far away.
[Percy Bysshe Shelley, 1817; published 1818]

keeping, and the production of a food surplus, the world's primary civilizations developed in Mesopotamia, in the Nile Valley of Egypt, the Indus Valley of Pakistan, northern China, the highlands and lowlands of Mesoamerica, and the mountain valleys of the Andes in South America. Other complex states and chiefdoms developed in southern Europe, Africa south of the Sahara, Kampuchea in Southeast Asia, and the North American Midwest.

The reasons postulated for the development of these societies have been varied: race, environment, invention, class struggle, the need for groups to subordinate themselves to authority, and warfare. There seems to be no point in suggesting a single cause for the development of civilizations in general, or even in individual cases. Civilizations are complex entities with complex explanations. Viable propositions include aspects of both conflict-based and integrative mechanisms. Thus, it is likely that in some world areas, as population grew, complex bureaucratic structures developed to facilitate group projects like the construction of city walls or irrigation networks; specialist classes originated to coordinate trade for materials unavailable locally; competition may have led to warfare with defeated groups becoming subordinate classes. As social distinctions developed, monumental projects became common as members of the newly emerged elite classes felt compelled to legitimate in some concrete ways the stratified social system. In this way, civilization, with all of its concomitants, quickly evolved in the world areas discussed in this chapter.

Study Questions

1. What are the key characteristics of the world's first civilizations, or state societies?
2. How are such monumental works as pyramids, great palaces, and temples part of a feedback system in the increasing investment of power in the hands of an elite; in other words, how are monumental works both an effect and a cause of the development of the state?
3. How have various scientists attempted to explain the rise of civilization? What appear to be essential commonalities wherever early civilization developed?
4. When and where did people first develop civilization? Was it rare or common? Did it occur independently in many areas, or was there a single source from which it spread into other regions?
5. How do conflict and integration models explain the evolution of early state societies?
6. Do state societies inevitably collapse? Is such collapse necessarily tragic for the people living in them?

Key Terms

civilization	Hassunan	central place
social stratification	Samarran	Olmec
state	Halafian	Chavin
chiefdom	Ubaid	repoussé
environmental	Uruk	Minoan
determinism	city-state	Mycenaean
ziggurat	rank societies	

For More Information

C. C. Lamberg-Karlovsky's and Jeremy A. Sabloff's (1995) *Ancient Civilizations: The Near East and Mesoamerica* provides excellent summaries of the various hypotheses presented to explain the development of state society. The book also contains in-depth discussions of the development of civilization in Mesopotamia, Egypt, the Indus Valley, and Mesoamerica. Though the time period discussed is a bit later than that focused on here, John Romer's *Ancient Lives: Daily Life in Egypt of the Pharaohs* provides remarkable insight into life in ancient Egypt. Graham Connah's *African Civilizations* provides the best recent discussion on the development of civilization on that continent. Muriel Porter Weaver's *The Aztecs, the Maya, and Their Predecessors: Archaeology of Mesoamerica* is a good source of information about the civilizations of Mesoamerica, as is Jeremy Sabloff's *The Cities of Ancient Mexico: Reconstructing a Lost World,* R. E. W. Adam's *Prehistoric Mesoamerica,* and, especially, Linda Schele and David Freidel's *A Forest of Kings: The Untold Story of the Ancient Maya.* Also see the series "Rediscovering the Maya" in various issues of *Natural History* magazine in 1991 and 1992.

K. C. Chang's (1986) *The Archaeology of Ancient China* is a good source of information on the Shang civilization. Thomas Patterson's *America's Past: A New World Archaeology* examines the development of the state in South America. *National Geographic* magazine has published fine articles on the cultures of Cahokia (December 1972 by George Stuart) and Angkor Wat (May 1982 by P. T. White). The *First Cities* volume (Hamblin 1973) of the Time-Life *Emergence of Man* series is still a good source for information about the early civilizations of Southwest Asia and India. Jonathan Haas's *The Evolution of the Prehistoric State* and Joseph Tainter's *The Collapse of Complex Societies* are especially useful treatments of the birth and death of civilizations.

An Evolutionary Afterword

---———— ⟋⟍ ————---

Lately it's occurred to me
What a long, strange trip it's been.
—The Grateful Dead

Stephen Jay Gould has depicted the evolution of all life on earth as a bush—enormous and incredibly complex. This image captures perfectly the way we now think evolution occurs: by the production of countless adaptive experiments called species, the twigs on the bush. Most are short-lived, but a few possess enough longevity to divide and give rise to still newer species, sprouting more twigs. In this book, we have focused on the story of the few twigs that make up the human part of the evolutionary bush.

Life, and the earth on which it evolved, can be seen as an integrated whole, just as a bush is intimately and inextricably part of the environment in which it is rooted. Species, past and present, and the environments in which they live, make up a living planet, on which each form of life depends for survival on its adaptation to the natural features of its environment. Although most of the species that have ever existed are now extinct, they are still part of that integrated whole. The evolutionary bush and our planet are as they are because these species once existed, just as the whole form of the bush depends on the specific pattern of its branching as it grows.

As you have seen, the hominids have been part of the evolutionary bush for a relatively short time. But one hominid, *Homo sapiens*, is now, in many ways, the dominant twig on the bush. Our twig is swollen far out of proportion to all others: There are nearly 6 billion of us. We live in every conceivable place on earth. We change the very face of the planet to suit our needs. And this success—if success it proves to be—is largely the result of an accident of evolution that has given us enormous and complex brains with the ability to store massive amounts of information and to use that information to think and reason.

Many see conscious thought as an indication that humans are superior to the other forms of life on the planet. What more advanced adaptation could there be, they ask, than the ability to think about things, including one's own origins? But such a philosophy creates an unbridgeable gulf between humans and other living things, a difference between "us" and "them" of kind rather than degree.

Such attitudes arise, of course, when a group of people have come to rely heavily on their ability to control natural resources in agricultural and civilized societies. These attitudes justify the manipulation and exploitation of nature that is necessitated by such cultural systems. This sense of human superiority is seldom found among hunter–gatherers, who see themselves as part of, rather than above and in control of, the natural world.

A belief in the superiority of our species is often incorporated into a society's religious system, where it is seen as having been bestowed by a higher authority and where it then easily influences, if not determines, the behavior of future generations. In the Judeo-Christian tradition, God clearly tells Noah and his sons that all the beasts of the earth, sea, and air are "delivered" into their hands and that "every moving thing that liveth shall be meat for you" (Genesis 9:2,3). So much did Europe rely on animals for food and labor that extensions of this attitude moved into philosophical-scientific areas. The famous French thinker René Descartes held that animals were mere machines, incapable of thought or even sensation.

We now have sufficient scientific information to understand that these ideas have no basis in fact and indeed are, to say the least, counterproductive. Our modern view of evolution as a bush shows us clearly that we are in no way the inevitable culmination of the process. Evolution could have happened in countless other ways. Our physical and genetic closeness to the other primates tells us that the differences between us and them are differences of degree, not kind. We must see our major adaptation—our brain—in the same light as we see the major adaptations of any living thing. The cheetah's swiftness, the eagle's visual acuity, the peppered moth's camouflage, and our complex brain are all simply the means of survival that evolution has provided our respective species, no more and no less.

Moreover, we also now understand the interrelated nature of all life on earth. The evolutionary bush persists because its twigs support one another according to the principles of ecological relationships. We may have the ability to understand and control many aspects of the natural world, but we must not forget that we arose from that world and are still a part of it, dependent ultimately on its resources and thus on its continuation.

In this regard, we believe, as do many, that evolution has placed on our shoulders not only a large brain but along with it the responsibility of guardianship over our planet. Our ability to exploit and control nature doesn't give us the right to do so without limits or moral considerations. Nor are such activities justified because they happen to fill our needs at the moment. Ironically, though, the growing recognition of this responsibility has come about at the very time we are accelerating our destruction of the earth—and of many other twigs on the evolutionary bush.

The list of species we have hunted to extinction is depressingly long. Not long after our species first arrived in the New World, hunting may have contributed to the complete demise of some thirty-five genera of American mammals. More recently, the dodo of Mauritius, the passenger pigeon of North America, and the Tasmanian wolf, to name but a few, have all been hunted to extinction. The list of species still living but currently endangered by human predation is even longer. It includes many of the African big-game animals, species we once thought so numerous as to be eternal.

Yet hunting is not nearly the most significant impact we have had on other species. Much more important is habitat destruction. If you think back over the story of our past, you see a clear trend. As we evolved bigger brains and greater intelligence, our cultures became more complex and our populations grew. We made greater demands on our environments. At first, we manipulated those environments simply. Our earliest ancestors knocked a few flakes off a rock, creating edges and points sharper and more durable than the teeth and nails biological evolution provided us. Such tools allowed us to procure more efficiently the plants and animals we used for food and as raw materials for various artifacts.

Our manipulation and exploitation of the environment took a great leap forward when later ancestors began to build shelters and control fire. More resources were required from the environment. Fire, along with better tools, allowed us to kill larger numbers of animals. Later still, with the shift from food gathering to food production, we began reshaping the landscape to human specifications.

Finally, in the development of civilization and the state, new patterns of social and political integration allowed for dense population aggregations and communal works like irrigation and road building, with associated environmental impacts never before possible. The history of culture has thus been one of increasing control, of the ever-greater human ability to rework and shape the world to fit our needs, real and perceived.

But the effects of these environmental impacts, even in ancient times, have been two-sided. For example, irrigation played a significant role in the development of Mesopotamian civilization, but resulting salinization of the soil rendered much of the land useless for agriculture.

More recently, short-term benefits have been derived from clearing tropical forests to create farmland, damming rivers to produce reservoirs, or rerouting them for irrigation, or carving up large sections of the earth to extract resources. But these activities can have dire results, including the extinction of other species. In the United States alone, some 300,000 acres per year of freshwater wetlands are drained for farming and building. Overall, 1 million acres of wildlife habitats are lost every year to development. Because we have no precise idea how many species of living things exist, estimates vary on the number of species becoming extinct, but they range from one plant or animal species per day to the incredible figure of one per hour. Indeed, the human twig on the evolutionary bush has become the dominant one at least in part through our destruction and replacement of other living things with which we once shared the earth.

The ultimate irony is that our understanding and control over nature may now lead to our bringing about the end of 4 billion years of evolution. Within the last century, we have come to understand the basic forces of the universe contained within the nucleus of the atom. We have tapped into those forces to generate electrical energy, diagnose and treat illnesses, and, tragically, to create weapons of terrifying destructive power. In a matter of minutes, we can destroy what evolution took billions of years to produce.

One significant conclusion to be drawn from the study of the past is that no species is permanent. All species undergo change, and all ultimately become extinct. The human species is no exception. We were not destined to evolve, and we are not destined to last forever. We share that fate with all other living things, past, present, and future.

An accident of evolution, our big brain, however, makes us capable of understanding our world to a degree far greater than that of any other species. We use our brain to exploit and manipulate nature, but we also have an obligation to use it to devise ways that we can survive—as we have a right to—and yet still protect our planet and share it with our fellow species.

We humans—the tip of a short twig—must live with the awesome knowledge that we have in our power the ability to uproot the rest of the bush of evolution that supports us. Only by fully understanding our world, as it is now and as it was in the past, can we hope to prevent that. Toward that hope, we have addressed this book.

For More Information

There are a number of organizations committed to educating the public and to addressing some of the threats we humans have posed to our world, and thus to ourselves. Here are some of the most successful.

The World Wildlife Fund (1250 Twenty-Fourth Street, NW, Washington, DC, 20037; http://www.panda.org), focusing on the protection of living creatures and their environments worldwide.

Greenpeace USA (1436 U Street, NW, Washington, DC 20009; http://www.greenpeace.org/greenpeace.html), aimed at protecting the environment, especially the oceans and marine animals.

The National Audubon Society (950 Third Avenue, New York, NY 10022; http://www.audubon.org/audubon/contents.html), one of the nation's oldest conservation organizations, dedicated to the protection of America's wildlife.

People for the Ethical Treatment of Animals (P.O. Box 42516, Washington, DC 20015; http://www.envirolink.org/arrs/peta/index.html), fighting any form of cruelty to animals and advocating the idea that our fellow creatures share our basic rights.

Survival International (2121 Decatur Place, NW, Washington, DC 20008; http://www.survival.org.uk/), dedicated to protecting the world's tribal peoples and their ways of life.

Amnesty International (322 Eighth Avenue, New York, NY 10001; http://www.organic.com/non-profits/amnesty/index.html), working to promote human rights for all the world's people.

The Jane Goodall Institute for Wildlife Research, Education and Conservation (P.O. Box 599, Ridgefield, CT 06877; http://www.wcsu. ctstateu.edu/cyberchimp/shoots.html), headed by the famous researcher on chimpanzee behavior and working to promote those things indicated in its title.

The Archaeological Conservancy (415 Orchard Drive, Santa Fe, NM 87501; http://www.govp.com/archcons/), committed to preserving America's past through the novel approach of buying land with significant archaeological resources.

There are many more organizations with similar goals. For more information on the work of any of the groups we have listed here, simply write to the addresses provided or look them up at their Web sites. Certainly, if evolution has provided us with the capability to destroy our planet, we are also endowed with the intelligence to preserve it. These organizations are a testament to that hope.

Glossary of Human and Nonhuman Primates

Adapidae (ah-da′-pih-day) A group of early primates from the then-connected landmass of North America and Europe dated to more than 50 mya and thought to be ancestral to prosimians such as lemurs and lorises.

Aegyptopithecus (ee-gyp′-toe-pith′-ah-cuss) An extinct monkey with several apelike traits. Discovered in Egypt and dating to more than 25 mya, it may represent a form of primate ancestral to Old World monkeys and apes.

Anthropoidea (an-throw-poi′-dee-ah) One of the two suborders of the order **Primates** (the other is **Prosimii**). Means "humanlike" and includes monkeys, apes, and hominids.

Ardipithecus ramidus (ar-di-pith′-ah-cuss rah′-mi-dus) A newly discovered hominid genus from Ethiopia dated at about 4.4 mya. It is based on skeletal fragments and teeth. Not yet fully documented or accepted, it is thought by its discoverers to represent the earliest hominid. Thus, the species name meaning "root" in the local language.

Australopithecus afarensis (os-tral-oh-pith′-ah-cuss ah-far-en′-sis) A fossil species from East Africa, a well-established species in the hominid line. Dated from 4 mya to 3 mya, afarensis had a small, chimp-sized brain but walked fully upright.

Australopithecus africanus (os-tral-oh-pith′-ah-cuss ah-frih-can′-us) A fossil hominid species from South Africa dated from about 3 mya to 2.3 mya. Similar to *A. afarensis*, it may well be a direct evolutionary descendant of that species. It retains the chimp-sized brain and is fully bipedal.

Australopithecus anamensis (os-tral-oh-pith′-ah-cuss ana-men′-sis) Found in Kenya and dating from 4.2 to 3.9 mya, it is the earliest well-documented fully bipedal hominid.

Australopithecus bahrelghazalia (os-tral-oh-pith′-ah-cuss bar-el-gah-zahl′-ya) A new species of this genus, based on a jaw and several teeth. Found in Chad and dated at 3 to 3.5 mya. The species name is based on an Arab name for a nearby riverbed. It is noteworthy as the only early hominid found outside of East or South Africa.

Catarrhini (cat-ah-rhine′-eye) One of two infraorders of suborder **Anthropoidea** (the other is infraorder **Platyrrhini**, the New World monkeys). Catarrhini is the infraorder of the Old World monkeys, apes, and hominids. Along with the geographical distinction, catarrhines can be distinguished from platyrrhines by their narrow nose shape, fewer premolar teeth, and lack of a prehensile tail.

Cercopithecidae (sir-co-pith-ah-sigh′-day) The taxonomic family of all monkeys of Europe, Africa, and Asia.

Cercopithecoidea (sir-co-pith-ah-coy′-dee-ah) The superfamily of all monkeys of Europe, Africa, and Asia.

Dryopithecus (dry-oh-pith′-ah-cuss) A genus of fossil apes from Europe dated from about 13 to 8 mya.

Eoanthropus (ee-oh-an′-throw-puss) "Dawn Man," the taxonomic name given the Piltdown fossil "discovered" in 1912. *Eoanthropus* had a very humanlike cranium but an apelike jaw, fulfilling the expectations of the time concerning the appearance of the earliest humans. It was later proven to be a fraud, and the name is no longer valid.

Gigantopithecus (ji-gan-toe-pith′-ah-cuss) A fossil ape genus from 12 to perhaps 1 mya in China, India, and Vietnam. The largest primate known, it may have reached a height of 12 feet when standing erect, and may have weighed 1200 pounds.

Hominidae (ho-mih′-nih-day) The family of modern and extinct human species, defined as the primates that are habitually bipedal. Members of this group are called "hominids."

Hominoidea (ho-min-oy'-dee-ah)   The superfamily that includes the large, tailless primates: apes and hominids, living and extinct.

Homo erectus (ho'-mow ee-wreck'-tuss)   A fossil hominid species dated from at least 1.8 mya to perhaps as late as 200,000 ya. First appearing in Africa, *H. erectus* was the first hominid species to expand beyond that continent. Fossils are found throughout Africa and Asia. There is abundant archaeological evidence and a few fossils indicating presence in Europe after 1 mya. Members of this species had an average brain size about two-thirds that of modern humans, made advances in stone tool technology, and late in their existence were able to control fire.

Homo ergaster (ho'-mow er-gas'-ter)   A proposed new species that includes the earliest *H. erectus* fossils from East Africa. These specimens are said by some experts to be different enough that they represent a separate species ancestral to both *H. erectus* and, later, *Homo sapiens*, but the idea is not widely accepted.

Homo habilis (ho'-mow ha'-bill-us)   A fossil hominid species dated from about 2.2 to 1.5 mya and found in East Africa. Fully bipedal and with an average brain size of 680 ml, *H. habilis* was the first confirmed hominid stone toolmaker. Because this was the first hominid with a brain larger than that of a chimpanzee and because of the association with stone tools, it is thought to be the earliest member of our genus, *Homo*.

Homo heidelbergensis (ho'-mow high-del-berg-en'-sis)   Early European hominids dated from at least 500,000 years ago to 200,000 years ago. Thought to be descended from the African hominid *Homo ergaster* by those who recognize that species.

Homo neanderthalensis (ho'-mow knee-an-dir-tall-en'-sis)   The name once applied to the Neandertals, indicating that they were a different species from *Homo sapiens*. In the past, this interpretation was based on an exaggeration of some of the differences between them and modern humans. At present, there is a debate as to whether or not Neandertals represent a separate species or are simply the European and Southwest Asian populations of **archaic** *Homo sapiens*. If they are indeed part of a distinct species, the name might be reinstituted. See *Homo sapiens neanderthalensis*.

Homo rudolfensis (ho'-mow rue-dolf-en'-sis)   Species name given by some authorities to certain specimens of *Homo habilis*, including the well-known skull ER 1470.

Homo sapiens (ho'-mow say'-pee-ens)   The taxonomic name for modern and some pre-modern (archaic) humans. There is some debate as to whether or not this name covers certain fossil forms. See *Homo sapiens*, **archaic** and *Homo sapiens*, **anatomically modern**.

Homo sapiens, **anatomically modern** (ho'-mow say'-pee-ens)   Humans with fully modern traits, who appeared sometime after 200,000 years ago in Africa and spread from there. The modern average human brain size is about 1400 ml, with a broad range of 1000 to 2200 ml for normal adults. It is now debated whether this group represents a separate species from **archaic** *Homo sapiens* or simply possesses modern traits.

Homo sapiens, **archaic** (ho'-mow say'-pee-ens)   Fossil hominids dated from 400,000 to about 35,000 years ago. Their average brain size of 1200 ml is only slightly less than modern humans, but they possess a number of primitive cranial features. The group is usually meant to include the Neandertals, who also had extremely robust postcranial skeletons, but some experts see that group as a separate species. See *Homo sapiens*, **anatomically modern** and *Homo neanderthalensis*.

Homo sapiens neanderthalensis (ho'-mow say'-pee-ens knee-an'-der-tall-en'-sis)   The name applied to the Neandertals, a human form dated from about 125,000 to about 35,000 years ago. They have been found in Europe and Southwest Asia. They have a mean brain size of 1500 ml and are generally more robust than modern humans. This name implies that they represent a subspecies of *Homo sapiens*. See *Homo neanderthalensis* for a different interpretation.

Homo sapiens sapiens (ho'-mow say'-pee-ens)   The same as *Homo sapiens*, **anatomically modern**.

Hylobatidae (high-low-bat'-ah-day)   The family that includes the gibbons and siamangs, the arboreal, so-called lesser apes of Southeast Asia. They are highly efficient brachiators.

Macaca (mah-cah'-cah)   A highly successful genus within family **Cercopithecidae** with representative species from North Africa to Europe to Japan.

Omomyidae (oh-mow-me'-ah-day)   A group of early primates that lived in the then-connected landmass of North America and Europe. Dated to more than 50 mya, they are thought to be ancestral to tarsiers and perhaps **Anthropoidea** as well.

Ouranopithecus (oo-ran'-oh-pith'-ah-cuss)   An ape form from Greece dated at 9 or 10 mya. With some hominidlike features, it is thought by some to be a member of the ape line that lead to the hominids.

Pan A genus within family **Pongidae** that includes the two chimpanzee species from Africa: *Pan troglodytes,* the common chimpanzee, and *Pan paniscus,* the bonobo or pygmy chimpanzee.

Papio (pah′-pee-oh) A genus within superfamily **Cercopithecoidea** (the Old World monkeys) comprised of the several species of baboons, large monkeys that live in social groups on the African savannas.

Paranthropus aethiopicus (par-an′-throw-pus ee-thee-o′-pih-cus) A hominid species from East Africa dated from 2.8 to 2.2 mya, the first of the so-called robust hominids, having large, rugged features associated with chewing. Its other features, including brain size, are so similar to members of genus *Australopithecus* that many authorities still include it in that genus. It is thought that the species was adapted to a diet of tough, gritty, hard vegetable foods. The most famous, and first, specimen is the "Black Skull."

Paranthropus boisei (par-an′-throw-pus boys′-ee-eye) A robust hominid of East Africa dated from 2.2 to 1 mya. It had large facial features associated with chewing, although less pronounced than in *P. aethiopicus.* The first specimen was "Zinjanthropus." Sometimes included in genus *Australopithecus.*

Paranthropus robustus (par-an′-throw-pus row-bus′-tus) A robust hominid of southern Africa dated from 2.2 to 1.5 mya. It is marked by robust chewing features, although less so than in either *P. aethiopicus* or *P. boisei.* The postcranial skeleton and the brain size remain similar to those of *Australopithecus.* It is sometimes included in that genus.

Pithecanthropus erectus (pith-ah-can′-throw-puss ee-wreck′-tus) Literally, the "upright ape-man," the original designation given to fossils found in Java ("Java Man") and China ("Peking Man") now labeled *Homo erectus.*

Platyrrhini (plat-ee-rhine′-eye) One of two infraorders of the suborder **Anthropoidea** (the other is suborder **Catarrhine,** the Old World monkeys, apes, and hominids). Platyrrhines include the New World monkeys. Members of this group can be differentiated from the catarrhines by their broad nose shape, greater number of premolar teeth, and, at least in several species, prehensile tails.

Pongidae (pon′-jih-day) The family of the so-called great apes, the orangutans of Southeast Asia and the gorillas, chimpanzees, and bonobos of Africa.

Primates (pry-mate′-ees) An order within class Mammalia consisting of large-brained, arboreal mammals with stereoscopic color vision and grasping hands (and sometimes feet). Includes prosimians, monkeys, apes, and hominids.

Prosimii (pro-sim′-ee-eye) One of two suborders of the order **Primates** (the other suborder is **Anthropoidea**). Prosimians are the more primitive of the two suborders; they retain features of some of the oldest primate fossils. Many lack color vision, are nocturnal, and have limited opposability of the thumb.

Sivapithecus (she′-vah-pith′-ah-cuss) The general group name of fossil ape forms from Africa, India, Pakistan, Turkey, Greece, Hungary, and China dated from 15 to 12 mya. Specifically, the genus thought to be ancestral to the orangutan.

Glossary of Terms

Terms in boldface type are defined elsewhere in the Glossary.

absolute dating   Any dating technique in which a specific age, year, or range of years can be assigned to an object or site. See **relative chronological sequence.**

Acheulian   A toolmaking tradition of *Homo erectus* in Europe and Africa. Includes hand axes, cleavers, and **flake tools.**

adaptation   The adjustment of an organism to a particular set of environmental conditions.

adapted   See **adaptation.**

Agricultural Revolution   See **Food-Producing Revolution.**

allele   A variant of a genetic **locus.** Most loci possess more than one allele, the different alleles conveying different instructions for the development of a certain **phenotype** (for example, blue eyes versus brown eyes and type O, A, or B blood).

allele frequency   The percentage of times a certain **allele** appears in a population relative to the other possible alleles at the same genetic **locus.**

amino acid   The chief component of proteins; the building block of all life.

analogy   In evolution, a trait that is similar in function in two or more species but that is unrelated evolutionarily. See **homology.**

anthropological linguistics   The anthropological study of language.

anthropology   The **holistic** and integrative study of people. Anthropology includes the study of human biology, human physical evolution, human cultural evolution, and human **adaptation.**

arboreal   **Adapted** to life in the trees.

archaeology   A branch of **anthropology** that focuses on cultural evolution through the study of the material remains of past societies.

Archaic   The time period in the New World that follows the **Paleo-Indian** period. The Archaic begins at the end of the **Pleistocene** and represents a period of cultural **adaptation** to the new post-glacial environment.

Arctic Small Tool Tradition   A stone tool tradition dating to about 4500 B.P. in the Arctic, characterized by small blades, less than 2.5 cm in length, used in cutting and carving, small **burins** for engraving bone and antler in the production of harpoons and sewing needles, small blades inset into bone and antler arrow and spear points, and even smaller microblades about 1 cm long set into handles and used for various tasks such as butchering and skinning animals and manufacturing watertight clothing from their skins.

artifact   Any object usually found at an archaeological site that was made by humans.

artificial selection   The process by which human beings choose those members of a plant or animal species that will live and reproduce and those that will not. The animals or plants selected are those that possess characteristics desirable to humans.

association   Objects found together in the same archaeological or geological stratum in proximity to one another are said to be in association.

Aurignacian   The stone tool technology associated with anatomically modern *Homo sapiens* in Europe beginning about 34,000 years ago. Includes long, narrow blade tools.

australopithecines   A small-brained **hominid** from 4.2 to 1 mya that represents the ancestors of all later **hominids** and several extinct hominid branches.

basicranium   The bones of the base of the skull.

biological anthropology   See **physical anthropology.**

biostratigraphy   The patterned appearance of plant and animal fossils in **strata.** The fossils of more ancient organisms are found in older, deeper strata, while those of more recent organisms are found in younger, generally higher layers.

bipedal   The ability to walk on two feet.

brachiate   The ability to swing through trees using arms and hands.

breeding population   A population within a species with some degree of genetic isolation from other populations of that species. See **deme.**

Bronze Age   The period in European prehistory when people began making bronze tools.

burin   A stone tool with a sharp, durable point, used in engraving bone, ivory, or antler.

carrying capacity   The number of organisms a given habitat or region can support.

catastrophist   An adherent to the hypothesis of catastrophism—that the world was produced through a series of catastrophic events, usually including Noah's flood. Compare to **uniformitarianism.**

central place   The geographic focal point of a political entity. A large city or ceremonial center with religious structures is often the central place of an ancient state or a chiefdom. Elites lived in central places.

Chavin   The artistic and iconographic style that appeared about 3000 ya and spread across groups that had been culturally separate and that lived in a series of river valleys in the western Andes in Peru. Chavin apparently set the stage for the development of larger, politically united entities in western South America.

Châtelperronian   A stone tool industry associated with late Neandertals in Europe. It appears to reflect an amalgam of the older Neandertal **Mousterian** industry and the **Aurignacian** of anatomically modern humans.

chiefdom   A level of sociopolitical integration more complex than the tribe but less so than the **state.** Chiefdoms are less rigidly structured than state societies and, without the formal structure of a government behind the office, a chief's power is less than that of a king or pharaoh.

chromosome   A strand of DNA in the nucleus of a cell that carries genetic information passed down to subsequent generations.

chronometric dating   A dating technique in which an actual age or range of years can be applied to archaeological objects or sites. Synonymous with **absolute dating.**

city-state   A large, politically complex entity, including a dense central population with surrounding villages owing allegiance to the city. Characteristic of the early civilization of Mesopotamia.

civilization   Used in this book for cultures with an agricultural surplus, social stratification, labor specialization, a formal government, rule by power, monumental construction projects, and a system of recordkeeping. Cultures evolved into early civilizations in a number of world areas from local **Neolithic** adaptations.

cline   A geographic continuum in the variation of a specific **phenotype.**

Clovis   A long, bifacially flaked stone spear point characterized by channels or flutes on both faces. Clovis points date to the period 11,700 to 11,000 years ago and are found throughout North America and parts of South America.

codominance   Used to describe the situation that occurs when neither allele of a **gene** pair is dominant and both are expressed in the organism.

codon   A section of the DNA molecule that codes for a particular **amino acid.**

comparative biology   The study of the similarities and differences among plants and animals.

comparative collection   An aggregation of modern specimens used in the identification of ancient remains found at archaeological or paleontological sites; for example, a comparative collection of seeds, wood types, or animal bones. An osteological comparative collection is a "bone library" useful not only in the identification of species but also the sex, age at death, and health status of the animal.

comparative osteology   Comparing the bones of different animal species.

competitive exclusion   The process by which one **species** outcompetes others for resources in a particular area.

core tool   A tool made by taking **flakes** off a stone nucleus.

creationist   One who believes that a supernatural power was directly or indirectly responsible for the origin of the universe, the earth, and all living things.

creation myth   A myth that explains the origin of the world and its inhabitants.

cultural anthropology   The branch of **anthropology** that focuses on cultural behavior. **Archaeology, ethnography,** and **anthropological linguistics** are included in cultural anthropology.

cultural evolution   Changes in cultural patterns through time.

cultural technique   A dating method based on cultural comparisons and the processes of culture change. A site may be dated based on the degree of similarity between the artifacts found there and those from other sites where absolute dates have been derived. Cultural dating techniques also include **seriation.**

culture   A nongenetic means of adaptation. Those things people invent or develop and then pass down, including political, social, technological, economic, and ideological systems.

deduction   A step in the scientific method. After developing a general explanation (a **hypothesis**) from specific observations through the process of **induction**, deduction is the step of suggesting those things that must be true (new data) if the hypothesis is valid.

deme   A genetically isolated population within a species; generally, the same as a breeding population and often physically distinguishable from other demes. See **breeding population, race, semispecies, subspecies.**

Denali Complex   A stone tool technology seen in the American Arctic consisting of **wedge-shaped cores,** microblades, bifacial knives, and **burins** and dated to about 10,000 years ago. Several features of the Denali Complex are reminiscent of elements of older complexes in northeast Asia, particularly that of Dyuktai Cave.

dendrochronology   A dating technique based on the unique, nonrepeating sequence of tree-ring widths.

deoxyribonucleic acid (DNA)   The molecule that contains the genetic code.

deviation amplification   The process by which a small change in one part of a cultural system results in larger changes in the rest of the culture, which then cause the original change to become increased. The development of agriculture and civilization reflect such processes.

diaphysis (plural *diaphyses*)   The shaft of a long bone— for example, femur, humerus, tibia.

differential reproduction   The process by which some individuals of a species are more successful than others at surviving, attracting mates, producing offspring, and hence passing down their characteristics. See **natural selection.**

diffusion   The geographic movement and sharing of cultural traits or ideas.

DNA hybridization   A method for establishing the biological distance between species based on the ability of strands of DNA from each species to bond to one another.

domesticate   To change, through **artificial selection** the wild form of a plant or animal to a form more useful to humans. The end product species is also called a domesticate.

dominance hierarchy   A social pattern seen in animal species in which certain individuals have preferential access to food, mates, and social activities.

dominant   Of a pair of **alleles,** the one that is expressed in the **heterozygous** condition.

egalitarian   Societies in which, within the same age–sex categories, all people are more or less equal in terms of wealth, social standing, and authority.

einkorn   A variety of wheat; *Tripsicum monococcum.* An important domesticate in the **Neolithic,** but not a significant agricultural crop today. (Compare to **emmer.**)

electron spin resonance (ESR) dating   A dating technique based on measuring the buildup of electrons in crystalline materials. Can be applied to sites from more than a few thousand to more than 10 million years old.

emmer   A variety of wheat; *Tripsicum turgidum.* An early domesticate of the **Neolithic** in southwest Asia and the source of cultivated wheat in the modern world. (Compare to **einkorn.**)

endocast   A natural or artificial cast or model of the interior of a fossil skull. In nature, loose material may fill a skull and harden, producing a model of the surface of the brain the skull housed. In the lab, latex or similar material can be poured into the skull or painted onto the interior surface, again producing a model of the surface of the brain.

endogamy   Marriages restricted to those within the same social group. Exogamy is marriage restricted to those outside the social group.

entoptic phenomena   Visual images that result from stimulation of the optic system during altered states of consciousness. Geometric designs in cave art of the **Upper Paleolithic** have been explained by some researchers as resulting from entoptic phenomena.

environmental determinism   The notion, popular in the nineteenth century, that the nature of the environment directly determines the technological level of a culture. Determinists assumed that more challenging environments produce more developed cultures.

enzyme   A **protein** in the body that causes and in part controls chemical processes.

epiphyseal union   The fusion during growth of the end of a long bone (**epiphysis**) to the shaft (**diaphysis**).

epiphysis   The end or cap of a long bone. Long bones have two epiphyses.

estrus   In many nonhuman mammals, the period during which a female is fertile; also, the signals indicating this condition to males of the species.

ethnoarchaeology   Conducting ethnographic research among a living people from the perspective of an archaeologist, focusing on the processes by which people's behavior becomes translated into the archaeological record.

ethnocentric   Judging another society's values in terms of one's own social values.

ethnography   A subfield within **cultural anthropology** that involves the intensive study of a human group. The ethnographer lives with a group of people, often for a number of years. Also applied to the written work produced by an ethnographer.

ethology   The study of the behavior of organisms under natural conditions.

evolution   Systematic change through time with reference to biological species and changes within cultural systems.

faunal analysis   The examination of animal remains from archaeological sites. Faunal analysis is helpful in the reconstruction of diet, seasonality, and subsistence technology.

feature   A nonportable element of a site, composed of **artifacts** or organic debris or both. Features reflect an activity or set of activities. Trash pits, fireplaces, graves, and tool-manufacturing stations are all examples of features.

field survey   The process whereby archaeological sites are discovered in the field. Surface walkovers, **test pits**, and aerial photography are important aspects of field survey.

fission   The division, or splitting up, of a **breeding population.**

flake   Stone fragment removed from a core. Flakes with sharp points or edges may be used as tools without modification or can be further shaped or sharpened for use.

flake tool   See **flake.**

flotation   A technique in which soil matrix and archaeological material is separated by the use of water. Some organic materials like seeds and charcoal will float and can be skimmed off the surface of standing water.

Food-Producing Revolution   The slow change, beginning after 12,000 ya, of a shift from **foraging** to food production among human groups, through the process of **domestication.** Also called **Agricultural Revolution.**

forager   See **hunter-gatherer.**

foramen magnum   The hole in the base of the skull through which the spinal cord emerges and around the outside of which the top vertebra articulates.

foraminifera   Microscopic marine organisms whose exoskeletons are used in the analysis of the oxygen isotope ratio in seawater. This ratio varies in proportion to the amount of the earth's water that is in land-based **glaciers.**

founder effect   Differences in an isolated population of a species caused by the characteristics of those individuals who randomly established the isolate.

gamete   The cells of sexual reproduction; for example, sperm and eggs.

gamete sampling   The form of **genetic drift** that operates when genes are passed to offspring in proportions that differ from those of the parental population.

gene   Generally, the portion of the DNA molecule that codes for a specific trait. **Locus** is now the preferred term.

gene flow   The exchange of genes among populations of a species through interbreeding.

gene pool   All **alleles** within a population.

genetic drift   The change in **allele frequencies** caused by random fluctuations within a population through time.

genetic engineering   Any intentional human manipulation of the mechanism of inheritance of some organism, especially of human beings.

genetic replacement hypothesis   A version of the replacement hypothesis for the evolution of anatomically modern *Homo sapiens*. In this view, modern humans evolved first in one place. By their migration and subsequent interbreeding with archaic humans with whom they came into contact, modern human genes replaced archaic ones. See **multiregional hypothesis** and **population replacement hypothesis.**

genetics   The study of the mechanism of inheritance and the physical results of that mechanism.

genome   The total genetic endowment of a species.

genotype   The **alleles** possessed by an organism.

glacial   See **glacial period.**

glacial period   Phases of the **Pleistocene Epoch** during which worldwide temperature dropped and substantial, long-term glacial expansion occurred. There have been as many as eighteen separate glacial periods during the last 1.6 million years, each lasting thousands of years. See **interglacial.**

glacier   A massive body of ice that, through a number of processes, can expand and move.

glume   The seed case in which an individual cereal grain is enclosed on the plant.

gradualism   The view in evolution that **speciation** is slow and steady with cumulative change. See **punctuated equilibrium.**

Gravettian   A toolmaking tradition of the Upper Paleolithic characterized by the production of small blades and denticulate knives. Dated from 27,000 to 21,000 B.P.

Greater Australia   Australia, New Guinea, and Tasmania. Another name for **Sahul.**

grooming   The practice among social primates in which one animal cleans the fur of another. Helps promote social cohesion.

Halafian   A **Neolithic** culture in Mesopotamia dating from 7500 to 6700 B.P. Halafian sites generally are small farming villages.

half-life   The amount of time it takes for half of a **radioactive isotope** to decay to a stable isotope.

hammerstone   A stone used to strike a stone core or nucleus in order either to shape the core into a tool or remove flakes, which can then serve as tools.

hand axe   A bifacial, all-purpose stone tool produced by *Homo erectus,* axelike in shape.

Hardy–Weinberg equilibrium   The formula that shows **genotypic** percentages within a population under hypothetical conditions of no evolutionary change.

Hassunan   A **Neolithic** culture in Mesopotamia dating from 8000 to 7200 B.P. Characterized by small farming villages where subsistence was based on the growing of wheat, barley, peas, and lentils. Hunting was still an important part of subsistence.

heterozygous   Possessing two different **alleles** in a gene pair.

holistic   A study that views its subject as a whole made up of integrated parts.

Holocene Epoch   The modern geological epoch, which began about 10,000 ya with the end of the **Pleistocene.**

hominid   Any member of the taxonomic family Hominidae. Modern humans and our ancestors; the bipedal primate.

hominid radiation   The expansion of the hominids out of Africa, where they initially evolved, into Asia beginning close to 2 mya and Europe after 1 mya.

homology   In evolution, a trait shared by two or more species through inheritance from a common ancestor. See **analogy.**

homozygous   Possessing two of the same **alleles** in a gene pair.

humerus (plural *humeri*)   The upper-arm bone.

hunter-gatherer   A society that relies on naturally occurring sources of food. Also called **forager.**

hyoid   A horseshoe-shaped bone in the front of the throat. Its form and position in fossil specimens may provide insights into the ability of members of a species to speak.

hypothesis   In the scientific method, a testable explanation of a phenomenon. See **theory.**

induction   A step in the **scientific method.** The process of developing a general explanation (called a **hypothesis**) from specific observations. See **deduction.**

inheritance of acquired characteristics   The incorrect idea that traits acquired by adaptation during an organism's lifetime could be passed to its offspring, once proposed as a mechanism for evolution.

in situ   In place. An **artifact,** organic remain, or **feature** that remains in its exact place of discovery is said to be in situ.

intelligence   The relative ability of an organism to take in, store, process, and utilize information from the environment.

interglacial   A long-term phase during the **Pleistocene** between glacial periods, when glacial ice receded and worldwide temperature increased.

interstadial   A short-term, relatively minor period of glacial retreat during longer phases of general glacial advance (**glacial periods**).

K/Ar dating (potassium/argon dating)   An **absolute dating** technique based on the decay of a **radioactive isotope** of potassium into argon. Often used to date volcanic rock that can be stratigraphically related to archaeological materials. The long **half-life** of the radioactive isotope of potassium renders the technique useful generally only for materials more than 100,000 years old. It is often applied to fossil hominid sites.

Laurasia   The former northern landmass made up of parts of present-day North America and Eurasia. Where primates first evolved 65 mya.

law of superposition   The stratigraphic law that the more recent layers are superimposed over the older ones.

legume   A large family of flowering plants that produce pods that contain seeds. Garden peas, snap beans, lima beans, lentils, and chick peas are all legumes domesticated during the **Neolithic.**

Levallois   A sophisticated and efficient tool technology involving striking uniform flakes from a prepared stone core. Began about 200,000 ya.

locus (plural, *loci*)   The location on a chromosome of the genetic code for a specific trait.

Lower Paleolithic   See **Paleolithic.**

Lower Pleistocene   The first part of the **Pleistocene Epoch** from 1.6 mya to 780,000 ya.

Lung-shan   The name given to the first fully agricultural people in China, dated to about 6000 ya.

macromutation   A change in a large number of genes or in a small number of important genes, with extensive physical results. See **mutation.**

Magdelanian   A late Paleolithic toolmaking culture in Europe dating from 16,000–11,000 B.P. Known from sites primarily in France and Spain, the Magdelanian material culture included finely made barbed harpoons, carved decorative objects, and cave paintings.

matrilocal   A type of society in which a married couple lives with the wife's family.

meiosis   The process of cell division in which **gametes** are produced, each with half the normal number of chromosomes for that species.

Mesolithic   The name given cultures in Europe at the end of the **Pleistocene** and before the **Food-Producing Revolution.** Adaptations of the Mesolithic usually reflect a change from those of the **Paleolithic** as plant and animal communities changed with the waning of the glaciers.

messenger ribonucleic acid (mRNA)   The form of ribonucleic acid that carries the genetic code out of the cell nucleus and into the cytoplasm where it is translated into proteins.

microblades   Small, usually extremely sharp, stone blades. Microblades were set into handles of bone, wood, antler, and so on.

midden   A pile of trash produced by the inhabitants of a settlement.

Middle Paleolithic   See **Paleolithic.**

Middle Pleistocene   The second phase of the **Pleistocene Epoch** from 780,000 to 200,000 ya.

Minoan   The earliest civilization in Europe. Centered on the island of Crete and beginning about 3900 ya, it appears to have been a city-state with Knossos as its capital.

mitochondrial DNA   Genetic material contained in the mitochondria of cells. Analysis of mitochondrial DNA (mtDNA) of modern humans has provided researchers with an estimate for the age of anatomically modern *Homo sapiens.*

mitosis   The process of cell division that produces exact copies of the original cell.

monogenic   A trait coded for by a single **locus.**

Mousterian   The **Middle Paleolithic** culture associated with the European Neandertals that included a unifacial flake tool technology.

Movius line   A geographic break between the manufacture of **hand axes** and that of simple stone chopping tools. Hand axes appear to the west of this line—located in eastern India—but not east of it.

multilinear   The accepted notion that different cultures pass through any one of a number of possible sequences of change.

multiregional hypothesis   The hypothesis that anatomically modern human beings evolved more or less independently in a number of different geographic areas. See **genetic replacement hypothesis** and **population replacement hypothesis.**

mutation   Any change in an organism's genetic material.

Mycenaean   The civilization in Greece that followed that of the Minoans and preceded that of the Greek city-states.

myth   A story, usually invoking the supernatural, to account for a society's origin and early history.

Natufian   The Late **Paleolithic**–Early **Neolithic** culture of Southwest Asia, dated from 12,000 to 10,000 ya.

natural selection   Evolution based on the relative reproductive success of individuals within a species, the degree of success determined by the individual's adaptive fitness. See **differential reproduction.**

Nenana Complex   Perhaps the oldest identified stone tool complex in Alaska, dating from 11,800 to 11,000 B.P. Predating the **Denali Complex,** Nenana includes bifacially flaked, unfluted spear points. Nenana bifaces are similar and perhaps related to tools made in eastern Russia about 14,000 years ago.

neocortex   The part of the brain of complex organisms responsible for memory and thought, in other words, for **intelligence.**

Neolithic   The "new stone age," now seen as the period characterized by **domestication** of plants and animals.

neoteny   Literally, "holding onto youth." The retention, in adults of one species of the juvenile features of an evolutionarily related species.

niche   The ecological address of an organism; the actual space inhabited by the organism as well as the organism's functional place in a community of organisms—where it lives as well as what it does to make a living.

notochord   A long cartilaginous rod that supports the body and protects the dorsal nerve. The evolutionary precursor of the vertebral column.

nuclear DNA   The genetic material contained in the nucleus of a cell. See **deoxyribonucleic acid.**

nuclear family   The family unit made up of parents and their offspring.

occipital   The bone of the rear of the skull. The occiput tends to be rounded and smooth in anatomically modern human beings, angled and rough in nonmodern hominids.

Oldowan   Tool technology associated with *Homo habilis* approximately 2.5 mya. Sharp-edged flakes were produced by striking a stone core.

Olmec   Dating to after about 3200 years ago in Mesoamerica, the Olmec peoples produced a number of large ceremonial centers with great earthworks, finely carved jade sculptures, and massive basalt carvings of human heads. The religious iconography of Olmec art seems to have served as a unifying element in ancient Mesoamerica.

opposability   The ability of the thumb to touch (oppose) the tips of the other digits.

paleoanthropologist   A **biological anthropologist** specializing in the study of human fossil remains.

paleoclimatologist   A specialist in ancient climatic conditions.

paleoethnography   The process of performing an **ethnography** of an archaeological culture; studying a people by excavating their material remains and attempting to reconstruct their lifestyle based on these remains.

paleofeces   Preserved fecal remains. Under the right circumstances, human feces can preserve for a long time period. Analysis of paleofeces can provide direct insights into ancient diet. Fossilized paleofeces are called coprolites.

Paleo-Indian   New World cultures, based on big-game hunting and characterized by fluted points, present from after 12,000 to 10,000 ya.

Paleolithic   The "old stone age," a time in which our most abundant archaeological artifactual evidence is stone tools. The Lower Paleolithic includes the stone tool industries of *Homo habilis* and *Homo erectus* from 2.5 mya to 250,000 ya. The Middle Paleolithic includes the stone tool industries of the archaic *Homo sapiens* from about 250,000 to 40,000 ya. The Upper Paleolithic includes the stone tool industries of anatomically modern *Homo sapiens* from about 40,000 to 10,000 ya.

paleopathology   The study of disease and nutritional deficiency in prehistoric populations, usually with reference to the study of their skeletons.

palynology   The identification of plants through the remains of their pollen grains.

Pangea   The supercontinent that included parts of all present-day landmasses, which began to break up about 138 mya.

parent material   The term used to indicate the source material of a particular soil. The parent material is often local bedrock that, through various processes of erosion, becomes soil.

parietals   The bones of the sides and top of the skull.

particulate   In the study of heredity, the idea that traits are controlled separately by individual particles rather than all together by a single agent. The genetic theory of heredity.

patrilocal   A type of society in which a married couple lives with the husband's family.

Peiligang   The earliest Neolithic culture in north China with well-established farming villages dated to 8500 to 7000 years ago. Cultigens included foxtail millet, broom-corn millet, and Chinese cabbage, but not rice. Domesticated animals include pig, dog, and chicken.

petrographic analysis   Examination of the morphology of a lithic source by the analysis of thin slices of rock. Can be used to determine the source of raw materials used by past people.

phalanges   Bones of the fingers and toes.

phenotype   Any physical or chemical trait that can be observed or measured. The expression of the genetic code.

physical anthropology   The branch of anthropology that focuses on humans as a biological species.

plate tectonics   The movement of the plates of the earth, caused by their interaction with the molten rock of the earth's interior. The cause of continental drifting.

Pleistocene Epoch   The geological time period, from about 1.6 mya to 10,000 ya, characterized by a series of glacial advances and retreats.

Pliocene Epoch   The geological time period dated from 5 million to 1.6 million years ago, during which the first **hominids** appeared in Africa.

point mutation   The **mutation** of a single **codon.**

polygenic   A trait coded for by more than one **locus.**

polymorphism   A trait showing variation within a **species** that is the result of genetic variation.

population   Any reproductive unit within a species; may be the species itself.

population replacement hypothesis   A version of the replacement hypothesis for the evolution of anatomically modern *Homo sapiens*. In this view, modern humans evolved first in one place and migrated throughout the rest of the world, where they physically replaced indigenous archaic human groups, which became extinct. There was no genetic admixture between the modern and archaic humans who came into contact. See **genetic replacement hypothesis** and **multiregional hypothesis.**

postnatal dependency   The period after birth when a young animal is dependent on adults for survival, which is relatively long among humans.

postorbital constriction   A narrowing of the skull behind the eyes, as viewed from above.

potassium/argon dating   See **K/Ar dating.**

prehensile   Grasping, with particular reference to the hands and feet of primates. The tails of a few New World monkeys are also prehensile.

primate   A large-brained, arboreal mammal with stereoscopic color vision and grasping hands and (often) feet.

primatologist   An anthropologist who studies **primates.**

prognathism   A protrusion of the lower portion of the face.

progressive   The now-rejected idea that evolution is always producing organisms that are better by current cultural standards.

prosimian   A member of the group of primates with the most primitive features, that is, that most resemble the earliest primates.

protein   One of a family of molecules that are the main constituent of cells and that carry out cellular functions. See **amino acid.**

protein synthesis   The process by which the genetic code puts together **proteins** in the cell.

provenience   The precise, measured location of archaeological artifacts.

punctuated equilibrium   The evolutionary theory that species remain stable for most of their history and that new species arise fairly suddenly as the result of mutations. See **gradualism; macromutation.**

quadrupedal   The ability to walk on four legs.

race   In biology, the same as **semispecies** or **subspecies.**

rachis   The area of attachment between seeds and other seeds or between seeds and other parts of a plant. A brittle rachis is an adaptive advantage in nature but selected against by humans in **artificial selection.**

radioactive isotope   An unstable form of an element that decays to a stable form, the rate of which can be used to date archaeological evidence.

radiocarbon dating   A **radiometric dating** technique using the decay rate of a **radioactive isotope** of carbon found in organic remains.

radiometric dating   A dating technique that uses the known rate of decay of radioactive elements found in the item to be dated.

random sample   A technique of archaeological survey in which certain areas within a region are randomly selected to test for the presence of sites in an attempt to obtain a representative selection of sites in the region.

rank societies   Nonegalitarian societies with a few sociopolitical levels filled by a relatively small number of people.

recessive   Of an **allele** pair, the one that is not expressed when combined in the heterozygous state with a dominant allele. See **dominant.**

recombination   The reconstitution of allele pairs at fertilization by the joining of the single alleles created in the process of producing **gametes.**

relative chronological sequence   A sequence of sites, events, or artifacts arranged in the relationship of older to younger. See **absolute dating** and **chronometric dating.**

remote sensing   A procedure in archaeological site survey in which sites are searched for and examined, once discovered, through noninvasive techniques, that is, without moving any soil.

replication   In experimental archaeology, facsimiles of archaeological specimens are produced and used in order to analyze how past peoples manufactured and utilized their **artifacts** and **features.**

repoussé   A method of decorating thin metal, including gold, in which the pattern is beaten up from the underside.

Sahul   The combined landmass of New Guinea, Tasmania, and Australia proper formed during periods of diminished sea level—the glacial maxima of the **Pleistocene.** Also called **Greater Australia.**

Samarran   A **Neolithic** culture of southern Mesopotamia. Samarran sites are located on the floodplain of the Tigris and Euphrates Rivers and date to less than 7500 years ago. There is evidence of communal works including the construction of irrigation canals, fortification walls, and communal grain storage structures.

savanna   A tropical grassland with trees scattered throughout. It is probably on the savanna that the hominid adaptation of bipedal locomotion first became adaptively significant.

scapula (plural *scapulae*)   The shoulder blade.

scavenge   Eating the remains of animals killed by other carnivores or that have died naturally.

science   The method of inquiry that attempts to explain phenomena through observation and the development and testing of hypotheses.

scientific creationism   The belief that scientific evidence exists that supports the religious claim that the universe is the product of divine creation.

scientific method   The process by which phenomena are explained through observation and the development and testing of **hypotheses.**

sedentary   A human settlement pattern in which people largely stay in one place or settlement year-round, although some members of the population may still be mobile in the search for food and raw materials.

segregation   The breaking up of **allele** pairs during the production of gametes. See **recombination.**

semispecies   Populations within a **species** that are isolated from one another but have not yet become truly different species. See **breeding population; deme; subspecies; race.**

seriation   A process of establishing a **relative chronological sequence** based on the statistical pattern of replacement of styles of a type of artifact.

settlement pattern   The distribution of archaeological sites and the analysis of their functions in relation to one another and to features of the environment.

sexual dimorphism   The differential physical appearance of the sexes of a species.

sexual selection   The form of selection in which mating partners are actively, rather than randomly, chosen by individuals within a population based on such things as appearance, presence of a nest site, and successful competition with other potential mates.

site   Any place that contains evidence of a past human presence.

social stratification   The presence of acknowledged differences in social status, political influence, and wealth among the people within a society.

Solutrean   An Upper **Paleolithic** culture of France and Spain, dating to 21,000–16,000 ya, that included the manufacture of finely made, leaf-shaped, bifacial spear points.

spatial context   The location and associations of an **artifact,** ecofact, or **feature.** Precisely where and with what something is found can provide information concerning how the object was made, used, or discarded.

speciation   The evolution of new species from existing species. See **species.**

species   A group of organisms that can produce fertile offspring among themselves but not with any other group. A closed genetic population, usually physically distinguishable from other populations and with a unique **gene pool.**

stadial   A short-term period of extreme cold and rapid glacial advance during a longer-term period of general, slow glacial expansion or retreat.

state   Class societies, often rigidly stratified into social levels, with a ruling class controlling the populace not by consensus but by coercion and force. The rulers in a state society have the power to levy and collect taxes, to establish and enforce laws, and to conscript people to do the work of the state.

stereoscopic vision   The ability to see in three dimensions; depth perception.

strata (singular, *stratum*)   Layers; here, distinct and distinguishable layers of rock and soil.

stratigraphy   The arrangement of soil in layers.

subspecies   Physically distinguishable populations within a **species.** A synonym for race. See **deme; semispecies; race.**

Sunda   The combined landmass of the modern islands of Java, Sumatra, Bali, and Borneo plus Southeast Asia, which joined during periods of glacial maxima and attendant lowered sea level during the **Pleistocene.**

suture   The line of contact between the bones that make up the skull, analysis of which can be used to provide an estimate for the age at death of an individual.

symbiosis   A close, prolonged relationship between two or more different organisms of different species that may be, but is not necessarily, beneficial to members of the different species.

taphonomy   The analysis of how organisms become part of the archaeological or paleontological record.

taxonomy   A systematic classification based on similarities and differences among the things being classified.

teosinte   Called "God's corn" by the Aztecs, the plant that is the wild ancestor for domesticated maize.

test boring   See **test pit.**

test pit   An exploratory, usually small, excavation made to establish the presence or absence of an archaeological site.

theory   A hypothesis that has been tested repeatedly and has been well supported by evidence and experimental testing is elevated to the status of theory.

torus   A continuous ridge of bone.

trace element analysis   A process in which the geographic source of a raw material can be determined through the analysis of small or trace amounts of impurities.

transect   A line of systematically located test pits.

transfer ribonucleic acid (tRNA)   The form of ribonucleic acid that lines up **amino acids** in their proper sequence along the **messenger RNA** to make proteins.

trephining   Cutting a hole in the skull.

tundra   A treeless expanse with low-growing vegetation and permanently frozen ground. Usually located in the Arctic, but during the **Pleistocene,** tundra conditions were found in the vicinity of **glaciers** in regions far to the south.

Ubaid   A site that lends its name to the culture of southern Mesopotamia at 6300 B.P. Irrigation canals constructed by the Ubaid people made agriculture possible and larger settlements developed on the Mesopotamian floodplain at this time. Evidence of the growing power of the religious elite is seen at these sites, with wealth becoming concentrated in the temples.

uniformitarianism   The concept that biological and geological processes that affected the earth in the past are still in operation today, and vice-versa. Compare to **catastrophist.**

unilinear   The now-discredited notion that all cultures pass through the same sequence of change.

Upper Paleolithic   See **Paleolithic.**

Upper Pleistocene   The final phase of the **Pleistocene Epoch** from 200,000 to 10,000 ya.

Uruk   The earliest city in Mesopotamia and, almost certainly, the world. It dates to about 5800 ya.

Venus figurines   Carved figures in stone, ivory, antler, and clay that depict women, often, but not always, with exaggerated secondary sexual characteristics. Among the first sculptures produced by humanity, the oldest date to 32,000 ya.

wear pattern   The mark left on stone tools as a result of their use. Such marks include polish, striations, chipping, and scarring. Analysis of wear patterns can provide information concerning how a tool was used and on what raw material.

wedge-shaped cores   Cores shaped like wedges from which blades are struck, found in sites in Siberia dating to after 20,000 years ago and as part of the **Denali Complex** in the American Arctic.

Yang-shao   The early **Neolithic** culture of China, dated to about 8000 ya.

ziggurat   Large mud brick structures built in Mesopotamia, among the earliest examples of monumental architectures in the world's earliest civilization.

zygote   A fertilized egg before cell division begins.

Bibliography

Adams, R. E. W. 1991. *Prehistoric Mesoamerica.* Norman: University of Oklahoma.

Adams, R. McC. and H. Nissen. 1972. *The Uruk Countryside.* Chicago: University of Chicago Press.

Adovasio, J. M., J. Donahue, K. Cushman, R. C. Carlisle, R. Stuckenrath, J. D. Gunn, and W. C. Johnson. 1983. Evidence from Meadowcroft Rockshelter. In *Early Man in the New World,* ed. R. Shutler, Jr., pp. 163–89. Beverly Hills, Calif.: Sage.

Aiello, L. C. 1993. The fossil evidence for modern human origins in Africa: A revised view. *American Anthropologist* 95: 73–96.

Allchin, B. and R. Allchin. 1982. *The Rise of Civilization in India and Pakistan.* Cambridge, Eng.: Cambridge University Press.

Allsworth-Jones, P. 1990. The Szeletian and the stratigraphic succession in central Europe and adjacent areas: Main trends, recent results and problems for resolution. In *The Emergence of Modern Humans: An Archaeological Perspective,* ed. P. Mellars, pp. 160–242. Ithaca, N.Y.: Cornell University Press.

Alva, W. and C. B. Donnan. 1993. *Royal Tombs of Sipan.* Los Angeles: Fowler Museum of Culture History.

Alva, W. and C. B. Donnan. 1994. Tales from a Peruvian crypt. *Natural History* 103(5): 26–34.

Anderson, E. 1952. *Plants, Life and Man.* Boston: Little, Brown.

———. 1956. Man as a maker of new plants and new plant communities. In *Man's Role in Changing the Face of the Earth,* Vol. 2, ed. W. L. Thomas, Jr., pp. 767–77. Chicago: University of Chicago Press.

Appleman, P. (ed.) 1970. *Darwin.* New York: Norton.

Arensburg, B., L. A. Schepartz, A. M. Tiller, B. Vandermeersch, and Y. Rak. 1990. A reappraisal of the anatomical basis for speech in Middle Paleolithic hominids. *American Journal of Physical Anthropology* 83: 137–46.

Arsuaga, J.-L., I. Martinez, A. Garcia, J.-M. Carretero, and E. Carbonell. 1993. Three new human skulls from the Sima de los Huesos Middle Pleistocene site in Sierra de Atapuerca, Spain. *Nature* 362: 534–37.

Asimov, I. 1969. *Asimov's Guide to the Bible.* New York: Avenel Books.

Attenborough, D. 1979. *Life on Earth.* Boston: Little, Brown.

Bahn, P. G. 1994. *Homo erectus* in Europe. *Archaeology* 47(6): 25.

———. 1996. Treasure of the Sierra Atapuerca. *Archaeology* 49(1) : 45–48.

Bailey, G. N. 1978. Shell middens as indicators of postglacial economies: A territorial perspective. In *The Early Postglacial Settlement of Northern Europe: An Ecological Perspective,* ed. P. Mellars, pp. 37–63. Pittsburgh: University of Pittsburgh Press.

Barbetti, M. and H. Allen. 1972. Prehistoric man at Lake Mungo, Australia, by 32,000 years B.P. *Nature* 240: 46–48.

Barinaga, M. 1992. "African Eve" backers beat a retreat. *Science* 255: 686–87.

Bartstra, G. J., S. Soegondho, and A. V. D. Wijk. 1988. Ngandong man: Age and artifacts. *Journal of Human Evolution* 17: 325–37.

Bass, W. 1971. *Human Osteology: A Laboratory and Field Manual of the Human Skeleton.* Columbia: Missouri Archaeological Society.

Beadle, G. 1977. The origin of *Zea Mays.* In *Origins of Agriculture,* ed. C. A. Reed, pp. 615–36. The Hague: Mouton.

Beaumont, P., H. deVilliers, and J. C. Vogel. 1978. Modern man in sub-Saharan Africa prior to 49,000 years B.P.: A review and evaluation with particular reference to Border Cave. *South African Journal of Science* 74: 409–19.

Bednarik, R. G. 1993. Oldest dated rock art in the world. *International Newsletter on Rock Art* 4: 5–6.

Begley, S. and F. Gleizes. 1989. My grandad, Neandertal? *Newsweek,* October 16, pp. 70–71.

Belfer-Cohen, A. and N. Goren-Inbar. 1994. Cognition and communication in the Levantine Lower Paleolithic. *World Archaeology* 26: 144–157.

Ben-Itzhak, S., P. Smith, and R. A. Bloom. 1988. Radiographic study of the humerus in Neandertals and *Homo sapiens sapiens. American Journal of Physical Anthropology* 77: 231–42.

Berreman, G. D. 1991. The incredible "Tasaday": Deconstructing the myth of a "stone-age" people. *Cultural Survival Quarterly* 51(1): 3–45.

Binford, L. 1968. Post-Pleistocene adaptations. In *New Perspectives in Archaeology,* eds. L. Binford and S. Binford, pp. 313–41. Chicago: Aldine.

———. 1978. *Nunamiut Ethnoarchaeology.* New York: Academic Press.

———. 1981. *Bones: Ancient Men and Modern Myths.* New York: Academic Press.

———. 1984. *Faunal Remains from Klasies River Mouth.* New York: Academic Press.

———. 1985. Ancestral life ways: The faunal record. *Anthroquest* 32: 1, 15–20.

Binford, L. and S. Binford. 1966. A preliminary analysis of functional variability in the Mousterian of Levallois facies. *American Anthropologist* 68: 239–95.

Binford, L. and K. Chuan. 1985. Taphonomy at a distance: Zhoukoudian, "The Cave Home of Beijing Man." *Current Anthropology* 26: 413–43.

Binford, L. and N. M. Stone. 1986. Zhoukoudian: A closer look. *Current Anthropology* 27: 453–76.

Binford, S. 1968. Variability and change in the Near Eastern Mousterian of Levallois facies. In *New Perspectives in Archaeology,* eds. L. Binford and S. Binford, pp. 49–60. Chicago: Aldine.

Birdsell, J. H. 1977. The recalibration of a paradigm for the first peopling of Greater Australia. In *Sunda and Sahul: Prehistoric Studies in Southeast Asia, Melanesia, and Australia,* eds. J. Allen, J. Golson, and R. Jones, pp. 113–67. New York: Academic Press.

Bischoff, J. L., N. Soler, J. Maroto, and R. Julià. 1989. Abrupt Mousterian/Aurignacian boundary at c. 40 ka bp: Accelerator 14C dates from l'Arbreda Cave (Catalunya, Spain). *Journal of Archaeological Science* 16: 563–76.

Blinderman, C. 1986. *The Piltdown Inquest.* Buffalo: Prometheus Books.

Boaz, N. T. 1988. Status of *Australopithecus afarensis. Yearbook of Physical Anthropology* 31: 85–113.

Boëda, E., J. Connan, D. Dessort, S. Muhesen, N. Mercier, H. Valladas, and N. Tisnérat. 1996. Bitumen as a hafting material on Middle Paleolithic artefacts. *Nature* 380: 336–38.

Boesch, C. and H. Boesch-Achermann. 1991. Dim forest, bright chimps. *Natural History* 100(3): 50–57.

Bonnichsen, R. and K. L. Turnmire. (eds.) 1991. *Clovis: Origins and Adaptations.* Corvallis, Ore.: Center for the Study of the First Americans.

Bordes, F. 1972. *A Tale of Two Caves.* New York: Harper & Row.

Boserup, E. 1965. *The Conditions of Agricultural Growth: The Economics of Agrarian Change Under Population Pressure.* Chicago: Aldine.

Boule, M. and H. V. Vallois. 1923. *Fossil Men.* 1957 ed. New York: Dryden Press.

Bouyssonie, A., J. Bouyssonie, and L. Bardon. 1908. Découverte d'un squelette humain mousterian à la Bouffia de la Chapelles-aux-Saints (Correze). *L'Anthropologie* 19: 513–18.

Bowdler, S. 1977. The coastal colonisation of Australia. In *Sunda and Sahul: Prehistoric Studies in Southeast Asia, Melanesia, and Australia,* eds. J. Allen, J. Golson, and R. Jones, pp. 205–46. New York: Academic Press.

———. 1990. Peopling Australasia: The "Coastal Colonization" hypothesis re-examined. In *The Emergence of Modern Humans: An Archaeological Perspective,* ed. P. Mellars, pp. 327–43. Ithaca, N.Y.: Cornell University Press.

Bowen, D. Q. 1979. Quarternary correlations. *Nature* 277: 171–72.

Bower, B. 1987a. Uncovering life by an ancient lake. *Science News* 131: 264.

———. 1987b. Stone age site gets pushed back in time. *Science News* 132: 199.

———. 1987c. Skeletal aging of New World settlers. *Science News* 133: 215.

———. 1989a. Ritual clues flow from prehistoric blood. *Science News* 136: 405.

———. 1989b. Stone blades yield early cultivation clues. *Science News* 135: 101.

———. 1989c. Talk of ages. *Science News* 136: 24–26.

———. 1990. Civilization and its discontents. *Science News* 137: 136–39.

———. 1995a. Fossil hints at hominids' European stall. *Science News* 147: 85.

———. 1995b. Human genetic origins go nuclear. *Science News* 148: 52.

Bowlby, J. 1990. *Charles Darwin: A New Life.* New York: Norton.

Bowler, J. M., R. Jones, H. Allen, and A. G. Thorne. 1970. Pleistocene human remains from Australia: A living site and human cremation from Lake Mungo, western New South Wales. *World Archaeology* 2: 39–60.

Bradley, R. S. 1985. *Quarternary Paleoclimatology: Methods of Paleoclimatological Reconstruction.* Boston: Allen and Unwin.

Braidwood, R. 1960. The agricultural revolution. *Scientific American* 203(3): 130–48.

———. 1975. *Prehistoric Men.* Glenview, Ill.: Scott, Foresman.

Bräuer, G. 1984. A craniological approach to the origin of anatomically modern *Homo sapiens.* In *The Origins of Modern Humans: A World Survey of the Fossil Evidence,* eds. F. H. Smith and F. Spencer, pp. 327–410. New York: Liss.

———. 1992. Africa's place in the evolution of *Homo sapiens.* In *Continuity or Replacement: Controversies in* Homo sapiens *Evolution,* eds. G. Bräuer and F. Smith, pp. 83–98. Rotterdam: Balkema.

Bräuer, G., H. J. Deacon, and F. Zipfel. 1992. Comments on the new maxillary finds from Klasies River Mouth, South Africa. *Journal of Human Evolution* 23: 419–22.

Breuil, H. 1952. *Four Hundred Centuries of Cave Art.* Montignac, France: Centre D'études et de Documentation Prehistorique.

Brice, W. R. 1982. Bishop Ussher, John Lightfoot, and the age of creation. *Journal of Geological Education* 30: 18–24.

Bridges, P. S. 1995. Skeletal biology and behavior of ancient humans. *Evolutionary Anthropology* 4(4): 112–20.

Brown, F., J. Harris, R. Leakey, and A. Walker. 1985. Early *Homo erectus* skeleton from West Lake Turkana. *Nature* 316: 788–92.

Bruhns, K. O. 1994. *Ancient South America.* Cambridge, Eng.: Cambridge University Press.

Burger, R. L. 1988. Unity and heterogeneity within the Chavin Horizon. In *Peruvian Prehistory,* ed. R. W. Keating, pp. 99–144. Cambridge, Eng.: Cambridge University Press.

Burger, R. L. 1992. *Chavin and the Origins of Andean Civilization.* New York: Thames and Hudson.

Buttrick, G. A. (ed.) 1952. *Interpreter's Bible.* New York: Abingdon Press.

Butzer, K. 1971. *Environmental Archaeology: An Ecological Approach to Prehistory.* New York: Aldine-Atherton.

———. 1982. *Archaeology as Human Ecology.* Cambridge, Eng.: Cambridge University Press.

Byrne, R. W. and J. M. Byrne. 1988. Leopard killers of Mahale. *Natural History* 97(3): 22–26.

Calder, N. 1983. *Timescale.* New York: Viking Press.

Callen, E. O. 1967. Analysis of the Tehuacán coprolites. In *The Prehistory of the Tehuacán Valley: Volume One—Environment and Subsistence,* ed. D. Byers, pp. 261–89. Austin: University of Texas Press.

Cann, R. L. 1992. A mitochondrial perspective on replacement or continuity in human evolution. In *Continuity or Replacement: Controversies in* Homo sapiens *Evolution,* eds. G. Bräuer and F. Smith, pp. 65–73. Rotterdam: Balkema.

Cann, R. L., M. Stoneking, and A. C. Wilson. 1987. Mitochondrial DNA and human evolution. *Nature* 325: 31–36.

Cann, R., O. Richards, and J. K. Lum. 1994. Mitochondrial DNA and human evolution: Our one lucky mother. In *Origins of Anatomically Modern Humans,* eds. M. H. Nitecki and D. V. Nitecki, pp. 135–48. New York: Plenum.

Carbonell, E., J. M. B. de Castro, J. L. Arsuaga, J. C. Díaz, A. Rosas, G. Cuenca-Bescós, R. Sala, M. Mosquera, and X. P. Rodriguez. 1995. Lower Pleistocene hominids and artifacts from Atapuerca-TD6 (Spain). *Science* 269: 826–30.

Carniero, R. 1970. A theory of the origin of the state. *Science* 169: 733–38.

Castleden, R. 1990. *The Knossos Labyrinth.* London: Routledge.

Cavalli-Sforza, L. L. 1991. Genes, peoples and languages. *Scientific American* 265(5): 104–10.

Cavallo, J. A. 1990. Cat in the human cradle. *Natural History* 99(2): 53–60.

Chagnon, N. 1977. *Yanomamö: The Fierce People,* 2nd ed. New York: Holt, Rinehart & Winston.

Chang, K. C. 1968. *The Archaeology of Ancient China.* New Haven, Conn.: Yale University Press.

Chang, K. C. 1986. *The Archaeology of Ancient China.* 2nd ed. New Haven, Conn.: Yale University Press.

Chapman, J., and G. D. Crites. 1987. Evidence for early maize (*Zea mays*) from Icehouse Bottom Site, Tennessee. *American Antiquity* 52: 318–29.

Chard, C. 1974. *Northeast Asia in Prehistory*. Madison: University of Wisconsin Press.

Chase, P. and H. Dibble. 1987. Middle Paleolithic symbolism: A review of current evidence and interpretations. *Journal of Anthropological Archaeology* 6: 263–96.

Chauvet, J.-M. 1996. *Dawn of Art: The Chauvet Cave*. New York: Abrams.

Chen T., Q. Yang, and E. Wu. 1994. Antiquity of *Homo sapiens* in China. *Nature* 368: 55–56.

Cherry, J. F. 1987. Island origins: The early prehistoric Cyclades. In *Origins: The Roots of European Civilisation*, ed. B. Cunliffe, pp. 16–29. Chicago: Dorsey Press.

Childe, V. G. 1942. *What Happened in History*. Baltimore: Pelican Books.

———. 1951. *Man Makes Himself*. New York: Mentor Books.

———. 1953. *New Light on the Most Ancient East*. New York: Norton.

Churchill, S. and E. Trinkaus. 1990. Neandertal scapular glenoid morphology. *American Journal of Physical Anthropology* 83: 147–60.

Cinque-Mars, J. 1978. Bluefish Cave I: A Late Pleistocene eastern Beringian cave deposit in the northern Yukon. *Canadian Journal of Anthropology* 3: 1–32.

Clark, J. D. 1976. Prehistoric population pressures favoring plant domestication in Africa. In *Origins of African Plant Domestication*, eds. J. R. Harlan, J. M. J. De Wet, and A. B. L. Stemler, pp. 67–106. The Hague: Mouton.

Clark, G. 1971. *Excavation at Star Carr*. Cambridge, Eng.: Cambridge University Press.

———. 1980. *Mesolithic Prelude*. Edinburgh: University of Edinburgh Press.

Clarke, D. 1978. *Analytical Archaeology*. New York: Columbia University Press.

Clottes, J. 1995. Rhinos and lions and bears (Oh, My!). *Natural History* 104(5): 30–35.

Coe, M. 1968. *America's First Civilization*. New York: Van Nostrand.

Cohen, M. 1977. *The Food Crisis in Prehistory*. New Haven, Conn.: Yale University Press.

Coltorti, M., M. Cremaschi, M. C. Delitala, D. Esu, M. Fornaseri, A. McPherron, M. Nicoletti, R. van Otterloo, C. Peretto, B. Sala, V. Schmidt, and J. Sevink. 1982. Reversed magnetic polarity in an early Lower Paleolithic site in central Italy. *Nature* 300: 173–76.

Conkey, M. 1978. Style and information in cultural evolution: Toward a predictive model for the Paleolithic. In *Social Archaeology: Beyond Subsistence and Dating*, eds. C. Redman, M. J. Berman, E. V. Curtin, W. T. Langhorne, N. M. Versaggi, and J. C. Wanser, pp. 61–85. New York: Academic Press.

———. 1980. The identification of prehistoric hunter-gatherer aggregation sites: The case of Altamira. *Current Anthropology* 21: 609–39.

———. 1981. A century of Paleolithic cave art. *Archaeology* 34(4): 20–28.

———. 1983. On the origins of Paleolithic art: A review and some critical thoughts. In *Mousterian Legacy*, ed. E. Trinkaus, pp. 201–27. Oxford, Eng.: British Archaeological Reports, International Series, 164.

Conklin, W. J. and M. E. Moseley. 1988. The patterns of art and power in the Early Intermediate period. In *Peruvian Prehistory*, ed. R. W. Keatinge, pp. 145–63. Cambridge, Eng.: Cambridge University Press.

Connah, G. 1987. *African Civilizations*. Cambridge, Eng.: Cambridge University Press.

Constable, G. and the Editors of Time-Life. 1973. *The Neanderthals*. New York: Time-Life Books.

Cook, J., C. B. Stringer, A. P. Current, H. P. Schwarcz, and A. G. Wintle. 1982. A review of the chronology of the European Middle Pleistocene hominid record. *Yearbook of Physical Anthropology* 25: 19–65.

Coon, C. S. 1962. *The Origin of Races*. New York: Knopf.

Coppens, Y. 1994. East side story: The origin of humankind. *Scientific American* 270: 88–95.

Cowan, C. W. and P. J. Watson. (eds.) 1992. *The Origins of Agriculture: An International Perspective*. Washington, D.C.: Smithsonian Institution Press.

Cowen, R. 1995. *History of Life*, 2nd ed. Boston: Blackwell Scientific Publications.

Crawford, G. W. 1992. Prehistoric plant domestication in East Asia. In *The Origins of Agriculture: An International Perspective*, eds. C. W. Cowan and P. J. Watson, pp. 7–38. Washington, D.C.: Smithsonian Institution Press.

Crawford, H. 1991. *Sumer and the Sumerians*. Cambridge, Eng.: Cambridge University Press.

Crelin, E. S. 1987. *The Human Vocal Tract: Anatomy, Function, Development, and Evolution*. New York: Vantage Press.

Cronin, J. E., N. T. Boaz, C. B. Stringer, and Y. Rak. 1981. Tempo and mode in hominid evolution. *Nature* 292: 113–22.

Dahlberg, F. 1981. *Woman the Gatherer*. New Haven, Conn.: Yale University Press.

Darwin, C. R. 1898. *On the Origin of Species by Means of Natural Selection*, 6th ed., 1872. New York: Appleton.

Davern, C. F. (ed.) 1981. *Genetics: Readings from Scientific American*. San Francisco: Freeman.

Day, M. H. 1971. Postcranial remains of *Homo erectus* from bed IV Olduvai Gorge, Tanzania. *Nature* 232: 283–87.

———. 1988. *Guide to Fossil Man,* 4th ed. Chicago: University of Chicago Press.

Deacon, H. J., and R. Shuurman. 1992. The origins of modern people: The evidence from Klasies River. In *Continuity or Replacement: Controversies in* Homo sapiens *Evolution,* eds. G. Bräuer and F. Smith, pp. 121–30. Rotterdam: Balkema.

Dean, M. C., C. B. Stringer, and T. G. Bromage. 1986. Age at death of the Neandertal child from Devil's Tower, Gibraltar and the implications for students of general growth and development in Neandertals. *American Journal of Physical Anthropology* 70: 301–9.

De Bonis, L. and G. D. Koufos. 1994. Our ancestor's ancestor: Ouranopithecus is a Greek link in human ancestry. *Evolutionary Anthropology* 3(3): 75–83.

Deetz, J. 1965. *The Dynamics of Stylistic Change in Arikara Ceramics.* Urbana: University of Illinois Series in Anthropology, No. 4.

de Lumley, H. 1969. A Paleolithic camp at Nice. *Scientific American* 220(5): 42–50.

———. 1975. Cultural evolution in France in its Paleolithic setting during the Middle Pleistocene. In *After the Australopithecines: Stratigraphy, Ecology and Culture Change in the Middle Pleistocene,* eds. K. Butzer and G. Issac, pp. 745–807. The Hague: Mouton.

Dennell, R. 1986. Needles and spear-throwers. *Natural History* 95(10): 70–78.

Dettwyler, K. A. 1991. Can paleopathology provide evidence for "compassion"? *American Journal of Physical Anthropology,* 84: 375–84.

de Waal, F. B. M. 1995. Bonobo sex and society. *Scientific American* 272(3): 82–88.

Diamond, J. 1987. The worst mistake in the history of the human race. *Discover* 8(5): 64–66.

———. 1989. The great leap forward. *Discover* 10(5): 50–60.

Dib, C., S. Fauré, C. Fizames, D. Samson, N. Drouot, A. Vignal, P. Millasseau, S. Marc, J. Hazan, E. Seboun, M. Lathrop, G. Gyapay, J. Morissette, and J. Weissenbach. 1996. A comprehensive genetic map of the human genome based on 5,264 microsatellites. *Nature* 380: 152–54.

Dibble, H. 1987. The interpretation of Middle Paleolithic scraper morphology. *American Antiquity* 52: 108–18.

Dickson, D. B. 1990. *The Dawn of Belief: Religion in the Upper Paleolithic of Southwestern Europe.* Tucson: University of Arizona Press.

Dikov, N. N. 1978. Ancestors of Paleoindians and proto-Eskimo-Aleuts in the Paleolithic of Kamchatka. In *Early Man in America from a Circum-Pacific Perspective,* ed. A. L. Bryan, pp. 68–69. Edmonton, Canada: Archaeological Researches International.

Dillehay, T. D. 1987. By the banks of the Chinchihuapi. *Natural History* 96(4): 8, 9–12.

———. 1989. *Monte Verde: A Late Pleistocene Settlement in Chile, Vol. 1: Paleoenvironment and Site Context.* Washington, D.C.: Smithsonian Institution Press.

Dillehay, T. D., and M. B. Collins. 1988. Early cultural evidence from Monte Verde in Chile. *Nature* 332: 150–52.

Dixon, E. J. 1993. *Quest for the Origins of the First Americans.* Albuquerque: University of New Mexico Press.

Donnelly, P., S. Tavaré, D. J. Balding, and R. C. Griffiths. 1996. Technical comments: Estimating the age of the common ancestor of men from the ZFY intron. *Science* 272: 1357–58.

Dorit, R. L., H. Akashi, and W. Gilbert. 1995. Absence of polymorphism at the ZFY locus on the human Y chromosome. *Science* 268: 1183–85.

Doyle, A. C. 1981. *The Celebrated Cases of Sherlock Holmes.* London: Octopus Books.

Editors of Time-Life. 1973. *The First Men.* New York: Time-Life Books.

Eldredge, N. and S. J. Gould. 1972. Punctuated equilibria: An alternative to phyletic gradualism. In *Models in Paleobiology,* ed. T. S. Schopf, pp. 82–115. San Francisco: Freeman, Cooper.

Elias, S., S. K. Short, C. H. Nelson, and H. H. Birks. 1996. Life and times of the Bering Land Bridge. *Nature* 382: 60–63.

Engels, F. 1942. *The Origin of the Family, Private Property and the State.* 1972 ed. Chicago: Kerr.

Facchini, A. and G. Guisberti. 1990. *Homo sapiens sapiens* remains from the island of Crete. In *Continuity or Replacement: Controversies in* Homo sapiens *Evolution,* eds. G. Bräuer and F. H. Smith. Rotterdam: Balkema.

Fagan, B. 1991. *In the Beginning: An Introduction to Archaeology.* Boston: Little, Brown.

Fairservis, W. A. 1975. *The Roots of India.* Chicago: University of Chicago Press.

Farnsworth, P., J. Brady, M. DeNiro, and R. S. MacNeish. 1985. A re-evaluation of the isotopic and archaeological reconstructions of diet in the Tehuacán Valley. *American Antiquity* 50: 102–16.

Feder, K. L. 1996. *Frauds, Myths, and Mysteries: Science and Pseudoscience in Archaeology,* 2nd ed. Mountain View, Calif.: Mayfield.

Fedigan, L. M. and L. Fedigan. 1988. Gender and the study of primates. *Curricular Module for the Project on Gender and Curriculum.* Washington, D.C.: American Anthropological Association.

Feibel, C. S., F. H. Brown, and I. McDougal. 1989. Stratigraphic context of fossil hominids from the Omo Group deposits: Northern Turkan basin, Kenya and Ethiopia. *American Journal of Physical Anthropology* 78: 595–622.

Ferris, T. 1988. *Coming of Age in the Milky Way.* New York: William Morrow and Co.

Fischman, J. 1992. Hard Evidence. *Discover* 13(2): 44–51.

Flannery, K. 1965. The ecology of early food production in Mesopotamia. *Science* 147: 1247–56.

———. 1967. Vertebrate fauna and hunting patterns. In *The Prehistory of the Tehuacán Valley: Volume One— Environment and Subsistence,* ed. D. Byers, pp. 132–77. Austin: University of Texas Press.

———. 1968. Archaeological systems theory in early Mesoamerica. In *Anthropological Archaeology in the Americas,* ed. B. J. Meggers. Washington, D.C.: Anthropological Society of Washington.

———. 1973. The origins of agriculture. *Annual Review of Anthropology* 2: 271–310.

Flint, R. F. 1971. *Glacial and Quarternary Geology.* New York: Wiley.

Flood, J. 1990. *Archaeology of the Dreamtime: The Story of Prehistoric Australia and Its People.* New Haven, Conn.: Yale University Press.

Ford, R. 1985. Patterns of prehistoric food production in North America. In *Prehistoric Food Production in North America,* ed. R. Ford, pp. 341–64. Anthropological Papers, Vol. 75. Ann Arbor: Museum of Anthropology, University of Michigan.

Fossey, D. 1983. *Gorillas in the Mist.* Boston: Houghton Mifflin.

Franciscus, R. G. and E. Trinkaus. 1988. Nasal morphology and the emergence of *Homo erectus. American Journal of Physical Anthropology* 75: 517–27.

Frayer, D. W., M. H. Wolpoff, A. G. Thorne, F. H. Smith, and G. G. Pope. 1993. Theories of modern human origins: The paleontological test. *American Anthropologist* 95: 14–50.

Freeman, L. G. 1973. The significance of mammalian faunas from Paleolithic occupations in Cantabrian Spain. *American Antiquity* 38: 3–44.

Freidel, D. 1979. Culture areas and interaction spheres: Contrasting approaches to the emergence of civilization in the Maya lowlands. *American Antiquity* 44: 6–54.

Frere, J. 1800. Account of flint weapons discovered in Hoxne in Suffolk. *Archaeologia* 13: 204–5.

Frison, G. B. (ed.) 1974. *The Casper Site.* New York: Academic Press.

Fritz, G. 1994. Are the first American farmers getting younger? *Current Anthropology* 35(3): 305–9.

Galdikas, B. 1995. *Reflections of Eden: My Years with the Orangutans of Borneo.* Boston: Little, Brown.

Gamble, C. 1982. Interaction and alliance in Paleolithic society. *Man* 17: 92–107.

———. 1983. Culture and society in the Upper Paleolithic of Europe. In *Hunter–Gatherer Economy in Prehistory: A European Perspective,* ed. G. Bailey, pp. 210–11. Cambridge, Eng.: Cambridge University Press.

———. 1986. *The Paleolithic Settlement of Europe.* Cambridge, Eng.: Cambridge University Press.

Gargett, R. H. 1989. Grave shortcomings: Evidence for Neandertal burial. *Current Anthropology* 30: 157–90.

Gernet, J. 1987. *A History of Chinese Civilization.* Cambridge, Eng.: Cambridge University Press.

Godfrey, L. R. and M. R. Sutherland. 1996. Paradox of peramorphic paedomorphosis: Heterochrony and human evolution. *American Journal of Physical Anthropology* 99: 17–42.

Goodall, J. 1971. *In the Shadow of Man.* Boston: Houghton Mifflin.

———. 1986. *The Chimpanzees of Gombe: Patterns of Behavior.* Cambridge, Mass.: Belknap Press.

———. 1990. *Through a Window: My Thirty Years with the Chimpanzees of Gombe.* Boston: Houghton Mifflin.

———. 1995. A message from Jane Goodall. *National Geographic* 187(6): 129.

Goodman, A. H. and G. Armelagos. 1985. Disease and death at Dr. Dickson's mound. *Natural History* 94(9): 12–18.

Gore, R. 1996. The Dawn of Humans: Neandertals. *National Geographic* 189(1): 2–35.

Gorman, C. 1969. Hoabinhian: A pebble-tool complex with early plant associations in Southeast Asia. *Science* 163: 671–73.

Gorman, C. 1972. Excavations at Spirit Cave, North Thailand: Some interim impressions. *Asian Perspectives* 13: 79–107.

Gould, S. J. 1977. *Ever Since Darwin.* New York: Norton.

———. 1980. *The Panda's Thumb.* New York: Norton.

———. 1983. Part 4: Teilhard and Piltdown. In *Hen's Teeth and Horse's Toes.* New York: Norton.

———. 1985a. Human equality is a contingent fact of history. In *The Flamingo's Smile.* New York: Norton.

———. 1985b. Darwin at sea—and the virtues of port. In *The Flamingo's Smile.* New York: Norton.

———. 1985c. *The Flamingo's Smile.* New York: Norton.

———. 1987a. Life's little joke. *Natural History* 96(4): 16–25.

———. 1987b. Empire of the apes. *Natural History* 96(5): 20–25.

———. 1987c. Bushes all the way down. *Natural History* 96(6): 12–19.

———. 1988. A novel notion of Neanderthal. *Natural History* 97(6): 16–21.

———. 1991. *Bully for Brontosaurus.* New York: Norton.

———. 1993a. *The Book of Life.* New York: Norton.

———. 1993b. *Eight Little Piggies.* New York: Norton.

———. 1995. *Dinosaur in a Haystack.* New York: Harmony Books.

Grayson, D. K. 1983. *The Establishment of Human Antiquity.* New York: Academic Press.

Greenberg, J., C. G. Turner II, and S. L. Zegura. 1986. The settlement of the Americas: A comparison of linguistic, dental, and genetic evidence. *Current Anthropology* 27(5): 477–94.

Greene, J. C. 1959. *The Death of Adam: Evolution and Its Impact on Western Thought.* Ames: Iowa State University Press.

Grine, F. E. (ed.) 1988a. *Evolutionary History of the "Robust" Australopithecines.* New York: Aldine de Gruyter.

Groube, L., J. Chappell, J. Muke, and D. Price. 1986. A 40,000 year-old human occupation site at Huon Peninsula, Papua New Guinea. *Nature* 324: 453–55.

Groves, C. P. 1989. A regional approach to the problem of the origin of modern humans in Australasia. In *The Human Revolution: Behavioural and Biological Perspectives in the Origins of Modern Humans,* eds. P. Mellars and C. Stringer, pp. 274–85. Princeton, N.J.: Princeton University Press.

Grün, R. 1993. Electron spin resonance dating in paleoanthropology. *Evolutionary Anthropology* 2(5): 172–81.

Grün, R., et al. 1996. Direct dating of Florisbad hominid. *Nature* 382: 500–501.

Grün, R., P. B. Beaumont, and C. B. Stringer. 1990. ESR dating evidence for early modern humans at Border Cave in South Africa. *Nature* 344: 537–39.

Grün, R. and C. B. Stringer. 1991. Electron spin resonance dating and the evolution of modern humans. *Archaeometry* 33: 153–99.

Guilbaud, M. 1993. Debitage from the Upper Câstelperronian Level at Saint-Césaire. In *Context of a Late Neandertal,* eds. F. Lévêque, A. M. Backer, and M. Guilbaud, pp. 39–58. Madison, Wisc.: Prehistory Press.

Guthrie, R. D. 1990. Late Pleistocene faunal revolution—New perspective on the extinction debate. In *Megafauna and Man: Discovery of America's Heartland,* eds. L. D. Agenbroad, J. I. Mead, and L. W. Nelson, pp. 42–53. Hot Springs, S.D.: The Mammoth Site of Hot Springs and Northern Arizona University.

Gutin, J. 1995. Do Kenya tools root birth of modern thought in Africa? *Science* 270: 1118–19.

Haas, J. 1982. *The Evolution of the Prehistoric State.* New York: New York University Press.

Habgood, P. J. 1992. The origin of anatomically modern humans in east Asia. In *Continuity or Replacement: Controversies in* Homo sapiens *Evolution,* eds. G. Bräuer and F. Smith, pp. 273–87. Rotterdam: Balkema.

Halverson, J. 1987. Art for art's sake in the Paleolithic. *Current Anthropology* 28: 63–71.

Hamblin, D. J. and the Editors of Time-Life. 1973. *The First Cities.* New York: Time-Life Books.

Hammond, N. 1974. Paleolithic mammalian faunas and parietal art in Cantabria: A comment on Freeman. *American Antiquity* 39: 618–19.

Hansen, J. M. 1991. *The Paleoethnobotany of Franchthi Cave, Greece.* Bloomington: Indiana University Press.

Harlan, J. 1992. Indigenous African Agriculture. In *The Origins of Agriculture: An International Perspective,* eds. C. W. Cowan and P. J. Watson, pp. 59–70. Washington, D.C.: Smithsonian Institution Press.

Harlan, J. R., J. M. J. De Wet, and A. Stemler. (eds.) 1976. Plant domestication and indigenous African agriculture. In *Origins of African Plant Domestication,* pp. 3–22. The Hague: Mouton.

Harlan, J. R., J. M. J. De Wet, A Stemler, and D. Zohary. 1966. Distribution of wild wheats and barley. *Science* 153: 1074–80.

Harmon, R., J. Glaze, and K. Nowak. 1980. ^{230}Th/^{234}U dating of travertines from the Bilzingsleben archaeological site. *Nature* 284: 132–35.

Harris, C. L. (ed.) 1981. *Evolution: Genesis and Revelations.* Albany: State University of New York Press.

Harris, D. 1977. Alternative strategies toward agriculture. In *Origins of Agriculture,* ed. C. A. Reed, pp. 179–243. The Hague: Mouton.

Harris, M. 1968. *The Rise of Anthropological Theory.* New York: Cromwell.

Harrold, F. B. 1980. A comparative analysis of Eurasian Paleolithic burials. *World Archaeology* 12: 195–211.

———. 1989. Mousterian, Châtelperronian and early Aurignacian in Western Europe: Continuity or Discontinuity. In *The Human Revolution: Behavioural and Biological Perspectives in the Origin of Modern Humans,* eds. P. Mellars and C. Stringer, pp. 677–713. Princeton, N.J.: Princeton University Press.

Hartl, D. L. 1977. *Our Uncertain Heritage: Genetics and Human Diversity.* New York: Lippincott.

Hedges, S. B., S. Kumar, K. Tamura, and M. Stoneking. 1992. Human origins and analysis of mitochondrial DNA sequences. *Science* 255: 737–39.

Heim, J. L. 1968. Les restes Neandertaliens de La Ferassie 1: Nouvelles données sur la stratigraphie et inventure de squelettes. *Computes Reneud de l'Academie del Sciences, Series D* 266: 576–78.

Henning, G. J., W. Herr, E. Weber, and N. I. Xirotiris. 1981. ESR-dating of the fossil hominid cranium from Petralona Cave, Greece. *Nature* 292: 533–36.

Henry, D. O. 1989. *From Foraging to Agriculture: The Levant at the End of the Ice Age.* Philadelphia: University of Pennsylvania Press.

Higham, C. 1989. *The Archaeology of Mainland Southeast Asia.* Cambridge, Eng.: Cambridge University Press.

Ho, P. 1977. The indigenous origins of Chinese agriculture. In *Origins of Agriculture,* ed. C. A. Reed, pp. 413–84. The Hague: Mouton.

Hoffman, M. 1979. *Egypt Before the Pharaohs.* New York: Knopf.

———. 1983. Where nations began. *Science 83* 4(8): 42–51.

Hole, F., K. Flannery, and J. A. Neely. 1969. *Prehistory and Human Ecology of the Deh Luran Plain: An Early Village Sequence from Khuzistan, Iran.* Ann Arbor: University of Michigan Press.

Holloway, R. 1980. Indonesian "Solo" (Ngandong) endocranial reconstructions: Preliminary observations and comparisons with Neandertal and *Homo erectus* groups. *American Journal of Physical Anthropology* 53: 285–95.

———. 1981. The Indonesian *Homo erectus* brain endocasts revisited. *American Journal of Physical Anthropology* 55: 503–21.

Hopkins, D. 1982. Aspects of the paleogeography of Beringia during the late Pleistocene. In *The Paleoecology of Beringia,* eds. D. M. Hopkins, J. V. Matthews Jr., C. E. Schweger, and S. B. Young, pp. 3–28. New York: Academic Press.

Hoppe, K. 1992. Antiquity of oldest American confirmed. *Science News* 142: 334.

Hovers, E., Y. Rak, and W. Kimbell. 1996. Neandertals of the Levant. *Archaeology* 49(1): 49–50.

Howard, R. W. 1975. *The Dawn Seekers: The First History of American Paleontology.* New York: Harcourt Brace Jovanovich.

Howell, F. C. 1960. European and northwest African Middle Pleistocene hominids. *Current Anthropology* 1: 195–232.

———. 1966. Observations on the earlier phases of the European Lower Paleolithic. Special publication of *American Anthropologist* 68: 88–201.

Howells, W. W. 1980. *Homo erectus*—who, when, and where: A survey. *Yearbook of Physical Anthropology* 23: 1–23.

Huang, W., R. Ciochon, Y. Gu, R. Larick, Q. Fang, H. Schwarcz, C. Yonge, J. de Vos, and W. Reinle. 1995. Early *Homo* and associated artefacts from Asia. *Nature* 378: 275–78.

Hublin, J.-J. 1996. The first Europeans. *Archaeology* 49(1): 36–44.

Hublin, J.-J., F. Spoor, M. Braun, F. Zonneveld, and S. Condemi. 1996. A late Neanderthal associated with Upper Paleolithic artefacts. *Nature* 381: 224–26.

Huddleston, L. E. 1967. *Origins of the American Indians: European Concepts 1492–1729.* Austin: University of Texas Press.

Huntington, E. 1924. *Civilization and Climate.* New Haven, Conn.: Yale University Press.

Ikeya, M. 1982. Petralona Cave dating controversy: Response to Henning et al. *Nature* 299: 281.

Ingmanson, E. J. and H. Ihobe. 1992. *Predation and meat eating by* Pan paniscus. Paper presented at the 61st Annual Meeting of the American Association of Physical Anthropology. Las Vegas.

Irving, W. 1978. Pleistocene archaeology in eastern Beringia. In *Early Man in America from a Circum-Pacific Perspective,* ed. A. L. Bryan, pp. 96–101. Occasional Papers of the Department of Anthropology, University of Alberta, vol. 1. Edmonton: Archaeological Researches International.

Isaac, G. 1977. *Olorgesailie: Archaeological Studies of a Middle Pleistocene Lake Basin in Kenya.* Chicago: University of Chicago Press.

James, S. 1989. Hominid use of fire in the Lower and Middle Pleistocene. *Current Anthropology* 30: 1–11.

Jia, L. and W. Huang. 1990. *The Story of Peking Man.* New York: Oxford University Press.

Jochim, M. 1983. Paleolithic cave art in ecological perspective. In *Hunter–Gatherer Economy in Prehistory: A*

European Perspective, ed. G. Bailey, pp. 212–19. Cambridge, Eng.: Cambridge University Press.

Johanson, D. and M. Edey. 1981. *Lucy: The Beginnings of Humankind.* New York: Simon & Schuster.

Johanson, D. and J. Shreeve. 1989. *Lucy's Child: The Discovery of a Human Ancestor.* New York: Morrow.

Jones, R. 1989. East of Wallace's Line: Issues and problems in the colonization of the Australian continent. In *The Human Revolution: Behavioural and Biological Perspectives in the Origins of Modern Humans,* eds. P. Mellars and C. Stringer, pp. 743–82. Princeton, N.J.: Princeton University Press.

Jones, R. 1987. Pleistocene life in the dead heart of Australia. *Nature* 328: 666.

Jones, R. 1992. The human colonisation of the Australian continent. In *Continuity or Replacement: Controversies in* Homo sapiens *Evolution,* eds. G. Bräuer and F. Smith, pp. 289–301. Rotterdam: Balkema.

Jordan, E. and F. S. Collins. 1996. A march of genetic maps. *Nature* 380: 111–12.

Kaiser, J. 1995. Blood from a stone: Tests for prehistoric blood cast doubt on earlier results. *Science News* 147: 376–77.

———. 1996. Were cattle domesticated in Africa? *Science* 272: 1105.

Kano, T. 1990. The bonobos' peaceable kingdom. *Natural History* 99(11): 62–71.

Kaplan, L., T. F. Lynch, and C. E. S. Smith, Jr. 1973. Early cultivated beans (*Phaseolus vulgaris*) from an intermontaine Peruvian valley. *Science* 179: 76–77.

Keeley, L. H. 1980. *Experimental Determination of Stone Tool Use: A Microwear Analysis.* Chicago: University of Chicago Press.

Kennedy, K. A. R. 1975. *Neanderthal Man.* Minneapolis: Burgess Press.

———. 1976. *Human Variation in Space and Time.* Dubuque, Iowa: Brown.

Kennedy, K. A. R., A. Sonakia, J. Chimet, and K. K. Verma. 1991. Is the Narmada hominid an Indian *Homo erectus? American Journal of Physical Anthropology* 86: 475–96.

Kent, J. 1987. The most ancient south: A review of the domestication of the Andean camelids. In *Studies in the Neolithic and Urban Revolutions,* ed. L. Manzanilla, pp. 169–84. Oxford, Eng.: British Archaeological Review.

Kenyon, K. 1954. Ancient Jericho. *Scientific American* 190(4): 76–82.

Kimbel, W. H., T. D. White, and D. C. Johanson. 1988. Implications for KNM-WT 17000 for the evolution of "robust" australopithecines. In *Evolutionary History*

of the "Robust" Australopithecines, ed. F. E. Grine, pp. 259–68. New York: Aldine.

Kingston, J. D., B. D. Marino, and A. Hill. 1994. Isotopic evidence for Neocene hominid paleoenvironments in the Kenya rift valley. *Science* 264: 955–59.

Klein, R. G. 1982. Age (mortality) profiles as a means of distinguishing hunted species from scavenged ones in Stone Age archaeological sites. *Paleobiology* 8: 151–58.

———. 1983. The Stone Age prehistory of southern Africa. *Annual Review of Anthropology* 12: 25–48.

———. 1989. *The Human Career: Human Biological and Cultural Origins.* Chicago: University of Chicago Press.

———. 1992. The archaeology of modern human origins. *Evolutionary Anthropology* 1(1): 5–14.

———. 1994. The problem of modern human origins. In *Origins of Anatomically Modern Humans,* eds. M. Nitecki and D. Nitecki, pp. 3–17. New York: Plenum.

Knecht, H., A. Pike-Tay, and R. White. 1993. Introduction. In *Before Lascaux: The Complex Record of the Early Upper Paleolithic,* eds. H. Knecht, A. Pike-Tay, and R. White, pp. 1–4. Boca Raton, Fla.: CRC Press.

Kramer, A. 1991. Modern human origins in Australasia: Replacement or evolution. *American Journal of Physical Anthropology* 86: 455–73.

———. 1993. Human taxonomic diversity in the Pleistocene: Does *Homo erectus* represent multiple hominid species? *American Journal of Physical Anthropology* 91: 161–71.

Kranzberg, M. 1984. Technological revolutions. *National Forum: The Phi Kappa Phi Journal* 64(3): 6–10.

Kurtén, B. 1968. *The Pleistocene Mammals of Europe.* London: Weiderfield and Nicholson.

Lack, D. 1947. *Darwin's Finches: An Essay on the General Biological Theory of Evolution.* Cambridge, Eng.: Cambridge University Press.

———. 1953. Darwin's finches. *Scientific American* 188(4): 65–72.

Laitman, J. and R. C. Heimbach. 1984. The basicranium and upper respiratory system of African *Homo erectus* and early *Homo sapiens. American Journal of Physical Anthropology* 63: 180.

Lamberg-Karlovsky, C. C. and J. A. Sabloff. 1995. *Ancient Civilizations: The Near East and Mesoamerica.* Prospect Heights, Ill.: Waveland Press.

Landau, M. 1991. *Narratives of Human Evolution.* New Haven, Conn.: Yale University Press.

Larick, R. and R. Ciochon. 1996. The first Asians. *Archaeology* 49(1): 51–53.

Larsen, C. S. and R. M. Matter. 1985. *Human Origins: The Fossil Record.* Prospect Heights, Ill.: Waveland Press.

Leakey, R. E. F. and A. Walker. 1985a. A fossil skeleton 1,600,000 years old: *Homo erectus* unearthed. *National Geographic* 168(5): 624–29.

———. 1985b. Further hominids from the Plio-Pleistocene of Koobi Fora, Kenya. *American Journal of Physical Anthropology* 67: 135–63.

Lee, R. 1979. *The !Kung San: Men, Women, and Work in a Foraging Society.* Cambridge, Eng.: Cambridge University Press.

Lee, R. B. and I. DeVore. 1968. *Man the Hunter.* Chicago: Aldine.

Leiberman, P. 1984. *The Biology and Evolution of Language.* Cambridge, Mass.: Harvard University Press.

Leigh, S. 1992. Cranial capacity evolution in *Homo erectus* and early *Homo sapiens. American Journal of Physical Anthropology* 87: 1–13.

Leroi-Gourhan, A. 1968. The evolution of Paleolithic art. *Scientific American* 218(2): 58–70.

———. 1982. *The Dawn of European Art: An Introduction to Paleolithic Cave Painting.* Cambridge, Eng.: Cambridge University Press.

Lévêque, F., A. M. Backer, and M. Guilbaud. (eds.) 1993. *Context of a Late Neandertal.* Monographs in World Archaeology. Volume 16. Madison, Wisc.: Prehistory Press.

Lewin, R. 1982. *Thread of Life: The Smithsonian Looks at Evolution.* Washington, D.C.: Smithsonian Books.

———. 1984. Unexpected anatomy of *Homo erectus. Science* 226: 529.

———. 1987a. Africa: Cradle of modern humans. *Science* 237: 1292–95.

———. 1987b. The unmasking of mitochondrial Eve. *Science* 238: 24–26.

———. 1987c. *Bones of Contention: Controversies in the Search for Human Origins.* New York: Simon & Schuster.

———. 1991. The biochemical route to human origins. *Mosaic* 22(3): 46–55.

Lewis-Williams, J. D. and T. A. Dowson. 1988. The signs of all times. *Current Anthropology* 29(2): 201–17.

Lewontin, R. 1982. *Human Diversity.* New York: Scientific American Library.

Lloyd, S. 1978. *The Archaeology of Mesopotamia.* London: Thames and Hudson.

Long, A., B. Benz, J. Donahue, A. Jull, and L. Toolin. 1989. First direct AMS dates on early maize from Tehuacán, Mexico. *Radiocarbon* 31: 1035–40.

Long, J. C., A. Chakravarti, C. Boehm, S. Antonarakis, and H. Kazazian. 1990. Phylogeny of human b-globin haplotypes and its implications for recent human evolution. *American Journal of Physical Anthropology* 81: 113–30.

Lovejoy, C. O. and E. Trinkaus. 1980. Strength and robusticity of the Neandertal tibia. *American Journal of Physical Anthropology* 53: 465–70.

Lowe, G. W. 1989. The heartland Olmec: Evolution of material culture. In *Regional Perspectives on the Olmec,* eds. R. J. Sharer and D. C. Grove, pp. 33–67. New York: Cambridge University Press.

Lu Zun'e. 1987. Cracking the evolutionary puzzle: Jinniushan Man. *China Pictorial* 4: 34–45.

Lyell, C. 1873. *The Geological Evidences of the Antiquity of Man.* London: Murray.

Lynch, T. F., R. Gillespie, J. A. J. Gowlett, and R. E. M. Hedges. 1985. Chronology of Guitarrero Cave, Peru. *Science* 229: 864–67.

MacNeish, R. S. 1964. Ancient Mesoamerican civilization. *Science* 143: 531–37.

———. 1967. An interdisciplinary approach to an archaeological problem. In *The Prehistory of the Tehuacán Valley: Volume One—Environment and Subsistence,* ed. D. Byers, pp. 14–23. Austin: University of Texas Press.

Maisels, C. K. 1990. *The Emergence of Civilization: From Hunting and Gathering to Agriculture, Cities, and the State in the Near East.* New York: Routledge.

Manglesdorf, P. 1958. Reconstructing the ancestor of corn. *Proceedings of the American Philosophical Society* 102: 454–63.

Marks, A. E. 1990. The Middle and Upper Paleolithic of the Near East and the Nile Valley: The problem of cultural transformations. In *The Emergence of Modern Humans: An Archaeological Perspective,* ed. P. Mellars, pp. 56–80. Ithaca: Cornell University Press.

Marks, A. E. 1993. The early Upper Paleolithic: The view from the Levant. In *Before Lascaux: The Complex Record of the Early Upper Paleolithic,* eds. H. Knecht, A. Pike-Tay, and R. White, pp. 5–21. Boca Raton, Fla.: CRC Press.

Marks, J. 1991. What's old and new in molecular phylogeny. *American Journal of Physical Anthropology* 85: 207–19.

———. 1995. *Human Biodiversity: Genes, Race, and History.* New York: Aldine.

Marshak, A. 1972a. *The Roots of Civilization.* New York: McGraw-Hill.

———. 1972b. Cognitive aspects of Upper Paleolithic engraving. *Current Anthropology* 13: 445–77.

Martin, P. S. 1982. The pattern of meaning of Holarctic mammoth extinction. In *Paleoecology of Beringia,* eds. D. Hopkins, J. Matthews, C. Schweger, and S. Young, pp. 399–408. New York: Academic Press.

Martin, R. D. 1990. *Primate Origins and Evolution: A Phylogenetic Reconstruction.* Princeton, N.J.: Princeton University Press.

Maxwell, M. 1993. Pioneers of the Arctic: The last of the habitable lands. In *The First Humans: Human Origins and History to 10,000 B.C.,* ed. G. Hurnehult, pp. 209–25. San Francisco: HarperSan Francisco.

McConnell, J. B. 1988. Whence we've come, where we're going, how we're going to get there. In *Biotechnology and the Human Genome,* eds. A. D. Woodhead and B. J. Barnhart, pp. 1–4. New York: Plenum.

McCrone, J. 1991. *The Ape That Spoke: Language and the Evolution of the Mind.* New York: Avon Books.

McDermott, F., R. Grün, C. B. Stringer, and C. J. Hawkesworth. 1993. Mass-spectrometric U-series dates for Israeli Neaderthal/early modern hominid sites. *Nature* 363: 252–55.

McIntosh, S. and R. McIntosh. 1982. Finding West Africa's oldest city. *National Geographic* 162(3): 396–418.

McKillop, H. 1994. Ancient Maya tree-cropping. *Ancient Mesoamerica* 5: 129–40.

Mellaart, J. 1965. *Earliest Civilizations of the Near East.* London: Thames and Hudson.

Mellars, P. (ed.) 1990. *The Emergence of Modern Humans: An Archaeological Perspective.* Ithaca, N.Y.: Cornell University Press.

Meltzer, D. J. 1989. Why don't we know when the first people came to North America? *American Antiquity* 54: 471–90.

———. 1993a. Pleistocene peopling of the Americas. *Evolutionary Anthropology,* pp. 157–69.

———. 1993b. *Search for the First Americans.* Washington, D.C.: Smithsonian Books.

Mercier, N., H. Valladas, J-L. Joron, J-L. Reyss, F. Léveque, and B. Vandermeersch. 1991. Thermoluminescence dating of the late Neanderthal remains from Saint-Césaire. *Nature* 351: 737–39.

Milisauskas, S. 1978. *European Prehistory.* New York: Academic Press.

Miller, N. 1992. The origins of plant cultivation in the Near East. In *The Origins of Agriculture: An International Perspective,* eds. C. W. Cowan and P. J. Watson, pp. 39–58. Washington, D.C.: Smithsonian Institution Press.

Miller, P. 1995. Jane Goodall. *National Geographic* 187(6): 102–28.

Million, R., B. Drewit, and G. Cowgill. 1973. *The Teotihuacan Map: Urbanization at Teotihuacan,* Vol. 1. Austin: University of Texas Press.

Molnar, S. 1975. *Human Variation: Races, Types, and Ethnic Groups.* Englewood Cliffs, N.J.: Prentice-Hall.

Monastersky, R. 1991. Tales from ice time: Two holes through Greenland offer a glimpse of climates past and future. *Science News* 140: 161–76.

———. 1992. New date resets geologic clocks. *Science News* 141: 14.

Montagu, A. (ed.) 1964. *The Concept of Race.* New York: Collier.

Morgan, L. H. 1877. *Ancient Society.* 1964 ed. Cambridge, Mass.: Belknap Press.

Morlan, R. E. 1978. Early man in northern Yukon Territory: Perspectives as of 1977. In *Early Man in America from a Circum-Pacific Perspective,* ed. A. L. Bryan, pp. 78–95. Occasional Papers of the Department of Anthropology, University of Alberta, vol. 1. Edmonton: Archaeological Researches International.

———. 1983. Pre-Clovis occupation north of the ice sheets. In *Early Man in the New World,* ed. R. Shutler, Jr., pp. 47–63. Beverly Hills: Sage.

Morse, D. 1969. *Ancient Disease in the Midwest.* Springfield: Illinois State Museum.

Morse, D., J. Duncan, and J. Stoutamire. (eds.) 1983. *Handbook of Forensic Archaeology and Anthropology.* Tallahassee, Fla.: Published by the editors, distributed by Bill's Bookstore.

Movius, H. 1953. The Mousterian cave of Teshik-Tash, south-central Uzbekistan, Central Asia. *Bulletin of the American School of Prehistorical Research* 17: 11–71.

Mowat, F. 1987. *Woman in the Mists.* New York: Warner Books.

Napier, J. R. and P. H. Napier. 1985. *The Natural History of the Primates.* London: British Museum (Natural History).

Natural History. 1991–1992. Rediscovering the Maya. *Natural History.*

Newcomer, M. 1971. Some quantitative experiments in handaxe manufacture. *World Archaeology* 3: 85–94.

Nichols, M., J. Goodall, G. B. Schaller, and M. G. Smith. 1993. *The Great Apes: Between Two Worlds.* Washington, D.C.: National Geographic Society.

Nova. 1993. *This Old Pyramid.* Boston: WGBH-TV.

O'Brien, E. M. 1984. What was the Acheulean hand ax? *Natural History* 93(7): 20–23.

O'Connor, D. 1993. *Ancient Nubia: Egypt's Rival in Africa.* Philadelphia: University Museum, University of Pennsylvania.

Oliva, M. 1993. The Aurignacian in Moravia. In *Before Lascaux: The Complex Record of the Early Upper Paleolithic,* eds. H. Knecht, A. Pike-Tay, and R. White, pp. 37–55. Boca Raton, Fla.: CRC Press.

Olsen, S. J. 1985. *Origins of the Domestic Dog.* Tucson: University of Arizona Press.

Ovey, C. (ed.) 1964. *The Swanscombe Skull: A Survey of Research on a Pleistocene Site.* Royal Anthropological Institute of Great Britain and Ireland, Occasional Paper 20.

Owen, R. 1984. The Americas: The case against an Ice-Age human population. In *The Origins of Modern Humans: A World Survey of the Fossil Evidence,* eds. F. H. Smith and F. Spencer, pp. 517–64. New York: Liss.

Parés, J. M. and A. Pérez-González. 1995. Paleomagnetic age for hominid fossils at Atapuerca archaeological site, Spain. *Science* 269: 830–32.

Park, M. A. 1979. *Dermatoglyphics as a Tool for Population Studies: An Example.* Unpublished doctoral dissertation. Bloomington: Indiana University Department of Anthropology.

Park, M. A. 1996. *Biological Anthropology.* Mountain View, Calif.: Mayfield.

Passingham, R. E. 1982. *The Human Primate.* Oxford, Eng.: Freeman.

Patterson, T. 1973. *America's Past: A New World Archaeology.* Glenview, Ill.: Scott, Foresman.

Pauketat, T. R. 1994. *The Ascent of Chiefs: Cahokia and Mississippian Politics in Native America.* Tuscaloosa: University of Alabama Press.

Pearsall, D. 1989. *Paleoethnobotany: A Handbook of Procedures.* New York: Academic Press.

Pfeiffer, J. E. 1969. *The Emergence of Man.* New York: Harper & Row.

———. 1982. *The Creative Explosion: An Inquiry into the Origins of Art and Religion.* New York: Harper & Row.

Phillipson, D. W. 1993. *African Archaeology.* Cambridge, Eng.: Cambridge University Press.

Pilbeam, D. 1984. The descent of the hominoids and hominids. *Scientific American* 250(3): 84–96.

———. 1986. Human origins. *David Skomp Distinguished Lecture in Anthropology.* Bloomington: Indiana University.

Pope, G. G. 1988. Recent advances in Far Eastern paleoanthropology. *Annual Reviews in Anthropology* 17: 43–77.

———. 1992. Craniofacial evidence for the origin of modern humans in China. *Yearbook of Physical Anthropology* 35: 243–98.

Possehl, G. L. 1980. *Indus Civilization in Saurashtra.* Delhi, India: B. R. Publishing.

Potts, R. 1984. Home bases and early hominids. *American Scientist* 72: 338–47.

Poulianos, A. N. 1971. Petralona: A Middle Pleistocene cave in Greece. *Archaeology* 24(1): 6–11.

Powers, W. R. and J. F. Hoffecker. 1989. Late Pleistocene settlement in the Nenana Valley, central Alaska. *American Antiquity* 54: 263–87.

Price, T. D. 1987. The Mesolithic of western Europe. *Journal of World Prehistory* 1: 225–305.

Price, T. D. 1991. The view from Europe: Concepts and questions about terminal Pleistocene societies. In *The First Americans: Search and Research,* eds. T. D. Dillehay and D. J. Meltzer, pp. 185–208. Boca Raton, Fla.: CRC Press.

Radner, D. and M. Radner. 1982. *Science and Unreason.* Belmont, Calif.: Wadsworth.

Rak, Y. 1990. On the differences between two pelvises of Mousterian context from the Qafzeh and Kebara Caves, Israel. *American Journal of Physical Anthropology* 81: 323–32.

Rak, Y. and B. Arensberg. 1987. Kebara 2 Neandertal pelvis: First look at a complete inlet. *American Journal of Physical Anthropology* 73: 227–31.

Ray, J. 1974. *The Wisdom of God Manifested in the Works of the Creation.* New York: Georg Olms Verlag.

Read-Martin, C. E. and D. W. Read. 1975. *Australopithecus* scavenging and human evolution: Approach from fauna analysis. *Current Anthropology* 16: 359–68.

Relethford, J. H. 1994. *The Human Species: An Introduction to Biological Anthropology,* 2nd ed. Mountain View, Calif.: Mayfield.

———. 1995. Genetics and modern human origins. *Evolutionary Anthropology* 4(2): 53–63.

Rensberger, B. 1981. Facing the past. *Science 81* 2(8): 40–51.

Rice, P. 1981. Prehistoric Venuses: Symbols of motherhood or womanhood. *Journal of Anthropological Research* 37: 402–14.

Rice, P. and Paterson, A. 1985. Cave art and bones: Exploring the interrelationships. *American Anthropologist* 87: 94–100.

———. 1986. Validating the cave art-archaeofaunal relationship in Cantabrian Spain. *American Anthropologist* 88: 658–67.

———. 1988. Anthropomorphs in cave art: An empirical assessment. *American Anthropologist* 90: 664–74.

Richard, A. F. 1985. *Primates in Nature.* New York: Freeman.

Ridley, M. 1993. *Evolution.* Boston: Blackwell Scientific Publications.

Rightmire, G. P. 1979. Cranial remains of *Homo erectus* from Beds II and IV, Olduvai Gorge, Tanzania. *American Journal of Physical Anthropology* 51: 99–116.

———. 1984. *Homo sapiens* in sub-Saharan Africa. In *The Origins of Modern Humans: A World Survey of the Fossil Evidence,* eds. F. H. Smith and F. Spencer, pp. 295–326. New York: Liss.

———. 1985. The tempo of change in the evolution of Mid-Pleistocene *Homo.* In *Ancestors: The Hard Evidence,* ed. E. Delson, pp. 255–64. New York: Liss.

———. 1990. *The Evolution of* Homo erectus: *Comparative Anatomical Studies of an Extinct Human Species.* New York: Cambridge University Press.

Rightmire, G. P. and H. Deacon. 1991. Comparative studies of Late Pleistocene human remains from Klasies River Mouth, South Africa. *Journal of Human Evolution* 20: 131–56.

Rindos, D. 1984. *The Origins of Agriculture: An Evolutionary Perspective.* Orlando, Fla.: Academic Press.

Roberts, R. G., R. Jones, and M. A. Smith. 1990. Thermoluminescence dating of a 50,000-year-old human occupation site in northern Australia. *Nature* 345: 153–56.

Robins, A. H. 1991. *Biological Perspectives on Human Pigmentation.* Cambridge: Cambridge University Press.

Rodden, R. J. 1965. The early Neolithic village in Greece. *Scientific American* 212(4): 83–91.

Romer, J. 1984. *Ancient Lives: Daily Life in Egypt of the Pharaohs.* New York: Holt, Rinehart and Winston.

———. 1988. *Testament: The Bible and History.* New York: Holt.

Roosevelt, A. C. et al. 1996. Paleoindian cave dwellers in the Amazon: The peopling of the Americas. *Science* 272: 373–84.

Rose, M. 1995. The last Neandertals. *Archaeology* 48(5): 12–13.

Roush, W. 1996. Corn: A lot of change from a little DNA. *Science* 272: 1873.

Ruff, C. B. 1993. Climatic adaptation and hominid evolution: The thermoregulatory imperative. *Evolutionary Anthropology* 2(2): 53–60.

Ruspoli, M. 1986. *The Cave of Lascaux: The Final Photographs.* New York: Abrams.

Sabloff, J. 1989. *The Cities of Ancient Mexico: Reconstructing a Lost World.* New York: Thames and Hudson.

Sabloff, J. 1994. *The New Archaeology and the Ancient Maya.* New York: Scientific American Library.

Sagan, C. 1980. *Cosmos.* New York: Random House.

Sanders, W. and B. Price. 1968. *Mesoamerica: The Evolution of a Civilization.* New York: Random House.

Sarich, V. 1971. A molecular approach to the question of human origins. In *Background for Man,* eds. P. Dolhinhow and V. M. Sarich, pp. 60–81. Boston: Little, Brown.

Sauer, C. 1969. *Seeds, Spades, Hearths, and Herds: The Domestication of Animals and Foodstuffs.* Cambridge, Mass.: MIT Press.

Savage-Rumbaugh, S. and R. Lewin. 1994. Ape at the brink. *Discover* 15(9): 91–98.

Savaria. 1965. *The Popol Vuh.* Guatemala: Publicaciones Turisticas.

Schele, L. and D. Freidel. 1990. *A Forest of Kings: The Untold Story of the Ancient Maya.* New York: Morrow.

Schick, K. D. and N. Toth. 1993. *Making Silent Stones Speak: Human Evolution and the Dawn of Technology.* New York: Simon and Schuster.

Schiffer, M. B. 1976. *Behavioral Archaeology.* Orlando: Academic Press.

Shackleton, N. J. and N. D. Opdyke. 1973. Oxygen isotope and paleomagnetic stratigraphy of equatorial Pacific core V28-238: Oxygen isotope temperatures and ice volumes on a 10^5 and 10^6 year scale. *Quaternary Research* 3: 39–55.

———. 1976. Oxygen-isotope and paleomagnetic stratigraphy of Pacific core V28-239 Late Pliocene and latest Pleistocene. In *Investigation of Late Quaternary Paleoceanography and Paleoclimatology,* eds. R. M. Cline and J. Hays, pp. 449–64, Vol. 145: Geological Society of America.

Shackleton, N., J. Backman, H. Zimmerman, D. V. Dent, M. A. Hall, D. G. Roberts, D. Schnitker, J. G. Baldauf, A. Despraires, R. Homrighausen, P. Huddleston, J. B. Keene, A. J. Kaltenback, K. A. O. Krumsiek, A. C. Morton, J. W. Murray, and J. Westberg-Smith. 1984. Oxygen isotope calibration of the onset of ice-rafting and history of glaciation in the North Atlantic region. *Nature* 307: 620–23.

Shapiro, H. L. 1974. *Peking Man.* New York: Simon & Schuster.

Sharer, R. and W. Ashmore. 1993. *Archaeology: Discovering Our Past,* 2nd ed. Mountain View, Calif.: Mayfield.

Shea, B. T. 1989. Heterochrony in human evolution: The case for neoteny reconsidered. *Yearbook of Physical Anthropology* 32: 69–101.

Shea, J. 1989. A functional study of the lithic industries associated with hominid fossils in Kebara and Qafzeh Caves, Israel. In *The Human Revolution: Behavioural and Biological Perspectives in the Origins of Modern Humans,* eds. P. Mellars and C. Stringer, pp. 611–25. Princeton, N.J.: Princeton University Press.

Shipman, P. April 1984. Scavenger hunt. *Natural History* 93(4): 20–27.

———. 1986. Scavenging or hunting in early hominids: Theoretical frameworks and tests. *American Anthropologist* 88: 27–43.

———. 1990. Old masters. *Discover* 11(7): 60–65.

Shipman, P. and J. Rose. 1983. Evidence of butchery and hominid activities at Torralba and Ambrona: An evaluation using microscopic techniques. *Journal of Archaeological Science* 10: 465–74.

Shreeve, J. 1990. Argument over a woman: Science searches for the mother of us all. *Discover* 11(8): 52–59.

———. 1996a. *The Neandertal Enigma: Solving the Mystery of Modern Human Origins.* New York: Viking.

———. 1996b. New skeleton gives path from trees to ground an odd turn. *Science* 272: 654.

———. 1996c. Sunset on the savanna. *Discover* 17(7): 116–25.

Sillen, A. and C. K. Brain. 1990. Old flame: Burned bones provide evidence of an early use of fire. *Natural History* 99(4): 6–10.

Simons, E. 1964. The early relatives of man. *Scientific American* 211(1): 50–62.

Simons, M. 1996. New species of early human reported found in Africa. *The New York Times.* May 23, p. A8.

Singer, R. and J. Wymer. 1982. *The Middle Stone Age at Klasies River Mouth in South Africa.* Chicago: University of Chicago Press.

Smith, B. 1989. Origins of agriculture in Eastern North America. *Science* 246: 1566–70.

———. 1992a. Prehistoric plant husbandry in eastern North America. In *The Origins of Agriculture: An International Perspective,* eds. C. W. Cowan and P. J. Watson, pp. 101–19. Washington, D.C.: Smithsonian Institution Press.

———. ed. 1992b. *Rivers of Change: Essays on Early Agriculture in Eastern North America.* Washington, D.C.: Smithsonian Institution Press.

———. 1995. *The Emergence of Agriculture.* New York: Scientific American Library.

Smith, B. H. 1993. The physiological age of KNM-WT 15000. In *The Nariokotome* Homo erectus *skeleton,* eds. A. Walker and R. Leakey, pp. 195–220. Cambridge, Mass.: Harvard University Press.

Smith, F. H. 1984. Fossil hominid from the Upper Pleistocene of central Europe and the origins of modern Europeans. In *The Origins of Modern Humans: A World Survey of the Fossil Evidence,* eds. F. H. Smith and F. Spencer, pp. 137–210. New York: Liss.

———. 1991. The Neandertals: Evolutionary dead ends or ancestors of modern people. *Journal of Anthropological Research* 47(2): 219–38.

———. 1992. The role of continuity in modern human origins. In *Continuity or Replacement: Controversies in* Homo sapiens *Evolution,* eds. G. Bräuer and F. Smith, pp. 145–58. Rotterdam: Balkema.

———. 1994. Samples, species, and speculations in the study of modern human origins. In *Origins of Anatomically Modern Humans,* eds. M. Nitecki and D. Nitecki, pp. 227–52. New York: Plenum.

Smith, F. H., A. B. Falsetti, and S. M. Donnelly. 1989. Modern human origins. *Yearbook of Physical Anthropology* 32: 35–68.

Smith, F. H. and F. Spencer (eds.) 1984. *The Origins of Modern Humans: A World Survey of the Fossil Evidence.* New York: Liss.

Smith, J. M. 1984. Science and myth. *Natural History* 93(11): 10–24.

Smith, M. A. 1987. Pleistocene occupation in arid Central Australia. *Nature* 328: 710–11.

Smuts, B. 1985. *Sex and Friendship in Baboons.* Hawthorne, N.Y.: Aldine.

Soffer, O. 1993. Upper-Paleolithic adaptations in central and eastern Europe and man-mammoth interactions. In *From Kostenki to Clovis: Upper Paleolithic-Paleoindian Adaptations,* eds. O. Soffer and N. Preslov, pp. 31–50. New York: Plenum.

Solecki, R. S. 1971. *Shanidar: The First Flower People.* New York: Knopf.

Solheim, W. 1972. An earlier agricultural revolution. *Scientific American* 226(4): 34–41.

Sowunmi, M. A. 1985. The beginnings of agriculture in West Africa: Botanical evidence. *Current Anthropology* 26: 127–29.

Spencer, F. 1990. *Piltdown: A Scientific Forgery.* New York: Oxford University Press.

Stanford, C. B. 1995. To catch a colobus. *Natural History,* 104(1): 48–55.

Steudel, K. 1996. Limb morphology, bipedal gait, and the energetics of hominid locomotion. *American Journal of Physical Anthropology* 99(2): 345–56.

Stiner, M. C. 1995. *Honor Among Thieves: A Zooarchaeological Study of Neandertal Ecology.* Princeton: Princeton University Press.

Stipp, J. J., J. H. A. Chappell, and I. McDougall. 1967. K/Ar age estimate of the Pliocene-Pleistocene boundary in New Zealand. *American Journal of Science* 265: 462–74.

Stoneking, M. 1993. DNA and recent human evolution. *Evolutionary Anthropology* 2(2): 60–73.

Stoneking, M. and R. L. Cann. 1989. African origin of human mitochondrial DNA. In *The Human Revolution: Behavioural and Biological Perspectives in the Origins of Modern Humans,* eds. P. Mellars and C. Stringer, pp. 17–30. Princeton, N.J.: Princeton University Press.

Straus, L. G. 1989. Age of the modern Europeans. *Nature* 342: 476–77.

Straus, W. L. and A. J. E. Cave. 1957. Pathology and the posture of Neandertal Man. *Quarterly Review of Biology* 32: 348–63.

Stringer, C. B. 1974. A multivariate study of the Petralona skull. *Journal of Human Evolution* 3: 397–404.

———. 1988. The dates of Eden. *Nature* 331: 565–66.

———. 1989. The origin of early modern humans: A comparison of the European and non-European evidence. In *The Human Revolution: Behavioural and Biological Perspectives in the Origins of Modern Humans,* eds. P. Mellars and C. Stringer, pp. 232–44. Princeton, N.J.: Princeton University Press.

———. 1990. The emergence of modern humans. *Scientific American* 263(6): 98–104.

———. 1992a. Reconstructing recent human evolution. *Philosophical Transactions of the Royal Society of London* (B) 337:217–24.

———. 1992b. Replacement, continuity, and the origin of *Homo sapiens.* In *Continuity or Replacement: Controversies in* Homo sapiens *Evolution,* eds. G. Bräuer and F. Smith, pp. 9–24. Rotterdam: Balkema.

———. 1993. Secrets of the pit of the bones. *Nature* 362: 501–2.

———. 1994. Out of Africa: A personal history. In *Origins of Anatomically Modern Humans,* eds. M. Nitecki and D. Nitecki, pp. 149–74. New York: Plenum.

Stringer, C. B. and P. Andrews. 1988. Genetic and fossil evidence for the origin of modern humans. *Science* 239: 1263–68.

Stringer, C. B. and C. Gamble. 1993. *In Search of the Neanderthals.* New York: Thames and Hudson.

Stringer, C. B. and R. Grün. 1991. Time for the last Neandertals. *Nature* 351: 701–2.

Stringer, C. B., R. Grün, H. P. Schwarcz, and P. Goldberg. 1989. ESR dates for the hominid burial site of Es Skhul in Israel. *Nature* 338: 756–58.

Stringer, C. B., F. C. Howell, and J. K. Melentis. 1979. The significance of the fossil hominid skull from Petralona, Greece. *Journal of Archaeological Science* 6: 235–53.

Stringer, C. B., J. J. Hublin, and B. Vandermeersch. 1984. The origin of anatomically modern humans in western Europe. In *The Origins of Modern Humans: A World Survey of the Fossil Evidence,* eds. F. H. Smith and F. Spencer, pp. 51–136. New York: Liss.

Stringer, C. and R. McKie. 1996. *African Exodus: The Origins of Modern Humanity.* Claremont, Ca.: Cape.

Struever, S. and F. A. Holton. 1979. *Koster: Americans in Search of Their Prehistoric Past.* Garden City, N.Y.: Anchor Press/Doubleday.

Strum, S. 1987. *Almost Human.* New York: Random House.

Stuart, G. E. 1972. Who were the "mound builders"? *National Geographic* 142(6): 783–801.

Svoboda, J. 1993. The complex origin of the Upper Paleolithic in the Czech and Slovak Republics. In *Before Lascaux: The Complex Record of the Early Upper Paleolithic,* eds. H. Knecht, A. Pike-Tay, and R. White, pp. 23–36. Boca Raton, Fla.: CRC Press.

Swisher, C. C., G. H. Curtis, T. Jacob, A. G. Getty, A. Suprijo, and Widiasmoro. 1994. Age of the earliest known hominids in Java, Indonesia. *Science* 263: 1118–21.

Szabo, B. and D. Collins. 1975. Ages of fossil bones from British interglacial sites. *Nature* 254: 680–82.

Szalay, F. S. and E. Delson. 1979. *Evolutionary History of the Primates.* New York: Academic Press.

Tainter, J. A. 1988. *The Collapse of Complex Societies.* Cambridge, Eng.: Cambridge University Press.

Tappen, N. C. 1985. The dentition of the "Old Man" of La Chapelle-aux-Saints and inferences concerning Neandertal behavior. *American Journal of Physical Anthropology* 67: 43–50.

Tattersall, I. 1993. *The Human Odyssey: Four Million Years of Human Evolution.* New York: Prentice Hall.

————. 1995a. *The Fossil Trail: How We Know What We Think We Know About Human Evolution.* New York: Oxford University Press.

————. 1995b. *The Last Neandertal: The Rise, Success, and Mysterious Extinction of Our Closest Human Relatives.* New York: Macmillan.

Taylor, R. E. 1991. Frameworks for dating the Late Pleistocene peopling of the Americas. In *The First Americans: Search and Research,* eds. T. D. Dillehay and D. J. Meltzer, pp. 77–111. Boca Raton, Fla.: CRC Press.

Templeton, A. R. 1993. The "Eve" hypothesis: A genetic critique and reanalysis. *American Anthropologist* 95: 51–72.

————. 1996. Gene lineages and human evolution. *Science* 272: 1363.

Thomas, D. H. 1989. *Archaeology,* 2nd ed. New York: Holt, Rinehart & Winston.

Thorne, A. G. and M. H. Wolpoff. 1992. The multiregional evolution of humans. *Scientific American* 266(4): 76–83.

Tishkoff, S. A., E. Dietzsch, W. Speed, A. J. Pakstis, J. R. Kidd, K. Cheung, B. Bonné-Tamir, A. S. Santachiara-Benerecetti, P. Moral, M. Krings, S. Pääbo, E. Watson, N. Risch, T. Jenkins, and K. K. Kidd. 1996. Global patterns of linkage disequilibrium at the CD4 locus and modern human origins. *Science* 271: 1380–87.

Tobias, P. V. 1987. The brain of *Homo habilis:* A new level of organization in cerebral evolution. *Journal of Human Evolution* 16: 741–61.

Todd, I. A. 1976. *Çatal Hüyük in Perspective.* Menlo Park, Calif.: Benjamin/Cummings.

Toth, N. 1985. The Oldowan reassessed: A close look at early stone artifacts. *Journal of Archaeological Science* 2: 101–20.

Trinkaus, E. (ed.) 1983a. Neanderthal postcrania and the adaptive shift to modern humans. In *The Mousterian Legacy,* pp. 165–200. Oxford: British Archaeological Reports, International Series, 164.

————. 1983b. *The Shanidar Neandertals.* New York: Academic Press.

————. 1984. Western Asia. In *The Origins of Modern Humans: A World Survey of the Fossil Evidence,* eds. F. H. Smith and F. Spencer, pp. 251–94. New York: Liss.

————. 1985. Pathology and the posture of the La Chapelle-aux-Saints Neandertal. *American Journal of Physical Anthropology* 67: 19–41.

————. 1986. The Neandertals and modern human origins. *Annual Review of Anthropology* 15: 193–218.

————. 1989. The Upper Pleistocene transition. In *The Emergence of Modern Humans: Biocultural Adaptations in the Later Pleistocene,* ed. E. Trinkaus, pp. 42–66. New York: Cambridge University Press.

Trinkaus, E. and P. Shipman. 1993. *The Neandertals: Changing Images of Mankind.* New York: Knopf.

Trinkaus, E. and D. D. Thompson. 1987. Femoral diaphyseal histophometric age determinators for the Shanidar 3, 4, 5 and 6 Neandertals and Neandertal longevity. *American Journal of Physical Anthropology* 72: 123–29.

Trinkaus, E. and I. Villemeur. 1991. Mechanical advantages of the Neandertal thumb in flexion: A test of an hypothesis. *American Journal of Physical Anthropology* 84: 249–60.

Turner, B. L. and P. Harrison. (eds.) 1983. *Pulltrouser Swamp: Ancient Maya Habitat, Agriculture, and Settlement in Northern Belize.* Austin: University of Texas Press.

Tuross, N. and T. D. Dillehay. 1995. The mechanism of organic preservation at Monte Verde, Chile and the use of biomolecules in archaeological interpretation. *Journal of Field Archaeology.* 22: 97–101.

Tylor, E. B. 1871. *Primitive Culture: Part I—The Origins of Culture.* 1958 ed. New York: Harper and Brothers.

Unger-Hamilton, R. 1989. The epi-Paleolithic southern Levant and the origins of cultivation. *Current Anthropology* 30: 88–103.

Valdes, V. C. and J. L. Bischoff. 1989. Accelerator ^{14}C dates for Early Upper Paleolithic (Basal Aurignacian) at El Castillo Cave (Spain). *Journal of Archaeological Science* 16: 577–84.

Valladas, H., J. L. Reyss, J. L. Joron, G. Valladas, O. Bar-Yosef, and B. Vandermeersch. 1988. Thermoluminescence dating of Mousterian "Proto-Cro-Magnon" remains from Israel and the origin of modern man. *Nature* 331: 614–16.

Van Peer, P. 1992. *The Levallois Reduction Strategy.* Monographs in World Archaeology. Volume 13. Madison, Wisc.: Prehistory Press.

Van Peer, P. and P. M. Vermeersch. 1990. Middle to Upper Paleolithic transition: The evidence for the Nile Valley. In *The Emergence of Modern Humans: An Archaeological Perspective,* ed. P. Mellars, pp. 139–59. Ithaca, N.Y.: Cornell University Press.

Van Riper, A. B. 1993. *Men Among the Mammoths: Victorian Science and the Discovery of Human Prehistory.* Chicago: University of Chicago Press.

Vietmeyer, N. 1992. Forgotten roots of the Incas. In *Chilies to Chocolate: Food the Americas Gave the World,* eds. N.

Foster and L. S. Cordell, pp. 95–104. Tucson: University of Arizona Press.

Vigilant, L., M. Stoneking, H. Hardpending, K. Hawkes, and A. Wilson. 1991. African populations and the evolution of human mitochondrial DNA. *Science* 253: 1503–08.

Villa, P. 1982. Conjoinable pieces and site formation processes. *American Antiquity* 47: 276–90.

Vrba, E. S. 1993. The pulse that produced us. *Natural History* 102(5): 47–51.

Walker, A. 1993. Perpectives on the Nariokotome discovery. In *The Nariokotome* Homo erectus *Skeleton,* eds. A. Walker and R. Leakey, pp. 411–30. Cambridge, Mass.: Harvard University Press.

Walker, A. and C. B. Ruff. 1993. The reconstruction of the pelvis. In *The Nariokotome* Homo erectus *Skeleton,* eds. A. Walker and R. Leakey, pp. 221–33. Cambridge, Mass.: Harvard University Press.

Walker, A. and R. Leakey (eds.) 1993. *The Nariokotome* Homo erectus *Skeleton.* Cambridge, Mass.: Harvard University Press.

Warren, P. 1975. *The Aegean Civilizations.* Oxford, Eng.: Elsevier Phaidon.

———. 1987. Crete: The Minoans and their gods. In *Origins: The Roots of European Civilisation,* ed. B. Cunliffe, pp. 30–41. Chicago: Dorsey Press.

Watson, J. D. 1968. *The Double Helix.* New York: Athenaeum.

Weaver, K. 1985. The search for our ancestors. *National Geographic* 168(5): 560–623.

Weaver, M. P. 1972. *The Aztecs, the Maya, and Their Predecessors: Archaeology of Mesoamerica.* New York: Seminar Press.

Weaver, R. F. 1984. Changing life's genetic blueprint. *National Geographic* 166(6): 818–47.

Weiner, J. 1994. *The Beak of the Finch: A Story of Evolution in Our Time.* New York: Knopf.

Weiner, J. S. 1955. *The Piltdown Forgery.* London: Oxford Press.

Weiner, J. S. and B. G. Campbell. 1964. The taxonomic status of the Swanscombe skull. In *The Swanscombe Skull: A Survey of Research on a Pleistocene Site,* ed. C. Ovey, pp. 175–209. Royal Institute of Great Britain and Ireland, Occasional Paper 20.

Weiss, G. and A. von Haeseler. 1996. Technical comments: Estimating the age of the common ancestor of men from the ZFY intron. *Science* 272: 1359–60.

Wendorf, F., A. E. Close, R. Schild, K. Wasylikowa, R. A. Housley, J. R. Harlan, and H. Królik. 1992. Saharan exploitation of plants 8,000 years B.P. *Nature* 359: 721–24.

Wheat, J. B. 1972. *The Olsen–Chubbuck Site: A Paleo-Indian Bison Kill.* Salt Lake City: Memoirs of the Society for American Archaeology, No. 26.

Wheatly, P. 1971. *The Pivot of the Four Quarters.* Chicago: Aldine.

White, J. P. and J. F. O'Connell. 1982. *A Prehistory of Australia, New Guinea, and Sahul.* New York: Academic Press.

White, P. T. 1982. The temples of Angkor: Ancient glory in stone. *National Geographic* 161(5): 552–89.

White, R. 1982. Rethinking the Middle-Upper Paleolithic transition. *Current Anthropology* 23(2): 169–92.

White, R. 1993. Technological and social dimensions of "Aurignacian-age" body ornaments across Europe. In *Before Lascaux: The Complex Record of the Early Upper Paleolithic,* eds. H. Knecht, A. Pike-Tay, and R. White, pp. 277–99. Boca Raton, Fla.: CRC Press.

White, T. 1986. Cut marks on the Bodo cranium: A case of prehistoric defleshing. *American Journal of Physical Anthropology* 69: 503–9.

White, T. D. and P. A. Folkens. 1991. *Human Osteology.* San Diego: Academic Press.

White, T. D., G. Suwa, and B. Asfaw. 1994. *Australopithecus ramidus,* a new species of early hominid from Aramis, Ethiopia. *Nature* 371: 306–12.

Whitley, D. S. and R. I. Dorn. 1993. New perspectives on the Clovis vs. pre-Clovis controversy. *American Antiquity* 58: 626–47.

Whittle, A. 1985. *Neolithic Europe: A Survey.* Cambridge, Eng.: Cambridge University Press.

Williams, S. 1991. *Fantastic Archaeology: The Wild Side of North American Prehistory.* Philadelphia: University of Pennsylvania Press.

Wilmsen, E. 1974. *Lindenmeier: A Pleistocene Hunting Society.* New York: Harper & Row.

Wilson, A. C. and R. L. Cann. 1992. The recent African genesis of humans. *Scientific American* 266(4): 68–73.

Wing, E. 1977. Animal domestication in the Andes. In *Origins of Agriculture,* ed. C. A. Reed, pp. 837–60. The Hague: Mouton.

Wittfogel, K. 1957. *Oriental Despotism: A Comparative Study of Total Power.* New Haven, Conn.: Yale University Press.

Wolpoff, M. 1980a. *Paleoanthropology.* New York: Knopf.

———. 1980b. Cultural remains of Middle Pleistocene hominids. *Journal of Human Evolution* 9: 339–58.

————. 1984. Evolution in *Homo erectus:* The question of stasis. *Paleobiology* 10: 389–406.

————. 1988. The place of the Neandertals in human evolution. In *The Emergence of Modern Humans: Biocultural Adaptations in the Later Pleistocene,* ed. E. Trinkaus, pp. 97–141. New York: Cambridge University Press.

————. 1989. Multiregional evolution: The fossil alternative to Eden. *The Human Revolution: Behavioural and Biological Perspectives in the Origins of Modern Humans,* eds. P. Mellars and C. Stringer, pp. 62–108. Princeton, N.J.: Princeton University Press.

————. 1992. Theories of modern human origins. In *Continuity or Replacement: Controversies in* Homo sapiens *Evolution,* eds. G. Bräuer and F. Smith, pp. 25–64. Rotterdam: Balkema.

Wolpoff, M. H., A. G. Thorne, F. H. Smith, D. W. Frayer, and G. G. Pope. 1994. Multiregional evolution: A worldwide source for modern human populations. In *Origins of Anatomically Modern Humans,* eds. M. Nitecki and D. Nitecki, pp. 175–99. New York: Plenum.

Wolpoff, M., X. Z. Wu, and A. G. Thorpe. 1984. Modern *Homo sapiens* origins: A general theory of hominid evolution involving the fossil evidence from East Asia. In *The Origins of Modern Humans: A World Survey of the Fossil Evidence,* eds. F. H. Smith and F. Spencer, pp. 411–84. New York: Liss.

Wood, B. A. 1984. The origin of *Homo erectus. Courier Forschungsinstitut Seckenberg* 69: 99–111.

Wood, B. A. 1992. Early hominid species and speciation. *Journal of Human Evolution* 22: 351–65.

Woodhead, A. D. and B. J. Barnhart. 1988. *Biotechnology and the Human Genome.* New York: Plenum.

Wright, G. 1971. Origins of food production in Southwestern Asia: A survey of ideas. *Current Anthropology* 12: 447–77.

Wu, R. (Woo Ju-kang). 1985. New Chinese *Homo erectus* and recent work at Zhoukoudian. In *Ancestors: The Hard Evidence,* ed. E. Delson, pp. 245–48. New York: Liss.

Wu, R. (Woo Ju-kang) and S. Lin. 1983. Peking Man. *Scientific American* 248(6): 86–94.

Yarnell, R. 1977. Native plant husbandry north of Mexico. In *Origins of Agriculture,* ed. C. A. Reed, pp. 861–78. The Hague: Mouton.

Yellen, J. E., A. S. Brooks, E. Cornelissen, M. J. Mehlman, and K. Stewart. 1995. A Middle Stone Age worked bone industry from Katanda, Upper Semliki Valley, Zaire. *Science* 268: 553–56.

Yi, S. and G. Clark. 1985. The "Dyuktai Culture" and New World origins. *Current Anthropology* 26: 1–13.

Yun-Xin, F. and W.-H. Li. 1996. Technical comments: Estimating the age of the common ancestor of men from the ZFY intron. *Science* 272: 1356–57.

Zimmer, C. 1994. Cows were in the air. *Discover* 15(9): 29.

Zohary, D. and M. Hopf. 1994. *Domestication of Plants in the Old World.* Oxford: Clarendon Press.

Index

527